CANADIAN LITERARY LANDMARKS

CANADIAN LITERARY LANDMARKS

John Robert Colombo

Hounslow Press

This book
is dedicated to
Philip Singer, B.A., M.L.S.

Hounslow Press
A Division of Anthony R. Hawke Limited
124 Parkview Avenue
Willowdale, Ontario, Canada
M2N 3Y5

ISBN 0-88882-073-9

Design: David Shaw & Associates Ltd.
Composition: Accurate Typesetting Ltd.
Printing: Tri-Graphic Printing (Ottawa) Limited

Publication was assisted by
the Canada Council and
the Ontario Arts Council.

Printed in Canada.

Contents

To have done this is to have lived, though fame
Remember us with no familiar name.

Archibald Lampman

Or find it, find it, find it commonplace
but effective, valid, real, the unity
in the family feature, the not unsimilar face?

A. M. Klein

The centre of reality is wherever one happens to be, and its
circumference is whatever one's imagination can make of it.

Northrop Frye

Preface

Canadian Literary Landmarks is an illustrated guide to places in the country with literary associations. It describes the literary sites, or landmarks, that are related to the lives or works of important or interesting writers of the past and present. There are over 1,200 references to more than 750 places associated with some 500 authors. There are more than 650 illustrations. The entries are arranged alphabetically within province or territory. Each place or site is briefly located and concisely described to root it in a region and to relate it to a literary work or a period in the life of an imaginative writer. The book is comprehensive and provides the reader with a geographical perspective on the country's literature and writers. It maps the Canadian literary imagination, and as such should enrich the reading experience of every literate Canadian.

Most of the major literary writers of the past are represented, along with a selection of noteworthy contemporary writers. Although the book concentrates on poets, storytellers, novelists, and dramatists, it does not neglect journalists, editors, historians, and others concerned with the world of books. Not all the information is strictly literary, for there are some architectural and historical details included, along with biographical information about all the members of the Group of Seven and some other literary-minded artists. Coverage is given to visiting foreign authors who had occasion to comment on Canadian locales.

The places for which there are entries include all major cities and a great many towns, villages, and settlements; important lakes and rivers; major regions; even imaginative locales. The sites embrace places of birth, principal residences, points of inspiration, locales transformed by imaginative acts, and final resting places. The entries are necessarily brief, but it is hoped that each entry will delight and inform.

It took close to two years to assemble the literary and geographical information in this book. The work did not start from scratch but was built on a quarter century of involvement in the world of letters. During the time I worked on this book I evolved two criteria for inclusion. I decided that if I included a piece of information it had to be either *important* or *interesting*. Allow me to discuss these two criteria in turn.

The criterion that the information be important in itself meant that the book had to include all the significant landmarks. For example, it had to include entries for Robert Service's cabin in the Yukon, Stephen Leacock's home in Orillia (known to readers as "Mariposa"), Gabrielle Roy's rue Deschambault in St. Boniface, and Margaret Laurence's Neepawa (or "Manawaka"). This familiar ground is well covered. Indeed, there are not single but multiple entries for famous writers and their landmarks. Hundreds of lesser-known landmarks, each significant in its own way, are also described. Some instances are Farley Mowat's Burgeo, Thomas H. Raddall's Liverpool, Frederick Philip Grove's Rapid City, Jack Hodgins' Nanaimo, Al Purdy's Pangnirtung (as well as the same poet's Ameliasburg).

The second criterion that the information be of interest permitted the broadening of the book to include, as well as famous writers, many lesser-known but nonetheless familiar writers, some interesting places, and some

A somewhat pensive John Robert Colombo considers what he will include in the preface to Canadian Literary Landmarks. *This photo by Ellen Tolmie was taken in the author's study in his suburban North York home at 42 Dell Park Avenue, Toronto. [Ellen Tolmie]*

out-of-the-ordinary bookish details. So the coverage extends to visiting foreign writers such as Rudyard Kipling and Ernest Hemingway, Mark Twain and William Faulkner, and to oddities such as Bertram Tennyson, the Canadian cousin of the poet laureate. Some of these entries should be taken with a grain of salt, perhaps, but salt does add savour, if not flavour.

It should be borne in mind that not all writers and literary works are illuminated when viewed geographically. For every Earle Birney, who writes about the here and now, there is a Margaret Avison whose life and work seem apart from the standard atlases and gazetteers. A writer like Mavis Gallant, who is an expatriate, has moved right off the Canadian map. Some books are rooted in regions, some not. Richard Rohmer's novels tell us little about locale, whereas those of Mordecai Richler are specific to the street on which the action takes place. Even within a writer's work there is a division based on geographical considerations. The prose of Margaret Atwood usually displays a strong sense of place, her poetry hardly any at all. Some writers set their works in generalized locales, being principally concerned with their characters' psychology; Alice Munro and Marie-Claire Blais are authors who may be approached by regional considerations but are best confronted along other avenues of approach.

The reader should bear in mind that the length of an entry has no necessary connection with its importance. Indeed, it often requires more words to explain a minor matter than it does a major concern. (There is an East Indian saying that the artist who wishes to paint both the elephant and the flea will find it necessary to decrease the size of the former and increase the size of the latter.) It is also true that the number of entries devoted to a single author gives no necessary indication of quality or importance. Multiple entries are more often indicative of geographical mobility than literary distinction. Thus L. M. Montgomery rates more entries than Hugh MacLennan. There are more statues of Robert Burns in this country than of any other literary figure (there are probably more memorials to him in Canada than there are in his native Scotland); this observation gives an indication of the affection felt for this man and his verse by Canadians of Scots origin, yesterday if not today.

Here are some considerations that kept the present work within manageable limits. The desire to represent an author was weighed against whether his or her work was in print or accessible in a collection or anthology. Attention was paid to publishers' catalogues and academic curricula to measure the desire to inform against the need to know. A plus factor was a presently standing building or plaque; a minus factor was a reference that could only be general — "in this town was born" — or to a parking lot. Generally the details that are highlighted are things the reader already knows a little about. Writers in French — whether Acadian, Manitoban, Ontarian, French-Canadian, or Québécois — are represented to the degree that their work has been translated into English and to the extent that it impinges on the consciousness of English-Canadian readers.

Who or what is Canadian has been generously interpreted. The adjective has been applied retrospectively and posthumously to include those who are early, new, old, or former Canadians, as well as birds of passage, not to mention English explorers and French missionaries, even Norsemen who wrote narratives about events that took place on what is now Canadian soil one thousand years ago. An equally wide view has been taken of what constitutes "literary." Generally it is taken to mean imaginative prose and poetry, but now and then it is extended to include writing and bookish material.

The representation given to native writers is perhaps more extensive than the average reader might expect. Inuit and Indian singers and narrators have made a distinct and dramatic contribution to the imagination of Canadians all out of proportion to their numbers. Wherever appropriate Indian authors have been related to their reserves and Inuit authors to their settlements or co-operatives, as these lands are places of memory, where the lore of the land has been handed down from generation to generation. Only in the last few decades have the oral traditions gone from lip to page. A related matter is non-native folklore which has been granted more space than might otherwise be anticipated.

Canadian Literary Landmarks is not a guide book in the sense that it gives tourist information. There is a general absence in these pages of such dated and detailed information as mileages, street addresses, telephone numbers, visiting hours of sites open to the public. Some information has been given for the principal literary landmarks, when appropriate, but not for all. It is assumed that the interested reader in planning an itinerary will use the telephone directory, the local library, or the district tourist bureau.

In most books of literary places the entries are arranged within a single alphabetical listing. In this book there are twelve separate alphabetical listings to correspond to the ten provinces and two territories. The provinces and territories have been arranged in a general way from East to West. There are so many sites of significance in the metropolitan areas that different principles of organization had to be found to deal with them. Some sites are arranged alphabetically within cities, others chronologically, still others thematically.

Two cities presented special problems. Montreal and Toronto together account for approximately 20 per cent of the population of the country. Coincidentally they account for about one-fifth of the references in this book. Both cities lend themselves to a two-part alphabetical division into Places and People. It will be apparent that a writer's chances of being noted are better if he or she resides in a small hamlet in Alberta rather than in an apartment or suburb in Montreal or Toronto. The reader may find rather more entries than anticipated for Ontario

Over eight hundred maroon-coloured bronze plaques, like this one which honours L. M. Montgomery at Green Gables, Cavendish, P.E.I., mark historic and sometimes literary sites across the country. [Parks Canada]

A homesick G.I., working on the Alaska Highway in 1943, posted at Watson Lake, Y.T., a sign giving the mileage to his home town. Hundreds of G.I.s followed suit. [Tourism Yukon]

and its capital Toronto. If so the reader might bear in mind that *Canadian Literary Landmarks* is being published in 1984, the year which marks the bicentennial of Ontario and the sesquicentennial of Toronto. They are also the province and city in which the author lives.

A special feature of this book, which might not be immediately apparent, is the treatment of place names derived from literary sources. There is an entry for any place of any size that bears an officially recognized name that derives from an author or a literary work. There are over two hundred such places. One thinks automatically of Stratford, Ont. Then come to mind Shelley, B.C., and perhaps even Chesterfield Inlet, N.W.T. The importance of such literary toponomy may not be immediately apparent. But would there be a world-renowned Shakespearian festival at Stratford today had the Ontario community retained its original name, Little Thames?

There are in 1984 over 850 maroon-and-bronze plaques with bilingual inscriptions erected across the country by the Historic Sites and Monuments Board of Canada. In addition there are innumerable plaques erected by provincial and municipal governments as well as special-interest groups. Perhaps 10 per cent of all these plaques have specific literary content. All sites with officially raised plaques have been considered for inclusion, but no special mention has been made of them. Also located and described are fictitious places — "Jalna," "Jubilee," "Crocus," "Manawaka," even "Kingdom of the Saguenay" — more often than not through "see" references to their real-life counterparts.

The impetus behind compiling this book is the belief, experienced by most people though almost impossible to formulate, that there exists in this country as elsewhere

on this planet the "genius of place." Each place has its own character. Artists are especially sensitive to such characteristics, and it is through literary and artistic works that these become apparent. An attempt has been made not so much to "mythologize" places as to disclose the myths in which they are enmeshed. As such, *Canadian Literary Landmarks* is an imaginative cartography, groundwork for a "mythography."

The work is also something of a "native odyssey." If there is one place in the country which sums up this book it is Watson Lake, Y.T., on the Alaska Highway, where hundreds of road signs point out principal places in every direction. In these pages the signs are imaginative signposts that summarize our hopes and our fears.

Literature deals directly with our hopes and fears. As Canadians we find that both Kafka and Callaghan, both Roth and Richler, tell us about ourselves. In the past Canadians have not paid all that much attention to the creative writers among them. When Rupert Brooke toured the country in 1913, he noted in particular the absence of "associations" in the landscape. No sword in the water, no one thinking about the prairies, and so on. When he toured Quebec, no one pointed out Crémazie's House, so immersed was his guide in material and historical matters.

We rattled up and down the steep streets, out among tidy fields, and back into the noisily sedate city again. We saw where Wolfe fell, where Montcalm fell, where Montgomery fell. Children played where the tides of war had ebbed and flowed. Mr. Norman Angell and his friends tell us that trade is superseding war; and pacifists declare that for the future countries will win their pride or shame from commercial treaties and tariffs and bounties, and no more from battles and sieges. And there is a part of Canadian patriotism that has progressed this way. But I wonder if the hearts of that remarkable race, posterity, will ever beat the harder when they are told, "Here Mr. Borden stood when he decided to double the duty on agricultural implements," or even "In this room Mr. Ritchie conceived the plan for removing the shilling on wheat." When that happens, Quebec will be a forgotten ruin. . . .

Quebec never did become Brooke's "forgotten ruin" perhaps because Crémazie and Garneau and others in the Quebec City he visited preserved some sense of the past in their lives and works and handed it down to future generations.

Brooke found friendliness and some fellowship across the country, but few if any places where the imagination could flourish. The prevailing view was, and has remained, that the landscape is hostile to the literary temperament and resistant to imaginative treatment. In *The Republic of Childhood* (1975), Sheila Egoff wrote about the relationship between fantasy-writing and landscape, but the point she makes applies not just to fantasy authors but to all imaginative authors:

It is this shift, with its implication of re-creation, that Canadian fantasists seem unable or unwilling to confront. Much can be blamed on the land itself; perhaps there is simply so much geographical space that the Canadian imagination cannot embrace it, reorder it — or escape it. The land also lacks traditional associations. Build a fantasy on King Arthur and place-names abound — from Mount Badon to Tintagel. Take a house that is centuries old, like Lucy Boston's "Green Knowe," and a mystery immediately becomes plausible. Without such aids the Canadian

landscape seems inhospitable or even inimical to fantasy, and so it all too often remains a framework for, rather than a participant in, the story; that is, it does not help to shape the events. The feeling of immensity and coldness that is generated is almost an antithesis to the nature of fantasy. In Canada, writers of fantasy have to make new things familiar.

Until recently, at least, all Canadian writers have struggled "to make new things familiar." Perhaps only now is it possible to remake the familiar, to realize the real, so to speak.

One way of transforming the familiar is to see it through eyes other than our own. In a modest way this work tries to do that. It scratches the surface — the literary surface — of the country. Like a relief map it indicates heights and depths, it shows areas of concentration, and it reveals unexpected shapes and contours, colours and textures. There is something surprising about seeing a site that has been written about; it is rather like meeting a celebrity. What one sees is interpreted in light of what one knows. Mark Twain had this element of surprise in mind when he has one of the characters in *Tom Sawyer Abroad* (1894) say to another when Tom is in Baghdad:

Mainly we laid on our backs and talked; we didn't want to go to sleep. Tom said we was right in the midst of the *Arabian Nights* now. He said it was right along here that one of the cutest things in that book happened; so we looked down and watched while he told about it, because there ain't anything that is so interesting to look at as a place that a book has talked about.

We remake the world when we see it simultaneously as a mark and as a landmark. This psychological and aesthetic act may well have been what the surrealists had in mind when they drew up their own map of the world.

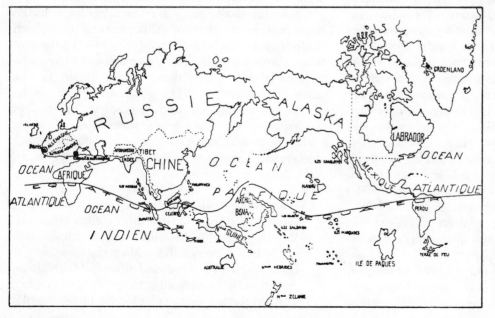

"The World at the Time of the Surrealists" is the title of this map which draws attention to places to the extent that they are of interest to surrealists. The map first appeared in the June 1929 issue of the Belgian magazine Variétés. *Although unsigned, it is considered the work of Yves Tanguy. It reflects surrealist concern for regions that produce so-called primitive art. Thus the Pacific Ocean, Russia, and Alaska are given prominence. Neither the United States nor Canada is identified, although Labrador and the Queen Charlotte Islands warrant attention. Somewhat similar to this map is the view of Canada the reader will receive from* Canadian Literary Landmarks, *which stresses those sites and settlements that have inspired the literary imagination.* [Wald / Zeller]

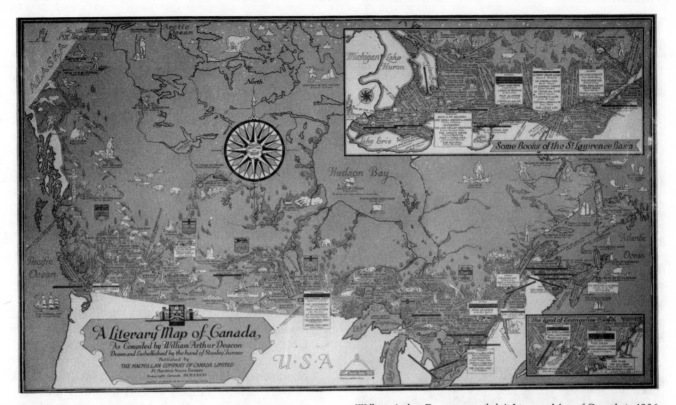

Le Monde au Temps des Surréalistes is a Mercator projection of the world but one in which the continents and countries and cities appear not as they do on standard maps but to the degree that they are of interest to surrealists. There is no Canada on this map, but plainly marked are both Labrador and the Queen Charlotte Islands, areas known to produce Eskimo and Indian art. The point the surrealists are making is that the world is manageable and rearrangeable, for it corresponds to some degree to our conceptions of it.

Over the years many detailed guides to literary places in the United States and the United Kingdom have been published, but there has been no guide for Canada. It is true that William Arthur Deacon oversaw the production of A Literary Map of Canada in 1936, the year the present writer was born, and that Morris Wolfe and David Macfarlane attempted the trick again in 1979; but neither map was more than a move in the right direction, being more decorative than dramatic. Why have Canadians had to wait so long?

The truth is that no one noticed its absence. No one felt he required a guide to literary places. There is no shortage of sites, as the present book shows, but perhaps there is a shortness of vision. There is no absence of authors, but there might be an absence of mind, a disinclination on the part of Canadians to imagine. In no ethnological or cultural sense could there be a Canadian people. But there are some notions that Canadians hold to be self-evident: the country is not really a country, certainly not an imaginative whole; the land and its peoples are too diverse, unmanageable, to be assimilable; the country is, below the federal surface, "a fling of a

William Arthur Deacon compiled A Literary Map of Canada *in 1936. It is a handsome production, with four-colour embellishments by Stanley Turner. This piece of literary cartography marks the first attempt to "put Canadian literature on the map." [Deacon Papers, Thomas Fisher Rare Book Library, University of Toronto / Karen Hendrick]*

nation" (in Earle Birney's phrase). After all, it was a Canadian, J. Tuzo Wilson, who argued successfully that the surface of the globe, far from being fixed, is sitting on a collection of plates in motion. This is the "mosaic" vision in action.

There is also the feeling that history, especially literary history, happened elsewhere. Nowhere today, except perhaps in the emotional responses of some of our imaginative writers and prophets like Margaret Laurence and Hugh MacLennan, is there the largeness of vision, the Whitmanesque exuberance found in a passage like this from Ocean to Ocean (1873) by George M. Grant:

But, no matter what may be said in its disparagement, it is a wide and goodly land, with manifold beauties of its own, with boundless resources that are only beginning to be developed, and with room and verge for Empire. Each Province has attractions for its children. One would need to live in it to understand how strong these attractions are. Only when you live among the country people do they reveal themselves. Strangers or tourists are not likely to have the faintest conception of their deepest feelings. Thus a man who lives in his study, or in a select coterie, or always in a city, may — no matter how great his ability — utterly misconceive the spirit of a province or nation and the vigour of its life. It has been my lot to live for a time in

This portrait of George Monro Grant appeared as the frontispiece to his inspired travel account Ocean to Ocean. [Metropolitan Toronto Library]

almost every one of our provinces, and to cross the whole Dominion, again and again, from ocean to ocean, by steamer or canoe, by rail and buck-board, on horse back and on foot, and I have found, in the remotest settlements, a remarkable acquaintance with public questions and much soundness of judgment and feeling in regard to them; a high average purity of individual and family life, and a steady growth of national sentiment. I have sat with the blackened toilers in the coal mines of Pictou and Cape Breton, the darkness made visible by the little lamps hanging from their sooty foreheads; have worshipped with pious Highlanders in log huts in fertile glens and on the hillsides, where the forest gives place slowly to the plough, and preached to assembled thousands, seated on grassy hillocks and prostrate trees; have fished and sailed with the hardy mariners, who find "every harbour, from Sable to Canseau, a home"; have ridden under the willows of Evangeline's country, and gazed from North and South Mountain on a sea of apple-blossoms; have talked with gold miners, fishermen, farmers, merchants, students, and have learned to respect my fellow countrymen and to sympathize with their provincial life, and to see that it was not antagonistic, but intended to be the handmaid to a true national life.

Go there, not altogether in the spirit of "Baddeck, and that sort of thing." Pass from Annapolis Royal into the Bay of Fundy, and then canoe up the rivers, shaded by the great trees of New Brunswick. Live a while with the habitants of Quebec, admire their industry, frugality and courtesy; hear their carols and songs, that blend the forgotten music of Normandy and Brittany with the music of Canadian woods; music and song, as well as language and religion, rooting in them devotion to "Our Language, our Laws, our Institutions." Live in historic Quebec, and experience the hospitality of Montreal. Pass through the Province of Ontario, itself possessing the resources of a kingdom. Sail on lakes great enough to be called seas, along rugged Laurentian coasts, or take the new Northwest passage by land, that the Canadian Pacific has opened up from the Upper Ottawa, through a thousand miles once declared impracticable for railways, and now yielding treasures of wood and copper and silver, till you come to that great prairie ocean, that sea of green and gold in this month of May, whose billows extend for nigh another thousand miles to the Rocky Mountains, out of which great Provinces like Minnesota and Dakota will be carved in the immediate future. And when you have reached the Pacific, and look back over all the panorama that unrolls itself before your mental vision, you will not doubt that the country is destined to have a future. You will thank God that you belong to a generation to whom the duty has been assigned of laying its foundations; and knowing that the solidity of any construction is in proportion to the faith, the virtue and the self-sacrifice that has been wrought into the foundation, you will pray that you for one may not be found wanting.

Plainly these are words from the past, but they express sentiments and feelings that are available to us and assimilable by us today. Each region has its writer, for the literary imagination is most concerned, as Northrop Frye noted, with particulars. It is at home in a region, not in a dominion. In fact, it may be most at home within a region, a district, a city, a town, a village, a settlement, a street, a house, a living room, a human being's head and heart and body. As Frye concluded in 1965:

It seems to me that Canadian sensibility has been profoundly disturbed, not so much by our famous problem of identity, important as that is, as by a series of paradoxes in what confronts that identity. It is less perplexed by the question "Who am I?" than by such riddle as "Where is here?"

It was to suggest some answers to the Zen-like riddle "Where is here?" that this book was researched and written.

Acknowledgements

This *omnium gatherum* may be the work of a single author yet it represents the labour of innumerable contributors. I am indebted to Philip Singer as a friend for his conviction that a book such as this one would serve a useful purpose. I am grateful to Philip Singer and Michael Richardson as librarians at the Bathurst Heights Area Branch of the North York Public Library system for their assistance in research, as well as to the freelance writer, Mark Fortier, who undertook much of the fact-checking. Alan Rayburn, Executive Secretary of the Canadian Permanent Committee on Geographical Names, Ottawa, made a remarkable contribution through literary toponomy. Gunther Abrahamson and John MacDonald of Indian Affairs and Northern Development assisted greatly with the northern representation. Edith Fowke, the folklorist, lent a helping hand in the field of folklore and song. Terrence Keough shared his detailed knowledge with me. I am also indebted to Diane Mew for her editorial acumen and to David Shaw for his typographical expertise. As for the illustrations, these come from the sources acknowledged where the illustrations are reproduced. The by-line Bill Brooks identifies the well-known Toronto-based photographer and writer. Research was conducted at the Metropolitan Toronto Library and at the John P. Robarts Research Library of the University of Toronto. To the librarians of these and other institutions, my heartfelt thanks. Let me express my gratitude to the officers of the Writers' Union of Canada, the League of Canadian Poets, and the Canadian Authors' Association for publicizing in their bulletins my project, thereby bringing it to the attention of readers and writers who shared their knowledge with me. In the preparation of the book I used a considerable array of sources, ranging from books to printouts, microprint to telephone conversations. I have endeavoured to bring all of this information, much of it new and never before published, in line with the following volumes: William Rose Benét's *The Reader's Encyclopedia* (1948); *The Encyclopedia Canadiana* (1958, 1963); William B. Hamilton's *The Macmillan Book of Canadian Place Names* (1978); Reader's Digest Association's *Explore Canada* (1974), *Scenic Wonders of Canada* (1976), *Heritage of Canada* (1978), *Canadian Book of the Road* (1979), and *Drive North America* (1983); Norah Story's *The Oxford Companion to Canadian History and Literature* (1967); William Toye's *Supplement to The Oxford Companion to Canadian History and Literature* (1973) and *The Oxford Companion to Canadian Literature* (1983). In addition I have made use of my own publications, notably *Colombo's Canadian Quotations* (1974), *Colombo's Canadian References* (1976), *Colombo's Book of Canada* (1978), *Colombo's Book of Marvels* (1979), and *Colombo's 101 Canadian Places* (1983).

Special acknowledgements are in order to the following men and women who assisted in the preparation of this book: R. C. Baird, National Postal Museum, Ottawa; Hugh A. Dempsey, Glenbow Centre, Calgary; Mrs. Cyrus Eaton, Islamorada, Florida; Mrs. Ken Hay, Kenora, Ont.; Linda Oliver, E. J. Pratt Library, Victoria University, Toronto; Louis Toth, Accurate Typesetting Limited, Toronto. In addition, I wish to acknowledge the use of four texts: *Seven Rivers of Canada* (1961) and *Rivers of Canada* (1974) by Hugh MacLennan; *Rupert Brooke in Canada* (1978) edited by Sandra Martin and Roger Hall; *Oscar Wilde in Canada* (1982) edited by Kevin O'Brien.

The list that follows is an attempt to acknowledge the assistance received from institutions and individuals in the preparation of this book. It is impossible to list all the names of those who have contributed to its text or illustration, but it is possible and desirable to name those institutions and individuals who have made contributions above and beyond the call of duty often at personal expense. I am grateful for this assistance and for the help I received from many others who go unnamed.

Dominion: Alliance of Canadian Cinema, Television and Radio Artists (ACTRA), Toronto; Canadian Actors' Equity, Toronto; Canadian Broadcasting Corporation, Creative Services, Toronto; Glenbow Centre, Calgary; Government of Canada: Regional Industrial Expansion, Department of Industry, Trade & Commerce; Canadian Government Office of Tourism; Energy, Mines & Resources Canada; Canadian Permanent Committee on Geographical Names, Ottawa; McClelland and Stewart Ltd., Toronto; National Film Board of Canada, Montreal and Toronto; National Library of Canada, Ottawa; National Postal Museum, Ottawa; Ontario Film Institute, Toronto; Parks Canada; Performing Arts Magazine; Public Archives of Canada; Royal Canadian Mounted Police, Ottawa; University of Calgary: Special Collections; Marie Baboyant, Montreal; Sherry Brethour, Don Mills; Bill Brooks, Scarborough; Richard Carver, Ottawa; Don Evans, Orillia; Barker Fairley, Toronto; Mark Fortier, Toronto; Edith Fowke, Toronto; Anthony R. Hawke, Willowdale; George Hencz, Toronto;

Marge Hodgeman, Scarborough; S. W. Horrall, Ottawa; Jeremy Katz, Toronto; Terrence Keough, Ottawa; Donna McGillis, Gore's Landing; Hugh MacLennan, Montreal; Gerald Pratley, Don Mills; Linda Rhéaume, Ottawa; Alan Rayburn, Ottawa; Philip Singer, Toronto.

Newfoundland: Department of Development, St. John's; William Gough, Burgeo and Toronto; M.E.A. Hall, Parks Canada, St. John's; Mary K. Ryan, St. John's.

Nova Scotia: Department of Government Services, Halifax; Silver Donald Cameron, D'Escousse; Lesley Choyce, Porters Lake; Harold Horwood, Annapolis Royal; Fraser Sutherland, Pictou and Toronto; Douglas Vaisey, Saint Mary's University, Halifax.

New Brunswick: Tourism New Brunswick, Fredericton; Provincial Archives, Fredericton; J. E. Belliveau, Shediac; Wayland Drew, Grand Manan; Raymond Fraser, Fredericton and Montreal; M. A. MacDonald, Rothesay; Michael O. Nowlan, Oromocto.

Prince Edward Island: Department of Finance and Tourism, Charlottetown; George Dewar, O'Leary; Moncrieff Williamson, Centennial Centre, Charlottetown.

Quebec: Ministère de l'Industrie, du Commerce et du Tourisme: Direction Générale du Tourisme, Direction du Marketing, Quebec City and Montreal; Marie Baboyant, Montreal; Joel Bonn, Montreal; Edgar Andrew Collard, Montreal; Louis Dudek, Montreal; Endré Farkas, Montreal; Hugh Hood, Montreal; Betty and Ralph Gustafson, North Hatley; Irving Layton, Montreal; Ross Leslie, Montreal; Ken Norris, Montreal; Marvin Orbach, Concordia University, Montreal; Mary Peate, Montreal; Howard Ryshpan, Montreal and Toronto; Peter Whalley, Morin Heights.

Ontario: Ministry of Tourism and Recreation, Toronto; Anglican Church of Canada: General Synod Archives, Toronto; United Church of Canada: Committee on Archives and History, Toronto; Julianne Beck, Toronto; John Bell, Ottawa; Kamala Bhatia, Hamilton; Earle Birney, Toronto; Jay Cody, Orillia; Paulette Collet, Toronto; Howard Engel, Toronto; John Fear, Kitchener; Doug Fetherling, Toronto; Mark Frank, Toronto; Greg Gatenby, Toronto; Marty Gervais, Windsor; Imogene Givens, Harley; Jim Harris, Hydro Glen; Karen Hendrick, Robarts Library, Toronto; William Humber, Toronto; Reg Innell, Toronto; Alootook Ipellie, Ottawa; Donald Jones, Toronto; Gwendolyn MacEwen, Toronto; Robert McMichael, Forest; Donald MacSween, Ottawa; Garry Manning, *Daily Mercury*, Guelph; Patricia Morley, Manotick; William F. E. Morley, Kingston; John Moss, Ottawa; Alice Neal, London; Linda Oliver, Toronto; Michael Power, Windsor; Steve Salmaniw, West Hill; Judith

and Milan Somborac, Collingwood; Albert Spratt, Mississauga; Robert Stacey, Toronto; Robert Sward, Toronto; Gladys Todd, Simcoe; William Toye, Toronto; Ronald Tripp, Thornhill; Jerry Tutunjian, Toronto; Hugh P. Walker, Scarborough; Jack Warwick, Toronto; Barbara and George Weider, Collingwood.

Manitoba: Department of Business Development and Tourism, Winnipeg; Provincial Archives, Winnipeg; Department of Cultural Affairs and Historical Resources, Winnipeg; Alexandre L. Amprimoz, St. John's College, Winnipeg; Tom Boreski, Cultural Affairs and Historical Resources, Winnipeg; Robert Kroetsch, Winnipeg.

Saskatchewan: Revenue, Supply and Services, Regina; Tourism and Small Business, Regina; Bill Harnum, Saskatoon; Morris C. Shumiatcher, Regina; Glen Sorestad, Saskatoon.

Alberta: Travel Alberta, Edmonton; Government Services: Public Affairs Bureau, Edmonton; Marlene Alt, Banff; Ted Davy, Calgary; Hugh Dempsey, Glenbow Centre, Calgary; Allan Shute, Edmonton; Rudy Wiebe, Edmonton.

British Columbia; Tourism British Columbia, Victoria; Greater Victoria Visitors Information Centre, Victoria; Diane Ackerman, Victoria; Mary Lile Benham, Victoria; Allan Fotheringham, Vancouver; Grace E. Funk, Vernon; Percilla Groves, Simon Fraser University, Burnaby; W.J. Learning, The Vancouver Playhouse, Vancouver; Susan Musgrave, Sidney; John Newlove, Nelson; George Noble, White Rock; Robin Skelton, Victoria; George Woodcock, Vancouver; J. Michael Yates, Burnaby.

Yukon Territory: Tourism Yukon, Whitehorse; Heritage and Cultural Resources, Whitehorse; Barbara McDougall, Whitehorse; Dick North, Whitehorse.

Northwest Territories: Travel Arctic, Yellowknife; Economic Development and Tourism, Frobisher Bay; Government Information, Yellowknife; Indian and Northern Affairs, Ottawa; Robin Gedalof, London; John MacDonald, Ottawa.

I should also acknowledge the Canada Council and the Ontario Arts Council. Although no requests were made on behalf of this book to these bodies, their assistance in the past permitted the amassing of much of the material that found its way into these pages. Anthony R. Hawke, publisher of Hounslow Press, assisted in many ways. Finally I must acknowledge my debt to my wife, Ruth Colombo, whose support, material and psychological, was indispensible.

Colombo's Literary Landmarks

Here is a list of three dozen of the top literary locales in the country. The selection of sites is necessarily subjective, yet it attempts to represent geographical, historical, social, and cultural concerns as well as strictly literary interests. Had this list been prepared by the editors of *Michelin Guide,* they would have added asterisks or stars to the entries:

*Interesting.

**Worth a detour.

***Worth a journey.

It is the opinion of the author of *Canadian Literary Landmarks* that all thirty-six sites are "Worth a journey." It is recognized that the average person is unlikely to visit No. 1, not to mention No. 36, but as these sites happen to be the first and last entries in the book, they mark a convenient and symbolic beginning and ending.

1. L'Anse aux Meadows, Epaves Bay, Nfld.
2. Haliburton House, Windsor, N.S.
3. Grand Pré National Park, Minas Basin, N.S.
4. Poets' Corner, Fredericton, N.B.
5. Green Gables, Cavendish, P.E.I.
6. Laure Conan Museum, Point-au-Pic, Que.
7. Bouchard House, Péribonca, Que.
8. Lower Town, Quebec City, Que.
9. Arts Building, McGill University, Montreal, Que.
10. St. Urbain Street, Montreal, Que.
11. Library of Parliament, Ottawa, Ont.
12. "Salterton," Kingston, Ont.
13. "Literary Lakefield," Lakefield, Ont.
14. Stephen Leacock's Home, Orillia, Ont.
15. "Jalna," Clarkson, Ont.
16. Victoria College, Toronto, Ont.
17. Cabbagetown, Toronto, Ont.
18. Massey College, Toronto, Ont.
19. Harbourfront, Toronto, Ont.
20. John McCrae's Home, Guelph, Ont.
21. Chiefswood, Onondaga, Ont.
22. Stratford Festival, Stratford, Ont.
23. Uncle Tom's Cabin, Dresden, Ont.
24. Riel's Gravesite, St. Boniface, Man.
25. Charles W. Gordon's House, Winnipeg, Man.
26. "Street of Riches," Winnipeg, Man.
27. Nellie McClung's House, La Rivière, Man.
28. "Manawaka," Neepawa, Man.
29. F. P. Grove's Gravesite, Rapid City, Man.
30. Grey Owl's Cabin, Prince Albert Provincial Park, Sask.
31. S. G. Stephansson's Homestead, Markerville, Alta.
32. "W. O. Mitchell Country," High River, Alta.
33. Dollarton Beach, Vancouver, B.C.
34. Siwash Rock, Stanley Park, Vancouver, B.C.
35. Robert Service's Cabin, Dawson, Y.T.
36. North Pole, N.W.T.

A close reading of the Greenlander's Saga and other early narratives led to the discovery of evidence of Norse settlement near the remote fishing village of L'Anse aux Meadows, Nfld. Eight house-sites, including a smithy, have been restored. [Parks Canada]

Newfoundland

L'Anse aux Meadows

Located on the northeastern tip of Newfoundland, north of St. Anthony, L'Anse aux Meadows is a National Historic Park and a Unesco World Heritage Site. Here the Norwegian explorer Helge Ingstad in the 1960s found the remains of a Viking settlement, confirming the words of the *Greenlander's Saga,* an Icelandic prose narrative by an unknown scribe, about Leif the Lucky's landfall around the year A.D. 1000: ". . . and Leif named the land for what it grew and called it Wineland." The *Saga* was translated by George Johnston (b.1913) in 1976. Al Purdy (b. 1918), who visited the Viking site, wrote movingly about it in "Over the Hills in the Rain, My Dear" in *Being Alive: Poems 1958-78* (1978).

L'Anse aux Meadows appears on the World Heritage List, a roster of sites that are recognized by Unesco as possessing natural and cultural properties of outstanding universal value. By 1984, 164 sites had been so recognized in 78 countries. In Canada there are eight World Heritage Sites and more are in the planning stage. The Canadian World Heritage Sites are listed here:

> L'Anse aux Meadows National Historic Park, Nfld.
> Dinosaur Provincial Park, Alta.
> Head-Smashed-in Bison Jump, Alta.
> Wood Buffalo National Park, Alta. & N.W.T.
> Anthony Island Provincial Park, B.C.
> Burgess Shale, Yoho National Park, B.C.
> Kluane National Park, Y.T.
> Nahanni National Park, N.W.T.

Avalon Peninsula

The Avalon Peninsula, the southeastern portion of Newfoundland, is the setting of *The Boat Who Wouldn't Float* (1969), an amusing book by Farley Mowat (b. 1921) who has lived in outports here. "She lay hauled out at Muddy Hole, a small fishing village on the east coast of the Avalon Peninsula — a coast that is rather inexplicably called the Southern Shore, perhaps because it lies south of St. John's and St. John's is, in its own eyes at least, the centre of the universe." Mowat continued, "Tourist maps show Muddy Hole as being connected to St. John's by road. This is a typical Newfoundland 'jolly.'"

"Baleena"   See BURGEO.

Bay Despair

Ship Hole is an outport near Bay Despair on the southern coast of Newfoundland. It is the home port of the *Black Joke* which was engaged in rum-running in the 1930s in Farley Mowat's *The Black Joke* (1963), possibly the only work of fiction written by a Canadian with scenes set in the ports of St. Pierre and Miquelon, French possessions off the southern tip of Newfoundland. In this juvenile adventure of the sea, there is a description of the outport. "Ship Hole stood revealed as a typical Newfoundland fishing village, with its handful of houses facing the waterfront, its small square church, and the more imposing and concentrated cluster of buildings and wharves belonging to the local merchant. There were no roads in Ship Hole or vehicles either. Narrow, twisting paths connected the various parts of the settlement; but the sea was the real highway, and the whole life of the inhabitants depended on the sea."

Bay Roberts

Bay Roberts, on Conception Bay, figures as "Peterport" in *The New Priest in Conception Bay* (1858), the first novel written about life in Newfoundland. The author, Boston-born Robert Traill Spence Lowell (1816-1891), based it on his experiences as a medical missionary of the English Society for the Propagation of the Gospel at Bay Roberts. Lowell was the brother of the American literary critic James Russell Lowell (1819-1891) and the grandfather of the American poet Robert Lowell (1917-1977).

Beachy Cove

Beachy Cove is a wild, cliff-ringed bay between Portugal Cove and St. Philips, on Conception Bay. The novelist Harold Horwood (b. 1923) has lived here and made it the locale of his novel *The Foxes of Beachy Cove* (1967). Horwood has written: "Farley Mowat wrote one of his books, *The Black Joke,* at my house in Beachy Cove. I wrote the penultimate version of *Tomorrow Will Be Sunday* at his house in Burgeo (several years before the whale)" — a reference to the whale "Moby Joe" whose death Mowat lamented in *A Whale for the Killing* (1972).

Brigus

The fishing village of Brigus, situated at the head of Conception Bay, was the birthplace of Robert A. Bartlett (1875-1946) — "Captain Bob" — the sea captain who commanded the *Karluk* on Vilhjalmur Stefansson's Arctic Expedition of 1914 and later published an account of his experiences. His home, Hawthorne Cottage, was declared a National Historic Site in 1982. He is buried in the nearby churchyard where a memorial marks his last resting place.

Rockwell Kent (1882-1971), the American realist painter of unconventional views, settled briefly with his family in Brigus. During World War One he was suspected of being a German spy and deported. In later years he was suspected by the American government of being a communist sympathizer. All things considered, he probably preferred the Newfoundlanders to his fellow Americans. He discusses life in Brigus in his autobiography, *It's Me O Lord* (1955). Kent appears as the artist Peter Keen in *The Eyes of the Gull* (1936), a novel by Margaret Iris Duley (1894-1968).

Bristol's Hope   See HARBOUR GRACE.

Burgeo

This isolated fishing community, on the southwest coast, may well be the only outport known by name to mainlanders. For it was here that Farley Mowat (b. 1921) and his wife Claire took up residence in 1962-67, becoming Burgeo's most popular "come-from-away" residents. Mowat was named custodian of the whale that was beached here from January 20 to February 6, 1967. When Mowat complained that outporters were shooting bullets into the whale (nicknamed "Moby Joe") his popularity declined. He wrote *A Whale for the Killing* (1972) which was filmed in 1981. Claire Mowat published a fictionalized memoir of life in "Baleena" titled *The Outport People* (1983).

Burgeo has a literary background that predates the residency of the Mowats. Clyde Rose (b. 1937), the

Farley Mowat and his wife Claire Mowat are one-time residents of Burgeo. Both have written books about outport life. [NFB / In Search of Farley Mowat; McCLelland & Stewart / Paul Orenstein]

publisher of Breakwater Books, was born and educated here. William Gough (b. 1945), poet and author of *Maud's House* (1984), lived here in 1953-55. His novel is set in "King's Cove," modelled in part on Burgeo.

Cape Bonaventure

Local tradition maintains that Cape Bonaventure, Trinity Bay, is the site of the landfall made by the explorer John Cabot on June 24, 1497. A plaque was raised by the Historic Sites and Monuments Board of Canada to mark the site. However, current opinion holds that Cabot made his landfall on the southern coast of Nova Scotia or on the coast of Maine. There is a plaque with a somewhat similar inscription at Cape North, N.S.

Cape Porcupine   See LABRADOR.

Cape St. Mary's

This small fishing community on the southwest tip of the Avalon Peninsula is celebrated in one of the most moving and popular of Newfoundland's folk songs. The song is called "Let Me Fish off Cape St. Mary's" and it was written in 1947 by Otto Kelland (b. 1904), the balladier and one-time resident of the outport. The final verse runs: "Take me back to that snug green cove / Where the seas roll up their thunder. / There let me rest in the earth's cool breast, / Where the stars shine out their wonder, / And the seas roll up their thunder."

Cape Spear

Cape Spear, on the Atlantic coast southeast of St. John's, is the most easterly point in North America. It is 3,223 miles or 5,187 km in a straight line across Canada to Mount St. Elias, Y.T. Terry Fox (1958-1981) commenced his "Marathon of Hope" at Cape Spear, jogging across the country to raise "one dollar for every Canadian" for cancer research.

Change Island

A native of this island, located in Notre Dame Bay on the north coast, is A. R. Scammell (b. 1913), writer and song-writer. He is well known for having composed in 1928, as a school assignment, the words and music of "The Squid-Jiggin' Ground," which perfectly captures the life and language of the fisherfolk of Change Island. The lyrics appear in Scammell's collection *My Newfoundland* (1966).

Churchill Falls   See LABRADOR.

Coley's Point

This small outport, on Conception Bay, is the birthplace of David French (b. 1939), the dramatist. He lived here until 1945 when the family moved to Toronto. Coley's Point acts as the setting or background for two of his most powerful plays, *Leaving Home* (1972) and *Of the Fields, Lately* (1975).

In this scene from the Festival '73 production of David French's Leaving Home *at the Arts and Culture Centre, St. John's, Mary was played by Joy Taylor, Billy by Len Madden, and Ben by Leslie Mulholland.* [Performing Arts / Richard Stoker]

Come-By-Chance

Come-By-Chance, south of Clarenville, may well have the loveliest name of any place in the country. It is the birthplace of humorist Ray Guy (b. 1939), who grew up in Arnold's Cove, Placentia Bay. While writing for the *St. John's Evening Telegram*, he poked fun at Joey Smallwood — creating or at least popularizing the tag "the only living father of Confederation" — and honed his skills as a satirist. One of his liveliest books is *You May Know Them As Sea Urchins, Ma'am* (1975), which displays his humour to advantage: witty, subtle and irreverent.

Corner Brook

The city of Corner Brook, on the west coast of the Island, appears as "Milltown" in *House of Hate* (1970), the powerful autobiographical novel by Percy Janes (b. 1922). The house of Saul Stone and his family is located on "Humber Heights." The description runs: "We did not live on a street. The straggling, stony lane, rising up from the beach to our house and beyond, pulled crazily from one side to the other by the staggered line of houses, was known simply as the hill."

Fermeuse Bay

Admiral's Cove, Fermeuse Bay, on the east coast of the Avalon Peninsula, was the birthplace of Richard Brothers (1757-1824), self-proclaimed mystic and British Israelite, whose notions influenced the British-Israel World Federation, founded in 1919. After a brief stint in the Royal Navy, Brothers settled in London in 1787 where he began to speak of his "Holy Mission." He wrote two prophetic works which outlined his many revelations and prophecies. Brothers was arrested in 1795 for prophesying his own ascension to the British throne. At one time he commanded a great reading audience in England, Ireland, the United States, and Continental Europe, but by the turn of the century he had slipped into obscurity. In 1806 he was released from the private asylum where he had been imprisoned and lived a relatively peaceful life until his death in 1824. As Harold Horwood noted in his travel book *Newfoundland* (1969), Brothers and his ideas were taken seriously almost everywhere except in his native Admiral's Cove.

Fogo

This small fishing community, on Fogo Island, off the northeastern coast, is mentioned by name in the popular folksong "I'se the B'y that Builds the Boat." The so-called Fogo Process was developed here in 1967 by the National Film Board and Memorial University. Film and video are used to stimulate individual and group action to foster desirable community change.

Fogo Island holds a special place in the mythology of the Flat Earth Society, members of which maintain that the Earth is shaped like a pancake with an Edge or Great Abyss which may be sighted (weather permitting) at the North Pole or off Fogo Island. This at least is the belief of the Flat Earth Society as reconstituted in Fredericton, N.B., in 1973. (The original Flat Earth Society of Great Britain fell into desuetude some time earlier.) The Canadian founders included poet Alden Nowlan, philosopher Leo Ferrari, and writer Raymond Fraser. Several hundred people are members, including Eugene Ionesco. It was the poet Al Pittman who first sighted "the Edge" off Fogo Island, and the intrepid Dr. Ferrari actually fell over the edge, or so he alleges, but saved himself by clutching on a projecting rock and pulling himself back, the only man alive known to have survived such an ordeal.

Picturesque view of Fogo Island. [Nfld. Department of Development]

Gambo

The small community of Gambo, near Bonavista Bay, is the birthplace of Joseph R. (Joey) Smallwood (b. 1900). He worked as a printer, typesetter, reporter and newspaper editor before he became known to his fellow Newfoundlanders as "the Barrelman" on radio in 1937-43. He made use of his popularity as a patriot and story-teller to enter politics. He brought Newfoundland — "screaming," some say — into Confederation, serving as the Island's first premier (1949-72). A prolific writer and speaker on behalf of "the Great Island," he edited *The Book of Newfoundland* (1937) and *Encyclopedia of Newfoundland and Labrador* (from 1981). Richard Gwyn (b. 1934) told his story in *Smallwood: The Unlikely Revolutionary* (1968, 1972), and Joey told his own story in his memoirs, *I Chose Canada* (1973), which waxes eloquent about his first career as a pig-farmer.

Grand Banks

The Grand Banks, a shallow area of the continental shelf in the Atlantic Ocean off Newfoundland, are one of the world's richest fishing grounds. A number of ballads about fishing and shipwrecks bear the title "The Banks of Newfoundland." The best novel set in this spawning area is *Captains Courageous* (1897) by Rudyard Kipling (1865-1936). Subtitled "A Story of the Grand Banks," it tells how a young fellow becomes a man aboard a fishing schooner. Kipling wrote the novel in Brattleboro, Vermont. He described the Grand Banks as "a triangle two hundred and fifty miles on each side — a waste of wallowing sea, cloaked with dank fog, vexed with gales, harried with drifting ice, scored by the tracks of reckless livers, and dotted with the sails of the fishing-fleet." *Captains Courageous,* directed by Victor Fleming, was filmed in 1938.

One of the greatest peacetime marine disasters occurred south of Newfoundland. This was the sinking of the White Star liner *Titanic* the evening of April 14, 1912.

Spencer Tracy won an Academy Award for his portrayal of a wise fisherman in Captains Courageous, *the film version of Rudyard Kipling's novel about a boy (Freddie Bartholomew) who learns to be a man off the Grand Banks. [Ontario Film Institute]*

Thomas Hardy (1840-1928) was inspired to write a poem, "The Convergence of the Twain" (1912), and E. J. Pratt (1882-1964) a narrative called "The Titanic" (1935) in which he described the iceberg that ripped into the *Titanic* as "calved from a glacier near Godhaven coast." Richard Brown, a marine biologist at the Bedford Institute of Oceanography, Halifax, wrote *Voyage of the Iceberg* (1983) which is subtitled "The Story of the Iceberg that Sank the Titanic."

Pratt set a second narrative poem in these waters. He turned to the North Atlantic off the northeastern coast of Newfoundland for "The Cachalot" (1925), his epic tale of the whale fishery. The fast-moving poem gives some inkling of the drama of the seas daily enacted by cold-blooded creatures.

Grand Falls

At Grand Falls, on the Exploits River, a plaque erected in 1980 commemorates the Beothuks, a small nation of Newfoundland natives exterminated by both the Micmac Indians and the white population. The Beothuks were the original "Red Indians," for they painted themselves with red ochre, and their fate informs such imaginative works as the novel *Riverrun* (1973) by Peter Such (b. 1939). The last known survivor of this nation was a young woman named Shanawdithit. She died in St. John's in June 1829 and was buried in the Church of England Cemetery on the Southside Hills. "Her grave, however, no longer exists," explained Pierre Berton in "The Last of the Red Indians" from *My Country: The Remarkable Past* (1976). "It was dug up to make way for a new road and so her bones, like those of all her people, are lost forever."

Gordon Pinsent wrote and starred in The Rowdyman. *The part of Estelle Wall, his sister, was played by Mary Cole. [Ontario Film Institute]*

Grand Falls is the birthplace of Gordon Pinsent (b. 1930), actor and writer. He wrote and starred in the 1972 movie *The Rowdyman* which he made into a novel two years later. He played Will Cole, a happy-go-lucky native of Corner Brook, who caused the death of his best friend.

Happy Valley   See LABRADOR.

Harbour Grace
The historic town of Harbour Grace, on Conception Bay, was first governed by the English poetaster Robert Hayman (1575-1629). Having little to occupy himself between 1618 and 1628, he composed epigrams in verse which celebrated life in the colony. "The Aire, in *New-found-Land* is wholesome, good," he wrote in *Quodlibets* (1628), with an eye on colonization. This collection of verse is said to be the first English book written in North America. The colony of which Hayman was governor was called Bristol's Hope.

Kelligrews
The village of Kelligrews, on the east coast of Conception Bay, was the inspiration and setting of the lively ballad "The Kelligrews' Soiree." Written by John Burke (1851-1930), the so-called Bard of Prescott Street, St. John's, it celebrates the "spree" here in which "there was birch rhine, tar twine, / Cherry wine and turpentine," etc.

Labrador
Labrador comprises a huge area which is geographically part of the Province of Quebec but politically associated with Newfoundland. It has twice the area of "the Great Island." Newfoundland's claim to the land drained by the rivers that flow into the Atlantic was confirmed by a decision of the Judicial Committee of the British Privy Council in 1926.

Surprisingly, Labrador is one of the two Canadian locations that appear on the Surrealists' Map of the World, drawn by Yves Tanguy and published in 1929. (The other location is the Queen Charlotte Islands, B.C.; no doubt they were chosen on account of their totem poles and Haida carvings.) No one is certain why the French surrealists were impressed — at a distance — by rocky Labrador. Perhaps Tanguy and others were familiar with the description of the land by Jacques Cartier (1491-1557). Sailing along the bleak coast of Labrador in 1534, he described the region as "the land God gave to Cain." This may well be the first literary description of a Canadian place. Certainly it is suitably demonic.

Cape Porcupine Cape Porcupine, on the coast of Labrador, was identified by the Norwegian explorer Helge Ingstad in the 1960s with Forest Land (or Markland) mentioned in the Icelandic prose narrative *The Greenlander's Saga*. Here, about A.D. 1001, Leif the Lucky is said to have exclaimed: "By its worth shall this land be named, and called Forest Land."

Churchill Falls Churchill Falls is a 245-foot cataract on the Churchill River in Labrador. The falls and river were named by Newfoundland Premier Joseph R. Smallwood after Sir Winston Churchill (1874-1965), British war leader and Nobel laureate in Literature. The Churchill Falls Power Project, the largest in the Western world, was completed in 1974.

Happy Valley The government building in Happy Valley, east of Goose Bay, Labrador, was named in 1980 after the author Elizabeth Goudie (1902-1982). One of the outstanding women of Newfoundland and Labrador, she contributed to the heritage of Labrador and was the first native of Labrador to have a book published. *Woman of Labrador* (1973) recounts her life as the wife of a trapper.

Nain The first Moravian mission was established at Nain, on the east coast, in 1771. Fluent in the language of the Greenland Eskimos, the Moravian missionaries began in the late eighteenth century to distribute passages from the Scriptures in the Eskimo language, using Roman orthography rather than the syllabic system which later found acceptance.

The small settlement is the setting of Harold Horwood's novel *The White Eskimo* (1972). Horwood, as well as being a novelist and journalist, served in 1949 in the Newfoundland House of Assembly as the first representative for Labrador. Other sites specifically mentioned in the novel are Okak and the Kiglapaite Mountains.

Maid Marion Falls
Maid Marion Falls is on the Naskaupi River, north of Churchill Falls. The name derives from the legend of Robin Hood, as does Robin Hood Bay.

"Milltown" See CORNER BROOK.

Milton
A plaque located at Milton, near Clarenville, Trinity Bay, was unveiled in 1959 to commemorate the celebrated expedition across the interior of Newfoundland made in 1822 by William Epps Cormack, with Joe Sylvester as his guide. Cormack, a native Newfoundlander, was the first to penetrate the interior of Newfoundland. His famous *Narrative of a Journey across the Island of Newfoundland* (1856) tells how he tried to establish contact with the Beothuk Indians, but failed as the nation was in decline. The trek took place from Shoal Harbour, Trinity Bay, in the east to St. George's Harbour in the west.

Nain See LABRADOR.

Pass Island
Pass Island, in Hermitage Bay, might be the model for "Pigeon Inlet," which is the setting of many of the stories written by Ted Russell (1904-1977), who was born at Coley's Point, Conception Bay, and began his career as a teacher at Pass Island. His best-known collections of stories of outport life are *The Holdin' Ground* (1970), *The Chronicles of Uncle Mose* (1975), and *Tales from Pigeon Inlet* (1977). His "Uncle Mose" stories were popular on CBC Radio on "the Great Island."

Peckford Island
"Before them lay open country covered with apple trees laden with fruit." So runs the description of the Earthly

Paradise said to be reached by St. Brendan the Navigator, the Irish abbot and missionary who flourished between 484 and 578. The description comes from the Latin account of St. Brendan's voyage, *Navigatio Sancti Brendani,* set down by an unknown scribe some three centuries later. It has been translated a number of times, notably by J. F. Webb as *The Voyage of St. Brendan* (1965).

It is not likely the Celtic imagination of the unknown scribe was inspired by bleak Peckford Island on the east coast of Newfoundland. Yet when the modern-day explorer and writer, Tim Severin, undertook to recreate St. Brendan's voyage from Ireland to America, via Iceland and Greenland, in a rudderless, leather-sewn *currah,* it was at Peckford Island that his little boat came to rest on June 26, 1977. Severin tells the full story in *The Brendan Voyage* (1978). St. Brendan, it seems, in search of the Earthly Paradise, found Newfoundland.

"Peterport" See BAY ROBERTS.

Port de Grave
Born at Port de Grave, south of Carbonear on Conception Bay, was Daniel Woodley Prowse (1834-1914). He was the author of *The History of Newfoundland* (1895), the first extensive modern account of "the Great Island."

Random Island
The comparative isolation of Random Island, in Trinity Bay, suits the temperament of the Anglo-Irish playwright, Michael Cook (b. 1933), who settled in Newfoundland in 1965. After teaching at Memorial University, St. John's, he moved in 1975 to Random Island to write radio, television, and stage plays. *Head Guts and Soundbone Dance* is a compassionate portrait of a fishing culture, and *Jacob's Wake* chronicles the collapse of a culture confronting the twentieth century.

Robin Hood Bay
Robin Hood Bay is on the west side of Trinity Bay, which is northwest of St. John's. The name derives, as does Maid Marion Falls, from the English legend of the outlaw of Sherwood Forest. There is an early reference to Robin Hood in the Middle English poem *The Vision of Piers Ploughman,* written between 1360 and 1399.

St. Anthony
Outside the Curtis Memorial Hospital in St. Anthony, on the northeast coast, a plaque was unveiled in 1980 to honour Sir Wilfred Grenfell (1865-1940), the English-born medical missionary who devoted his life to the health and well-being of the fishermen of Newfoundland and Labrador. A man of many talents, Dr. Grenfell wrote such works of fiction about his experiences as *The Harvest of the Sea* (1905), *Down to the Sea* (1910), and *Tales of the Labrador* (1916). Tradition has it that the novelist Norman Duncan (1871-1916) used Dr. Grenfell as the model for the hero of his popular novel *Dr. Luke of The Labrador* (1904), although Duncan himself always denied this. The ashes of the missionary and his wife are buried under a granite rock at Fox Farm Hill which overlooks the St. Anthony hospital. The International Grenfell Association, founded in 1912, continues the missionary's work.

Sir Wilfred Grenfell, 5¢ stamp, 1965. [Canada Post Corporation]

Statue of Sir Wilfred Grenfell, St. Anthony. [Nfld. Department of Development]

St. John's
The historic city of St. John's is the capital of Newfoundland which once was Britain's oldest colony but now is Canada's youngest province, having joined Confederation in 1949. Water Street, one of St. John's principal thoroughfares, has been called "the oldest street in North America." There are many descriptions of the colony and city from the earliest of times to the present, but perhaps the most vivid evocation of the city today is "The Wind through St. John's," a poem included by Earle Birney (b. 1904) in his collection *Fall by Fury* (1978).

John Burke John Burke (1851-1930) was known as "The Bard of Prescott Street." He was born in St. John's, probably at 10 Kings Road, and was a clerk in the O'Dyer firm on Water Street. He wrote songs to make extra money. "The Kelligrews' Soiree" (which Joey Smallwood has called "a classic folklore song known throughout Newfoundland") was written as a take-off on snobbery among the upper classes. Other popular songs are "Wedding in Renews" and "Betsy Brennan's Blue Hen." The texts of these appear in Paul Mercer's collection *The Ballads of Johnny Burke* (1974). He lived at 74 Prescott Street for many years, but from the early 1900s to his death his home was the house at 62 Prescott Street.

Bowring Park Among the monuments and memorials erected in Bowring Park in downtown St. John's stands a statue of Peter Pan, the embodiment of youth in the children's fantasy *Peter Pan* (1904) by the Scottish dramatist and novelist J. M. Barrie (1860-1937). It is a replica of the statue commissioned by the author and erected in Kensington Gardens, London. It was presented to the city by Sir Edgar R. Bowring in memory of a young girl who drowned in the *Florizel* disaster on February 19, 1918. This disaster is the subject of *A Winter's Tale: The Wreck of the Florizel* (1976) by Cassie Brown (b. 1919).

Statue of Peter Pan, Bowring Park, St. John's [Nfld. Department of Development]

The Newfoundland Museum in St. John's. [Nfld. Department of Development]

Newfoundland Museum The most poignant exhibit in the Newfoundland Museum's Beothuk collection is the caribou-skin coat made and worn by Shanawdithit, the last of the Beothuks, who died in St. John's in 1829. "The Beothuks were among the first native people of North America to be seen by European explorers," runs the wording on the plaque raised in St. John's in their honour. "The destruction of the nation was a direct consequence of European intrusions." Al Purdy (b. 1918) has a poem called "Beothuck Indian Skeleton in Glass Case, St. John's Museum" in *Bursting into Song* (1982).

Confederation Building On the grounds of the Confederation Building, the seat of the Provincial Legislature, a plaque acknowledges "Newfoundland's Entry in Confederation," which occurred on March 31, 1949. Thus it

Confederation Building, St. John's. [Nfld. Department of Development]

draws attention to Joseph R. (Joey) Smallwood (b. 1900), former premier and "only living father of Confederation," who was born at Gambo. On the grounds is a statue of Sir Wilfred Grenfell (1865-1940), the medical missionary whose main monument stands at St. Anthony. The Confederation Building is the setting for some sections of the political novel *Clapp's Rock* (1983) by William Rowe (b. 1942), a lawyer and former member of the Legislature.

Harold Horwood The novelist and journalist Harold Horwood was born in St. John's in 1923 and grew up at 134 Campbell Avenue in the house built by Captain John Horwood, whom Harold calls "the family's first writer," and occupied in the 1980s by his grandson, Charles Horwood, also a writer. Harold was associated with the movement to bring Newfoundland into Confederation and in 1949 he became the first member to sit in the House of Assembly for Labrador. He has written such

Author Harold Horwood emerges from a mukluk in this drawing by Don Evans who draws as Isaac Bickerstaff. [Special Collections, University of Calgary Libraries]

novels as *Tomorrow Will Be Sunday* (1966), which is set in an outport called "Caplin Bight," *The Foxes of Beachy Cove*, (1967), and *The White Eskimo* (1972).

St. John's Evening Telegram The *St. John's Evening Telegram* is one of the province's two principal newspapers, the other being the *St. John's Daily News*. The *Evening Telegram*, which calls itself "The People's Paper," was founded in 1879. Before its sale to the Thomson empire its columns were noted for some of the most spirited writing in Canadian journalism. Contributors in the pre-Thomson days have included Michael Cook (b. 1933), Harold Horwood (who was a columnist in 1952-58), and Ray Guy (b. 1939) who shifted from straight reportage to satire in the 1960s.

Memorial University Memorial University, at St. John's, was founded in 1925 as a memorial to the men of New-foundland and Labrador who died in the First World War and is the principal university on the Island. In 1981 a new university building was named the Captain Robert A. Bartlett Building to honour "Captain Bob" of Brigus.

The Memorial University of Newfoundland Folklore and Language Archive, one of the most exciting in the country, was created in 1968 by the American-born scholar Herbert Halpert (b. 1911). The collection embraces 6,700 original sound recordings, 5,000 separate manuscripts, 10,000 photographs, plus other materials including video. While serving in 1946 with the U.S. Army in Gander, Halpert met Joey Smallwood who assured him that there was no more Newfoundland folklore to collect, that Smallwood had collected it all!

The Queen Elizabeth II Library of Memorial University houses the Centre for Newfoundland Studies which has begun to acquire the work of Newfoundland authors. Its holdings include the literary papers of Phoebe Florence Miller (1889-1979), "poet and postmistress" of Topsail; scripts of the "Barrelman Radio Programs" between 1937 and 1955; typescripts of the film and novel versions of *The Rowdyman,* by the actor-writer Gordon Pinsent; and the work-in-progress of the poet Alastair Macdonald.

A National Historic Plaque, unveiled in 1981 in the Library, honours Margaret Iris Duley (1894-1968), a native of St. John's, who wrote four novels — *The Eyes of the Gull* (1936), *Cold Pastoral* (1938), *Highway to Valour* (1941), and *Novelty on Earth* (1942) — as well as a work of non-fiction, *The Caribou Hut* (1949). Her work is noted for its vivid portrayal of Newfoundland and its people. She lived on Monkstown Road and is buried in the General Protestant Cemetery, Wakeford Bridge Road.

A number of writers are associated with the English Department of Memorial University, which is headed by Patrick O'Flaherty who, with Peter F. Neary, edited *By Great Waters: A Newfoundland and Labrador Anthology* (1974). Clyde Rose (b. 1937), who established Break-water Books with the poet Al Pittman (b. 1940), has edited such collections as *The Blasty Bough* (1976) and *Baffles of Wind and Tide* (1973).

A grand undertaking of noble proportions was the twenty-year compilation and publication of *Dictionary of Newfoundland English* (1982), edited by George M. Story, W. J. Kirwin, and J. D. A. Widdowson of the Department of English. It documents the characteristic vocabulary of Newfoundlanders from "Aaron's Rod" to "Zad" (local pronunciation for the last letter of the alphabet."

Leaning against the motor car is the poet E. J. Pratt. Seated on the running board are his wife Viola (left) and his sister Charlotte (middle). Taken near Holyrood, Conception Bay, 1925. [Viola and Claire Pratt]

Sally's Cove
It was at Sally's Cove, in Gros Morne National Park, that Elisabeth Bristol Greenleaf, then a Grenfell mission teacher, began to collect folklore in 1920. Nine years later, with Grace Yarrow Mansfield, she formed the Vasser College Folklore Expedition to this area. The result of their work was the publication of *Ballads and Sea Songs of Newfoundland* (1933).

Toslow
"Straight through the Channel to Toslow we'll go," runs the last line of the chorus of "The Ryans and the Pittmans," the popular Newfoundland folk song which begins: "We'll rant and we'll roar like true Newfound-landers. . . ." Toslow is a small outport community on Placentia Bay. It is located on Burin Peninsula, opposite Argentia. In the folk song it is the home of the girl who is "the nicest of all." The song appears in *The Penguin Book of Canadian Folk Songs* (1973) edited by Edith Fowke.

"Wachna"   See SCHEFFERVILLE, Que.

Western Bay
E. J. Pratt (1882-1964), the narrative poet, was born in this small outport on the shore of Conception Bay. He spent his early years here and in half a dozen fishing villages up and down the coast where his father served as a clergyman. At the age of fifteen, he left for St. John's where he received his early education. In 1903, he taught and preached in various outports. Four years later he decided to continue his education at Victoria College, University of Toronto. His major publications include *Newfoundland Verse* (1923), *Brébeuf and His Brethren* (1940), *Towards the Last Spike* (1952), and his *Collected Poems* (1958). In the words of the National Historic Sites and Monuments Board's plaque, unveiled on the Post Office Grounds in 1978: "His poetry deals with grand themes such as evolution, the heroic in history, and man's struggle with the forces of nature. In many poems the images of sea and rock echo his Newfoundland beginnings."

Writers Island
Writers Island is in Bonavista Bay, south of Brown Fox Island, Little Fox Island, and Silver Fox Island. The Canadian Permanent Committee on Geographical Names offers no explanation for this place name which is officially spelled (like Peggys Cove, N.S.) without an apostrophe.

Nova Scotia

Afton River

This river, which flows midway between Antigonish and Port Hawkesbury, was named after the river in Scotland celebrated by Robert Burns (1759-1796) in the song which begins, "Flow gently, sweet Afton, among thy green braes. . . ." There is also an Upper Afton and an Afton Indian Reserve.

Amherst

The town of Amherst is close to the New Brunswick border. At the corner of Princess and Church streets there stood a two-storey, yellow-painted cottage which in its day was Canada's most haunted house. Between 1878 and 1880, strange things happened here. Raps and knockings were heard, furniture moved on its own, fires broke out, objects flew about, words ("Esther Cox, you are mine to kill") formed on walls without visible hands to print them. (The phenomena were connected with the presence in the house of an 18-year-old girl by that name, and they ceased when she left.) Walter Hubbell's account, *The Haunted House* (1879), went through ten editions. Psychic investigators Hereward Carrington and Walter F. Prince studied "the Great Amherst Mystery," which R. S. Lambert in *Exploring the Supernatural* (1955) called "a classic case of poltergeist haunting, rarely equalled in any part of the world."

Also in Amherst, Oscar Wilde lectured on aesthetics at the Academy of Music in 1882. He told a local reporter that Canada's leading poets were Louis Fréchette, Charles G. D. Roberts, and Pelham Mulvany ("a man once well known at Trinity College").

Leon Trotsky, the Russian revolutionary, was held in a prisoner-of-war camp near Amherst from April 3 to 29, 1917. In his autobiography, *My Life* (1931), he contrasted the conditions of his incarceration unfavourably with those experienced in the Peter-Paul Fortress of St. Petersburg.

By a quirk of fate, the writer and artist Wyndham Lewis (1882-1957) was born on his father's yacht off Amherst. On the basis of this, and because he had an American father and an English mother, Lewis claimed status as an Anglo-Canadian and, indeed, served in the First World War with the Canadian War Artists. He spent much of the Second World War living in Toronto and Windsor, Ont., to his infinite regret.

The settlement of the Amherst area by farming folk from England is the theme of the fiction of Will R. Bird (1891-1984), notably his historical novel *Here Stays Good Yorkshire* (1945). Stories collected under the title *Sunrise for Peter* (1946) also evoke the area.

Annapolis Royal   See LOWER GRANVILLE.

Annapolis Valley   See BRIDGEWATER.

Antigonish

The town of Antigonish, midway between Halifax and Sydney, is internationally known as the home of the Antigonish Movement, a cooperative, self-help organization that grew out of the extension program of St. Francis Xavier University. The project was started in 1921 by Father James J. Tompkins (1870-1955) and Father Moses Michael Coady (1882-1959), both of whom wrote of the need to help men and women to become "masters of their own destiny." The university has published a literary journal, *The Antigonish Review*, since 1971.

General view of the campus of Saint Francis Xavier University, Antigonish. [Nova Scotia Department of Government Services Photograph]

Coady's work influenced a number of writers and public figures, including Conservative leader Brian Mulroney (b. 1939), author of *Where I Stand* (1983). The title poem of *O'Malley to the Reds and Other Poems* (1972), by Kenneth Leslie (1892-1974), is a tribute to Coady and his Christian Socialism.

Inspired by reports of a haunted house in Antigonish,

the American versifier Hughes Mearns wrote an amusing little quatrain called "Antigonish" (1899), which runs: "As I was going up the stair / I met a man who wasn't there! / He wasn't there again today! / I wish, I wish he'd stay away."

At Glen Bard, in Antigonish County, there is a plaque on the grounds of the local church erected in 1961 by the Antigonish Highland Society to Iain MacGille-Eathain (1787-1848), "The Bard MacLean, one of the most famous Gaelic poets who ever lived in this land. He was born in the Island of Tiree, Scotland, and came with his family to this country in the year 1819. He settled near this location. . . . 'Lone, brooding mid the gloom of forest ventures, my moods are fitful and my soul is wan.'"

Auburndale

Auburndale, northwest of Bridgewater in Lunenburg County, was named after the imaginary village of Auburn in *The Deserted Village* (1770) by the Anglo-Irish man of letters, Oliver Goldsmith (1728-1774).

Baddeck

Baddeck, in the beautiful Bras d'Or region of Cape Breton Island, is associated with the life and work of Alexander Graham Bell (1847-1922), the Scots-born scientist and inventor of, among other things, the telephone. He summered here at the estate he called *Beinn Bhreagh*, Gaelic for "beautiful mountain," which overlooks Bras d'Or, an inland sea that resembles a Scottish loch. Here he conducted experiments with airplanes and hydrofoils. His estate remains in private hands — owned by the Grosvenor family, publishers of the *National Geographic* magazine — but his gravesite may be visited, as well as the Bell Museum of Technological Design.

Modernistic exterior and interior of the Alexander Graham Bell Museum, Baddeck, N.S. [Dept. of Regional Industrial Expansion]

Alexander Graham Bell, 4¢ stamp, 1947. [Canada Post Corporation]

"Barringford"   See SHELBURNE.

Bridgewater

For many years the novelist Ernest Buckler (1908-1984) lived on a farm outside Bridgewater, in the Annapolis Valley. The valley and the surrounding hills are described in a general, poetic way in Buckler's novel, *The Mountain and the Valley* (1952). "Entremont" is the author's name for the farm in the novel. The Annapolis Valley is also the setting for Buckler's book of essays, *Ox Bells and Fireflies* (1968), and some of the stories that make up *The Rebellion of Young David* (1975). Buckler was born at Dalhousie West.

Ernest Buckler was caught between "the mountain and the valley" in this caricature by Isaac Bickerstaff (nom de plume of Don Evans). [Special Collections, University of Calgary Libraries]

Cape Blomidon

North of the village of Blomidon, on the shore of Minas Basin, is Cape Blomidon, a rocky region said to be the abode of Glooscap, the hero of Micmac legend. Folklorist Cyrus Macmillan (1880-1953) published two collections of Algonkian tales in 1918 and 1922; a selection was reprinted as *Glooscap's Country and Other Indian Tales* (1956). Kay Hill (b. 1917) has written *Glooscap and His Magic* (1963) and *More Glooscap Stories* (1970).

Cape North

At Cape North, on the northeastern tip of Cape Breton Island, stands a round stone tower six feet high. It is surmounted by a bust of the explorer John Cabot and a plaque below carries the following inscription: "Cabot's Landfall. On 24th June, 1497, in the *Matthew* out of Bristol, England, with a crew of eighteen men, John Cabot discovered the continent of North America. His landfall, *First Land Seen*, was in this vicinity, and is believed to have been the lofty headland of North Cape Breton. It is to commemorate this important event that this monument has been erected by the Cape Breton Historical Society." There is a somewhat similar inscription on a plaque at Cape Bonaventure, Nfld.

Chester

The summer home of retired diplomat and diarist Charles Ritchie (b. 1906) is at Chester, on Mahone Bay, southwest of Halifax. He extols the beauty and serenity of the region in *Storm Signals: More Undiplomatic Diaries, 1962-1971* (1983): "This south shore of Nova Scotia with its mixture of small fishing villages and sea inlets, sparkling in sun and wind, squat white farmhouses sheltered by trees and set in rough meadows, has a flavour all its own, never pinned on paper by painter or writer." Elsewhere in the same volume he considers the role of literature in adding "a dimension to living in Canada. One thing that makes for thinness in the air at home is just the lack of this dimension. A cityscape remains a private world until it has been put into words. But winter Montreal, thanks to Callaghan, and Halifax, thanks to Hugh MacLennan, are now on the literary map."

Dartmouth

Dartmouth is situated on the east side of Halifax harbour, and is known as the city with twenty-six lakes, surely a record number.

Joseph Howe (1804-1873), statesman and journalist, is recalled in the Howe Room of the Dartmouth Heritage Museum, which has re-created his study and contains such personal possessions as his watch, pipe, snuffbox and Micmac dictionary.

Helen Creighton (b.1899), well-loved collector of Maritime lore, lived from 1920 to 1978 at "Evergreen," 26 Newcastle Street. The house has two storeys and a turret and dates back to 1867. In 1978 it was acquired by the city as an historic site. It was Creighton who first collected the popular song "Farewell to Nova Scotia," subsequently adopted by Catherine McKinnon as her signature song.

Helen Creighton is shown here recording the reminiscences of a Lunenburg fisherman. [Edith Fowke]

D'Escousse

"Two general stores, a garage, a big, new church, a brick

school-house, a community hall, wharf: downtown D'Escousse." So did Silver Donald Cameron (b. 1937) describe his adopted village, on Isle Madame, facing the shore of Cape Breton Island. Although born in Toronto, the journalist and novelist has lived here since 1971, latterly in the village's only flat-roofed house. It has a view of the wharf, harbour, and Lennox Passage. His novel *Dragon Lady* (1980) is set in "Nectar Harbour," which would be D'Escousse if this village were situated on Petpeswick Inlet, near Halifax. "Belltower Lake" in the novel is derived from Belfry Lake, near Gabarus. After five years in D'Escousse, Cameron added to his name. Tired of being confused with other Donald Camerons, he began signing his articles Silver Donald Cameron, the "silver" being an allusion to the colour of his hair.

East Mapleton

East Mapleton, southwest of Pictou, is the birthplace of Will R. Bird (1891-1984). One of the province's most loved authors, he set his novels about farming life among English immigrants in this district. These include *Here Stays Good Yorkshire* (1945), *Judgment Glen* (1947), and *The Shy Yorkshireman* (1955). He recalled his childhood years nostalgically in *Ghosts Have Warm Hands* (1968). Perhaps he is most widely known for his short stories, collected in *Sunrise for Peter* (1946).

"Entremont" See BRIDGEWATER.

Eskasoni Island

Eskasoni is an island off East Bay, Cape Breton Island, and the home of the Micmac poet Rita Joe (b. 1931), author of the autobiographical poems in Micmac and English included in *Poems by Rita Joe* (1978).

Glace Bay

The mining community of Glace Bay is located on Cape Breton Island northeast of Sydney. Hugh MacLennan (b. 1907) was born here "in a small house, encircled by a brook, perched atop a grassy knoll a mile or so inland from the coast" (in the words of his biographer Elspeth Cameron). MacLennan was deeply influenced by his Cape Breton background and set his novel *Each Man's Son* (1951) in one of its small but unspecified communities.

Also born in Glace Bay were the labour versifier Dawn Fraser (1888-1968) and broadcaster and drama critic Nathan Cohen (1923-1971). In the 1920s Fraser read his protest poems at political meetings held in the Savoy and Russell theatres in Glace Bay — poems like "I Write Not What I Wish to Write but Rather What I Must" and "The Case of Jim McLachlan," collected in *Echoes from Labour's War* (1976). Cohen was educated at Mount Allison University and returned to Glace Bay to edit the one-man labour paper, *Glace Bay Gazette* (1942-44), published by his father, before commencing his career as an arts commentator and drama critic in Toronto.

Henry Wadsworth Longfellow, American poet whose North American themes brought him honour in Canada, photographed by Sarony, N.Y. [C-51933 / Public Archives Canada]

The statue of Evangeline (left) with the Church of St. Charles, is the heart of Grand Pré National Park, N.S. [Nova Scotia Department of Government Services Photograph] A detailed view of the Statue of Evangeline (right) at Grand Pré National Park. [Bill Brooks]

Longfellow's poetic tale of separated lovers has been popular with movie-goers. All that remains of the Evangeline made in 1913 by the Canadian Bioscope Company are stills, like the one on the left. On the right is a poster from the Fox Film Corporation's Evangeline of 1919. [Ontario Film Institute]

Grand Pré

The community of Grand Pré, at the head of the Bay of Fundy, will be forever associated with the Acadians who lived here until the order of Expulsion of 1755 drove them into exile. The community is the gateway to Grand Pré National Historic Park, the centrepiece of which is the Church of St. Charles which serves as a memorial museum. In front of the church stands the bronze statue of Evangeline. Begun by Philippe Hébert and completed by his son Henri, it depicts the Acadian heroine as a happy young girl or as a sad older woman, depending on the vantage point. Nearby is Evangeline's Well, which dates back to the period of English occupation and has been restored. Close by is a plaster bust of Henry Wadsworth Longfellow (1807-1882), the American poet whose narrative poem *Evangeline: A Tale of Acadie* (1847) gave classic expression to this tragic event. In the words of the plaque fastened to the memorial, he told millions of readers "the poignant tale of the exiled Acadian lovers of Grand Pré." Longfellow's version of the events was the basis of the first Canadian feature film, *Evangeline*, which

was released in 1914 to critical and financial acclaim. Unfortunately all known negatives and prints of this silent film have been lost or destroyed.

Longfellow was not alone in telling the story of the Expulsion in literary form. The title poem of *Low Tide on Grand Pré* (1893), the first book of lyrics by Bliss Carman (1861-1929), while it does not deal with the narrative, captures the solemn sadness of the locale. Sir Charles G. D. Roberts (1860-1943) told the Acadian side of events in two prose romances, *The Forge in the Forest* (1896) and *A Sister to Evangeline* (1898).

The picturesque region around Grand Pré has inevitably become known as Evangeline Country. Longfellow modelled his heroine on an actual Acadian woman, Emmeline Labiche; he modelled Gabriel, her inconstant lover, on Louis Arceneaux. To follow in their footsteps, one must trek beyond Evangeline Country, and indeed beyond the borders of Canada. The trail leads to St. Martinville, a town on the Bayou Teche, in the heart of Louisiana's Cajun country. In real life Emmeline and Louis found their separate ways to St. Martinville. Beneath Evangeline Oak, at the end of Port Street, the lovers who were long separated recognized one another. The grave of Emmeline Labiche may be found in the churchyard of St. Martin of Tours Catholic Church, 133

South Main Street; above the grave rises the statue of Evangeline, posed for by actress Dolores del Rio, who was the star of the movie *Evangeline,* filmed at nearby Catahoula Lake and released by Hollywood in 1929. North of St. Martinville, in Longfellow-Evangeline State Park, is the Acadian House Museum, which is reputed to be the cottage in which Louis Arceneaux lived with his wife.

Granville Ferry

The short-story writer and novelist H. R. Percy (b.1920) settled at Granville Ferry, near Annapolis Royal, in 1952 after a career in the Royal Canadian Navy. He writes in a cottage across the road from "The Moorings," which he has operated for bed and breakfast with his wife since 1973. He has written about the Annapolis Valley in such books as *The Timeless Island* (1960), *Flotsam* (1978), and *Painted Ladies* (1983).

Percy is not Granville Ferry's sole literary figure. His neighbour is the novelist and journalist Harold Horwood (b. 1923) who has written that "the most beautiful literary landmark in eastern Canada is 'The Moorings,' a Victorian house at Granville Ferry, almost within sight of my own home on Annapolis Basin."

Great Village

Great Village, at the head of the Bay of Fundy, is known as the "village of white" because the majority of its buildings are painted a dazzling white. Here the American poet Elizabeth Bishop (1911-1979) spent her childhood years. In such poems as "First Death in Nova Scotia," "Cape Breton," and "In the Village" from *The Complete Poems: 1927-1979* (1982), she captures perfectly Maritime characteristics. As she wrote in "The Map," "The names of seashore towns run out to sea, / the names of cities cross the neighbouring mountains. . . ."

Halifax

Halifax is the capital of Nova Scotia and the central city of the Atlantic provinces. Aware of the city's imperial past and its strategic naval importance, Rudyard Kipling (1865-1936) referred to it as "the warden of the north" in "The Song of the Cities" from *The Seven Seas* (1896): "Into the mist my guardian prows put forth, / Behind the mist my virgin ramparts lie, / The Warden of the Honour of the North, / Sleepless and veiled am I." The novelist Thomas H. Raddall (b. 1903), who was raised in Halifax, made use of the phrase in the title of his popular history, *Halifax: Warden of the North* (1948, 1965).

Joseph Howe's Halifax The life of Joseph Howe (1804-1873) is interwoven with the history of Halifax. Had he not been such a prominent political figure in his day, he would have been even more celebrated as a man of letters. Yet this "Tribune of Nova Scotia" left a varied and vivid literary legacy, as witness the continued popularity of such volumes as *The Speeches and Public Letters* (1858), *Poems*

Joseph Howe, 8¢ stamp, 1972. [Canada Post Corporation]

The statue of Joseph Howe (top left) on the grounds of Province House, Halifax. [Nova Scotia Department of Government Services Photograph] Province House with the statue of Joseph Howe in the park, Halifax. [Nova Scotia Communication & Information Centre]

C. W. Jefferys' drawing of Joseph Howe (bottom) Speaking at an Open Air Meeting. [C-73666 / Public Archives Canada]

and *Essays* (1874), and *Western and Eastern Rambles* (1973).

The small cottage in which Howe was born has long been a thing of the past. But a small cairn and plaque mark the spot where the cottage stood at 5956 Emscote Drive. In the Public Archives of Nova Scotia, on South Street, may be viewed the printing press on which he printed the *Novascotian,* the spirited newspaper which carried the first of Nova Scotian humorist T. C. Haliburton's "Sam Slick" narratives.

Charged with criminal libel, he delivered his famous, two-day speech in defence of an "unshackled press" in the old Courthouse in March 1835. This handsome Georgian building, now called Province House, on George Street, is the oldest legislative building in Canada. Howe was acquitted and acquired the status of a folk hero. He served as a member of the Legislature for twenty-five years and, from 1860 to 1863, as premier. A plaster statue depicting him with his right arm out-thrust stands in the Legislative Library. The original, in bronze, stands outside the Legislative Building on the south end of the Lower Parade.

Government House, the grey and graceful building located between Barrington and Hollis streets, was build in 1800. It was called a "palace" by T. C. Haliburton who described the New Year's Day Levée in *The Old Judge* (1849). Howe was summoned here in 1840 to expound his views on Responsible Government. He returned to Government House for a few brief weeks in 1873, to serve as Lieutenant-Governor. The building now serves as the residence of the Lieutenant-Governor.

Howe died in 1873 and his body lies under a shaft of Nova Scotia granite in historic Camp Hill Cemetery. A plaque marks the final resting place of this great patriot. Howe felt the sad absence of legend and tradition in everyday life. "But these things are not for us," he wrote in "Kentville Falls" (1828), included by M. G. Parks in his edition of *Western and Eastern Rambles*. "Our wild and beautiful scenes cannot draw for enchantment on legendary lore, and like penniless maidens, must be loved for themselves alone." But he was not one to take a back seat for anyone. "Boys, brag of your country," he once said. "When I'm abroad, I brag of everything that Nova Scotia is, has, or can produce; and when they beat me at everything else, I turn round on them and say, 'How high does your tide rise?'"

There is a week-long Joseph Howe Festival held in Halifax in late September.

Halifax Citadel A star-shaped fortress, Halifax Citadel sits atop Citadel Hill overlooking the city and the harbour. It dates back to 1749, though the present fortifications (the fourth on the site) date from the time of Prince Edward, Duke of Kent, Commander-in-Chief of the British forces (1794-1800), and the years thereafter. The duke directed the reconstruction of the Citadel and other military installations in the town. The Halifax Citadel became a National Historic Park in 1956. In one of its museums there is a life-size model of Angus McAskill, the Cape Breton Giant, as well as one of his actual boots.

The Old Town Clock A Halifax landmark, the Old Town Clock was erected by order of the Duke of Kent but completed in 1803 three years after his return to England. The clock itself has four faces and the tower was restored in 1962. From here, each day, the "noon gun" is fired. So

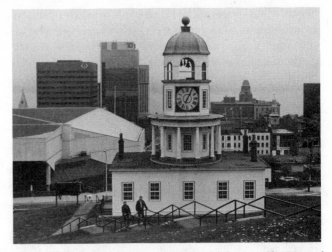

The Old Town Clock, Halifax, around which tales are told. [Dept. of Regional Industrial Expansion]

central is the Old Town Clock to Halifax life that when William Borrett (1894-1983), the writer and broadcaster, published between 1942 and 1948 five collections of talks and tales he titled or subtitled them *Tales Told Under the Old Town Clock*. Borrett tells the sad story of the love of the Duke of Kent and Madame de St. Laurent, as well as the tragic tale of "Miss Lewly," the name adopted by Dédé Hugo (1830-1915), the French novelist Victor Hugo's daughter, who lived in Halifax from 1861 to 1864 hoping to attract the British officer Albert Pinsen. Her lapse into madness became the basis of the movie *The Story of Adèle H.*, directed by François Truffaut in 1975.

Province House This legislative building on George Street, described in the section on Joseph Howe, has a wall plaque which commemorates the first printing press introduced into British North America. The first issue of the *Halifax Gazette* bears the date March 23, 1752. The two-page weekly was "printed by John Bushnell at the Printing Office, Grafton St., where advertisements are taken in." Not only is the *Halifax Gazette* Canada's first newspaper, it is still being published; since 1867 it has appeared as the *Nova Scotia Royal Gazette*, the official government publication. On his North American travels, Charles Dickens (1812-1870) spent time in Halifax and described the opening of the legislature in 1842. "It was like looking at Westminster through the wrong end of the telescope," he noted.

Prince's Lodge All that recalls the lodge erected by Prince Edward, Duke of Kent, is the Prince's Lodge. This round-domed music room, originally built in 1794, has been reconstructed. It overlooks a heart-shaped pool. The site which overlooks Bedford Basin recalls the great Canadian romance of the English prince and his French mistress, Madame de St. Laurent. The couple separated when the duke was summoned back to England. He married and became the father of Queen Victoria. The tale of Edward and Julie de St. Laurent has been told in romantic fiction many times.

Nova Scotia College of Art and Design Here a gallery in the College has been named in honour of Anna Leonowens (1834-1915), one of the founders of the Nova Scotia College of Art in 1887. Leonowens worked as a tutor in the Royal Palace in Siam (now Thailand) in 1862-68 and recalled her experiences in *The English Governess at the Siamese Court* (1870). The book was the basis of the film *Anna and the King of Siam* in 1946, and the Rodgers and Hammerstein musical *The King and I* of 1951, which in turn was filmed in 1956. She lived in Halifax from 1878 to 1897, then moved to Montreal where she taught Sanskrit at McGill.

Hugh MacLennan's Halifax Hugh MacLennan (b. 1907), the novelist and essayist, was born at Glace Bay, Cape Breton Island. The family moved to Sydney in 1914 and, the following year, to Halifax where young MacLennan attended Tower Road School. He was ten years old and about to leave for school from the family home — a two-storey Victorian residence at 197 South Park Street — when, at 9:05 a.m., on December 6, 1917, the Norwegian freighter *Imo,* and the French munitions ship *Mont Blanc* collided in the Narrows of Halifax harbour, causing the latter to catch fire. The resulting explosion largely destroyed the north end of the city, killing an estimated two thousand people and injuring another nine thousand. Damage caused by the Halifax Explosion was still being pointed out to tourists sixty years later, and the Halifax Relief Committee, established in 1918, was not

Hugh MacLennan with Halifax harbour in the distance. [Special Collections, University of Calgary Libraries]

The title page of Barometer Rising *(1941), Hugh MacLennan's first published novel. [Macmillan of Canada]*

finally wound up until 1975. More than two decades after the event MacLennan completed *Barometer Rising* (1941), his first novel, the definitive fictional presentation of the disaster. The "Wain House" mentioned in the novel is said to be modelled on the old Odell House which stood at the top of Ked Street, next to Fort Massey Church (which served as a makeshift hospital), since demolished. MacLennan presents a panorama of the city through the eyes of his hero, Neil Macrae, who is standing on Citadel Hill: "Halifax covers the whole of an oval peninsula, and the Citadel is about in the centre of it. He could look south to the open Atlantic and see where the park at the end of the town thrusts its nose directly into the outer harbour. At the park the water divides, spreading around the town on either side; to the west the inlet is called the Northwest Arm, to the east it is called the Stream, and it is here that the docks and ocean terminals are built." Seldom in literature have a subject, a city, and an author's experience and style coalesced into as satisfying a novel as they have in *Barometer Rising.* MacLennan graduated from Dalhousie University and a Rhodes scholarship took him to Oxford.

Fairview Cemetery In this cemetery, in the north end of Halifax, are the numbered graves of 125 persons who lost their lives in the sinking of the *Titanic,* which struck an iceberg south of Newfoundland on its maiden voyage, April 14, 1912. The disaster, the greatest peacetime maritime disaster, attracted the attention of E. J. Pratt (1882-1964) who published his narrative poem *The Titanic* in 1935.

In the same cemetery, memorials mark the common grave of the victims of the Halifax Explosion, December 6, 1917.

Two Statues On South Park Street, opposite the Lord Nelson Hotel, erected in 1928, are two gifts from the local chapter of the North British Society to the citizens of Halifax: a statue of Robert Burns (1759-1796), the Scottish poet, and a bust of Sir Walter Scott (1771-1832), the novelist. Ray Smith (b.1941), the fiction writer, has set a series of linked stories in the tavern of the Lord Nelson Hotel. Indeed, the collection is called *Lord Nelson Tavern* (1974).

Neptune Theatre The Neptune Theatre, which opened in the renamed Garrick Theatre at 5216 Sackville Street in 1963, was felicitously called after *Le Théâtre de Neptune,* the masque staged at Port Royal in 1606. The founder and first artistic director was Leon Major. Opening productions were Shaw's *Major Barbara* and an historical play, *Louisbourg,* by Jack Gray (b. 1927).

University of King's College The oldest literary association on the continent is said to be the Haliburton Club, established for faculty and students in 1884 on the campus of the University of King's College. The university, the oldest in the British Commonwealth outside the British Isles, was established in 1789 at Windsor, the hometown

Barometer Rising

HUGH MacLENNAN

DUELL, SLOAN AND PEARCE
NEW YORK

of Thomas Chandler Haliburton (1796-1865), in whose honour the club was named. In 1923, the university was relocated and now shares a campus with Dalhousie University. The Haliburton Club, which was once presided over by Sir Charles G. D. Roberts, meets infrequently.

Dalhousie University Dalhousie University, founded in 1818, is the largest in Atlantic Canada. Since 1920 it has published *The Dalhousie Review,* an academic quarterly. The Folklore Department has a library of lore collected by Helen Creighton. Among the distinguished faculty members are two social philosophers, George P. Grant (b. 1918) and Edgar Z. Friedenberg (b. 1921).

The Killam Library of Dalhousie University houses the University Archives and Special Collections. In the Archives are the private papers of such authors as James de Mille, Archibald MacMechan, Thomas H. Raddall, Frank P. Day, Charles Bruce, Will R. Bird, Spider Robinson, as well as the records of the Neptune Theatre. The Special Collections contain the Bacon Collection (four hundred works by and about Sir Francis Bacon, including a unique copy of his 1680 *Essays*) and the five-thousand-item Kipling Collection, housed in the O. E. Smith wing of the Macdonald Science Library. The Kipling Collection grew out of correspondence between Dr. John G. MacDougall, a Halifax surgeon, and the English man of letters. It was augmented in 1956 by forty literary manuscripts and ninety original illustrations for Kipling's published works and over eight hundred letters bequeathed by James McGregor Stewart, a prominent Halifax lawyer. Thus Dalhousie is the "warden" of Kipling in Canada.

Of Passing Note The poet, John Malcolm Brinnin (b. 1916), was born of American parents in Halifax. At the age of four he was taken back to the United States. He is best known for his book *Dylan Thomas in America* (1956).

Part of the action of The Story of Adèle H.*, directed in 1975 by François Truffaut, was set in Halifax. The film concerns the love of Victor Hugo's daughter, Dédé, played by Isabelle Adjani, for an English lieutenant who spurned her obsessive attentions. [Ontario Film Institute]*

A number of poems in *Selected Poems* (1963) touch upon his Maritime upbringing.

Although traces of the Africville section of Halifax are fast fading, the pride of the black community of Halifax informs the poems of George Elliott Clarke (b. 1960). Born in the Black Loyalist community of Windsor Plains but raised in Africville and elsewhere in Halifax, Clarke is the author of *Saltwater Spirituals and Deeper Blues* (1983) which begins with a section called "Soul Songs" devoted to poems about twelve different Black churches.

Hawthorne

The community of Hawthorne, southeast of Port Hood, was named in honour of the American novelist Nathaniel Hawthorne (1804-1864).

Lawrencetown

Lawrencetown, at Lawrencetown Beach, east of Dartmouth on the eastern shore (not to be confused with the community of the same name in the Annapolis Valley), may boast Nova Scotia's single literary press. This is Pottersfield Press which was established by Lesley Choyce in 1979 to issue the first volume of *The Pottersfield Portfolio,* an annual anthology of poetry and fiction from Atlantic Canada. More than a dozen books of limited commercial but strong literary interest have since appeared. The press operates from a two-hundred-year-old farmhouse, the oldest structure in the community.

The restored home of Simeon Perkins, shipbuilder and diarist, is now a museum at Liverpool. [Nova Scotia Department of Government Services Photograph]

Liverpool

Liverpool is situated at the mouth of the Mersey River on the province's southeast coast. The Perkins House has been restored and furnished in the style of the eighteenth century. It was built in 1766 and occupied by shipbuilder Simeon Perkins (1735-1812), whose three-volume diary, published in 1948-61, covers the years from 1766 to 1790.

Perkins's diary was discovered and edited by the novelist Thomas H. Raddall (b. 1903) who bought a

A sign fastened to the sill of one of the front windows identifies the frame house erected by the popular novelist Thomas H. Raddall at Liverpool. [Nova Scotia Department of Government Services Photograph]

house in 1933 on Park Street and has lived here ever since. In his autobiography *In My Time* (1976), he describes the two-storey wooden house. "It gave me a large study lighted by five windows and with household and telephone chatter sealed off by soundproof walls and double doors with an air space between them." Here he wrote for *Blackwood's* and *Saturday Evening Post* before plucking up the courage to write historical romances such as *His Majesty's Yankees* (1942) — in which Simeon Perkins figures — *Roger Sudden* (1944), *The Nymph and the Lamp* (1950), and *The Governor's Lady* (1960), all with eastern seaboard settings.

Lockeport

In the cemetery at Lockeport, a town on the east coast southwest of Liverpool, is the grave of John Sutherland (1919-1956). A native of Liverpool, N.S., Sutherland established himself as an editor, critic and poet in Montreal in the 1940s. Miriam Waddington edited his writings in 1973. From 1971 to 1976, Tomi Ungerer, artist and satirist, was a farmer near Lockeport. *Far Out Isn't Far Enough* (1984) is his visual and verbal tribute.

John Sutherland, noted essayist and editor, with his sister Betty. Betty married Irving Layton. John's half-brother is Donald Sutherland, the actor. [Miriam Waddington]

Louisbourg

Literature almost bypassed Louisbourg, on the east coast of Cape Breton Island. The immense citadel built in 1713 by order of the Sun King, Louis XIV of France, fell to the English on two occasions and was finally demolished in 1760 by sappers commanded by Captain John Byron, future father of the English poet, George Gordon, Lord Byron (1788-1824). The vast reconstruction undertaken at Louisbourg National Historic Park will, when completed, see one-quarter of the original citadel returned to its late eighteenth-century glory. Next to Colonial Williamsburg, the reconstruction of Louisbourg is the largest such undertaking in North America.

In its day the King's Bastion Barracks, now restored as part of the Fortress of Louisbourg, was the largest building in the New World. [Parks Canada / S. Mackenzie]

Louisbourg is the setting of Thomas Raddall's 1944 novel *Roger Sudden*. The American historical novelist, F. Van Wyck Mason (1901-1978), used the locale in *The Young Titan* (1959). James de Mille (1833-1880) set his romantic novel *The Lily and the Cross* (1874) in Louisbourg. Biographies of common people who lived and worked here are related in *Louisbourg Patriots* (1982) by Christopher Moore (b. 1950).

Lower Granville

Lower Granville, near Annapolis Royal, is the gateway to Port Royal National Historic Park, which features the reconstruction of the wooden Habitation built by Samuel de Champlain in 1605. The French explorer called this

A tourist emerges from a reconstruction of the Habitation built by Samuel de Champlain at Port Royal in 1605. [Parks Canada / J. Steeves]

C. W. Jefferys' drawing of the First Play in Canada, 1606.
[C-29560 / Public Archives Canada]

early settlement — the first permanent European settlement north of Florida — Port Royal, and Katherine Hale (1878-1956) clearly had this building in mind when she wrote in *Historic Houses of Canada* (1952): "Standing at the Basin's edge where it all occurred, looking out at the hills sheltering the water, I could see the little train of canoes setting out — the God of the Sea in full regalia, drawn by the six Tritons rising from the ocean to represent his horses, followed by the useful Indians 'bearing gifts.' I could hear the ringing, punctilious inflection of those clear-cut French voices delivering the first dramatic verse ever uttered on this continent. Then, to the sound of cannon and bugle, I could picture the return to the Fort, over whose gates the arms of France had been encircled with crowns of laurel and Latin mottoes, the 'welcoming assemblage,' and the end of the spectacle in a brief dramatic epilogue." What she is describing is the pageant written by Marc Lescarbot (1570-1642), the French lawyer and poetaster who spent the winter of 1606-7 at Port Royal. The pageant was performed at the water's edge on November 14, 1606, to greet the return of the colonist Sieur de Poutrincourt, and it constitutes the first theatrical production in North American history. Lescarbot published it as a masque called *Le Théâtre de Neptune* in *Les Muses de la Nouvelle France* (1609).

A plaque in the park honours Harriette Taber Richardson, a student of history from Cambridge, Massachusetts, who in 1928 organized the Associates of Port Royal to rebuild the Habitation. She felt it was only justice that the palisaded fortress should be reconstructed by descendants of the New Englanders and Virginians who had destroyed the original fort in 1613. It was not reconstructed until 1939. Harriette Richardson was the first person to translate *Le Théâtre de Neptune* into English. Since then it has been rendered into English a number of times, most notably by the poet F. R. Scott.

Lunenburg

The historic port of Lunenburg, on the east coast, is the focus of Lunenburg County, a region rich in folklore. The traditions of the county's German and other settlers have been collected in *Folklore of Lunenburg County* (1950) by Helen Creighton (b. 1899). Murray Beck, the author of the two-volume study *Joseph Howe* (1982, 1983), lives in Lunenburg.

Mabou

Mabou, a village on the west coast of Cape Breton Island, is the birthplace of Ray Smith (b. 1941) who makes much of the fact in his imaginative work *Cape Breton is the Thought Control Centre of Canada* (1969). The village, with its fiddlers, is called "Moidart" in the radio play "The Big Coffin Reel" by Silver Donald Cameron (b. 1937).

Mantua

East of Windsor is Mantua which was named after the birthplace of Virgil (70-19 B.C.), who was known as "the Mantuan Swan."

Milton

There are two Miltons in Nova Scotia: one in Queens County, the other in Yarmouth County. The names derive from "Mill Town" or "Milltown" and not from the English poet John Milton.

Born in the village of Milton, in Queens County, was Marshall Saunders (1861-1947), the author of *Beautiful Joe* (1894). At the unveiling of the plaque in her honour in 1953, Watson Kirkconnell (1895-1977), then president of Acadia University, pointed out that Saunders was the first Canadian to write a book that sold more than one million copies.

Mulgrave   See PORT SHOREHAM.

Nerissa

A former locality in Guysborough County, northeast of the community of Guysborough, Nerissa is remembered in the name Nerissa Round Lake. Nerissa is the name of Portia's waiting-woman in Shakespeare's *The Merchant of Venice*.

New Albany

New Albany, east of Bridgetown, was the birthplace of Alden Whitman (b. 1913), who served as chief obituary writer for *The New York Times* from 1964 to his retirement in 1976. Whitman originated the practice of interviewing public figures for obituary purposes prior to need. He reprinted thirty-four of the four hundred or so obituaries he wrote in the collection *Come to Judgment* (1980).

New Annan

The giantess Anna Swan (1846-1888) was born in New Annan, Colchester County. At seventeen she was 7'6" tall, and P. T. Barnum displayed her as "the tallest girl in the world." He exaggerated her height by posing her beside Commodore Nutt, the smallest man in the world. In later life she married Captain Van Buren Bates, the

Kentucky giant, and they had two children, who weighed twenty pounds apiece at birth. A contemporary author with the same last name as the giantess, Susan Swan (b. 1945), has written a novel about Anna Swan, *The Biggest Modern Woman of the World* (1983). There is even a play called *Giant Anna* (1978) by Donna Smyth (b. 1943) which is enacted with life-sized puppets.

New Glasgow

New Glasgow, southeast of Pictou, was the birthplace of the poet George Frederick Cameron (1854-1885). His single collection, *Lyrics on Freedom, Love and Death* (1887), appeared posthumously. A plaque was raised in his honour in the Post Office.

Tourists view the fabled "money pit" of Oak Island, Mahone Bay. [Nova Scotia Department of Government Services Photograph]

Oak Island

Oak Island, one of three hundred or so islands in Mahone Bay southwest of Halifax, has long been associated with tales of treasure buried by the infamous Captain Kidd, who was hanged for piracy in 1701. Since 1795 searches have been made for the fabled "money pit." Thomas H. Raddall (b. 1903) has dismissed such speculation in his essay "A Matter of History," but the British writer Rupert Furneaux (b. 1908) keeps the tradition alive with *Money Pit: The Mystery of Oak Island* (1972), in which he draws a parallel between the characteristics of Oak Island and details of the setting of "The Gold Bug" (1843), the celebrated short story by Edgar Allan Poe (1809-1849). Probably more books and articles have been written about Oak Island than about any other Canadian island (excluding Newfoundland and Vancouver Island).

Pictou

Pictou, on the north shore, is associated with Thomas McCulloch (1776-1843), Presbyterian minister and satirist, who settled here in 1803 and founded the Pictou Academy (1838-43) before assuming the presidency of Dalhousie University in Halifax. McCulloch is the author of the first work of Canadian humour, a series of

letters published as "Letters of Mephibosheth Stepsure" in the *Acadian Recorder* in 1821-23, reprinted in book form in 1862, and republished as *The Stepsure Letters* (1960). Here is a sample of his dry humour: "Amidst the infirmities of age, it is a great comfort to old folks, that, whatever destruction time works in their memory, they never find it affecting their judgment." The Thomas McCulloch House, built in 1806 of bricks imported from Scotland, is a museum.

C. W. Jefferys' drawing of Thomas McCulloch, D.D. [C-69877 / Public Archives Canada]

A pioneer in the Barney's River area of Pictou County near the border with Antigonish County was John MacLean (1787-1848), called "The Bard MacLean." He wrote in the Gaelic in the manner of the Highland bards of old and was widely admired for his forceful poems about clearing the forests.

Pleasant Bay

Pleasant Bay, on the Cabot Trail, is immediately north of Cape Breton Highlands National Park. Here stands the stone replica of a Scottish crofter's hut. Its erection was inspired by a lyrical poem, "Canadian Boat-Song," published in a Scottish magazine in 1829. Authorship of the composition has been ascribed to David Macbeth Moir (1789-1839), a Scottish physician and versifier who never

The Crofter's Hut, sometimes called the Lone Shieling, on the Cabot Trail, Cape Breton Island. [Bill Brooks]

visited North America. It has also been attributed to his correspondent, John Galt (1799-1839), colonist and novelist, who spent a number of years in early Canada. The poem is the lament of the Highlanders from the Hebrides exiled in North America. The widely quoted refrain runs: "Fair these broad meads — these hoary woods are grand; / But we are exiles from our fathers' land." There is no specific reference to Pleasant Bay in *The Blood is Strong* (1956), the play by Lister Sinclair (b. 1921), but the action is set in "a settler's cabin on Cape Breton Island in the early 19th century."

Port Royal   See LOWER GRANVILLE.

Port Shoreham

In this fishing community on Chedabucto Bay, south of Mulgrave, was born Charles Bruce (1906-1971) who wrote in prose and verse about the lives of farmers and fishermen in rural Nova Scotia. His best-known books are *The Mulgrave Road* (1951), a collection of lyrics; *The Channel Shore* (1954), a novel; and *The Township of Time* (1959), a series of linked stories covering the years 1786-1950. For many years he was general manager of Canadian Press in Toronto. Harry Bruce (b. 1934), his son, is also a journalist and author. He recently acquired the family farmstead in the Port Shoreham area.

Pubnico

Near the southern tip of the province is Pubnico, and nearby is Lower East Pubnico, the home of Dorothy Gilman (b. 1923), the popular American novelist and author of *The Unexpected Mrs. Pollifax* (1966) and its sequels. She also wrote about her travels here and elsewhere in *A New Kind of Country* (1978).

Pugwash

Pugwash is a hamlet on an inlet of Northumberland Strait, east of Amherst. Lord Bertrand Russell (1872-

Chatting informally by the shores of the Pugwash River are (left to right): Sir Julian Huxley, the distinguished scientist, educator, and older brother of Aldous Huxley; Dr. F. Cyril James, then Principal and Vice Chancellor of McGill University; and Cyrus Eaton, industrialist and founder of the Pugwash Conferences. This photograph was taken during the 1957 Pugwash Conference. [Mrs. Cyrus Eaton]

1970), the distinguished mathematician and philosopher and recipient of the Nobel Prize for Literature in 1950, invited nuclear scientists from ten nations, including the United States and the Soviet Union, to meet here and discuss world peace. The First Pugwash Conference of Nuclear Scientists was held in July 1957; subsequent conferences have been held here and elsewhere in the world. Julian Huxley and others resided at the rustic Thinker's Lodge built in the 1830s and owned by Cyrus Eaton, the Pugwash-born, Cleveland-based millionaire industrialist and peace advocate. Russell advised the scientists to "remember your humanity and forget the rest."

River John

Northwest of Pictou is the small community of River John, the birthplace of Roy Mackenzie (1883-1957), the first major Anglo-Canadian collector of folklore. He tells the story of his collecting in *The Quest of the Ballad* (1919). Most of his collecting of songs took place in Pictou County, where he is buried.

Wild ponies and tall, wind-blown grass are characteristic of Sable Island, N.S. [Nova Scotia Department of Government Services Photograph]

Sable Island

This treeless strip of sand and submerged shoals in the Atlantic Ocean east of Halifax is known as "the graveyard of the Atlantic" for the many ships wrecked here. It is called "Marina" in Thomas Raddall's *The Nymph and the Lamp* (1950), a romantic novel about the love of the island's lighthouse-keeper for a girl from the mainland. The author had once been a wireless operator at Cape Sable. Some two hundred horses run wild on the island. Their freedom has been celebrated in a fine poem by Al Purdy (b. 1918).

It was off Sable Island that Sir Humphrey Gilbert (1539-1583) drowned, after claiming Newfoundland as England's first overseas colony. His dying words, uttered while reading Sir Thomas More's *Utopia* (1516), were said to be words of encouragement to himself and his crew aboard the *Squirrel:* "We are as near to heaven by sea as by land!"

The storm that claimed Sir Humphrey's life also took that of Stephen Parmenius (1541-1583), the Hungarian poet and traveller who was a friend of Richard

Hakluyt and the author of verses in Latin. He is the first Magyar known to have visited America, and his tragic death deprived the world of the epic poem he planned to write about his voyage of discovery.

St. Anns

On the Cabot Trail northeast of Baddeck, St. Anns is the seat of the Gaelic College of Celtic Folk Art, the only centre for Gaelic studies in North America. St. Anns was also the home of Angus McAskill (1825-1863), the so-called "Cape Breton Giant," who stood 7′9″ and weighed 425 pounds. He died here but is buried in nearby Englishtown. His oversize chair is on view at the Giant McAskill-Highland Pioneers Museum at St. Anns. His gigantic boot may be seen in the Nova Scotia Museum in the Halifax Citadel. The life and legend of McAskill are the substance of James P. Gillis's *The Cape Breton Giant: A Truthful Memoir* (1898), an inadvertently amusing biography. It has such passages as "I was twice in the United States; I do not say so for the sake of boast" and "Early in life I came to conclusions some of which I notice in present books of geometry." Gillis was also a versifier: "And lovely girls / In pink ado / With costumes swell / Enrich the view." A summer event at St. Anns is the Gaelic Mod.

Shelburne

Loyalists established this small town east of Yarmouth. Required to leave the United States in 1791, the versifier Joseph Stansbury (1740-1809) settled here. He remained for two unhappy years before returning to New York in 1793. While in Shelburne he wrote "To Cordelia," in *The Loyal Verses of Joseph Stansbury and Dr. Jonathan Odell* (1860), which begins: "Believe me, Love, this vagrant life / O'er Nova Scotia's wilds to roam, / While far from children, friends, or wife, / Or places that I can call a home / Delights not me; — another way / My treasures, pleasures, wishes lay."

Shelburne's first mayor, when the town was incorporated in 1907, was John Hood, grandfather of the novelist Hugh Hood (b. 1928). The novelist modelled his fictional "Barringford" on Shelburne in his first novel *White Figure, White Ground* (1964). There is a nearby Barrington, which may have inspired the literary name, though Hood has noted: "The name 'Barringford' has a number of allegorical associations which are obvious when one speaks the name aloud. 'The sundering flood.'"

Spencer's Island

Here, on the shore of Minas Basin, near Parrsborough, in 1861, a twin-masted brigantine named *Amazon* was built. Renamed the *Mary Celeste*, she was found abandoned on December 5, 1872, drifting ghost-like at a point between the Azores and the Portuguese coast. This incident remains one of the great mysteries of the sea. Sir Arthur Conan Doyle (1859-1930) called it the *Marie Celeste* in his short story "J. Habakuk Jephson's Statement" in *The Captain of the Pole-Star* (1890). Thomas H. Raddall (b. 1903) discusses the ship in *Footsteps on Old Floors* (1968); in his research, he found the burial place of the ship's first captain in the village of Economy, and a grandson of the ship's builder living in the village of Advocate. A cairn on the waterfront contains a plaque about "the world's most famous mystery ship." Bela Lugosi starred in the Hollywood film *The Mystery of the Marie Celeste*, released in 1935.

Springhill

Seventy-four miners died at Springhill, the mining town near the New Brunswick border, in the cave-in of the Cumberland Mine, October 23, 1958. The disaster inspired Ewan MacColl (b. 1919) and Peggy Seeger (b. 1935) to compose "The Ballad of Springhill," with the haunting refrain, "In the town of Springhill, Nova Scotia, / Down in the dark of the Cumberland Mine, / There's blood on the coal and the miners lie / In the roads that never saw sun nor sky, / Roads that never saw sun nor sky."

The poet Fraser Sutherland (b. 1946), a native of Pictou, has written a poem "Leamington Cemetery" inspired by the graveyard on the outskirts of Springhill.

Stellarton

At Stellarton, south of Pictou, a plaque honours the noted nationalist George Munro Grant (1835-1902). Born at nearby Albion Mines, Grant accompanied Sir Sandford Fleming on an exploratory journey from the Great Lakes to the Pacific Ocean in search of a route for a transcontinental railway. His narrative, *Ocean to Ocean* (1873), inspired a generation of Canadians. He served as Principal of Queen's University, Kingston, Ont., from 1877 to his death. His son, William L. Grant (1872-1935), was headmaster of Upper Canada College from 1917 to his death. His grandson, George P. Grant (b. 1918), has enjoyed a notable academic career and has written a number of influential works of philosophy, including *Lament for a Nation* (1965).

Walden

Walden is located north of Bridgewater in Lunenburg County. It was named after *Walden* (1854), the account by Henry David Thoreau (1817-1862) of his interlude at Walden Pond, Concord, Massachusetts.

Waverley

The small community of Waverley, north of Halifax, was named after the so-called Waverley Novels of the Scots novelist Sir Walter Scott (1771-1832).

Windsor

Thomas Chandler Haliburton (1796-1865), a native of Windsor in the central part of the province, erected an attractive wooden villa here in 1836. He named it "Clifton" but it is now known as Haliburton House. Since

Front view of Haliburton House at Windsor, N.S. The one-time home of T. C. Haliburton is Nova Scotia's best-known literary residence. [Nova Scotia Department of Government Services Photograph]

Thomas Chandler Haliburton, with clock in background, drawn by Don Evans (as Isaac Bickerstaff). [Special Collections, University of Calgary Libraries]

1939 it has been designated an historic site. The original gardens were depicted by W. H. Bartlett in his *Canadian Scenery Illustrated* (1840); the grounds today comprise an estate of twenty-five acres.

Haliburton, a man of many accomplishments, who was a judge as well as a satirist, wrote his masterpiece, *The Clockmaker* (1836), at "Clifton." This first volume was so successful that it was followed by five sequels. These satires, which earned Haliburton the distinction of being the first Canadian author to reach an international readership, are rich in local lore and colour. In the pages of his books, Canadian readers come across the first use in print of such everyday expressions as "an ounce of prevention is worth a pound of cure," "a miss is as good as a mile," "you can't get blood out of stone," "it's raining cats and dogs," "the early bird gets the worm," "he drank like a fish," "as quick as a wink," "six of one and half a dozen of the other," and "this country is going to the dogs."

Attached to the Blockhouse is a plaque to commemorate Flora Macdonald (1722-1790), the Scottish Jacobite and heroine. According to the plaque, she was "the

preserver of Bonnie Prince Charlie" following the Battle of Culloden who "spent the winter of 1779 here with her husband" for "her loyalty and devotion in the midst of troubled days have long been told in Scottish story and song." The plaque goes on to quote Samuel Johnson: "A name that will be mentioned in history, and if courage and fidelity be virtues, mentioned with honour."

Sir Charles G. D. Roberts (1860-1943) taught at King's College in 1885-95 and was joined here by his cousin, Bliss Carman (1861-1929). Roberts wrote about the region in the poems of *In Divers Tones* (1886) and the novel *By the Marshes of Minas* (1900).

Alden Nowlan (1933-1983), the poet, was born on a farm in the vicinity of Windsor. He wrote about life in small towns in the Maritimes with unparalleled conviction and strength.

C. W. Jefferys' drawing of James de Mille. [C-69351 / Public Archives Canada]

Wolfville

Wolfville is a small town on Minas Basin and the seat of Acadia University, founded by Baptists in 1838. The novelist James de Mille (1833-1880) was educated at Wolfville and taught classics at Acadia from 1864 to his death. He wrote some thirty books, including his most famous, *A Strange Manuscript Found in a Copper Cylinder* (1888).

De Mille's energy found its echo in Watson Kirkconnell (1895-1977) who served as president of Acadia from 1948 to his retirement. A scholar of some distinction, he spoke some fifty languages and translated verses from many of them, including in 1962 the Polish epic poem *Pan Tadeusz*. He was perhaps the most prolific of all Canadian scholars and poets. It is claimed Kirkconnell learned to write with his left hand so that he could continue to write while shaking hands with his right.

Earle Birney (b. 1904) has written a sound poem "Arrivals — Wolfville" (1962) which recreates the sounds of the train ride from Haifax to Wolfville.

Yarmouth

At Yarmouth, on the southwest coast, is the Yarmouth County Historical Museum. On display is the so-called Yarmouth Stone, found here in 1812. The 400-pound stone has marks which have been variously interpreted and translated. They may be Viking or even Carthaginian inscriptions, but it is more likely they are of Micmac origin or the result of natural erosion.

New Brunswick

Baie de Chaleur

According to Maritime legend, a spectral ship sails the turbulent waters of the Baie de Chaleur, in the Gulf of St. Lawrence, between the Gaspé Peninsula and the north coast of New Brunswick. The legend is told in ballad form as "The Phantom Light of the Baie de Chaleurs" by Arthur Wentworth Hamilton Eaton (1849-1937), the Kentville-born poet and author of *Acadian Legends and Lyrics* (1889) and *Acadian Ballads and Lyrics in Many Moods* (1930). The poem begins: "This is the tale of the phantom light / That fills the mariner's heart, at night. . . ."

Bay of Fundy

The Bay of Fundy, between New Brunswick and Nova Scotia, has inspired a number of poems. One of the sweetest of them is "Rivers of Canada" by Bliss Carman (1861-1929), the concluding couplet of which runs: "And all the pleasant rivers that seek the Fundy foam, / They call me and call me to follow them home."

Boiestown

This small community on the Miramichi River is mentioned in the final verse of "Peter Emberley," one of the best-known Maritime folk songs. It purports to be the dying words of Emberley, who left his native Prince Edward Island in 1884 and died as the result of a logging accident on the Miramichi. He requests blessings: "Near by the city of Boiestown where my mouldering bones do lay, / A-waiting for my Saviour's call on that great Judgement Day." It may be read in *The Penguin Book of Canadian Folk Songs* (1973) edited by Edith Fowke. Boiestown is also the locale of the folk song "Duffy's Hotel."

Buctouche

This fishing village, on the east coast, north of Moncton, dates back to Acadian days, and is the birthplace and summer residence of Antonine Maillet (b. 1929), the folklorist whose tales of La Sagouine, the slatternly charwoman who speaks a rich seventeenth-century Acadian argot, have brought her an immense following. Maillet's books include *La Sagouine* (1971), *Don L'Orignal* (1978), and *Pélagie* (1982). "I have avenged my ancestors," Maillet said after writing the last title, which won for its author

France's Prix Goncourt. It recreates the conditions of the arduous return of a group of exiled Acadians some time after the Expulsion of 1755. So popular is the author among her native Acadians that rue Maillet in Buctouche was named in her honour, and a large signboard with a painting of La Sagouine was erected near the entrance to the town.

Actress Viola Léger as La Sagouine, "the slattern," created by Antonine Maillet. [CBC]

Campbellton

Campbellton, on the south side of the Restigouche River estuary, is the town to which Hugh Garner (1912-1979) reported to claim his $17 weekly unemployment cheque during the summer of 1949. He did not reside in the New Brunswick town but on his wife's family farm near Aniqui, Que., in the Gaspé. Here he wrote the story "Red Racer" and the novel *Present Reckoning* (1950).

Campobello Island

The southern portion of this picturesque island in the Bay of Fundy, close to the coast of Maine, has been preserved as Roosevelt Campobello International Park. Here is the thirty-two room, Dutch Colonial style summer home of the Roosevelt family, where U.S. President Franklin Delano Roosevelt (1882-1945) spent his youthful summers. The idyll ended in his thirty-ninth year when he contracted polio after swimming in the cold waters of the Bay of Fundy. He returned once to his "Beloved Island" as President. The heartbreak of these years is the substance

Canadian and American flags hang from the front porch of Roosevelt Cottage, boyhood home of Franklin Delano Roosevelt, Campobello Island, N.B. [Tourism New Brunswick]

of Dore Schary's 1958 Broadway play, *Sunrise at Campobello*. The first of three acts takes place between August and September 1921: "We are in the large living room of the Franklin Delano Roosevelt summer home at Campobello, New Brunswick, Canada. It is a homey, sprawling summer lodge. Picture windows reveal the firs and pines of the forest and allow us to view part of the bay." Schary adapted the play for the 1960 Hollywood movie, staring Ralph Bellamy as F.D.R. and Greer Garson as Eleanor Roosevelt. The poet Alden Nowlan relates much of the lore and history of the Island in his *Campobello* (1975).

Caraquet

The high point of the annual Acadian Festival, held for eight days in August in Caraquet, the town on the province's north shore, occurs when two students are crowned Evangeline and Gabriel, after the tragic lovers of Longfellow's narrative poem *Evangeline: A Tale of Acadie* (1847). Close to Caraquet is the Acadian Historic Village, a reconstructed French settlement of some fifty buildings which recall the period prior to the Expulsion of 1755.

Chatham

Chatham, on the Miramichi River, northeast of Newcastle, is associated with Michael Whelan (1858-1937), the so-called poet of the Renous. He was born at Grainfield, on the Renous River, which he celebrated in his ballads and songs. Best known is his version of "The Dungarvon Whopper," a popular Miramichi folksong. He is buried in St. Michael's Cemetery, Chatham, where interested citizens erected a fitting grave marker in 1981.

Cocagne

The settlement of Cocagne, located on the east coast north of Shediac, recalls the fabled Land of Cockaigne of medieval literature, where no one needs to work. The American novelist James Branch Cabell (1879-1958) revived an interest in Cocagne in his once-popular satire *Jurgen* (1919).

Evangeline

This Acadian community, southeast of Caraquet, was named in honour of the heroine of Longfellow's poem *Evangeline: A Tale of Acadie* (1847).

Fredericton

Fredericton, the capital of New Brunswick, has many literary associations. It was founded by Loyalists, the most literate and literary-minded of immigrants, and it attracted unusual people, such as William Cobbett (1762-1835), the English journalist. He was stationed at the British garrison here in 1784-91, and he included his views of Fredericton in his reminiscences published as *The Life and Adventures of Peter Porcupine* (1796) and *Advice to Young Men* (1830).

In recent years Fredericton and its environments have served as the setting of popular novels. There are references to the Saint John River, the Federal Buildings, and the Paradise Gardens Restaurant in the novel *Shacking Up* (1980), by Kent Thompson (b. 1936), which takes place in a motel on the outskirts of town.

The Green In this park, which overlooks the St. John River, will be found a statue of the poet Robert Burns (1759-1796).

Carman's Birthplace and House The frame house at 809 George Street has a back portion with a separate entrance. It is believed Bliss Carman (1861-1929) was born in the back portion. Built around 1840, the frame house at 83 Shore Street is Carman's boyhood home. The front of the house faces the garden with its enormous elms.

"The old homestead in Fredericton, which had been Bliss Carman's home since early childhood until his removal to the United States in the early nineties, is a plain old-fashioned house situated within a hundred yards of the river. The view from the garden in the rear is the most attractive and shows a verandah extending across almost its entire width and two small balconies at the upstairs windows. From his room the poet could overlook the green fields beyond the garden and a superb line of elms along the great blue river in the distance. In this garden the youthful Carman kept his canoe, carrying it to and

This is the house in which Bliss Carman was born and raised. It was photographed about 1908. [Provincial Archives]

The poet Bliss Carman is dressed as a little boy in this drawing by Don Evans signed Isaac Bickerstaff. [Special Collections, University of Calgary Libraries]

The old Rectory at Fredericton, N.B., where Sir Charles G. D. Roberts spent his youth, looked like this in 1908. [Metropolitan Toronto Library]

from the water almost daily. It is doubtless to the outdoor life and freedom of these early years that he owes his splendid physical equipment and that exuberant joy in mere living that is so strongly marked in his literary work." This description of the childhood home was written by E. J. Hathaway in "Canadian Literary Homes," *The Canadian Magazine*, January 1908.

Jonathan Odell House The large frame house at 808 Brunswick Street was the residence of Jonathan Odell (1737-1818), the Loyalist who settled here in 1784. Odell was multi-talented, being a surgeon, divine, captain, provincial secretary, and versifier of note. His poems were first collected in *The Loyal Verses of Joseph Stansbury and Dr. Jonathan Odell* (1860). A plaque has been erected in his honour on the "Deanery."

Roberts House The redbrick house "of good old Georgian design" (according to Katherine Hale in *Historic Houses of Canada* [1952]) at 734 George Street was the rectory occupied by the parents of the poets Sir Charles G. D. Roberts (1860-1943) and Theodore Goodridge Roberts (1877-1953), his younger brother. A frequent visitor was their cousin Bliss Carman (1861-1929). As Hale noted, "In summer weather the great old-fashioned

This vintage photograph shows the pipe-smoking poet Bliss Carman and his cousin the man-of-letters Charles G. D. Roberts. [Provincial Archives]

garden, haunt of all fragrant and time-honoured flowers, was the favourite spot."

Sir Charles G. D. Roberts spent his youth at the old Rectory at Fredericton. As E. J. Hathaway wrote in "Canadian Literary Homes" in *The Canadian Magazine*, January 1908, it "has been his home since 1874, when his father, Rev. Canon Roberts, removed from Westcock. His mother and younger brother live there now, and it is still looked upon as the family headquarters. Here under parental guidance he first felt the impulse of the poetic gift, and here as a lad of twenty he put forth his first modest book, *Orion and Other Poems*."

Three Poets' House The nineteenth-century frame house at 895 Charlotte Street has been occupied by three poets: Theodore Goodridge Roberts (1877-1953), his daughter Dorothy Roberts (b. 1903), and Alfred G. Bailey (b. 1905)

The Old Burying Ground Many Loyalists are buried here. At the corner of Sunbury and George streets will be found the grave of Julia Catherine Hart (1796-1867), the author of *St. Ursula's Convent* (1824), the first work of fiction to be written and published in Canada. It was issued in two volumes by subscription in Kingston. Her father, it is interesting to note, was a partner of Benedict Arnold.

Officers Square In this small park is an acknowledgement of how much Fredericton benefitted from the largesse of Lord Beaverbrook (1879-1964). To mark the British press lord's eightieth birthday, the city erected a bronze statue of the man, sculpted by Vincent Apap, and two giant beavers, carved in stone by the Acadian sculptor Claude Roussel.

Legislative Building In the library of the Legislative Building is a 1785 edition of the *Domesday Book*, the compilation of which was ordered by William the Conqueror in 1086.

Alden Nowlan Alden Nowlan (1933-1983) was appointed writer-in-residence at the University of New Brunswick in 1969. He lived in the pleasant house at 676 Windsor Street and with his wife hosted many visiting poets and writers. Here he discussed the writer's lot and, with friends, considered the pros and cons of the theories of the Flat Earth Society. He once wrote a short poem called "Epitaph" which runs: "This is the tragedy that

The snapshot shows Alden Nowlan mowing the lawn of his Fredericton house in the 1970s. [Claudine Nowlan / Michael O. Nowlan]

hounds and batters: / Not that we die, but that it seldom matters." He was a person who did matter.

University of New Brunswick The University of New Brunswick, founded in 1785, is the second-oldest in the country, and the Arts Building is the oldest university building still in active use.

A plaque on campus draws attention to Fredericton-born author Julia Catherine Hart (1796-1867). Her *St. Ursula's Convent* (1824), the first novel published in what is today Canada, was written in Fredericton. It is largely of historical interest, but it does contain some "scenes from real life."

The Observatory is a small building on campus which houses the offices of *The Fiddlehead*, founded by the Bliss Carman Society of Fredericton in 1945 and said to be "the oldest living literary magazine in the country." Poetry readings are given in the Ice House.

Among the poets and fiction-writers associated with the English Department now and in the recent past are A. G. Bailey, Fred Cogswell, Robert Gibbs, Desmond Pacey, and Kent Thompson. Alden Nowlan was the long-time writer-in-residence.

In the Harriet Irving Library of the University of New Brunswick, the Rufus Hathaway Collection of Canadian Literature offers researchers first editions and complete

works of such writers as Bliss Carman, Charles G. D. Roberts, Duncan Campbell Scott, and Francis Sherman. It also offers literary manuscripts by A. G. Bailey, Cid Corman, Louis Arthur Cunningham, Julia Catherine Hart, Harry Howith, Dorothy Roberts, Alden Nowlan, Desmond Pacey, John Reade, Charles G. D. Roberts, Lloyd Roberts, Theodore Goodridge Roberts, Francis Sherman, and Raymond Souster. Included, as well, are the manuscripts and correspondence of Fred Cogswell connected with the publication of *The Fiddlehead* in 1945-83. The Beaverbrook Special Collections has the manuscripts of *Don Fernando* and *Points of View* by W. Somerset Maugham (1874-1965) and memorabilia associated with Rudyard Kipling.

The Poets' Corner of Canada The Historic Sites and Monuments Board of Canada erected on May 15, 1947, a monument on the campus of the University of New

Three buildings on the campus of the University of New Brunswick. The Old Arts Building (left), the oldest university building in Canada still used for institutional purposes, is associated with Bliss Carman, Sir Charles G. D. Roberts, and Alfred Bailey. The Brydon Jack Observatory (upper) is the editorial office for The Fiddlehead, the country's oldest literary magazine, founded in 1945 by Alfred G. Bailey. The Poets' Corner of Canada (above) is so identified by an Historic Sites and Monuments Board plaque in front of the Harriet Irving Library. [University of New Brunswick]

Brunswick to honour three poets. The plaque stands in front of the Harriet Irving Library. The three poets are Francis Sherman (1871-1926), Bliss Carman (1861-1929), and Sir Charles G. D. Roberts (1860-1943). All three had close connections with Fredericton and the rest of the province. The designation "Poets' Corner" is taken to apply to the city of Fredericton, not just to the university campus. The notion of honouring the city's poets originated with Alfred G. Bailey (b. 1905), poet and professor. Other poets of the past associated with Fredericton are Jonathan Odell (1737-1818), the Loyalist, and James Hogg (1800-1866), said to be related to the Scottish poet of the same name. Since the Second World War, Fredericton, and in particular the University of New Brunswick, has favoured the muse by creating an environment conducive to the flourishing of the literary arts, particularly poetry.

Alfred G. Bailey, poet and professor, plants a scarlet maple tree alongside the grave of Bliss Carman in Forest Hill Cemetery, Fredericton. This was done on May 13, 1954, in fulfillment of a wish expressed by the deceased poet in a poem titled "The Grave-Tree." Standing on the left is Professor Louis Sehult; on the extreme right, Colin B. Mackay, President of the University of New Brunswick; next to the President is Professor Desmond Pacey, critic and writer. [Alfred G. Bailey / Michael O. Nowlan]

Forest Hill Cemetery Here, on the outskirts of Fredericton, on a wind-swept knoll, are memorials to three poets: Bliss Carman (1861-1929), Sir Charles G. D. Roberts (1860-1943), and Francis Joseph Sherman (1871-1926). The ashes of the first and the bodies of the second and third are interred here. All three were born in Fredericton, Carman and Roberts being cousins. Time has diminished Sherman's reputation, which rests on *The Complete Poems* (1935), edited by Lorne Pierce.

Today a maple tree rises above Carman's plot. This was not always so. Carman once wrote: "Let me have a scarlet maple / For the gravestone at my head...." These lines were recalled by J. Alex. Edmison when he visited the grave in 1954. He was surprised and disappointed to find no maple tree. Addressing the Fredericton

branch of the Canadian Club later that day, he complained about the missing maple tree. The premier of New Brunswick and the president of the University of New Brunswick were in the audience and both pledged their support. So it came about, on May 13, 1954, the twenty-fifth anniversary of Carman's death, that Alfred G. Bailey planted and dedicated the maple tree, in conformity with Carman's expressed wish.

There is a fresh grave behind that of Carman, that of Alden Nowlan (1933-1983), who wrote in his poem "Star Light, Star Bright": "I never told this before. / I'm telling you because / you're like me: silly / and afraid of the dark. / Bend closer. / I know a far greater secret. / Everyone else is too."

The Toronto poet Raymond Souster (b. 1921) visited the cemetery and in his poem "Fredericton" (1954) was hard on the three poets. "All Latin'd and Greek'd here," he wrote, "Not one of them / with very much to say, / but dressed it up, faking it."

Perhaps the last words should be Carman's, for as he wrote in "Envoi": "Have little care that Life is brief, / And less that art is long. / Success is in the silences, / Though fame is in the song."

Grand Manan Island

Grand Manan is the largest of the islands at the mouth of the Bay of Fundy and a noted resort area with an appeal to naturalists, photographers, and writers. Perhaps the most famous writer to be identified with the island is Willa Cather (1876-1947), the American novelist, who first came to the Island in 1922 and three years later built a summer home here which she used off and on for years. Outside North Head, on a wooded hillside overlooking the Bay of Fundy, stands Cather Cottage which is a frame bungalow of salt-box construction. "Luminous space prevails," wrote Wayland Drew (b. 1932), the novelist, who has lived in Cather Cottage. Indeed, his ruminative work, *Brown's Weir* (1983), which he wrote with his wife Gwendolyn, describes the weir immediately in front of the cottage. The only novel Cather set on Canadian soil is *Shadows on the Rock* (1931), which dramatizes the clash of the French and the English in the wilderness of New France at the end of the seventeenth century. Willa Cather and her residency on Grand Manan are matters of moment in the story "Dulse" in *The Moons of Jupiter* (1982) by Alice Munro (b. 1931).

Hampton

Hampton, northeast of Saint John, has been the home of Stuart Trueman (b. 1911) since 1983 when he and his wife moved here from nearby Rothesay where they had lived for some three decades. A former newspaper editor, a discoverer of Moncton's so-called Magnetic Hill, a Leacock Award winner for humour, Trueman has more than a dozen books in print. He has been called — after the romance writer W. E. Dan Ross — the best selling author in New Brunswick.

Alden Nowlan is providing a touch-up to his newspaper office in Hartland, about 1960. [Claudine Nowlan / Michael O. Nowlan]

"Marriage!" cries the preacher (played by Robin Gammell) while his devoted wife (Dawn Greenhalgh) and choir members look on, Miracle at Indian River is a 1972 CBC-TV production based on Alden Nowlan's story. [Memory Lane]

Hartland

Spanning the St. John River at Hartland, northwest of Fredericton, is the world's longest covered bridge. From 1952 to 1962, Hartland was home to Alden Nowlan (1933-1983), who worked first as a reporter and then as the editor of the weekly *Observer*. He wrote many of his early poems here, as well as some of the stories collected in *Miracle at Indian River* (1968).

Inglewood Manor

Inglewood Manor was a 32,000-acre grant of land to Moses Perley in the area of Loch Alva west of Saint John

The Lake Utopia monster is said to inhabit Lake Utopia, a small loch northeast of St. George. The fabulous sea serpent, reported at intervals, is depicted in an engraving from the Canadian Illustrated News, *November 30, 1872. The lake was named by Sir Guy Carleton in a dystopian mood when he learned that farm lots, assigned to Loyalists in 1783, were really underwater and hence of "utopian" use. [New Brunswick Museum]*

in 1832. Perley derived the name from the novel *Rob Roy* (1817) by Sir Walter Scott (1771-1832). North of Loch Alva is Robin Hood Lake, and west of it is Sherwood Lake.

Lake Utopia

A small body of water in Charlotte County, west of Saint John, Lake Utopia bears a grand name. It was so named by Sir Guy Carleton in a dystopian mood after the political romance *Utopia* (1516), by the English writer and statesman Sir Thomas More (1478-1535), when he learned that farm lots, assigned to Loyalists in 1783, were really underwater and hence of "utopian" use. Lake Utopia is blessed — or cursed — with a sea serpent, the so-called Lake Utopia Monster, first reported in 1867.

Miramichi River   See NEWCASTLE.

Photograph of Oscar Wilde taken on his North American tour, 1882. [Mander & Mitchenson]

The tidal bore (which so impressed Joseph Howe) and the Magnetic Hill (popularized by Stuart Trueman) are among the attractions of Moncton, N.B. [Tourism New Brunswick]

Moncton

Moncton, on the Petitcodiac River, is the transportation hub of the Maritimes. When Oscar Wilde lectured on aesthetics here, on October 12, 1882, the sheriff served him with a writ. The action had nothing to do with the subject of his lecture but with a disagreement between local sponsors. Irritated at the time, Wilde was more philosophical back in Boston. "The whole thing illustrates the illegality of most law and the immorality of most moral institutions," he wrote in a letter. "True, it afforded me an interesting insight into certainly not a very favourable side of Canadian ordinary life, and for experience one would go through a great deal, even to a sudden visit from the sheriff."

Although born in Sherbrooke, Que., the eminent literary critic Northrop Frye (b. 1912) was raised in Moncton and graduated from Aberdeen High School (where he stood first). In the mid-1920s the family occupied a modest home at 340 High Street. Frye's father was manager of the Moncton Supply Co., a plumbing and hardware supplies firm; his mother, the daughter of a clergyman, had taught at Stanstead College, Stanstead, Que.

Mount Murdoch

Located in the north-central part of the province, Mount Murdoch bears the last name of Beamish Murdoch (1800-1876), Maritime historian and author of *History of Nova Scotia* (1865-67).

Mount St. Nicholas

Mount St. Nicholas is located between Newcastle and Grand Falls. It was so named in 1964, the inspiration being two names — North Pole Stream and North Pole Mountain — already assigned to local features.

Eight mountains in the vicinity bear the names of Santa's reindeer, inspired by the ballad "A Visit from St. Nicholas" (1822) by the American versifier Clement C. Moore (1779-1863): "More rapid than eagles his coursers they came / And he whistled and shouted, and called them by name: / 'Now, Dasher! now, Dancer! now, Prancer and Vixen! / On Comet! on, Cupid! on, Donder and Blitzen! / To the top of the porch, to the top of the wall! / Now dash away, dash away, dash away all!'"

The ninth peak was slated to be called Mount Rudolph, in honour of Rudolph the Red-nosed Reindeer, but the Canadian Permanent Committee on Geographical Names rejected the suggestion, approving the substitute, Mount St. Nicholas.

Newcastle

The Miramichi Folk Song Festival has been held every summer since 1958 at Newcastle, a town near the mouth of the Miramichi River. It was founded by Louise Manny (b. 1890), historian and folklorist, who collected the songs of the river's loggers and published them as *Songs of Miramichi* (1968). The region is rich in traditional song and story.

Max Aitken, Lord Beaverbrook (1879-1964), was raised here, in the Old Manse adjacent to St. James Church, now a library and museum. His bronze bust stands on a pedestal in the Town Square, his ashes housed in the base of the monument. When his will was probated it was learned that Newcastle was "the town where my heart lies." Beaverbrook took his title from the Acadian hamlet of Beaver Brook Station, north of Newcastle. It is

Lord Beaverbrook's boyhood home is now a museum at Newcastle. [Bill Brooks]

The features of Lord Beaverbrook — half imp, half gnome — survey Newcastle's Town Square. [Bill Brooks]

Michael O. Nowlan and his son Peter are shown in 1982, relaxing at his summer cottage on the Miramichi, the source of much of Nowlan's fiction and poetry. [Michael O. Nowlan / Edward C. O'Reilly]

impossible to travel far in New Brunswick without encountering the benefactions of The Beaver. Indeed, even the traditional songs collected by Louise Manny were published at The Beaver's expense.

The novelist David Adams Richards (b. 1950) was born in Newcastle and has lived off and on in the vicinity. He has set his three novels — *The Coming of Winter* (1974), *Blood Ties* (1976), *Lives of Short Duration* (1981) — in a vaguely defined Maritime setting near the mouth of the Miramichi.

Raymond Fraser (b. 1941) made use of a local landmark and watering hole when he called his book of stories *The Black Horse Tavern* (1972).

Passamaquoddy Bay

Passamaquoddy Bay is an inlet of the Bay of Fundy between Maine and New Brunswick. The word is said to be Micmac for "where the pollock are." It was the euphony of the name and not the beauty of the bay that most appealed to James de Mille (1833-1880) who wrote the amusing and musical verse "Sweet Maiden of Quoddy" (1870) whch includes such lines as: ". . . in New Brunswick we'll find it — / A sweetly sequestered nook / Where the swift gliding Skoodawabskook-sis / Unites with the Skoodawabskook."

Robin Hood Lake   See INGLEWOOD MANOR.

Sackville

Sackville, in the eastern part of the province close to the Nova Scotia border, brings to mind the magic realist canvases of Alex Colville (b. 1920), the artist, who once studied and then taught at Mount Allison University, where among his students was Christopher Pratt, the magic realist of Newfoundland. Nearby is the array of antennae of Radio Canada International, the CBC's voice to the world. Sackville overlooks to the west the Tantramar Marshes, an eighty-square-mile area of marshland, the sight of which inspired Sir Charles G. D. Roberts (1860-1943) to write one of his finest lyric poems, "The Tantramar Revisited" (1886). The marshes have inspired innumerable poetic reveries and tributes, including the lyrics in *High Marsh Road* (1980) by Douglas Lochhead (b. 1922) and *At the Edge of the Chopping There Are No Secrets* (1978) and *Stilt Jack* (1978), both by John Thompson (1938-1976).

St. Andrews

In the southwestern part of the province, close to the border with Maine, is St. Andrews. A plaque in the Post Office Building honours Oliver Goldsmith (1794-1861), a son of St. Andrews, who worked as a colonial administrator in Halifax and wrote *The Rising Village* (1825, 1834), a narrative poem that deals with the sufferings of the Loyalists. Goldsmith wrote it in imitation of the style of *The Deserted Village* (1770) by his great-uncle and namesake, Oliver Goldsmith (1728-1774).

In the vicinity of St. Andrews is the home of the novelist David Walker (b. 1911), who came to Canada in 1938 as an aide-de-camp to the Governor General, Lord Tweedsmuir (author John Buchan). He achieved wide popularity with *Geordie* (1950) and *Come Back Geordie* (1966), both of which were made into successful films. His other novels include *Where the High Winds Blow* (1960), set in part in the Arctic; *Mallabec* (1965), set in the Maritimes; and *The Lord's Pink Ocean* (1972), set in a New Brunswick-like locale in the future.

Saint John

Shipbuilding was once the mainstay of this industrial city, located at the mouth of the St. John River. On the waterfront a green mound, surmounted by a flag, is all that recalls the dramatic story of the defence and fall of Fort La Tour in April 1645. The gallant defence was led by Françoise Jacquelin, wife of General Charles de la Tour. The event is the subject of a poem by Marjorie Pickthall

One guide book describes the Tantramar Marshes as "vast, barn-dotted . . . the world's biggest hayfield." The melancholy marshes have inspired generations of poets. [Tourism New Brunswick]

What remains of Fort La Tour is the "green mound" on the harbour front, with the city of Saint John in the distance. [M. A. MacDonald]

(1883-1922) and a study by George Frederick Clarke (1850-1905). M. A. MacDonald is the author of *Fortune and La Tour: The Civil War in Acadia* (1983), a gripping account of the affair.

The North End of the city was the scene of a famous romance in 1785. William Cobbett (1762-1835) the polemicist, was a soldier in his early twenties stationed at Fort Howe, which stood on a limestone ridge directly behind the waterfront site of the old French Fort La Tour. Cobbett fell in love with Ann Reid, a thirteen-year-old sergeant's daughter, and he courted her by Jenny's Spring, a natural spring named after a local settler. The site, now built over, is on First Street. When his regiment was transferred to Fredericton, Cobbett entrusted her with his savings — 150 golden guineas. Several years later he found her again in England, working as a domestic in an officer's house; she gave him back the gold, untouched. A long and happy marriage, with seven children, followed.

The city's past is evoked in the lovely children's poem "The Ships of Saint John" by Bliss Carman (1861-1929) which begins: "Where are the ships I used to know, / That came to port on the Fundy tide / Half a century ago, / In beauty and stately pride?"

There is a plaque in the New Brunswick Museum to honour James de Mille (1836-1880), the author of more than thirty books who was born in Saint John. He is remembered mainly as the author of *A Strange Manuscript Found in a Copper Cylinder* (1888), a seminal novel in the history of Canadian fantastic literature.

The poet Alden Nowlan (1933-1983) lived in Saint John from 1963 to 1968 when he worked as reporter and then editor of the *Telegraph-Journal. Bread, Wine and Salt* (1966) was published while he lived in this city.

Canada's most prolific writer must be W. E. Dan Ross (b. 1912), who has written over three hundred mass-market paperbacks in the last quarter-century, as well as some seven hundred short stories in the last two decades. This boast is not unsubstantiated, for his work is collected and catalogued by the Mugar Memorial Library of Boston University. (The exact count was 342

novels published in the 1963-78 period under dozens of pseudonyms. Twenty-two of the "Barnabas Collins" novels, inspired by the ABC-TV gothic soap opera *Dark Shadows*, appeared as by Marilyn Ross.) The author lives in a beautiful home overlooking the Kennebecasis River just outside his native Saint John.

St. John River

The peaceful, poetic-appearing St. John River is the principal river of New Brunswick. It rises in the State of Maine and for some miles forms the international boundary. It empties into the Bay of Fundy at Saint John. It was this river that Fred Cogswell (b. 1917), born at East Centreville, had in mind when he wrote, in the poem "Valley-Folk," included in *The Long Apprenticeship* (1980), "narrow is the house where we were born" in contrast to "the wider regions where the river goes." The poem "St. John River" by Alden Nowlan (1933-1983) begins: "The colour of a bayonet this river. . . ."

Hugh MacLennan (b. 1907) has expressed his feelings about the St. John River in *The Rivers of Canada* (1961): "Happiness is the word which always comes to my mind when I think of the River St. John. It is the shortest of our principal streams, being only about 420 miles long, and its system is a small one. Yet it offers so much variety of scenery that a stranger travelling along it encounters a surprise every twenty miles or so. The St. John is intimate and very beautiful."

The moody St. John River, N.B. [Dept. of Regional Industrial Expansion]

Shediac

Shediac is located on the east coast of the province, northeast of Moncton. In the town square a plaque on a stone cairn bears the inscription "Hommes des Lettres." It commemorates three Acadian men of letters from Shediac and environs: Pascal Poirier (1852-1933), author of works on Acadian customs and first Acadian senator; John Clarence Webster (1863-1950), author of many historical works and said to be author of the first book on obstetrics written in North America; and Placide Gaudet

(1850-1930), historian and genealogist. The inscription also acknowledges the importance of the first journal, *Moniteur Acadien,* founded in 1867 by Israel Landry and then edited by Ferdinand Robidoux.

Sherwood Lake   See INGLEWOOD MANOR.

Tantramar Marshes   See SACKVILLE.

Tatamagouche

Near Tatamagouche, west of Pictou, there is a stone road marker which identifies the birthplace of the great astronomer, Simon Newcomb (1835-1909), who became first president of the Astronomical and Astrophysical Society of America. He is remembered by non-astronomers as the author of the science-fiction novel *His Wisdom, the Defender* (1900) and as a false forecaster (in 1902 he wrote that "flight by machines heavier than air is unpractical and insignificant, if not utterly impossible").

Westcock

Westcock, a small community south of Sackville near the mouth of the Tantramar River, was considered by William Arthur Deacon (1895-1977), who was then compiling *A Literary Map of Canada* (1936), to be "one of the smallest but most important literary places in Canada." Near here, at Douglas, was born Sir Charles G. D. Roberts (1860-1943), who wrote about Westcock and region in such autobiographical novels as *The Heart that Knows* (1906). "His animal stories are located between this vicinity and that of Fredericton," continued Deacon. Such poems as "The Tantramar Revisited" and "Westcock Hill" describe the region memorably. Westcock inspired Roberts' finest stories, poems, and novels, and on this inspiration has Deacon based his claim on Westcock's importance.

Prince Edward Island

Alberton

The area around Cascumpeque Bay, in the northwest part of the province, is associated with the poetaster, John Hunter-Duvar (1821-1899). A native of Scotland, he settled in 1857 on a tract of land on the Mill River near here, calling the estate Hernewood and acquiring the sobriquet the Bard of Hernewood. He is mainly remembered for *The Emigration of the Fairies* (1888), a long fanciful poem that tells how the "little people" from his native Scotland clung to a clump of earth and crossed the ocean to their second home at Hernewood. His estate is now the Mill River Golf Course. Memorabilia of the poet are displayed at the Hernewood Junior High School, and the community of Duvar, near Hernewood, was named in his honour. He is buried in the churchyard of St. Luke's Anglican Church at O'Leary Corner, west of Summerside.

This photograph of the poet John Hunter-Duvar is reproduced from L. George Dewar's Hernewood. *[Margaret Mallett]*

Avonlea See CAVENDISH.

Bay Fortune

Bay Fortune, located on the east coast of the Island southwest of Souris, is noted for its beauty. Captain Frederick Marryat (1792-1848) of the HMS *Aeolus* anchored here in the spring of 1811, and described the harbour in his first novel *Frank Mildmay, or the Naval Officer* (1829).

The peace of Bay Fortune attracted theatrical folk

Jane Wyman pushes a wheelbarrow of potatoes in Johnny Belinda, *which was filmed in 1948 on Cape Breton Island rather than on Prince Edward Island. [Ontario Film Institute]*

from New York who summered here, among them the actor Charles Coghlan (1841-1899). Coghlan died on tour and was buried in Galveston, Texas. A flood loosed his coffin and the Gulf Stream floated his remains to Bay Fortune in June 1901. At least this is the account popularized in "Ripley's Believe It or Not!" column of September 15, 1927. Ripley based his story on the reminiscences of Sir Johnston Forbes-Robertson and Lily Langtry.

The actor Charles P. Flockton was another summer resident. His ashes were brought here in 1904 and buried beneath a sundial erected in his memory at Abells Cape (sometimes called Flockton's Cape) by the actress Mrs. Leslie Carter and her manager David Belasco. The inscription on the sundial reads: THE CREEPING SHADOWS MARK ANOTHER HOUR OF ABSENCE.

The playwright Elmer Harris (1878-1966), summering here in the 1930s, heard of an incident that took place before the turn of the century at Dingwells Mills involving the rape of a deaf mute, the birth of a baby boy, and the separation of the mother and child. This became the basis of his play *Johnny Belinda* which was premiered on Broadway in 1940. The play takes place in 1900 in Souris (which is described as "a bleak little village at the eastern end of the island"). The 1948 Hollywood film starring Jane Wyman was photographed on Cape Breton Island, N.S. The musical *Johnny Belinda*, which premiered in Charlottetown in 1968, was based on the play, with words by Mavor Moore and music by John Fenwick. The name is also commemorated in Johnny Belinda Pond, a small body of water at Dingwells Mills, between St. Peters and Souris.

Bill Cole as the Doctor teaches sign language to Amanda Hancox as Belinda in the CBC-TV version of the musical Johnny Belinda, *with words and music by Mavor Moore and John Fenwick based on the Elmer Harris play.* [Ontario Film Institute]

Cavendish

The most famous literary shrine in the country will be found in the village of Cavendish, on the Island's north shore, in Prince Edward Island National Park. As well as being the most famous, it is the most loved of the country's literary landmarks. As the novelist Edward McCourt recalled in *The Road Across Canada* (1965): "I have visited only one other shrine so crowded with devotees — the Brontë parsonage in Haworth. The gloom-ridden, spectre-haunted home of that tragic sisterhood is a far cry indeed from Green Gables, where all is sunlight and good cheer. . . ."

Cavendish is the locale of Green Gables. The white frame house with green trimming is at once the one-time home of the author L. M. Montgomery (1877-1942) and the setting of her children's classic, *Anne of Green Gables* (1908), and some of its seven sequels. The farmhouse has been fully restored and furnished to represent the time around the turn of the century when Anne Shirley, the imaginative orphan, was adopted and raised by a strict but kindly brother and sister who lived in a farmhouse on the outskirts of the village of Avonlea, modelled on Cavendish.

Lucy Maud Montgomery was born in nearby New London, but was raised by her maternal grandparents, David and Margaret MacNeill, in this farmhouse. Here she wrote *Anne of Green Gables*, which has never been out of print since its original publication in 1908, and here she lived until 1911 when she married the Reverend Ewan Macdonald and moved to Ontario.

In the vicinity are sites familiar to readers of the "Anne" books: the Babbling Brook, the Haunted Woods, Lover's Lane, and the Lake of Shining Waters. From Green Gables, peering across the rolling hill, one may see the neat little cemetery where L. M. Montgomery is buried, together with her husband who died in 1943.

Childhood comes alive again at Green Gables in Cavendish in Prince Edward Island National Park. This farm house is the world-famous setting of L. M. Montgomery's childhood classic, Anne of Green Gables. *The house is fully restored and furnished as it would have been in Anne's day.* [Dept. of Regional Industrial Expansion]

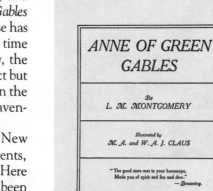

Anne's bedroom at Green Gables. [Dept. of Regional Industrial Expansion]

ANNE OF GREEN GABLES

By
L. M. MONTGOMERY

Illustrated by
M. A. and W. A. J. CLAUS

"The good stars met in your horoscope,
Made you of spirit and fire and dew."
—*Browning.*

BOSTON ❖ L. C. PAGE & COMPANY ❖ MDCCCCVIII

Title page of the first edition of Anne of Green Gables. *The children's classic by L. M. Montgomery was rejected by five firms before it was finally published in 1908.* [Metropolitan Toronto Library]

Photographic portrait of L. M. Montgomery with signature.
[C-11299 / Public Archives Canada]

L. M. Montgomery, 8¢ stamp, 1975. [Canada Post Corporation]

Charlottetown

Charlottetown is the capital city — indeed, the only city — of the province. Dorothy Livesay (b. 1909) began her poem "Prince Edward Island," in *Signpost* (1929-32), with these words: "They shut out evenings from their eyes, / These people of the farms." John Buchan (1875-1940), Governor General Lord Tweedsmuir, delivered an eloquent address in Charlottetown in September 1937. The address was titled "Island Magic" and it refers to P.E.I. as "this delectable island."

St. Paul's Anglican Church Students of Thomas Carlyle (1795-1881) will recall the beautiful Blumine, the "Rose Goddess" of the Scottish writer's autobiographical work *Sartor Resartus* (1833-34). The author was a schoolteacher in Scotland when, in 1816, he met Margaret Elizabeth Gordon, a Charlottetown-born beauty, then in her eighteenth year. They fell in love but soon parted. Carlyle never forgot Margaret, for she turns up as Blumine who is loved by Diogenes Teufelsdröckh in *Sartor Resartus*. In this work she spurns Diogenes for a more promising suitor. Margaret did the same, for she returned to Charlottetown as Lady Bannerman, wife of the Lieutenant-Governor of the province. All this is recalled by the entry for Margaret in the baptismal registry kept in St. Paul's Anglican Church, established 1747.

Province House Charlottetown is known as the "Cradle of Confederation," for in 1864 the Charlottetown Conference, the first of the three pre-Confederational conferences, was convened here. The meeting of the future Fathers of Confederation took place in Province House, the handsome sandstone building erected in 1847. Lovers of words will relish the wording of the plaque erected in the Confederation Chamber in 1927 to mark the site of the historic meeting. It reads: PROVIDENCE BEING THEIR GUIDE / THEY BUILDED BETTER THAN THEY KNEW. The

Not far from Green Gables, on Route 6, is Rainbow Valley, a recreation area that features a cottage reminiscent of the one described in *Rainbow Valley* (1919), the book in which Anne watches her children grow up.

Anne of Green Gables has been filmed twice — the first time in a silent version released in 1919 with Mary Miles Minter, the second time in a sound version in 1934 with an actress who so identified with the role she called herself Anne Shirley. In 1941, there was a sequel, *Anne of Windy Poplars*, with the same actress. The musical based on the novel was written by Don Harron and Norman Campbell; it premiered in 1954 and has been revived at the Charlottetown Summer Festival every year since 1965. Green Gables was acquired by the federal government, restored, and officially opened in 1973. Montgomery herself wrote: "Cavendish was 'Avonlea' to a certain extent, 'Lover's Lane' was a very beautiful lane through the woods on a neighbour's farm. It was a beloved haunt of mine from my earliest days. The 'Shore Road' has a real existence, between Cavendish and Rustico. But the 'White Way of Delight,' 'Wiltonmere,' and 'Violet Vale' were transplanted from the estates of my castles in Spain. 'The Lake of Shining Waters' is generally supposed to be Cavendish Pond. That is not so. The pond I had in mind is the one at Park Corner . . . Anne's habit of naming places was an old one of my own. I named all the pretty nooks and corners about the old farm."

The summer spirit of the Island and the ambience of Montgomery's fiction are explored by Francis W. P. Bolger and others in *Spirit of Place: Lucy Maud Montgomery and Prince Edward Island* (1983).

Of tangential interest is the fact that L. M. Montgomery is the author of the words to a quasi-anthem called "The Island Hymn" which was sung to the tune of "God Save the King" until L. W. Watson, organist of St. Peter's Anglican Cathedral, wrote new music for it. The first verse runs: "Fair Island of the sea, / We raise our song to thee, / The bright and blest; / Loyally now we stand / As brothers, hand in hand, / And sing God save the land / We love the best."

Province House, in Charlottetown, boasts the historic Confederation Chamber in which federal union of the British North American colonies was discussed. [Parks Canada / T. Grant]

Confederation Chamber in Province House has been called "the Birthplace of Canada" for here the so-called Fathers of Confederation met in 1864 to build a nation. On the wall may be seen the plaque that merges the words of Milton and Emerson. [P.E.I. Tourism]

wording is a powerful pastiche of lines from John Milton's *Paradise Lost* (1667) and Ralph Waldo Emerson's poem "The Problem" from *Poems* (1847) — a fine combination of the Old World and the New.

The Confederation Centre of the Arts This modern-looking building in downtown Charlottetown was opened in 1964 to mark the centenary of the Charlottetown Conference. The first director of the Art Gallery and Museum in the complex was Moncrieff Williamson (b. 1915), author of the standard biography of Robert Harris, the Charlottetown-based artist who painted the group portrait *The Fathers of Confederation*, a sketch of which is exhibited here. The other prize possession of the Art Gallery and Museum is the holograph manuscript of *Anne of Green Gables*. The Centre has staged, annually since July 1965, the musical comedy *Anne of Green Gables* based on the childhood classic with words by Don Harron and music by Norman Campbell.

A modernistic sculpture "Centennial Dimension" by Henry Purdy complements the contemporary architecture of the Confederation Centre of the Arts in the auditorium of which is annually staged the musical version of Anne of Green Gables. [P.E.I. Tourism]

Prince of Wales College This educational institution dates back to 1834, and one of its outstanding students was the youthful L. M. Montgomery (1877-1942). When the new women's residence and student's centre was completed in 1961, it was named Montgomery Hall.

Milton Acorn Milton Acorn (b. 1923), who was born in Charlottetown and attended Spring Park and West Kent schools, sold his carpenter's tools in 1958 and devoted his life to poetry. There are a number of poems about the Island in *I've Tasted My Blood* (1969), which earned him the sobriquet "The People's Poet," and *The Island Means Minago* (1975), which he has called "the poet's revolutionary analysis of this province's past and present."

Milton Acorn, "The People's Poet." [McClelland & Stewart / Herbert Lee]

Clifton See NEW LONDON.

Dingwells Mills See BAY FORTUNE.

French River
Anne's House of Dreams is located at French River, on New London Bay, west of Cavendish. This white frame

All of Avonlea approves of Anne Shirley (played by Susan Cuthbert) in Anne of Green Gables, the musical by Don Harron (words) and Norman Campbell (music), which is produced annually by the Charlottetown Festival at the Confederation Centre of the Arts. [Charlottetown Festival / George Zimbel]

Anne's House of Dreams was erected on Route 20, at French River, near Cavendish, to depict the home of Anne and Gilbert as newlyweds in the "Anne" books. The furnishings are turn-of-the-century, and a granite stone was erected nearby in 1973 to honour the literary heroine. [P.E.I. Tourism / Richard Furlong]

L. M. Montgomery was born in this cottage at New London. It is now a museum. Among its treasured items are a replica of "the old blue chest" made famous in her writings, the author's wedding dress, and her personal scrapbook. [P.E.I. Tourism]

house, furnished in turn-of-the-century style, was modelled on the first home occupied by Anne, her husband Gilbert, and their young child Rilla in L. M. Montgomery's *Anne's House of Dreams* (1918). The heroine, Anne Shirley, is honoured by a granite monument erected in 1973. There are also scale models of other sites mentioned in the Anne books, Diana Barry's House and the Old Presbyterian Church in Cavendish.

Green Gables

Green Gables is the official name of the post office at Cavendish. It was so named in 1953, after *Anne of Green Gables* (1908) by L. M. Montgomery who lived and wrote in Cavendish.

Johnny Belinda Pond   See BAY FORTUNE.

Lake of Shining Waters

This is the official name of a small lake located at Cavendish. The name is derived from *Anne of Green Gables* (1908), the children's book by L. M. Montgomery.

Milton Station

Located northwest of Charlottetown, Milton Station was not named after the English poet, John Milton, but for the birthplace in Scotland of the celebrated Jacobite heroine Flora Macdonald. As well, there are a number of mills at Milton Station.

New London

New London, southwest of Cavendish, boasts L. M. Montgomery's birthplace. In this small white cottage with green trimmings was born one of the world's most loved authors. Visitors to the cottage see the Blue Chest described in the Anne books, the author's personal scrapbook, as well as her wedding dress, veil, and shoes. New London was known in the 1870s as Clifton.

Orwell Cove

The birthplace of Sir Andrew MacPhail (1864-1938), physician and man-of-letters, may be visited at Orwell Cove, east of Charlottetown. MacPhail aided Marjorie Pickthall in the publication of her first book, *The Drift of Pinions* (1913), and he edited John McCrae's posthumous volume *In Flanders Fields* (1919). He evoked the pioneering life of his mother in his biography, *The Master's Wife* (1939). Located north of Orwell Cove is Sir Andrew MacPhail Provincial Park.

Park Corner

The Anne of Green Gables Museum is situated here at Silver Bush, near the French Shore, west of French River. Following the death of her parents, the young L. M. Montgomery lived in the modest home of her aunt and

Author L. M. Montgomery (whose photograph may be seen on the wall) was married in this room, now part of Anne of Green Gables Museum at Silver Bush, Park Corner, on July 5, 1911. The bookcase in the corner, which holds nineteen autographed first editions, is the one described in Anne of Green Gables. [P.E.I. Tourism / Gord Johnston]

uncle. Here, on July 5, 1911, she married Ewan Macdonald, a Presbyterian minister. In later years she described it as "a most quaint and delightful old place." Events that occurred in the vicinity are fictionalized in *The Story Girl* (1911) and *Pat of Silver Bush* (1933). The museum, owned and operated by descendants of her aunt and cousins, includes the bookcase described in *Anne of Green Gables* (1908) and handicrafts once owned by the author.

Ruskin

Ruskin was the name of a post office in Riverton from 1891 to 1913. Riverton is south of Morell. Ruskin was named after the English essayist John Ruskin (1819-1900).

St. Peter's

On a farm at Fortune Road, east of St. Peter's, lived Lawrence Doyle (1847-1907), the composer of such popular songs as "The Picnic at Groshaut" and "Prince Edward Isle, Adieu." Edward D. (Sandy) Ives wrote *Lawrence Doyle: The Farmer-Poet of Prince Edward Island* (1971).

Souris　See BAY FORTUNE.

Summerside

Summerside is sometimes called "the western capital of the province." Here was born Mark Strand (b. 1934), the American poet and translator, author of such collections of surrealist poems as *Reasons for Moving* (1968) and *The Story of Our Lives* (1973).

Trilby

Trilby was the designation of a post office from 1894 to 1912 in North Milton, northwest of Charlottetown. The name recalled that of Trilby O'Ferrall, the heroine of the novel *Trilby* (1894) by the English novelist George du Maurier (1834-1896), grandfather of the novelist Daphne du Maurier (b. 1907).

Trout River

The celebrated folksinger Larry Gorman (1846-1917) was born at Trout River, near Grand River, in the Tyne Valley. He is the subject of *The Man Who Made the Songs* (1964) by Edward D. (Sandy) Ives (b. 1925). Gorman's best-known song is probably "The Skull on Cowden Shore" written about his lumbering experiences in the Miramichi.

Quebec

Abitibi

The rugged Abitibi District of Northern Quebec, southeast of James Bay, is perhaps the key locale of *The Drama of the Forest* (1921) by author and artist Arthur Heming (1870-1940). The key word is "perhaps" because the naturalist was under some pressure to admit to a key locale. William Arthur Deacon was researching *A Literary Map of Canada* in September 1936 and in a series of letters pressed the naturalist for a specific setting. "*The Drama of the Forest* principally describes the life that is typical of Northern Alberta, Northern Saskatchewan, Northern Manitoba, and Northern Ontario," he maintained. "When I wrote the book I had so many places in mind that it would be a mistake to nail it down to one locality." He concluded aptly, "To mark one spot with an X to represent the book would be almost like marking one spot to represent a history of Canada." Nevertheless he was appreciative of the editor's problem. After reminding Deacon that the book was based on thirty years of wilderness experience and twenty-three trips into the wilds, being set in "The Great Northern Forest" in 1895, Heming surrendered and said, "But if you like mark Abitibi and let it go at that."

Ancienne-Lorette

Here, at Sainte-Marie-de-la-Beauce, west of Quebec City, the young folklorist Marius Barbeau (1883-1969) began his career as a collector of traditional lore among the Huron Indians. The Jesuit mission of Notre-Dame-de-Lorette, on the St. Charles River, dates back to 1673. Here was sung "Jesous Ahatonhia," the so-called "Huron Carol," written by the French missionary Jean de Brébeuf (1593-1649) about 1641 at Huronia and brought by the Christian Hurons to Ancienne-Lorette where it may still be heard sung in the language of the Hurons. There are actually two Huron reserves west of Quebec City at Loretteville.

Asbestos

The world's largest asbestos mine is located, south of Sherbrooke, in the Eastern Townships. Workers mining the non-inflammable mineral struck on February 14, 1949. The strike divided Quebec society. Pierre Elliott Trudeau (b. 1919) edited a collection of essays, *La Grève*

de l'Amiante (1956), on the subject; it was translated by James Boake as *The Asbestos Strike* (1974). The playwright John McDonough (b. 1924) wrote *Charbonneau and Le Chef* (1968) about the dramatic confrontation of the Catholic Bishop Joseph Charbonneau and the Quebec Premier Maurice Duplessis.

Life in a small asbestos-mining town before the advent of unions is lovingly depicted in Claude Jutra's Mon Oncle Antoine. *Here young Benoit (played by Jacques Gagnon) and Antoine (Jean Duceppe) take a sleigh ride together.* [Ontario Film Institute]

Baie-Saint-Paul

The frame house at Baie-Saint-Paul, on the north shore, once occupied by the painter Clarence Gagnon (1881-1942), is still standing. He lived here from 1909 until his death. Here he illustrated a famous edition of Louis Hémon's classic novel *Maria Chapdelaine* (1933). This picturesque region of the province is a favourite with painters for its scenic beauty.

Beaconsfield

The Montreal suburb of Beaconsfield, located west of Dorval on Montreal Island, was named after Benjamin Disraeli (1804-1881), First Earl of Beaconsfield, political novelist of some distinction.

Beauharnois

A farm in the Beauharnois region, south of Montreal, is the setting of the once-controversial novel *La Scouine* (1918) by Albert Laberge (1877-1960). The novel describes the life of a family in the region between 1813 and 1863. The author, who was born in Beauharnois, described the region in such realistic terms that his account was denounced as pornographic and only sixty copies were published. The novel was translated by Conrad Dion as *Bitter Bread* (1977).

Beauport

It was in Beauport, between Quebec City and Montmorency Falls, in 1850 that Henry David Thoreau (1817-1862) and a travelling companion, first realized that Quebec was different. The following account comes from Thoreau's *A Yankee in Canada* (1866).

"We were now fairly in the village of Beauport, though there was still but one road. The houses stood close upon this, without any front yards, and at an angle with it, as if they had dropped down, being set with more reference to the road which the sun travels. It being about sundown, and the falls not far off, we began to look round for lodging, for we preferred to put up at a private house, that we might see more of the inhabitants. We inquired first at the most promising-looking houses, — if, indeed, any were promising. When we knocked, they shouted some French word for come in, perhaps *Entrez,* and we asked for a lodging in English; but we found, unexpectedly, that they spoke French only. Then we went along and tried another house, being generally saluted by a rush of two or three little curs, which readily distinguished a foreigner, and which we were prepared now to hear bark in French. Our first question would be 'Parlez-vous Anglais?' but the invariable answer was 'Non, monsieur';" and we soon found that the inhabitants were exclusively French Canadians, and nobody spoke English at all, any more than in France; that, in fact, we were in a foreign country, where the inhabitants uttered not one familiar sound to us. Then we tried by turns to talk French with them, in which we succeeded sometimes pretty well, but for the most part pretty ill."

Novelist Yves Thériault wears an Eskimo-like hood in this sketch by Isaac Bickerstaff (artist Don Evans). [Special Collections, University of Calgary Libraries]

Bersimis Reserve

The Bersimis Reserve is on the north shore, southwest of Baie-Comeau. Ashini, the last of the Montagnais chiefs, in *Ashini* (1960), the powerful novel by Yves Thériault (1915-1983), journeys from Bersimis to Ottawa to parlay with the prime minister.

Bic

Located on the south shore, southwest of Rimouski, the resort village of Bic is mentioned in the epistolary novel *The History of Emily Montague* (1769) by Frances Brooke (1724-1789). There is a legend told about Bic. On the last day of creation, the angel in charge of decorating the world had a surplus of mountains and islands. They were scattered around Bic.

The highest points of Bic are the church spire and crucifix atop the mount. The resort town figures in Micmac legend and Frances Brooke's epistolary novel. [Direction générale du Tourisme-Québec]

"Bralington"   See SAINTE-JUSTINE-DE-DORCHESTER.

Carillon

At the foot of the Long Sault Rapids, near present-day Carillon, which is located on the Ottawa River northwest of Montreal, a monument marks the supposed site of the last stand of Adam Dollard des Ormeaux and his sixteen companions against the Iroquois attack on May 1, 1660. A second monument in Parc Dollard des Ormeaux, near the Carillon Canal, pays tribute to these heroes of New France. The battle inspired French-Canadian patriots, like Lionel-Adolphe Groulx (1878-1967), and the narrative poem *At the Long Sault* (1943) by Archibald Lampman (1861-1899).

Caughnawaga

Located southwest of Montreal on the south shore, the Caughnawaga Reserve for Christian Iroquois dates back to 1680. It has caught the eye of innumerable writers, only a few of whom may be mentioned here. "Where are the braves, the faces like autumn fruit, / who stared at the child from the coloured frontispiece?" questioned A. M. Klein (1909-1972) in "Indian Reservation: Caughnawaga." The American essayist Edmund Wilson (1895-1972) expressed a fascination with the Mohawk highsteel-workers in his study *Apologies to the Iroquois* (1959). And Leonard Cohen (b. 1934) rhapsodized over the Mohawk Christian saint Kateri Tekakwitha (1656-

This is the altar of the Mission Church of St. François-Xavier where Kateri Tekakwitha is buried, Caughnawaga. [Direction générale du Tourisme-Québec]

Bishop's University was established at Lennoxville in 1843 by George Mountain, third Bishop of Quebec. [Direction générale du Tourisme-Québec]

1680) in his exuberant novel *Beautiful Losers* (1966). Outside Tekakwitha School on the Reserve stands a statue raised in honour of the "Lily of the Mohawks." Her remains lie in a white marble tomb in the Mission Church of St. Francis Xavier, erected in 1717.

Chapman

West of Lac Saint-Jean is the Canton de Chapman, which bears the name of the journalist and poet William Chapman (1850-1917). A *canton* is the equivalent of a township, the use in Quebec being based on that of Switzerland.

Chicoutimi

The city of Chicoutimi is located on the Saguenay River and is recalled in the nickname of the hockey player Georges Vézina — the Chicoutimi Cucumber. It is also recalled in the short rhyme "Chicoutimi Town" by Dennis Lee (b. 1939) from *Jelly Belly* (1983) which runs: "Which is the way to Chicoutimi town, / Left foot up, and right foot down. / Right foot up and left foot down, / That is the way to Chicoutimi town."

Cloridorme   See GASPÉ.

Disraeli

The community of Disraeli, south of Thetford Mills, was named in honour of Benjamin Disraeli (1804-1881), Prime Minister of Great Britain and author of such political novels as *Coningsby* (1844), *Sybil* (1845), and *Tancred* (1847).

Eastern Townships

The collective name of the eleven townships, south of the St. Lawrence and east of the Richelieu, is the Eastern Townships, or Les Cantons de l'Estrie. The largest city in the Townships is Sherbrooke. The region is renowned for its rural charm.

Foster was home to John Glassco (1909-1981), man of letters, who settled here for reasons of health in 1935. He lived on Jamaica Farm, served as village mayor, and founded the annual horse show in 1951. He celebrated rural excellences in his *Selected Poems* (1971), once defining his existence here as "no way of living but a mode of life."

Frelighsburg is associated with André Langevin (b. 1927), the novelist and playwright, who lives here year-round.

Lennoxville is the seat of Bishop's University, founded in 1843. Champlain College was established on Bishop's campus in 1971. Festival Lennoxville, which was devoted to the staging of Canadian plays and entertainments, operated out of Bishop's Centennial Theatre. The Festival opened in 1972 with a revival of *The Ottawa Man*, an adaptation by Mavor Moore (b. 1919) of Nikolai Gogol's *The Inspector General* (1837), newly set in Northwest Manitoba. The Festival closed is doors in 1982. A long-time member of Bishop's faculty is the poet Ralph Gustafson.

Magog is a pleasant town. Mordecai Richler has his summer home not too far from the town, on the shore of Lake Memphremagog.

The University of Sherbrooke is the largest educational institution in the Eastern Townships. [Direction générale du Tourisme-Québec]

Hugh MacLennan writing in his study at Stone Hedge, North Hatley, from the NFB film Hugh MacLennan: Portrait of a Writer. *[NFB]*

North Hatley is, according to Ralph Gustafson (b. 1909), the literary centre of the Eastern Townships. He lives here, on Houghton Street, as do Ronald Sutherland and D. G. Jones. Not far away are the summer homes of Hugh MacLennan (b. 1907) and F. R. Scott (b. 1899). With the royalties from *Two Solitudes*, MacLennan in 1945 bought a cottage called "Stone Hedge" which overlooks a little lake named Massawippi. Life during the summer months is relaxed, at least as he described it in his essay "Everyone Knows the Rules" (1951). Scott and his wife the painter Marion Scott acquired a summer home close by; their neighbours were Mason Wade (b. 1913), the historian, and Bernard DeVoto (1897-1955), the American literary critic. Scott's friend from McGill and literary collaborator, A. J. M. Smith, drove each year from his home at East Lansing, Michigan, to spend the summer at his cottage at Drummond Point on Lake Memphremagog.

Saint-Elie-d'Orford was the birthplace of Alfred Desrochers (1901-1978), whose Parnassian sonnets in *A l'ombre d'Orford* (1929) celebrate the life of those of *le terroir*, the homeland.

Sherbrooke is the home of the Université de Sherbrooke which goes back to 1879. Two faculty members who write in English and translate from the French are the poet D. G. Jones (b. 1929) and the critic Ronald Sutherland (b. 1933). The Bibliothèque générale of the University has manuscript collections of Jean-Charles Harvey (1891-1967) and Monseigneur Emile Chartier (1876-1963). *Ellipse*, the bilingual journal founded in 1969, is published from the university.

At the Musée de Séminaire de Sherbrooke are preserved two limestone boulders, found in nearby Bromptonville in the 1900s, that bear inscriptions which have been variously interpreted and translated. One school of thought maintains that the characters are of recent creation; another feels they are in the Libyan

language and date back 500 years before the Vikings, proof of a Phoenician expedition to this region of North America. This school of thought translates them to read: "Thus far our expedition travelled in service of our revered Lord Hiram to conquer land."

Way's Mills is a village near Mount Orford. Louis Dudek and his wife Aileen Collins have their summer home here.

R. G. Everson held a lunch for poets and others associated with CIV/n magazine at Ripple Cove Inn, Ayer's Cliff, Que. The event took place on October 9, 1963, and the diners (left to right) are: Louis Dudek, Aileen Dudek, Ralph Gustafson, Buddy Rozynski, Lorna Everson, R. G. Everson, and Wanda Rozynski. [Betty Gustafson Literary Collection]

Celebrities gather at Louis Dudek's home at Way's Mills, Que. Top (left) to right): Darryl Hine, Ralph Gustafson, John Glassco. Middle: Monique Jones, A. J. M. Smith, D. G. Jones, Marian McCormick (Glassco). Front: Louis Dudek, Avrum Malus, Aileen Collins (Dudek), R. G. Everson. The photograph was taken by Betty Gustafson. [Dudek Collection]

Antoine Gérin-Lajoie (1824-1882) was attracted to the Townships. He described farming life and prospects in the region in his two-part novel, *Jean Rivard* (1874, 1876).

Other authors associated with the Townships are W. H. Drummond, Frank Oliver Call, and Louise Morley Bowman. As Ralph Gustafson wrote: "Is there any other centre in Canada with such a winter, summer, coagulation of congregated conspicuous creators?"

Fréchette

West of Lac Saint-Jean is the Canton de Fréchette, named after the celebrated poet Louis-Honoré Fréchette (1839-1908).

Gaspé

The Gaspé region on the south shore of the St. Lawrence is one of the most historic and picturesque in the country. On July 24, 1534, the explorer Jacques Cartier planted a cross on the peninsula. As Stephen Leacock wrote in *Canada: The Foundations of Its Future* (1941): "He skirted the New Brunswick coast and beyond it, on the Gaspé Peninsula set up a tall wooden cross, thirty feet high, carrying a shield and three fleurs-de-lis, and at the top the legend VIVE LE ROI DE FRANCE. The scene remains in our history, a picture that never fades." The cross has long since been replaced by a permanent monument.

Cloridorme, on the northeastern tip of the Gaspé Peninsula, resembles many other coastal villages. Associated with it, however, is the legend of Rose Latulippe, the girl who danced with the Devil but was saved by the power of love. The legend, which is called "L'Etranger" in *L'Influence d'un Livre* (1837) by Philippe Aubert de Gaspé (1814-1841), has been dated to 1740. It was adapted by Brian Macdonald and set to music by Harry Freedman as *Rose Latulippe*, the first full-length ballet on a Canadian theme. It premiered at the Stratford Festival, August 16, 1966.

André Breton (1896-1966), the French surrealist, was one of a number of French artists and intellectuals who weathered the Second World War in the United States. Between August and October 1944 he travelled throughout Quebec, spending part of the time in the Gaspé. He recorded his ideas and impressions in *Arcane 17* (1947). The title of this unusual work, which has yet to be translated from the French, derives from the Major Arcana of the Tarot Pack, the seventeenth being The Star which may represent loss and abandonment or hope and bright prospects. "Today the isolation of the Gaspé is

Samuel de Champlain called this rocky promontory "pierced" rock. It was the surrealist André Breton who likened it to a razor blade. [*Direction générale du Tourisme-Québec*]

as hopeless and as grand as can be," Breton notices. "This region of Canada is living today, in effect, off its particular status, and despite everything it lies a little on history's margin because, incorporated into the English Dominion, it has yet guarded something of its Frenchness."

Breton's eye was caught by Le Rocher Percé, off the Gaspé coast. He was not alone in this for Percé Rock — it was named "percé" by Samuel de Champlain in 1607; the word means "pierced," a reference to the gap in the enormous block of low-lying limestone — has caught the eye of innumerable travellers and tourists. Breton caught something of its mystery. In *Arcane 17* he called it a razor blade rising out of the water, an image ever imperious and commanding, a marvellous iceberg of moonstone. He admitted that "to a distracted observer, Percé Rock is but the nesting place of birds." Yet he affirmed its worth: "I carry some of it very far."

The commemorative plaque erected in honour of Napoléon-Alexandre Comeau at Godbout reads: "Humble Child of Nature, He Knew How to Read with Authority in the Great Book of Nature while Serving His Fellows and His Country." [*Direction générale du Tourisme-Québec*]

Godbout

On the north shore, northeast of Baie-Comeau, lived for some forty years Napoléon-Alexandre Comeau. The

Cloridorme and other villages of the Gaspésie, like Grande Vallée pictured here, are rich in atmosphere and charm. [*Direction générale du Tourisme-Québec*]

physician, naturalist, and hunter wrote *Life and Sport on the North Shore* (1909). There is a plaque raised in his honour and his remains are in the commemorative mausoleum. Baie-Comeau was named for him.

Granby

Granby, west of Sherbrooke, is the location of the well-known Granby Zoo. The city was once the home of Palmer Cox (1840-1924), the artist, who created imaginary creatures with large heads and diminutive bodies, called Brownies. The large house Cox occupied, at 125 rue Elgin, is privately owned. But La Maison Vittie, 66 rue Dufferin, the office of Les Amis de Palmer Cox, may be visited. Cox is buried in the Granby Cemetery, his place marked by a humped brown stone called the "Thumbstone." The inscription reads: "Palmer Cox (1840-1924). In creating the Brownies he bestowed an inestimable heritage on childhood." Some of the Brownie books are still in print.

Palmer Cox was a popular cartoonist in his day. He lived from 1905 on in the Brownie Castle — Château Brownies — still standing in the lovely city of Granby in the Eastern Townships. His seventeen-room house came complete with a four-storied octagonal tower which housed his studio. The house, depicted here in a painting signed "Pearson," is still standing. [Galerie d'Art Mena'sen, Sherbrooke]

To a generation raised on the Muppets and the Smurfs, the Brownies should not look very peculiar. This panel from "The Brownies Trip Abroad" is pen and ink over graphite. [National Gallery of Canada]

Hémon

Northwest of Lac Saint-Jean is the Canton de Hémon, which celebrates the French journalist, Louis Hémon (1880-1913), author of the classic novel of the Lac Saint-Jean region, *Maria Chapdelaine* (1916).

Ile d'Orléans

The Isle of Orléans, situated in the St. Lawrence northeast of Quebec City, is called the "Isle of the Sorceress" in

Les Anciens Canadiens (1863) by Philippe-Joseph Aubert de Gaspé (1786-1871). Here, according to tradition, the murderess La Corriveau held a witches' sabbath, and since then she has shrieked through the air in her iron cage in search of victims. A resident of the island is Félix Leclerc (b. 1914), the first of the *chansonniers*, whose tales and songs celebrate traditional values.

Ile des Demons

The tale of the abandonment of Marguerite de la Rocque on this desolate island, in the St. Lawrence near the mouth of Rivière Saint-Paul, was first told by Marguerite d'Angoulême (1492-1549), Queen of Navarre, in *The Heptameron* (1558). The romantic tale is based on an incident that occurred on the 1542 voyage to New France of the explorer Roberval, uncle of Marguerite, who abandoned his niece to the elements because she had fallen in love with an unworthy man.

Inukjuaq

Markoosie (b. 1943), the author of the first Inuit novel, was born in the small community of Inukjuaq, on the north coast of the Ungava Peninsula. At Resolute, N.W.T., where he was raised, he wrote *Harpoon of the Hunter* (1970) in his native language. This novel, about his experiences living in the traditional manner at Inukjuaq, has been translated into English, French, and ten other languages.

A view of the resort town of Kamouraska as it appears today, not as it was described by Anne Hébert in her well-known novel. [Direction générale du Tourisme-Québec]

Kamouraska, Anne Hébert's atmospheric novel about obsession leading to murder in the south shore village of Kamouraska, was filmed by Claude Jutra, with Geneviève Bujold and Philippe Léotard as the lovers. [Ontario Film Institute]

Isaac Bickerstaff (artist Don Evans) transformed author Anne Hébert into one of the witches of her novel Children of the Black Sabbath. [*Special Collections, University of Calgary Libraries*]

View of the Cloisters, Kingsmere, Gatineau, Que. [National Capital Commission]

Kamouraska

The south-shore resort town of Kamouraska is southwest of Rivière-du-Loup. It is the setting of *Kamouraska* (1970), the dramatic novel by Anne Hébert (b. 1916). Here, in the 1840s, Elisabeth Tassy fell in love with Dr. Morel and their liaison resulted in murder. Hébert described the "petrified landscape" of Kamouraska to great effect. The novel was filmed in 1973, partly in the Maison Langlais, an old home with four chimneys.

"The Kingdom of the Saguenay"

The goal of Jacques Cartier's voyage of 1535 was the "Kingdom of the Saguenay," the fabulous region, rich in gold, silver, and copper, at the head of the Saguenay River. Cartier's two Indian guides, Domagaya and Taignoagny, led him to believe that "there are immense quantities of gold, rubies, and other things . . . the men there are white as in France and go clothed in woollens . . . marvels too long to relate." Cartier found no such region, much to his sorrow. It is a sign of the lack of imagination of succeeding generations that no poet or story-teller embellished the belief in the "Kingdom of the Saguenay."

Kingsmere

In the rolling Gatineau Hills north of Ottawa is nestled Kingsmere, the summer home of W. L. Mackenzie King (1874-1950), who bequeathed it to successive prime ministers. Between 1902 and 1950, he deliberately created an array of ruins here, called the Cloisters. During the war, Lester B. Pearson was an external affairs officer in London. He was surprised to be wakened one night in 1941 with an urgent request: collect some of the rubble from the bombed Palace of Westminster, and dispatch it by diplomatic pouch to Ottawa. The stones may be seen in the Cloisters. The archway here is a gateway into the magical kingdom of "the forest" in the poetic prose of "Kingsmere," included by Gwendolyn MacEwen (b.

1941) in *Noman* (1972). In her novel *Julian the Magician* (1961), the magician walks through this archway into a new past and a new future.

Lac Balzac

West of Baie-Comeau is Lac Balzac, which bears the name of the great French novelist Honoré de Balzac (1799-1850).

Lac Bergson

Lac Bergson, west of Baie-Comeau, was so named to honour the French philosopher, Henri Bergson (1859-1941).

Lac Hémon

Lac Hémon, north of Lac Saint-Jean and west of Baie-Comeau, was named in honour of the French writer Louis Hémon (1880-1913), author of the classic novel *Maria Chapdelaine* (1916).

Lac Le Franc

This small lake in the Mont Tremblant district was named in honour of Marie Le Franc (1879-1964), the novelist from Brittany who lived in Westmount in 1906-26 before returning to France. She set a number of her novels in Quebec, notably *La Rivière Solitaire* (1934) in Temiskaming and *Pêcheurs de Gaspésie* (1938) in the Gaspé Peninsula.

Lac Long John

West of Schefferville is Lac Long John which was named after the one-legged pirate Long John Silver in *Treasure Island* (1883), the popular adventure novel by Robert Louis Stevenson (1850-1894).

Lac Manicouagan

Lac Manicouagan is drained by the Manicouagan River which flows into the St. Lawrence southwest of Baie-Comeau. The flow is regulated by seven hydro-electric dams, the largest of which is officially known as the Daniel Johnson Dam, after the Quebec premier; unofficially it is called Manic 5, being the fifth built across the Manicouagan River in 1968. It is a point of pride in Quebec that this structure, the world's highest multiple-arch concrete dam, was built entirely by French-speaking Quebeckers. Manic 5 has inspired such popular songs as "La Manicouagan" by the chanteuse Pauline Julien (b. 1933).

Lac Maria-Chapdelaine

North of Lac Saint-Jean and west of Baie-Comeau is Lac Maria-Chapdelaine, named after the heroine of Louis Hémon's novel *Maria Chapdelaine* (1916). A regional municipality in the Lac Saint-Jean area is also named Maria-Chapdelaine.

Lac Quasimodo

The name of this lake, northwest of Lac Saint-Jean, is that of Quasimodo, the crippled bell-ringer in *The Hunchback of Notre Dame* (1831) by Victor Hugo (1802-1885).

Lac Rivard

North of Mont-Laurier is Lac Rivard, named for the *littérateur* Adjutor Rivard (1868-1945). Canton de Rivard was named after another Rivard, not the author.

Lac Saint-Jean

"One hundred and twenty-five miles from Quebec as the loon flies, almost due north over unbroken spruce forests, lies Lake St. John, the cradle of the terrible Saguenay," wrote the American naturalist John Burroughs (1837-1921) in "The Halcyon in Canada" from *Locusts and Wild Honey* (1879). "On the map it looks like a great cuttlefish with its numerous arms and tentacula reaching out in all directions into the wilds. It is a large oval body of water thirty miles in its greatest diameter."

The Lac Saint-Jean region, especially the area around Péribonca, is identified with the novel *Maria Chapdelaine*

The Lac Saint-Jean district, so lovingly described by Louis Hémon, is less isolated today than it was when the author lived here and wrote his classic novel Maria Chapdelaine. This monument in his honour stands in a small park. [Direction générale du Tourisme-Québec]

(1916), by Louis Hémon (1880-1913). In the novel the Chapdelaines farmed the land near the lake.

Lac Saint-Pierre

This lake, east of Sorel, will be long associated with what happened "wan dark night" when the *Julie Plante* sank, as described in the dialect poem "The Wreck of the *Julie Plante*: A Legend of Lac St. Pierre" from *The Habitant and Other French-Canadian Poems* (1897) by William Henry Drummond (1854-1907). The moral of the poem is "You can't get drown on Lac St. Pierre / So long you stay on shore." The poem is based on an incident told to Drummond when, as a youth, he worked in the lumbering village of Bord-à-Plouffe, on the Rivière-des-Prairies, on the north shore of Montreal Island.

Lac Voltaire

Lac Voltaire, west of Baie-Comeau, recalls the famous French satirist François Marie Arouet (1694-1778), who wrote as Voltaire.

Lac Zola

Lac Zola, west of Baie-Comeau, commemorates the French novelist Emile Zola (1840-1902).

Lachine

Now part of Metropolitan Montreal, Lachine on the south shore of Montreal Island was named in mockery of La Salle's dream of discovering a route to China in the 1660s. It was also a point of departure for the fur brigades.

Poetry readers will recall the mysterious poem by A. J. M. Smith (1902-1980) called "The Sorcerer." It begins: "There is a sorcerer in Lachine / Who for a small fee will put a spell / On my beloved. . . ."

Saul Bellow (b. 1915), the American novelist and Nobel laureate, was born in Lachine. He lived here until he was three; from three to nine, he lived in downtown Montreal, on rue Sainte-Dominique, near Warshaw's supermarket, where he became fluent in English, French, Yiddish, and Hebrew. Then he accompanied his parents to Chicago where he has lived ever since. He was presented with an honourary degree by McGill University in 1973. The public library at Lachine was renamed the Bibliothèque Municipale Saul Bellow on June 10, 1984, the author's sixty-ninth birthday.

Irving Layton (b. 1912) has described the urbanized landscape in his poem "Lachine, Que."

Lemay

West of Lac Saint-Jean is the Canton de Lemay, which commemorates Pamphile Lemay (1837-1918), patriot, poet, and translator.

Lennoxville   See EASTERN TOWNSHIPS.

Lévis

Lévis is located on the south shore, across from Quebec

Lloyd Bochner played Inspector Carpenter, the man obsessed with bringing Donald Morrison to justice, in the made-for-TV film The Megantic Outlaw, directed by Ron Kelly [Ontario Film Institute]

City. At Saint-David-de-l'Auberivière may be visited the house in which was born Louis Fréchette (1839-1908), the most famous French-Canadian poet of his day and the first French-Canadian literary figure honoured by the Académie française. His *Poésies choisies* appeared in 1908. His restored home is located at 22 rue Saint-Laurent.

At Pointe-Lévy (Lauzon), the body of the murderess Marie-Josephte Corriveau (1733-1763) was exposed in an iron cage at a crossroads. The cage is exhibited in the Château Ramezay, Montreal. La Corriveau continues to haunt Quebec lore and literature; Corriveau is the name, for instance, of the dead soldier in *La Guerre, Yes Sir!* (1968) by Roch Carrier (b. 1937).

Lièvre River

According to Hugh MacLennan (b. 1907), writing in *The Rivers of Canada* (1961), the Lièvre is the second-longest tributary of the Ottawa River and a dangerous and lonely river to canoe. "Locally the Lièvre is pronounced in French as 'Lever' because, after its original discovery and naming by French explorers, nothing was done with it until some Scotch people came to it after the Conquest. The Scotch mispronounced the French name, and when French Canadians moved in later, they accepted the

Idyllic scene from Morning on the Lièvre, the NFB film based on the Lampman poem. [NFB]

mispronunciation. The Ottawa story is charged with anomalies like this and with forgotten episodes."

The haunting beauty of the Lièvre River, as it winds past maple-wooded hills in late September, is the subject of two poems by Archibald Lampman (1861-1899). "Morning on the Lièvre" from *Among the Millet* (1888) has refrain-like lines which run "Slowly as a cloud we go, / Sky above and sky below." The director of the short film *Morning on the Lièvre*, produced by the National Film Board in 1961, made good use of the refrain. Lampman also wrote the sonnet "Dawn on the Lièvre."

Lorette   See ANCIENNE-LORETTE.

Lozeau

Northeast of Matagami, which is north of Rouyn-Noranda, is the Canton de Lozeau. It was named in honour of the poet Albert Lozeau (1878-1924).

Malbaie, La   See POINTE-AU-PIC.

Megantic County

Associated with this county in the Eastern Townships is the Megantic Outlaw, the sobriquet of Donald Morrison (1858-1894) who accidentally killed an inspector and was sheltered by the Scottish settlers during a two-year manhunt. Much has been written about the fugitive, a recent novel being *The Outlaw of Megantic* (1973) by Bernard Epps (b. 1936).

Tiptoeing through the fleurs-de-lis (in this drawing by Don Evans as Isaac Bickerstaff) is the poet Louis Fréchette. [Special Collections, University of Calgary Libraries]

Mirabel

Mirabel International Airport is located here, northwest of Montreal. The world's largest airport in area, it was opened in 1975, displacing a number of old communities. Plans for the airport caught the attention of F. R. Scott (b. 1899) who wrote "La Révolution Tranquille" (1969), which begins: "Goodbye, Ste. Scholastique, / Goodbye, St. Jerusalem. . . ."

Montebello

At Montebello, on the north shore of the Ottawa River west of Montreal, Louis-Joseph Papineau (1786-1871), the leader of the Rebellion of 1837, built "Montebello," his manor home. It was erected in 1850 and may now be visited on the grounds of Le Château Montebello, a Canadian Pacific hotel.

Montmorency Falls

"It is a splendid introduction to the scenery of Quebec," wrote Henry David Thoreau (1817-1862) of the Montmorency Falls which he beheld in 1850. The Falls are located north of Quebec City close to where the Montmorency River empties into the St. Lawrence. "The falls of Montmorency are obviously one of the greatest of the beauties of nature," wrote Henry James (1843-1916), "but I hope it is not beside the mark to say that of all the beauties of nature, 'falls' are to me the least satisfying."

The Montmorency Falls were so named by Samuel de Champlain. The 274-foot cataract has attracted innumerable tourists and writers. [Direction générale du Tourisme-Québec]

Montreal

Montreal is the world's largest French-speaking city (after Paris). It may boast more churches than any other city on the earth (after Rome). Today it has 2.5 million inhabitants and a mix of francophones, anglophones, and allophones that makes it unique in the world. It was not always so impressive. "Montreal is an exceedingly good commercial town, and business there is brisk," wrote Anthony Trollope in North America (1862). "It has now 85,000 inhabitants. Having said that of it, I do not know what more there is left to say." Mark Twain lived in Montreal for six months to secure British copyright for his books. He noted: "This is the first time I was ever in a city where you couldn't throw a brick without breaking a church window." Brendan Behan, the Irish playwright, visited Montreal in the 1960s. "This is the only place where a good French accent isn't a social asset," he quipped.

Quips aside, modern Canadian literature came of age in Montreal through the efforts of writers on the McGill campus in the late 1920s and early 1930s. It remains congenial to individuality in the arts to this day. Louis Dudek is quoted, in the introduction to the anthology

View of Montreal and the St. Lawrence River from Westmount Lookout. [Direction générale du Tourisme-Québec]

Montreal: English Poetry of the Seventies (1977), edited by Endré Farkas and Ken Norris, as boasting: "It is the destiny of Montreal to show the country from time to time what poetry is."

Montreal — or Montréal, as Saturday Night magazine and the Parti Québécois would spell it — has a greater francophone than anglophone population. There should be a gazetteer for French-language literature in Canada. The present one represents the "French fact" to the extent that it impinges — through translation and events — on the literary consciousness of English-speaking Canadians. The Gallic charm of the city was most concisely caught by A. M. Klein (1909-1972) in his bilingual poem "Montreal" which resounds with such lines as "O city metropole, isle riverain!" and "Bilinguefact your air!"

Places

Baron Byng High School Baron Byng High School is the most celebrated secondary school in the country. It bears the name of Viscount Byng of Vimy, Governor General from 1921 to 1926, and it was built in 1921 in the Jewish quarter, 4251 St. Urbain Street, near Rachel. A. M. Klein (1909-1972) attended in the 1920s and formed the Sholem Aleichem Club — named after the Hebrew salutation adopted as a pseudonym by the writer Solomon Rabinowitz (1859-1916) — which was joined by the young David Lewis (1909-1981), former leader of the NDP, who reminisced about these years in his autobiography The Good Fight (1981). Lewis noted that although the student body was predominantly Jewish the faculty and staff were resolutely Anglo-Saxon. Irving Layton (b. 1912) studied here in the mid-1920s, and Mordecai Richler (b. 1931) in the late 1940s and early 1950s. Richler, who noted that the school displayed the flags of the nations of the world, but not that of the newly declared State of Israel, despite protests from the students. He caught the school with skewers in his classic novel The Apprenticeship of Duddy Kravitz (1959), where it appears as "Fletcher's Field," deriving that name from

Baron Byng High School, on St. Urbain Street, is arguably the most celebrated high school in the country. It now serves the community as a youth centre. [Arden Ryshpan]

the popular name of nearby Mount Royal Park. The St. Urbain Street area has changed its character from immigrant Jewish to immigrant Greek and Portuguese, and Baron Byng High School has been closed since the late 1970s. The building is now used as the headquarters for the Sun Youth Organization.

Ben's Delicatessen   This restaurant (now known as Bens) has been a Montreal institution since 1908 when it was founded by the late Benjamin Kravitz. It is now operated by his sons and grandsons at the intersection of Metcalfe and De Maisonneuve. Its smoked-meat sandwiches are popular with the late-night, early morning crowd (being open twenty-three hours a day) as well as with McGill students and writers including Leonard Cohen and Hugh MacLennan. Framed photos of celebrities adorn the walls. There is even a "Poets' Corner / Le Cour des Poètes" with framed and signed photos of A. M. Klein, Louis Dudek, Irving Layton, F. R. Scott, Ralph Gustafson, Phyllis Webb, and other bards.

Bibliothèque Nationale du Québec   The National Library of Quebec is the deposit library for the province. Its special collections, located in the Edifice Marie-Claire Daveluy, 125 rue Sherbrooke ouest, include the manuscripts of Claude-Henri Grignon, the popular radio and television writer; the papers of Gabriel Nadeau which embrace those of Louis Dantin; and manuscripts by such authors as Yves Thériault, Rina Lasnier, Emile Nelligan, Alfred Desrochers, and Alain Grandbois.

Bonsecours Market   Marché Bonsecours, which housed the Parliament of Canada from 1849 to 1852, and now contains the city's planning department, is the centre of Old Montreal. This is how the area looked to the American author William Dean Howells (1837-1920) in his novel *Their Wedding Journey* (1871): ". . . pausing on their way to alight and walk through the Bonsecours Market, where the *habitans* have all come in their carts, with their various stores of poultry, fruit, and vegetables,

and where every cart is a study. Here is a simple-faced young peasant-couple with butter and eggs and chickens ravishingly displayed; here is a smooth-cheeked, black-eyed, black-haired young girl, looking as if an infusion of Indian blood had darkened the red of her cheeks, presiding over a stock of onions, potatoes, beets, and turnips; there an old woman with a face carved like a walnut, behind a flattering array of cherries and pears; yonder a whole family trafficking in loaves of brown-bread and maple-sugar in many shapes of pious and grotesque device. . . ."

Historic Bonsecours Market in Old Montreal as it appears today. [Direction générale du Tourisme-Québec]

Cemeteries   Of Montreal's centrally located cemeteries, two are of particular interest to lovers of literature.

Mount Royal Cemetery is the Protestant burial ground, beautifully situated on the slope of Mount Royal. Among the graves are those of the explorer David Thompson (1770-1857) and Mrs. Anna Leonowens (1834-1915), the original Anna of "Anna and the King of Siam" (whose story is told in the entry on Halifax). Believed buried here are the remains of Charles Heavysege (1816-1876), poet and playwright; Longfellow called him "the greatest dramatist since Shakespeare," though history has been less kind and Robertson Davies ridiculed his writing in his novel *Leaven of Malice* (1954). Also buried here are William Henry Drummond (1854-1907), the "habitant poet," and R. Stanley Weir (1856-1926), lawyer and poet, mainly recalled as the author of the English words to the national anthem "O Canada!" which first appeared in his volume *After Ypres and Other Verse* (1917). It was Weir who incorporated the "True North" phrase from Tennyson's *Idylls of the King* (1872). Irving Layton (b.1912) has a poem about "these iambic stones" called "Cemetery in August."

Notre-Dame-des-Neiges Cemetery, adjoining Mount Royal Cemetery, is the Catholic burial ground. Irving Layton's poem "Côte des Neiges Cemetery" describes its irregular terrain and monuments and includes the lines: "On slope and summit the statuary is vain /

And senatorial." Buried here is Calixa Lavallée (1842-1891) who composed the music of the national anthem "O Canada!" The Union des Artistes has reserved a section for performers on stage, screen, radio, and television. Among the literary notables are, almost at random: Sir George-Etienne Cartier, Louis Fréchette, Pamphile Lemay, Thomas D'Arcy McGee, Emile Nelligan, and Philippe Panneton ("Ringuet"). Also buried here are Camillien Houde (1889-1958), the colourful and controversial mayor of Montreal, Joseph Guibord (the printer whose death in 1869 led to the so-called Guibord Incident), and Pierre Laporte, murdered by the FLQ in October 1970.

Centaur Theatre Company   Located in the Old Exchange Arts Centre, 453 rue Saint-François-Xavier, the Centaur Theatre Company is Quebec's main English-language theatre company. It was founded in 1969 by Maurice Podbrey and Herbert C. Auerbach. Among its interesting premieres are *The Great White Computer* by Peter Desbarats, *The Divine Sarah* by Jacques Beyderwellen, *Montparnasse* by Marcy Kahan, and *Balconville* and other plays by David Fennario.

Plays by David Fennario and others are premiered by the Centaur Theatre, which is located in the old Montreal Stock Exchange building, 453 St. François Xavier, erected in 1903. [Ross Leslie]

David Fennario, playwright. [Performing Arts]

The Château Ramezay, originally built in 1705, has served as a governor's residence, a military headquarters, a literary meeting place, and now a museum. [Direction générale du Tourisme-Québec]

Château Ramezay   La Musée du Château Ramezay is housed in the old stone building of pleasing proportions at 280 rue Notre-Dame ouest that has known so many uses in the last two and three-quarter centuries. Originally built in 1705 by Governor Claude de Ramezay, it served from 1727 as the official residence of the Intendant. When Montreal was occupied by American forces, it served as occupation headquarters. As commander of the city, Benedict Arnold received within these walls, on April 27, 1776, the elderly Benjamin Franklin (1706-1790), who as a representative of the Continental Congress was charged with the task of reporting on conditions in occupied Quebec. Franklin established the first regular postal service in Quebec and brought in the first printer, Fleury Mesplet. The château housed the Université Laval in 1895 and was the meeting place in 1896-99 of l'Ecole Littéraire de Montréal, a school of nationalistic-minded writers and poets. Among their number were Jean Charbonneau, Paul de Martigny, Emile Nelligan, Albert Lozeau, Louis Dantin, Gonsalve Desaulniers, and Charles Gill.

Lily St. Cyr, the ecdysiast, performed at the Gaiety Theatre, 84 St. Catherine Street West. The onetime home of the Comédie-Canadienne, it is currently the home of the Théâtre du Nouveau Monde. [Ross Leslie]

Comédie-Canadienne Le Théâtre de la Comédie-Canadienne had its home in the Gaiety Theatre, an old vaudeville house on rue Sainte Catherine est near the Place des Arts. It operated from 1958 to 1966, under the direction of Gratien Gélinas (b. 1909), whose trilogy of plays, *Tit-Coq, Bousille and the Just,* and *Yesterday the Children Were Dancing,* were all premiered here. Gélinas was well loved for his comic character Fridolin, who delivered monologues at the Cabaret Mon Paris each May between 1938 and 1946; the monologues, now published, ridiculed in a loving manner Quebec society and its shibboleths.

Concordia University Concordia University was formed in 1974 through the amalgamation of two colleges, Sir George Williams University, established in downtown Montreal in 1873, and Loyola College, established in the city's west end in 1899. It is the largest educational institution in the province.

Among the writers associated with Concordia there are two poets, Henry Beissel and Gary Geddes, and two novelists, John Buell and Elizabeth Spencer. John Buell (b. 1927) is the author of *The Pyx* (1959) and *The Shrewsdale Exit* (1972), among other serious thrillers; Elizabeth Spencer (b. 1921) is widely admired for her short stories which are set in the southern United States.

The Norris Library on the Sir George Williams campus has a special collection devoted to works by and about Irving Layton (b. 1912). It includes manuscripts of most of Layton's books, unpublished correspondence, criticism, audio and video tapes of readings and other public appearances, limited editions, etc. In addition to the Layton Collection, there is the Concordia Centre for Broadcasting Studies, which houses the Canadian National Theatre on the Air, some 14,000 CBC and other scripts dating from 1925 to 1961. It was first organized by Howard Fink in 1972.

Karen Black plays a call girl and Christopher Plummer a police detective in The Pyx, *the psychological thriller with religious overtones based on John Buell's novel set in Montreal.* [Ontario Film Institute]

Crémazie Monument There is a small monument to Octave Crémazie (1827-1879), the *littérateur* of Quebec City, in the mini-park situated at the corner of rue Saint-Laurent and rue Crémazie which was named in his honour. Originally it stood at the Carré Saint-Louis, St. Louis Square, erected there in 1906, but it was moved to its present site in 1973.

The Discobolus The English satirist Samuel Butler (1835-1902) spent some months in Montreal in 1874-75. He visited the city in an attempt to resuscitate the failing Canada Tanning Extract Company in which he held equity. He did not succeed in his endeavours but in his journal he recorded his impressions of Montreal. On the premises of the Montreal Natural History Society he came upon a poor plaster cast of the Discobolus. It was relegated to the "lumber room" because the naked disc-thrower "has neither vest nor pants with which to cover his limbs." The original was sculpted by the celebrated Greek sculptor Myron who lived in the fifth century before Christ. The original is lost but copies are in the Vatican Museum and the British Museum. Plaster casts were once displayed in museums and employed as models of the male physique in art schools throughout the Western world — but not in Montreal where it was considered indecent. Out of the experience Butler wrote his famous satire "A Psalm of Montreal" with its one-line refrain: "O God! O Montreal." Butler's friend Matthew Arnold so enjoyed the verse he arranged to have it published in *The Spectator* on May 18, 1878. So popular was the satire, with its implied putdown of Montreal, that in 1913, when Rupert Brooke visited the city, he sought out the Discobolus. "I made my investigations in Montreal," he wrote. "I have to report that the Discobolus is very well, and, nowadays, looks the whole world in the face, almost quite unabashed." He found it in the gallery of the Art Association of Montreal, then in Phillips Square. It would be pleasant to report that visitors to Montreal in the mid-eighties are able to view the Discobolus but that pleasure is denied. The statue was part of the collection of the Montreal Museum of Fine Arts until the mid-sixties, when it was loaned, without authorization, for display to a commercial enterprise. It has been untraceable since then. Perhaps it languishes in some Montreal company's "lumber room."

Dominion Square More statues have been erected to honour Robert Burns (1759-1796) in cities across the country than any other literary figure. Montreal's statue to the Scots poet stands in Dominion Square, near the Sun Life Building. Irving Layton has written "Woman in the Square," a poem about emerging into Dominion Square from the old Windsor Hotel.

The Double Hook Montreal's English-language Canadiana bookstore, The Double Hook, was opened at 1235A rue Greene on October 17, 1974, by Joan Blake,

Judy Mappin, and the novelist Hélène Holden. It is "a drop-in centre for Canlit fans from all over the city, literary figures passing through, and of course a fun place for the neighbourhood as well, especially on Saturdays when coffee and cookies are served." The bookstore was named after Sheila Watson's novel, *The Double Hook* (1959), copies of which are always in stock.

Elizabeth Square   There is a statue of Louis Cyr (1863-1912), sculpted by Robert Pelletier, standing in Elizabeth Square. Cyr was known as "the strongest man in the world." He weighed some 300 pounds and once lifted a 551-pound weight with one finger. He is more folk figure than a literary figure, perhaps, but he struck a responsive chord in Montrealers' hearts. In his early years he was employed as a policeman and patrolled this area of the city.

Fletcher's Field   See MOUNT ROYAL.

This drawing shows the old Hôtel Dieu Hospital in 1821, the building described — but never visited — by the notorious Maria Monk. Built in 1644, it was demolished about 1861, when its successor the Hôtel-Dieu, was opened at Pine Avenue and Parc Jeanne-Mance.

Hôtel-Dieu   The Hôtel-Dieu, at 209 avenue Pine ouest, completed in 1860, brings to mind an earlier Hôtel-Dieu, a Catholic convent and hospital on rue Saint Paul that was a familiar building in the early nineteenth century. It became the centre of a storm of controversy when one Maria Monk (1817-1849) arrived in New York in a pregnant state. She maintained she had been a "Black Nun" who was held against her will in the Hôtel-Dieu from which she had after five years managed to make her escape. She was joined in her anti-Catholic cause by George Bourne, a Presbyterian minister, who wrote or co-wrote *The Awful Disclosures of Maria Monk* (1836). To dispel the falsehoods and brand Maria Monk an impostor, the nuns opened the doors of the Hôtel-Dieu to prove that the author or authors of the book had never been inside its walls. Years later one Mrs. Lizzie St. John Eckel published a purported autobiography titled *Maria Monk's Daughter* (1874).

L'Institut Canadien   In Place Vanquelin there is a plaque which marks the site of the Institut Canadien. An important literary and scientific society founded in 1866, despite clerical opposition, it espoused free inquiry in the humanities and sciences. Members included Louis-Joseph Papineau and Sir Wilfrid Laurier. When Bishop Bourget refused Christian burial to Joseph Guibord, the Institut's printer in 1869, it sparked the Guibord Incident.

The Jewish Public Library   Both a lending library and a centre for Jewish learning and literature, the Jewish Public Library was founded in 1914 and is located in modern quarters at 5151 chemin de la Côte Sainte Catherine. From 1953 to 1966 it was at 4499 rue Esplanade. The JPL has collections of prose and poetry in four languages — Hebrew, Yiddish, French, English — and sponsors lectures and readings on an on-going basis. It draws attention to the outstanding school of Yiddish-language poets in Montreal, which included Y. Y. Segal (1896-1954), Melech Ravitch (1893-1976), Rachel Korn (1898-1982), as well as Sholem Shtern (b. 1903) and Chaveh Rosenfarb (b. 1923).

Lafontaine Park   Parc Lafontaine is an old park with such attractions as an illuminated fountain and a storybook garden with biblical scenes. Over the years it has been the scene of many a separatist protest. Of literary interest is the fact that it was while strolling through the park that Breavman in *The Favourite Game* (1963), by Leonard Cohen (b. 1934), ponders the past and the future: "Some say that no one ever leaves Montreal, for that city, like Canada itself, is designed to perceive the past, a past that happened somewhere else."

Longueuil   Longueuil now includes Ville Jacques-Cartier, a working-class suburb on the south shore. Jacques Ferron (b. 1921), the author of such stories and novels as *Tales from the Uncertain Country* (1972) and *Dr. Cotnoir* (1973), is a medical doctor in general practice at 1285 Chambly. He is known as "an honest man." In 1963 he founded the Rhinoceros Party — its motto is "From One Pond to Another" — to ridicule the platforms of the mainline political parties. He was named by the FLQ terrorists to act as an intermediary during the October Crisis of 1970.

Jacques Ferron, author, physician, and founder of the Rhinoceros Party, drawn by Don Evans who signs his work Isaac Bickerstaff. [Special Collections, University of Calgary Libraries]

McGill University "It is an island of quiet in the city's roar," wrote Hugh MacLennan (b. 1907) of McGill University, "and at night an island of darkness in the city's blaze." The campus is situated in downtown Montreal; indeed, a boulder standing in the foyer of the Dawson Building marks the site of the Indian village of Hochelaga. Since it was chartered in 1821, McGill has played a leading role in the country's — and the world's — intellectual life.

Macdonald Physics Laboratory Advanced work in radioactivity and atomic physics, undertaken in 1898-1907 at the laboratory in the Macdonald Physics Building, led to the awarding of Nobel Prizes in Chemistry to Ernest Rutherford in 1908 and to Frederick Soddy in 1921. (When Rutherford taught at McGill he lived at 3702 Sainte-Famille.) The Macdonald Physics Building, as well as the Macdonald Chemistry Building and the Macdonald Engineering Building, were donated by Sir William Macdonald, philanthropist and tobacco manufacturer.

The Arts Building Innumerable scholars and authors have maintained offices in the Arts Building, the first structure to be erected on the campus. It was built in 1839. Stephen Leacock (1869-1944), who is sometimes called "the laughing economist," taught political science and economics in its halls from 1903 to his retirement in 1936. He was known by his students as "leaky steamcock." As a colleague wrote: "And he, before Winston Churchill, saved the British Empire every Monday, Wednesday, and Friday at three o'clock in Room 20." He helped to establish the *McGill Fortnightly Review*, which appeared in 1925-27 and provided a literary vehicle for such talented students as A. J. M. Smith, Leon Edel, and F. R. Scott who launched the so-called Montreal Movement. Hugh MacLennan taught here from 1951 to 1979. Louis Dudek maintained an office at Arts 240, teaching from 1951 to his retirement in 1984. Close to the Arts Building is the modern-looking building, completed in 1965, called the Stephen Leacock Building.

Montreal Neurological Institute The founder and first director of the Montreal Neurological Institute from 1934 to his retirement in 1960 was Wilder Penfield (1891-1976), the distinguished surgeon who undertook the systematic mapping of the human brain. In addition to innumerable scientific papers, he is the author of an autobiography and two novels, *No Other Gods* (1954) about Moses and *The Torch* (1960) about Hippocrates. McGregor Avenue, between McGill University and Mount Royal, was renamed Rue Docteur Penfield.

Libraries There are twenty-two libraries on the McGill campus. The main library is the **MacLennan Library** which has a limited but illustrious collection of manuscript material. Half of Stephen Leacock's literary effects were bequeathed to the library, and the Leacock Room, which contains many inscribed first editions of his collections, is constructed of oak panelling from a private

The Arts Building (top) *and the Leacock Building* (bottom) *on the campus of McGill University.* [McGill University]

library where he once worked. There is also a substantial collection of the personal papers of Hugh MacLennan. In addition, the library has manuscripts and correspondence from Charles Sangster, Archibald Lampman, Sir Charles G. D. Roberts, Leslie Gordon Barnard, and John Glassco. John Buchan, as Governor General Lord Tweedsmuir, presented the library with the elegantly mounted and bound manuscript of his biography, *Augustus* (1937). Kipling did the same with his *Traffics and*

Discoveries (1904). In addition, there are letters from David Hume and John Ruskin, as well as two letters from Rainer Maria Rilke. Rare Canadiana is part of the Laurence Lande Collection of Canadiana prior to 1867.

Two other libraries that must be mentioned are the **McCord Museum** and the **Osler Library** of the History of Medicine. The McCord Museum, at 690 rue Sherbrooke ouest, housed in the old McGill Union building which was erected in 1907, has many enthnographic and artistic treasures. Of particular interest is the Notman Photographic Archives, which consist of some 700,000 glass negatives and proofs of photographs taken by the Scotsborn photographer William Notman (1826-1891).

The Osler Library of the History of Medicine grew out of the bequest to the university of his personal library by Sir William Osler (1849-1919), the famous physician and writer and McGill graduate. Sir William once maintained, "It is easier to buy books than to read them and easier to read them than to absorb them." Indeed, many of the eight thousand books in his personal library still had uncut pages, as they were rare volumes of historical interest.

Sir William Osler, 10¢ stamp, 1969. [Canada Post Corporation]

Stephen Leacock photographed on the McGill campus about 1925. [McGill University]

F. R. Scott, "the compleat Canadian." [McClelland & Stewart]

A brand-new Canadian flag was designed for My Fur Lady in 1957 by R. Gordon Webber. The McGill musical revue was created by Brian Macdonald, Timothy Porteous, James Domville, Donald MacSween, and Erik Wang. [Donald MacSween / Max Sauer]

The Main   The wide street that is called The Main by the English is known to the French as Boulevard Saint-Laurent. It runs north and south and divides Montreal Island into the east end (supposedly French) and the west end (supposedly English).

When the heroine of *The Book of Eve* (1973), by Constance Beresford-Howe (b. 1922), receives her old age pension, she leaves her home on avenue Monkland in Notre-Dame-de-Grâce and crosses The Main to rent a room in the east end of the city where she finds romance with a Hungarian.

The ethnic mix of the district is described by Rodney Whitaker, the American academic who writes as Trevanian in his bestselling thriller *The Main* (1976).

Maison Cormier   Maison Cormier, at 1418 avenue Pine, was designed in the Art Deco manner and erected in 1930 by the architect Ernest Cormier as his personal residence. In the late 1970s it was acquired by Pierre Elliott Trudeau (b. 1919), whose role as Prime Minister from 1968 to 1984 has upstaged his contributions as an essayist and thinker. He was a founder of *Cité Libre*, which was concerned with civil liberties and social problems and published from 1950 to 1966. Among his publications are: *The Asbestos Strike* (1956; translated 1974), *Two Innocents in Red China* (with Jacques Hébert, 1961; translated 1968), *Federalism and the French Canadians* (1968), *Approaches to Politics* (1970), and *Conversations with Canadians* (1972).

Maison de Radio-Canada   Maison de Radio-Canada, at 1400 rue Dorchester ouest, was opened in 1974 to consolidate the Canadian Broadcasting Corporation's operations in Montreal. The futuristic-looking building houses the head offices and production centres of French-language radio and television, as well as the regional and local English-language operations, not to mention the facilities of Radio Canada International, the Corporation's foreign service.

Maison Papineau   The stone residence at 440 rue Bonsecours was once occupied by Louis-Joseph Papineau

(1786-1871), the rebel leader of the Rebellion of 1837 in Lower Canada, and owned by the family from 1847 to 1920. The building was erected in 1758. Papineau's grandson, Henri Bourassa (1868-1952), nationalist and co-founder of *Le Devoir,* was born here. It was restored and occupied by the music critic Eric McLean in 1960. In his restoration, McLean had to strip nineteen layers of wallpaper from its four-foot-thick walls.

Man and His World   Man and His World, on Ile Sainte-Hélène, is the continuation of Expo 67, the brilliantly successful World's Fair, which marked both the centenary of Confederation and the greening of Québec. It was held from April 28 to October 27 and drew some fifty million visitors.

Francophone and Anglophone authors read at LaRonde, but the main literary event was La Rencontre Mondiale de Poésie, the Expo World Poetry Conference, organized by Guy Sylvestre (b. 1918). It drew more than thirty poets from around the world for four days and nights of discussion and dining. Meetings took place in Expo's Dupont Auditorium and the theme was "The Poet and the World of Man." Among those poets in attendance were Earle Birney, Jean-Guy Pilon, Irving Layton, George Barker, Robert Lowell, Denise Levertov, and Czeslaw Milosz. Ezra Pound, invited by Louis Dudek, agreed to come but cancelled at the eleventh hour.

Aerial view of LaRonde, the amusement park of Man and His World/Terre des Homme, with Jacques Cartier Bridge. [Direction générale du Tourisme-Québec]

Mechanics' Hall   Among the distinguished visiting writers to deliver public lectures here at 204 St. James Street West, now at 360 rue Saint-Jacques, was Charles Kingsley (1819-1876), the author of *Westward Ho!* (1855) and *Water Babies* (1863). On March 23, 1874, he spoke on Westminster Abbey, suggesting it should be a memorial to the Empire and the burial place of illustrious Canadians; the following evening, he discussed the Scandinavian discoverers of North America and praised their courage. The lectures were sponsored by McGill's University Literary Society.

The Montreal Forum   Le Forum de Montréal, at avenue Atwater and rue Sainte-Catherine, is the home of the Club de Hockey Canadien, the Montreal Canadiens, the team affectionately known as "the Habs." Innumerable books have been devoted to this famous team which dates back to 1909. The Forum building, built in 1924, enlarged 1949, and renovated 1968, has a seating capacity of 16,076 (plus an area for 2,000 standees). There is a memorable account of a "hockey night" at the Forum, with Maurice "Rocket" Richard performing on ice in *The Loved and the Lost* (1951), the novel by Morley Callaghan (b. 1903).

The Monument National, 1182 St. Laurent, was built in 1894. It was one of Montreal's first theatres. Gratien Gélinas' Tit-Coq was premiered here. Since the 1970s the building has been used by the National Theatre School. [Ross Leslie]

Monument National   One of the earliest of Montreal's civic theatres, the Monument National was erected in 1894. The handsome building is located at 1182 rue Saint-Laurent. Here, on the evening of May 22, 1948, Gratien Gélinas (b. 1909) starred in his play *Tit-Coq.* It ran for over five hundred performances and was filmed in 1953. In recent years the theatre has been used for productions mounted by the National Theatre School of Canada. This institution — colingual rather than bilingual — was founded in 1960 and is located at 5030 rue Saint-Denis.

The National Theatre School has its headquarters in a former juvenile court building at 5030 Saint-Denis. It was founded in Montreal in 1960 as a colingual (rather than a bilingual) institution for the professional training of actors and other theatre personnel. [Ross Leslie]

Mount Royal   Mount Royal, named by Jacques Cartier in 1535, rises 764 feet above sea level. An illuminated cross, erected in 1924, glows on its eastern flank. In his Montreal lecture on May 15, 1882, Oscar Wilde casually referred to Mount Royal as a "hill," causing consternation and resentment.

Sir Arthur Conan Doyle (1859-1930), lecturing in the city on Spiritualism, was inspired by its history. "It was a joy to feel the glamour of history once more as we entered Montreal. On the first day we ascended the mountain and looked down on what is one of the most wonderful views in the world— and I can speak now with some knowledge," he said in *Our Second American Adventure* (1923). "And here, under our eyes, as we stand on Mount Royal, we could have seen eighteen men landing from a small ship which lay out in the stream. The leader, Maisonneuve, unbuckles his great sword, takes off his broad-brimmed hat, and kneels down at the river edge, with his faithful seventeen behind him. That was the birth of Montreal."

References to "the Mountain" appear in many novels and poems. In *The Loved and the Lost* (1951), Morley Callaghan describes the influential publisher Joseph Carver as living on "the Mountain" in "the Château," whereas Jim McAlpine lives at the Ritz Hotel, and Peggy Sanderson in a monastic cell of a basement apartment not far from the Negro quarter of Saint-Antoine.

The title story of *Flying a Red Kite* (1962), the collection by Hugh Hood (b. 1928), takes place on the summit and the slopes, the locale of the NFB film *The Red Kite* based on the story in 1965. Hood's collection of "Scenes from Montreal Life" is called *Around the Mountain* (1967). Both F. R. Scott and Irving Layton have written poems called "Mount Royal" about the scene and setting.

Mount Royal Park has been the official name since 1874 of the parkland on the northern slope of Mount Royal. To the English the park is known as Fletcher's Field, to the French it is Parc Jeanne-Mance, although neither name is an official designation.

A. M. Klein (1909-1972) has a poem, "Winter Night: Mount Royal Lookout" (1941-47), which describes the cross "which bleeds / into the 50 miles of night." In the park there is a statue of Sir George-Etienne Cartier (1814-1874), a Father of Confederation and a composer of popular songs. The statue was sculpted by George Hill and includes the figure of an angel.

The park is known to readers of *The Apprenticeship of Duddy Kravitz* (1959) by Mordecai Richler (b. 1931) as Fletcher's Field (which doubles as the name of Baron Byng High School). Not far away is Wilensky's Light Lunch, 5165 rue Clark, which also figures in the novel.

Richler is not the only writer to make use of the park for fictional purposes. Michel Tremblay (b. 1942), who was born close by, on rue Fabre, has written a number of autobiographical novels set in the 1940s under the general title *Chroniques du Plateau Mont-Royal*. Sheila Fischman translated two of them as *The Fat Woman Next Door Is Pregnant* (1981) and *Thérèse and Pierrette at the Ecole des Saintes Anges* (1982).

The National Film Board of Canada   The head offices and principal production studios of the NFB are located at 3155 chemin Côte-de-Liesse, Ville Saint-Laurent. The Board, established by John Grierson in 1939, is the largest government film unit in the world. "Designed to interpret Canada to Canadians and to other nations," it has filmed numerous poems, stories, and novels by Canadian and foreign writers. Among the English-language producers and writers with offices here are Donald Brittain (b. 1928), Norman McLaren (b. 1914), and William Weintraub (b. 1926). A leading French-language producer and writer with the ONF — Office National du Film du Canada — is Jacques Godbout (b. 1933).

John Grierson, cigarette in hand, examines a World War II poster for the NFB film 1944: Year of Decision. [NFB]

Greed turns a man into a beast in Neighbours, created by Norman McLaren. [NFB]

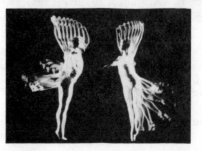

Multiple movement of dancers in Norman McLaren's incredibly beautiful short film Pas de Deux. [NFB]

Jacques Godbout, littérateur and cinéaste, when the NFB released his feature film YUL 871 in 1966. (The title refers to the Montreal-Paris flight designation.) [Ontario Film Institute]

Brian Moore, novelist. [McClelland & Stewart]

Newspapers "Newspapers are born free," F. R. Scott once quipped, "and everywhere they are in chains."

Montreal's first publisher was none other than Benjamin Franklin (1706-1790), the American printer and man of letters, who arrived in 1776 during the American occupation. He arranged for the printer Fleury Mesplet to settle in Montreal with his press, paper, and fonts of type. Two years later Mesplet's press produced the first issue of *La Gazette de Commerce et Littéraire*, the bilingual ancestor of the *Montreal Gazette*. A plaque on rue de la Capitole, off Place d'Armes, identifies the site of Mesplet's pioneer printing house.

Today's two principal French-language newspapers are *Le Devoir* and *La Presse*. The former was founded in 1910 by the intellectual Henri Bourassa, and it is published mornings at 211 rue du Saint-Sacrement. The latter, founded in 1884, is published evenings from 7 rue Saint-Jacques. Reputations are made and remade in the pages of *Le Devoir*, but *La Presse* — published in the 1970s by the novelist Roger Lemelin — boasts the largest circulation of any French-language newspaper outside France.

The principal English-language daily newspaper is the *Montreal Gazette*. As it dates back to 1778, it may claim Benjamin Franklin as its first publisher or founder. It is issued from 250 rue Saint-Antoine ouest. Brian Moore (b. 1921), then an immigrant from Ireland, worked as proofreader on the paper in the 1950s. In his novel *The Luck of Ginger Coffey* (1960), James Francis Coffey is an employee of "The Tribune." In the novel and the 1964 movie based on it, "The Tribune" resembles the *Montreal Gazette*.

Montrealers mourn the demise, within living memory, of four important newspapers: The *Montreal Herald* appeared between 1811 and 1957. Life at the *Herald* is recalled in the pages of *Why Rock the Boat?* (1961), the comic novel by William Weintraub (b. 1926), which was filmed in 1974. The *Montreal Standard* was published weekly from 1904 to 1951 when it was absorbed by *Weekend Magazine*. Mavis Gallant (b. 1922) worked on the *Standard* in 1944-50 when she left Montreal for Paris. She wrote about this period of

Robert Shaw and Mary Ure were the principals in The Luck of Ginger Coffey, *about the plight of a middle-aged Dubliner who tries his luck in Montreal. The film was based on Brian Moore's novel.* [Ontario Film Institute]

Stuart Gillard (right) plays the naive cub reporter, Sean Sullivan (left) the weary city editor, and Henry Beckman (centre) the brutal managing editor in Why Rock the Boat? *based on the comic novel by William Weintraub.* [Ontario Film Institute]

Mavis Gallant, who exchanged the St. Lawrence River for the Seine, is seen through the eyes of Isaac Bickerstaff (artist Don Evans). [Special Collections, University of Calgary Libraries]

her life in the preface and stories that comprise *The End of the World and Other Stories* (1974). *Le Nouveau Journal* signalled the "new wave" in nationalistic Quebec journalism, but it was short-lived. Founded by Jean-Louis Gagnon in 1961, it folded the following year. Among its columnists was the novelist Yves Thériault. Lastly, the *Montreal Star*, founded in 1867 by Hugh Graham, later Lord Atholstan, was once the largest English-language daily newspaper in Canada. When it folded in 1979 it was being published from 245 rue Saint-Jacques.

Nordheimer's Hall   Following his controversial luncheon speech at the Windsor Hotel, Matthew Arnold (1822-1904) delivered two evening addresses at Nordheimer's Hall, then at 207-15 St. James Street West, now at 363. The English man of letters spoke without notes on February 22, 1884, on "Numbers." Edgar Andrew Collard summarized the speech in *Canadian Yesterdays* (1955, 1963) as a complaint about the materialization of the upper class, the vulgarization of the middle class, and the brutalization of the lower class. The following evening he spoke on "Literature and Science" and how only the former answers the deepest human questions of goodness, truth, and beauty. "Quebec is the most interesting thing by much that I have seen on this continent," he later wrote about his North American lecture tour, "and I think I would sooner be a poor priest in Quebec than a rich hog-merchant in Chicago."

Notre-Dame-de-Grâce   The west-end district of NDG comes alive as a residential quarter in the memoir, *Girl in a Red River Coat* (1970), by Mary Peate (b. 1927). The author lived on avenue Harvard and attended St. Augustine of Canterbury School and the church of the same name on Côte Saint-Antoine at Marcil. Her girlhood was a period rich in emotion and excitement. The author now lives in California.

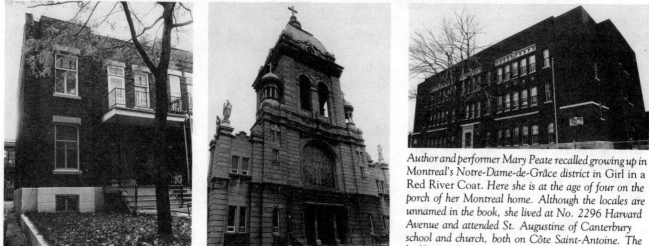

Author and performer Mary Peate recalled growing up in Montreal's Notre-Dame-de-Grâce district in Girl in a Red River Coat. *Here she is at the age of four on the porch of her Montreal home. Although the locales are unnamed in the book, she lived at No. 2296 Harvard Avenue and attended St. Augustine of Canterbury school and church, both on Côte Saint-Antoine. The buildings today look much as they did in the 1930s. [Rick Kerrigan]*

74

The twin towers of the historic church of Notre-Dame-de-Montréal (right) rise high above Place d'Armes. The crypt of the original structure was the burial place of the original Noble Savage. Across the square stands the Bank of Montreal (left). The frieze of its pediment depicts the sauvage rejecting the blandishments of civilization. [Direction générale du Tourisme-Québec]

Notre-Dame-de-Montréal The Church of Notre-Dame de Montréal, erected in Place d'Armes in the Gothic Revival style in 1824-28, elicited much comment from travellers. Its twin towers, 227 feet (69.2 metres) high, were dubbed Temperance and Perseverance. "But I was impressed by the quiet religious atmosphere of the place," wrote Henry David Thoreau (1817-1862), following his visit in 1850, in *A Yankee in Canada* (1866). "It was a great cave in the midst of a city; and what were the altars and the tinsel but the sparkling stalactics, into which you entered in a moment, and where the still atmosphere and the sombre light disposed to serious and profitable thought?"

Harriet Beecher Stowe (1811-1896) was more guarded in 1869: "In our very neighbourhood, the wondrous sound of the great bells of Notre Dame tell us of services going on there, which doubtless bring peace to many pious souls who have been led by the ancient pathways of Rome."

William Dean Howells (1837-1920), who visited Montreal twice, in 1860 and 1870, wrote in *Their Wedding Journey* (1871) that he found that the prospect of Montreal from the tower shows a city "which has less that is merely mean in it than any other city on our continent," but he went on to note: "At the cathedral there are, perhaps, the worst paintings in the world, and the massive pine-board pillars are unscrupulously smoked to look like marble; but our tourists enjoyed it as if it had been St. Peter's; in fact it has something of the barn-like immensity and impressiveness of St. Peter's."

In fact, it was modelled on Notre-Dame in Paris. It was built beside La Paroisse, the old parish church of Notre-Dame of 1672, in the crypt of which was buried the body of the great Huron Indian chief Koniaronk (1649-1701), nicknamed The Rat. When Baron de La Hontan (1666-1715) expressed unorthodox opinions about New France in *New Voyages to North America*, written in 1703 and translated by R. G. Thwaites in 1905, he had them issue from the lips of Adario, a fictitious Huron chief modelled on The Rat and the prototype of the Noble Savage. Adario stands at the head of a long line of "children of nature" in the works of such authors as Chateaubriand, Voltaire, James Fenimore Cooper, and even Alexander Pope (who wrote: "Lo, the poor Indian . . . "). No trace remains of The Rat, but the Noble Savage lives on.

In fact, the Nobel Savage is depicted on the façade of the Bank of Montreal building across the Square from the church. In the bas-relief of the pediment appear images of the Bank's coat of arms, a sailor, a colonist, and symbols of music and literature, as well as two Amerindians, one of which rejects what the Europeans have to offer.

Notre-Dame-de-Montréal is the church that inspired Irving Layton (b. 1912) to compose one of his most popular poems. "On Seeing the Statuettes of Ezekiel and Jeremiah in the Church of Notre Dame" has the lines about "my hot Hebrew heart / as passionate as your own." Perhaps the Nobel Savage still lives.

Sam Tata's celebrated photographic portrait of Irving Layton. [Concordia University Library, Layton Collection]

Ouimetoscope The first building to be designed and erected as a movie theatre in North America is the Ouimetoscope at 1206 rue Sainte-Catherine est. The 1,000-seat theatre was built by film exhibitor Léo-Ernest Ouimet in 1907 and named the Ouimetoscope. It still operates under that name as a repertory movie house.

Outremont   The desirable residential district of Outremont boasts F. X. Garneau Park, named in honour of François-Xavier Garneau (1809-1866), the distinguished historian of the three-volume *Histoire du Canada* (1845-48).

Parc Jeanne-Mance   See MOUNT ROYAL.

Place d'Armes   This historic square in Old Montreal marks the site where Maisonneuve founded the colony of Ville-Marie in 1641. The imposing Church of Notre-Dame-de-Montréal is in Place d'Armes. The square supplied the writer Scott Symons (b. 1933) with the title of his 1967 novel about life in Montreal.

Place des Arts   Place des Arts, Montreal's arts centre, was opened in 1965. The centre's smallest stage, La Théâtre Port-Royale, is the permanent home of La Théâtre du Nouveau Monde, the well-known repertory company founded in 1951 by Jean Gascon, Jean-Louis Roux, and Guy Hoffman. The TNM first occupied the old Orpheum Theatre. The stage was named after the theatrical entertainment provided by Marc Lescarbot at Port Royale (for which see Lower Granville, N.S.).

Place Jacques-Cartier   The centrepiece of this square in the heart of Old Montreal is the Nelson Column, erected in 1809 in honour of Lord Horatio Nelson. It is the oldest standing monument in Montreal and the first tribute paid anywhere to the English Admiral who was victorious over the French. The Nelson Hotel, at 421, has associations going back to the 1837 rebellion, and the *boîtes* in the neighbourhood are congenial to *chansonnières*.

Nelson's Column, rising over Place Jacques-Cartier, with the dome of Bonsecours Market in the background. [Direction générale du Tourisme-Québec]

Place Norman-Bethune   This small square was created on de Maisonneuve and Guy in 1978 to accommodate the gift from the People's Republic of China — a life-size statue of the controversial, charismatic medical doctor, Norman Bethune (1890-1939). Bethune's life and ideals have inspired diverse books and films, and Bethune himself was a close observer and vigorous writer of articles and

The white stone statue of Norman Bethune in downtown Montreal was donated by the People's Republic of China. [Arden Ryshpan]

letters and a keen amateur painter. During his Montreal years he practised medicine at the Royal Victoria Hospital (1928-33) and Sacré-Coeur Hospital (1933-36) at Cartierville. He lived in apartments on Baile Street, Fort Street, and for six months in 1936 in a third-floor flat at 1154 Beaver Hall Square where he conducted children's art classes. Then he left for Spain and his ultimate destination, China.

Pointe Saint-Charles   Pointe Saint-Charles is the English-speaking and Catholic working-class district between Saint-Henri and Verdun. As such it is the setting of plays by David Fennario (b. 1947) who was born and raised in the district. In fact, he wrote his first dramatic sketches never having seen a theatrical presentation. *Balconville* (1980) is set on adjoining balconies of walk-ups in the district. It is the first bilingual Canadian play. *Nothing to Lose* (1977) takes place in a local tavern, and *On the Job* (1976) in a dress factory. In his poem "Boardwalk at Verdun," the poet Irving Layton (b. 1912) describes the flight of birds over the river. The poem ends: "World, you are a brilliant madman / and these your fervid notions."

Le Parisien 5, at 480 St. Catherine Street West, was once called the Princess Theatre. In the dressing room backstage, the magician and escape artist Houdini received a blow to the stomach, delivered by a McGill student and college boxing champ. Houdini died ten days later in Detroit. [Ross Leslie]

Princess Theatre The most dramatic incident to take place at the Princess Theatre, on rue Sainte-Catherine west of Bleury, occurred not on the stage but in the dressing room. In the late morning of October 21, 1926, the magician and escape artist Houdini (1874-1926), while preparing for his matinée performance, gave an interview to some McGill students. Among the group was J. Gordon Whitehead, a college boxer, who punched Houdini in the stomach to test his reflexes. Caught unaware, Houdini had no time to tighten his stomach muscles and suffered a ruptured appendix which led to peritonitis and his death nine days later in Detroit.

Sketch of Houdini, the world-famous escape artist. [Ontario Film Institute]

Rasco's Hotel A leading hotel in the mid-nineteenth century, Rasco's was located in the building at 295 rue Saint-Paul est. Erected in 1836, the building now serves as government offices. Perhaps its most celebrated guest was Charles Dickens (1812-1870) who stayed here with his wife in 1842 and acted with members of the Garrison

in his theatrical works at the Théâtre Royal. A short street east of the hotel was named in his honour but goes unmarked today. The building was restored and identified as Hôtel Rasco in 1982.

Ritz-Carlton Hotel The Ritz-Carlton Hotel, at the southwest corner of Drummond and Sherbrooke, was designed in 1911. It retains some of its former elegance and remains a favourite with visiting writers. One of these was William Butler Yeats (1865-1939) who was in Montreal in 1932 to give a recital of his poems. In his hotel suite it was the task of poet R. G. Everson (b. 1903) to introduce Stephen Leacock to Yeats. Everson began: "Dr. Leacock, professor of Economics —" Leacock interjected: "I write too." Yeats responded: "A pity. So few read." Everson describes the encounter in his poem "The Confrontation" in *Indian Summer* (1976). There is a description of the Ritz in *The Loved and the Lost* (1951) by Morley Callaghan (b. 1903).

The Theatre Royal stood on this site in 1842 when Charles Dickens visited the city and acted here. Since 1845 the site has been occupied by one wing of the Bonsecours Market. The City of Montreal's planning authority now occupies the building. [Ross Leslie]

Rasco's Hotel, built in 1836, was among North America's finest hostelries. Among its guests were Charles Dickens and his wife. The building at 295 rue Saint-Paul in Old Montreal was restored in 1982, renamed Hôtel Rasco, and leased to the federal Department of Communications. [Ross Leslie]

Charles Dickens was so popular with Montrealers that they gave his name to a short lane behind Rasco's Hotel. The locale of Charles Dickens Lane, off Gosford Street, behind the Hotel (to the left) is shown here. It ceased to be a lane many years ago and today goes unmarked, which is something of a shame. [Ross Leslie]

Saint-Antoine Rue Saint-Antoine, which has the reputation of being a rough street, is in part the setting of Morley Callaghan's *The Loved and the Lost* (1951). Some of the action takes place in the "Café St. Antoine," a nightclub modelled on Rockhead's Paradise, opened in 1928 and still operating (since 1980 as the Rising Sun). Rockhead's had a Black clientele and flourished from 1928 to the 1950s. Callaghan's *The Many Coloured Coat* (1960) also takes place in the vicinity, with a specific mention of "Dorfman's Bar." There is a poem by Miriam Waddington (b. 1917) called "Saint Antoine Street" in *Driving Home* (1972).

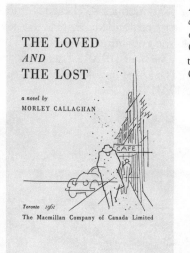

THE LOVED
AND
THE LOST

a novel by
MORLEY CALLAGHAN

Toronto 1961
The Macmillan Company of Canada Limited

A sketch by an unidentified artist appears on the title page of the first edition of Morley Callaghan's The Loved and the Lost. *[Macmillan of Canada]*

Saint-Denis Rue Saint-Denis is often called Montreal's "Latin Quarter," as sections of the street are frequented by students and bohemians, writers and artists. The Théâtre Saint-Denis, constructed in 1916, is the second-largest concert hall in the city. Perhaps the most celebrated performer to appear on its stage was Sarah Bernhardt (1845-1923), the great French actress, on one of her many "farewell tours." The "divine Sarah" made her first appearance on a Canadian stage not here but at the Academy of Music, on Victoria Street, now Eaton's. A delegation of Montrealers travelled by train to St. Alban's in Vermont, to accompany her over "the line." At St. Alban's Louis-Honoré Fréchette (1839-1908) declaimed the verse he wrote for the occasion. It included the lines: "Salut donc, O Sarah! salut, O dona Sol: / Lorsque ton pied mignon vient fouler notre Sol. . . ."

Quebec's oldest repertory theatre, the Théâtre du Rideau Vert, founded in 1948, is located at 4664 rue Saint-Denis. Here have been staged premieres of many plays by Michel Tremblay (b. 1942), some of which are set in the district of Saint-Henri.

Parti Pris, the socialist and separatist journal, was founded in 1963 and published until 1968 at the former Ecole d'Opérette, 3774 rue Saint-Denis. Among the founders were such writers as Pierre Maheu, André Major, and Paul Chamberland. La Librairie Champigny, the popular bookstore, is located at 4474 rue Saint-Denis. It figures in the fantasy-adventure novel *Le Matou* (1981) by Yves Beauchemin (b. 1941). The writer André Carpentier (b. 1947) called his collection of fantastic tales *Rue Saint Denis* (1978); it consists of nine tales, not unlike those of Edgar Allan Poe, which turn the street into a diabolical avenue.

Saint-Henri The French working-class district of Saint-Henri, below Westmount, has been memorably described by Gabrielle Roy (1909-1983). Her novel *Bonheur d'Occasion* (1945), translated by Hannah Josephson as *The Tin Flute* (1947), traces the fortunes of the Lacasse family. The novel, which was filmed in 1983, catches the quality of pinched lives brought about by poverty and unrelenting labour.

The vitality of the district is contained in the poems written in joual by Jean Narrache, pen name of Emile Coderre (1893-1970), the pharmacist who set up shop in Saint-Henri and wrote poems that appeared in such books as *Quand j'parl' tout seul* (1932). He caught the colour and romance of the people, rather in the manner of W. H. Drummond. Louis Dudek has done translations of his poems.

GABRIELLE ROY

BONHEUR
D'OCCASION

I
10ᵉ mille

Société des Editions Pascal
1498 ouest, rue Dorchester
Montréal

Title page of the first reprint edition of Bonheur d'Occasion *(1945), by Gabrielle Roy. It is known in English as* The Tin Flute. *[Société des Editions Pascal]*

Actress Mireille Deyglun adds an infectious smile to the role of the waitress in the film version of Gabrielle Roy's The Tin Flute. *[Ontario Film Institute]*

St. Joseph's Oratory Despite the fact that it has been a Montreal landmark since 1924 (although completed only in 1967) there are surprisingly few descriptions or depictions in prose or poetry, French or English, of the Oratoire Saint-Joseph, 3800 rue Queen Mary. It was conceived in 1904 by Brother André who is buried here and whose heart was on display until someone stole it from the Oratory in 1973. (It was recovered the following year.) It is said ninety-nine steps lead from the street level to the shrine where miraculous cures have been reported. A. M. Klein (1909-1972) refers to the steps as "St. Joseph's ladder" in his poem "The Cripples" (1941-47) in his *Collected Poems* (1975).

St. Lawrence Boulevard See THE MAIN.

St. Patrick's Church The baroque interior of St. Patrick's Church, on rue Saint-Alexandre, built in Gothic and Roman style in 1847 to serve Montreal's Irish community, has in the vestibule two plaques of literary interest. One plaque recalls that Thomas D'Arcy McGee (1825-1868), Father of Confederation and writer, worshipped here; indeed, his pew is identified. Another plaque notes that in this church was baptized Emile Nelligan (1879-1941), the poet, whose father was Irish and mother French-Canadian. After writing his breathtaking poems, he lapsed into silence, then displayed remote indifference to the world. From his twenty-sixth year he was hospitalized, dying at the Hôpital Saint-Jean-de-Dieu, on the outskirts of Montreal. His best-known poem, "Le Vaisseau d'or" ("The Ship of Gold"), supplied Jean Drapeau, Mayor of Montreal, with the name of his restaurant in the 1960s.

St. Urbain Street St. Urbain Street, or rue Saint-Urbain, is a street near The Main whch was settled at the turn of the century by Jews from Eastern Europe. It found its Balzac in Mordecai Richler (b. 1931), who was born and educated here, as was his hero, Duddy Kravitz, whose coming of age in the late 1940s and early 1950s serves as

Actor Richard Dreyfuss, everybody's image of Duddy, plays the young man on the make whose desire is to become a "somebody" in the film version of Mordecai Richler's novel The Apprenticeship of Duddy Kravitz. *[Ontario Film Institute]*

A scene from The Street, *the NFB short film animated by Caroline Leaf and based on Mordecai Richler's story. [NFB]*

the subject of *The Apprenticeship of Duddy Kravitz* (1959). The novel, which was filmed in the district in 1973, has splendid descriptions of St. Urbain Street and of Baron Byng High School which appears as "Fletcher's Field," the English name for Mount Royal Park located in the vicinity.

St. Urbain Street is the dominant symbol in *St. Urbain's Horseman* (1971) in which Richler's hero, the writer Jack Hersh who lives in London; returns to Montreal, revisits the Street, frequents Tansky's Cigar & Soda (modelled on Wilensky's Light Lunch, 5167 rue Clark), and dines at Hy's Delicatessen on The Main.

Richler discusses the mystique of St. Urbain Street in *The Street* (1969), a collection of essays, in which he points out that the area, once predominantly Jewish, is now largely Greek and Portuguese. Yet the area retains its Jewish reputation, in literature if not in reality. As a literal-minded observer has noted, the initial letters of parallel streets in the neighbourhood spell out the acronym JEWS. The streets are Jeanne-Mance, Esplanade, Waverly, and St. Urbain.

Sainte-Catherine Rue Sainte-Catherine, which runs roughly east and west through the centre of the city, may not be as fashionable as Sherbrooke, which runs more or less parallel to it, but it is more human. It has been celebrated in poetry and song and mentioned in story and novel. Jean Narrache (1893-1970) began his poem "Soir d'Hiver dans la Rue Ste-Catherine" (1932) with these lines: "A soir, sur la rue St'-Cath'rine, / Tout l'mond' patauge et puis s'débat / En s'bousculant d'vant les vitrines, / Les pieds dans d'la neig' chocolat." In 1963, André Major (b. 1942) published "O Rue Ste-Catherine" which concludes: "rue Ste-Catherine ombre changeante de ce que sera / notre cri de guerre / car le fer d'un peuple à venir y inscrit déjà / la nervosité de son amour."

Sherbrooke Street Rue Sherbrooke runs east and west through the city, as does its companion street, Sainte-Catherine. In his essay "The Best-Loved Street in Canada," from *Thirty and Three* (1954), Hugh Mac-Lennan (b. 1907) celebrates this street. His prose reaches a climax: "At University, quite suddenly, the sky opens out above the mountain. There is the spacious, lovely green of McGill campus with its fountains of elms, the Arts Building, grey and low at the end of a long shaded walk, and the grey stone piles of the Royal Victoria Hospital towering higher still. Over all the buildings is the cross on the brow of Mount Royal and over everything is the sky. All the way to Côte des Neiges, twelve city blocks in all, this climactic quality continues. It looks so settled, so sure of itself, this mortal heart of Montreal."

In MacLennan's novel *The Watch that Ends the Night* (1959), George Stewart says: "I love Montreal on a fine winter night and I was looking forward to the walk home along Sherbrooke Street with the evening star in the gap at the corner of Guy. . . ."

On a more pedestrian level, rue Sherbrooke has been called the longest street in the world within city limits, for it runs some twenty-two miles from Pointe aux Trembles to Montreal West.

Square Saint-Louis The houses here date from the 1870s, the trees even earlier. The poet Michel Bujold painted a poem on the side of the house at 33 Square Saint-Louis. Men and women prominent in French-Canadian or Québécois literature and the arts who lived or today live in the square include poets Albert Lozeau, Louis Fréchette, Gaston Miron, and Emile Nelligan; composer André Gagnon; singer Pauline Julien; film-maker Claude Jutra.

Square Saint-Louis, off Saint-Denis and above Sherbrooke, is one of Montreal's most beautiful residential squares. It was opened in 1879 and many members of the city's artistic community live or have lived within a stone's throw of St. Louis Square, including Emile Nelligan, Gaston Miron, Claude Jutra, and Pauline Julien. [Ross Leslie]

Sun Life Building The Sun Life Building, with its immense columns and twenty-six stories, has dominated Dominion Square and downtown Montreal since its construction, in stages, between 1918 and 1933, when it was Montreal's first skyscraper, its palladium of business, and Canada's largest building. So it came as a

symbolic as well as an economic blow to the city when the Sun Life Assurance Company announced in 1980 that it was moving its executive offices to Toronto. The joke that went the rounds has it that the Sun Life Building, once a life insurance centre, is now an unemployment insurance centre. Perhaps it is a coincidence that prior to the announcement William Weintraub (b. 1926) published his futuristic novel *The Underdogs* (1979) in which a key locale is the Sun Life Building which in an independent Quebec has become a hydroponic garden centre tended by anglophones who are unable to pass the francophone proficiency tests.

Montreal's first skyscraper was the massive Sun Life Building. [Direction générale du Tourisme-Québec]

Tattersall The industrialist Max Aitken, later Lord Beaverbrook (1879-1964), ran his Canadian holding companies from the offices at Tattersall, 244 rue Saint-Jacques, until 1910, when he left Montreal to seek fame and fortune in London.

Théâtre du Rideau Vert Quebec's oldest repertory theatre was founded in 1948 by Yvette Brind'Amour. It specializes in light commercial plays. One memorable evening was the premiere, on August 28, 1968, of *Les Belles-Soeurs* by Michel Tremblay (b. 1942). The atelier is located at 355 rue Gilford.

Université de Montréal L'Université de Montréal, founded in 1878 and dramatically sited on the northwest slope of Outremont, has the distinction of being the largest French university in the world outside France. It would be invidious to name some distinguished faculty members at the expense of others who are equally distinguished; yet the occasion cannot pass without noting the names of three faculty members of the past and present well-known to English Canadians; these are Lionel-Adolphe Groulx (1878-1967), the historian; Hans Selye (1907-1982), the medical scientist and authority on stress; and Gustave Gingras (b. 1918), a world authority on rehabilitation.

The distinguished psychiatrist and author, Karl

Aerial View of the Université de Montréal on the slope of Mount Royal.
[Direction générale du Tourisme-Québec]

Stern (1906-1975), was a member of the Department of Psychiatry at the Université de Montréal from 1955 to his death. Among his books are *The Pillar of Fire* (1951), *The Third Revolution* (1954), *Through the Dooms of Love* (1960), and *The Flight from Woman* (1965). He lived at 3800 avenue Grey and served, from 1958 to 1968, as psychiatrist-in-chief at St. Mary's Hospital.

Among the French-language writers and critics who teach at "the U. of M." are André Vachon, Gilles Marcotte, François Hébert, Monique Bosco, Jacques Brault, and Jean-Léo Godin. Hugh Hood, the English-language novelist and story-writer, has taught in the English department since 1961.

The poet A. M. Klein (1909-1972) has celebrated the situation and spirit of the educational institution in his poem "Université de Montréal" (1941-47) included in his *Collected Poems* (1975).

The university's Service des Archives, in the Pavillon Principal, has large holdings of interest to students of Quebec literature and society. Included in the manuscript collection are the letters of Hector de Saint-Denys-Garneau, Gérard Parizeau, Victor Morin, Jean Bruchési, Jean Beraud, and Louis Hémon (including the manuscript of the novel *Maria Chapdelaine*).

Véhicule The poetry scene in English in Montreal in the 1970s was enlivened by the activities of the Véhicule poets: Endré Farkas (b. 1948), Artie Gold (b. 1947), Tom Konyves (b. 1947), Claudia Lapp (b. 1946), John McAuley (b. 1947), Stephen Morrissey (b. 1950), and Ken Norris (b. 1951). The Véhicule Art Gallery was opened at 61 rue Sainte-Catherine ouest in 1972; the following year Véhicule Press was established in its print shop. The Gallery was the venue for poetry readings until 1977, when the Press moved to 1000 rue Clark in the Chinatown area. This period was de-

scribed in the novel *Murders in the Welcome Cafe* (1977) by Farkas. The Press moved again in 1979 to 307 rue Sainte-Catherine ouest and the following year its final exhibition (of Concrete Poetry) was held. The Véhicule Poets officially dispersed in 1981, the Art Gallery collapsed two years later, but the Véhicule Press continues at the residence of Simon Dardick, 218 Roy Street East. The Véhicule era was one of innovation and engagement.

The camera catches (left to right) Artie Gold, Ken Norris, and Endré Farkas at the 1977 launching of Montreal English Poetry of the Seventies *edited by Norris and Farkas. [Farkas Collection]*

Verdun See POINTE SAINT-CHARLES.

Ville Jacques-Cartier See LONGUEUIL.

Villeray The Villeray district of northeastern Montreal is where Claude Jasmin (b. 1930) was raised. He has written about the district in *La Petite Patrie* (1972), the first volume in a series of autobiographical sketches upon which the 75-part Radio Canada TV series was based. Jasmin is best known in English Canada for his novel *Ethel and the Terrorist* (1965), based on the first FLQ bombings in April 1963. Its sequel, *Revoir Ethel* (1976), which has yet to be translated, concerns an attempt to set off a bomb in the Olympic Stadium.

Westmount This residential district on the western slope of Mount Royal has long been considered the heart of Anglo-Saxon Montreal. William Douw Lighthall (1857-1954), *littérateur* and author of numerous books in various genres, was Mayor of Westmount in 1900-13. Several of Hugh MacLennan's novels have scenes set in dining rooms and drawing rooms in Westmount mansions. The spectacular view of the rest of the city from Westmount Lookout is described by Gwethalyn Graham (1913-1965) in her novel *Earth and High Heaven* (1944), which deals with covert anti-semitism. Perhaps the poem best descriptive of Westmount attitudes was written by F. R. Scott (b. 1899) who lives on Clark Street. Called "Calamity" (1953), it tells how a laundry truck crashed into "my maple tree" and created such a disturbance that "for a while we were quite human."

Westmount Lookout, with its impressive view of Montreal and the St. Lawrence and the mountains in the distance, is described by Gwethalyn Graham in her novel Earth and High Heaven. *Plates imbedded in the cement railing point out notable features of the scene. The Lookout is located off Summit Circle, Westmount. Enjoying the view is Montreal theatre-performer Ross Leslie.* [Howard Ryshpan]

The Westmount Public Library has been called "the site where modern Canadian poetry began." As A. J. M. Smith explained in "The Confessions of a Compulsive Anthologist" in *On Poetry and Poets* (1977): "In Westmount High and at McGill in the twenties no modern poetry (except Kipling) was taught — and little Canadian poetry (except Carman).... I had to discover modern poetry for myself — more or less by chance. In the Westmount Public Library I came upon *The New Poetry* edited by Harriet Monroe and Alice Corbin Henderson, published in 1917. Here I read with delight and fascination the new poetry of Ezra Pound, Wallace Stevens, T. S. Eliot, Yeats... Conrad Aiken, and H.D."

The October Crisis of 1970 commenced in Westmount with the kidnapping on October 5 of the British consular official James Cross from his home at 1297 Redpath Crescent. He was kept hostage at 18945 rue des Récollets until December 3 when he was released at Dorval Airport. Less fortunate was the Quebec government minister, Pierre Laporte, who was abducted on October 10 from his home at 725 rue Robitaille, Saint-Lambert, and held captive at 5630 rue Armstrong. His body was recovered on October 17 in the trunk of a car abandoned at the Saint-Hubert Airport. The most gripping account of these events is the documentary novel *The Revolution Script* (1971) by Brian Moore (b. 1921) which was subsequently filmed.

Windsor Hotel Although no longer the grand hotel it once was, the Windsor Hotel remains standing at 1170 rue des Récollets until December 3 when he was its former glory as Montreal's leading hostelry and magnet for literary lights.

Oscar Wilde (1856-1900) was a guest there in May 1882 and he recorded in a letter that when he looked out the window of his suite he could see a billboard advertising his lecture. He included a sketch of the billboard in one of his letters. While in Montreal,

Wilde sought out Louis-Honoré Fréchette (1839-1908), Quebec's leading poet, but Fréchette gave Wilde short shrift, finding his aestheticism and amorality pagan.

When he looked out the window of his suite in the Windsor Hotel, Oscar Wilde saw "one's own name in alternate colours of Albert blue and magenta and six feet high." He sketched the scene and concluded, in his letter to a friend, May 12, 1882: "I feel I have not lived in vain." [Rupert Hart-Davis]

Something of a scandal surrounded the luncheon address to the members of the Athenaeum Club in the hotel's main dining room. The address was delivered by Matthew Arnold (1822-1904) on February 21, 1884. The English poet, critic, and scholar spoke to a distinguished group that included Sir William Osler (1849-1919) and the above-mentioned Fréchette who recited a verse of welcome. For his part, Arnold attacked the defects of Protestantism, and then proceeded to do the same for Catholicism. Fréchette rose from the table and stomped out of the room. Arnold merely adjusted his eyeglasses.

There was an altogether different reaction to Sir Arthur Conan Doyle (1859-1930), the creator of Sherlock Holmes, who addressed a luncheon meeting of the Canadian Club in the hotel's Rose Room, June 4, 1914. In his speech titled "The Future of Canadian Literature," Doyle advised Canadians that they need not worry about their lack of literary development. "There are better things to do than dream," he said, for "the great deed that is accomplished is more glorious than the great sonnet." The message endeared him to the businessmen present.

It was in the basement of the Windsor Hotel during the centennial year that Mayor Jean Drapeau opened his publicized but short-lived restaurant, which he named "Le Vaisseau d'or" ("The Ship of Gold"), after the popular poem by Emile Nelligan (1879-1941). The text of the poem was reproduced on the wall of the restaurant in the original French and in A. J. M. Smith's English translation.

People

Ted Allan (b. 1916), playwright and biographer, grew up on St. Urbain Street. He described his childhood in a series of uncollected short stories which provided the basis for the film *Lies My Father Told Me*, directed by Jan Kadar in 1975. In the stories and film, the locale is

Ted Allan, the writer, played the part of the tailor Baumgarten in the 1975 feature film Lies My Father Told Me. *In this still from the production Allan is seen (second from right). The Israeli actor Yossi Yadin, with full beard, is seated opposite him. Montreal actor Howard Ryshpan is seated to Allan's right.* [Ginette Sauvé]

Here, on the grounds of Villa-Maria, 4245 Decarie, the deranged novelist Hubert Aquin committed suicide, March 15, 1977. Beyond the trees Villa-Maria is visible. The grounds were once Monklands, the official residence of Governor General Lord Monk. [Ross Leslie]

Cadieux Street, subsequently renamed De Bullion, above Sherbrooke. Scenes in the film were shot on De Bullion. The cemetery sequences were taken in the Jewish Cemetery on rue De La Savanne in the Town of Mount Royal, where A. M. Klein reposes.

Hubert Aquin (1929-1977), the novelist, was born near Lafontaine Park and studied, as did Emile Nelligan before him, at the Ecole Olier. During a four-month detention in 1964 in the Albert Prévost Psychiatric Institute, he wrote his first novel, *Prochain Episode* (1965). (He was under detention for the illegal possession of firearms, but was eventually found not guilty.) Violence fascinated him, and he shot himself to death on March 15, 1977, on the grounds of Villa-Maria, a private secondary school for girls, not far from the vice-regal country residence of Monklands. He left a suicide note which said in part, "I have lived intensely, and now it is over." His body was burned and his ashes are kept at the Montreal East Cemetery, 6893 rue Sherbrooke.

Multiple images of Hubert Aquin, the revolutionary novelist, from the NFB film Deux Episodes dans la Vie d'Hubert Aquin *directed by Jacques Godbout.* [NFB]

Don Bell (b. 1936) has turned journalism into an art in two books about life in Montreal in the 1960s and 1970s. The focus of *Saturday Night at the Bagel Factory* (1972, 1983) may be the Bagel Factory, at Saint-Viateur, near avenue Park, but the pieces range more widely. One particularly effective piece is "The Walk-Talk Tour of Old Montreal" which overlays the old buildings with new chatter. Bell's neglected classic is *Pocketman* (1979), a series of anecdotes, fables, stories, insights, etc., involving the unnamed "Pocketman," a Sufi-like character who could be found at "The Bistro" (actually Chez Lou Lou Bacchantes, on rue Mountain) where Bell met the gypsy writer Ron "Yanko" Lee, poet Eddie (Do Nothing) Baker, journalist Tom Wolfe, and artist Armand Vaillancourt. "Pocketman" is in reality Roy McDonald who in the 1980s is more often found at his neighbourhood McDonald's in London, Ont.

Paul-Emile Borduas (1905-1960), although a painter, is the principal author of perhaps the most important aesthetic manifesto in Canadian history, *Refus global.* Borduas largely wrote and printed four hundred copies of this declaration on August 9, 1948. It called for the liberation of man's spirit from society and convention. It demanded surrealism and automatism: "Make way for magic! Make way for objective mystery!" *Refus global,* along with his autobiographical essay *Projections libérantes* (1949), was reprinted in 1972. The long-range result of issuing the manifesto was the release of Borduas' own creative energy. The short-term effect was his dismissal from his teaching post at the Ecole du Meuble, then located at 506 rue Dorchester est.

Sir George-Etienne Cartier (1814-1873), Sir John A. Macdonald's "Quebec lieutenant" and a Father of Confederation, was noted in his day as the composer of two popular songs. These are "Avant tout je suis Canadien" (Before all I am a Canadian), a marching song for the Rebellion of 1837, and "O Canada, mon pays, mes amours" (O Canada, my country, my love), a quasi-anthem. There are many sites in Quebec and the rest of

Canada associated with him; here are the principal ones in Montreal. His residence and office is now called Cartier House; it is a three-storey stone building erected in 1840, now restored, on Berri in the Bonsecours area. Another residence on rue Saint-Vincent is plaqued. A bronze statue was raised in his honour in Mount Royal Park. These attest to the affection of French Canadians for the statesmen who brought Lower Canada into Confederation.

Composer-singer-poet Leonard Cohen. [CBC]

Leonard Cohen (b. 1934), the poet and singer, spends perhaps half of each year in his home town. He once lived on Hydra, an island in the Aegean, and he has been known to take refuge in a monastery in California. At the time of the publication of *The Spice-Box of Earth* (1961), he told an interviewer: "But I have to keep coming back to Montreal to renew my neurotic affiliations."

The Montreal he returns to is not that of the family home on Belmont Avenue Road in Upper Westmount. He lives by choice in a renovated, second-storey flat on rue Saint-Dominic in the low-rental east end. Around the corner, on rue Marie-Anne, in a small renovated house, lives his celebrated Suzanne. "I choose the rooms I live in with care, / There's only one table and only one chair," he claimed in "Tonight Will Be Fine" from his album *Songs from a Room*.

Cohen's "downward mobility" from Upper Westmount to the east end, Irving Layton once observed, is the reverse of his own "upward mobility" from the east end to Notre-Dame-de-Grâce, if not Westmount.

There is no shortage of references to Montreal in Cohen's poems and novels. Indeed, *The Favourite Game* (1963) hops about the city like the knight in chess. *Beautiful Losers* (1966) celebrates the Mohawk saint Kateri Tekakwitha of the nearby Caughnawaga Indian Reserve. In 1981, he told an interviewer: "I've been suggesting Montreal separate from Quebec and Canada. Montreal is a special kind of city-state. We shouldn't tie our destinies to either Quebec or Canada. It's not like either of them. The Free State of Montreal."

William Henry Drummond (1854-1907), the "habitant poet," lived from 1894 to his death, which occured in Cobalt, Ont., in a stately home at 1181 Mountain Street. The house, which gave shelter to Jefferson Davis, the leader of the U.S. Confederacy, in the spring and summer of 1867, has since been demolished. "His city residence was the modest unpretentious home of a practising physician: his real life was in the all-out-doors, which he knew and loved so well," wrote E. J. Hathaway in "Canadian Literary Homes," *The Canadian Magazine,* January 1908. In his youth Drummond worked as a telegrapher at Bord-à-Plouffe, Rivières des Prairies, between Montreal Island and the north shore, and it was here that he heard the mixture of French, Scots, Irish, and English that became the basis of his dialect poems.

W. H. Drummond's residence in Montreal is shown as it appeared in 1908. [Metropolitan Toronto Library]

Louis Dudek (b. 1918), who has made so marked a contribution to the literary life of Montreal, was born to Polish parents in the east end of the city. His birthplace was a third-floor flat at 2360 Bercy Street where he lived until his twenties with his family. He attended Lansdowne School and graduated from McGill University in 1939. He studied and taught in New York until 1951 when he returned to McGill where he taught until retirement in 1984. His office, Arts 240, in the Arts Building, was a Mecca for young poets.

In 1943, on the promenade of the Jacques Cartier Bridge (which Montrealers sometimes call "the Jimmy Carter Bridge"), where it overlooks St. Catherine Street, Dudek and fellow poet Irving Layton promenaded and planned together the transformation of Canadian poetry. From the bridge may be seen the site of Lansdowne School, now occupied by a supermarket, and the region Dudek described in the poems that

Louis Dudek is standing in front of the Westmount Public Library which he has called "the site where modern Canadian poetry began." [Louis Dudek]

make up *East of the City* (1946) — from St. Catherine down toward Notre Dame Street. The "bronze foundry" was on the east side of Delorimier Street, near Dorchester, where John Sutherland was employed. The "boiler factory" was on Lafontaine Street, east of Delorimier, which Dudek passed on his way home from school. Dudek frequented the printing office of *First Statement*, published by John Sutherland in 1942-45, located on the second floor of the building on the northeast corner of rue St. Antoine and rue Jeanne-Mance opposite the present offices and plant of *The Gazette*. The old *First Statement* office is now occupied by the Montreal Newspaper Guild, Local III.

A quarter-mile east of the village of Charlemagne, which is east of Montreal Island, will be found the Rozynski farm still owned by Dudek's relatives. Here, in 1951, Dudek was visited by John Sutherland and Raymond Souster who introduced him to the poetry of Charles Olson and Robert Creeley. "I'll always remember the day on the farm on the Little Jesus River," wrote Souster, "with Louis Dudek throwing the first two issues of Cid Corman's *Origin* down on the picnic table and saying, 'This is typical of what the nuts in New York are doing these days.'"

Dudek and his wife Aileen Collins spend as much time as possible in their summer home at the edge of the village of Way's Mills, near Mount Orford, their "Shangri-La," in the Eastern Townships. In Montreal they live at 5 Ingleside Avenue where *Delta* magazine, Delta Canada Press, and DC Books flourished in the 1950s and 1960s.

François-Xavier Garneau (1809-1866), the historian, is remembered in the naming in 1924 of F. X. Garneau Park, blvd. Monk and rue Briand, Saint-Paul district. Goaded by the passage of Lord Durham's *Report* (1839),

which dismissed French Canadians as "a people with no history, and no literature," he set himself the task of writing his *Histoire du Canada* (1845-48) in three volumes. The house in which he researched and wrote his mammoth history is in Quebec City. His great-grandson was the poet Hector de Saint-Denys-Garneau (1912-1943).

Hugh Hood (b. 1928), novelist and story writer, has taught in the English Department of the Université de Montréal since 1961, when he came here from Toronto. He prepared himself for the task of preserving, in a Proustian manner, that city's thoughts and textures in a series of twelve novels collectively called "The New Age," yet his earliest and perhaps most characteristic stories were set not in his native city but in his adopted city. The title story of *Flying a Red Kite* (1962), which was filmed as *The Red Kite* by the NFB in 1965, is set on the summit and slopes of Mount Royal. He found consciences to probe and tales to tell in each of the twelve quarters of the city in *Around the Mountain* (1967), subtitled "Scenes from Montreal Life." Since September 1967 he has lived in the residential district of Notre-Dame-de-Grâce at 4242 avenue Hampton.

Hugh Hood, the author of Dark Glasses, *is depicted by Don Evans, the artist who signs his drawings Isaac Bickerstaff. [Special Collections, University of Calgary Libraries]*

A. M. Klein (1909-1972), among the greatly gifted of poets, always maintained he was Montreal-born, but in truth his birthplace was Ratno, Poland, and he was brought to Montreal when he was one year old. He attended Baron Byng High School and in 1924 formed, with David Lewis and others, its Sholem Aleichem Club which was named after the well-loved Yiddish writer. At McGill University, he was part of the poetry scene, publishing alongside F. R. Scott, A. J. M. Smith, and others.

Klein lived in a succession of houses: 30 St. Charles Borromée, south of rue Vitre (1910-14); 4071 Hôtel de Ville, between Duluth and Rachel (1914-18); 4267 Clarke (1918-30); 4455 St. Urbain (1930-33); 4353 St. Urbain, when he married (1933-36); apartment at

117 rue Mount Royal ouest (1938-40); 4857 Hutchison, near St. Joseph Boulevard (1940-50); 236 avenue Querbes, Outremont (from 1950 to his death).

He maintained a second-floor study at this last address, and was visited here by Leon Edel, Irving Layton, A. J. M. Smith, among others, but he did little if any creative work from the early 1950s to his death. He died in his sleep in this house and is buried in Baron de Hirsch Affiliated Cemeteries, Section Montesiore Hebrew Protective, 5015 rue De La Savanne, where his tombstone describes him as "a beloved father and grandfather." In his "Requiem for A. M. Klein," in *The Pole-Vaulter* (1974), Irving Layton (b. 1912) wrote: "You were a medieval troubadour / Who somehow wandered into a lawyer's office / and could not find your way back again. . . ."

Klein wrote memorably and emotionally about Montreal, and especially about the races that met but did not mingle in the city. A minor but exceptionally sweet poem, "For the Sisters of the Hotel Dieu," celebrates the nursing nuns — addressed "O biblic birds" — who attended to his needs at the local hospital when he broke his leg while learning to skate. Other poems about the city are "Pastoral of the City Streets" and "Autobiographical" which begins: "Out of the ghetto streets where a Jewboy / Dreamed pavement into pleasant Bible-land. . . ."

Irving Layton (b. 1912), the poet, was born in the Romanian village of Pietra-Neamtz. At some future point a plaque may well be raised to mark the place; in the meantime there are numerous sites to note in the city of Montreal where he was brought by his mother at the age of one. There are two childhood homes of note. The first is the house at 183 rue Sainte-Elizabeth, demolished as part of the Dozois Plan, where his mother ran a grocery store with her four sons. (Not far away another immigrant woman, Ida Steinberg, opened her own delicatessen, and turned the family

Irving Layton in the 1980s: poet and prophet. [McClelland & Stewart / Sherry Collins]

business into a business empire.) The Laytons lived there from 1914 to 1925.

Still standing is the second of the two childhood homes. From 1925 to 1929, the family operated a grocery store and lived in the old house at 4158 City Hall Avenue. Layton wrote about the district in the poem "The Yard" which begins "No one prospers outside my door. . . ."

Layton attended Baron Byng High School behind the generation of A. M. Klein but ahead of the generation of Mordecai Richler. Then he studied at Macdonald College in Sainte-Anne-de-Bellevue and McGill University. "Philosophy 34" was written about studies at McGill. From 1946 to 1960, Layton taught at Herzliah, on Esplanade, now a French-language school, then a high school run by the United Talmud Torah. Such poems as "Schoolteacher in Late November" and "To the Girls of My Graduating Class" were inspired by this experience.

Layton and his wife, the painter Betty Sutherland, lived in a two-storey "cozy cottage" at 8035 Kildare Avenue in Côte Saint-Luc from 1950 to 1958. This marked a period of great creativity and sociability. Advance copies of two of his collections — *In the Midst of My Fever* and *The Long Pea-Shooter* — arrived from different publishers in the same mail delivery one day in 1954. Such popular poems as "On Seeing" and "Song of Naomi" date from this period. Friday evenings were reserved for poetry gatherings, and on one occasion in 1955 Leonard Cohen read his latest poems to a group that included F. R. Scott and Louis Dudek. Dudek agreed to publish Cohen's first collection on condition they could find a lively title. They instantly agreed on the line "Let us compare mythologies" from one of the poems. A somewhat intoxicated guest on another occasion was Dylan Thomas (1914-1953) who, despite his condition, spoke "Thomasese" for fifteen minutes before lapsing into unconsciousness.

Another creative period was spent in Apartment 6, 4391 avenue Somerled, Notre-Dame-de-Grâce.

At the bat is Irving Layton, popular teacher at Herzliah high school in Montreal, Spring 1952. [Concordia University Library, Layton Collection / H. S. Adler]

Layton lived here from 1960 to 1969 with his wife, the writer Aviva Layton (b. 1933), and here he wrote such poems as "I saw a Fawn," "Redemption," "A Dedication," and "Winter Light." Aviva Layton's novel, *Nobody's Daughter* (1982), although written later, has many points in common with this period in their life.

Layton announced "The Channukah lights are going out" — prophetically in light of the October Crisis two years in the future — and took a position of writer-in-residence at the University of Guelph and then moved to Toronto and vicinity for the next fourteen years. In November 1983 he returned to Montreal to a two-storey "writer's cottage" with oak panelling and a sunroom at 6897 avenue Monkland in Notre-Dame-de-Grâce.

Stephen Leacock (1869-1944), the humorist, was the country's most widely read author of the day. He taught in and then headed McGill University's Department of Political Science from 1903 to his retirement in 1936. He was attached to McGill and loath to leave it. "Indeed I have always found that the only thing in regard to Toronto which faraway people know for certain is that McGill University is in it," he wrote in *My Discovery of the West* (1937). Fellow political economists maintain there was more humour in his lectures and textbooks than in his speeches and books. He did much of his writing at his summer home in Orillia.

He loved McGill and Montreal — in that order. He wrote a book apiece about the university and the metropolis, and he was surprisingly tough on his adopted city in regard to the arts. In a long study, *Montreal: Seaport and City* (1942), he maintained: "It is not possible in such limited compass to say much of Montreal as the home of arts and letters. Nor is there much to say."

Leacock's favourite haunt was the University Club

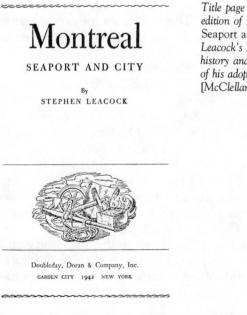

Montreal

SEAPORT AND CITY

By

STEPHEN LEACOCK

Doubleday, Doran & Company, Inc.
GARDEN CITY 1942 NEW YORK

Title page of the first edition of Montreal: Seaport and City, *Leacock's 340-page history and appreciation of his adopted city.* [McClelland & Stewart]

where he hosted dinners, played billiards, drank at the bar, and read newspapers. He was one of the charter members and helped found this men's faculty club in 1908, first in an old residence on Dorchester Street then, five years later, at its present location on Mansfield Street. Today there is a "Leacock Corner," with a portrait by Richard Jack that looks down on a small table flanked by two armchairs. At one notable dinner hosted by Leacock, B. K. Sandwell, John Murray Gibbon, and Pelham Edgar discussed the Canadian Copyright Act and their discussion was so animated they agreed to continue it in a series of meetings that eventually led to the founding convention in Montreal in 1921 of the Canadian Authors' Association. The University Club did not serve as the model for the "Mausoleum Club" described in *Arcadian Adventures with the Idle Rich* (1914). That distinction belongs to the Mount Royal Club, established in 1906 and located on Sherbrooke Street which is called "Plutoria Avenue" in this collection of humorous sketches.

With the earnings from *Nonsense Novels* (1911), he acquired a large three-storey residence on the lower slope of Mount Royal. The residence at 165 rue Côte-des-Neiges, since demolished, was near the Montreal General Hospital and within walking distance of McGill. As he wrote in the introduction to Vilhjalmur Stefansson's *Unsolved Mysteries of the Arctic* (1938): "With the help perhaps of an odd glass of hot toddy kept warm on the hearth, I can face any Arctic winter that ever was. No igloo was ever snugger than my study-library on the Côte-des-Neiges road, with a volume of Arctic adventure to centre its warmth and comfort."

Thomas D'Arcy McGee (1825-1868), patriot, poet, and Father of Confederation, lived in a limestone house in Montmorenci Terrace, at the southeast corner of rue Sainte-Catherine and Drummond. A gift of constituents, it had shamrocks carved in the stone windowsills. Following his assassination in Ottawa on April 7, 1868, his body lay in state for three days in the dining room here, before being conveyed to St. Patrick's Church on Easter Monday, which would have been his forty-third birthday. He is buried in Notre-Dame-des-Neiges Cemetery.

Hugh MacLennan (b. 1907) may have his roots in the Maritimes but his branches are in Montreal. He was twenty-eight when he came here to teach Classics at Lower Canada College in Notre-Dame-de-Grâce, from 1935 to 1945. During this period he lived at 5265 rue Côte-Saint-Luc where he wrote his first two novels, *Barometer Rising* (1941) and *Two Solitudes* (1945). Earnings from the latter encouraged him to become a full-time writer and to divide his time between Montreal and the summer cottage he acquired in the Eastern Townships. This period ended when he became a part-time instructor at McGill University in 1951, full-time

Hugh MacLennan in a mood intranquil. [Peter Paterson]

TWO
SOLITUDES

By Hugh MacLennan

COLLINS
70 BOND STREET, TORONTO

The title page of the first edition of Two Solitudes (1945) is austere by contemporary standards. [Hugh MacLennan]

Embodiments of the "two solitudes" are Jean-Claude Tallant (played by Jean-Pierre Aumont) and Huntley McQueen (played by Stacey Keach) in the movie based on Hugh MacLennan's novel Two Solitudes. [Ontario Film Institute]

in 1954, until retirement in 1979. He lived at 1535 avenue Summerhill, where he wrote *The Watch that Ends the Night* (1959), in the late 1950s and early 1960s.

MacLennan's work has a strong sense of place. He created the parish setting of *Two Solitudes*, explaining in the Author's Foreword: "The parish known in the story as Saint-Marc-des-Erables is also imaginary. There may be other Saint-Marcs in the province of Quebec, but they are not mine." The novel was adapted for the stage in 1957 and filmed in 1978. Montreal in the 1930s and 1940s is the setting of *The Watch that Ends the Night* (1959) which is concerned with the return as if from the dead of "Jerome Martell" (whose experiences recall those of Montrealer Norman Bethune).

More than any other novelist who comes to mind, MacLennan has written fiction that is part and parcel of Canada. As a social historian, but also as a psychologist, he has delved into the Canadian psyche as has no other writer. His novels will long remain in print for nationalist as well as literary reasons. So here is a list of them with sites specifically mentioned.

Barometer Rising (1941), about the Halifax Explosion, takes place between December 2 and December 10, 1917, and has specific mentions of the Citadel, Northwest Arm, the Stream, the Narrows, Bedford Basin, McNab Island, George's Island, Barrington Street, Granville Street, Hollis Street, George Street, the Parade, Water Street, York Redoubt, Sandwich Battery, North Street Station, Richmond Bluff, St. Mary's Cathedral.

Two Solitudes (1945) is set in the imaginary parish of Saint-Marc-des-Erables, near Montreal, between 1917 and 1939. There are references to Mount Royal, Dorval, Lac Saint-Louis, Halifax, etc. The title, of course, derives from a letter of Rainer Maria Rilke, and refers to the French and the English in Quebec.

The Precipice (1948), based on Anthony Tudor's

ballet *Pillar of Fire* which the author saw in New York in 1946, is set in "Grenville," Ont., an amalgam of Port Hope, Cobourg, and Belleville, Ont.

Each Man's Son (1951), set on Cape Breton Island, takes place in the colliery near the town of "Broughton," N.S. There are mentions of Moncton and Sydney, and the Prologue gives a history of settlement of Cape Breton Island.

The Watch that Ends the Night (1959) is set in Montreal in the 1930s and has references to Sherbrooke Street, Côte des Nieges, Dorval, Lake Saint-Louis, Dorchester Street, St. Catherine Street, Guy Street, as well as Ottawa and Halifax. The spectre of Norman Bethune looms over the novel, intriguingly.

Return of the Sphinx (1967), a generational novel, is set in Ottawa and Montreal and deals directly with separatism. Montreal references include Simpson Street, Sherbrooke Street, and the Ritz. In Ottawa it is the Rideau Canal that is referred to.

Voices in Time (1980) is set in the future but firmly anchored in the past. The locale is the environs of "Metro," as Montreal is known in the post-holocaust future, and perhaps owes something in conception to

E. M. Forster's "The Machine Stops." The year is 2039, with backward glances to the two world wars and the 1960s and 1970s when morality went into decline.

Gaston Miron (b. 1928) is the poet of the city of Montreal, according to many, though he was born not here but in Sainte-Agathe-des-Monts. In 1953 he helped found Les Editions de l'Héxagone, with its offices at Librairie Déom, on rue Saint-Denis, and since the 1960s has directed this literary publishing house which has issued works by such writers as Jean-Guy Pilon, Fernand Ouellette, and Paul-Marie Lapointe. Héxagone is now at rue Ontario est. Jacques Brault called the poet and publisher "Miron le Magnifique."

Emile Nelligan (1879-1941), the poet, was born in Montreal and baptized in St. Patrick's Church where a plaque was raised in his honour. He studied at the Ecole Olier and Mont Saint-Louis, then at the Collège de Montréal and the Collège Sainte-Marie, finally quitting at the age of seventeen. He made a handful of public appearances with the group known as the Ecole Littéraire de Montréal in 1899, then lapsed into insanity. He was committed to the Saint-Benoît asylum and, in 1925, to the public ward of the Jean-de-Dieu hospital, spending more than forty years in institutions. His *Poésies Complètes* (1952) was edited by Luc Lacourcière.

Emile Nelligan as a handsome young man, drawn by Isaac Bickerstaff (artist Don Evans). [Special Collections, University of Calgary Libraries]

Emile Nelligan, 17¢ stamp, 1979. [Canada Post Corporation]

Mordecai Richler (b. 1931) was born and raised in the St. Urbain Street area of the city and graduated from Baron Byng High School. He attended Sir George Williams College (now Concordia University) and worked for the CBC before moving to London, England, in 1959. He returned in 1972 and now lives in Westmount. His first novel, *The Acrobats* (1954), is set in post-war Spain. *Son of a Smaller Hero* (1955) explores the St. Urbain Street area, including the Main. A *Choice of Enemies* (1957) returns to Europe in the 1950s. *The Apprenticeship of Duddy Kravitz* (1959), which begins in 1947, is set in the St. Urbain Street area as well as the Laurentian resort town of Sainte-Adèle. *The Incomparable Atuk* (1963) describes the Toronto cultural scene in the 1960s, notably the Park Plaza Hotel and the University of Toronto, with excursions to Montreal and Baffin Island. *Cocksure* (1968) has the London literary scene in the early 1960s as its locale. *The Street* (1969) is a collection of stories about the St. Urbain Street ghetto. *St. Urbain's Horseman* (1971), set in London, has flashbacks to St. Urbain Street (notably "Tansky's Cigar and Soda") and an account of Duddy Kravitz in Toronto. *Joshua Then and Now* (1980) jumps from a cottage on Lake Memphremagog (where the author has a summer home) to a townhouse in Westmount, with passing references to the Montreal General Hospital, the Ritz-Carlton Hotel, etc.

Mordecai Richler visits the St. Urbain Street shooting of The Apprenticeship of Duddy Kravitz *and chats with Jack Warden (centre) who plays Max and Richard Dreyfuss (right) who plays Duddy. [Ontario Film Institute]*

Gabrielle Roy (1909-1983) made Montreal uniquely her own with her first novel, *The Tin Flute* (1947), despite the fact that she spent her early years at St. Boniface, Man., and her later years in Quebec City. She settled in Montreal following her first trip to Europe and from her flat on rue Dorchester explored the working-class district of Saint-Henri. Along the old Lachine Canal, she wrote, "I discovered the people that was my own, and its tragedy, and its sadness, and its gaiety too." She told the story of the Lacasse family, and set it amid familiar places: "There was nothing more peaceful than St. Ambroise Street on a winter night. . . the house where John lived was opposite the drawbridge at the corner of St. Augustin Street."

Michel Tremblay (b. 1942), the playwright, was born and raised on rue Fabre, a lesser-known street in the Plateau Mont-Royal district, east of The Main. It is the setting of many of his plays, as is the more ethnically and socially diverse Main. In 1974, he settled amid the more prosperous inhabitants of Outremont, which he wrote about in *The Impromptu of Outremont* (1980; English translation 1981). Tremblay's major plays are divided into those set in the Plateau Mont-Royal district and those set in The Main–Boulevard Saint-Laurent.

Located on rue Fabre in the Plateau Mont-Royal district of the author's youth are *Les Belles-Soeurs* (1968, 1974), *Forever Yours, Marie-Lou* (1971, 1973), *Bonjour la, Bonjour* (1974, 1975), and *Damnée Manon, Sacrée Sandra* (1977). In addition, his prose works are "chronicles" of life in the district: *The Fat Woman Next Door Is Pregnant* (1978, 1981) and *Thérèse and Pierrette at the Ecole de Saintes* (1980, 1982).

Located in The Main, the district of gay bars, cabarets, and bachelor apartments, are such plays as *La Duchesse de Langeais* (1970, 1976), *Demain Montréal m'Attend* (1972), *Hosanna* (1973, 1974), and *Sainte Carmen de la Main* (1976, 1981).

Michel Tremblay, playwright of Plateau Mont-Royal.
[*Performing Arts*]

"La Morte Rouge"

An imaginary village in rural Quebec, "La Morte Rouge" is the locale of the 1944 film *The Scarlet Claw*, which starred Basil Rathbone as Sherlock Holmes and Nigel Bruce as Dr. Watson. Holmes and Watson, attending a conference on criminology in Montreal, are summoned to this remote village where they find Lord Penrose (played by Paul Cavanagh) dead. His death is attributed to the century-old "monster of the marshes." Holmes proves the legend to be an invention and brings the murderer to justice. The action is loosely based on Sir Arthur Conan Doyle's novel *The Hound of the Baskervilles* (1902), which had earlier been successfully filmed; nevertheless, *The Scarlet Claw* is considered to be one of the most dramatic of Holmes movies. It concludes with a wartime message; Holmes quotes Sir Winston Churchill's description of Canada as "the linch-pin of the English-speaking world."

No log cabin was ever as sumptuous as the one depicted in The Scarlet Claw, the Sherlock Holmes movie set in Quebec. It starred Basil Rathbone as Sherlock Holmes and Nigel Bruce as Dr. Watson. [*Ontario Film Institute*]

Natashquan

This tiny fishing village on the north shore of the Gulf of St. Lawrence, opposite Anticosti Island, has emotional repercussions for a generation of *Québécois*, as it was the birthplace of Gilles Vigneault (b. 1928), the poet and chansonnier, who sings of Natashquan in many of his moving songs. Vigneault is best known as the composer and singer of "Mon Pays" (1964) and "Gens du Pays" (1976). A small Indian reserve is also located at Natashquan.

New Richmond

Stanley House, located outside New Richmond on the Baie des Chaleurs, is a rustic retreat that serves as a meeting place for artists and scholars. It was built as a salmon-fishing lodge about 1888 by Governor General Lord Stanley. Donated to the Canada Council by a subsequent owner in 1961, it is used during July and August for meeting purposes, and has accommodation for up to fifteen guests.

North Hatley   See EASTERN TOWNSHIPS.

Oka

The Trappist monks at the Cistercian monastery which overlooks the Lake of Two Mountains, at Oka, west of Montreal, make the delicious Oka cheese. Gratien Gélinas (b. 1909), the man of the theatre, has a summer home not far from the monastery.

Ottawa Valley   See OTTAWA RIVER AND VALLEY, Ont.

Percé Rock   See GASPÉ.

Péribonca

The village of Péribonca, in the Lac Saint-Jean region, was made famous by Louis Hémon (1880-1913), the French journalist and novelist, in his posthumously published novel of rural Quebec, *Maria Chapdelaine* (1916). To research the lives of the farming community, Hémon

Maria Chapdelaine *has been filmed three times. This is a still from the 1934 version directed by Julien Duvivier, starring Jean Gabin, Madeleine Renaud, and Jean-Pierre Aumont.* [PAC / National Film, Television and Sound Archives]

Maria Chapdelaine, *with Carole Laure as Maria and Nick Mancuso as her French lover, was directed by Gilles Carle. This was the third version of this French-Canadian classic. Julien Duvivier directed Madeleine Renaud and Jean Gabin in 1934; Marc Allegret did the same with Michèle Morgan and Philippe Lemaître in 1949. Carle's version was filmed in the picturesque Lac Baskatong area.* [Ontario Film Institute]

worked as a farm hand (at $8 a month) on the farm of Samuel and Laura Bédard. He kept notes throughout the summer of 1912, and in the fall revised them at a boarding house at Saint-Gédéon, on the southeast shore of Lac Saint-Jean. He completed the novel in the spring of 1913 in Montreal. Later that year he was killed in a railway accident at Chapleau, Ont.

The Bouchard house in which Hémon lived is now a museum. Here one may ponder the choice that Maria must make. Should she marry François Paradis, the trapper, and live the lives of her ancestors; or should she move to Boston with Lorenzo Suprenant? She keeps faith with her ancestors, the French settlers of Quebec. "In this land of Quebec naught shall die and naught change," runs the familiar peroration of the novel in W. H. Blake's translation of 1921. The novel has three times been made into a film, most recently in 1983.

Naught shall change? As Jean-Charles Falardeau, the

LOUIS HÉMON

MARIA CHAPDELAINE

illustrations de

CLARENCE GAGNON

ÉDITIONS MORNAY
8, RUE DE L'ARRIVÉE, PARIS-XV
1933

Title page of the 1933 edition of Maria Chapdelaine *illustrated by Clarence Gagnon.* [Hawkshead Services]

Louis Hémon, 8¢ stamp, 1975. [Canada Post Corporation]

social scientist, wrote in 1953: "The daughter of Maria Chapdelaine who was an ammunition-factory worker at Valcartier during the war now lives with her own family of five children in the Rosemount ward of Montreal. Maria's married brothers are employees of the Aluminum Company at Arvida and Shipshaw after having been workers at the Jonquière pulp plant."

In the Lac Saint-Jean area may be found: the Canton de Hémon, Lac Hémon, Lac Maria-Chapdelaine, and the municipality of Maria-Chapdelaine, the naming of which testifies to the imaginative and social impact of Hémon's classic novel.

Petit Rocher   See CALUMET ISLAND, Ont.

Pointe-au-Pic

Beautifully situated on the north shore of the St. Lawrence, Pointe-au-Pic was established in 1760 and is often described as North America's oldest resort. Born at nearby La Malbaie was Félicité Angers (1845-1924), who wrote under the pen name of Laure Conan and is regarded as the first French-Canadian woman novelist. Her finest work, *Angéline de Montbrun* (1884), which was translated

Laure Conan as a woman of style, drawn by Isaac Bickerstaff, pen name of Don Evans. [Special Collections, University of Calgary Libraries]

Laure Conan, 32¢ stamp, 1983. [Canada Post Corporaion]

by Yves Brunelle in 1975, is a novel set on the estate of "Vabriant" on the north shore. Her home is now a museum with some of her personal effects, not to mention Sitting Bull's rifle and the cassock of Lionel-Adolphe Groulx, the historian. Close by, in the Protestant cemetery at Murray Bay, is the grave of W. H. Blake (1861-1924), essayist and translator of Louis Hémon's *Maria Chapdelaine* (1921) and Adjutor Rivard's *Chez nous: Our Quebec Home* (1924). The Musée Charlevoix at La Malbaie, located in a moored ferry boat, has some of Laure Conan's personal effects.

Povungnituk

This tiny Inuit settlement, on the east side of Hudson Bay in the Ungava region of northern Quebec, is rich in myth and legend. Some traditional lore was collected by Zebedee Nungak (b. 1951) and Eugene Arima in *Eskimo Stories from Povungnituk, Quebec* (1969). Povungnituk — or Pov for short — means "place of bad smells." Pov is the home of the Povungnituk Co-operative.

Provancher

West of Lac Saint-Jean is the Canton de Provancher, the name of which commemorates the work of priest and naturalist Léon Provancher (1820-1892).

Quebec City

Quebec City, as well as being the capital of the Province of Quebec, is the most historic of Canadian cities. It was Hugh MacLennan (b. 1907) who made the fundamental observation: "Quebec, to me at least, has the air of a city that never was young. No community in America, few in Europe, give out such a feeling of intense, rain-washed antiquity as does Quebec's Lower Town." It is the only walled city in North America (north of Mexico). No less a traveller than Henry James (1843-1916), on his visit in 1871, observed "these idle ramparts" of the Old City and wrote: "Our clear American air is hostile to these mellow deposits and

incrustations which enrich the venerable surfaces of Europe. Still, they are walls; till but a short time ago they quite encircled the town; they are garnished with little slits for musketry and big embrasures for cannon; they offer here and there to the strolling bourgeoisie a stretch of grassy rampart; and they make the whole place definite and personal."

Aux Anciens Canadiens This restaurant specializes in authentic French-Canadian cuisine. It is located in Jacquet House, 34 rue Saint-Louis, the oldest house in Quebec City, built in 1675-76. In 1815-24, the thick-walled residence was occupied by Philippe-Joseph Aubert de Gaspé (1786-1871), then a struggling lawyer. Although appointed sheriff of the town, he ran up debts raising his thirteen children. In 1822 he retired to Saint-Jean-Port-Joli where he wrote his famous novel *Les Anciens Canadiens* (1863).

Cape Diamond Towering over the St. Lawrence is Cape Diamond, and crowning the cape is the Citadel, a polygonal stone fort which dates back to the French fort of 1693. In the main it was built by the British in 1823-32. "This is altogether superb," wrote Henry James of the view, "and if Quebec is not the most picturesque city in America, this is no fault of its incomparable site. Perched on its mountain of rock, washed by a river as free and ample as an ocean-gulf, sweeping from its embattled crest, the villages, the forests, the blue undulations of the imperial province of which it is warden — as it has managed from our scanty annals to squeeze out a past, you pray in the name of all that's majestic that it may have a future." This account was published in *Portraits of Places* (1884).

Château Frontenac This grand hotel, with green copper towers and turrets, was designed in 1890 (copied from plans for the lunatic asylum in Buffalo, N.Y.). It has added a sense of adventure to the skyline of Quebec City for close to a century. It was constructed on the site of the Château St. Louis, the residences of the

The Château Frontenac commands the St. Lawrence River like a mighty fortress. Tourists enjoy the spectacular view from Dufferin Terrace. [*Direction générale du Tourisme-Québec*]

governors of New France and of British North America. Earlier it had been the site of Fort St. Louis, begun by Champlain in 1620, torn down, and rebuilt by Frontenac in 1694. In 1942 and 1943 the Château Frontenac was the venue for the two wartime Quebec Conferences held by the Allies with Prime Minister Mackenzie King as "host." The Château Frontenac seems not to have inspired a work of fiction, yet how many human dramas have been enacted in its many suites!

Dufferin Terrace This wide boardwalk, southeast of the Château Frontenac, was begun in 1838 under Governor Lord Durham, author of the famous *Report;* the terrace bore his name until it was renamed for Governor General Lord Dufferin who ordered its extension with pavilions. The view is breathtaking and inspired F. R. Scott (b. 1899) to compose his lyric meditation on history and nationality called "On the Terrace, Quebec" (1970).

L'Anse au Foulon Located on the north shore of the St. Lawrence about two miles above Quebec City, L'Anse au Foulon has been known as Wolfe's Cove since the night of September 12-3, 1759, when General James Wolfe (1727-1759) made a landing here and led his troops to a track up the cliffs, where they formed upon the Plains of Abraham. Prior to the landing, the story goes, Wolfe recited Gray's "Elegy, Written in a Country Churchyard" (1749), adding: "Gentlemen, I would rather have written those lines than take Quebec tomorrow." The most familiar line of the poem runs, "The paths of glory lead but to the grave." Wolfe's impromptu poetry recital aboard ship on the St. Lawrence is the most celebrated in the history of Canada and perhaps of the continent.

Plains of Abraham The name has biblical overtones, but as meaningful as these may be, they are misleading. The expanse of land beyond the walls of the old city was originally owned by a ship's pilot, Abraham Martin, who sold part of it in 1635. The expanse retained his name.

The most decisive battle in the history of North America was fought here. It took place on September 13, 1759, and as described by the historian Francis Parkman (1823-1893) in *Montcalm and Wolfe* (1884): "In twenty minutes the battle was over, with the British victorious, the French in retreat. Brigadier-General James Wolfe was dead, the Marquis de Montcalm was dying. The scene remains the single central tableau in the minds of Canadians of English (if not of French) background."

There are many accounts of the battle in books by scholars, novelists, and poets. Perhaps the most memorable evocation of the event is the traditional song "Bold Wolfe," the lyrics of which are included by Edith Fowke in her edition of *The Penguin Book of*

Aerial view of the Plains of Abraham upon which the fate of nations was decided. In the Governor's Garden stands the Wolfe-Montcalm Monument with its celebrated unilingual inscription — in Latin. [Direction générale du Tourisme-Québec]

Canadian Folk Songs (1973). One of the most surprising accounts of the battle on the Plains of Abraham turns up in *The Books of My Life* (1956) by the well-known American writer Henry Miller (1891-1980) who treats it as a "cluster of images."

Here is Henry James on the site more than a century after the epic confrontation: "A battlefield remains a battlefield, whatever may be done to it; but the scene of Wolfe's victory has been profaned by the erection of a vulgar prison, and this memento of human infirmities does much to efface the meagre column which, with its neat inscription 'Here died Wolfe, victorious,' stands there as a symbol of exceptional virtue."

The Plains of Abraham are now part of 220 acres of Battlefields Park. On many occasions the inscription

The Death of General Wolfe, painted by Benjamin West in 1779, was the first major historical canvas in which the figures are garbed in the dress of the day rather than in togas. [National Gallery of Canada, Ottawa]

prized by James was defaced with the final word "victorious" scratched away.

Wolfe-Montcalm Monument There is a single monument to the two generals who died in battle, James Wolfe and the Marquis de Montcalm, erected in the Governor's Garden which adjoins the Château Frontenac. It bears an uncommonly concise and accommodating text, chosen following a competition won in 1828 by the Quebec journalist John C. Fisher (1794-1849). Fisher's text consists of eight words in Latin: MORTEM VIRTUS COMMUNEM / FAMAM HISTORIA / MONUMENTUM POSTERITAS DEBIT. The English translation is somewhat wordier though no less moving: "Valour gave them a common death; history a common fame; posterity a common monument."

The Golden Dog The popularity of the legend of the Golden Dog comes from the once-popular novel by William Kirby (1817-1906) called, inevitably, *The Golden Dog (Le Chien d'or)* (1877, 1896), which is set in

The famed Golden Dog inscription, the subject of legend and literature. [Direction générale du Tourisme-Québec]

Quebec City following 1748. Kirby weaves his tangled tale of family intrigue around the bas-relief figure of a dog gnawing a bone with a rhyming inscription which reads, in translation: "I am a dog that gnaws his bone / I crouch and gnaw it all alone / The time will come which is not yet / When I'll bite him by whom I'm bit." The figure was once part of a commercial establishment on rue du Fort. The site is now occupied by the Upper Town Post Office, used as government offices, where the Golden Dog may be seen above the peristyle.

Mrs. Frances Brooke The society of Quebec following the Conquest of 1759 is the subject of *The History of Emily Montague* (1769), an epistolary novel by Mrs. Frances Brooke (1724-1789), the wife of the military chaplain to the Quebec garrison. Mrs. Brooke moved in illustrious circles before she came to Quebec in 1763 for five years and set up residence in Sillery. James Boswell and Samuel Johnson attended a party held in her honour prior to her departure. In her novel, the first to be written in North America, there are descriptions of Quebec — "a scene perhaps not to be matched in the world" — but the focus is on the love interest, the highlight being a sleighride over the frozen St. Lawrence.

Portrait of the novelist Frances Brooke by Catherine Read (1723-1778). [PAC C 117373]

St. Matthew's Anglican Church In this church's ancient burial-ground on St. John Street may be found the headstone of Thomas Scott (d. 1823), favourite brother of the poet and novelist Sir Walter Scott (1771-1832). Sir Walter wrote of his brother, paymaster of the British regiment, that he was "a man of infinite humour and excellent parts, but he was unfortunate." (It seems Thomas was a chronic debtor.)

A large marble cross in the same cemetery commemorates Robert Wood (1792-1847). Identified as a lumber merchant, he was said to be the love child of Prince Edward, fourth son of George III and military commander of Quebec from 1791 to 1802, and his mistress, Madame de St. Laurent. It ended unhappily with Edward Augus-

The cemetery here predates the erection of St. Matthew's Anglican Church in 1872. [Direction générale du Tourisme-Québec]

tus, as the Duke of Kent, marrying Victoria Maria Louise and producing, in 1819, an heir to the British throne, Victoria.

Spencer Wood   The official residence of the Governor and then of the Lieutenant-Governor of the Province of Quebec was called Spencer Wood until 1950 when it was renamed Bois de Coulonge. The residence itself was built in 1780 on the bank of the St. Lawrence River near Sillery. Katherine Hale (1878-1956) wrote in *Canadian Houses of Romance* (1926): "What The Grange was to Toronto, Spencer Wood was to the Quebec of fifty years ago: its literary mecca, the place where scholars met, the home of one of the most delightful of essayists and raconteurs." She could be referring to any number of incumbents, but names none.

"Booksellers' Windows"   "Something assures one that Quebec must be a city of gossip; for evidently it is not a city of culture. A glance at the few booksellers' windows gives evidence of this. A few Catholic statuettes and prints, two or three Catholic publications, a festoon or so of rosaries, a volume of Lamartine, a supply of ink and matches, form the principal stock." So observed Henry James in 1871.

Basilica of Notre-Dame de Québec   This massive, grey stone cathedral caught the eye of Richard Henry Dana (1815-1882), author of *Two Years Before the Mast* (1840), on his tour of 1853, for he recorded in his journal: ". . . into the Cath. Cathedral. I was astounded at its beauty & effect. Not so large as that of Montreal, it far exceeds it in beauty & interest. There is much more design & effect. Here, too, were worshippers, scattered about, at random, saying their prayers in the silent Church." The American lawyer and writer was particularly struck by the Chapel of the Seminary, which he visited twice.

Octave Crémazie   Outside 42 rue de la Fabrique, a bronze plaque identifies the house in which Octave

Crémazie (1827-1879) was born. A poet who celebrated the past glories of Quebec, he operated a bookstore at 15 rue Saint-Joseph (from January to May 1844), at rue Sainte-Famille (1844-47), and at 12 rue de la Fabrique (1847-62), when it went out of business and Crémazie left for France. In the 1850s the premises of his store was the meeting place of the Mouvement Littéraire de Québec which was also known as the Ecole Patriotique de Québec. "If we spoke Huron or Iroquois, the works of our writers would attract the attention of the old world," he wrote; and he complained, "I have come too soon into too young a country."

Poet Octave Crémazie assumes a Napoleonic manner in this drawing by Don Evans (signed Isaac Bickerstaff). [Special Collections, University of Calgary Libraries]

This bronze plaque was erected in 1932 by La Société des Poètes at 42 rue de la Fabrique to mark the poet's birthplace and bookstore. [Hawkshead Services]

L'Institut canadien   L'Institut canadien de Québec was established in 1847 as a branch of the Montreal literary and scientific society which had been founded three years earlier. The branch in Quebec City was located on the site of the old Wesley Church, at rue Dauphine and rue Saint-Stanislas. The society maintained an excellent library and sponsored a series of public lectures. It published an annual yearbook of historical interest. The society ran into trouble in 1869 when it was condemned by the Vatican.

Opposite the old Wesley Church, in old Morrin College, Lord Dalhousie founded in 1824 the Quebec Literary and Historical Society. It was the first cultural society in the British Empire.

François-Xavier Garneau A plaque marks the old stone house where Lord Durham (1792-1840) briefly resided while gathering information for his celebrated *Report* (1839) which described the French in Lower Canada as "a people with no history, and no literature," and where, stung by the criticism or canard, the historian François-Xavier Garneau (1809-1866) resided while writing his classic *Histoire du Canada* (1845-48), initially undertaken to prove Durham wrong. His work inspired a generation of poets, novelists, folklorists, journalists, and scholars. The four-storey house is at 14 rue Saint-Flavien.

This monument to Sir George-Etienne Cartier, hand outstretched, stands in Montmorency Park, Quebec City. [Direction générale du Tourisme-Québec]

The sleek structure is Université Laval's Pavillon de l'éducation physique et des sports, erected in 1971. [Direction générale du Tourisme-Québec]

The celebrated historian François-Xavier Garneau as drawn by Isaac Bickerstaff (artist Don Evans). [Special Collections, University of Calgary Libraries]

Le Parc Montmorency This scenic and historic park, with its view of the St. Lawrence and the Laurentians, has a monument to Sir George-Etienne Cartier (1814-1873). In addition to his role as a public figure, he was something of a singer and composer and wrote the patriotic lyric "O Canada, Mon Pays, Mes Amours," which he set to an old French air. One anti-British stanza was removed when it was reset by Ernest Gagnon in 1860.

Jesuit Martyrs Relics of the Jesuit Martyrs of Huronia are preserved at the Résidence des Pères Jésuites, 14 rue Dauphine, the chapel of which dates back to 1817. In the Sanctuary of the Blessed Canadian Martyrs are the remains of those three of the eight martyrs that were preserved. The bones of Gabriel Lalemant and Charles Garnier are here, as well as half the skull of Jean de Brébeuf (1593-1649). The other half of his skull is in the possession of the Hôtel-Dieu.

Université Laval Laval is North America's oldest French-language university. Originally founded by Bishop Laval in 1663, it was only named after him in 1852. The university is noted for its department of modern languages, its department of folklore which was founded by Luc Lacourcière, and its department of social studies (the oldest in the country) established in 1938 by Father Georges-Henri Lévesque (b. 1903) and headed by him until retirement in 1963. It was Lévesque who encouraged a young student, Marie-Claire Blais (b. 1939), who went on to write such novels as *Mad Shadows* (1950).

The Division des Archives of the Bibliothèque de l'Université Laval houses many special collections, including the papers of poet Germain Beaulieu, archivist Arthur Maheux, writer Napoléon Bourassa, novelist Georges Bugnet, journalist Emile Castonguay, poet Rosaire Dion-Lévesque, poet Amédée Denault, historian Thomas Chapais, writer Albert Laberge, archivist Jean-Jacques Lefèbvre, and an extensive collection of the papers and works of the writer Félix-Antoine Savard. Les Archives de Folklore, founded in 1944 by Luc Lacourcière (b. 1910), has some hundred thousand items devoted to the traditional culture of the francophones of North America.

Gabrielle Roy, novelist. [McClelland & Stewart / John Reeves]

The Plouffe Family (1950) — among the tenements that make up the parish of St. Joseph. Such members of the Plouffe family as Papa Théophile, Mama Josephine, Napoléon, Ovide, Guillaume, and Cécile became familiar to two generations of Québécois through the popular novels, radio and television series based on them, and finally the feature film *Les Plouffe*, released in 1981. Lemelin caught up with the Plouffe family in the third volume of the saga, *Le Crime d'Ovide Plouffe* (1983), translated in 1984.

Roberval

The town of Roberval, on the southeast shore of Lac Saint-Jean, boasts the Parc Saint-Jean-de-Brébeuf, the centrepiece of which is a monument in the form of life-sized statues of the eight Jesuit martyrs. The park was named in honour of the French-born missionary, Jean de Brébeuf (1593-1649), who was killed by the Iroquois at the mission of Saint-Ignace in Huronia. He composed the "Huron Carol" and his two accounts of his missionary activities were first published in the Jesuit *Relations* (1632-73).

Saguenay River

The Saguenay River, which flows from Lac Saint-Jean into the St. Lawrence River at Tadoussac, passes through a spectacular mountainous canyon in the Laurentian Shield. Here early explorers searched in vain for the fabled Kingdom of the Saguenay. Tourists arrived in 1849 with the first excursions by boat. Rupert Brooke (1887-1915), the English poet who travelled across the country in 1913, was immensely affected by the demonic elements in the scene. He wrote in *Letters from America* (1916): "There are no banks to this river, for the most part; only these walls, rising sheer from the water to the height of two thousand feet, going down sheer beneath it, or rather by the side of it, to many times that depth. The water was

Gabrielle Roy   The well-loved novelist Gabrielle Roy (1909-1983), who wrote so nostalgically about her childhood in St. Boniface and her youth in rural Manitoba, lived in Quebec City from 1947, when she married a Quebec City physician. They resided in a brick apartment building on the Grand-Allée. She died on July 13, 1983, and her body was cremated. The ashes are kept at Columbarium du Jardin du Repos, Sainte-Foy, Quebec. *Enchanted Summer* (1967) is set in Charlevoix County northeast of Quebec City. The novel refers to specific places: Grande-Pointe, Baie-Saint-Paul, Baie-des-Rochers, Montmagny, and the islands in the St. Lawrence between Ile d'Orléans and Ile aux Coudres.

Roger Lemelin   Roger Lemelin (b. 1919) was born in the working-class district of Saint-Sauveur de Québec. In reading his work, one is made aware that there are two societies in Quebec City: that of Upper Town and that of Lower Town. Lemelin, who was one of ten children, became the Balzac of Lower Town when he set his first two novels — translated as *The Town Below* (1948) and

Les Plouffe was brilliantly cast by director Gilles Carle. In the kitchen scene appear Théophile Plouffe (Emile Genest), Joséphine Plouffe (Juliette Huot), Guillaume (Serge Dupire) and Napoléon (Pierre Curzi). On the dance floor Ovide (Gabriel Arcand) is apprehensive of the charms of Rita Toulouse (Anne Létourneau). [Ontario Film Institute]

of some colour blacker than black. Even by daylight it is inky and sinister. It flows without foam or ripple. No white showed in the wake of the boat. The ominous shores were without sign of life, save for a rare light every few miles, to mark some bend in the chasm. Once a canoe with two Indians shot out of the shadows, passed under our stern, and vanished silently down stream. We all became hushed and apprehensive. The night was gigantic and terrible. There were a few stars, but the flood slid along too swiftly to reflect them. The whole scene seemed some Stygian imagination of Dante. As we drew further and further into that lightless land, little twists and curls of vapour wriggled over the black river-surface. Our homeless, irrelevant, tiny steamer seemed to hang between two abysms. One became suddenly aware of the miles of dark water beneath. I found that under a prolonged gaze the face of the river began to writhe and eddy, as if from some horrible suppressed emotion. It seemed likely that something might appear. I reflected that if the river failed us, all hope was gone; and that anyhow this region was the abode of devils. I went to bed." See also "The Kingdom of the Saguenay."

Saint-Denis

Saint-Denis, northeast of Montreal, was a scene of fighting during the Rebellion of 1837. A statue of a *patriote* commemorates the loss of nine lives on November 23, 1837. A monument, near his former home, honours Sir Thomas Chapais (1858-1946), a leading historian and public figure.

Saint-Irénée

Saint-Irénée, on the north shore south of La Malbaie, has a monument to Sir Adolphe-Basile Routhier (1839-1920) who published in *Les Echos* (1882) the thirty-two line verse "Chant national" which was set to music by Calixa Lavallée in 1880 and is known today in its English version as "O Canada!"

Saint-Jean-Port-Joli

On the south shore of the St. Lawrence northeast of Quebec City, Saint-Jean-Port-Joli is now celebrated as a village of artisans. A plaque on the outskirts of the village marks the site of the manor of Philippe-Joseph Aubert de Gaspé (1786-1871), the last of the seigneurial line, who is remembered for his novel *Les Anciens Canadiens* (1863). Translated by Sir Charles G. D. Roberts as *Canadians of Old* (1890), it recreates the period between 1757 and the early 1800s and celebrates the friendship of a Highlander and a habitant, Archie Cameron of Lochiel and Jules d'Haberville. The manor was burned twice, by the British in 1759 and by accident in 1909. Aubert de Gaspé is interred in a marble tomb in the beautiful stone church, erected in 1776.

Saint-Joachim

The community of Saint-Joachim, on the north shore

northeast of Quebec City, is the setting of the novel *Not for Every Eye* (1962) by Gérard Bessette (b. 1902). It takes place in the local bookstore where there is an attempt to suppress a book by that dangerous French author Voltaire.

Saint-Joseph-de-la-Rive

This community, on the north shore northeast of Baie-Saint-Paul, is the home of Félix-Antoine Savard (b. 1896), novelist and folklorist. He is best known in English as the author of *Boss of the River* (1947), translated by Alan Sullivan, about the effects of foreign ownership on the lives of French Canadians. He established La Papetière Saint-Gilles, the only paper mill in the country capable of producing specialty, parchment papers.

St. Lawrence River

"The great river" was Jacques Cartier's description of the St. Lawrence in 1535. Later it was specifically called "the river of Canada." Although not the longest river in the country — it is exceeded in length by six hundred miles by the Mackenzie — it remains the most important. "An imperial river — the St. Lawrence has always been that," noted Hugh MacLennan (b. 1907) in *The Rivers of Canada* (1961). He went on to say: "Yet the St. Lawrence is more than a river, more even than a system of waters. It has made nations. It has been the moulder of the lives of millions — perhaps by now of hundreds of millions — in a multitude of different ways. At some point in my middle years, I realized that I myself belonged to the people whose lives the river had affected."

Saint-Placide

A plaque marks the birthplace in Saint-Placide, on the north shore of the Ottawa River west of Montreal, of Sir Adolphe-Basile Routhier (1839-1920). Routhier wrote the French lyrics of "O Canada!" and published them two years later in *Les Echos* (1882). The lyrics were set to music by Calixa Lavallée (1842-1891), the composer who was born in Quebec City.

Sainte-Adèle

The resort town of Saint-Adèle is located in the Laurentians north of Montreal. Near the town is the Village of Séraphin, with its general store, blacksmith shop, school, doctor's office, and church. The Village is an historical reconstruction inspired by *Un Homme et Son Péché* (1933), the novel by Claude-Henri Grignon (1894-1976) about Séraphin Poudrier who is beset by the sin of avarice and his long-suffering and childless wife Donalda. The novel became the basis of a daily radio serial and a weekly television series. Grignon lived in Sainte-Adèle and served briefly as its mayor.

Sainte-Agathe-des-Monts

A resort town in the Laurentians northwest of Montreal, Sainte-Agathe-des-Monts is the birthplace of Gaston Miron (b. 1928). Called "the first bard of the Québécois

Holding hands and running through the fields of the Laurentians are Duddy (played by Richard Dreyfuss) and Yvette (Micheline Lanctot) in the film The Apprenticeship of Duddy Kravitz, *based on Mordecai Richler's novel.* [Ontario Film Institute]

nation," Miron is a Montreal resident who, nevertheless, when he feels the regions of Quebec are being slighted, has been known to say: "But there's also Sainte-Agathe."

Here the French surrealist André Breton (1896-1966) completed *Arcane 17* (1947), the account of his visit to Quebec, August-October 1944. It includes evocative comments on the Gaspé and in particular Percé Rock.

The resort town figures in *The Apprenticeship of Duddy Kravitz* (1959) by Mordecai Richler (b. 1931). In the novel Duddy acquires land in the Sainte-Agathe area, and the 1973 movie based on the novel and directed by Ted Kotcheff was shot here.

Sainte-Agathe-des-Monts appears as "Val Laurent" in the psychological thriller, *Four Days* (1962), by John Buell (b. 1927).

Fiction and history merge in the Village de Séraphin at Sainte-Adèle. [Direction générale du Tourisme-Québec]

Sainte-Anne-de-Beaupré

The shrine located here, northeast of Quebec City, is dedicated to St. Anne, mother of the Virgin Mary, and has been a place of pilgrimage since 1659. It is a Canadian Lourdes to Roman Catholics. Inside the twin-spired Basilica will be seen a collection of crutches. They were observed by Henry David Thoreau (1817-

1862) on his visit in 1850: "I ran over to the Church of La Bonne Ste. Anne, whose matin bell we had heard, it being Sunday morning. Our book said that this church had 'long been an object of interest, from the miraculous cures said to have been wrought on visitors to the shrine.' There was a profusion of gilding, and I counted more than twenty-five crutches suspended on the walls, some for grown persons, some for children, from which it was to be inferred so many sick had been able to dispense with; but they looked as if they had been made to order by the carpenter who had made the church." Who was it who observed that at shrines one may see a profusion of crutches and canes but not a single prosthesis?

Sainte-Anne-de-Bellevue

Here, on the western tip of Montreal Island, in the home of Simon Fraser, fur trader and partner in the North West Company (it was his namesake who explored the Fraser River), the Irish poet Thomas Moore (1779-1852) was a guest in the summer of 1804. Fraser's two-storey stone house, which dates from 1798, still stands and is now operated by the Victorian Order of Nurses as a restaurant, Au P'tit Café, 153 Sainte-Anne-de-Bellevue. Moore penned "A Canadian Boat Song: Written on the River St. Lawrence" while a guest. The tune is a traditional voyageur melody used as a "parting hymn," but the lovely words are Moore's. The song ends: "Blow, breezes, blow, the stream runs fast, / The Rapids are near and the daylight's past." Nearby is the voyageurs' church, erected on the foundations of the chapel where voyageurs starting out for the Northwest paused to pray.

"We drove up the beautiful shores of the St. Lawrence, and saw the villages and villas which adorn them," wrote Sir Arthur Conan Doyle (1859-1930) in *Our Second American Adventure* (1923). "One small house of stone was pointed out in which Tom Moore dwelt and where he wrote the 'Canadian Boat Song.' No medallion marks it. This I have endeavoured to amend by a letter to the press. I must confess that I never knew before that Moore had been to Canada."

Sainte-Antoine

This small community on the south shore, near Verchères, was the birthplace of Sir George-Etienne Cartier (1814-1873), not only one of Quebec's leading statesmen and a chief architect of Confederation but also a many-talented composer and writer. Two of his songs are still sung: "O Canada, Mon Pays, Mes Amours" and "Avant Tout, Je Suis Canadien." A plaque marks the site of the house in which the patriot was born.

Sainte-Catherine-de-Fossambault

In the seigneurial manor here, northwest of Quebec City, the poet Hector de Saint-Denys Garneau (1912-

1943) was raised. Reclusive by nature, Garneau retired to the family estate a few years before his early death. He kept a journal in which he recorded his deepest thoughts and composed many of his most moving poems. Both *The Journal* (1962) and the *Complete Poems* (1975) exist in sensitive translations by John Glassco (1909-1981). Garneau's cousin, Anne Hébert (b. 1916), was born here, and for many years she summered at the family estate. Her poem "Manor Life" seems to reflect the ancestral experience. It was translated by Alan Brown (b. 1920) in her *Poems* (1975).

Sainte-Justine-de-Dorchester

The novelist Roch Carrier (b. 1937) was born in this remote village in the Beauce region. It haunts his imagination, for his novels and stories are usually set here, in a "microcosm" where, as he once explained, are to be found "all those forces which were in the French Canadian." The isolated village is usually called "Bralington" in his trilogy of novels: *La Guerre, Yes Sir!* (1970), *Floralie, Where Are You?* (1971), and *Is It the Sun, Philibert?* (1972), all translated by Sheila Fischman. The title story of *The Hockey Sweater and Other Stories* (1979), in which a young boy must cope with Eaton's delivering a Toronto Maple Leaf instead of a Montreal Canadien sweater, is set here.

A scene from The Sweater, *the NFB's animated film based on Roch Carrier's celebrated short story about the youngster in rural Quebec whose life is turned upside-down when Eaton's sends him a Maple Leaf hockey sweater rather than a Canadiens sweater.* [NFB]

Sainte-Marie-de-Monnoir

The seigneury of this small community in the Richelieu district is the subject of the novel *The Curé of St. Philippe* (1899), written in a realistic manner in English by Francis William Grey (1860-1939). The seigneury was owned by the Rolland family, into which Grey, an Englishman, married. The novel is subtitled "A Story of French-Canadian Politics."

Schefferville

Schefferville, the town in New Quebec close to the Labrador border, is the mining community where Quebec Premier Maurice Duplessis died in 1959. It is a place of survival in *The Chrysalids* (1955), the science-fiction novel by British author John Wyndham (1903-1969). Called *Re-Birth* in the United States, the novel is set in the future following a nuclear holocaust — "the Tribulation." Survival is possible in isolated farming communities like the religious society at "Wachna," which bears resemblances to Schefferville. Some distance away is the village of Rigo, apparently Rigolet, Labrador; and across the strait is a port called Lark, likely Lark Harbour, Nfld. Much farther to the south are the so-called Black Coasts (of the northeastern United States), but close at hand are "the Fringes" or "the Badlands about which nobody knows anything." The land is mostly radioactive. In this bleak world a young telepath comes of age.

Sherbrooke   See EASTERN TOWNSHIPS.

Sorel

There is a description of Sorel, on the St. Lawrence at the mouth of the Richelieu River, in the mid-nineteenth century in the novel *Kamouraska* (1970) by Anne Hébert (b. 1916). "Why this calm? Why this soft, gentle light spreading over a little deserted town? Sorel. Its streets with their beautiful houses. Wooden houses. Brick houses. Square Royal. Rue Charlotte. Rue Georges. The corner of Rue Augusta and Rue Philippe. Close by, the river flows between its level banks. The long green islands, property of the parish, where cows and horses, sheep and goats are grazing."

The novelist Germaine Guèvremont (1900-1968) lived in Sorel. Her novel *The Outlander* (1978), translated by Eric Sutton, is set in the 1950s near here.

Sulte

West of Lac Saint-Jean is the Canton de Sulte, called after the French-Canadian historian Benjamin Sulte (1841-1923).

Tadoussac

This village, on the east shore of the Saguenay River near its mouth on the St. Lawrence, was an important trading post in its day. It became a popular tourist resort in the mid-nineteenth century.

"I stopped here for a day or two," wrote Rupert Brooke (1887-1915) in a letter to the actress Cathleen Nesbitt, July 3, 1913, "& I'm glad I did. I'm sick of large towns, this is a small wee seaside resort, just a village, no railway & a steamer a day. A large hotel & cottages. It's at the corner where the Saguenay flows into the St. Lawrence — & such a lovely place, & I'm so peaceful & happy — & this afternoon I stole out & bathed — it *was* cold water & lay on the rocks & composed a Hymn. . . . It's rather nice being entirely unconnected & planless."

Témiscouata

In this wilderness region, southeast of Rivière-du-Loup on the south shore, the naturalist and author Grey Owl (1888-1938) settled with his wife Anahareo from 1925 to 1931. He resided for some time at Cabano, on Lac Témiscouata, and renounced trapping in 1928, dedicating his hunting and literary skills to furthering the cause of conservation. With the publication of his first book, *The Men of the Last Frontier* (1931), he came to the attention of the federal government and was hired by the National Parks Branch and sent to Alberta's Riding Mountain National Park to save the beaver.

Thetford Mines

Asbestos was discovered here, in the Megantic area, in 1876. Thetford Mines is called "Macklin" in the novel *Dust Over the City* (1955) by André Langevin (b. 1927).

Trois-Rivières

Trois-Rivières, on the north shore between Montreal and Quebec City, has many historical and some literary associations.

The historian Benjamin Sulte (1841-1923) was born in Trois-Rivières. There is a plaque in his honour in the City Hall, but the principal monument to the historian and author of over twenty volumes is the oversized bust in Champlain Park. At the base of the monument are plaques to commemorate the novelist Antoine Gérin-Lajoie (1824-1882), the poet Nérée Beauchemin (1850-1931), the historian Edmond Boisvert de Nevers (1862-1906), and Ludger Duvernay (1799-1852), patriot and founder of the Saint-Jean-Baptiste Society in 1834.

Also born at Trois-Rivières was Philippe Panneton (1895-1960) who, under the pseudonym Ringuet, wrote *Thirty Acres* (1938). Although he left the region at the age of eighteen, he returned for some time to practise as an eye specialist with offices in Trois-Rivières and Joliette to the southwest. It is in this vicinity that he set the land grant of *trente arpents* farmed by Euchariste Moisan in his celebrated novel of habitant life from the late nineteenth century to the 1930s. His patients supplied him with the little details of life in the region which he patiently transcribed while aboard trains travelling between his offices and to and from Montreal.

Ungava

The world's first full-length documentary film was shot on location at Inoucdjouac in the Ungava region of northern Quebec. The film was *Nanook of the North*, premiered in 1922, by the prospector-turned-director Robert Flaherty (1884-1951). It has set the style and standard for real-life features ever since. Flaherty drew on his Ungava experiences in writing two novels, *The Captain's Chair* (1938) and *White Master* (1939).

Perhaps the most powerful novel ever set in the Ungava Peninsula, where it borders on Labrador, is *Agaguk* (1958) by Yves Thériault (1915-1983) who wrote about the Montagnais Indians and himself claimed to be part Montagnais. It lyrically yet realistically depicts the traditional life of the Inuit hunter, focusing on the relationship between Agaguk and his wife Iriook. He returned some years later to the same locale with *Tayaout, fils d'Agaguk* (1969), to depict the great changes that occurred in the traditional lifestyles.

Gabrielle Roy (1909-1983) visited the remote region in the late 1950s and set part of her novel *The Hidden Mountain* (1961) here where "bald mountains of gneiss and schist, which, because of their intense colouration and the light they reflect, can be equalled in splendour, perhaps, nowhere in the world."

The southern tip of one of the Iles Radisson, in Ungava Bay, was named in honour of George Bernard Shaw (1856-1950). The rocky tip bears a striking resemblance to the high brow and shaggy beard of the Irish playwright. Pointe Bernard Shaw was approved as a name in 1983; the announcement was made to coincide with the opening of Shaw's play *The Simpleton of the Unexpected Isles* (1934) at the Shaw Festival, Niagara-on-the-Lake, Ont.

The Shaw Festival was instrumental in having a point on one of the Iles Radisson, in Ungava Bay, Que., named for the playwright George Bernard Shaw. The announcement coincided with the opening of The Simpleton of the Unexpected Isles *on July 4, 1983. No one is certain who first spotted the resemblance between the rock (left) and the bearded author (right). The feature is officially called Pointe Bernard Shaw.* [Canadian Press]

Vaudreuil

Located west of Montreal, Vaudreuil is the birthplace of nationalist and historian Lionel-Adolphe Groulx

(1878-1967), known as l'abbé Groulx, who adopted the maxim *Notre Maître le passé* ("our master the past"). One of Groulx's achievements was the rehabilitation of Adam Dollard des Ormeaux and his sixteen companions, the defenders of the Long Sault against the Iroquois in 1660, as saviours of New France.

Monument to Madeleine de Verchères at Verchères, Que. [Direction générale du Tourisme-Québec]

Verchères

Here, on the south shore of the St. Lawrence northeast of Montreal, the fourteen-year-old Madeleine de Verchères (1678-1747) led the defence of her father's seigneurial fort. Philippe Hébert's statue of the young heroine stands here, overlooking the St. Lawrence. William Henry Drummond (1854-1907) caught the excitement of the defence in his poem "Madeleine Verchères" in his *Complete Poems* (1926). The heroine herself wrote two accounts of her eight-day ordeal.

Viger

The village of Viger, on the south shore northeast of Rivière-du-Loup, is the setting of a number of stories by Duncan Campbell Scott (1862-1947) collected in the volume *In the Village of Viger* (1896) which treat of human nature and the habitant life.

Yamachiche

Located on Lac Saint-Pierre, southwest of Trois-Rivières, Yamachiche is associated with Antoine Gérin-Lajoie (1824-1882), man of letters and public figure. He was born at Sainte-Anne-de-Yamachiche; a plaque identifies his house and reproduces the well-loved words of his song "Un Canadien Errant" (1842) in the original French and the English translation of John Murray Gibbon. He also wrote the two-volume novel *Jean Rivard* (1874-76) which is set in the Eastern Townships. Also honoured with a plaque on his former home is Nérée Beauchemin (1850-1931), physician and poet, and author of *Patrie Intime* (1928), a collection of personal lyrics about love of the land and its people.

Ontario

Agawa Bay

Mysterious ochre figures, centuries old, adorn the face of Inscription Rock, in Agawa Bay, on the eastern shore of Lake Superior, at the edge of Lake Superior Provincial Park. The meaning of these figures — a mounted man, a horned panther, a crested serpent, and other Algonkian symbols and designs — has been lost. Yet the existence of Inscription Rock was part of Ojibwa tradition, as noted in 1851 by Henry R. Schoolcraft (1793-1864), although the American Indian agent and ethnologist had never set eyes on the site and had no clues as to its precise location. His account of Inscription Rock inspired Henry Wadsworth Longfellow (1807-1882) to credit his hero Hiawatha in *The Song of Hiawatha* (1855) with the invention of "picture-writing" during "the great, mysterious darkness / Of the speechless days. . . ." It was not until the summer of 1958 that native-art specialist Selwyn Dewdney (1909-1979), armed with Schoolcraft's account and a detailed knowledge of the natural world and native ways, rediscovered Inscription Rock in Agawa Bay after a fourteen-month search. He recounts his experience in *Indian Rock Painting of the Great Lakes* (1962).

The significance of the petroglyphs and the experience of seeing them are the subjects of the poem "The Horsemen of Agawa" by Al Purdy (b. 1918) in *Being Alive: Poems 1958-78* (1978).

Alexandria

Near Alexandria, northeast of Cornwall, was born the poetaster James MacRae (1849-1900) who called himself "A Native of County Glengarry." His work was satirized by William Arthur Deacon in *The Four Jameses* (1927), who quotes the following couplet: "Let me find the cause most fruitful of the sins of married folk, / Of the miseries and troubles that make rough their galling yoke." A sometime resident of the Alexandria region is the poet and playwright Henry Beissel (b. 1929).

Algoma

The lake-dotted Algoma District, the administrative centre of which is Sault Ste. Marie, was frequently painted by members of the Group of Seven. The best-known work of fiction set in Algoma is the novella *Bear* (1976), by Marian Engel (b. 1933). The fictitious setting is "Cary's Island," on which "Colonel Cary," a veteran of the Napoleonic Wars, erected an octagonal house, having selected the island after opening an atlas of North America, closing his eyes, and sticking a pin at random. On this island the librarian known as Lou spends a memorable summer with a chained bear. Engel locates the island: turn off Highway 17 at "Fisher's Falls," drive along Country Road 6, to the village of "Brody," where one needs a motor boat or launch.

No one knows when the rock art at Agawa Bay was painted. The figures in ochre are of a manned canoe, serpents, and a fabulous horned beast. [Bill Brooks]

BEAR

A Novel by

Marian Engel

McClelland and Stewart Limited

Title page of the first edition of Bear (1976), Marian Engel's fable-like novel set on a northern island. [McClelland & Stewart]

Sir Arthur Conan Doyle in his later years. [John Murray]

The life of Tom Thomson inspired The Far Shore, *the feature film directed by Joyce Wieland. Here Celine Lomez and Frank Moore explore the "far shore" of love. [Ontario Film Institute]*

Algonquin Park

Sir Arthur Conan Doyle (1859-1930) was a guest at The Highland Inn, Algonquin Park, when he wrote a poem called "The Athabaska Trail." From the Inn, on June 26, 1916, he mailed it to the editor of the *Montreal Gazette* to publish in its Dominion Day issue, marking it "No rights reserved." A tribute to a vast but young country, the twenty-four line poem concludes: "Mother of a mighty manhood, Land of glamour and of hope, / From the eastward sea-swept islands to the sunny western slope, / Ever more my heart is with you, ever more till life shall fail, / I'll be out with pack and packer on the Athabaska Trail."

Algonquin Park, Ontario's oldest, at the southern edge of the Canadian Shield, is associated with the painter Tom Thomson (1877-1917) who drowned in Canoe Lake, July 17. "He lived humbly but passionately with the wild," runs the inscription on the plaque written by J. E. H. MacDonald. "It made him brother to all unnamed things of nature." Thomson's ghost is said to haunt the lake, a belief mentioned by Arthur S. Bourinot (1893-1969) in the title poem of *Tom Thomson and Other Poems* (1954).

Alliston

The novelist Graeme Gibson (b. 1934) lived for some years in the 1970s on a farm in the vicinity of Alliston, a town southwest of Barrie. The district may well have inspired the rural locale of his novel *Perpetual Motion* (1982) which takes place in and around the town of "Mad River." In the novel a farmer unearths the skeleton of a woolly mammoth, a find unique to the region, and he devotes much energy to perfecting a perpetual-motion machine, a self-defeating notion. Gibson shared the farm with the author Margaret Atwood (b. 1939) and their daughter.

Tom Thomson, child of the wild, in a pen-and-ink sketch by Isaac Bickerstaff, artist Don Evans. [Special Collections, University of Calgary Libraries]

Graeme Gibson, novelist, photographer, teacher, philosopher. [McClelland & Stewart / Peter Paterson]

R. Tait McKenzie's Mill of Kintail, at Almonte, is now a museum devoted to his sculpture. [Terry Keough]

Almonte

North of Almonte, southwest of Ottawa, is Mill of Kintail, a grist mill restored as a home in the 1930s by the sculptor R. Tait McKenzie (1867-1938), now a museum devoted to his works. He executed the medallion on the Ottawa grave of the poet William Wilfred Campbell (1858-1918), now missing, and plaques of the poet Archibald Lampman (1861-1899) in the Library of Parliament in Ottawa and in the Convocation Hall of Trinity College, University of Toronto. Between Almonte and the Mill of Kintail is a roadside plaque commemorating Dr. James Naismith (1861-1939), the inventor of the game of basketball, who was born near here.

Ameliasburg

Ameliasburg, a small community associated with the poet Al Purdy (b. 1918), is located southwest of Belleville. Here, on the shore of Roblin Lake, Purdy built

Al Purdy gone Indian, sketched by Don Evans (signed by Isaac Bickerstaff). [Special Collections, University of Calgary Libraries]

a cottage that he has counted his home since 1957. "As much as any place in the world / I claim this snake fence village / of A-burg as part of myself. . . ." This is how he began the poem "Gateway" (1976), which concludes with the poet "walking thru the nineteenth-century village / with a kind of jubilation." The settler after whom Roblin Lake and Roblin's Mills were named is the ostensible subject of the poet's search for roots in the long poem, *In Search of Owen Roblin* (1974). Other characteristic poems, rich in regional reference, are "Roblin's Mills," "Wilderness Gothic," and "The Country North of Belleville." In 1965, Earle Birney (b. 1904) visited Purdy at his cottage and wrote "In Purdy's Ameliasburg" about "this round pond man" whose cottage has "a backyard of stones."

Amherstburg

The town of Amherstburg, south of Windsor, saw action in the War of 1812 and the Rebellion of 1837. Major John Richardson (1796-1852) served as a volunteer at Fort Malden and was taken prisoner by the Americans at Moraviantown. Widely read in his day, were his narrative poem *Tecumseh* (1828) and his romantic novel *Wacousta* (1832) which was dramatized by James Reaney (b. 1926) in 1979. Richardson described the region in his novel *The Canadian Brothers* (1840), and a plaque in Amherstburg was raised in his honour.

Angler

Angler, near the town of Marathon, on the north shore of Lake Superior, was the site of an internment camp during the Second World War. Here the evacuee, poet Takeo Ujo Nakano (b. 1903), was interned from August 1942 to November 1943. He came from the work camp at Yellowhead, B.C., and would leave for a factory assignment in Toronto. In his diary, the basis of his memoir *Within the Barbed Wire Fence* (1980), he wrote of the tedium of camp life. "The circumstances of confinement made for the production of many highly subjective haiku." Fifteen Japanese internees formed a Haiku Club and met weekly to read and discuss each other's poems on assigned themes. Some of the poems were haiku (three lines, seventeen syllables); others were tanka (five lines, thirty-one syllables). Nakano specialized in the latter, and wrote the following tanka about his work experiences: "Primeval forest! / Feeling as though in violation, / Cutting down standing trees / Before watchful guards. / Cutting firewood." The evacuees even compiled an anthology of Japanese-language haiku and tanka called *Loneliness Within the Barbed Wire Fence*. They patiently copied by hand three dozen copies of the two-hundred-page anthology, "a considerable job," he wrote many years later. "We who are fortunate enough to possess a copy hold one page of Japanese Canadian wartime history." Upon his release, Nakano was joined by his wife and daughter and continued as a poet in Toronto. In 1964, a tanka he had written was one of twelve chosen from 46,886 entries in the annual Imperial Poetry Contest. He went to Tokyo to be present at the recitation of the winning poems before Emperor Hirohito and Empress Nagako. His poem speaks volumes: "As final resting place, / Canada is chosen. / On citizenship paper, / Signing / Hand trembles."

Nakano refers in his diary to the recent graves of two German prisoners of war who attempted to escape from Angler in 1941. The full story of this unsuccessful prison break is told by John Melady in *Escape from Canada!* (1981).

Appin

Born on a farm near Appin, west of St. Thomas, was the once-popular essayist Peter McArthur (1866-1924). Appin is located in Ekfrid Township, so McArthur was known as the Sage of Ekfrid. His satiric columns on farming life appeared in the Toronto *Globe* and the *Farmer's Advocate* and were collected in numerous volumes beginning with *In Pastures Green* (1915). In 1967, Alec Lucas edited *The Best of Peter McArthur*, a pleasant collection. The farmhouse in which McArthur wrote has been moved to Doon Pioneer Village, but a plaque commemorates his achievement at the roadside park on Highway No. 2 just west of Appin.

Aramis Lake

This lake in the Atikokan area was named after the Aramis who is one of the original swashbucklers in *The Three Musketeers* (1844), the romance by Alexandre Dumas (1802-1870).

Aurora

This small community, north of Richmond Hill, hosted a rally of the Liberal Party on October 3, 1874. This comes to mind because the Liberals were addressed by Edward Blake (1833-1912), a former cabinet minister and the future Liberal Party leader, who delivered a rousing speech on the need for a reconsideration of Canada's colonial status, Senate reform, compulsory voting, proportional representation, and above all the growth of a national feeling. "The future of Canada, I believe, depends very largely upon the cultivation of a national spirit." His address is now known as the Aurora Speech and is a landmark in Canadian politics. It could be maintained, though with some difficulty, that the Aurora Speech had the same relation to Canadian nationalism as the battleship *Aurora* had to the Bolshevik Revolution.

Baldoon

There is a plaque on the bank of the Chenal Écarté, in Kent County, near Lake St. Clair, to mark the site of the ill-fated Highland colony of Baldoon, established here by

Lord Selkirk in 1804. The plaque makes no mention of "the Baldoon Mystery," the three-year-long haunting of the farmhouse of John McDonald between 1829 and 1831. No reasonable explanation was ever offered for the poltergeist-like disturbances. When John Frederick Troyer, the witch-doctor from Long Point, on Lake Erie, was brought in, the disturbances ceased. The haunting became the basis of the play *Baldoon* (1976), by James Reaney (b. 1926) and C. H. (Marty) Gervais (b. 1946), which premiered in Toronto.

The haunting at Baldoon took place in this lonely farmhouse depicted about 1850. The pen-and-ink drawing is signed "Nick." [Frank Mann]

Bancroft

North of Bancroft, near the village of Maple Leaf, is the restored stone farmhouse occupied by Sarnia-born R. Murray Schafer (b. 1933), the composer and author of the seminal work *The Tuning of the World* (1977). Out the back is an old barn which includes the composer's "sound-sculpture" — a collection of locally collected junk — which was "played" in the TV series *The Music of Man*.

Barry's Bay

The community of Barry's Bay, on the bay of the same name, an inlet of Lake Kamaniskeg, southwest of Pembroke, has attracted Polish immigrants from Pomerania since the 1870s. The community has been studied by J. L. Perowski in *A Kashubian Idiolect* (1969), which focused on folk beliefs and was denounced in the House of Commons as promoting the notion that the Kashubs believe in vampires; and by three anthropologists, F. A. Lorentz, A. Fischer, and T. Lehr-Splawinski in *The Cassubian Civilization* (1935). Gail Henley is the author of a novel set in the district called *Where the Cherries End Up* (1978).

Beardmore

The Ojibwa artist Norval Morrisseau (b. 1932), who was born in Fort William and raised at the Sandy Lake Reserve on Lake Nipigon, was twice "discovered" at Beardmore, east of Lake Nipigon. The first time it was by native-art specialist Selwyn Dewdney; the second time by

Norval Morrisseau and his art are inseparable in this pen-and-ink drawing by Don Evans (signed Isaac Bickerstaff). [Special Collections, University of Calgary Libraries]

Sir Gilbert Parker spent his youthful years in this home in Belleville, Ont. It is reproduced from "Canadian Literary Homes" in The Canadian Magazine, January 1908, where E. J. Hathaway explained: "His mother and sister still occupy the attractive old homestead in Belleville, which the sons bought for their parents many years ago." [Metropolitan Toronto Library]

Sir Gilbert Parker as seen by artist Don Evans (who signs his work Isaac Bickerstaff). [Special Collections, University of Calgary Libraries]

art dealer Jack Pollock. Pollock arranged Morrisseau's first exhibition in Toronto in 1962 and Dewdney edited Morrisseau's *Legends of My People* (1965) which preserves the traditional Ojibway legends and myths. The artist's Indian name is Copper Thunderbird.

The community has lent its name to the "Beardmore relics," a cache of Norse weapons dating from A.D. 1000, supposedly unearthed here in 1930, acquired and displayed by the Royal Ontario Museum and now kept under wraps. Although there is little question of the authenticity of the rusting sword, axehead, and other iron fragments, there was considerable controversy over the location of the find and the implied presence of Vikings in northern Ontario. James W. Curran, publisher of the Sault *Daily Star*, lectured on the theme "A Norseman died in Ontario 900 years ago" and published a book titled *Here Was Vinland* (1939). He also maintained, in *Wolves Don't Bite* (1940), that "any man that says he's been et by a wolf is a liar."

Bedivere Lake
Bedivere Lake, located east of Atikokan, was named after the knight of the Round Table. Sir Bedivere, one of Arthur's attendants, threw the sword Excalibur into the lake.

Belleville
Belleville, on the Bay of Quinte, came as a relief to Susanna Moodie (1803-1885) and her husband John Moodie after years of backwoods farming in the Peterborough area. They lived in the house at 114 Bridge Street West from 1840 to John's death in 1869. Then Susanna spent part of the year with her sister, Catharine Parr Traill (1802-1899), at "Westove" in Lakefield, and the rest of the year with her daughter in Toronto, where she died. She is buried in the Belleville Cemetery next to her husband.

Here she wrote *Roughing It in the Bush* (1852), about her exhausting years in the Peterborough area, and *Life in the Clearings* (1853), about society in Belleville. With her husband she published twelve issues of *Victorian Magazine* (1847-48). She called her Bridge Street West home "the haven of rest to which Providence has conducted me after the storms and trials of many years." Today it is known as "Bradfarrow," having been restored by Leo Simpson (b. 1934), the novelist who wrote *The Peacock Papers* (1973) and *Kowalski's Last Chance* (1980).

A plaque in the Corby Public Library honours Sir Gilbert Parker (1862-1932), the historical novelist. He was a benefactor of the library, and at its dedication in 1902 he spoke of himself as the son of "the limestone ridges," having been born at nearby Camden East. Although a voluminous writer, who saw the publication of his novels in a uniform edition, he is principally remembered as a public figure and as the author of a single historical romance, *The Seats of the Mighty* (1896), about the fall of New France.

On Bridge Street, near the Armories, stands the statue of Sir Mackenzie Bowell, Prime Minister in 1894-96, who died here in 1917. It inspired Al Purdy (b. 1918) to write "The Statue in Belleville" (1976) about the politician known as "The Fixer" for his dealings.

Earle Birney (b. 1904) wrote a sound poem, "Trawna Tuh Belvul" (1978), which captures the sounds of a journey by train made between Toronto and Belleville.

Farley Mowat (b. 1921) was born in Belleville, where his father, the writer Angus Mowat, was the public librarian.

Bellrock

The small community of Bellrock is close to Verona which is northwest of Kingston. The painter Kim Ondaatje has a summer home at Bellrock and here Michael Ondaatje (b. 1943) and D. G. Jones (b. 1928) have written some of their finest poems. Other residents of the region are two academic critics, Stan Dragland (b. 1942), author of the autobiographical novel *Peckertracks: A Chronicle* (1978), and John Moss (b. 1940), author of *A Reader's Guide to the Canadian Novel* (1983). The novelist Matt Cohen (b. 1942) lives in nearby Verona, features of which appear in his fiction as "Salem."

A view of the Scriven Memorial, near Bewdley, Ont. [Bill Brooks]

Bewdley

There is a granite memorial to Joseph Medlicott Scriven (1819-1886) in the Pengelley burial ground near Bewdley, north of Port Hope. An Irish-born teacher, Scriven wrote about 1857 the words to the popular evangelical hymn "What a Friend We Have in Jesus" which begins: "What a Friend we have in Jesus, / All our sins and griefs to bear! / What a privilege to carry / Everything to God in prayer!" He drowned in Rice Lake and was found, in the words of the memorial, "in the attitude of prayer."

Bill Lake

Bill Lake is located on the Ontario-Quebec border north of Lake Abitibi. The journalist Stephen Franklin (b. 1922) selected it as the site of the community of libraries named Knowledge Park. Here the collective memory of mankind will be housed in the Igloos of Minerva, twelve theme libraries of modernistic design, according to his futuristic documentary, *Knowledge Park* (1972).

"Birdseye Centre"   See SCUGOG ISLAND.

Blair

The village of Blair, southeast of Kitchener, is associated with the writer Jessie L. Beattie (b. 1896). She is the author of almost twenty books, including an autobiography, *A Walk through Yesterday* (1976). She was born at a farmhouse, still standing on Dickie Settlement Road, and grew up at the family home nearby at Old Mill Road. She lived for many years in Hamilton and, when she went blind, was forced to dictate her novels.

Blewett Township

Blewett Township, northwest of Sudbury, bears the name of the once-popular children's writer, Jean Blewett (1862-1934).

Bobcaygeon

The village of Bobcaygeon is east of Fenelon Falls. Here, on the shore of Sturgeon Lake, E. J. Pratt (1882-1964) built a cottage in which the family summered from 1920 to 1936 when it was sold. On the verandah and in the green-painted den he penned *The Witches' Brew* (1925) and other poetical works. The cottage is still standing.

These snapshots were taken in the summer of 1933 at Bobcaygeon by Claire Pratt, daughter of the poet E. J. Pratt. The poet is shown at ease in a lawn chair and with guests. The guests include William Arthur Deacon (right) and his wife Sally Townsend (to the left of the poet) and their two children Mary and Dierdre. The identity of the woman on the left is unknown. [Viola and Claire Pratt]

Bohemia Island

On this island in Muskoka, at the juncture of Lake Rosseau, Lake Muskoka, and Lake Joseph, the English horror-story writer Algernon Blackwood (1869-1951), spent the summer of 1892. He wrote about his experiences here in his autobiography, *Episodes before Thirty* (1923), and in fictional form in such stories as "A Haunted Island" (1906).

This idyllic sunset appeared on the letterhead and publications of the Whitman Club of Bon Echo which was founded by Flora MacDonald Denison in 1917. [Cyril Greenland]

Bon Echo Provincial Park

The centrepiece of Bon Echo Provincial Park, near Kaladar, north of Kingston, is "Old Walt," the immense Precambrian rock one mile long (1.6 km) and 400 feet high (120 m) that rises above Upper Mazinaw Lake. It was dedicated to the "democratic ideals" of Walt Whitman (1819-1892) by Flora MacDonald Denison (1867-1921), journalist and suffragette, who felt inspired by the great American poet's vision of democracy, and Horace L. Traubel (1858-1919), one of Whitman's literary executors and biographers. The dedication ceremony took place on August 25, 1919. After experiencing visions of "Old Walt," Traubel expired the next month within sight of the rock. Engraved in the face of the rock in foot-high letters are the following lines from Whitman's poem "Song of Myself": "My foothold is tenon'd and mortised in granite / I laugh at what you call dissolution / And I know the amplitude of time." At water level Algonkian Indians long ago painted 135 ochre images, the meaning of which has been lost. Present at the original dedication was Flora's son, playwright and company historian Merrill Denison (1893-1975), who following his mother's death operated Bon Echo Inn as an exclusive resort. Arthur Heming, Yousuf Karsh, A. Y. Jackson and other writers

In the film based on Margaret Atwood's novel Surfacing, *Kate was played by Kathleen Beller. Although the novel is set in the Quebec woods, the movie was shot in two locales in Ontario — Barry's Bay and Bon Echo Provincial Park. [Ontario Film Institute]*

and artists holidayed here. Denison's book of sketches, *Boobs in the Woods* (1927), recounts some of his experiences managing the resort. "Old Walt" was rededicated by Denison on June 29, 1955, to mark the centenary of publication of Whitman's *Leaves of Grass* (1855) and the launching of the *Encyclopedia Canadiana*. Denison deeded the land to the Ontario people and the park was formally opened in 1961. "Old Walt" remains a unique memorial to a great poet and to the spirit of democracy.

Bond Head

The most distinguished native of Bond Head, a village north of Toronto, was Sir William Osler (1849-1919), the famous physician and noted essayist on medical and other matters. Among his many non-medical publications is *Aequanimitas and Other Addresses* (1904). "Humanists have not enough Science," he complained, "and Science sadly lacks the Humanities." He was the personal physician of Walt Whitman in 1884-89. Osler's father was rector of Trinity Anglican Church, built 1845; to this day the church holds each year a special service for physicians and surgeons.

Bowmanville

The town of Bowmanville, east of Oshawa, is the setting of the novella "Ancient Lineage" in *A Native Argosy* (1929) by the novelist Morley Callaghan (b. 1903) who summered in the region. It was also the site of a German prisoner-of-war camp during the Second World War from which a daring escape was made.

Bracebridge

Bracebridge is east of Lake Muskoka and named after the title piece of *Bracebridge Hall, or the Humorists* (1822), a collection of tales and sketches written by the American literary figure, Washington Irving (1783-1859). The town of Gravenhurst, Ont., owes its name to the same work.

Brantford

The city of Brantford, situated southwest of Hamilton, is an historic city with numerous literary associations. Some associations, like those connected with the poet Pauline Johnson (1861-1913), are treated in the entry on the Six Nations Reserve, the 44,800-acre reservation located southeast of Brantford.

Her Majesty's Chapel of the Mohawks This historic chapel, also known as St. Paul's, was built in 1785. It was the first Protestant church in today's Ontario. One of its stained-glass windows depicts the legendary Iroquois hero Dekanahwideh presiding over planting of the Great Tree of Peace.

Alexander Graham Bell The Bell Family Homestead is a sturdy stone residence at 94 Tutela Heights Drive, now a museum that honours Alexander Graham Bell (1847-1922), the inventor of the telephone. The homestead was bought in 1870 by Melville Bell (1819-

Alexander Graham Bell Homestead, Tutela Heights, Brantford. Behind the house is Bell's "dreaming place." [Ontario Ministry of Tourism and Recreation]

1905), a specialist in speech who lectured at Edinburgh University before coming to Canada for health reasons. His son Alexander resided here for one year before leaving for Boston, but he spent long summer vacations at Tutelo Heights. The house was sold in 1881 when Melville Bell moved to Boston to be closer to his son. Alexander had what he called his "dreaming place" by the cliff's edge at the rear of the property. He once wrote, "The telephone was conceived in Brantford in 1874, and born in Boston in 1875." The first long-distance call was placed between Brantford and nearby Paris in 1876; it was three hours long. When Melville Bell taught at Edinburgh, one of his pupils was Sir Arthur Conan Doyle (1859-1930), then a medical student. It has been stated that Melville Bell and his scientific method were the models on which Doyle based his fictional detective Sherlock Holmes and his deductionist reasoning.

The honoured guest at the dedication of the Bell Memorial, on October 24, 1917, was Alexander Graham Bell himself. [Ontario Ministry of Tourism and Recreation]

Sara Jeannette Duncan   A plaque on the grounds of the First Baptist Church, 70 West Street, commemorates novelist and journalist Sara Jeannette Duncan (1862-1922), who was born in the house at 96 West Street, now Thorpe's Funeral Home. A graduate of the Brantford Collegiate Institute, she wrote nineteen novels, only one of which has a Canadian setting. *The Imperialist* (1904) is set in an Ontario town called "Elgin," which closely resembles Brantford in its social, political, and cultural references.

Sara Jeannette Duncan, author of The Imperialist, is so depicted by Isaac Bickerstaff, artist Don Evans. [Special Collections, University of Calgary Libraries]

000000000000000000000000

SON OF A HUNDRED KINGS

A Novel of the Nineties

by

THOMAS B. COSTAIN

DOUBLEDAY & COMPANY, INC.
Garden City, New York

000000000000000000000000

One of Thomas B. Costain's least popular — and least successful — novels was the only one set in his native Canada. Son of a Hundred Kings (1950) takes place in the Brantford area. [Doubleday Canada Limited]

Thomas B. Costain   The Thomas B. Costain School was named in honour of the historical novelist and native son, Thomas B. Costain (1885-1965), whose name was at one time a byword in the world of letters. Costain served as editor of *Maclean's* (1915-20), associate editor of *Saturday Evening Post* (1920-34), story editor for Twentieth Century-Fox (1934-36), advisory editor for Doubleday (1939-65). He did not write his first book until his fifty-seventh year, but in the next twenty-three, he published thirteen novels, two biographies, five histories, and five anthologies. His historical novel, *The Black Rose* (1945), was the basis of a successful movie. *High Towers* (1953) is set in the Montreal of the 1700s; *Son of a Hundred Kings* (1950) is set in a village called "Balfour" in the Brantford area in the 1890s. Costain was responsible for Doubleday publishing the "Canadian History Series," a popular re-telling of Canada's development in six volumes.

Brant Historical Society Museum   Among the many displays devoted to native materials and local history are items of interest connected with Alexander Graham Bell, Joseph Brant, Thomas B. Costain, and Pauline Johnson.

Brighton
Brighton is best known as the gateway to Presqu'ile Provincial Park. It has a literary association but no legitimate landmark. The novelist and journalist Harold Horwood (b. 1923) has written: "There is a cabin near but not exactly on Lake Ontario, near Brighton, built by Angus Mowat and used both by Farley Mowat and myself as a place to disappear and work. I did most of the work on *The White Eskimo* (1972) in this cabin, though I finished it in an apartment building in Toronto. Farley wrote *The Rock within the Sea* (1968) among other things there. The place is called 'Indian Summer,' and the only problem it presents, as a landmark, is that nobody can find it."

Brockville
Brockville, on the St. Lawrence River northeast of Kingston, appears as "Stoverville" in various works by Hugh Hood (b. 1928). At least the fictional town recreates many characteristics of Brockville which is the author's wife's hometown. Use is made of Stoverville in "Three Halves of a House" (1961), "Bicultural Angela" (1967), *A Game of Touch* (1970), *A New Athens* (1977), and *The Scenic Art* (1984). In the second-last of these novels the Stoverville district is turned into a pastoral place with a beautiful passage describing a ghost train and ghost boat in the ice at Brown's Bay.

Callander
The Dionne Quintuplets were born at Callander, southeast of North Bay, on May 28, 1934. Journalists had a field day with the births to Oliva and Elzire Dionne of five daughters — Yvonne, Annette, Cecile, Emilie, and Marie. Their physician, Dr. Alan Roy Dafoe, became a popular hero and was portrayed in three Hollywood films that exploited popular interest in the multiple births. Wilson MacDonald (1880-1967) wrote two poems, "Quintrains" and "Doc Dafoe," about the Quints, and

Pierre Berton (b. 1920) called the episode "a thirties melodrama" in *The Dionne Years* (1977). The original Dionne homestead has been moved to North Bay where it will be opened as a Quints museum. The eighteen-room mansion subsequently occupied by the Dionnes is now the Nipissing Manor Nursing Home.

The house in which the Dionne Quints were born at Callander, Ont., has been transformed into the Dionne Museum. [Ontario Ministry of Tourism and Recreation]

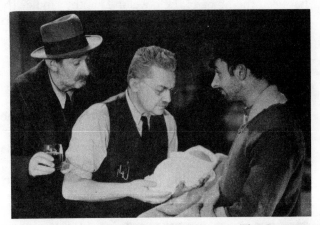

Jean Hersholt played Dr. Dafoe in the 1936 movie The Country Doctor, *the first of three Hollywood films based on the early life of the Dionne Quints.* [Ontario Film Institute]

Calumet Island
The region around Calumet Island in the Ottawa River, northwest of Ottawa, is associated with the legend of the "Lament of Cadieux." At Petit Rocher, or Little Rock, below Calumet Island, the voyageur Jean Cadieux (d. 1709) stood his ground against a band of Iroquois. Although mortally wounded, he scooped out a shallow grave and before expiring penned in his own blood on birchbark the "Lament of Cadieux." The English translation of the first verse runs: "Little rock of the high mount / I've come here to end my days / O, sweet echoes, hear my sigh / I'm sinking fast and going to die." The popular folk song is said to be the first about an incident that occurred in this country.

Cambridge   See GALT.

Camden East

In this village on the Napanee River, north of Kingston, was born Sir Gilbert Parker (1862-1932), historical novelist and member of the British House of Commons (1900-18). Among his novels are *The Seats of the Mighty* (1896), *Pierre and His People* (1892), and *When Valmond Came to Pontiac* (1895). The house in which he was born stood near the highway bridge over the Napanee River. A plaque was unveiled in 1958 on the grounds of St. Luke's Anglican Church, County Road No. 4.

Two important national magazines are published here by Camden House Publishing Limited. James and Elinor Lawrence launched *Harrowsmith* in 1976. The magazine, devoted to ecological concerns, was named after the nearby village of Harrowsmith. In 1981, James Lawrence launched *Equinox*, which is devoted to world exploration.

Camp X See OSHAWA.

Cannington

A farming community east of Lake Simcoe, Cannington is the location of the fifty-acre farm which, since 1964, has been the home of the novelist Timothy Findley (b. 1930). He is the author of two bestsellers, *The Wars* (1977) and *Famous Last Words* (1981), both of which were written here.

Cape Croker Reserve

On this reserve on the Bruce Peninsula, near Wiarton, was born and raised Basil H. Johnston (b. 1929) who learned the traditional lore of the Ojibway people from the lips of his grandmother. Johnston, a lecturer in the Department of Ethnology of the Royal Ontario Museum, is the author of *Ojibway Heritage* (1976) and *Ojibway Ceremonies* (1983).

Basil H. Johnston, author and folklorist. [McClelland & Stewart]

Carlyle Lake

North of Kirkland Lake is Carlyle Lake, named after the Scots-born, English writer Thomas Carlyle (1795-1881).

"Cary's Island" See ALGOMA.

Cedar Springs

A small community on the north shore of Lake Erie, Cedar Springs was the "old homestead" of Arthur Stringer (1874-1950). The once-popular novelist lived here from 1903 to 1921 before he moved permanently to New Jersey. In a letter of September 20, 1936, Stringer explained to William Arthur Deacon, who was researching A *Literary Map of Canada*, that he had recently tried to reacquire the "old homestead" but had failed in the attempt. Stringer is recalled as the one-time husband of Jobyna Howland, the original "Gibson Girl"; as the scriptwriter of the silent film *The Perils of Pauline*; as the writer of crime adventure novels; and as the author of "The Prairie Stories" centred around Calgary.

Chalk River

Located on the Ottawa River, northwest of Ottawa, Chalk River was selected in 1944 as the site for Canada's first nuclear reactor — the first in the world outside the United States. Atomic Energy of Canada operates the Chalk River Nuclear Laboratories and pays a grant in lieu of taxes for the nearby residential community of Deep River. Surprisingly, no literature (of a non-technical nature, it seems) has come out of Chalk River except for a juvenile novel, *Dale of the Mounted: Atomic Plot* (1959) by Joe Holliday, (b. 1910), which has the Laboratories as the setting.

Chapleau

The tragic death of Louis Hémon (1880-1913), the French journalist and author of *Maria Chapdelaine*, occurred at Chapleau, northeast of Sault Ste. Marie. He was walking along the train tracks about two miles north of the town when he was struck by a CPR express and instantly killed. He is buried in the Roman Catholic Cemetery at Chapleau. A stone monument was raised in his honour at Chapleau Centennial Park, across Dufferin Street from the CPR Station. Hémon did not live to see the publication in 1916 of his great novel about life in the farming community of Péribonca. It has been translated twice into English and into a dozen or more European languages. Three films have been based on it, the most recent in 1983.

The monument at Chapleau figures in the nightmare-like story "Mr. Sleepwalker" in *Mrs. Golightly and Other Stories* (1961) by Ethel Wilson (1890-1980) in which the following passage appears: "The train stopped at Chapleau for twenty minutes. Mary got out, and wandered, as she always did at Chapleau station, to the small stone memorial that

Photograph of Louis Hémon. [Archives Nationales du Québec, Collection Initiale]

Thoreau MacDonald's title page for the 1958 edition of Louis Hémon's classic novel Maria Chapdelaine. *[Macmillan of Canada]*

bears the name of Louis Hémon. Why, she wondered, did Louis Hémon come to Canada, write his book which, although unknown to most young Canadians, had already dimmed to a reputation faintly classic, and die? And why did Louis Hémon die, still young, at Chapleau, straggling rawly beside its railway station and its forests? A young man stood beside her and studied the carved words. Mary looked up at him and spoke tentatively. 'Do you know why Louis Hémon came here?' she asked."

Chatham

At what is now the First Baptist Church in Chatham, southeast of Sarnia, a meeting to plan for an anti-slavery government for the United States was held in May 1858. The leader elected was the American abolitionist, John Brown (1800-1859), who led the attack on Harper's Ferry, West Virginia. Although hanged, he lives on in the words of the hymn and Union song from the American Civil War, which begins: "John Brown's body lies a-mouldering in his grave, / His soul is marching on!" A number of American writers, including John Greenleaf Whittier, Henry David Thoreau, and Stephen Vincent Benét, have written about John Brown and his exploit, planned in Chatham.

There is a plaque in the Chatham Public Library to honour Jean Blewett (1862-1934), journalist and poet, who died in Chatham. Her volume of patriotic tales for children, *Heart Stories* (1919), was circulated by the Imperial Order of the Daughters of the Empire.

The Chatham-Kent Museum has a number of exhibits connected with the life of Josiah Henson (1789-1883), the original "Uncle Tom" who lived in a tulip-wood cabin at Dresden.

Chatsworth

Nellie McClung (1873-1951), prominent feminist, was born in Chatsworth, south of Owen Sound. Like so many other Ontario farming families, the McClungs moved West. In 1880, the family homesteaded in Manitoba's Souris Valley. McClung continued her westward migration by moving to Edmonton, Calgary, and finally Victoria. She tells the story of her life in *In Times Like These* (1913), *Clearing in the West* (1935), and *The Stream Runs Fast* (1945).

Chaucer Lake

Chaucer Lake and Tales Lake are both located northeast of Lake Nipigon. Their names recall the great English poet Geoffrey Chaucer (1340-1400) and his work *The Canterbury Tales* (1388).

Cheapside

Wilson MacDonald (1880-1967), poet and literary personality, was born in the village of Cheapside, east of Simcoe. He studied at the Port Dover Public School, Woodstock College, and McMaster University. He is principally remembered as the author of "The Song of the Ski" (1926), which he recited with great animation in high-school auditoriums across the country long before such poetry recitals were commonplace. In 1953 the Toronto and Cleveland chapters of the Wilson MacDonald Poetry Society were founded to promote his work and presented him each year with a new automobile.

The Wilson MacDonald Memorial School Museum was opened in 1965 in the one-room, red-brick school house in which the poet studied as a youngster. Displayed here are copies of collections such as *Out of the Wilderness* (1926) and the poet's unique, embellished manuscripts. The museum is located on Rainham Road near the intersection of the Cheapside Road.

Christopher Robin Lake

In Renfrew County, northwest of Pembroke, may be found nine features with names derived from the stories and poems of A. A. Milne (1882-1956), namely: Christopher Robin Lake, Eeyore Lake, Kanga Lake, Owl Lake, Piglet Lake, Pooh Lake, Rabbit Lake, Roo Lake, Tigger Lake. The names were adopted between 1948 and 1980.

Clarkson

The most famous country home in Canadian literature

will be found at 1503 Clarkson Road North, opposite the Church of St. Bride (Anglican), in the town of Clarkson which is between Mississauga and Oakville. The country home is known as Benares, but better known as the original of Jalna.

This elegant stone house was built in 1857 by Captain James B. Harris, formerly of the East India Company's 24th Foot Regiment, on the foundations of a house erected by a Loyalist in 1835. Harris called his country home Benares after the city in India where he had served. Descendants of the Harris family have owned and occupied Benares ever since. Deeded to the Ontario Heritage Foundation, someday it will serve as a museum.

Benares inspired the novelist Mazo de la Roche (1879-1961) when she created Jalna, the fictional home of her Whiteoaks family. Mazo found the name in a gazetteer that listed British posts in India. Her novel *Jalna* (1927) was the first of fifteen in the family saga. Members of the Harris family served as models for the Whiteoaks, and the poet Robert Finch (b. 1900) became the Finch of the novels.

The modest cottage occupied by Mazo de la Roche and her cousin Caroline Clement, who lived nearby, has long since disappeared. It was named Trail Cottage and it adjoined Woodlot, which still stands. Woodlot was owned by the Livesay family, and young Dorothy Livesay (b. 1909) enjoyed overhearing the conversations between Mazo and her father J. F. B. Livesay, a journalist. In an essay "The Making of Jalna: A Reminiscence" (1965), Livesay wrote: "Jalna, to us, meant Benares: that gracious, square brick house with the wide front porch and a long scullery at the back built of stone." The country home and its fictional counterpart are not identical — for instance, Benares has two stories, Jalna three — but they look enough alike that Benares could serve for exterior shots of Jalna in the CBC-TV series *Whiteoaks of Jalna*. There is no evidence that Mazo ever was invited inside the country home of the Harrises.

Dorothy Livesay added further details in *The Documentaries* (1968): "At Clarkson I was especially fascinated by a neighbour's house, *Benares*, with its solid dignity of brick and stone, its coach house, stable and orchards. There on a spring Sunday my father, J. F. B. Livesay, took me to 'high tea,' enabling me to have a glimpse of a lost Victorian world of mahogany furniture, gilt mirrors, family portraits.

"That house still stands today but its orchards and rolling meadows have been stripped away for housing estates. Now, the whole of Clarkson is little more than a suburb of Toronto, its cherry and apple trees turned into pavement, its lakeshore beaches bulldozed into oil refineries. The only happy fact for me is that the house my father built in the Thirties still hides quietly on the wooded knoll next to the property where Mazo de la Roche wrote *Jalna;* and the daffodils, irises and wild

This graceful country home, built by James B. Harris in 1857, is still occupied by his descendants. Harris called his home "Benares," and it inspired Mazo de la Roche's "Jalna." [CBC]

Old Adeline was played by Kate Reid and Renny by Paul Harding in the CBC-TV production of The Whiteoaks of Jalna. [CBC]

This still is taken from the RKO Radio Pictures' production of Jalna, *directed in 1935 by John Cromwell. The film starred Ian Hunter, Peggy Wood, C. Aubrey Smith, Kay Johnson, Nigel Bruce, and David Manners.* [PAC / National Film, Television and Sound Archives]

"Myself — London 1936" is Mazo de la Roche's caption to the frontispiece photograph of her autobiography, Ringing the Changes. *The successful novelist was fifty-seven at the time.* [Macmillan of Canada]

trilliums planted by my father still bloom each spring, along the creekside amongst white birches."

J. F. B. Livesay, journalist and father of Dorothy, is buried in St. Peter's Cemetery, Erindale, Ont.

Clinton

Since the late 1970s, the town of Clinton, southeast of Goderich, has been the home of author Alice Munro (b. 1931). Clinton and a clutch of other towns in Huron and nearby counties are depicted as "Dalgleish" in the stories that make up *The Moons of Jupiter* (1982).

Clinton is also associated with Steven Truscott who at the age of fourteen was sentenced to hang for the rape-murder of twelve-year-old Lynne Harper in 1959. The sentence was commuted to life imprisonment and Truscott was paroled in 1969. The case generated some notable books, begining with *The Trial of Steven Truscott* (1966) by Isabel Lebourdais and ending with *Who Killed Lynne Harper?* (1979) by Bill Trent.

Christopher Pratt's painting, a detail of which appeared on the cover of the Macmillan edition of The Moons of Jupiter, *captures the intimate quality of Alice Munro's stories.* [Art Gallery of Hamilton]

Cobalt

The mining community of Cobalt, southeast of Kirkland Lake, attracted William Henry Drummond (1854-1907), who wrote *The Habitant and Other French-Canadian Poems* (1897) in the broken English of the French-speaking lumbermen, canoemen, and farmers he knew from his early years at Lac Megantic, Que. In 1905, with his brothers, he established Drummond Mines, a silver-mining operation, at Kerr Lake, southeast of the town. All that remains of his cabin on the mining property is the original stone fireplace. He died here but was buried in Montreal.

Among Drummond's last poems are "The Calcite Vein — A Tale of Cobalt" and "Bloom — A Song of Cobalt" which concludes: "The bloom upon the cobalt — that's the only bloom for me." In 1933, a plaque was erected with an inscription from "Le Vieux Temps" which runs: "An w'en he fin' we ready, for mak' de longue voyage / He guide me t'roo de wood hesef upon ma las' portage." In 1969, a second plaque was erected, this one in the public park at the corner of Silver Street and Prospect Avenue in Cobalt.

On the outskirts of Cobalt is located the Highway Book Shop, a bookstore and publishing house. The proprietor has been known to advertise his operation as located at "200,000 Yonge Street," Cobalt being located due north of Toronto on Highway 11, an extension of Toronto's Yonge Street.

The inscription on the monument to Willet Green Miller, First Provincial Geologist of Ontario in 1902-23, is surprisingly literate: "To Cobalt he gave its name and a place among the great mining camps of the world. He read the secret of the rocks, and opened the portal for the outpouring of their wonderful riches. His monument is New Ontario." [Ontario Ministry of Tourism and Recreation]

Coboconk

Coboconk is a village near Lindsay. The name is Algonkian for "swift water." Phillips Thompson (1843-1933) made use of the odd name for the series of satiric letters he signed as if by one Jimuel Briggs, D.B., graduate of Coboconk University, supposedly reprinted from the *Coboconk Irradiator.* They appear in Thompson's book *The Political Experiences of Jimuel Briggs, D.B.* (1873). Thompson is best remembered as the author of *The Politics of Labour* (1887). He is the grandfather of the well-known author Pierre Berton.

The young Archibald Lampman lived in this house at 37 King Street East, Cobourg, from 1874. His father was curate of St. Peter's Anglican Church. [Terry Keough]

Dressler House, in Cobourg, was the birthplace and childhood home of Marie Dressler (1869-1934), star of stage and screen. She was born in the northeast room of this cottage-style house, built in 1833, maintained in the manner of the 1860s, and now operated as a stylish restaurant. Her father was the organist for St. Peter's Anglican Church next door. Dressler starred with Wallace Beery in Tugboat Annie *(1933), the creation of former Torontonian Norman Reilly Raine, and is credited with two autobiographies,* The Life Story of an Ugly Duckling *(1924) and* My Own Story *(1934). [Kevin C. Parker]*

Cobourg

The resort town of Cobourg, on Lake Ontario east of Oshawa, was the birthplace of silent screen star Marie Dressler (1869-1934). The house in which she was born, restored to the style of the 1930s, is now a restaurant and tavern. Outside St. Peter's Anglican Church there is a plaque raised in her honour. In her autobiography, *The Life Story of an Ugly Duckling* (1924), she wrote: "And as for my birthplace — Cobourg, Canada — I can give you only my word that I was born in a house and had a complete set of parents. Certainly no president could claim a more humble birthplace."

A farm on the outskirts of Cobourg in June 1914 was the meeting place of two theatre personalities. It was here that the youthful Raymond Massey (1896-1983) met a "young lady from Buffalo" who "was the most beautiful creature I had ever seen." So reminisced Massey in the second volume of his autobiography, *A Hundred Different Lives* (1979). She announced that she was going to New York. "I shall become a professional actress. On the stage — on Broadway." He explained, "I think I'll make farm machinery or something," but dreamed that he would some day become an actor and appear opposite her on Broadway. Twenty-six years later he appeared on Broadway with this "young lady," the actress Katharine Cornell.

Coleridge

Coleridge, a former locality northwest of Orangeville, was named after the English poet Samuel Taylor Coleridge (1772-1834).

Collingwood

Collingwood is situated at the foot of Blue Mountain and the shore of Georgian Bay and is not lacking in literary associations.

Edna Jaques (1891-1978), author of more than a dozen collections of homespun verse, was born in the two-storey brick house built by her father at 130 4th Street. She recalls growing up here, attending the old Methodist Church on Maple Street, and studying at the old Central School, in her autobiography *Uphill All the Way* (1977). In 1902, the family went West to homestead southeast of Moose Jaw. She is mainly remembered for "In Flanders Now," from *Beside Still Waters* (1938), which is her "answer" to the "question" posed by John McCrae in his famous poem "In Flanders Fields."

Fanciers of verse could do worse than read A. G. Churchill's *Poetical Directory of Collingwood* (1876) which begins: "From yonder Blue Mountains, historians look down / On Collingwood harbour — that beautiful town . . ." and continues with descriptive verses on the butcher, the saddle-maker, the hotel-keeper, the captain of the *Waubuno*, etc. Selections appear in *Reflections: An Historical Anthology of Collingwood* (1983).

Collingwood is the setting of a novel by Morley Callaghan (b. 1903). This is *Luke Baldwin's Vow* (1948), which is about a young boy and his dog. The Callaghan family summered in the region.

Many of the country's leading poets came to Collingwood to recite from their work and conduct workshops as part of the Great Canadian Poetry Weekends. These were sponsored each June by the Blue Mountain Foundation for the Arts and co-ordinated by Barbara Weider and Denis Mildon from 1976 to 1982.

A visitor to a small community southwest of Collingwood was Alexander Solzhenitsyn (b. 1918). The Russian dissident novelist drove alone from his residence at Cavendish, Vermont, to visit a local resident who had been an officer in the Czar's army, as part of his research for his historical work *August 1914* (1972). He remained one night and said that the countryside reminded him of his native Russia.

Combermere

Born in Combermere, northeast of Bancroft, was John W. Dafoe (1868-1944), the long-time and widely respected editor of the Winnipeg *Free Press*. There is a commemorative plaque northeast of the nearby community of Purdy.

Couchiching   See ORILLIA.

Crusoe Island
A small island in Lake Muskoka, Crusoe Island was named after the hero of *Robinson Crusoe* (1719) by Daniel Defoe (1659-1731). In the same lake is Friday Island, named after Crusoe's "man Friday."

Crusoe Lake
Crusoe Lake and Robinson Lake are located east of Kenora, and were named after the famous novel *Robinson Crusoe* (1719) by Daniel Defoe (1659-1731).

Dacre
Dacre, southwest of Renfrew, is the location of Ontario's Magnetic Hill where automobiles appear to coast uphill. Matawatchan, southwest of Dacre, is the home of Duke Redbird (b. 1939), the native performer, poet, and writer. Born of Métis ancestry on the Saugeen Indian Reserve, near Southampton, Redbird was raised in the Matawatchan area and, in 1983, bought an old frame farmhouse in the region. Among his publications are *We Are Métis* (1979), a history of his people, and *Loveshine and Redwine* (1981), a collection of songs and poems.

Daisy Mae Lake
North of Sault Ste. Marie and west of Chapleau is Daisy Mae Lake, called after the sweetheart in the Li'l Abner comic strip created by cartoonist Al Capp (1909-1979).

"Dalgleish"   See CLINTON.

Darwin Lake
The fame of the English naturalist, Charles Darwin (1809-1882), is perpetuated in the naming of this lake near Cobalt.

Defoe Lake
South of Lake Abitibi will be found Defoe Lake, named after the English writer Daniel Defoe (1659-1731). Nearby will be found other features with literary associations: Trollope Lake, Carlyle Lake, Mount Smollett, and Mount Goldsmith.

Delhi
The tobacco fields of Delhi, northwest of Simcoe, are the setting of "Hunky," the widely anthologized short story by Hugh Garner (1913-1979) about an itinerant Hungarian-born tobacco-picker.

Delta
On the grounds of the Delta United Church on Highway

Society's indifference to the Indians is the subject of Hugh Garner's story "One, Two, Three Little Indians." Here Tom (Daniel Grigg) comforts his young wife (Marie Mimford) in the CBC-TV dramatization of the story in 1971. [Memory Lane]

42, northeast of Gananoque, a plaque was raised in 1962 to honour Lorne Pierce (1890-1961) who was born in Delta. As well as an ordained minister, Pierce was the long-time editor (from 1920 to 1960) of the Ryerson Press in Toronto. At the age of thirty-six, he endowed the Royal Society of Canada with funds to present annually in perpetuity the Lorne Pierce Medal for Distinguished Contribution to Canadian Literature.

"Deptford"   See THAMESVILLE.

Doon
Doon Pioneer Village, located in the village of Doon, southeast of Kitchener, pays tribute to the early settlers of southern Ontario. Peter McArthur's house was brought here from the family land near Appin, Ekfrid Township, in western Ontario. Peter McArthur (1866-1924) is mainly remembered as a fine satirist, as a glance at *The Best of Peter McArthur* (1967), edited by Alec Lucas will,

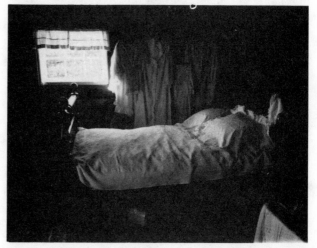

View of the bedroom with nightdresses of Peter McArthur's House in Doon Pioneer Village. [Bill Brooks]

show. He was born in Ekfrid Township and worked as a journalist in New York and London before settling on the family farm in 1908 and writing casual essays published in newspapers and collected in books beginning with *In Pastures Green* (1915). "I like to keep my feet on the earth — in good Canadian mud," he wrote. He had a deft touch: "A satirist is a man who discovers unpleasant things about himself and then says them about other people." "Disaster precedes reform." "Success invariably makes a man philosophical."

Adjacent to the village is Homer Watson Memorial Park, named in honour of the painter whom Oscar Wilde admired and called "the Canadian Constable." South of the village is the field-stone house, built in 1835, occupied by Watson from 1881 to his death in 1936.

Uncle Tom's Cabin, as well as being the title of Stowe's world-famous book, is the name of the tulipwood cabin, near Dresden, occupied by Josiah Henson, the original Uncle Tom. He is buried near his celebrated home. [Ontario Ministry of Tourism and Recreation]

Dresden

At Dresden, north of Chatham, is the Josiah Henson House, better known as Uncle Tom's Cabin. The two-storey homestead was built of tulipwood about 1842 by Josiah Henson (1789-1883), the most famous of all fugitive slaves. He boarded the so-called Underground Railroad in Kentucky with his wife and four children and escaped to freedom in Upper Canada in 1830. Ten years later he met Harriet Beecher Stowe (1811-1896) at Andover, Massachusetts, and the American novelist made use of his descriptions and experiences in her abolitionist novel *Uncle Tom's Cabin* (1852). The homestead is one of seven buildings in the museum complex. Henson is buried in the family plot near the homestead.

Uncle Tom's Cabin, which Mrs. Stowe wrote in Brunswick, Maine, was one of the most popular and influential books of the nineteenth century, being praised by Lord Macaulay, George Sand, Leo Tolstoy, and countless others. Readers of the novel recall not only the freedom of Uncle Tom's Cabin but the slavery of Simon Legree's Plantation. The latter site may be found in the

town of Chopin, Louisiana. According to Rita Stein in *A Literary Tour Guide to the United States: South and West* (1979), in the town of Chopin is the Little Eva Plantation once owned by Robert McAlpin, a New England kinsman of Mrs. Stowe. Legend has it that McAlpin was the prototype of Simon Legree in *Uncle Tom's Cabin*, a tradition the Louisiana novelist Kate Chopin (1851-1904), whose father bought the plantation from McAlpin, touched upon in her first novel *At Fault* (1890). It has never been established that Mrs. Stowe visited this part of Louisiana; she may have had reports from her brother Charles Beecher. So if Canada has Uncle Tom's Cabin, the United States has Simon Legree's Plantation.

A well-written novel for younger readers about the movement of former slaves is *Underground to Canada* (1977) by Barbara Smucker (b. 1915).

Ellengowan

The community of Ellengowan, west of Chesley, bears the name of the estate in the romantic novel *Guy Mannering* (1815) by Sir Walter Scott (1771-1832).

Elliot Lake

Elliot Lake, north of Blind River, is the site of Ontario's uranium fields. Peter Such (b. 1939) worked here as a student miner and described the locale and the work in his first novel *Fallout* (1969).

Emo

Here, near Fort Frances in the Lake of the Woods area, the American anthropologist Ruth Landes (b. 1908) lived for seven months in the early 1930s, interviewing Mrs. Maggie Wilson, a Cree woman then in her late fifties who possessed a remarkable memory of Ojibway lifestyles and traditions. Using Mrs. Wilson as informant, Landes published two books, *Ojibwa Sociology* (1937) and *The Ojibwa Woman* (1938).

Erin

The village of Erin, southeast of Orangeville, has become the small-press capital of Canada. Novelists Dave and Ellen Godfrey founded here in 1972 their own publishing house, Press Porcépic, as an imprint for literary books of limited but vital interest. Three years later, their printer and designer, Tim Inkster, with his wife Elke, established a new imprint, The Porcupine's Quill, Inc., for the private-press quality printing and publishing of *belles lettres*. Independently, in 1974, Jim Filby, his wife Jean, and two partners joined forces to publish illustrated volumes of local history under The Boston Mills Press imprint. Erin has more publishing houses than most cities have bookstores.

The most popular native poet in nineteenth-century Canada was probably Alexander McLachlan (1818-1896), known in his day as "the Burns of Canada" and hardly remembered a century later. He farmed in Perth County but in 1850 moved to Erin where he supported himself and his family by opening a tailor shop. He published five books of vigorous verse, including *The Emigrant and Other Poems* (1861), and died in Orangeville.

Fort William   See THUNDER BAY.

Friday Island   See CRUSOE ISLAND.

Galt

The city of Galt amalgamated with the towns of Hespeler and Preston in 1973 and became Cambridge. The settlement of Galt, located northwest of Hamilton, was founded and named in 1827 to honour the superintendent of the Canada Company, John Galt (1779-1839). When he returned to his native Scotland, Galt turned to literature and turned out a series of novels and biographies. He described the lot of the Scottish settler in Upper Canada in his novel *Lawrie Todd* (1830), and he is usually credited with the authorship of the once-popular "Canadian Boat Song" (1829), which inspired the erection of a stone replica of a crofter's hut in Pleasant Bay, N.S.

Mazo de la Roche (1879-1961) lived with her family in Galt between 1891 and 1895.

Gargantua   See RABELAIS CREEK.

Geneva Park   See ORILLIA.

Georgian Bay

The poet William Wilfred Campbell (1858-1918) referred to Georgian Bay as the Lake District and wrote about it in his finest poems. "How One Winter Came in the Lake Region" from *The Dread Voyage* (1893) is particularly evocative of the wind-swept region. Campbell was born in Kitchener, when it was called Berlin, but at the age of six weeks brought to Wiarton. In 1867 the family moved to Meaford and remained there for five years, returning to Wiarton. In later years Campbell lived in Ottawa. He yearned to be the poet of a "vaster Britain" and, indeed, "poet-laureate of the British Empire."

Ruth Nichols (b. 1948), the children's writer, set one of her delightful fantasies *beneath* the waters of Georgian Bay. It seems this aquatic domain is home to the dwarfish "Mer-people" of *The Marrow of the World* (1972).

Glengarry County

The recorder without equal of life in Glengarry County was Charles William Gordon (1860-1937), the clergyman and novelist who wrote under the pen name Ralph Connor. Born in Glengarry County, at St. Elmo, northeast of Cornwall in southeastern Ontario, he lies buried in the St. Elmo Cemetery. In 1959, a plaque was unveiled on the grounds of the Presbyterian Church where his father had served as the minister. The church is located at the corner of Concession Road 19 and County Road 20 in St. Elmo.

A kilted Charles W. Gordon (novelist Ralph Connor) throws the caber in this drawing by Isaac Bickerstaff (artist Don Evans). [Special Collections, University of Calgary Libraries]

The Glengarry Schoolhouse at Upper Canada Village, Morrisburg. [Bill Brooks]

Gordon wrote more than two dozen novels, many of them set in the West. Two of his most popular remain *The Man from Glengarry* (1901), which depicts life among the Highland lumberman in 1860-71, and *Glengarry School Days* (1902), whch makes use of his own experiences in telling the story of the schooling of a youngster in the 1870s. A log schoolhouse that resembles the one described in this novel may be found at Upper Canada Village, at Morrisburg.

The widely anthologized title story of *Old Man Savarin and Other Stories* (1895) by Edward William Thomson (1849-1924) is set in Glengarry County.

Goderich

Colonist, physician, and writer, William "Tiger" Dunlop (1792-1848) founded Goderich on the eastern shore of Lake Huron in 1827. Here he built his country home Gairbraid on the Maitland River. The Lizars sisters,

The many accomplishments of William "Tiger" Dunlop are listed on this plaque. He is described as "a man of surpassing talent, knowledge, and benevolence." [Terry Keough]

Kathleen (d. 1931) and Robina (d. 1918), described the colonial-style country home in their anecdotal *In the Days of the Canada Company* (1896) in terms of "warmth, fires, a dining-room with a shining table, and cabinets of coloured china and bright silver, Indian ornaments and hangings, a black butler and his assistant, and more wonderful food than the poor settlers ever dreamed of." All this is gone, for as Katherine Hale (1878-1956) lamented in *Historic Houses of Canada* (1952): "Going! It had gone long ago — hardly its ghost remains. Slightly below the site of the house, which stands on the brow of the hill, lies the private burial ground of the three Dunlops. It is now completely overgrown with rank grass and weeds, and seems to be part of a rubbish heap. Who would think that the community which Tiger Dunlop fathered could so neglect the legendary house in which he lived!" Dunlop's memory is held in esteem on account of his notorious — or hilarious — last will and testament which included such bequests as the following: "I leave my brother Alan my big silver snuff-box, as I am informed he is rather a decent Christian, with a swag belly and a jolly face." His tomb is off Highway 21, north of Goderich. A plaque mounted in the New Huron County Court Building, Goderich, honours Sir J. S. Willison (1856-1927), born at Hills Green. An editor and political correspondent, he became in 1913 the first Canadian journalist to be knighted.

Gore's Landing   See LAKEFIELD.

Grand River Reserve   See SIX NATIONS RESERVE.

"Grantham"   See ST. CATHARINES.

Gravel Gertie Island
Gravel Gertie Island, south of Dryden, recalls the likeable but ugly-looking character created by the American cartoonist Chester Gould (b.1900) in his comic strip "Dick Tracy."

Gravenhurst
Gravenhurst, at the southern tip of Lake Muskoka, was named after a reference in the title story in *Bracebridge Hall, or the Humorists* (1822), a collection of tales and sketches by the American writer Washington Irving (1783-1859). The reference is to a location in England which turns out to be non-existent. Bracebridge, Ont., was named after the title piece.

Norman Bethune was born in the manse of Trinity United Church in Gravenhurst. The plaque erected by the Historic Sites and Monuments Board of Canada is inscribed in Chinese characters. [Parks Canada / F. Cattroll]

Gravenhurst was the birthplace of Norman Bethune (1890-1939) who is identified (on the official plaque) as "an internationally famed humanitarian, surgeon and revolutionary." He was born in the manse of Knox Presbyterian Church, now Trinity United Church, a two-storey frame house erected in 1880 on John Street that is now a museum, but raised in a succession of small towns, and cities, including Beaverton, Blind River, Aylmer, Sault Ste. Marie, Toronto, and Owen Sound. He graduated from Jesse Ketchum Public School in Toronto and from Owen Sound Collegiate Institute.

There are a number of memorials to Dr. Bethune in the People's Republic of China, where he died, but there are only two in Canada. (The other is Place Norman-Bethune in Montreal.) "We must all learn from him the

Norman Bethune in Spain in 1936 and in China in 1939, from the NFB documentary Bethune. *[NFB]*

spirit that is so completely free from selfishness," explained Mao Tse-tung in his essay "In Memory of Norman Bethune" which was reprinted in part in *Quotations from Chairman Mao Tse-Tung* (1966), "The Little Red Book," edited by Lin Piao.

Many of Bethune's traits may be seen in the finely drawn character of Jerome Martell, the brilliant surgeon and idealist in Hugh MacLennan's novel *The Watch that Ends the Night* (1959). Ted Allan and Sydney Gordon wrote the first biography of Bethune called *The Scalpel, The Sword* (1952, 1971). The documentary film *Bethune,* released by the NFB in 1964, inspired Roderick Stewart to write the standard biography, *Bethune* (1973), and take up a teaching post in China. A feature-length film was made in China in the late 1970s, and Bethune (a fine writer in his own right) has inspired countless poems.

The Great Lakes

These five freshwater lakes are the largest group of lakes in the world. They were first referred to as "these great lakes" by Pierre-Esprit Radisson in 1665. In order of size they are Lake Superior, Lake Michigan, Lake Huron, Lake Erie, and Lake Ontario.

"The Great Lakes," wrote the French traveller Alexis de Tocqueville (1805-1859) in *Democracy in America* (1835), translated by George Lawrence in 1966, "are not framed, as are most lakes in the Old World, by hills or rocks; their banks are level, hardly rising more than a few feet above the water. So each is like a huge cup filled to the brim. The slightest change of global structure would tilt their waters to the pole or to the tropics." The fact that they are not "framed" may explain the verdict of Henry James (1843-1916) in *Portraits of Places* (1883): "The scene tends to offer, as one may say, a sort of marine effect missed."

The scene upset Rupert Brooke (1887-1915) who noted in a letter written in 1913 while sailing on "the cold magnificence of Lake Superior": "I have a perpetual feeling that a lake ought not to be this size. A river and a little lake and an ocean are natural; but not these creatures. They are too big, and too smooth, and too sunny; like an American business man."

It seems the first Canadian poet to write about all five bodies of water was James Reaney (b. 1926) in "The Great Lakes Suite" in *The Red Heart* (1949). Here is how he begins his tribute to the largest of the lakes: "I am Lake Superior / Cold and gray. / I have no superior. . . ."

The poet David McFadden (b. 1940), who was born in Hamilton, on Lake Ontario, has set himself the goal of driving the circumference of each lake and describing his experiences. Nothing much happens, but there is a lot of local colour in *A Trip around Lake Huron* and *A Trip around Lake Erie,* both published in 1980.

Guelph

Guelph, northeast of Kitchener, was founded in 1827 by the Scots colonist and novelist John Galt (1779-1839).

He was at the time superintendent of the Canada Company and he described in his *Autobiography* (1833) how he and his fellow colonist and author, William "Tiger" Dunlop (1792-1848), marked the occasion by felling a maple tree and emptying a flask of whisky. "The name was chosen in compliment to the royal family, both because I thought it auspicious in itself and because I could not recollect that it had ever been before used in all the king's dominions."

James Gay The best "good bad poet" in Canadian literature is James Gay (1810-1891). An umbrella-maker and eccentric versifier, he styled himself "Poet Laureate of Canada and Master of All Poets, Royal City of Guelph, Ontario." Upon the death of Henry Wadsworth Longfellow in 1882, he wrote to Lord Tennyson and suggested "now Longfellow is gone there are only two of us left. There ought to be no rivalry between us." His inadvertently amusing verse is collected in a volume called *Canada's Poet* (1884). He is sometimes credited with the deathless couplet: "Hail our Great Queen in her regalia; / One foot in Canada, the other in Australia."

John McCrae Guelph was the birthplace and hometown of John McCrae (1872-1918), physician, soldier, and poet. McCrae will long be remembered for the

Adjoining the John McCrae Memorial Home (top) at Guelph, Ont., are the Memorial Gardens (bottom), where a gigantic book of bronze lies open to display the text of "In Flanders Fields" [Ontario Ministry of Tourism and Recreation]

121

Major John McCrae, officer Commanding 16th Battery, C.F.A., at Guelph, 1902-1904. [C-19919 / Public Archives Canada]

John McCrae, 5¢ stamp, 1968. [Canada Post Corporation]

fifteen-line poem "In Flanders Fields" which he wrote in Flanders in 1915. It is the most famous poem of World War One and one of the most moving and popular of elegies in the English language.

John McCrae House, the stone cottage in which he was born on Water Street, displays memorabilia associated with his life and work, especially his military and medical career, and particularly a holograph of his famous poem. Adjacent to the cottage are the Memorial Gardens, dedicated to the memory of the war dead, with as focal point the bronze replica of an open book displaying the text of "In Flanders Fields."

The lament, which exhorts the living not to "break faith" with the dead, was composed in twenty minutes on May 5, 1915, during the Second Battle of Ypres. The author was mourning the death of a friend. It first appeared anonymously in *Punch*, December 8, 1915. Its fame and familiarity stem from its recital at the first Armistice Day service on November 11, 1918. The standard text, introduced by Sir Andrew MacPhail (1864-1938), appears in the volume *In Flanders Fields and Other Poems* (1919).

McCrae fell in battle in the last year of the Great War. He was buried in the military graveyard at Wimereaux, in northern France.

The Communist Party of Canada

The founding convention of the Communist Party of Canada was held in the strictest secrecy in a barn (since demolished) behind a small farm house then owned by Albert Frederick Farley, an early CCP member, on the outskirts of Guelph. The farm house is still standing at 257 Metcalfe Street. The meeting on May 28-9, 1921, was attended by twenty-two delegates of various Socialist, Marxist, and Communist groups. They adopted a constitution and recognized the leadership of the Communist International.

The farm house is in private hands and surrounded by a housing development. In 1972, the owners, renovating their front porch, discovered a cache of documents and items hidden by Farley and his comrades. The material predicted the overthrow of the capitalist system by the new "Cooperative commonwealth." This "time capsule" was donated in 1979 to the Guelph Civic Museum, 6 Dublin Street South, and artifacts from it are on permanent display.

University of Guelph

The University of Guelph was formed in 1964, being earlier known as the Ontario Agricultural College. Arguably the most illustrious alumnus of OAC is the author and economist, John Kenneth Galbraith (b. 1908), who was invited to deliver the first convocation address at the new university. In various articles, interviews, and books, Galbraith has described his years at OAC in the early 1930s. He makes light of them, despite the fact that it took him an extra year to complete the regular course of study.

Housed in the Macdonald Stewart Room of the McLaughlin Library are a number of special collections. The L. M. Montgomery Collection includes the diaries and private scrapbook of L. M. Montgomery (1874-1942) which are closed to public access until 1992. The Shaw Festival Archives and the Tarragon Theatre Archives are depository collections, as is the Porcupine's Quill Collection devoted to the work of designer-printer-poet, Tim Inkster.

Other Associations

It is an odd fact that Zane Grey (1875-1939), who became famous for his Western novels, wrote a short story about a baseball game in Guelph. In the title story of *The Red Headed Outfield and Other Stories* (1912), a game is played between the Boston Red Stockings, then the best American baseball team, and the Guelph Maple Leafs, then Canada's leading team, in which the latter won despite the fact that the former introduced into play a "live ball." The story is based on an actual game (which the visiting team won) played by Grey's brother Romer in 1873.

One of the most effective of Canadian plays depicts conditions in the Guelph Reformatory. John Herbert (b. 1926) wrote *Fortune and Men's Eyes* based on his experiences as an inmate. The comedy-drama is set in an unnamed Ontario reformatory. It had its Broadway premiere in 1967 and resulted in the formation of the Fortune Society to help in the rehabilitation of former inmates. The play was filmed in 1971.

Raised on a farm at Summer Hill, outside Guelph,

Queenie (played by Michael Greer) descends the ladder and begins his flamboyant dance number before his fellow inmates in Fortune and Men's Eyes, the film version of John Herbert's play. Directed by Harvey Hart, it was filmed at the Prison de Québec on the Plains of Abraham. [Ontario Film Institute]

was the redoubtable Elinor Glyn (1864-1943), the English-born romantic novelist and Hollywood scriptwriter. After the publication of her daring novel *Three Weeks* (1907), the following verse was popular: "Would you like to sin / With Elinor Glyn / On a tiger-skin? / Or would you prefer / To err / With her / On some other fur?" Her novel was filmed in Hollywood in 1924, and four years later her short story "It" appeared in *Cosmopolitan*. The story turned the neuter pronoun into an euphemism for sex appeal. Glyn created vechicles for Clara Bow, the so-called It Girl. Lenore Coffee in *Storyline* (1973) describes the introduction of Glyn and Sir Gilbert Parker who became amorous, attempting to hold Glyn in his arms. She replied, "You may kiss my hand. All emotion begins at the wrist." In her autobiography, *Romantic Adventure* (1936), she explained: "The years of my childhood, spent at Summer Hill, developed my character, moulded my tastes, and coloured my point of view for life." A chance aquaintance in the Guelph area was a youthful farmer, the future father of poet Earle Birney.

Haileybury

Leslie McFarlane (1903-1977), the freelance writer, was raised in Haileybury; he returned to this mining community northeast of Cobalt in 1926 to answer the question, posed in his autobiography, *Ghost of the Hardy Boys* (1976), "Can a young man of unproven talents, living in the northern woods, finance a career in authorship?" He answered the question himself. "Definitely, he could. For a few months anyway."

Here in an office above a bank he wrote the early volumes in the Hardy Boys series for the Stratemeyer Syndicate which supplied outlines. The first volume, *The Tower Treasure*, was written on a secondhand Underwood in a cabin on Lake Ramsey, near Sudbury; but in Haileybury, McFarlane completed *The House on the Cliff, The Secret of the Old Mill*, and many others in the popular series. The house name was "Franklin W. Dixon." (McFarlane also wrote as "Roy Rockwood" and "Carolyn Keene.") The setting of the adventures of Frank and Joe Hardy, youthful detectives, is Bayport, on Barmet Bay, on the Atlantic coast.

McFarlane wrote his last Hardy Boy book, *The Phantom Freighter*, in Nova Scotia in 1946. He spent his retirement years in the town of Whitby. It was always a surprise to him that the Hardy Boys series — one of the most successful of all time — secured him a niche in the annals of Canadian writing.

Haliburton

The village of Haliburton and Haliburton County, northeast of Lake Simcoe, were named after Thomas Chandler Haliburton (1796-1865), the satirist, who was the first chairman of the Canadian Land and Emigration Company which bought about one million acres of land within the boundaries of the present county in 1861.

Hamilton

"Foundries breweries asylums universities" is how the poet Earle Birney (b. 1904) summed up Hamilton, at the western end of Lake Ontario, in his poem "To a Hamilton (Ont.) Lady Thinking to Travel." Foundries and breweries are outside the scope of this inquiry, but asylums and universities fall within it.

The Hamilton Psychiatric Hospital, on the brow of Hamilton Mountain, is a collection of new buildings on the site of the old Hamilton Asylum, of which Richard Maurice Bucke (1837-1902), the writer and friend of Walt

Marshall McLuhan inaugurated the first Multicultural Conference at Mohawk College, Hamilton, in May 1977. Many writers, including Hugh MacLennan and Gratien Gélinas, came for Mohawk's Canada Days, and in the last year of his life Glenn Gould conducted members of the Hamilton Symphony Orchestra in private concerts in the Auditorium of Mohawk College. [Kamala Bhatia]

Miriam Waddington, Hugh Garner, and Lovat Dickson are caught by the camera of Helen Hughes at Canada Day at Mohawk College, Hamilton, 1977. [Miriam Waddington]

W. Blair Bruce's "The Phantom Hunter" was painted in 1888 after reading Charles Dawson Shanley's poem "The Walker of the Snow" which is about a spectre that haunts the Quebec countryside. The large canvas is perhaps the most popular painting in the Art Gallery of Hamilton, Bruce's native city. [Art Gallery of Hamilton, Bruce Memorial, 1914]

Whitman, was briefly superintendent in 1876. Not far from the hospital is Mohawk College of Applied Arts and Sciences where James (Jim) Foley (b. 1922), writer and Canadiana enthusiast, has taught since 1976. Here he founded the short-lived Academy of Canadian Writers to celebrate literary achievement in the country. It was through his efforts in 1978 that Mohawk became the first community college to appoint a writer-in-residence.

McMaster University, with its innovative Medical School, goes back to 1887. For two decades the chairman of the Department of Religion was George P. Grant (b. 1918), who lived in a stately old residence on wooded grounds in nearby Dundas. Appalled at being hectored from the pulpit to vote for "majority government" (which implied the Liberal Party), he penned his classic text *Lament for a Nation* (1965), subtitled "The Defeat of Canadian Nationalism." A member of the English Department is Graham Petrie (b. 1939), the author of widely published surreal stories and the novel *Seahorse* (1980).

McMaster's Mills Memorial Library, under the leadership of librarian and writer William Ready (1914-1981), began to acquire literary papers in a major way. Ready was instrumental in the 1960s in gaining the Bertrand Russell papers for Canada. He also added the selected papers of Samuel Beckett, Vera Brittain, Anthony Burgess, Sir George Catlin, and Thomas Carlyle. Canadian writers whose literary papers reside at Mills include Pierre Berton, John Robert Colombo, John Coulter, Margaret Laurence, David McFadden, Farley Mowat, and Peter C. Newman. In addition, Mills has acquired the archives of McClelland and Stewart, Oberon Press, and the Writers' Union of Canada.

The columnist and correspondent Kathleen "Kit" Coleman (1864-1915) died and is buried in Hamilton. She covered the Spanish-American War in 1898 as the world's first accredited female war correspondent. She was also Canada's first syndicated columnist, as Ted Ferguson noted in his biography *Kit Coleman, Queen of Hearts* (1978).

Hamilton appears as "Mill City" in the autobiographical novel *Pandora* (1972) by Sylvia Fraser (b. 1935). The author was born in Hamilton. Set in the 1940s, the novel mentions "Laura Secord Public School" and "No. 13 Oriental Avenue."

Harrowsmith   See CAMDEN EAST.

Havergal
The community of Havergal, near Bancroft, was named after Frances Ridley Havergal (1836-1879), English author of hymns and other religious verse.

Hiawatha Island
The Song of Hiawatha (1855), the popular narrative poem by Henry Wadsworth Longfellow (1807-1882), was the inspiration for the name of this small island in Lake Muskoka.

Hiawatha Reserve
On the northwest shore of Rice Lake, southeast of Peterborough, is the Hiawatha Reserve. It bears the name of the hero of *The Song of Hiawatha* (1855) by Henry Wadsworth Longfellow (1807-1882).

Huronia   See MIDLAND.

Ibsen Lake
The Norwegian dramatist, Henrik Ibsen (1828-1906), has this lake named after him in the Cobalt area.

Ingersoll
The town of Ingersoll, northeast of London, was named for Major Thomas Ingersoll, the father of Laura Secord (1775-1868). Canada's first cheese factory was established here in 1864, as the plaque mounted in the Post Office Building attests. The town will forever be associated with "Ode on the Mammoth Cheese, Weighing over 7,000 Pounds" published in *Musings on the Banks of Canadian Thames* (1884) by James McIntyre (1827-1906), the Scottish-born casket-maker and poetaster who lived here. It begins: "We have seen the Queen of cheese, / Laying quietly at your ease. . . ."

At Salford, south of Ingersoll, Aimee Semple McPherson (1890-1923) was born and raised in a farmhouse that has since burnt down. The flamboyant evangelist founded the Angelus Temple of the Church of the Foursquare Gospel in 1923 in Echo Park, Los Angeles. A museum in Echo Park displays her white cape, her Bible, and her jewelled rhinestone cross. She is buried in Forest Lawn Cemetery. She appears in the novel *Elmer Gantry* (1927) by Sinclair Lewis (1885-1951). The reporter Gordon Sinclair (1900-1984) covered her occasional return visits to the Ingersoll region, and Earle Birney composed the poem "Mammorial Stunzas for Aimee Simple McFarcin" (1931).

Inscription Rock   See AGAWA BAY

Iona Station

John Kenneth Galbraith (b. 1908), the noted economist and public figure, was born on a farm outside Iona Station, a small community located south of London and north of Lake Erie, in Elgin County. In his memoir *The Scotch* (1964), he locates the farmhouse on Hogg Street, not three miles west of Iona Station. "Hogg Street is in Dunwich Township some five or six miles from the Lake, and it runs parallel to the shore for some six miles from the Currie Road to the Southwold Township town line. Not even in the Western Isles are the Scotch to be found in more concentrated solution." The author described Iona Station in his youth as a market centre of twenty-five souls, its principal buildings being McBride's store and McIntyre House. Galbraith wrote *The Scotch* in Delhi while U.S. Ambassador to India. He considers it his finest book, and it is certainly one of the best Canadian memoirs. The title bothered his British publishers who refused to release it, arguing that his ancestors were Scots, not the Scotch. Galbraith countered by noting that "the Scotch" harkens back to an earlier usage. But this is one battle he lost, for he agreed to have it published in hardcovers in Britain as *Made to Last*. His paperback publishers were unhappy with that and retitled it *The Non-Potable Scotch*. Galbraith admitted that three titles for one short book were two too many.

He wrote with less affection about Elgin County in his autobiography, *A Life in Our Times* (1981). When others noted his propensity for hard intellectual labour, he commented: "A long day following a plodding, increasingly reluctant team behind a harrow endlessly back and forth over the uninspiring Ontario terrain persuaded one that all other work was easy." He took five years to complete a four-year-course in animal husbandry at the Ontario Agricultural College, now the University of Guelph. In his autobiography he wrote that "Canada might be a mother, but Michigan was a mistress." He went on to say, "I have never understood why one's affections must be confined, as once with women, to a single country." In an interview he has described himself as an advisory rather than as a practising Canadian.

Jackson's Point   See SUTTON.

"Jubilee"   See WINGHAM.

"Juniper Junction"   See SCUGOG ISLAND.

Kanata

Kanata, an incorporated municipality west of Ottawa, bears a doubly symbolic name. The name recalls the Algonkian word *kanata*, meaning "collection of huts," from which Canada was derived. It also relates to

Canada's post-industrial future, as here are clustered more than 250 companies concerned with telecommunications, computers, and microtechnology. It seems likely in the future works of fiction will limn Kanata.

Keats Lake

Keats Lake, like Shelley Lake, is located southeast of Atikokan. It bears the surname of the English poet John Keats (1795-1821).

Keewatin

West of Kenora, in the Lake of the Woods area, is the town of Keewatin. Here the Lake of the Woods Flour Mills inspired "the rambling, wooden mill at the foot of the rapids" in *The Master of the Mill* (1944) by Frederick Philip Grove (1879-1948). In the novel the mill is located at "Langholm" on the "North River," likely the Saskatchewan community of Langham on the North Saskatchewan River.

Kempenfelt Bay

Part of Georgian Bay, this body of water is home to Kempenfelt Kelly, a frequently sighted sea serpent. Dennis Lee (b. 1939) has an amusing poem in *Alligator Pie* (1974) called "The Fishes of Kempenfelt Bay."

Kenora

Kenora, in the Lake of the Woods area, is a region haunted by the Windigo, the spirit of cannibalism among the Algonkian-speaking Indians. At least such a belief was recorded by David Thompson (1770-1857) in his *Narrative of His Explorations in Western North America 1784-1812* (1916) and by Sir William Francis Butler (1838-1910) in *The Great Lone Land* (1872). The English writer Algernon Blackwood (1869-1951), who visited the area in 1898, was inspired to write the classic story "The Wendigo," included in his collection *The Lost Valley and Other Stories* (1910). In that story Kenora

Kenora could be called the Wendigo capital of the world. From the Lake of the Woods region there come more descriptions, in fact and in fiction, of the dread Algonkian spirit of cannibalism than from any other. Algernon Blackwood visited Kenora in 1898 and set his famous story "The Wendigo" in the area. This drawing by Matt Fox comes from a reprint of the 1910 tale in Famous Fantastic Mysteries, *June 1944.*

figures as Rat Portage, its pre-1905 name.

Some Ojibwa lore from the Lake of the Woods region, including traditional "tales of power," are retold by James Redsky (b. 1899) in *Great Leader of the Ojibway: Mis-qwona-queb* (1972), edited by James R. Stevens. In all there are eight Indian reserves in the vicinity of Kenora.

Gordon Island is situated in Lake of the Woods, due south (through Devil's Gap) of Kenora. It was named after Charles W. Gordon (1860-1937), the novelist who wrote as Ralph Connor. He summered here with his family in a cottage with a tower where he wrote.

Paul I. Wellman (1898-1966), the American novelist, described Portage Bay, Deadman's Portage, and other local features in his popular novel *Portage Bay* (1957), which was inspired, in part, by Portage Bay Camp, which still operates as a fishing resort.

Kettle Point Reserve

The children of Kettle Point Reserve, located at the south end of Lake Huron, northeast of Sarnia, provided the delightful illustrations that appear in the *Alphabet Book* (1960) compiled by Ann Wyse. The letters of the alphabet were illustrated in black and white by Ojibwa children between the ages of five and eight who attended Kettle Point Reserve School, at Forest. They also contributed to *The One to Fifty Book* (1973), compiled by Ann and Alex Wyse.

Kingston

Kingston, on the St. Lawrence at the eastern end of Lake Ontario, was built to be the capital of Canada. It did not work out that way, but the handsome stone architecture remains. "It may be said of Kingston, that one half of it appears to be burnt down, and the other half not to be built up," observed Charles Dickens (1812-1870) in *American Notes* (1842).

"A little after daybreak the steamer stopped at the Canadian city of Kingston, a handsome place, substantial to the water's edge, and giving a sense of English solidity by the stone of which it is largely built." So wrote the American novelist William Dean Howells (1837-1920) in his novel *Their Wedding Journey* (1871). Howells visited Kingston on at least two occasions, in 1860 and 1870.

Cataraqui Cemetery This historic cemetery, on the outskirts of Kingston, is the resting place of Sir John A. Macdonald (1815-1891), the first Prime Minister of Canada. He was educated and articled in law at Kingston and represented the district in the House of Assembly of the Province of Canada. Of all federal politicians, he is the one whose memoirs, had he written them, would be required reading today! He was wary of print, and once advised a friend never to write a letter and never to destroy one.

Statue of Sir John A. Macdonald, Parliament Hill, Ottawa. [National Capital Commission]

The gravesite of Sir John A. Macdonald prompts thoughts of mortality and immortality (the literary variety anyway). There have been sixteen prime ministers of Canada from Confederation to January 1, 1984. Fourteen are dead and buried; yet among the quick are Joe Clark and Pierre Elliott Trudeau. Most of these men are authors in their own right, some have written autobiographies, and every one of them has been the subject of a biography or a study. (Mackenzie King seems to have engendered a literary-historical industry.) So it is perhaps appropriate here to list the prime ministers, roughly in the order of their administrations. As well as the name, for each is given years of birth and death followed by his final resting place.

Sir John A. Macdonald (1815-1891): Cataraqui Cemetery, Kingston, Ont.

Alexander Mackenzie (1822-1892): Lakeview Cemetery, Sarnia, Ont.

Sir John Abbott (1821-1893): Mount Royal Cemetery, Montreal, Que.

Sir John S. Thompson (1844-1894): Holy Cross Cemetery of All Saints Cathedral, Halifax, N.S.

Sir Mackenzie Bowell (1823-1917): Belleville Cemetery, Belleville, Ont.

Sir Charles Tupper (1821-1915): St. John's Anglican Cemetery, Halifax, N.S.

Sir Wilfrid Laurier (1841-1919): Notre Dame Cemetery, Ottawa, Ont.

Sir Robert Borden (1854-1937) Beechwood Cemetery, Ottawa, Ont.

Arthur Meighen (1874-1960): St. Mary's Cemetery, St. Mary's, Ont.

R. B. Bennett (1870-1947): Graveyard, St. Michael's Anglican Church, Mickleham, Surrey, England.

W. L. Mackenzie King (1874-1950): Mount Pleasant Cemetery, Toronto, Ont.

Louis St. Laurent (1882-1973): Cemetery of St. Thomas Aquinas, Compton, Que.

John G. Diefenbaker (1895-1979): Grounds of the Diefenbaker Centre, University of Saskatchewan, Saskatoon, Sask.

Lester B. Pearson (1897-1972): Maclaren Cemetery Wakefield, Que.

Historical Plaques There are historical plaques to commemorate the lives of two writers with Kingston connections.

Charles Sangster (1822-1893), the poet, is honoured with a plaque raised on the Barrie Street side of the Cricket Field, near Court Street. He was born at the Naval Yard, Point Frederick, and worked at the Ordinance Office, Fort Henry. He published his two books, *The St. Lawrence and the Saguenay* (1856) and *Hesperus and Other Poems and Lyrics* (1860), in Kingston. He worked with the Post Office Department in Ottawa from 1868 to 1886, when he returned to Kingston and lived with his nephew in a small white frame cottage on Barrie Street. He died here and is buried in the Cataraqui Cemetery. Sangster is variously considered "The Canadian Wordsworth" and "The Father of Canadian Poetry."

C. W. Jefferys' sketch of Charles Sangster. [C-69347 / Public Archives Canada]

Grant Allen (1848-1899), the novelist, was born at Aldwington House, Wolfe Island. A plaque, raised here in 1952, honours the man and his achievement. At the age of thirteen, he accompanied his family to the United States. In later years he established himself in England as one of the leading Anglo-American novelists and science popularizers. He was so well known to the reading public that H. G. Wells referred to him by name in *The Time Machine* (1893). Among his dozens of novels and hundreds of short stories is *The British Barbarians* (1895), a satiric view of England from the vantagepoint of the twenty-fifth century. One of his neighbours at Hindhead, Surrey, where he died, was Sir Arthur Conan Doyle, who completed Allen's final novel, *Hilda Wade* (1900).

Kingston Penitentiary What is now called the Kingston Penitentiary was established in 1835. The oldest in Canada, it attracted the attention of Charles Dickens (1812-1870) on his tour of eastern Canada in 1842. In his *American Notes* (1905), he wrote vividly about a prisoner he spotted in one of the cells. It is the stuff of fiction.

"There is an admirable gaol here, well and wisely governed, and excellently regulated in every respect. The men were employed as shoemakers, rope-makers, blacksmiths, tailors, carpenters, and stone-cutters; and in building a new prison, which was pretty far advanced towards completion. The female prisoners were occupied in needlework. Among them was a beautiful girl of twenty, who had been there nearly three years. She acted as bearer of secret dispatches for the self-styled Patriots on Navy Island during the Canadian Insurrection: sometimes dressed as a girl, and carrying them in her stays; sometimes attiring herself as a boy, and secreting them in the lining of her hat. In the latter character she always rode as a boy would, which was nothing to her, for she could govern any horse that any man could ride, and could drive four-in-hand with the best whip in those parts. Setting forth on one of her patriotic missions, she appropriated to herself the first horse she could lay her hands on; and this offence had brought her where I saw her. She had quite a lovely face, though, as the reader may suppose from this sketch of her history, there was a lurking devil in her bright eye, which looked out pretty sharply from between her prison bars."

Through prison records the prisoner who enchanted Dickens has been identified as Eunice Whiting, aged seventeen at the time of her conviction for horse-stealing on June 1, 1839. She had auburn hair, fair complexion, and came from the Gore (Hamilton). She was discharged on June 8, 1842.

Somewhat later Susanna Moodie (1803-1885) visited the jail and desribed the experience in *Life in the Clearings* (1853). She was intrigued by one inmate, Grace Marks, an Irish serving girl who had goaded a hired hand into murdering their masters. For this act she was serving a life sentence. When she went mad she was sent to the mental asylum in Toronto where she was again questioned by Mrs. Moodie.

In modern times prisoners of conscience have served time in the Kingston Penitentiary and written of their experiences. One is Tim Buck (1891-1973), long-time leader of the Communist Party of Canada, who was jailed under the notorious Section 92 of the Criminal Code. An attempt was made on his life in 1932, as he recorded in his autobiography.

In the 1960s, local writers David Helwig (b. 1938) and Tom Marshall (b. 1938) conducted creative writing workshops in the penitentiary.

Roger Caron (b. 1938) received the Governor General's Award for Non-Fiction for *Go-Boy! Memoirs of a Life Behind Bars* (1978), which was written here and in other prisons across the country while serving a sixteen-year sentence for bank robbery and jail break. In all, Caron spent twenty-three of his first thirty-nine years behind bars. He discusses the riot on April 14, 1971. He wrote: "Kingston Penitentiary seen through a winter blizzard was enough to strike terror into the bravest heart."

Douglas Library, Queen's University, Kingston, [Queen's University]

Queen's University Queen's University figures as "Waverley University" in the so-called Salterton novels of Robertson Davies. Queen's was chartered by Queen Victoria in 1841 and has played a prominent role in post-secondary education in Canada West, Ontario, and Canada ever since, especially during the principalship from 1877 to his death of the noted nationalist George M. Grant (1835-1902).

Queen's University was the first university to award Arthur Koestler (1905-1983) an honourary degree. This occurred in November 1968 and the Anglo-Hungarian man of letters was extremely grateful as he felt neglected by the academic communities of the Western world. George Whalley (1915-1983) had a long association with the English Department. He was the subject of the satiric poem "Anglo Canadian," written by Irving Layton (b. 1912), which lampoons "a native of Kingston, Ont.," whose accent (acquired in a few years at Oxford) "makes even Englishmen . . . feel / unspeakably colonial."

As valuable as they are varied, the Queen's University Archives, in Kathleen Ryan Hall, include the personal papers of John Buchan (secured through the intercession of Leonard Brockington) and approximately forty running feet of material from George Woodcock. Other major collections are those of Lorne Pierce (who as the editor of the Ryerson Press corresponded with most literary figures in the country), Bliss Carman, Sir Charles G. D. Roberts, and Oberon Press. There are literary papers here from George Bowering, Hugh Garner, Ralph Gustafson, Dorothy Livesay, and Al Purdy, not to mention Marjorie Pickthall, Wilson

MacDonald, Merrill Denison, and the original manuscript of William Kirby's *The Golden Dog.*

Although writers from across the country meet regularly, this was not so before the mid-1960s. Among the first of the modern conferences was the Kingston Writers' Conference which brought together on the university campus in the summer of 1955 about fifty contemporary writers and literary professionals, including F. R. Scott, A. J. M. Smith, Morley Callaghan, Robert Weaver, Desmond Pacey, Malcolm Ross, Ralph Allen, Phyllis Webb, and John Morgan Gray. The conference was funded by the Rockefeller Foundation — this was in pre-Canada Council days — and the proceedings were published by Macmillan's. The conference marked a coming of age of the literary community. Hugh Garner made much of the occasion in his autobiography *One Damn Thing after Another* (1974).

Two writers who are members of the Department of English are David Helwig (b. 1938) and Tom Marshall (b. 1938). For a time the latter edited *Quarry,* an undergraduate magazine founded in 1951 which became, in 1965, a recognized "little magazine." The university also publishes *Queen's Quarterly,* an academic journal with an interest in Canadian letters, which was established in 1893.

Salterton Much has been written about the relationship between the very real Kingston and the very imaginary "Salterton," the community created by Robertson Davies (b. 1913) as the setting for three comic novels, *Tempest-Tost* (1951), *Leaven of Malice* (1954), and *A Mixture of Frailties* (1958). Salterton boasts (to limit the equivalences to the first novel) two cathedrals — St. Michael's (Catholic) and St. Nicholas (Anglican) — a Waverley University, a Court House, "and one of Her Majesty's largest and most forbidding prisons." Might these be St. Mary's and St. George's, the Doric-columned City Hall, Queen's University, and the Kingston Penitentiary?

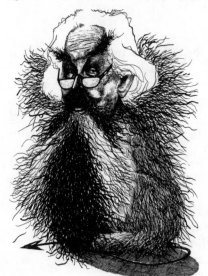

Robertson Davies is depicted by Isaac Bickerstaff (artist Don Evans) as a bearded creature [Special Collections, University of Calgary Libraries]

The author was born at Thamesville but raised in Kingston in a residence no longer standing. His father was publisher of *The Kingston Whig-Standard*. In a television program in 1984, Davies recalled that being the publisher's son he heard not read "all the news that isn't fit to print" for a newspaper's editorial office is "a gigantic gossip-shop."

Matt Cohen, novelist and chronicler of life in the fictitious Ontario community of Salem. [McClelland & Stewart]

Two Quartets   Two authors of fiction who have written linked novels set in Kingston and vicinity are David Helwig (b. 1938), who was born in Toronto and teaches at Queen's University, and Matt Cohen (b. 1942), a native of Kingston. Life in the city is unfulfilling; at least this seems to be so in Helwig's quartet: *The Glass Knight* (1976), *Jennifer* (1979), *It Is Always Summer* (1982), and *A Sound Like Laughter* (1983). Life in the town of "Salem," a rural area north of Kingston, rather like Verona, where the author lives on a farm, is rather more exciting and exhausting for four generations of the Thomas family, in the quartet by Cohen: *The Disinherited* (1974), *The Colours of War* (1977), *The Sweet Second Summer of Kitty Malone* (1979), and *Flowers of Darkness* (1981). Salem is presented as "as small town that closed its eyes to the present, let alone the future."

Abbey Dawn   Abbey Dawn was the name of the five-hundred-acre "Wild Life and Native Indian Sanctuary" owned by Wallace Havelock Robb (1888-1976) who called himself the Abbé of Abbey Dawn. On his farm, off Highway 2 a few miles east of Kingston, was a ceremonial bell which was struck only when a poet or pregnant woman came to visit. One visiting Montreal bard, Hyman Edelstein, died within minutes of striking the bell. Al Purdy was luckier, for he dropped in unexpectedly in 1957 and Robb never got around to offering Purdy the honour. As a versifier, Robb was partial to Indian themes and motifs. He would sign his letters in red ink with a feather design. He closed the Abbey in 1962.

Wallace Havelock Robb, wearing his poet's robe, poses alongside the Granite Sculpture at Abbey Dawn, Ont. The Granite Sculpture is a portrait and memorial in stone to Robert Holmes, painter of wildflowers, done from life by the Montreal-based sculptor John Byers in 1930. With the closing of Abbey Dawn in 1962, the Granite Sculpture was re-erected at The Guild Inn, Toronto. [Spencer Clark]

Kingsville

Ornithologists, naturalists, and conservationists — as well as wild birds — flock to the Jack Miner Bird Sanctuary, near Kingsville, on Lake Erie, west of Point Pelee National Park. The 2,000-acre sanctuary dates back to 1904, the banding of birds to 1909. Jack Miner (1865-1944) told his story in *Wild Goose Jack* (1969), which doubles as the title of the 1982 film biography produced and directed by Michael Dana Murphy.

Part of the action of *The Galton Case* (1959), a Lew Archer mystery novel by Ross Macdonald (1915-1983), takes place on the grounds of a summer home at Kingsville and in the fictitious community of "Pitt" not far away.

Kipling Reef

Southwest of Manitoulin Island is Kipling Reef, named to honour the English poet and writer, Rudyard Kipling (1865-1936).

Kirkland Lake

Kirkland Lake, southeast of Timmins, is associated with the fortunes of Sir Harry Oakes (1874-1943) who, as a penniless prospector, staked a gold claim here in 1912 which established Tough-Oakes Mines and Lake Shore Mines. For some years he resided in Oak Hall, a thirty-seven-room mansion overlooking Niagara Falls, a museum since 1965. In 1939, he moved to the Bahamas. He was found brutally murdered in his villa outside Nassau on July 8, 1943. The murder was never solved, despite extensive inquiries and more than a dozen books on the life and death of Sir Harry. He figures as a major character in *Famous Last Words* (1981), the novel by Timothy Findley (b. 1930). Gene Hackman plays the multi-millionaire tycoon in *Eureka*, a film released in 1984. There is a bronze bust of Sir Harry in Kirkland Lake's Museum of Northern History. Perhaps James Wreford (b. 1915), the poet, when he wrote the satiric poem "Kirkland Lake" in *Of Time and the Lover* (1950), had Sir Harry in mind when he penned the lines: "Under the dark industrial sky / we wonder why we have to die. . . ."

Kitchener

The "twin cities" of Kitchener and Waterloo are located northeast of London. In the main hall of the Kitchener-Waterloo Collegiate there are plaques to commemorate two writers born in Kitchener when it was called Berlin: Archibald MacMechan (1862-1933), scholar, critic, editor, essayist, historian, poet, and story-writer; and W. W. Campbell (1858-1918), the poet who wrote "Indian Summer" (1889) and aspired to be "poet-laureate of the British Empire." Local tradition, noted Carl Klinck, puts Campbell's birthplace at a house which once stood at the corner of Duke and Young streets. The corner is now occupied by a parking lot, Forsyth Shirt Company, St. Mary's School, and Albert Hall. At the age of six weeks, young Campbell was taken to Wiarton in the "lake district" he loved to write about.

At some future time plaques may be erected alongside those of MacMechan and Campbell to honour two fine writers of mystery fiction, Margaret Millar (b. 1915) and Kenneth Millar (1915-1983), who attended KCI as students and even taught here. Margaret Millar was born Margaret Strum in Kitchener, and while attending high school she met Kenneth Millar who, though born in Los Gatos, California, of Canadian parents, was raised orphan-like in a succession of towns and cities, including Vancouver, Wiarton, Winnipeg, Medicine Hat, and Kitchener. In Sep-

This photograph of mystery-story writer Ross Macdonald and Toronto editor Jerry Tutunjian was taken by the lifeguard on the beach at Santa Barbara, California, in February 1973. [Jerry Tutunjian]

tember 1930 he enrolled at KCI where he met Margaret Strum. Millar graduated in 1932 and attended the University of Western Ontario. The couple married in June 1938 and the following year taught English and History at KCI. Thereafter they lived in the United States, ultimately settling at Los Gatos. Margaret Millar was the first to come to prominence with psychological detective fiction. *Beast in View* (1955) is among her finest novels. Kenneth Millar published as Ross Macdonald and came into his own with *The Galton Case* (1959). He created the private detective Lew Archer, (Hollywood renamed the detective Harper; he was played by actor Paul Newman in a number of films based on Macdonald's books.) In Kitchener, Margaret Strum lived on Homewood Avenue; Kenneth Millar lived on Brubacher Street near Lancaster Street. Both were encouraged in their reading — if not their writing — by the librarian Mabel Dunham.

The history and character of Waterloo County informed the writing of Mabel Dunham (1881-1957), Ontario's first professional librarian. In *The Trail of the Conestoga* (1924), she dramatized the settlement along the Grand River by the Pennsylvania Dutch; in *Kristli's Trees* (1948), she entered into the mind of a Mennonite farm boy. She helped establish the Kitchener Public Library, an excellent public library once housed in a Carnegie building where in the late 1940s and early 1950s a frequent borrower was the author of the present work. Her portrait hangs in the new library; she is buried in the cemetery beside the First Mennonite Church, 800 King Street East, Kitchener.

Kleinburg

The McMichael Canadian Collection was founded in 1954 by Robert and Signe McMichael as a memorial to the Group of Seven in the village of Kleinburg, north of Toronto. The collection consists of paintings and drawings by members of the Group and other artists of the time as well as Indian and Inuit arts and crafts. The Gallery has the original illustrations by Clarence Gagnon to the 1933 edition of Hémon's *Maria Chapdelaine*. The shack in which Tom Thomson painted was moved from behind the Studio Building in Toronto to this setting. Buried on the grounds are five members of the Group: Lawren Harris, A. Y. Jackson, Frank H. Johnston, Arthur Lismer, and F. H. Varley, all of whom were vivid writers as well as splendid painters. In fact, if the Group represented any single ideal, it was that the vision of the North of these landscape painters could be expressed in both shapes and sounds.

The residences of two notable literary figures are outside the village of Kleinburg. East of Binder Twine Park are the homes on adjoining properties of Pierre Berton (b. 1920), author and media personality, and J. G. (Jack) McClelland (b. 1922), publisher of McClelland and Stewart Limited. They are close personal friends as well as business associates.

The McMichael Canadian Collection: The Entranceway (top), the Tom Thomson Shack (middle), and A. Y. Jackson, artist-in-residence in his later years (bottom). [The McMichael Canadian Collection, Kleinburg, Ontario]

Lake Couchiching See ORILLIA.

Lake Superior Provincial Park

This scenic park, on the eastern shore of Lake Superior south of Wawa, has attracted more painters than writers. Paul Kane (1810-1871) painted here in 1846, and members of the Group of Seven — Lawren Harris, A. Y. Jackson, Frank H. Johnston, J. E. H. MacDonald — travelled and painted the landscape courtesy of the Algoma Central Railway. Areas within the park have generated legends. Devil's Chair Island, near Cape Gargantua, is said to be the spot where the giant Nanabozho, protector of the Ojibwa people, rested after leaping over the lake. Devil's Warehouse Island is believed to be the source for the ochre employed by the Ojibwa in the decoration of body-parts and rock-surfaces. Lake Superior is the "Big-Sea-Water" of *The Song of Hiawatha* (1855) by Henry Wadsworth Longfellow (1807-1882).

Lakefield

The town of Lakefield, on the Otonabee River north of Peterborough, begs the adjective "literary." Attracted to the backwoods of "literary Lakefield" in the early nineteenth century were three writers, all related: Colonel Samuel Strickland (1804-1867) and his two sisters, Catharine Parr Traill (1802-1899) and Susanna Moodie (1803-1885). The poet Isabella Valancy Crawford (1850-1887) lived here briefly, as well.

Samuel Strickland Samuel Strickland was in the employ of the Canada Company, with the novelist John Galt and the colonist William "Tiger" Dunlop, for some years before he acquired uncleared land in 1831 on the shores of Katchewanook Lake. With his wife Emma, he became a backwoods pioneer in Douro Township, near Lakefield. He wrote about his experiences in *Twenty-Seven Years in Canada West* (1853). In 1855 he settled in Lakefield, where he had helped to build the Old Christ Church (Anglican), 62 Queen Street, North Douro. He is buried in the churchyard adjoining the church. The church has been restored to its original appearance, and a plaque commemorates the life of this pioneer author.

Catharine Parr Traill Samuel Strickland was joined in 1832 by his sister Catharine Parr Traill and her husband Lieutenant Thomas Traill, a half-pay officer. They received a grant of land next to Strickland's and took up farming in 1846 in three locales near Gore's Landing, Rice Lake: at "Wolf Tower," so described in *The Canadian Crusoes* (1852), now Tower Manour Resort, a trailer camp near Bewdley; on a rented farm called "Mount Ararat," west of Gore's Landing; and for eight years at "Oaklands," Concession 8, Lot 11. They lived here until 1857 when their farmhouse burnt down. With the subsequent death of her husband, Catharine moved into "Westove," 16 Smith Street, Lakefield.

Catharine Parr Traill was sketched with maple leaf by Don Evans as Isaac Bickerstaff. [Special Collections, University of Calgary Libraries]

Here she resided, frequently visited by her sister Susanna Moodie, from 1862 until her death. This house is privately owned but identified by a plaque. Catharine wrote many books, including *The Backwoods of Canada* (1836) and *The Female Emigrant's Guide* (1854). Because of her longevity — she died in her 98th year — she was regarded as the oldest author in the British Empire. In 1975 a plaque was erected at Young's Point Lock Station, near Lakefield, to mark the connection of this remarkable woman with Lakefield.

Susanna Moodie   Susanna Moodie and her husband, half-pay officer John Moodie, immigrated in 1832 and briefly took up backwoods farming on their grant of land in Douro Township alongside that of Strickland and the Traills. The following year, after an extended stay at the Steamboat Hotel in Cobourg, they occupied a one-room log shanty on a farm bought by Moodie in

Hamilton Township, northeast of Port Hope, which they named "Malsetter" after her Orkney home. A plaque marks the site at Concession 4, Lot 32. Unhappy here, they returned in 1834 to the original grant in Douro Township and farmed here for six years. In 1840, Moodie was appointed sheriff of what is now Hastings County, requiring their departure for Belleville, where Mrs. Moodie's literary career flourished. A plaque commemorates Susanna Moodie in Cenotaph Park, on the north side of Water Street, east of Bridge Street, in Lakefield. Her principal books, based on her experiences as a backwoods pioneer, are *Roughing It in the Bush* (1852) and *Life in the Clearings* (1853). On these two books Margaret Atwood (b. 1939) based *The Journals of Susanna Moodie* (1970).

The two Strickland sisters are characters in the historical play by Robertson Davies (b. 1913) called *At My Heart's Core* (1950), whch is set at the time of the Rebellion of 1837 in Douro Township, Upper Canada.

Isabella Valancy Crawford   There is no plaque in Lakefield to mark the home of Isabella Valancy Crawford. The Crawford family moved here in 1864 from Paisley, and lived in a cottage near Stoney River Reserve until 1869, when the family left for neighbouring Peterborough. Crawford thus spent here the years between her eighteenth and her twenty-second year.

Margaret Laurence   Lakefield's most disinguished living writer is Margaret Laurence (b. 1926) who has lived in the region since 1970. For some time she occupied a cottage on the Otonabee River, outside Peterborough, but lately she has resided in a yellow brick house across the street from a church in Lakefield. When she still lived in Peterborough she glanced north and gleaned the following impressions, in "Down East" from *Heart of a Stranger* (1976): "In nearby Lakefield, you can buy a

Susanna Moodie, who felt ill at ease in the backwoods of Upper Canada, was drawn by Isaac Bickerstaff (Don Evans). [Special Collections, University of Calgary Libraries]

Margaret Laurence with a divining rod, drawn in pen and ink by Don Evans (who signs his sketches Isaac Bickerstaff). [Special Collections, University of Calgary Libraries]

pine blanket chest made by someone's great-grandfather, and if you're lucky you can hear a old-timer reminiscing about the last of the great paddlewheel steamers that used to ply these waters. In Lakefield, too, they make excellent cheese. You can buy it, in three degrees of sharpness, from the place where it is produced, and the giant cheese wheels smell and taste like your childhood. There is also a place where they still make their own ice-cream, in a dozen flavours." She has been called "the First Lady of Lakefield."

Lammermoor

The name of Lammermoor, northwest of Perth in Lanark County, was inspired by the *Bride of Lammermoor* (1819), the historical novel by Sir Walter Scott (1771-1832). In the novel the bride is named Lucy Ashton; in the Donizetti opera based on the story she is named Lucia.

The poet Charles Mair was born in this handsome stone home at Lanark, Ont. The house once had a verandah. [Terry Keough]

Lanark

Lanark, southwest of Ottawa, is the birthplace of the poet Charles Mair (1838-1927), whose house stands today as Store No. 3 of the Glenayre Kitten Factory Outlet, located on the main street. Farther north, in the Lanark Town Hall, is a plaque that commemorates the poet and nationalist.

Leaskdale

L. M. Montgomery (1874-1942) lived in the pleasant but unpretentious manse of St. Paul's Presbyterian Church in Leaskdale, northeast of Newmarket, for fifteen years. Here she wrote eleven of her twenty-three books, including *Anne of the Island* (1915) and *Anne's House of Dreams* (1918), as well as the "Emily" books. She resided here from 1911, following her marriage to the Reverend Ewan Macdonald at Park Corner, P.E.I., to 1926 when the couple moved to Norval and then to Toronto. Here she did much of her own housekeeping, collected her mail in a basket,

worked in the den or in the study (where two desks faced one another), knitted socks for the Red Cross during the First World War, and wrote her well-loved books. Some details of her domestic arrangements at Leaskdale appear in *L. M. Montgomery as Mrs. Ewan Macdonald* (1965) by Margaret H. Mustard, who includes this account of a meeting of the Young People's Guild in 1922: "On the evening of March 22nd, the Young People's Guild met in the church. The topic for the evening was 'Canadian Authors.' Leader — Margaret Leask. The meeting opened by singing Hymn 197. The scripture reading was the 23rd Psalm, followed by prayer by Mr. Macdonald. Hymn 404. Reading on 'Canadian Authors' by Mrs. Macdonald. Recitation — 'Cremation of Sam McGee' — Robert Service — by Margaret Leask; Reading — 'My Financial Career' — Stephen Leacock — by Harvey Shier; 'The Wasp Chorus' — Marion Keith — by Mrs. E. Macdonald. 'He was Scotch and So was She' — Jean Blewett — by Margaret Leask; 'Soft Sawder' — from Sam Slick — by Miss F. Rundle; 'A Ride for Life' — Ralph Connor — by Chester Macdonald; 'Did You Ever' by Stuart Macdonald. After the program the members took the opportunity of presenting Mrs. Macdonald, L. M. Montgomery, author of the 'Anne' Books, with a bouquet of Killarney Roses. . . ."

Lindsay

At Lindsay, northwest of Peterborough, a plaque on the grounds of the Victoria County Historical Society Museum notes that the naturalist and author Ernest Thompson Seton (1860-1946) lived here when he was a youngster. The Seton family came from England in 1866 and stayed here for four years before moving to Toronto. Seton's semi-autobiographical novel *Two Little Savages* (1906) is set in the Lindsay area.

Locksley

Locksley is a small community south of Pembroke. It bears the name of an imaginary place described by Alfred Lord Tennyson (1809-1892) in his famous poem "Locksley Hall" (1842) in which he declares: "Better fifty years of Europe than a cycle of Cathay."

London

In the nineteenth century, London was known as "London the Lesser." When the Irish playwright Brendan Behan (1923-1964) learned there was a London, Ont., he exclaimed: "Why, the very name is an impertinence in itself!"

London Psychiatric Hospital Located in the North Complex of the London Psychiatric Hospital, 850 Highbury Avenue, is the Teaching and the Research Museum. Here has been recreated the Superintendent's Office, decorated and furnished to recall the period of occupancy of Richard Maurice Bucke (1837-1902),

The Asylum for the Insane in London, Ont., 1880. [Griffin-Greenland Collection]

Walt Whitman, "the good gray poet," posed for the camera of the Edy Bros., portrait photographers in London, Ont. Whitman signed and dated the photograph which has been reproduced from the frontispiece of the Diary (1904). [Cyril Greenland]

Dr. Richard Maurice Bucke is shown behind his large oak desk in the Superintendent's office of the Asylum for the Insane, London, Ont. The photograph was taken by Elliot of London in 1899. It was in this office that Bucke conversed with his house guest, Walt Whitman, in 1880. [University of Western Ontario Libraries]

alienist and author. The heavy oak desk and other memorabilia belonged to Dr. Bucke who occupied the original Superintendent's Office from 1877 to his death. Over this desk he chatted with his house guest in the summer of 1880, the American poet Walt Whitman (1819-1892), edited four of Whitman's posthumous publications, and completed his own books, including the classic volume Cosmic Consciousness (1901). None of the buildings on the grounds dates from Whitman's time. The old chapel, now named the Chapel of Hope and being restored, was erected three years later. Bucke is buried at Mount Pleasant Cemetery, London.

Dr. Bucke died the year following the publication of his magnum opus Cosmic Consciousness (1901). He is buried, along with his wife and other family members, in the Bucke plot, Mount Pleasant Cemetery, London. [Alice Neal]

Arthur Stringer's House In the dignified, yellow-brick house, at 64 Elmwood Avenue, the novelist Arthur Stringer (1874-1950) was raised. He lived here with his family from his tenth year until he left London to attend the University of Toronto. He is credited with the script of the 1914 silent film The Perils of Pauline. His trilogy of prairie novels consists of The Prairie Wife (1915), The Prairie Mother (1920), and The Prairie Child (1921).

Dewdney Residence Selwyn Dewdney (1909-1979), a man of many talents, lived at 26 Erie Avenue. For some years he taught art at Beal Technical School; among his students were the young artists Jack Chambers (1931-1978) and Greg Curnoe (b. 1936). Henry R. Schoolcraft's description of Inscription Rock in 1851 led him to the lost site at Agawa Bay in 1958. His novel, Wind Without Rain (1946), an exposé of the teaching profession, is still relevant. His son is the poet Christopher Dewdney (b. 1951), author of a scientifically named poetic work, A Palaeozoic Geology of London, Ontario (1973).

James Reaney James Reaney (b. 1926) and his wife poet Colleen Thibaudeau (b. 1925) have lived in a modest home at 276 Huron Street since 1961 when Reaney joined the English Department of Middlesex College, University of Western Ontario. His suite of poems, The Dance of Death at London, Ontario (1963), has a number of local references. Here between 1960 and 1971 the Reaneys handset their "little magazine" called Alphabet.

"James Reaney I regard as a genius with the unique ability to write innocently about things not innocent," observed Barker Fairley who painted this portrait of the poet and playwright in the 1960s. [Barker Fairley]

University of Western Ontario   Housed in the D. B. Weldon Library of the University of Western Ontario are a number of major collections, including the unpublished plays of Sara Jeanette Duncan, the papers of Peter McArthur, the letters of Bliss Carman to Margaret Lawrence Greene, the papers of Walter Bauer, and the literary effects of Richard Maurice Bucke.

For many years Carl F. Klinck (b. 1908), scholar and general editor of *Literary History of Canada* (1965), headed the English Department here. Among the best-known writers who teach on the campus are the poets James Reaney (b. 1926) and Don Gutteridge (b. 1937) and the novelist Larry Garber (b. 1937).

Tolpuddle Martyrs   Northeast of London, off Fanshaw Road, is Siloam Cemetery, the burial place of some of the original Tolpuddle Martyrs. Farmers exiled from England for "illegal combination," they settled in 1844 on farms in London. Every May Day trade unionists and others lay wreaths on the white marble monument erected in memory of their leader George Loveless. The inscription reads: "Our victory is certain." They kept their immediate descendants in ignorance of their "disgrace."

Plaque and Tombstone of George Loveless, leader of the Tolpuddle Martyrs, and his wife Elizabeth, in Siloam Cemetery. The white marble stone is inscribed: "These are they which came out of great tribulation and have washed their robes, and made them white in the name of the Lamb." [Ken McGuffin]

Other Notable Sites   Roy Macdonald (b. 1937) would be something of a local character except that he is a national character. A segment of his ongoing diary has been published as *Living: A London Journal* (1978), and it shows his talent for making the insignificant meaningful. "Existence itself is The Extraordinary Miracle," he writes. He has in real life some of the Zen-like characteristics attributed to him in *Pocketman* (1979), the unacknowledged underground classic by Don Bell (b. 1936). Macdonald's base of operations is the McDonald's, on Wellington Road at Baseline, and the Wellington Country-Style Donut Shop, on Wellington.

The Grand Theatre, built in 1880, rebuilt in 1901, was once owned by Ambrose Small, the Toronto millionaire theatre-manager who disappeared mysteriously in 1919. Small's ghost is said to haunt the theatre, the home of the Grand Theatre Company which, under director Robin Phillips, launched its first (and sole) season in September 1983.

Long Point

The spirit of Dr. John Frederick Troyer (1753-1842) continues to haunt, imaginatively speaking, the windswept spit of Long Point, which extends into Lake Erie, south of Simcoe. Legends linger about the self-styled doctor — the first permanent resident of what is now Norfolk County — the herbalist-cum-witch-doctor who with a magical "moonstone" and a "witch trap" halted the "haunting" at Baldoon.

In *Canadian Houses of Romance* (1926), Katherine Hale (1878-1956) described her attempt to locate the ruins of the witch-doctor's house: "Step softly over the grass, this is a Witch House, a little tumble-down shed behind a hidden road, weed-choked, and desolate. There is nothing to see, unless a trace of folk-lore is a sight, or an old legend."

Although Troyer's log cabin no longer stands, the site — Troyer's Flats, approximately 2 kilometres east of Port Rowan on the Bay — (Lot 20 in First Concession of Walsingham) is visible from the Sidney Aker farm. At the Eva Brook Donly Museum, one may view his cabin door (with its heavy lock), his "witch trap" (actually an old bear-trap), and his favourite rifle.

The strange doings of Dr. Troyer are the subject of the children's book by C. H. (Marty) Gervais (b. 1946), *Doctor Troyer and the Secret of the Moonstone* (1976). With James Reaney (b. 1926), Gervais has written the play *Baldoon* (1976), which tells the story of the haunting in the Scottish settlement and Troyer's part in settling the disturbance.

Long Sault

At Long Sault, west of Cornwall, Adam Dollard des Ormeaux heroically halted the Iroquois advance on Montreal, May 2, 1660. The week-long resistance inspired the lyric poet, Archibald Lampman (1861-1899), during the last months of his life to attempt a narrative poem. He never did complete "At the Long Sault: May, 1660," which includes the lovely lines: "The numberless stars out of heaven / Look down with a pitiful glance; / And the lilies asleep in the forest / Are closed like the lilies of France."

Longfellow Lake
This lake in the Cobalt area honours the memory of the poet Henry Wadsworth Longfellow (1807-1882).

Lucan
In St. Patrick's Cemetery, in Lucan, northwest of London, the headstone with the large letters "Donnelly" recalls the Irish blood feud that erupted the night of February 4, 1880, in the slaughter of members of the Donnelly family on their farm on the outskirts of Lucan. More articles and books have been devoted to this tragedy than to most military battles. The original black gravestone, which stated that the Donnellys had been murdered, was replaced in 1966 with a granite marker that identified them as having died. *The Donnellys* (1975-77) is the overall title of three plays written by James Reaney (b. 1926) about the blood feud that brought about almost thirty violent deaths.

Featured on the cover of the 1980 reprint of Thomas P. Kelley's The Black Donnellys — *"the true story of Canada's most barbaric feud" — is a drawing of the old Donnelly tombstone at Lucan, Ont. [Pagurian Press Limited]*

Engraving of Thomas Donnelly used in the production of Sticks and Stones, the first of the three Donnelly plays written by James Reaney. [Tarragon Theatre]

Mackinac See SAULT STE. MARIE.

Manitoulin Island
Manitoulin Island in Lake Huron made the *Guinness Book of World Records* (1983), compiled by Norris McWhirter (b. 1925). The entry reads: "The largest island in a lake is Manitoulin Island (1,068 sq. mi.) in the Canadian (Ontario) section of Lake Huron. The island itself has a lake of 41.09 sq. mi. on it, called Manitou Lake, which is the world's largest lake within a lake, and in that lake are a number of islands."

On the northeastern tip of Manitoulin Island is located the Wikwemikong Reserve. Here the Indians have preserved many of their traditions, both visual and oral. The Odawa artist and writer Daphne Odjig (b. 1925) has made use of these in her illustrations for *Tales from the Smokehouse* (1974) written by Herbert T. Schwarz. Odjig both told and illustrated the ten stories that make up *Legends of Nanabush* (1971).

Art collector Robert McMichael visited the reserve in 1975 in search of local artists. Told of a very young artist named James Simon, he visited him in the family home. McMichael was struck by the Dali-like design of Simon's painting "Autumn Spirit" and asked Simon if he knew about Salvador Dali. "Salvador Dali?" Simon replied. "I think I know that guy's name. What reservation is he on?"

Maple
Lord Beaverbrook was born William Maxwell Aitken (1879-1964) in the manse of the St. James Presbyterian Church at Maple, north of Toronto. For half a century he was a force with which to be reckoned on London's Fleet Street. He reserved his affections and philanthropies for Newcastle, N.B., where he was raised.

Marmion
Marmion, between Hanover and Owen Sound, was named after Lord Marmion, the central figure in the romantic narrative poem *Marmion: A Tale of Flodden Field* (1808) by Sir Walter Scott (1771-1832). There is also a Marmion Lake, near Atikokan.

Mattagami Lake
The region around Mattagami Lake, north of Timmins, inspired Duncan Campbell Scott (1862-1947) on northern journeys in 1905 and 1906 to compose two fine poems. These are "Night Burial in the Forest" (1906) and "The Height of Land" (1915) which describe the point where the waters divide into those that flow south towards Lake Superior and those that flow north towards Hudson Bay. The Mattagami Reserve is located on the north shore of Kenogamissi Lake, southwest of Timmins.

Meaford
Meaford is a picturesque town on Georgian Bay, east of Owen Sound, which was once visited by Marshall Saunders (1861-1947). Here the novelist met a local miller, William Moore, who told her how he had rescued a homely puppy from a brutal master who had clipped its ears and tail. The miller gave the poor dog a good home. Inspired by the incident (and by a reading of Anna Sewell's *Black Beauty*), Saunders wrote her

Frontispiece illustration of Marshall Saunders' Beautiful Joe, new and revised edition published in 1934. The illustration is signed Kenneth W. With. [Metropolitan Toronto Library]

popular novel, *Beautiful Joe: An Autobiography* (1894). It won a prize offered by the American Humane Society and in half a century sold over seven million copies in more than ten languages. There is a plaque to honour Saunders in Beautiful Joe Park, on Victoria Crescent.

Saunders never lived in Meaford. Born in Milton, N.S., she settled permanently in Toronto in 1914. Her large home in the Lawrence Park area of the city was a refuge for a variety of animals. She dropped her first name, Margaret, and published as Marshall Saunders to avoid the public antipathy to female novelists.

Medonte Township

In the vicinity of Georgian Bay lies Medonte Township, Simcoe County, and here, at "Owl Pen," a run-down farm between Moonstone and Coldwater Valleys, the journalist Kenneth McNeill Wells (b. 1905) took up farming following service in the Second World War. The humorous articles he wrote about his farming experiences in this "Canadian Eden" appeared in four collections and were selected in a fifth, *The Owl Pen Reader* (1969), illustrated by his wife Lucille Oille. Inscribed on the farmhouse mantle were the words: "Our dreams are all we own."

Here is the log house built and occupied by Kenneth McNeill Wells and his wife in Medonte Township, between Barrie and Orillia. He called it his "Owl Pen." [Jim Harris]

Mercutio River

The Mercutio River in the Atikokan area bears the name of Romeo's friend in Shakespeare's *Romeo and Juliet* (1597).

Merivale

The name of a former community in the city of Nepean, Merivale was named after the English writer and actor Philip Merivale (1886-1946). The name is now recalled in Merivale Road, one of the main thoroughfares of Nepean.

Merlin

It seems the village of Merlin, in Kent County, near Chatham, was so named in 1860 after a village near Edinburgh, Scotland. Perhaps that village was named after the enchanter of Arthurian romance.

Merrill Lake

Merrill Lake, named after the author Merrill Denison (1893-1975), is west of Bon Echo, the "wilderness estate" that he donated to the people of Ontario as a provincial park.

Michilimackinac   See SAULT STE. MARIE.

Middleville

At Middleville, southwest of Ottawa, was born the novelist Robert Stead (1880-1959), whose family left here for Manitoba when he was two years old. The begining of his novel *Neighbours* (1922) is set in the late 1880s at a place reminiscent of Herron Mills close by.

Midland

The town of Midland, on Georgian Bay, is the heart of Huronia, the region in which the Jesuits established their mission to the Huron Indians and the site of the first European settlement in the interior of early Canada. The Jesuits built the palisaded settlement here on the bank of the Wye River in 1639, and ten years later burnt it before abandoning it. It was meticulously reconstructed in the 1960s and is now a major teaching and tourist attraction called Sainte-Marie-among-the-Hurons. Among the points of interest is the Indian chapel which contains the bones of the founder of the Jesuit mission, Jean de Brébeuf (1593-1649).

Brébeuf and the other missionaries who died at the hands of the Iroquois are honoured in the building and naming of the twin-spired, limestone church known as the Martyrs' Shrine. This Catholic church was erected in 1926, anticipating by four years the canonization of Brébeuf and the other "martyr-saints." On the grounds is a grotto dedicated to Our Lady of Huronia, patroness of Sainte-Marie and the Jesuit martyrs.

Sainte-Marie-among-the-Hurons and the Martyrs' Shrine, which is close by, bring to mind *Brébeuf and His Brethren* (1940). This narrative poem was written by E. J.

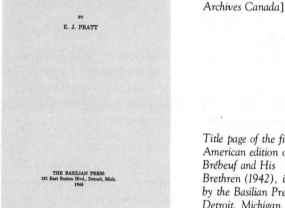

Brébeuf and His Brethren
(The North American Martyrs)

BY

E. J. PRATT

THE BASILIAN PRESS
181 East Boston Blvd., Detroit, Mich.
1942

C. W. Jefferys' drawing of the Martyrdom of Brébeuf and Lalemant, 1649. [C-46282 / Public Archives Canada]

Title page of the first American edition of Brébeuf and His Brethren (1942), issued by the Basilian Press in Detroit, Michigan. [Macmillan of Canada]

Pratt (1882-1964), an ordained Methodist minister as well as outstanding poet and teacher, and it evokes the seventeenth century and the wilderness of the region. Pratt reaches great heights when he describes the martyrdom of the Jesuits in terms of: ". . . the sound of invisible trumpets blowing / Around two slabs of board, right-angled, hammered / By Roman nails and hung on a Jewish hill." Yet a note of scepticism was sounded by the poet F. R. Scott (b. 1899), the son of an Anglican archbishop, who noted that the Spaniards were burning Incas in Latin America at roughly the same time as the Iroquois were burning Frenchmen in North America, so he wrote the squib "Brébeuf and His Brethren" (1941) which concludes: "Then is priest savage, or Red Indian priest?"

Associated with Brébeuf and his mission in Huronia is the "Huron Carol." Sometimes referred to by its Huron title "Jesous Ahatonhia," this hymn has been sung in Huron, in French, and in English. The English version, which begins "'Twas in the moon of winter time," was published in 1926 by the versifier J.E. Middleton (1872-1960). A children's book about the mission, which tells the story of the composition of the carol, is *O Children of the Wind and Pines* (1967) by the American author Laura Nelson Baker (b. 1911).

In the town of Midland, Huron Indian Village has been reconstructed in Little Lake Park to give some notion of how the agricultural Hurons lived. The town itself did not cause the poet Raymond Souster (b. 1921) to pause and ponder. In a ten-line poem called "Midland" (1962), he described the place and concluded: "Record this: the poet / was hard pressed to write / ten poor lines about you."

Milton

The village of Milton, southwest of Toronto, recalls the English poet John Milton (1608-1674), but the origin of the name is more prosaic than poetic. It relates to a settler named Martin Mills; Milltown appears on early maps.

Milton Lake

Milton Lake, north of Atikokan, was named in honour of the English poet John Milton (1608-1674). It is near Hogarth Lake, which similarly honours the English artist William Hogarth (1697-1764).

Minnehaha Point

Minnehaha Point is the most easterly point of Beausoleil Island, part of Georgian Bay Islands National Park, north of Midland. Minnehaha is the bride of Hiawatha in Longfellow's famous poem *The Song of Hiawatha* (1855). There is also a Minnehaha Lake in Algonquin Park.

Mississauga

In the district of Mississauga, west of Metropolitan Toronto, an historic home became the site of the most publicized murder in recent years. On July 18, 1973, the

In this still from I Miss You, Hugs and Kisses, *based on the Demeter murder case, Charles Kruschen (played by Donald Pilon) rubs noses with Magdelaine (Elke Sommer). [Ontario Film Institute]*

battered body of Christine Demeter, the former model and wife of developer Peter Demeter, was found in the garage adjoining the rambling Demeter home at 1437 Dundas Crescent, a dead-end street. The house was built in the 1820s by a Dr. Beaumont Dixie; a photograph appears in *The Governor's Road* (1982) by Mary Byers and Margaret McBurney. The Demeter murder and subsequent trial was the subject of *By Persons Unknown* (1977) by George Jonas and Barbara Amiel, a winner of the Edgar, the award of the Mystery Writers of America.

Moby Dick Rock

Near Pointe au Baril in the Thirty Thousand Islands is Moby Dick Rock, which recalls *Moby Dick* (1851) by Herman Melville (1819-1891).

Modo Lake

Modo Lake, in the Atikokan area, was named after the fiend named Modo in Shakespeare's *King Lear* (1605).

Modred Lake

The name of this lake, in the Atikokan area, recalls that of the treacherous knight of the Round Table in Tennyson's *Idylls of the King* (1859-72).

Mono Mills

The area around Mono Mills, east of Orangeville, is the setting of *The Yellow Briar* (1933), the sensitive story of an Irish orphan growing up in a farming community. It was written by Patrick Slater (1880-1951), a lawyer who published as John Mitchell. Slater is buried in Spring Creek Cemetery, Clarkson, where his gravestone is inscribed with lines from *The Yellow Briar*.

Monte Cristo Island

This small island, in Lake Muskoka, was named in 1892 by one George Sibbett who, when he received his Crown grant, was reading the romantic novel *The Count of Monte Cristo* (1844) by Alexandre Dumas (1802-1870).

The Museum of Revillion Frères may be visited at Moosonee. The French fur company, it will be recalled, financed the filming of Nanook of the North. *[Ontario Ministry of Tourism and Recreation]*

Moose Factory

Erected as a fur fort by the Hudson's Bay Company in 1673, Moose Factory is the first English settlement in what is now known as Ontario. Moose Factory grew into Moosonee. Here, in 1856, two missionaries, John Horden and E. A. Watkins, produced the first written materials, based on passages from Scriptures, in the syllabic system for use among the Eskimos. They employed the orthography devised in 1841 by James Evans, at Norway House, Man., as modified in 1853 by Robert Hunt at Lac La Ronge, Sask. The Horden-Watkins system was adapted by E. J. Peck at Blacklead Island, N.W.T. In modified form it continues in use among the Inuit to this day. The Inuit writer Peter Pitseolak (1902-1973) once exclaimed: "We were so stupid. We should have thought of writing on sealskins."

According to Dennis Lee (b. 1939), who wrote the poem "Homage to Moose Factory, Ont.," in *Nicholas Knock* (1974), the world's wonders are "flashy trash" and "a bore beside the lore / Of old Moose Factory!"

Archibald Lampman was born at Morpeth, Ont. His father was the clergyman at Trinity Church. This cairn was raised in 1930 to honour the poet. [Terry Keough]

Morpeth

Archibald Lampman (1861-1899) was born in the rectory at Morpeth, on Lake Erie, east of Chatham. Long gone is the rectory, a fact lamented by an unidentified fan of the poet writing in *Canadian Magazine*, December 1906. "The house in which he was born is, as may be seen, the plain, old-fashioned frame structure, familiar in small towns of this continent. It was then the Church of England parsonage. There were old trees near it, and we hope there was a garden. The lake, so sudden in storms, and so beguiling in calm, was not far away. Thus, however brief may have been the poet's experience of quaint old Morpeth, its memories may have lived in his lines. The house remained standing until a few years ago, when it was torn down to give place to a more modern, up-to-date structure. It is matter for regret that some steps are not taken to preserve places like this — connected in sentiment at least with the beginnings of our Canadian literature. In the broken-down village of Morpeth there are scores of building lots that might have been secured for a new parsonage site almost for the asking, without interfering with a building which should now be the property of the nation." East of the village, on the grounds of Trinity Anglican Church, there is a memorial cairn placed there in 1930 at the instigation of Lampman's friend, Duncan Campbell Scott (1862-1947). At the unveiling Wilson MacDonald (1880-1967) recited his poem "The Cairn at Morpeth."

Morrisburg

Upper Canada Village, at Morrisburg, southwest of Cornwall, is a collection of some fifty renovated or reconstructed buildings furnished to recreate the ambience of mid-nineteenth century Ontario. One of these structures is a schoolhouse that resembles the one described by Ralph Connor (1860-1937) in *Glengarry School Days* (1902), complete with copybooks, leather strap, and birch rod.

Mount Goldsmith

South of Lake Abitibi will be found Mount Goldsmith, named after the Irish-born English author and playwright, Oliver Goldsmith (1728-1774).

Mount Hope

Three miles west of Mount Hope, which is south of Hamilton, was the childhood home of Maggie Clark who, as a student at Glanford Section School No. 5, inspired her teacher, George Washington Johnson (1839-1917), to compose the ballad "When You and I Were Young, Maggie." Johnson published it in his collection of poems *Maple Leaves* (1864), the year Maggie and George were married. Maggie died the following year and is buried here. In 1866, the ballad was set to music by J. A. Butterfield, an English composer, and it was an instant hit. Maggie's childhood home, in front of which a plaque has been erected, is a stone house; just north of the house, on Twenty Mile Creek, was located the "creeking old mill" mentioned in the poem. The mill, Maggie, and George are gone, but the creek remains.

Mount Oliver Goldsmith

Mount Oliver Goldsmith, north of Kirkland Lake, bears the name of Oliver Goldsmith (1728-1774), the Irish-born English author, not his Canadian namesake.

Mount Smollett

Mount Smollett, south of Lake Abitibi, bears the name of the Scots-born English novelist, Tobias Smollett (1721-1771), author of the popular novel *The Expedition of Humphry Clinker* (1771). It is near Mount Goldsmith, Trollope Lake, and Carlyle Lake.

Muskoka

The first Summer School of Canadian Literature was held at the Epworth Inn on Lake Rosseau, in Muskoka, during the summer of 1926. Guests of honour included Sir Charles G. D. Roberts (1860-1943) and Sir Gilbert Parker (1862-1932). A bystander overheard the former cautioning the latter not to be too formal.

Pauline Johnson (1861-1913) wrote her single most famous poem, "The Song My Paddle Sings," in Toronto, January 1-16, 1892, after a canoeing trip on Lake Muskoka.

Canada has lacked a writer's colony like Yaddo or McDowell in the United States, although one flourished during the summer at Tamwood Lodge on Lake Muskoka during the 1970s. It was established at the suggestion of Gerry Lampert of the League of Canadian Poets and subsidized by the Ontario Arts Council through the Writers' Development Trust. Tamwood Lodge hosted a dozen or so writers at a time for visits of one or two weeks' duration from 1976 to 1981. Such poets as Robert Sward, biographers as Marian Fowler, and journalists as Betty Jane Wylie relaxed and wrote amid the beauties of Muskoka.

Navy Island

Navy Island lies in the Niagara River above the Falls and was occupied by William Lyon Mackenzie and fellow rebels during the Rebellion of 1837. The French novelist Jules Verne (1828-1905) has Navy Island occupied by French-Canadian patriots in his sensational novel *Family without a Name* (1889), and he has a lively if fanciful description of the Patriot supply ship *Caroline* plunging over the brink of Niagara Falls. One of Mackenzie's accomplices, Eunice Whiting, was caught and imprisoned for three years. She acted as a courier for the Rebels, and Charles Dickens (1812-1870) chatted with her when he toured the Kingston Penitentiary in 1842.

Newmarket

A plaque to commemorate Mazo de la Roche (1879-1961) was erected at Wesley Brooks Conservation Park in Newmarket, north of Toronto. The novelist was born in Newmarket.

Niagara Falls

Many waterfalls are higher than Niagara Falls, but none approach it in volume. It is the prime tourist attraction of North America, and has prompted descriptions, both positive and negative, since the missionary Louis Hennepin (1626-1705) first described it on December 6, 1678, as "an incredible Cataract or Waterfall, which has no equal." "Niagara Falls must be the second major disappointment of American married life," quipped Oscar Wilde (1856-1900) in 1882. The following year, in *Portraits of Places* (1883), Henry James (1843-1916) judged it "the most beautiful object in the world." Hugh MacLennan (b. 1907) has written, "The Niagara is the best-known river on earth and the second most-famous," noting that it is only thirty-four miles long.

C. W. Jefferys' drawing of Father Hennepin at Niagara Falls, 1678.
[C-70245 / Public Archives Canada]

Mighty Cataracts, Mighty Thoughts Virtually every writer who visited the North American continent has made his pilgrimage to Niagara Falls to behold the twin cataracts. Rupert Brooke (1887-1915) was no exception. He viewed the Falls in 1913 and described his reaction in private letters and in *Letters from America* (1916). On a sheet of paper wet with the spray of the Falls, he penned these words to a friend: "I'm so impressed by Niagara. I hoped not to be. But I horribly am. The colour of the water, the strength of it, and the clouds of spray — I'm afraid I'm a Victorian at heart after all. Please don't breathe a word of it; I want to keep such shreds of reputation as I have left. Yet it's true. For I sit and stare at the thing and have the purest Nineteenth Century grandiose thoughts, about the Destiny of Man, the Irresistibility of Fate, the Doom of Nations, the fact that Death awaits us All, and so forth. Wordsworth Redivivus. Oh dear! Oh dear!" He made a striking observation about the spray and mist in his published volume: "The Victorian lies very close below the surface in every man. There one can sit and let great cloudy thoughts of destiny and the passage of empires drift through the mind; for such dreams are at home by Niagara. I could not get out of my mind the thought of a friend, who said that the rainbows over the Falls were like the arts and beauty and goodness, with regard to the stream of life — caused by it, thrown upon its spray, but unable to stay or direct or affect it, and ceasing when it ceased."

Official Plaques Among the official plaques mounted on the escarpment overlooking the Canadian and American Falls there are two of literary interest. The first honours Louis Hennepin (1626-1705), the missionary who wrote the first description of the Falls on December 6, 1678. Hennepin overestimated its height by three hundred per cent. The second plaque honours, curiously, José Maria de Heredia (1842-1905), the Cuban-born French poet and Parnassian who wrote an ode to the mighty Niagara.

Lundy's Lane The Battle of Lundy's Lane, a decisive incident in the War of 1812, took place on July 25, 1814. The American invaders were forced to withdraw. Soldiers from both sides, as well as Laura Secord (1775-1868), the heroine of the war, are buried in Drummond Hill Cemetery which occupies part of the battlefield. Lundy's Lane is now part of the city of Niagara Falls. The battle is celebrated in the title poem of *Lundy's Lane and Other Poems* (1916) by Duncan Campbell Scott (1862-1947).

So renowned was the victory at Lundy's Lane that Tennyson wrote "Have we not stood together in the van: / Whether at Queenston Heights, or Lundy's Lane?" Alas, the Tennyson who wrote that couplet — from "Canada to Britain" included in *The Land of Napioa and Other Essays in Prose and Verse* (1896) — was not the poet-laureate Alfred Lord Tennyson but his Canadian nephew, Bertram Tennyson who died about 1903 in Moosomin, Sask.

Maid of the Mist The steamer that from May to October takes tourists close to the base of the Falls is called the *Maid of the Mist,* a reference to the Iroquois legend of an Indian maiden who, preferring death to unhappiness, sailed her birchbark canoe over the brink of the Falls, only to be saved from certain death by the god He-no, whom she married. Lore has it that the Maid of the Mist may sometimes be glimpsed in the spray and mist of "the Mighty Thunderer." The best-known rendering of the legend in verse form is "The White Canoe: A Legend of Niagara Falls" in the *Poetical Works* (1881) of Rosanna Eleanor Leprohon (1832-1879).

Sir Harry Oakes Oak Garden Theatre, the outdoor park, and Oak Hall, the thirty-seven-room residence overlooking the Falls, are named after Sir Harry Oakes (1874-1943), the millionaire mining magnate who lived here before moving to the Bahamas. His brutal and unsolved murder in Nassau occasioned at least four books and innumerable magazine and newspaper articles.

Goat Island Separating the Canadian and American Falls is Goat Island. In "The Goat Island Poetry Conference" (1958), Raymond Souster (b. 1921) wrote about a "conference to end poetry" during which twenty minor poets are swept over the Horseshoe Falls.

Clifton Gate Pioneer Memorial Arch To mark the one hundredth anniversary of the Rebellion of 1837-38, a fifty-foot stone archway was erected by the Niagara Parks Commission between the Oakes Garden and the Souvenir Shop overlooking the Niagara Gorge. Designed by C. W. Jefferys, it was decorated with engravings and inscriptions by the sculptor Emanuel Hahn. The main carving depicted W. L. Mackenzie presenting the Seventh Report of Grievances to the House of Assembly in 1835. The Clifton Gate Pioneer Memorial Arch, unveiled in 1938 in the presence of W. L. Mackenzie King and Mitchell Hepburn, stood until 1968 when it was declared a "traffic hazard" and unceremoniously dismantled by the Niagara Parks Commission to en-

The Clifton Gate Pioneer Memorial Arch, before the unveiling in 1938, looked as mysterious as the Kaaba Stone in Mecca. Today only traces of it remain on the pavement of the parking lot between the Oakes Garden and the Souvenir Shop. [Ontario Archives; Mark Frank]

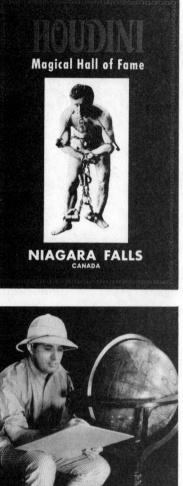

The Houdini Magical Hall of Fame opened in Niagara Falls in 1968. Visitors may examine manacles, strait-jackets, and trunks from which the Escape Artist freed himself. Some of the effects were once owned by Joseph Dunninger, the mentalist. Houdini's death resulted from a blow received backstage at the Princess Theatre in Montreal. [The Houdini Hall of Fame]

Robert L. Ripley of "Believe It or Not!" fame is shown wearing a pith helmet, as befits a world traveller. He included Canada in his travels, addressing the Canadian Club in Toronto in 1932. [Ripley International Ltd.]

large the parking lot. The stones went into storage; a number of inscriptions were lost. Some carvings have been re-erected at Mackenzie House in Toronto, mainly due to the efforts of researcher Mark Frank who refers to the incident as "the case of the fallen arch."

Commercial Attractions Downtown Niagara Falls abounds in commercial attractions. Setting aside the wax museums named after the actor Boris Karloff (who chose his professional name in 1911 on a train between Kamloops and Nelson, B.C.) and the monster Frankenstein (who met his end at the North Pole, in Mary Shelley's novel), there are two attractions with vestiges of literary interest. These are the Houdini Hall of Fame and Ripley's Believe It or Not! Museum.

The Houdini Hall of Fame, opened in 1968, displays props and paraphernalia associated with Houdini (1874-1926), the most famous of all magicians and escape artists. He died on Halloween in 1926, as the result of a freak accident in the dressing room of the Princess Theatre in Montreal. On the anniversaries of his death, well-publicized seances have been held in the Hall in an attempt to communicate with the spirit of the departed Houdini, despite the fact that he devoted much of his professional life to denying the possibility of life after

death and debunking spiritualists and spiritualism. The writer Gwendolyn MacEwen (b. 1941) has written a number of poems about the man whose death-defying acts plainly continue to fascinate so many.

Ripley's Believe It or Not! Museum, opened in 1963, features displays suggested by the cartoons of the American artist and journalist, Robert L. Ripley (1893-1949), the "modern Marco Polo" whose life has been described as "an odyssey of incredible oddities." An item from the first "Believe It or Not!" cartoon in The New York Globe, December 19, 1918, featured a Canadian: "A. Forrester of Toronto — ran 100 yds. backwards in 14 seconds." In 1977, Ripley International Limited was acquired by Toronto entrepreneur T. Alec Rigby. Here are some Canadian Ripleyisms: "The Douglas fir, also known as the Douglas spruce, is neither a fir nor a spruce — but a pine tree." "The Canadian River rises in New Mexico, flows through Texas and Oklahoma to Arkansas, but does not come near Canada." "The Canadian Jumping Fern travels by rooting fresh plants at the ends of its fronds." "The Canada Goose flies only north and south. It never migrates laterally." "The International Opera House, Rock Island, Quebec — Its stage is in Canada and the audience sits in the United States." "The Canada Goose to move its feathers uses 1,200 muscles." "Frank Jones of

Simcoe, Ontario, has worn the same overcoat for 43 yrs." "The oldest Legislator in history — Senator David Wark (1804-1905) of New Brunswick, was still an active member of the Senate in Canada at the age of 101." "The map of New Brunswick, Canada's 'Picture Province,' when viewed upside down forms a likeness of Jacques Cartier — discoverer of the St. Lawrence River." "The alphabet used by the Eskimos of the Canadian Arctic consists of only 4 vowels and 10 consonants — which can be written 4 different ways." "The Canadian jackfish eats ducks." There is an affectionate tribute to Ripley called "An Odyssey of Incredible Oddities" in *Translations from the English* (1974), a collection of poems by John Robert Colombo (b. 1936).

C. W. Jefferys' sketch of William Kirby. [C-69349 / Public Archives Canada]

"The Passion of Christ"

The most extensive and impressive series of illustrations based on the printed word on public display in Canada is the series called "The Passion of Christ." This is exhibited in the Niagara Falls Art Gallery and Museum, located at the McLeod Intersection, which was opened in 1971 to exhibit this work, which consists of 160 watercolours by the artist William Kurelek (1927-1977) to illustrate the entire Gospel according to St. Matthew.

Kurelek executed the series at the rate of one panel a week over a period of three years, following his visit in 1959 to the sites associated with the last days of Jesus of Nazareth. The watercolours are historically accurate except when the artist deliberately extended the message of the Passion into other times and places. The entire series is reproduced in full colour in *The Passion of Christ According to St. Matthew* (1975), issued by the Niagara Falls Art Gallery and Museum which was built by Olha and Mykola Kolankiwsky, Ukrainian-born Canadians. Mykola Kolankiwsky is the editor and publisher of *We and the World*, a Ukrainian-language periodical established in 1950.

Niagara-on-the-Lake

The picturesque town of Niagara-on-the-Lake is situated on the south shore of Lake Ontario, north of Niagara Falls. There is much of historic interest here, plus a number of points of literary interest.

Fort George

Fort George, now part of Fort George National Historic Park, was built in 1796-99. Here Sir Isaac Brock entertained the visiting Irish poet, Thomas Moore (1779-1852), on the latter's North American tour of 1804. Moore penned a number of poems in the Canadas, including "The Woodpecker," "To the Lady Charlotte Rawdon, from the Banks of the St. Lawrence," and "A Canadian Boat Song," but all seem to have been written at Lachine, Que., not Niagara-on-the-Lake.

Old Kirby House

There is a plaque to identify the home occupied by the novelist and historian William Kirby (1817-1906) between 1857 and his death. The Georgian-style townhouse, of whitewashed stucco, is located at 130 Front Street. Kirby is principally recalled as the author of *The Golden Dog* (1877), a romantic historical novel set in Quebec during the days of Louis XV. Writing in *Canadian Houses of Romance* (1926), Katherine Hale (1878-1956) described the condition of Kirby's study at the time of his death. "And accumulating in his desk, afterwards to be stowed away for years in the attic, were diaries and documents and letters of considerable importance. Here are copies of Indian treaties, and observations as to the doings of the countryside, with some perspective of the outer world; and letters conveying the pleasure of Queen Victoria in *Le Chien d'Or*, and from Lord Tennyson and the Duke of Argyll and others." As unlikely as it seems, the Old Kirby House was also occupied by the novelist Malcolm Lowry.

Malcolm Lowry

One does not immediately associate the novelist Malcolm Lowry (1909-1957) with Niagara-on-the-Lake. Yet during the Second World War he lived here with his wife Margerie Bonner. In June 1944, when their shack at Dollarton, B.C., was levelled, the Lowrys headed east and stayed with their friends the Noxons, who lived for a time in Oakville and then in the Old Kirby House in Niagara-on-the-Lake. There are descriptions of locales in Niagara-on-the-Lake in "The Element Follows You Around, Sir" (1964), which occupies two chapters in *October Ferry to Gabriola* (1970).

The Lowrys spent the summer and fall with the Noxons in the Old Kirby House and then moved into a room at the Riverside Inn where, on Christmas Eve 1944, he completed his masterpiece, *Under the Volcano* (1947), filmed by John Huston in 1984. The Riverside Inn, located at 35 Melville Street, is now known as the Dew Drop Harbour Inn. Conflagrations fascinated him. The "element" which followed him around was fire, and one of his most effective poems — "A Lament — June 1944" included in *Selected Poems* (1962) — was written in Niagara-on-the-Lake. It refers to the fire that mysteriously broke out and burnt down his house, concluding:

"But our house is gone. / And the world burns on." In February 1945, the Lowrys returned to British Columbia.

One other writer has resided in both Oakville and Niagara-on-the-Lake and he is Irving Layton (b. 1912). Lowry lived in Oakville before Niagara-on-the-Lake; Layton reversed the order, establishing his residence with his wife Harriet at 9 Castlereagh Street in Niagara-on-the-Lake in 1979 and then moving into a white house in 1982 at 395 Lakeshore Road East, Oakville.

Mystery Lady A resident of Victoria Street in Niagara-on-the-Lake is Mrs. A. G. Bowen-Judd (b. 1922), the English-born author who writes mystery novels about the lawyer detective Antony Maitland under the pen name of Sara Woods. Two of her many popular novels are *Bloody Instructions* (1962) and *Call Back Yesterday* (1982).

George Bernard Shaw The Shaw Festival is the only theatre in the world dedicated to the production of the plays of George Bernard Shaw (1856-1950). Founded in 1962, the Festival's first productions were staged in the historic Court House, which dates from 1848. The modern Festival Theatre was opened in 1973. In the lobby of the modern building there is a bust of G.B.S. by Jacob Epstein and a bust of the Festival's founder, Brian Doherty (1906-1974), by Jacobine Jones. Books by and about Shaw, with quotations from his works, may be viewed in the Doherty/Stelco Library off the foyer. The library featu. es a copy of the Samuel French acting edition of Doherty's Broadway success, *Father Malachy's Miracle* (1937), based on Bruce Marshall's 1931 novel. One New York critic described his discovery of the Shaw Festival in Niagara-on-the-Lake as "coming upon a Watteau at a country auction."

George Bernard Shaw brings delight to theatre-goers in Niagara-on-the-Lake. Top: His plays are performed in both the new Festival Theatre and the old Court House Theatre. Bottom: The Shaw Festival was founded by Brian Doherty (left). G.B.S. is honoured in the Festival Theatre's foyer with this bust by Sir Jacob Epstein (centre). Heath Lamberts played the lead in the widely acclaimed 1983 production of Cyrano de Bergerac *(right). [Shaw Festival]*

Nickleby Lake

In the Atikokan area are geographical features with names derived from the characters and locales created by Charles Dickens (1812-1870). These are Squeers Lake, Snodgrass Lake, Gads Hill, and Nickleby Lake.

Nipigon

It was at Nipigon, on the north shore of Lake Superior, that the poet Duncan Campbell Scott (1862-1947) heard from a Hudson's Bay Company factor two stories about the endurance of the Indians in the wilderness. He retold these in 1905 as "On the Way to the Mission" and "The Forsaken," two of his most powerful poems. From the same period comes "Night Hymns on Lake Nipigon" which evokes "the lonely, loon-haunted Nipigon reaches." Scott wrote about his experience at the trading post called Nipigon House in his essay "The Last of the Indian Treaties" (1906). The north country between here and the Ottawa River impressed him so much that he made this the locale of the stories in *The Witching of Elspie* (1923).

The popular children's book, *Paddle-to-the-Sea* (1941), written by the American author Holling C. Holling (b. 1900), begins in a cabin on the shore of Lake Nipigon in which an Indian boy is carving out of wood a tiny Indian seated in a canoe. When he releases it, the figure in the canoe sails around the Great Lakes, tumbles over Niagara Falls, flows down the St. Lawrence, and is rescued by a fisherman who takes it with him to France. The book was filmed by the NFB in 1966.

Nokomis Lake

There are three lakes in Ontario that bear this name. In Longfellow's *The Song of Hiawatha* (1855), Nokomis is the daughter of the Moon, the mother of Wenonah, and the grandmother of Hiawatha. Each lake perhaps reflects an aspect of this mythological personality.

The first Nokomis Lake is in Algonquin Park, northeast of Huntsville (east of it is Minnehaha Lake). The second Nokomis Lake is west of Kirkland Lake and southeast of Timmins. The third Nokomis Lake is southwest of Chapleau. Nearby are Poetry Lake and Verse Lake.

Norval

L. M. Montgomery (1874-1942) called Norval "a pretty little village in the valley of the River Credit." It is located west of Brampton. The author of *Anne of Green Gables* (1908) lived here with her husband in the two-storey manse of the Presbyterian church from 1926 to 1935. Here she wrote such novels as *Pat of Silver Bush* (1933) and *Anne of Windy Poplars* (1936).

Oakville

At Oakville, which is midway between Hamilton and Toronto, the Ukrainian community has developed the T. H. Shevchenko Museum and Memorial Park. It was designed for Ukrainian community use and it pays honour to Taras H. Shevchenko (1814-1861), the poet and patriot of Ukraine. A museum on the grounds has exhibits of memorabilia associated with the man and his turbulent times. Watson Kirkconnell (1895-1977) translated *The Poetical Works of Taras Shevchenko* (1964).

Malcolm Lowry (1909-1957), the novelist, resided briefly in Oakville. This was in the summer of 1944 and he and his wife stayed with their friends the Noxons. The Noxons, it seems, were summer visitors, for research has failed to identify their residence here. Lowry described in *October Ferry to Gabriola* (1970) the Oakville Public Library, which was situated on the site of the present 198 Lakeshore Road East. He refers to an "old tollbooth" and to a librarian named "Miss Braithwaite," but these too have eluded verification. Here he evokes the Oakville Public Library: "It was an interesting little library, in the old tollbooth, beneath the police station; the volumes mostly of the Victorian era, with complete sets of Howells, Meredith, Mark Twain, Mark Rutherford, and a startling array of translations from the nineteenth-century French classics: the Goncourt Brothers, Zola, Flaubert; *Crime and Punishment* was there, in Constance Garnett's translation; so was Lawrence's *Studies in Classic American Literature*; but twentieth-century fiction seemed scarcely represented save by the seven-day books, current best sellers, lying on a shelf above Miss Braithwaite's head." It is possible the details are figments of Lowry's imagination.

Irving Layton (b. 1912) resided in the white house at 395 Lakeshore Road East from November 1982 to November 1983 when he returned home — to Montreal.

Orangeville

The town of Orangeville, north of Guelph, was the birthplace of O. D. Skelton (1878-1941), Ottawa mandarin in the 1920s and 1930s. Alexander McLachlan (1818-1896), known as the "Canadian Burns," died here at his home on Elizabeth Street, after having lived on a farm 10 kilometres west of here in 1877-95. McLachlan is buried in Greenwood Cemetery beneath a monument erected in 1900 by public subscription.

Archibald Lampman (1861-1899) taught school here from September to December 1882, and the experience was not a happy one. "The pedagogue, like the poet, is born and not made," Lampman wrote to a college friend.

A resident of Orangeville from 1956 to 1969 was the writer Max Braithwaite (b. 1911), who joined the Rotary Club and sat on the Town Council. He wrote about his experiences with tongue in cheek in his novel *A Privilege and a Pleasure* (1974). In his travel book *Max Braithwaite's Ontario* (1974), he explained: "Orangeville in many ways is typical of towns within a fifty-mile radius of Toronto."

Orillia

The town of Orillia is situated on the south end of Lake Couchiching in the vicinity of Lake Simcoe. It has a number of literary associations.

The Stephen Leacock Home at Orillia, Ont. [Bill Brooks]

"I count none but sunny hours" appears on the face of the sundial set in white cracked concrete in the English garden of Stephen Leacock's home. [Jim Harris]

Stephen Leacock, "the laughing philosopher," as photographed by Notman & Son. [Stephen Leacock Memorial Home]

Stephen Leacock The Stephen Leacock Memorial Home was for many years the summer home of Stephen Leacock (1869-1944), the celebrated humorist. It is located on the south shore of Lake Couchiching's Old Brewery Bay, in the east end of Orillia. The author of thirty-four volumes of humour as well as twenty-seven books of history, biography, criticism, economics, and political science, Leacock has more books in print than any other Canadian author, living or dead. After L. M. Montgomery's Green Gables at Cavendish, P.E.I., the Stephen Leacock Memorial Home is the country's leading literary shrine.

Leacock's roots run deep in the region. Although born in England, he was raised on a backwoods farm from the age of six. The one-hundred-acre farm — the house burnt down in the 1960s — is now part of the Howard Anderson farm. It is visible looking northwest from the red brick schoolhouse at Egypt, Georgina Township. The farm was four miles from the village of Sutton. Young Leacock was taken each Sunday to St. George's Anglican Church which overlooks Lake Simcoe.

He was educated in Egypt, a settlement in the area, and as a twelve-year-old became a boarder at Upper Canada College, Toronto. From 1887 to 1891, he taught high school at Strathroy (where one of his pupils was Sir Arthur Currie) and Uxbridge. He then attended the University of Toronto and taught French and German from 1891 to 1899 at Upper Canada College. He attended the University of Chicago, graduating with a doctorate in economics in 1903, when he joined the Department of Economics at McGill University, Montreal. He was a popular professor, teaching from 1901 to retirement in 1936.

Leacock acquired thirty-three acres of land on a small point on Lake Couchiching in 1908, following a world lecture tour. He called it Old Brewery Bay, after the nearby ruins of a stone brewhouse. He erected a cottage and boathouse with a studio above it. In 1929, he erected the spacious residence that is standing here today. Leacock died in 1944 and the residence was sold. It was owned by Louis Ruby, publisher of the sensational tabloid *Flash,* who sold it to the city in 1957. It was formally opened on July 5, 1958, and is now one of the country's prime literary attractions. There are plans to rebuild the boathouse in which Leacock wrote many of his books.

The Stephen Leacock Memorial Home is open daily from mid-June until Labour Day, 10:00 a.m. to 5:00 p.m., and other times by appointment. Furnishings and memorabilia associated with the life of "the Baron of Brewery Bay" are on display, including the original, handwritten manuscript of *Sunshine Sketches of a Little Town* (1912). The "little town" of the title is called Mariposa in the book, but it was modelled on Orillia. "Mariposa is not a real town," he warned his readers. "On the contrary, it is about seventy or eighty of them. You may find them all the way from Lake Superior to the sea, with the same square streets and the same maple trees and the same churches and hotels, and everywhere the sunshine of the land of hope."

The house includes a special exhibit called "Leacock's

Grant Macdonald illustrated the "Mariposa Belle" for the 1948 edition of Leacock's Sunshine Sketches of a Little Town. [Grant Macdonald]

Orillia, Ontario ..._July 25 41._..

To the Orillia Public Library :

I here recommend granting the privileges of the Library

to _Stephen Lushington Leacock_

and guarantee the return to the Library, in good condition, of all books drawn upon the applicant's card.

Signature _Stephen Leacock_

To borrow books from the Orillia Public Library in the 1940s, one needed an "Endorsement." Here is Stephen Leacock's signature endorsing his son Stephen Lushington Leacock's request for a library card. [Orillia Public Library / Jim Harris]

Life-size bust of Stephen Leacock by Elizabeth Wyn Wood in the foyer of the Orillia Public Library. [Jim Harris]

Mariposa," which draws parallels between sites and citizens of Orillia and places and people in Mariposa. (Both Mariposa and Orillia, by the way, are Spanish names. Mariposa means "butterfly," Orillia means "river bank." They were selected in 1820 by Sir Peregrine Maitland, the Lieutenant-Governor, who had formerly served in Spain — Orillia for the town, Mariposa for the Township in Victoria County.)

For many years the curator of the Home was Ralph L. Curry, of Georgetown University, Kentucky, author of _Stephen Leacock: Humorist and Humanist_ (1959), the first biography, and editor of _The Leacock Medal Treasury: Three Decades of the Best Canadian Humour_ (1976). The Leacock Medal for Humour, established in 1947, is awarded here annually. The Stephen Leacock Associates, a group of friends, meet in the Orillia Public Library, which has a collection of his works as well as a bronze bust of "the laughing economist" by the noted sculptor Elizabeth Wyn Wood unveiled in 1949. Visitors to the home should note the sundial in the garden with its inscription "I count none but sunny hours," which is as true of a sundial as it is of Leacock's humour.

Leacock died at the Toronto General Hospital on March 28, 1944, his last words to a nurse being, "I was a good boy, wasn't I?" His ashes are buried in the family plot in St. George's churchyard. The Ontario government, in the 1970s, opened Stephen Leacock Provincial Park, a recreation area of 162 acres on Lake Simcoe, some miles southeast of Old Brewery Bay. Leacock once wrote: "I have known that name, the Old Brewery Bay, to make people feel thirsty by correspondence as far away as Nevada."

Champlain's Statue   In Couchiching Beach Park there is a fine statue of Samuel de Champlain by the sculptor Vernon March. It was erected in 1925 to commemorate Champlain's visit to the region in 1615. Raymond Souster (b. 1921) has written in his poem "Words Before a Statue of Champlain" (1962): "The sculptor, no Rodin, / has at least caught / the look of vision / shining from the eyes, / the gleam of unrest. . . ."

Geneva Park   Each year the Couchiching Conferences are held at Geneva Park, as the conference centre is called (the name being worthy of the League of Nations). Geneva Park is located on Lake Couchiching, an extension of Lake Simcoe, 9 miles (14 kilometres) north of Orillia. The Couchiching Conferences are sponsored by the Canadian Institute on Public Affairs and "provide an open forum for discussion of Canadian social and economic problems in an international setting." Summer conferences have been convened since 1932, winter since 1954. The proceedings are usually newsworthy and cov-

The Champlain Monument at Couchiching Beach, Orillia, was sculpted by Vernon Marsh. [Ontario Ministry of Tourism and Recreation]

Stephen Vizinczey, author of In Praise of Older Women, which was written in Toronto, and An Innocent Millionaire, portions of which were written in Gravenhurst and Toronto. [McClelland & Stewart]

Don Evans, the Orillia-based caricaturist, as seen by Isaac Bickerstaff, his alter ego. [Special Collections, University of Calgary Libraries]

ered by the media but have yet to attract the attention of a sharp-witted novelist — with one exception. Stephen Vizinczey (b. 1933), the Hungarian-born writer, in his novel, *In Praise of Older Women* (1965), has his hero an academic who attends one of the "Couch" conferences. He finds it a bacchanal by night and, by avoiding the formal sessions, an orgy by day.

Also Notable   Orillia was briefly the home of Mazo de la Roche (1879-1961). Her father was a commercial traveller and moved here with his family in the late 1880s. In 1892, the future novelist was admitted (as "Maizo Roche") to the Orillia Collegiate. The family moved to Toronto the following year.

The Anglo-Canadian playwright George Hulme (b. 1931) was born in Orillia. His best-known comedy is *The Lionel Touch* (1969).

Satire still thrives in Orillia, for the city is the home of the caricaturist Don Evans (b. 1936), noted for his drawings of Canadian writers.

Oshawa

The city of Oshawa, east of Toronto, has numerous associations with the automobile manufacturer and philanthropist Colonel Sam McLaughlin but few with Canadian letters. The city did occasion the classic observation of Xaviera Hollander, the so-called Happy Hooker. "You know what I think Oshawa needs?" she asked during a book promotion tour in 1973. "A good brothel."

Oshawa is not far from the site of Camp X, the code name for the important training camp and communications centre for guerilla warfare and intelligence operations run by the Allies during the Second World War. It was given cover by the Canadian Broadcasting Corporation and directed by Sir William Stephenson (b. 1896), once known as "the Quiet Canadian" but now (that he has been the subject of two bestselling biographies by William Stevenson) known as "the Man Called Intrepid."

Camp X was located on isolated farmland on the north shore of Lake Ontario. The closely guarded site was occupied by some eight buildings, the largest of which was an immense concrete-block transmitting station. The location, which will receive an Ontario historic plaque in the near future, is on Boundary Road south of the immense warehouse built by the Liquor Control Board of Ontario.

Intriguing references to Camp X crop up in William Stevenson's *A Man Called Intrepid* (1976) and its sequel *Intrepid's Last Case* (1983). In the television dramatization of the former book, a would-be terrorist is shot in a glamourized Camp X setting. The faking and forging of documents was a routine operation at Station M (for Magic): the underground transmitter in contact with intelligence stations throughout Europe was called Hydra; the world's biggest radio-communications system was dubbed Aspidistra; the training camp was here for Leopards (Winston Churchill's term for Canadian commandos). Ian Fleming (1908-1964) learned espionage tricks at Camp X which he later worked into his James Bond books. He also disobeyed orders and refused to "murder" an operative in a Toronto hotel.

When the book about Camp X is written, it will make fascinating reading. At least one writer, the poet R. G. Everson, knew the camp inside and out. Memorabilia associated with Camp X is on display on weekends at the Oshawa Airport Museum in the Quoncet hut near the main hangar.

Ottawa

"Ottawa is a sub-arctic lumber-village converted by royal mandate into a political cockpit." This often-reprinted observation on the nation's capital was made by Goldwin Smith (1823-1910), the essayist and political scientist. Less popular is the fine tribute paid to the city by the English poet Rupert Brooke (1887-1915) who wrote, following a visit in 1913: "But what Ottawa leaves in the mind is a certain graciousness — dim, for it expresses a barely materialized national spirit — and sight of kindly English-looking faces, and the rather lovely sound of the soft Canadian accent in the streets."

The Centre Block and Peace Tower, Parliament Hill, Ottawa. [NFB Photothèque / Hans Blohm]

The most honoured book in the country: the Book of Remembrance in its twenty-four karat gold frame, ornamented with the Royal Arms and the Arms of Canada, quartered with angels kneeling in prayer in the Memorial Chamber of the Peace Tower. The name of each Canadian soldier who gave his life in the service of his country is inscribed in the Book, the pages of which are turned each day. [W. J. L. Gibbons]

Parliament Hill Parliament Hill is the promontory overlooking the Ottawa River in downtown Ottawa upon which are situated the Parliament Buildings. Dominating the Hill is the Centre Block with its 291-foot Peace Tower which was dedicated in 1927. The lower level of the Tower has a Memorial Chamber.

Inscribed in the four Books of Remembrance, which lie open on altars in the Memorial Chamber of the Peace Tower, are the names of those Canadians who died in the South African War, World War I, World War II, and the Korean War. Inscribed on white marble tablets on the walls are suitable passages of prose and poetry by a mélange of authors, including Laurence Binyon, John Bunyan, Victor Hugo, Rudyard Kipling, and John McCrae — or they were, until 1982, when a committee convened by the Seargeant-at-Arms replaced the original tablets with new ones to represent equally both official languages. In 1983 there was agitation to have the Books of Remembrance — essentially lists of names of those who died in action — rescripted "bilingually." Conspicuous by its absence is the inscription composed by Rudyard Kipling: "They are too near / To be great / But our children / Shall understand / When and how our / Fate was changed / And by whose hand." It is anticipated that the original tablets, like this one, will be displayed in the Senate Chamber along with the war paintings donated by Lord Beaverbrook.

Those who lived through the Second World War will recall that Sir Winston Churchill (1874-1965) delivered his celebrated "Some chicken! Some neck!" address before a joint sitting of the Senate and the House of Commons, December 30, 1941. Then he was led to the Speaker's Chambers where Yousuf Karsh snapped his famous "bulldog" portrait of Sir Winston, having first snatched the cigar from his mouth.

The sitting of the House of Commons was suspended at 2:15 p.m. May 18, 1965, after "a loud explosion was

Sir Winston Churchill, 5¢ stamp, 1965. [Canada Post Corporation]

heard in the chamber." The epicentre of the blast was the men's public washroom on the third floor near the entrance to the Visitor's Gallery. The blast was caused by the premature explosion of the homemade bomb being prepared by Paul Joseph Chartier, an unemployed truck driver from Alberta, who was preparing to pitch it into the Commons chamber. He was killed in the explosion. Found on his body was a speech which begins: "Mr. Speaker, Gentlemen, I might as well give you a blast to wake you up." Gary Geddes (b. 1940) has written *War and Other Measures* (1976) about the incident.

Library of Parliament   The memorable domed chamber with sixteen sides of the Library of Parliament was designed by Thomas Fuller and completed in 1866. The building survived a succession of fires in 1813, 1842, 1849, 1854, 1916 and 1952. Over the gothic entranceway is engraved the image of the Golden Dog (popularized by the author William Kirby) with the inscription: "Je suis un chien qui rouge un os" ("I am a dog who gnaws a bone").

The books (reserved for the use of elected and appointed officials) number almost half a million. Lord

Tweesdmuir made good use of the collection, as did historian Francis Parkman and writer Wyndham Lewis (although the latter two were neither elected nor appointed officials). The first woman employed in the Library was the widow of the poet Archibald Lampman; she subsequently died at her desk. Among the literary manuscripts held by the Library are holographs by Archibald Lampman of the poems "Alcyone" and "David and Abigail."

The poet Raymond Souster (b. 1921) has written "Parliamentary Library, Ottawa" (1958) in which he notes that in this chamber "no one gets to carve Kilroy was here."

Sir Galahad   At the foot of Parliament Hill stands the statue to Sir Galahad, the knight of the Round Table, erected in memory of Henry A. Harper who drowned in the Ottawa River while trying to save Miss Bessie Blair, December 6, 1901. Inscribed on the base of the romantic-looking statue, erected in 1905, is the noble sentiment from "The Holy Grail" by Alfred Lord Tennyson (1809-1892): "If I lose myself, I save myself." A prime mover in promoting the erection of the monument to personal heroism and sacrifice was W. L. Mackenzie King (1874-1950) who devoted an essay to it called "The Secret of Heroism." W. W. Campbell (1858-1918) has a poem "Henry A. Harper" in his *Collected Poems* (1905) which includes the lines: "There lurks a godlike impulse in the world, / And men are greater than they idly dream."

Sir Galahad, the spirit of youth, with the Parliament Buildings in the background. [National Capital Commission]

The Library of Parliament with the white marble statue of Queen Victoria, Parliament Hill, Ottawa. [Dept. of Regional Industrial Expansion]

Statue of Sir George-Etienne Cartier, Parliament Hill, Ottawa. [National Capital Commission]

Statue of Thomas D'Arcy McGee, Parliament Hill, Ottawa. [Dept. of Regional Industrial Expansion]

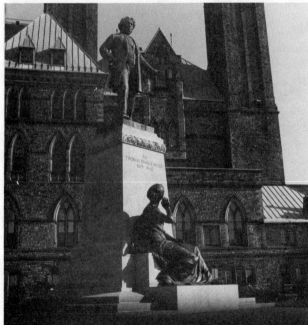

Statues   Among the statues that adorn the grounds of Parliament Hill are those of Thomas D'Arcy McGee (1825-1868) and Sir George-Etienne Cartier (1814-1873).

Centennial Year   National buoyancy was perhaps highest in the centennial year. One associates Parliament Hill on July 1, 1967, with the song "CA-NA-DA," written and performed by Bobby Gimby (b. 1921). One of its catchy lines goes: "Merrily we roll along / Together all the way." Judy LaMarsh (1924-1980), the minister in charge of these celebrations, wrote in her autobiography that this patriotic song "was the only thing associated with the Centennial Commission, so far as I am aware, that was not chosen by a committee after a contest."

Confederation Square   There are very few depictions in prose or poetry of the National War Memorial in Confed-

eration Square, the scene of the ceremonies on Remembrance Day. The gigantic arch, with the allegorical figures of Peace and Freedom, was designed by Vernon March and dedicated in 1939 by King George VI. The poem "National War Memorial" (1969) by Raymond Souster (b. 1921) does evoke the monument.

South of Confederation Square, near Laurier Street, stands a sculpture that consists of an arrangement of four rectangular steel pillars, ten feet tall, coloured red, blue, green, and yellow. The sculpture, installed in 1970 by Guido Molinari, is called "Homage to Samuel Beckett." It is laconic, like Beckett.

Detail of the National War Memorial, Confederation Square, Ottawa. [NFB Photothèque / Ted Grant]

National Arts Centre, designed by Fred Lebensold and opened in 1969, Confederation Square, Ottawa. [Hawkshead Services]

Supreme Court of Canada   Although not large and built in recent times, the Supreme Court of Canada is an impressive building. Here one recalls that the poet and lawyer F. R. Scott (b. 1899) defended the right of Canadians to import copies of the novel *Lady Chatterley's*

Lover (1928) by D. H. Lawrence (1885-1930). As he wrote in "A Lass in Wonderland" (1956): "I went to bat for the Lady Chatte / Dressed in my bib and gown. / The judges three glared down at me / The priests patrolled the town."

National Library and Public Archives Building The National Library of Canada and the Public Archives of Canada have, since 1967, shared the premises of a building of uninspired design at 395 Wellington Street.

The most extensive collection of Canadian books in the world is housed in the National Library of Canada. Since 1953, when it was formally established, two copies of every book published in the country have had to be deposited with the library. The holdings of the Literary Manuscripts Collection are extensive. Through purchase or donation it has acquired manuscripts by more than seventy authors. Represented are (almost at random): Robertson Davies, Gratien Gélinas, John Glassco, Marie Le Franc, Roger Lemelin, Markoosie, Claire Martin, Gabrielle Roy, Benjamin Sulte, Phyllis Webb, Ethel Wilson, and J. Michael Yates.

Panels on the main floor of the National Library depict the written and spoken word, and at the entrance to the Rare Book Room there are figures of Shakespeare, Molière, Dante, and Cervantes. Panels on the second floor are devoted to the nine Muses and Apollo. Two murals executed by Charles Comfort are on the second floor. These are titled *Legacy*, which symbolizes Canadian writers, and *Heritage*, which represents non-Canadian writers. Also on the second floor are murals by Alfred Pellan and other artists, as well as Lawren Harris Jr.'s portrait of W. Kaye Lamb, National Librarian from 1953 to 1968. On the third floor, glass panels depict men prominent in the country's history from the time of Jacques Cartier to Confederation.

The Public Archives of Canada is the national collection of documents relating to the history of the country. On the terrace behind the building stands the statue of Sir Arthur Doughty (1860-1936), Dominion Archivist (1904-35), which was commenced by R. Tait McKenzie and completed by Emanuel Hahn in 1940. The

The National Library of Canada (top) is shown from the Garden of the Provinces. The foyer (middle) features "Three Way Piece-Points," the Henry Moore sculpture donated by the British Government when the Library opened in 1976. The "Heritage" mural by Charles Comfort adds a note of interest to the Reading Room (lower left). The terrace (lower right) includes the bronze statue of Sir Arthur Doughty, Dominion Archivist (1904-35), commenced by R. Tait McKenzie, completed by Emanuel Hann in 1940. [National Library of Canada]

features are somewhat acerbic: the Doughty motto is reproduced *Palma non sine pulvere* ("No success without a struggle").

The Public Archives houses a large collection of literary manuscripts in order to preserve a complete and varied record of all aspects of the country's literary history. Among the larger collections are the papers of Catharine Parr Traill, Susanna Moodie, Louis-Honoré Fréchette, W. W. Campbell, Archibald Lampman, Duncan Campbell Scott, E. K. Brown, L. M. Montgomery, Grey Owl, Emily Carr, Alain Grandbois, A. M. Klein, F. R. Scott, Lovat Dickson, John Glassco, George Johnston, Jay Macpherson, Miriam Waddington, Joe Rosenblatt, and Richard Rohmer. It has, as well, the records of the Canadian Authors' Association, the Canadian Writers' Foundation, and the League of Canadian Poets. Letters of Matthew Arnold are among the Mackenzie King Papers. Among outstanding single acquisitions are a holograph copy of "In Flanders Fields" by John McCrae and holograph religious and political verse by Louis Riel. In 1984 the papers of Marshall McLuhan were acquired.

National Museum of Man The National Museum of Man is one of the four museums under the rubric the National Museums of Canada. It includes the Canadian War Museum, the Archaeological Survey of Canada, and the Centre for Folk Culture Studies. The latter was founded by Marius Barbeau (1883-1969) and includes cylinders, records, and tapes of some 10,000 Inuit, Indian, French, English, and ethnic songs.

Rideau Hall Rideau Hall is the popular name of Government House, the stone mansion originally erected in 1838 which, since Confederation, has been the official residence of the Governor General. One does not readily associate Rideau Hall with literary considerations, yet one distinguished guest was Matthew Arnold, who stayed here in February 1884, and at least four representatives of the Crown have left literary legacies.

Lord Dufferin (1826-1902), who served in 1872-78, made many speeches (which Goldwin Smith caricaturized as "elegant flummery"). But it was his wife, Lady Dufferin, who sounded a national note with *My Canadian Diary* (1891) in which she referred to the country as "this Canada of ours."

Lord Lorne (1845-1914), who served in 1878-83, was a poetaster who composed a poem on the occasion of his naming of the new province of Alberta after his wife. It begins: "In token of the love which thou hast shown / For this wide land of freedom, I have named / A province vast, and for its beauty famed, / By thy dear name to be hereafter known." On another occasion he was inspired by the Rocky Mountains to compose the popular hymn "Unto the Hills."

Lord Tweedsmuir (1875-1940), who served from 1935 to his death, was without question the *littérateur* of Rideau Hall. He was famous as John Buchan, the author of adventure thrillers like *The Thirty-Nine Steps* (1915),

The flag of the Governor General flies above Rideau Hall, Ottawa. [*Hawkshead Services*]

before he assumed vice-regal office. He helped to establish the Governor General's Awards for Literature (awarded annually since 1936). At Rideau Hall he dictated two posthumously published novels: *Lake of Gold* (1940) for children; *Sick Heart River* (1941) for adults. He may have referred to "the governor generalities" of his office, and to himself as a joke as a *littérateur* (to historian C. P. Stacey), yet he was in his day the best-known author in the country. The Quebec writer Fernand Rinfret paid him a graceful compliment when he noted: "There is someone reading Proust in Rideau Hall." His addresses in *Canadian Occasions* (1940) are worth reading today, and his *Memory Hold-the-Door* (1940) is a classic autobiography (and was one of President John F. Kennedy's favourite books).

Vincent Massey (1887-1967), who served in 1952-59, the first Canadian to do so, chaired the important Massey Commission (1949-51). His speeches appeared in *On Being Canadian* (1948) and in his autobiography *What's Past Is Prologue* (1963). It was his feeling that he "made the Crown Canadian."

Former Governor General Vincent Massey. [PAC (C 1015)]

Former Governor General Lord Tweedsmuir. [PAC (C 8507)]

Former Prime Minister John G. Diefenbaker enjoyed a brief chat with Sir John A. Macdonald (in the person of actor William Hutt) during a break in the filming of CBC-TV's The National Dream *series in Ottawa, in 1973. [Memory Lane]*

Edward Schreyer (b. 1935), who served in 1979-83, delivered his first address to the House of Commons and the Senate in English, French, and Ukrainian, where it so appears in Roman and Cyrillic typefaces.

24 Sussex Drive   The official residence of the Prime Minister, located at 24 Sussex Drive, kitty-corner to Rideau Hall, is a grey stone mansion built in 1867. It is off-limits to tourists who are not even permitted to photograph it from the sidewalk. It differs from Number 10 Downing Street and the White House in this if not in other regards. The single artistic work that is set within these walls — in part, at least — is the one-woman revue *Maggie and Pierre* (1980), written and performed by Linda Griffiths (b. 1953) to much acclaim across the country. It was based on the widely publicized marriage and separation of two authors, Pierre Elliott Trudeau (b. 1919) and Margaret Trudeau (b. 1948).

Actress Linda Griffiths impersonated both the prime minister and his increasingly estranged wife in Maggie and Pierre, *the 1980 dramatic revue directed by Paul Thompson for Theatre Passe Muraille. It took the audience inside 24 Sussex Drive. [Theatre Passe Muraille]*

Official residence of the Prime Minister, 24 Sussex Drive, Ottawa. [NFB Photothèque / Cedric Pearson]

Thomas D'Arcy McGee   A plaque marks the spot on Sparks Street Mall near where an assassin's bullet ended the life of Thomas D'Arcy McGee (1825-1868) on April 7, 1868. McGee was a popular and controversial parliamentarian, but also a man of letters. At one time every schoolchild knew the opening lines of his verse "Jacques Cartier" which run: "In the seaport of St. Malo, 'twas a smiling morn in May, / When the Commodore Jacques Cartier to the westward sailed away." Progressive education has done away with popular verse. A number of books have been written about the assassination by a disgruntled Fenian, and Al Purdy (b.1918) has contributed two lively poems which were inspired by the incident: "Murder of D'Arcy McGee" in *Sundance at Dusk* (1976) and "Who Killed D'Arcy McGee?" in *The Stone Bird* (1981). On Parliament Hill a statue of McGee stands near the Library of Parliament.

Archibald Lampman   For many, Archibald Lampman (1861-1899) is the poet of nature condemned to a sedentary existence in Ottawa. As befits a poet of nature, Lampman was ever on the move. He was born in 1861 in the rectory (now demolished) of Trinity Anglican Church, Morpeth. There followed four family moves: to Perrytown, near Port Hope, in 1866; to Gore's Landing, on Rice Lake, in 1867, where visits were paid by Susanna Moodie and Catharine Parr Traill; to Cobourg, in 1874, where he attended the Cobourg Collegiate Institute; and to Port Hope, in 1876, where he enrolled at Trinity College School. Lampman then studied at the old Trinity College, Toronto, in 1879-82, and taught high school in

Photograph and specimen signature of Archibald Lampman, the Canadian Keats. [NFB]

One of Archibald Lampman's many Ottawa residences was Philomen Terrace on Daly Avenue. [Terry Keough]

Duncan Campbell Scott is depicted by Isaac Bickerstaff (artist Don Evans) as a contributor to "At the Mermaid Inn." The other contributors to the column are Archibald Lampman and W. W. Campbell. [Special Collections, University of Calgary Libraries]

born in a parsonage that used to stand near the corner of Queen and Metcalfe streets, across from the Dominion Methodist Church where his father was minister. For many years he occupied a comfortable red brick house at 108 Lisgar Street, where the Edwards Building now stands. A plaque in the building honours the poet but fails to recreate the ambience of Scott's residence. Here, in July 1913, he entertained the youthful poet Rupert Brooke (1887-1915), who came armed with a letter of introduction from the English poet John Masefield (and another letter of introduction to Sir Wilfrid Laurier which resulted in lunch with the Prime Minister). Brooke wrote to fellow poet Wilfred Gibson of his meeting with Scott: "The only poet in Canada was very nice to me in Ottawa...nobody cares if he writes or doesn't."

In later years Scott reminisced about his friendship with Archibald Lampman and his decades with the Indian Affairs Department for the benefit of critic E. K. Brown (1905-1951) who caught the warmth of their friendship in his preface to Scott's *The Circle of Affection* (1947). The complete Scott-Brown correspondence has been published under the title *The Poet and the Critic* (1984), edited by Robert L. McDougall of Carleton University. Scott was unjustly neglected as a poet in his own day; the same is true today, though decreasingly so.

Orangeville in September-December 1882, when he left for Ottawa.

In the nation's capital he worked as a postal clerk from 1883 to his death in 1899. He boarded at 67 O'Connor Street, then moved into the family home (since demolished) at 144 Nicholas Street. He lived at three locations in Philomen Terrace on Daly Avenue: at No. 363 in 1886; at No. 369 in 1892-94; and at No. 375 in 1894-96. From then until his death he resided at 187 Bay Street, since demolished. He lies in Beechwood Cemetery.

Duncan Campbell Scott The distinguished poet and civil servant Duncan Campbell Scott (1862-1947) was

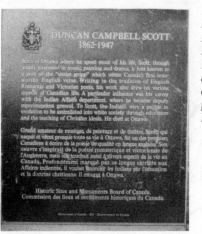

In the foyer of the office building that occupies the site of Duncan Campbell Scott's old home, 108 Lisgar, the Historic Sites and Monuments Board of Canada erected this plaque in 1963. [Terry Keough]

Double portrait of A. Y. Jackson and Marius Barbeau, 1925, painted in pen and black ink over pencil by Arthur Lismer. [PAC C-102019]

Norman Levine builds a snowman in this caricature drawn by Don Evans (who signs his work Isaac Bickerstaff). [Special Collections, University of Calgary Libraries]

Marius Barbeau The folklorist Marius Barbeau (1883-1969) lived from the 1950s on at 260 McLaren Avenue. Those who visited him at his home reported that it was a miniature museum, festooned with Indian, Eskimo, and French-Canadian artifacts and handicrafts. He wrote more than one hundred books and reports, and he was in his day the country's leading folklorist.

Two Authors The prairie novels of Robert Stead (1880-1959) were widely read in his day but they were not profitable enough to permit him the luxury of full-time writing. He worked in the Parks and Resources division of the Department of Mines and Resources. He lived in two houses in Ottawa: in 1919, at 253 Daly Avenue; in 1920-59, 193 2nd Avenue.

Three residences in Ottawa are associated with William Wilfred Campbell (1858-1918). The poet worked for various government departments and lived in the following residences: in 1900-1, at 281 Bronson (Concession) Avenue; in 1902-5, at 38 Charles Street; in 1906-7, at 280 O'Connor Street.

Norman Levine "As a child and a young man Murray Street was 'home,'" wrote Norman Levine (b. 1924) in his travel memoir Canada Made Me (1958, 1979). "Not the entire street, but the one block next to Anglesea Square where most of the fruit and vegetable and rag pedlars of Ottawa lived." He went on to say, "It cuts right through Lower Town. At one end is Anglesea Square (a treeless, grassless, dusty playground); the Bishop's Palace with the young priests pacing up and down the stone porch; the two Catholic schools. East of the Square is a small park, a large barn, the end of a streetcar line. Not much further is the Rideau River. At the other end of the street, past the synagogue, the Boulevard, are the wooden shacks, the poor French, the rough taverns. This end of the street ends the same as the other with a park and a river. And clustered near it is the centre of Ottawa the tourist knows: the Chateau Laurier, the Parliament Buildings, the By Ward Market, and the Basilica."

The author Robert Stead was drawn by Goodridge Roberts. [PAC C-104569]

Josef Stalin beams, not comprehending that Igor Gouzenko (played by Dana Andrews) harbours traitorous thoughts which he will not share with his comrade (actor Peter Whitney) in the 1948 Hollywood film The Iron Curtain. [Ontario Film Institute]

Soviet Embassy The severe limestone building at 285 Charlotte Street dates from 1956 and replaces the old Embassy building which burnt down. It was from the old building that Igor Gouzenko (1919-1982) defected the evening of September 5, 1945, taking with him documents that established the existence of Soviet spy rings operating in North America. Gouzenko told his story in *This Was My Choice* (1948) which was filmed later that year as *The Iron Curtain* in which Dana Andrews played the defector. The only other book Gouzenko wrote was *The Fall of a Titan* (1953), a highly readable novel about a Stalin-like dictator, which won the Governor General's Award for Literature.

Posing for the camera at the Klein Symposium at the Université d'Ottawa, May 5, 1974, are the following participants (left to right): Ralph Gustafson, David Lewis, Marya Fiamengo, F. R. Scott, Phyllis Gotlieb, Guy Sylvestre, P. K. Page, Louis Dudek, A. J. M. Smith, Dorothy Livesay, Irving Layton, Seymour Mayne. The portrait on the wall between Sylvestre and Page is that of A. M. Klein. [Concordia University Library, Layton Collection]

Université d'Ottawa This bilingual university, originally founded in 1848, is located in downtown Ottawa. The Morisset Library has an exemplary collection of manuscripts of leading French authors of the nineteenth and twentieth centuries. Available for research purposes are holographs by one hundred or so eminent writers, including the following names (limited to twenty-five): Guillaume Apollinaire, Honoré de Balzac, Charles Baudelaire, Henri Bergson, André Breton, Albert Camus, Paul Claudel, Jean Cocteau, Colette, Gustave Flaubert, André Gide, Victor Hugo, Max Jacob, Stéphane Mallarmé, André Malraux, Guy de Maupassant, François Mauriac, Charles Péguy, Marcel Proust, Arthur Rimbaud, George Sand, Jean-Paul Sartre, Paul Valéry, Paul Verlaine, Emile Zola.

The holdings of the Archives du Centre de Recherche en civilisation Canadienne-française are about evenly divided between material relating to Franco-Ontarians and to Quebec literature and fine arts. Writers who are collected include: William Chapman, Jean Charbonneau, Albert Ferland, Albert Laberge, Jules Tremblay, Rémi Tremblay. Among the historians are Jean Bruchési, Thomas Chapais, and Gustave Lanctôt. The Centre belongs to the School of Graduate Studies and houses research projects concerned with producing a critical edition of the works of François-Xavier Garneau and a new edition of the *Dictionnaire pratique des auteurs québécois.*

Associated with the English Department of the Université d'Ottawa since 1973 is the poet and editor, Seymour Mayne (b. 1944).

Carleton University Carleton University, which was founded in 1942, has been located on its present campus on the outskirts of Ottawa since 1959. It is the home of the Institute of Canadian Studies which, since 1963, has issued the Carleton Library series of reprinted and original paperbacks devoted to Canadian anthropology, economics, geography, history, law, political science, and sociology. The series editor is Michael Gnarowski. Less serious is Carleton's reputation as the "graffiti capital of Canada." It seems more graffiti is reported from its walls and halls than from anywhere else in the country.

Fantasy Capital Despite the description of Ottawa as a lacklustre city and the world's coldest capital after Ulan Bator, the city is not lacking in elements of fantasy. These go beyond the neo-gothic gargoyles on Parliament Hill and the neo-classical ruins at Kingsmere in the Gatineau Hills. The city is home to a school of youngish fantasy writers who meet at the House of Speculative Fiction, 101 Fourth Avenue, a bookstore opened in 1979 that specializes in the literature of the fantastic, managed by the writer Galad Elflandsson (b. 1951), which features works by Charles R. Saunders (b. 1946), Charles de Lint (b. 1951), Gordon Derevanchuk (b. 1952), and bibliographer John Bell (b. 1952). No other city has such a concentration of new writers who specialize in High Fantasy. Montreal comes a close but critical second, with such academic critics as Darko Suvin, David Ketterer, Robert M. Philmus, and Marc Angenot, who publish regularly in *Science-Fiction Studies*. The Ottawa group sponsored the World Fantasy Convention in October 1984.

The Ottawa Fantasists (left to right): Charles de Lint, Gordon Derevanchuk, John Bell, Charles R. Saunders. [Su Rogers]

Archibald Lampman lies in Beechwood Cemetery, Ottawa. The boulder, engraved "LAMPMAN," draws attention to two headstones, both of which have sunken somewhat into the ground. The marker on the left is that of the poet, the one on the right that of his son, born May 1894, died August 1895. [Donna Brouillard]

Beechwood Cemetery   At the entrance to Beechwood Cemetery in Rockcliffe Park is a plaque which reproduces a sonnet, "In Beechwood Cemetery" (1894), the first line of which runs: "Here the dead sleep — the quiet dead. . . ." The poem was written by Archibald Lampman (1861-1899), who lies buried here, as does his friend and fellow poet Duncan Campbell Scott (1862-1947) who wrote of Lampman's burial site: "Above one's unrealizing head the snow will sift, the small ferns rise and the birds come back in nesting time . . . the sternest wind from under the pole star will blow unconfined over his grave, above it the first hepatics will gather in fragile companies, the vesper sparrow will return to nest in the grass, and from a branch of maple to sing in the cool dusk." Also buried in Beechwood Cemetery is the poet W. W. Campbell (1858-1918), whose portrait plaque was stolen from his memorial. Although not buried here, Nicholas Flood Davin (1843-1901), journalist and public figure, has an imposing memorial in Beechwood Cemetery.

"Flowes of dream will spring eternal," reads part of the inscription on the stone bench that marks the grave of William Wilfred Campbell in Beechwood Cemetery, Ottawa. Missing is the medallion of the poet by R. Tait McKenzie. [Terry Keough]

Grave of Duncan Campbell Scott, Beechwood Cemetery, Ottawa. The inscription lacks the traditional dates of birth and death. [Terry Keough]

Ottawa River and Valley
"Today, of course, the Ottawa is regarded as the chief tributary of the St. Lawrence system. Yet *la grande rivière,* which once was itself the master stream of a great system, has retained a genuine air of independence." These are the thoughts of Hugh MacLennan (b. 1907) writing in *The Rivers of Canada* (1961).

The Ottawa River, which is one of the principal tributaries of the St. Lawrence River, acts for some 400 miles of its course as the boundary between the provinces of Ontario and Quebec. Some features of the river and its valley — like Calumet Island, Ont., and the Lièvre, Que. — have strong historic and literary associations. Archibald Lampman (1861-1899) has written two sonnets, "To the Ottawa" and "To the Ottawa River," which evoke the mighty watercourse. Some tales of the mythical lumberjack Paul Bunyan have been localized to the Ottawa valley by John D. Robins in *Logging with Paul Bunyan* (1957). Bernie Bedore (b. 1923), born in Arnprior, has popularized another backwoods strongman, Big Joe Mufferaw, in a series of books beginning with *Tall Tales of Joe Mufferaw* (1966). Stompin' Tom Connors composed the song "Big Joe Mufferaw" (1970) which includes the lines: "The best man we ever saw / Was Big Joe Mufferaw. . . ."

Bernie Bedore lives in McNab Township between Arnprior and Renfrew. A resident of Renfrew is Joan Finnigan (b. 1925), the author of a number of collections of poems, books about the lore of the valley, and the poetic screenplay to the NFB film *The Best Damn Fiddler from Calabogie to Kaladar* (1969).

Henry Wentworth Monck (1859-1896), the visionary, came from March Township in Carleton County. He was called "the Prophet of March" and, according to R. S. Lambert (1894-1981), in *For the Time Is at Hand* (1947), he issued various manifestoes in the 1870s and 1880s calling for the abolition of war and the establishment of a united Christendom with a central government and police force centred in Palestine in the "Land of Israel." He has been credited with first using the phrase

"United Nations." He sat for the figure of Christ in Holman Hunt's painting "Christ in the Temple."

A native of "Gallop" in the Ottawa valley is Bartholomew Bandy, the anti-hero of a series of comic novels by Donald Lamont Jack (b.1924) that commenced with *Three Cheers for Me* (1962) and by 1983 had reached five volumes.

Owen Sound

Buried on the outskirts of Owen Sound, on Georgian Bay, is Tom Thomson (1877-1917), the celebrated painter, who was born in Claremont and raised in Owen Sound. Some paintings by this artist, whose vision of the northern woods inspired the Group of Seven and the literary nationalism of the 1920s and 1930s, are displayed at the Tom Thomson Memorial Gallery and Museum of Fine Art.

Near the Museum is a plaque that honours William "Billy" Bishop (1894-1956), whose experiences as a World War I flying ace served as the basis for the one-man musical revue *Billy Bishop Goes to War* (1981), written by John Gray (b. 1946) and performed by actor Eric Peterson. Buried in the Owen Sound cemetery is Mary Esther MacGregor (1876-1961) who, as Marion Keith, wrote such regional novels as *Duncan Polite* (1905) and *The Silver Maple* (1906).

Paisley

A plaque raised to commemorate the poet Isabella Valancy Crawford (1850-1887) stands in front of the Old Hose Tower, Queen and Goldie streets, in Paisley, southwest of Owen Sound. She was twelve years old in 1858 when she was brought to Paisley by her family, and she lived here for six years. In 1864 the family moved to Lakefield and then Peterborough. Following the death of her father in 1875, with her mother and sister she lived in Toronto where she published at her own expense the single volume of poems to appear during her lifetime, *Old Spookses' Pass, Malcolm's Katie, and Other Poems* (1884). She possessed "the most remarkable mythopoeic imagination in Canadian poetry," wrote Northrop Frye.

Palgrave

Palgrave, north of Brampton, was named after Francis Turner Palgrave (1824-1897), best known for his anthology *The Golden Treasury of the Best Songs and Lyrical Poems in the English Language* (1861), one of the most influential of all anthologies.

The artist and writer David Milne (1882-1953) lived here in 1930-33 and painted and sketched some of his most characteristic work.

Parry Sound

Parry Sound, on Georgian Bay, was the home of Leslie A. Crouch (1915-1969), the country's leading science-fiction fan. Excited about rocket ships before they became space ships, and aliens when they were known as bug-

Parry Sound was named after the Arctic explorer Sir W. E. Parry, but the town had an explorer of even more remote regions in the person of its radio and television repairman, Leslie A. Crouch, whose imagination embraced both space and time. Taken in 1937, these photographs show Crouch, then aged 22, and the family home, with a sign that reads "Crouch Radio Service." Although the sign has been removed, the house still stands. [Ruby Crouch]

eyed monsters, Crouch issued, from the two-storey family home at 41 Waubeek Street, his own science-fiction magazine. He called it *Light* and issued it in mimeographed form to other fans for more than two decades. The full story is told in *Years of Light* (1982) by John Robert Colombo (b. 1936).

Actor and writer Don Harron (b. 1924) created the hick farmer Charlie Farquharson who comes from Parry Sound for the 1952 production of the musical *Spring*

Charlie Farquharson, the hick from Parry Sound, played by Don Harron, drawn by Don Evans who signs his work Isaac Bickerstaff. [Special Collections, University of Calgary Libraries]

Thaw. Charlie is the putative author of Harron's books of humour, beginning with *Charlie Farquharson's History of Canada* (1972) and *Charlie Farquharson's Jogfree of Canada* (1974).

The scholar Kathleen Coburn (b. 1905) acquired the island designated as B578 in Georgian Bay, southwest of Parry Sound, as a summer home in 1939. Here through many hot summers she edited the manuscripts of Samuel Taylor Coleridge (1772-1834). She wrote in her memoir, *In Pursuit of Coleridge* (1977): "As for the editorial process through which Coleridge puts me, I have long thought that the two best places for it have been the British Museum and Georgian Bay. The BM is the one and only library for Coleridge work. . . . But why Georgian Bay? I suppose it is that whereas in other places, in Toronto, in London, any city, the rhythms of life and the rhythm of work are often felt to be in conflict; here on the island, where I am now writing, they seem peculiarly to interact as one harmony, and have been doing so from the beginning and will to the end."

Petawawa

Petawawa, on the Ottawa River between Pembroke and Deep River, is a military camp with prison compound established in 1905. The name is said to be an Indian word meaning "where one hears the noise of the waters." Perhaps the most notable (certainly the most poetic) inmate of Petawawa's prison was the Communist bard Joe Wallace (1895-1975) who was detained in March 1941 under the Defence of Canada Regulations. He was imprisoned until the fall of the following year. He spent twenty-eight days in solitary confinement and the experience was responsible for one of his most vivid poems, "How High, How Wide," which runs: "My prison window is not large, / Five inches high, six inches wide, / Perhaps seven. / Yet it is large enough to show / The whole unfettered to and fro / Of heaven. How high, how wide, is heaven? / Five inches high, six inches wide, / Perhaps seven."

Joe Wallace had his portrait painted by Barker Fairley who commented on the Communist writer: "He stood for something, which is not a bad thing in a poet. . . ." [Barker Fairley]

Peterborough

Peterborough is picturesquely located on the Otonabee River in central Ontario. Lakefield, immediately to the north, is associated with three literary pioneers, Colonel Samuel Strickland (1804-1867) and his two sisters, Catharine Parr Traill (1802-1899) and Susanna Moodie (1803-1885).

Isabella Valancy Crawford A plaque identifies the house at 350 Water Street, at the corner of Charlotte Street, which was occupied by the poet Isabella Valancy Crawford (1850-1887) and her family. They lived here from 1869, following their move from Lakefield, to the death of the physician father in 1875, when Isabella and her mother and sister moved to Toronto. It was in Peterborough that she began to publish her mythopoeic poems. She died in Toronto but is buried in Little Lake Cemetery, Peterborough. Her marker takes the form of a Celtic cross seven feet high on a marble base; the inscription reads "Poet by the Gift of God."

Isabella Valancy Crawford, poet of high romance, in this drawing by Isaac Bickerstaff (artist Don Evans). [Special Collections, University of Calgary Libraries]

Robertson Davies The man-of-letters Robertson Davies (b. 1913) is a man of many parts, who has an allegiance to three communities in Ontario. A number of his novels are set in "Salterton" which has many of the characteristics of Kingston; he served as the first Master of Massey College in Toronto; and from 1942 to 1960 he lived in Peterborough where he was editor and then publisher of the Peterborough *Examiner*, a newspaper owned by the author's father, Senator Davies. He contributed many columns, essays, and editorials (including the only Canadian editorial note on the death of the psychoanalyst Carl Jung) to the pages of the *Examiner*, and no doubt many of his contributions surprised the newspaper's readers if not the Peterborough "clerisy" (those who read books not because they are professionally involved with them but for pleasure and profit).

Davies created the curmudgeonly Samuel Marchbanks for the newspaper's readers. Marchbanks was born at "Skunk's Misery, Ont." an "undetermined number of years ago" and is "a masculinist (as opposed to a feminist)." His views are set forth in three collections: *The Diary of Samuel Marchbanks* (1947), *The Table Talk of Samuel Marchbanks* (1949), and *Marchbanks' Almanack* (1967). Essays originally published in the newspaper's columns reappeared in *A Voice from the Attic* (1961) and such recent compilations as *One Half of Robertson Davies* (1977) and *The Enthusiasms of Robertson Davies* (1979).

Nearby Douro Township is the setting of Davies' historical play *At My Heart's Core* (1950).

Hugh Kenner Hugh Kenner (b. 1923), the literary critic, was born in Peterborough and educated at the University of Toronto where he contributed to student publications. He took his M.A. in 1946 and then taught at Assumption College, now the University of Windsor. In 1948 he left for the United States where he has enjoyed a notable career as an apologist for Modernist literature, especially the work of Ezra Pound. Kenner Collegiate Vocational Institute on Monaghan Road South was named in his honour.

Margaret Laurence The novelist Margaret Laurence (b. 1926) settled in 1970 in an old house on the outskirts of Peterborough and served as chancellor of Trent University. She wrote *The Diviners* (1975) in a small cedar cabin on the Otonabee River. She called it "The Shack" in *Heart of a Stranger* (1976) where she wrote: "My best place at the moment is very different, although I guess it has some of the attributes of that long-ago place. It is a small cedar cabin on the Otonabee river in southern Ontario. I've lived three summers there, writing, bird-watching, river-watching. I sometimes feel sorry for the people in speedboats who spend their weekends zinging up and down the river at about a million miles an hour. For all they're able to see, the riverbanks might just as well be green concrete and the river itself flowing with molten plastic."

For a time she called this shack "Manawaka" after the fictional community based on Neepawa, Man. She subsequently moved to Lakefield. She has written on the subject of Peterborough in "Down East" in *Heart of a Stranger* (1976): "To me, this small city on the Otonabee river meant Robertson Davies' country — some of his books, *The Diary of Samuel Marchbanks* and others, and himself those years ago as the fiery editor of the Peterborough *Examiner*. The area remains so related, but now I see it as the historical home of Susanna Moodie as well, that snobbish composer of dreadful patriotic poems and writer of *Roughing It in the Bush*, that genteel and self-dramatizing English lady who never really came to terms with what was a very raw land when she settled here in the 1830s. More especially the area now evokes Catharine Parr Traill, who made this land her own, who named many of the wildflowers, and who lived hereabouts until she died at a very old age — a woman both gentle and strong."

Trent University Is there a university in the world more attractively situated than Trent University, with its campus on the gentle Otonabee River to the north of Peterborough? Trent was founded in 1963 and patterned after Oxford's tutorial and seminar system. Since 1966 it has published the *Journal of Canadian Studies,* and its first president, Thomas H. B. Symons, was chairman of the Commission on Canadian Studies. The two-volume report was called *To Know Ourselves* (1975) and it argued: "The most valid and compelling argument for Canadian studies is the importance of self-knowledge, the need to know and to understand ourselves; who we are; where we are in time and space; where we have been; where we are going; what we possess; what our responsibilities are to ourselves and others." The one-volume version was titled *The Symons Report* (1978).

The Thomas J. Bata Library of Trent University has a number of special collections. There is correspondence from Robert W. Service and Frances Stewart and manuscript material of the historian Edwin C. Guillet. The Shell Canada Fund for Canadian Literature made possible the purchase of the library of modern Canadian poetry and the personal papers of A.J.M. Smith. These are located in the A.J.M. Smith Conference Room.

Few universities anywhere in the world are more pleasingly situated than Trent University on the Otonabee River. [Ontario Ministry of Tourism and Recreation]

Poetry Lake See NOKOMIS LAKE.

Port Arthur See THUNDER BAY.

Port Burwell

The naturalist and writer Fred Bodsworth (b. 1918) was born in Port Burwell, on Lake Erie. Among his novels set in the wilds are *The Strange One* (1959), *The Atonement of Ashley Morden* (1964), *The Sparrow's Fall* (1967), and *Last of the Curlews* (1972).

Port Colborne

The first "Canada Day" was held in the spring of 1970 in Port Colborne, at the Lake Erie end of the Welland Canal. It was organized by James (Jim) Foley, an English teacher and Canadian literature enthusiast at the Port Colborne High School, to celebrate Canadian sovereignty and literature. A busload of writers arrived from Toronto and surrounding areas to recite their work, address teachers and students, and conduct teaching and writing workshops. Since 1973 Foley has been a member of the faculty of Mohawk College, Hamilton.

Port Dover

The poet and writer Raymond Knister (1899-1932) is buried in Port Dover Cemetery which is located on the Blue Line road at Highway 6 which leads into the town of Port Dover on Lake Erie. The plot is marked by a flat slab on which is inscribed the full text of his moving poem "Change" which concludes: "I shall not wonder more, then, / But I shall know. Leaves change, and birds, flowers, / And after years are still the same." Knister, born in a farmhouse near what is today known as Ruscom Station, between Leamington on Lake Erie and Stoney Point on Lake St. Clair, was raised in Comber, Cedar Springs, and Norwood, villages generally east of Ruscom Station. His poems evoke these farming communities. He lived on a farm in the Port Dover area in 1929-31, and drowned off Stoney Point. His death was a major loss to Canadian literature. He once wrote: "We have wanted to discover and create a new heaven and a new earth here in Canada, and to make others see it."

Port Hope

Port Hope is a picturesque town on Lake Ontario east of Oshawa. In the churchyard of St. Mark's Anglican Church, erected in 1822, lie the remains of Vincent Massey (1887-1967), the first native-born Governor General (1952-59). Like his younger brother, the actor Raymond Massey, the different roles he played in public life have been variously interpreted. He was appointed chairman of the Massey Commission, and its famous *Report* (1951) laid the foundation for the creation of the Canada Council in 1957. Massey died at "Batterwood," his country estate on the outskirts of Port Hope. Here, in his twenty-five-room mansion, was held the Port Hope Conference of 1933 which dedicated the Liberal Party to social change.

Also dedicated to social change, but of another order, is the author Farley Mowat (b. 1921), who has lived with his writer wife Claire Mowat in Port Hope since the early 1970s.

Port Rowan   See LONG POINT.

Prescott

Northeast of Brockville on the St. Lawrence is situated Prescott where Fort Wellington, now part of the National Park, saw action during the War of 1812 and the Rebellion of 1837. The English novelist Anthony Trollope (1815-1882) felt Prescott was not worth fighting for, at least in 1861. He wrote in *North America* (1862): "From Ottawa we went by rail to Prescott, which is surely one of the most wretched little places to be found in any country."

The newspaper editor and author Bruce Hutchison (b. 1920) was born on Dibble Street in Prescott but raised in Cranbrook, B.C., and then Merritt and finally Victoria. The exuberant nationalism of *The Unknown Country* (1942) and *The Incredible Canadian* (1953) about Mackenzie King inspired a generation of readers. He edited successively the Winnipeg *Free*

This is the last known photograph of Raymond Knister, Port Dover, August 1932. The poet is holding his daughter Imogen. [Imogen Givens]

The poet Raymond Knister is buried in the cemetery between Simcoe and Port Dover. "The stone is blue marble," noted his daughter Imogen Givens. "My father used to quote poetry constantly and of his favourites was (as Mother recalls it): 'A poet needs three things — space around his feelings, contemplation that desires enough, and a well-wrought grave.' Mother thought of that quotation when she chose the large flat blue marble stone. It must be about six feet long. She had them carve a sketch of his head in the marble from a pen-and-ink sketch she had made when they were first married in 1927. It was her idea to have the poem 'Change' inscribed. Many young writers and students have come to see the grave. Len Gasparini of Windsor wrote a poem about it called 'At Raymond Knister's Grave.'" [Imogen Givens]

Press, the *Victoria Times*, and the *Vancouver Sun*. His autobiography appeared as *The Far Side of the Street* (1976). He lives in retirement in Victoria, B.C.

Queenston

Queenston, on the Niagara River north of Niagara Falls, is historic ground. On these slopes, on October 13, 1812, the Battle of Queenston Heights was fought. The American invaders retreated. The British leader, Sir Isaac Brock, killed in action, lies buried beneath the impressive monument that towers over the countryside, erected in 1824 and re-erected in 1854, inspiring Charles Sangster (1822-1893) to compose his tribute "Brock" which begins: "One voice, one people, one in heart. . . ."

If Brock is the "hero" of the War of 1812, the "heroine" is Laura Secord, the Loyalist lady who was in her late thirties when she made the midnight trek through the woods from Queenston to Beaver Dam to warn the British of the impending American attack. Although she showed her heroism in June 1813, it was not until 1861 that her act of loyalty was recognized by the visiting Prince of Wales, later Edward VII. She is buried in Drummond Hill Cemetery. There is a monument to her at Queenston Heights, dedicated in 1910, and her frame house at Queenston was restored by the Laura Secord candy company in 1969.

Close to Laura Secord's house is the two-storey stone house occupied by William Lyon Mackenzie (1795-1861). Here, in 1824, he founded the weekly *Colonial Advocate* which he continued to publish from Toronto, then called York. Mackenzie's house has been restored, and among the displays are the desks that belonged to the newspaper publisher and the novelist William Kirby (1817-1906).

On the grounds of the Laura Secord Memorial School, 45 Princess Street, was unveiled a plaque to commemorate Major John Richardson (1796-1852), pioneer historian, author and soldier. Born in Queenston, he wrote *Tecumseh* (1828), a poem, and *Wacousta* (1832), a novel about the capture of Fort Detroit.

C.W. Jefferys' drawing of Laura Secord Telling Her Story to Fitzgibbon, 1813. [C-70253 / Public Archives Canada]

Laura Secord Homestead with an Ontario Historic Sites Board plaque, Queenston, Ont. [Ontario Ministry of Tourism and Recreation]

Inspired by Brock's monument, Francis Sparshott (b. 1926) wrote "The Ballad of Queenston Heights" in *The Naming of the Beasts* (1979). One verse runs: "Who is that sweating officer / waving a useless sword? / That's General Sir Isaac Brock / who wants to be a Lord."

Rabelais Creek

Rabelais Creek, north of Sault Ste. Marie, brings to mind the French satirist, François Rabelais (1494-1553). Nearby are two associated sites, Cape Gargantua and Pantagruel Bay, named after the gigantic hero and heroine of his burlesque *Gargantua and Pantagruel* (1530). Apparently the shape of Cape Gargantua accounts for its name. Associated features in the vicinity are Gargantua Bay, Gargantua Island, Gargantua Lake, Gargantua Harbour, and even a dispersed rural community named, simply, Gargantua. The first recorded use of the giant's name in the region is on a map of 1826.

Brock's Monument, which overlooks the gardens of Queenston Heights Park, has occasioned much versification. [Parks Canada / F. Cattroll]

Red Rock

Northeast of Thunder Bay, at Red Rock, was the site of the largest of the eight internment camps for the 2,290 refugees from Germany and Austria who were deported from England to Canada and were mistakenly treated by the Ministry of Defence as enemy aliens rather than as friendly aliens. They were interned between 1940 and 1943, with more than half going to Red Rock. The rest were sent to smaller camps located at Monteith, Ont.; Quebec City, Ile-aux-Noix, Sherbrooke, Farnham, and Trois-Rivières, Que.; and Little River, N.B.

The novelist Eric Koch (b. 1919) was one of the refugees, and in his study of this episode, *Deemed Suspect: A Wartime Blunder* (1980), he described conditions at Red Rock and at the other internment camps. Noting the intelligence, talent, and sophistication of these men — there were no women among them — he observed their subsequent careers and the fact that many elected to become Canadian citizens. What follows is a list of twenty-two of the refugees who achieved success in literature and the arts — or notoriety.

Gregory Baum (religious thinker), Helmut Blume (musicologist), Ernest Borneman (sociologist), Oscar Cahen (artist), Emile Fackenheim (philosopher), Klaus Fuchs (atomic scientist, spy), Freddy Grant (composer; his hit song "You'll Get Used to It" premiered on a prison ship), Ernest "Putzi" Hanfstaengl (Hitler's favourite pianist, socialite), William B. Heckscher (art historian), F. D. Hoeniger (English professor), Walter Homburger (manager of the Toronto Symphony Orchestra), Hans Kahle (former commander of the XIth International Brigade, Spanish Civil War; original of "General Hans" in Ernest Hemingway's *For Whom the Bell Tolls*), Helmut Kallmann (musicologist), Walter Klinkhoff (Montreal art dealer), Eric Koch (TV executive, novelist), Franz Kraemer (musical director), Henry Kreisel (novelist), Kaspar Naegele (sociologist), John Newmark (pianist), Kurt Swinton (publishing executive), Arturo Vivante (short-story writer; released through the intervention of the actress Ruth Draper, Vivante described the episode and life in Toronto in stories published in *The New Yorker*), Charles Wasserman (journalist, broadcaster, novelist).

Renfrew

Here, west of Ottawa, an accident turned a hobo into a poet. Hopping a freight train that was pulling out of Renfrew, W. H. Davies (1871-1940), a Welsh-born hobo and peddlar, fell on the tracks. His right leg was so crushed it had to be amputated at the knee. His wanderings curtailed, Davies settled for a more sedentary life in London, England, where he went on to write some three dozen books, including *The Autobiography of a Super-Tramp* (1908), with a preface by George Bernard Shaw. Davies is principally remembered for his *Autobiography*, for his pleasant poem "Leisure," which begins: "What is this life if, full of care, / We have no time to stand and stare?"

Ridgeway

Here, west of Fort Erie, took place the Battle of Ridgeway in which, in June 1886, the Canadian volunteers repulsed the Fenian raiders from the United States. Set in Buffalo, Fort Erie, and Ridgeway is the novel *In the Midst of Alarms* (1894), by Robert Barr (1850-1912), which tells the story of the invasion in human terms.

Rob Roy

Rob Roy, southwest of Collingwood, was named after the Scottish outlaw whose exploits inspired Sir Walter Scott (1771-1832) to write the romantic novel *Rob Roy* (1817). There is a Rob Roy Island in Skeleton Lake, Muskoka.

Robinson Lake   See CRUSOE LAKE.

Roblin Lake   See AMELIASBURG.

Rockton

Rockton, west of Dundas, is the birthplace and burial place of the journalist and versifier Robert Kirkland Kernighan (1857-1926) who called himself "The Khan" and wrote from "The Wigwam," the log cabin he built at Rushdale Farm. His best-known verse is "The Men of the Northern Zone" which begins: "This is the land of the true and the leaf, / Where freedom is bred in the bone — / The Southerner never shall place his heel / On the men of the Northern Zone." It appears in his collection *The Khan's Book of Verse* (1925).

Rockwood

Rockwood is a village northeast of Guelph. Here flourished the Rockwood Academy between 1850 and 1882. The daughter of the principal of this private school was the poet Agnes Ethelwyn Wetherald (1857-1940), whose work has not weathered well. A plaque marks the

C.W. Jefferys' drawing of the Rockwood Academy and Principal Wetherald. [C-69073 / *Public Archives Canada*]

building which is now privately owned. Educated at the Academy was Archibald MacMurchy (1832-1912), author of *Handbook of Canadian Literature* (1906).

St. Augustine

Born in the small community of St. Augustine, northwest of Goderich, was Harry J. Boyle (b. 1915), broadcaster and author, who recreates his rural Irish-Catholic boyhood in such humorous books as *Mostly in Clover* (1961), *Homebrew and Patches* (1963), *Memories of a Catholic Boyhood* (1973), and *The Luck of the Irish* (1975).

St. Catharines

St. Catharines is situated by the Welland Canal, northwest of Niagara Falls. Among other things it is the birthplace of the playwright Bernard Slade (b. 1930), author of *Same Time, Next Year* (1975) and *Tribute* (1978).

Downtown St. Catharines will feel familiar to fans of the detective novels of Howard Engel (b. 1931). The author was raised in the city which appears as "Grantham" in the Benny Cooperman mysteries which include, to date: *The Suicide Murders* (1980), *The Ransom Game* (1981), *Murder on Location* (1982), and *Murder in Algonquin Park* (1983). Cooperman has an office located above a woman's clothing store at "200 St. Andrew's Street." (There is a women's clothing store at 200 St. Paul Street.) Cooperman frequents the cafeteria in the "United Cigar Store" on the north side of the same street. (There is an eatery called Bubbles not far from the women's clothing store.) The mystery fan could find many other parallels between Benny Cooperman's turf and the terrain of St. Catharines.

St. Elmo   See GLENGARRY COUNTY.

St. Thomas

Struck down and killed by a Grand Trunk train at St. Thomas, south of London, was Jumbo, the best-loved circus elephant of all time. The mammoth, African-born pachyderm was a featured performer with the Barnum and Bailey Circus (The Greatest Show on Earth) when the accident occurred, September 15, 1885. A plaque in St. Thomas recalls the tragic event. Editorial writers of the day quoted the following lines from Shakespeare's *Macbeth* (1606): "Hath borne his faculties so meek, hath been / So mild in his great office, that his virtues / Will plead like angels, trumpet-tongued, against / The deep damnation of his taking-off." The word "jumbo," as a synonym for great size, derives from the African reference to Mumbo Jumbo, but was popularized by the elephant Jumbo (1861-1885). Tom Thumb, one of Barnum's featured performers, was also hit by the train and suffered a broken leg. The stuffed carcass of Jumbo was displayed and eventually ended up in the Tufts University Museum, near Boston, where a fire in 1975 destroyed both the carcass and the museum. Jumbo's skeleton is displayed at the Museum of Natural History in New York. The huge bones are covered with graffiti.

In the Elgin County Court House at St. Thomas, south of London, a plaque honours the historian George M. Wrong (1860-1948) who was born in nearby Gravesend. He became the first Professor of Modern History at the University of Toronto in 1895. In the words of the plaque, "A believer in the historian's moral duty to interpret the past for society's present needs, he viewed Canadian history in terms of the country's British and French origins, and the American presence."

Sainte-Marie-among-the-Hurons   See MIDLAND.

Sandy Lake Reserve

The traditions of the Plains Crees are maintained at the Sandy Lake Reserve which is located in the vicinity of Lake Nipigon. Although born in Fort William, the Ojibwa artist Norval Morrisseau (b. 1932) was raised by his grandfather on this Reserve where, as Copper Thunderbird, he learned the secular and sacred lore. He wrote and illustrated *Legends of My People, the Great Ojibway* (1965) and illustrated *Windigo and Other Tales of the Ojibway* (1969) by Herbert T. Schwarz.

Born on the Sandy Lake Reserve was Carl Ray (1943-1978), the Ojibwa artist. The grandson of a Cree medicine man, he illustrated *Sacred Legends of the Sandy Lake Cree* (1971) by James R. Stevens (b. 1940). Also born here was Edward Ahenakew (1885-1961) who preserved the legends of his people in *Voices of the Plains Cree* (1973).

Sappho Island

Sappho Island, in Lake Muskoka, was named in honour of the celebrated Greek poetess, Sappho. It is the only place in Canada that recalls the poetess from Lesbos who lived about 600 B.C.

Sarnia

Situated at the southern tip of Lake Huron, Sarnia became the setting of the denouement of the real-life drama

Morley Callaghan (centre) chats with director Ron Weyman and actor John Vernon on the set of the CBC-TV production More Joy in Heaven, *telecast August 17, 1973.* [PAC /National Film, Television and Sound Archives]

involving Norman "Red" Ryan (1895-1936), the celebrated bank robber, who was killed in a gun battle with the local police when he tried to rob a liquor store in the city, May 24, 1936. Ryan was supposedly rehabilitated, and this irony led Morley Callaghan (b. 1903) to ponder the vagaries of human nature in the person of Kip Caley in his novel *More Joy in Heaven* (1937).

Sault Ste. Marie

The Soo, as the city between Lake Superior and Lake Huron is popularly known, occasioned the following generalization made by Norman Levine (b. 1924) in *Canada Made Me* (1958, 1979): "No one is really a stranger in Canada if he was brought up in a small town. They remain so much the same across the country: a vast repetition, not only of the Main Street, the side streets, the railway track, the river; but the same dullness and boredom."

Morley Torgov (b. 1928) did not find this to be so. In his fictional memoir, *A Good Place to Come From* (1974), he celebrated the thirty or forty Jewish families who lived near the intersection of Queen and Bruce streets in downtown Sault Ste. Marie in the late 1930s and early 1940s. "The Soo" figures as Steelton in *The Outside Chance of Maximilian Glick* (1982), in which an ultra-orthodox rabbi is dispatched to serve the needs of a conservative congregation. The humorous novel is based on an actual incident that occurred in Moncton, N.B.

One remembers Henry Wadsworth Longfellow (1807-1882) and *The Song of Hiawatha* (1855) in the 240-acre Hiawatha Park. But to recall more of the Indian past of this region, one must cross the border by bridge and visit Sault Ste. Marie, Michigan. The American city may be smaller than the Canadian one, but it offers a site of interest to Canadians: the house once occupied by Henry Rowe Schoolcraft (1793-1864), the American Indian agent who was married to the daughter of an Ojibwa chief. Schoolcraft was among the first to translate native songs into English. In one of this ethnological publications, he confused the legendary Hiawatha with the mythical Nanabozho, and in the process misled Longfel-

Henry Wadsworth Longfellow, engraved by S. Hollyier. [PAC C-12178]

low in the composition of *The Song of Hiawatha*. Longfellow acknowledged his debt for "curious Indian legends, drawn chiefly from the various and valuable writings of Mr. Schoolcraft, to whom the literary world is greatly indebted for his indefatigable zeal in rescuing from oblivion so much of the legendary lore of the Indians."

Schoolcraft's house was moved from 705 East Portage Avenue to the grounds of the Edison Sault Power Company. In this house, now open as a museum, but much altered from its original appearance, Schoolcraft entertained Anna Brownell Jameson (1794-1860) who described the meeting in *Winter Studies and Summer Rambles in Canada* (1838). They visited a Chippewa tribe and Jameson was adopted by it.

Mackinac is a modern abbreviation of the older name Michilimackinac, which applies to both the Island and the Straits that provide a channel between Lake Michigan and Lake Huron. The Mackinac area, ceded to the United States by the Treaty of Ghent, is now part of upperstate Michigan. The area lies generally south of Sault Ste. Marie, Ont.

In a celebrated incident during the Conspiracy of Pontiac, the British fort on the south shore was entered by Ojibwas through the ruse of playing lacrosse and seized. The event occurred on June 2, 1763, and it caught the eye of the historical novelist Sir Gilbert Parker (1862-1932) who tells the story of the seizure in *When Valmond Came to Pontiac* (1895).

On Mackinac Island, the State Park has many historic buildings and displays, including an Indian Dormitory with a mural that portrays scenes from *Hiawatha*. Of related interest is Minnehaha Park in Minneapolis, Minnesota, with its Minnehaha Falls and its statues of Hiawatha and his beloved Minnehaha.

Scugog Island

Lake Scugog lies southwest of Peterborough. On Scugog Island, on the grounds of the Scugog Shores Historical Museum, about one kilometre north of Highway 7A, there is a plaque to honour James (Jimmy) Frise (1891-1948), the popular cartoonist who was born here and educated at Myrtle, Seagrave, and Port Perry. He is best remembered for the weekly half-page cartoon feature, called "Birdseye Centre," which depicted life among farmers and fishermen, urchins and dogs, in a fictional community set somewhere in Ontario. It was created by Frise, originally as "Life's Little Comedies," and carried by the *Star Weekly* (1921-47) and as "Juniper Junction" by *Weekend Magazine* (1947-48). His friend and sometime collaborator Greg Clark (1892-1977) introduced *Birdseye Centre* (1973), a selection of Frise's visual — and sometimes verbal — humour.

Shakespeare

Some miles southeast of the city of Stratford is the village of Shakespeare, named in honour of William Shakespeare (1564-1616).

Actor Robert Christie played the part of David Willson, *the religious leader who built the Sharon Temple, in the CBC-TV special* Music at Sharon Temple. [CBC]

Frederick Philip Grove from the frontispiece of In Search of Myself *(1946). [C-36086 / Public Archives Canada]*

Sharon

The village of Sharon is located north of Newmarket. The King James Version of the Bible, which dates from 1611, influenced the name of the village and the design and decor of the Temple of Peace at Sharon. This three-storey building of unusual design was erected for the purposes of worship in 1825-31 by David Willson (1778-1866), leader of the Children of Peace. An offshoot of the Quakers, this group was inspired by music and the symbolism of the Bible. The building, constructed along the lines of Solomon's Temple, includes a walnut reconstruction of the Ark of the Covenant and a many-stepped Jacob's Ladder. In 1918, the Sharon Temple was restored as a museum, and it is now the setting for an annual music festival.

Shelley Lake

Southeast of Atikokan may be found Shelley Lake, named after the English poet Percy Bysshe Shelley (1792-1822). Close by is Keats Lake.

Sibbald Point   See SUTTON.

Simcoe

A plaque in the Eva Brook Donly Museum in Simcoe, south of Brantford, recalls the life and work of Egerton Ryerson (1803-1882), one-time editor of the *Christian Guardian* and chief superintendent of education for Upper Canada (1844-76). In the wording of the plaque, "He was largely responsible for shaping On-tario's present school system." Of literary interest are his autobiography, *The Story of My Life* (1883), and *My Dearest Sophie* (1955), letters to his daughter edited by C. B. Sissons.

North of Simcoe, on Highway 24, is the small farm owned by the novelist Frederick Philip Grove (1879-1948) and occupied by him and his family from 1930 to his death. Here he wrote *Two Generations* (1939) which is "a story of present-day Ontario" set in "Sleepy Hollow," a district modelled on Spooky Hollow discussed by Harry B. Barrett (b. 1922) in *Lore and Legends of Long Point* (1977). While here he also wrote *The Master of the Mill* (1944). The farmhouse is located on the northwest corner of the intersection of Highway 24 and Concession Road 13, approximately two miles north of Simcoe. The house, which dates back to 1830, with additions in the late 1800s and by Grove in 1930-33, is still owned by the family and used as a "country retreat."

On a tobacco farm some ten miles west of Simcoe, the young Hugh Garner (1913-1979) worked as a primer for $3 a day in 1939, until the outbreak of World War Two. The experience served him well, supplying the settings and characterizations behind two of his most anthologized short stories, "The Conversion of Willie Heaps" and "Hunky."

Six Nations Reserve

The tales and traditions of the 9,500 Indians who live on the Six Nations Reserve on the Grand River, southeast of Brantford, have been preserved in numerous books. The most powerful tradition concerns the establishment of the Great Peace, as the Iroquois Confederacy is called, among the warlike Six Nations (Mohawk, Oneida, Onondaga, Cayuga, Seneca, Tuscarora). Its power and importance have been noted by observers as dissimilar as Friedrich Engels (1820-1895) and Edmund Wilson (1895-1972). The tradition is descriptive of events "which as far as can be ascertained took place about the year 1390," according to Duncan Campbell Scott (1862-1947), the poet and later deputy superintendent of the Indian Affairs branch of the Dominion government, presenting the text of the "Traditional History of the Iroquois" to the Royal Society of Canada on May 16, 1911.

A ceremonial event is enacted at the Six Nations Reserve, the country's largest, near Brantford. [Ontario Ministry of Tourism and Recreation]

The Confederacy and Longfellow The traditional founder of the Confederacy is the semi-legendary Iroquois prophet, statesman, and lawgiver named Dekanahwideh. After establishing the Great Peace, he spoke these last words: "If the Great Peace should fail, call on my name in the bushes, and I will return." Then he sailed away in his stone canoe. He was assisted by the semi-legendary Hiawatha who, thanks to Henry Wadsworth Longfellow (1807-1882) and his narrative *The Song of Hiawatha* (1855), is the world's best-known North American Indian. The Iroquois chief was born an Onondagan, raised a Huron, and adopted by Mohawks. Longfellow merged his identity with that of the mythical Nanabozho, the Algonkian culture hero. According to the latter tradition, as recounted by Charles M. Skinner in *Myths and Legends of Our Own Land* (1896), when Hiawatha completed his task he stepped into his stone canoe and disappeared "in the spaces of the sky." There is no memorial to Longfellow at the Six Nations Reserve, though there is a marble bust of the poet at Grand Pré, N.S., in gratitude for his poetic narrative of Acadian life. There is a bust of the poet in Westminster Abbey, London, and his principal home — The Longfellow-Craigie House, 105 Brattle Street, Boston — has the upright desk in the study where he wrote many of his poetic narratives.

Chiefswood, the childhood home of Pauline Johnson, was erected in 1853 by Chief G. H. M. Johnson of the Six Nations as a wedding present for his English bride, Emily S. Howells, a relation of the distinguished Boston literary family. This brochure dates from the restoration of Chiefswood, officially opened on June 8, 1960. [Ontario Ministry of Tourism and Recreation]

Pauline Johnson The finest residence on the reserve is Chiefswood, where Pauline Johnson (1861-1913), the Mohawk poet, was born. This stately, two-storey residence was erected in 1853 by the poet's father on the north bank of the Grand River between the villages of Onondaga and Middleport and restored in 1963. The Prince of Wales visited Chiefswood and Alexander Graham Bell, who lived in Brantford, was a frequent guest a decade or so later. Pauline Johnson wrote her earliest poems here and only left in 1884 to live in nearby Brantford. After many years on tour she retired to Vancouver in 1909. Chiefswood, now a museum, has been restored to recall the 1870s. Among the memorabilia and mementos of a more leisured age is the writing desk on which she penned her first poems.

Traditional Tales The Indian reserves may be seen as national resources, as they are repositories of traditions that, from time to time, are revealed through word of mouth, the medium of print, or more recently in drawings and paintings. A great many legends and tales told on the Six Nations Reserve have been anchored in print, but a bibliography of them here is beside the point. Ojibwa traditions have been told by Patronella Johnston in *Tales of Nokomis* (1970), and Alma Greene (1896-1984) has recorded Mohawk traditional lore in *Forbidden Voice* (1971) and *Tales of the Mohawks* (1975).

Slough of Despond

Christian must pass through the "miry" Slough of

Despond, described in *Pilgrim's Progress* (1678) by John Bunyan (1628-1688). There is another Slough of Despond in Keppel Township, Grey County.

Southampton
Anglican rector at Southampton, on Lake Huron, was William Wilfred Campbell (1858-1918), the poet, from 1889 to 1891, after which he left the Church and became a civil servant in Ottawa.

Stoney Point
About midway between Chatham and Windsor is Stoney Point. Here, in the waters of Lake St. Clair, drowned Raymond Knister (1899-1932), the poet and story writer.

"Stoverville"   See BROCKVILLE.

Stratford
Stratford is pleasantly situated on the banks of the Avon River which is a tributary of the Thames River. The city owes its name to William "Tiger" Dunlop (1792-1848), author and agent of the Canada Company, who decided in 1831 that the tiny settlement on the banks of the Avon deserved a more imposing name than Little Thames. So he called it after Stratford-upon-Avon, the birthplace of England's leading dramatist, William Shakespeare (1564-1616). If he had left the name as it was, would there be today a Stratford Festival at Little Thames?

The name and association with the Bard of Avon so intrigued Tom Patterson (b. 1920), a Stratford-born, Toronto-based trade-magazine editor, that he devoted all his efforts to creating in his native city a summer theatre devoted to the works of the classical repertoire. His obsession became a reality on the evening of July 13, 1953, when Alec Guinness made a dramatic entrance onto the makeshift stage under the canvas tent, reciting the opening lines of *Richard III* which begin: "Now is the winter of our discontent / Made glorious summer by this son of York." The first seasons were directed by Tyrone Guthrie (1900-1971). The permanent Festival Theatre came into use in 1957, the reconditioned Avon Theatre

The silhouette of the original Stratford Festival Tent, photographed in 1954, inspired the architect Robert Fairfax's design for the Stratford Festival Theatre, opened three years later. [Stratford Festival /Peter Smith, Robert C. Ragsdale]

Alec Guinness on the Stratford Stage as the hunchback king, Richard III. [Startford Festival]

Droeshout's celebrated engraving of William Shakespeare from the First Folio. [Metropolitan Toronto Library]

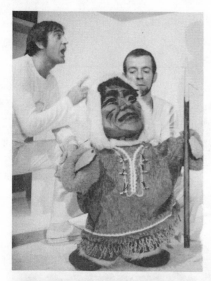

Inook, the marionette, is adjusted by puppeteers prior to the 1973 premier of Henry Beissel's poetic play Inook and the Sun. *[Stratford Festival / Robert C. Ragsdale]*

The cast of James Reaney's Colours in the Dark, *produced in 1967, included Douglas Rain, Martha Henry, Sandy Webster, Mary Hitch, and Heath Lamberts. [Stratford Festival / Douglas Spillane]*

Maggie Smith played the Queen of Egypt in the 1976 production of Antony and Cleopatra. *[Stratford Festival / Zoe Dominic]*

and the experimental Third Stage in 1971. Thus was born the famous Stratford Festival.

There are busts in the foyer of the Festival Theatre of the founder, Tom Patterson (by Alan Jarvis), and of the first artistic director, Tyrone Guthrie (by Ursula Hanes). Guthrie collaborated with artist Grant Macdonald and Robertson Davies (b. 1913) on three books devoted to the Festival seasons. These are *Renown at Stratford* (1953), *Twice Have the Trumpets Sounded* (1954), and *Thrice the Brinded Cat Hath Mew'd* (1955). Guthrie's own autobiography, *A Life in the Theatre* (1959), contains a chapter on the beginnings of Stratford.

Although devoted to the classical repertoire, the Festival has comissioned original plays. *Colours in the Dark,* premiered in 1967, was among the earliest of these. It was written by the poet and dramatist James Reaney (b. 1926) who was born on the family farm on the outskirts of Stratford. The location of the farm was Lot 39, Concessions I and II, South Easthope, Perth County. "Our farm had the most complex history imaginable," wrote the poet, who has visualized it in an emblem poem called "The Farm."

Reaney's writing is rich in regional memories and images. In "The Royal Visit" (1949) he poetically celebrated the visit of King George VI and Queen Elizabeth in 1939: "I'll remember it to my dying day." A *Suit of Nettles* (1958) is a suite of poems set in an Ontario barnyard. An Ontario town not unlike Stratford is the setting of *Night-Blooming Cereus* (1959), the chamber opera with music by John Beckwith. *The Killdeer* (1960), his verse drama, is set on a small Ontario farm. The Stratford Festival presented his play *Colours in the Dark* in 1967. Reaney's most moving tribute to Stratford remains *Twelve Letters to a Small Town* (1962), a suite of poems which begins with an evocation of the Avon River: "What did the Indians call you? / For you do not flow / With English accents." Local references — to the High School, Public Library, King William Street, Shakespearian Gardens — abound.

Born at Stratford were Kathleen Lizars (d. 1931) and her sister Robina Lizars (d. 1918) who together wrote a number of books including *In the Days of the Canada Company* (1896), *Humours of '37* (1897), and *Committed to His Charge* (1900). The latter catches the ambience of a community like Stratford.

Theatre-goers may well ponder the lines of James McIntyre (1827-1906), poet and furniture dealer and author of *Musings on the Banks of the Canadian Thames* (1884), who rhymed wretchedly: "For here in Stratford every ward / Is named from dramas of great bard, / Here you may roam o'er Romeo, / Or glance on Juliet bestow."

Sudbury

The image that comes to mind when one thinks of Sudbury, west of North Bay, is the thirty-foot Big

Nickel which rises above the Canadian Centennial Numismatic Park outside the mining centre. It towers over its neighbours, including the Copper Penny, the Twenty-Dollar Gold Piece, the 1964 "Kennedy" Fifty-cent Piece, and the U.S. Penny.

Raymond Souster (b. 1921) wrote "Very Short Poem" (1969) which runs, in its entirety: ". . . But only God can make a tree. / (He'll never try it in Sudbury.)" Miriam Waddington (b. 1917) wrote in "Dead Lakes" in *Driving Home* (1972): "And I search / for the living water / in the dead lakes / of Sudbury / and I search / for a living element / in the dead places / of my country."

Laurentian University, the bilingual institution founded in Sudbury in 1960, is a federation of church-related educational institutions with three affiliated colleges, Algoma College in Sault Ste. Marie, Nipissing College in North Bay, and Collège de Hearst in Hearst. Laurentian has a department of folklore, founded by Germain Lemieux, which specializes in Indian, French, and English songs.

In the 1960s, NASA leased an area of land to the west of Sudbury as a training ground for astronauts who were scheduled to go to the moon. The site was believed to be geologically similar to the moon since a meteor had come to earth here, creating the Sudbury basin and the mineral mix that gave the town its basic industry.

In no way connected with NASA's use of the land is its employment by the Strugatsky brothers — the Russian science-fiction writing team of Arkady Strugatsky (b. 1925) and Boris Strugatsky (b. 1931) — who used Sudbury as a model community in their thought-provoking short novel *Roadside Picnic* (1972, 1977). The city of Harmont has a good many of the characteristics of Sudbury. Here in the novel is located a branch of the International Institute for Extraterrestrial Culture, for Harmont is one of the world's six Visitation Zones — a dumping ground for alien artifacts with inexplicable properties. The novel concerns the changes brought about by the introduction of these items into society through the illegal services of "stalkers." It leaves Sudbury one of the scariest places on earth. •

Sundridge

On the outskirts of Sundridge, northeast of Parry Sound, is High Rock Park, on a knoll overlooking Lake Bernard. In the park is a memorial cairn to Mary S. Edgar (b. 1889), a versifier, mainly remembered as the author of two hymns "God Who Touchest Earth with Beauty" and "God of all the Many Lands" included in the *United Church Hymn Book* (1972). Edgar was born in Sundridge. She became deaf at an early age and ran the Bernard Lake Camp for Girls.

Sutton

The graveyard of St. George's Anglican Church, at

Two tombstones in the Churchyard of St. George the Martyr, Sibbald's Point: Mazo de la Roche (1879-1961) and Stephen Butler Leacock (1869-1944). [Jim Harris]

These stained-glass windows in the Church of St. George the Martyr, at Sibbald's Point, were installed "in abiding memory of Mazo de la Roche . . . 'He groweth best who loveth best, / All things both great and small.'" [Jim Harris]

Sibbald Point, near Jackson's Point, east of Sutton, south of Lake Simcoe, is the final resting place of two famous writers, both of whom were raised in the region.

The ashes of Stephen Leacock (1869-1944) are buried in the family plot, sheltered by an umbrella elm. He once wrote of the site that would include his gravesite: "The Church, the graveyard, and the sweep of land that runs down to Eildon Hall and the Lake, with a background of bay and island, a forest sunk in the waters, possess a wistful loveliness that no artificial beauty of the landscape can emulate or approach."

Also buried here is Mazo de la Roche (1879-1961), the novelist, whose headstone punningly reads: "Mon Dieu Est Ma Roche." There is a stained-glass window with a memorial to the novelist in St. George's Anglican Church, built of stone in 1877 to replace the wooden church erected in 1839.

Swastika

Swastika is the name given to a small mining community near Kirkland Lake in 1906. It is now part of

Kirkland Lake, northwest of Timmins. Ontario's use of "swastika" — the Sanskrit word for a twisted cross — predates by at least two decades the selection of this sign as the emblem of the Nazi Party by Adolf Hitler. In 1940 there was a movement to rename the community "Winston" to honour the wartime leader Sir Winston Churchill, but the townfolk objected, maintaining that they were, despite their name, as patriotic as the next man. Yet it is possible that the Ontario place name may have influenced Hitler in his choice of the Nazi emblem. The link is the Mitfords.

Local tradition has it that in his youth the eccentric British peer Lord Redesdale prospected the area, living for some time in a log cabin just ouside Swastika. The feeling is that he drew attention to the twisted cross in conversation with his daughters, the Mitford sisters, who were better known than he. Jessica and Nancy Mitford took to literature and Unity took to fascism, becoming Hitler's "nordic goddess." Unity could have apprised Hitler of the twisted cross. Thus an Ontario place name may have been perverted into the most hated of all symbols.

Temagami

In the Finlayson Point Provincial Camping Grounds, off Highway 11, near the village of Temagami, southwest of Cobalt, there is a plaque to honour the life and work of Archibald S. Belaney (1888-1938), the naturalist and author who became internationally known as Grey Owl.

An Englishman who immigrated to Ontario in 1905, Belaney found employment the following year as a guide in the Temagami area. He joined a band of Ojibwa at Bear Island in Lake Temagami and acquired from them a detailed knowledge of native ways and the natural world. He was adopted by the band and named "Washaquonasin" or Grey Owl. In 1912, he joined the Mississauga Reserve in the Biscocastasing area of Algoma and, with time out for service in the Great War, he lived here until 1925. He lived with the Iroquois girl Anahareo from 1926 and commenced a life devoted to the conservation of the beaver. This period of Grey Owl's life is the subject of *Grey Owl's Favourite Wilderness* (1983) by Allison Mitcham. In 1926, he relocated at Cabano, in Northern Quebec, described in *Pilgrims of the Wild* (1930). His publications brought him to the attention of the federal authorities who appointed him Honorary Park Warden first at Riding Mountain National Park in Manitoba and then at Prince Albert National Park in Saskatchewan.

Temagami appealed to the poet Archibald Lampman (1861-1899) who has written a lovely sonnet "On Lake Temiscamingue" in which he evokes "the weird magic of old Indian tales" at Temagami.

At Rabbit Chutes, near Temagami, the self-styled Indian spokesman Buffalo Child Long Lance (1890-1932) starred in the Hollywood film *The Silent Enemy*.

It was shot on location and released in 1930. The "silent enemy" was the hunger experienced by the Indians of the region. Here Long Lance met Agnes Belaney, Ojibwa daughter of Grey Owl, who played a small part in the film.

Tennyson

The small community of Tennyson, east of Perth, is named after the English poet Alfred Lord Tennyson (1809-1892).

Thackeray Township

Thackeray Township, north of Kirkland Lake, was named in honour of William Makepeace Thackeray (1811-1863), the English novelist.

Thamesville

Thamesville is located on the Thames River northeast of Chatham. At Moraviantown, just west of Thamesville, the Shawnee chief Tecumseh (1768-1813) fell in battle on October 5, 1813. There is a plaque to mark the spot. His death elicited many literary treatments. Francis Hall waxed poetic in *Travels in Canada and the United States* (1818). Major John Richardson (1796-1852), captured during the battle, wrote about the incident in *War of 1812* (1842) and in a poem in four cantos, *Tecumseh* (1828). Charles Mair (1838-1927) contributed a poetic drama, *Tecumseh* (1926). The list could be extended.

Robertson Davies (b. 1913), the man of letters, was born in the village of Thamesville. He spent five years here before being taken to Renfrew and then Kingston. Thamesville may well have served as the model of "Deptford," the small community that is the locus of the action in "The Deptford Trilogy," which consists of *Fifth Business* (1970), *The Manticore* (1972), and *World of Wonders* (1975). The snowball that was thrown on December 27, 1908, by Percy Boyd Staunton at Dunstable Ramsay but which hit Mrs. Dempster had incal-

A medallion, a pictograph, and the word "TECUMSEH" are part of the Tecumseh Memorial at Thamesville. [Terry Keough]

Plaque erected in 1971 on the outskirts of Thamesville, Ont. [Terry Keough]

The penetrating and discerning eyes are those of Robertson Davies. [McClelland & Stewart]

culable consequences. It seems that Deptford is "on the Thames River about fifteen miles east of Pittstown." According to *Fifth Business* the inhabitants were "serious people, missing nothing in our community and feeling ourselves in no way inferior to larger places. We did, however, look with pitying amusement on Bowles Corners, four miles distant and with a population of one hundred and fifty. To live in Bowles Corners, we felt, was to be rustic beyond redemption."

Thousand Islands

This cluster of more than 1,500 islands in the St. Lawrence River at the eastern end of Lake Ontario has impressed every traveller, tourist, or resident who has considered them aesthetically. Walt Whitman (1819-1892), in 1880, called them "the most beautiful extensive region of lakes and islands one can probably see on earth." Blaise Cendrars (1887-1961), the French writer, on his tour of North America in 1919, wrote a poem "The Thousand Islands" which concludes: "What a beautiful evening murmur Andrée and Frédérique sitting side by side on the terrace of a chateau out of the Middle Ages / And ten thousand motor boats respond to their ecstasy."

To the Indians of the region the Thousand Islands are remnants of paradise thrown down by the creator. To Claude Aubry (b. 1914), in his children's fantasy *The King of the Thousand Islands* (1963), the region is the realm of Maha Maha II, King of the Yellow Ants. What caught the eye of Raymond Souster (b. 1921) was the Rhenish castle on Heart Island, built by an American millionaire who never occupied it, described in the poem "Boldt's Castle" (1967).

Pine Island, a two-acre island on the American side of the border, is owned by John Keats (b. 1920), the American social critic, who wrote about twenty years of insular existence in his memoir, *Of Time and an Island* (1974), which begins: "Our house is built on a rock in a river. The rock is one of the oldest known to exist. . . ."

Thunder Bay

Thunder Bay is the amalgamation of Fort William and Port Arthur at the northern tip of Lake Superior.

Fort William, the greatest of the fur forts managed by the North West Company, has been reconstructed to approximate its appearance in 1816. In the Great Hall of the fort, traders hosted the partners from Montreal with extravagant displays of wealth. There is a memorable description of these annual revels in *Astoria* (1836), commissioned by John Jacob Astor and written by Washington Irving (1783-1859). "Such was the North West Company in its powerful and prosperous days, when it held a kind of feudal sway over a vast domain of lake and forest," wrote the American author. "We have sat at the hospitable boards of the 'mighty Northwesters,' the lords of the ascendant at Montreal, and gazed with wondering and inexperienced eye at the baronial wassailing, and listened with astonished ear to their tales of hardships and adventures." Irving concluded, sadly, that "the feudal state of Fort William is at an end; its council chamber is silent and deserted; its banquet hall no longer echoes to the burst of loyalty, or the 'auld world' ditty; the lords of the lakes and forests have passed away; and the hospitable magnates of Montreal — where are they?"

From Hillcrest Park there is a fine view of the bay and the long peninsula which culminates in the cape called the Sleeping Giant for its resemblance to a prone figure. This is part of Sibley Provincial Park. The Sleeping Giant has been likened by the Ojibwa to Nanabozho, the mythical giant whose return has been prophesied by native tradition. Pauline Johnson has a poem "The Sleeping Giant" (1912) about the recumbent being.

Sir Arthur Conan Doyle (1859-1930) wrote about approaching Port Arthur in *Our Second American Adventure* (1923): "Long before one reaches it one sees the mountainous wheat elevators in which much of the western harvest is stored until it can be shipped eastwards. They have been called the 'Castles of Com-

The silhouette in the distance is the faint outline of the Sleeping Giant, Thunder Bay. [Dept. of Regional Industrial Expansion]

The Incredible Journey was filmed by Walt Disney with a fine cast headed by radio veteran John Drainie. The story of how three pets find their way back home was written by Sheila Burnford. [Ontario film Institute]

merce,' and from a distance they look like a combination of the great keep of a Norman fortress, with the pillars of Luxor built into it. There is one which is alone sufficient to hold the bread-supply of the whole population of the United Kingdom for five days."

Stephen Leacock (1869-1944) in *My Discovery of the West* (1937) anticipated the amalgamation of the cities. "When I say Fort William I include with it the adjoining city of Port Arthur. They ought to be joined and called Fwather, or Port Arthliam. One can't keep saying both. But under any name it is quite literally what you would call a *gigantic* place. . . . Everything is planned to be a mile away from everything else."

For many years Sheila Burnford (1918-1984) lived and wrote at her summer home at Pass Lake, east of Thunder Bay. Still widely read is her children's book *The Incredible Journey* (1960) about two dogs and a cat

that made a 250-mile trek through the wilderness of Northern Ontario. The novel was filmed in 1963.

At the Terry Fox Scenic Lookout, on Highway 11 east of Thunder Bay, the statue of Terry Fox (1958-1981) was unveiled on June 26, 1982. Sculpted by Manfred Pirwitz, the nine-foot bronze statue atop a granite base depicts the one-legged marathon runner facing West. It stands not far from the spot where the brave young man was forced to conclude his cross-country "Marathon of Hope" in aid of cancer research.

Timmins

The mining community of Timmins, southwest of Cochrane, may have a literary association or two, but what the town brings to mind is the story "A Little Dinner at Timmins's" (1848), by William Makepeace Thackeray (1811-1863), in which an easy-going barrister, Fitzroy Timmins, is induced by his wife, Rosa, to give a dinner-party beyond their means.

Toronto

"Toronto as a city is not generally attractive to a traveller," wrote the English novelist Anthony Trollope (1815-1882) in *North America* (1862). "The streets are all parallelogramical, and there is not a single curvature to rest the eye." The list of those eminent writers who have voiced their opinions of the capital of Ontario goes from Brendan Behan (who got drunk here) and John Cheever (who admired the clear light) to Edmund Wilson (who grumbled about the driving) and Yevgeni Yevtushenko (who maintained at Maple Leaf Gardens that Canada's best poet is Phil Esposito). Perhaps it was the poet Rupert Brooke who, after a few days here in 1913, summed up the city best when he wrote, "Toronto, soul of Canada, is wealthy, busy, commercial. . . ." The city affected Jan Morris, the British traveller and writer, in much the same way more than seventy years later. 'Cheer up!" she advised Torontonians in *Saturday Night*, June 1984. "You have drawn a second prize, I would say, in the Lottario of Life." It was founded and named York by John Graves Simcoe, Tradition holds that stepping ashore, May 13, 1793, he quoted Shakespeare's *Henry VI, Part 3:* "Let's harbour here at York." York was renamed Toronto in 1834 under its first mayor, William Lyon Mackenzie.

Places

A Space An artist-run centre with a multidisciplinary program, A Space was established in 1970 and operated from a coachouse at 85 St. Nicholas Street, not many steps north of the old Bohemian Embassy. Under the direction of poet Victor Coleman (b. 1944), it sponsored literary readings and performances by such writers and groups as William Burroughs, John Giorno, Michael Ondaatje, and the Four Horsemen. It occupied office space in the old Ryerson Press building, 299 Queen Street

West, from 1978 to November 1983, when it moved to a ground-floor area at 204 Spadina Avenue. In recent years its orientation has been more visual than verbal.

Allan Gardens   There is a statue of Robert Burns (1759-1796) in Allan Gardens, on the Sherbourne Street side. Designed by the Scottish sculptor T. W. Stevenson and erected in 1906, it depicts the handsome Scottish poet as a somewhat benign statesman. At the foot of this statue, a group of poets "liberated" the city's parks for poetry readings in the early 1960s. Led by Milton Acorn (b. 1923), they gave unauthorized recitals of their poems. This was in contravention of the city's bylaws, which they succeeded in amending to permit public poetry readings in parks. Since then there have been hardly any public readings in parks.

Burns is Canada's most honoured poet or writer. There are more statues erected to his memory across the country then to any other author, living or dead, Canadian or other. The nearest competitors for statuary honours would appear to be Sir George-Etienne Cartier and Sir Winston S. Churchill, both of whom are more notable as statesmen than as creative artists. There are statues, monuments, memorials, or reminders of Burns's popularity as a poet and a man in the following places: Halifax, N.S.; Fredericton, N.B.; Burlington, P.E.I.; Montreal, Que.; Toronto, Ont.; Winnipeg, Man.; Vancouver, B.C.; Victoria, B.C.

Statue of Robert Burns, the country's most publicly hounoured poet, in Allan Gardens. [Mark Fortier]

The Annex   The Annex is the area of large houses, many of which were (and are) rooming houses, north and west of Bloor Street and Avenue Road. The action of *Silence on the Shore* (1962), the novel by Hugh Garner (1913-1979), takes place in one run by a Mrs. Hill who has an affair with an alcoholic boarder named Gordon Lightfoot (in the first edition but altered to George Lightfoot in the 1971 edition). The street names are slightly disguised in the novel: 120 "Adford Road," the location of the boarding house, is patently 120 Bedford Road; "Berther Avenue" is Bernard Avenue; "Lownard Avenue" is Lowther Avenue; "Parklawn Hotel" is the Park Plaza, etc.

There is a bust of the Finnish composer Jan Sibelius in Sibelius Park in the Annex. "Sibelius Park" is the title of a two-part meditation on "the years of desperate affirmation" in *Civil Elegies and Other Poems* (1972) by Dennis Lee (b. 1939).

Artists Alliance Building   The painter Charles Pachter developed the warehouse building at 24 Ryerson Avenue, near Bathurst and Queen, turning it into an arts centre with the name Artists Alliance Building in the 1960s. Here are the head offices of a group of artistic organizations, including the Writers' Union of Canada, the League of Canadian Poets, the Periodical Writer's Association of Canada, and the Writers' Development Trust.

The Arts and Letters Club   The Arts and Letters Club is a Toronto institution that goes back to 1908, when it was founded as an English-style club for male members in the old Assizes Building, formerly the Court House, on Adelaide Street. Among active early members were Hector Charlesworth and Bertram Brooker. Members were exuberant hosts of the young poet Rupert Brooke (1887-1915) who was so impressed with the bonhommie of his visit in July 1913 that he wrote to Edward Marsh: "They're really a quite up-to-date lot, and very cheery and pleasant. . . . Oh, Eddie, one fellow actually possessed my *Poems*. Awful. Triumph." Seven years later, the Club sponsored the first exhibition of the newly formed Group of Seven. Over the years plays by Merrill Denison and John Coulter, among others, were performed, often premiered. In the 1950s and 1960s the Club attracted personnel from the Macmillan and Ryerson publishing houses, including Macmillan's John Morgan Gray and John Webster Grant, Lorne Pierce's successor at Ryerson. Charles Bruce, novelist and journalist, and Lovat Dickson, biographer, frequently dined here. Since 1920 the Club has occupied premises in St. George's Hall, 14 Elm Street.

St. George's Hall, 14 Elm Street, is the home of the Arts and Letters Club. [Mark Fortier]

Avenue Park The centrepiece of this small park, at the intersection of Avenue Road and St. Clair Avenue, is the fanciful statue of Peter Pan. This is the city's single statue to a literary character. It is a copy of the statue that stands in Kensington Gardens, London, which was sculpted by Sir George Frampton in 1912 at the personal expense of Sir James M. Barrie (1860-1937), playwright and author of the play *Peter Pan* (1904). It symbolizes the spirit of eternal youth and was erected "To the Spirit of Children at Play" by a local citizen's group in 1929.

St. Clair Avenue, west of Avenue Park, has so many psychiatrists' offices it has been dubbed "the Mental Block." In *The Journals of Susanna Moodie* (1970), Margaret Atwood (b. 1939) has a poem "A Bus Along St. Clair: December" in which the pioneer woman thinks: "there is no city; / this is the centre of a forest."

Statue of Peter Pan, "the spirit of eternal youth," in Avenue Park. [Mark Fortier]

Black Creek Pioneer Village Located in the northwest part of Metropolitan Toronto and opened in 1967, Black Creek Pioneer Village is the reconstruction of a nineteenth-century, Upper Canadian village. It includes the original Roblin's Mill, transported here from the Belleville area. Al Purdy (b. 1918) has written two poems, included in his *Selected Poems* (1972), about Roblin's Mill, one of which expresses regret that it was moved from Eastern Ontario to its present locale.

The Bohemian Embassy This now-legendary coffee house was located in a loft above 7 St. Nicholas Street, near the intersection of Wellesley and Yonge streets, and it flourished under the direction of writer-performer Don Cullen from 1960 to 1966. In addition to jazz and folksinging by Ian and Sylvia it featured weekly poetry readings by Milton Acorn, Margaret Atwood, David Donnell, Gwendolyn MacEwen, and many others, organized by John Robert Colombo. One year "La BoEm" was mistakenly listed in the Toronto Telephone Directory under "Consulates." Raymond Souster's poem "Gwendolyn MacEwen at the Bohemian Embassy" (1965) captures the atmosphere.

Longhouse Book Shop Ltd. at its new location, 626 Yonge Street, Toronto. [Mark Fortier]

Bookstores There are more than two hundred stores for new books and some sixty stores for used books in the city, according to the Yellow Pages. Here is information on four of them, one of which is no longer in operation.

The Albert Britnell Book Shop, at 765 Yonge Street, has been a Toronto landmark since 1893. It has served patrons at its present location since 1928. It is family owned and operated and considered by many book buyers to be the finest all-round bookstore in the country.

Dora Hood's Book Room was located at 34 Ross Street when it closed its doors in 1962. The premier antiquarian Canadiana book service, it was founded by the Toronto widow and author Dora Hood in the back room of her house on Spadina Avenue in 1928. It had a succession of owners, including the scholar, librarian, and historian W. Stewart Wallace (1884-1971).

Longhouse Book Shop, 630 Yonge Street, was established in 1972 as the first retail store to devote itself exclusively to Canadian books (plus children's literature). In July 1984, Longhouse moved to 626 Yonge Street. The proprietors are Beth Appeldoorn and Susan Sandler.

The World's Biggest Book Store, 20 Edward Street just off Yonge Street, is, as its name suggests, the world's largest. It offers seventeen miles of shelves of new and remaindered books. It was designed like a supermarket by Coles founder Jack Cole and opened by him personally in the fall of 1980.

Boys and Girls House Boys and Girls House, 40 St. George Street, is the home of the Toronto Public Library's special collection of children's literature. It was originally established in 1909 and was the first such collection in the British Commonwealth. The present collection was founded by the librarian Lillian H. Smith in 1922, and the present building was opened in 1964.

Two special reference collections are housed at Boys and Girls House. The one is devoted to rare children's literature; the other, to science fiction. The Osborne

Collection of Early Children's Books, augmented by the Lillian H. Smith Collection of more recent titles, is a valuable resource of approximately 20,000 items, and a number of popular and scholarly publications have resulted from the collection. The librarians arrange interesting displays of new and old acquisitions.

The science-fiction collection is called the Spaced Out Library, and it is based on books and magazines donated by Judith Merril (b. 1923). The collection now includes some 20,000 titles, making it the world's largest public collection. It also has the world's largest collection of Canadian SF (in English), as well as specimens of "space art" by Jon Lomberg, Toronto resident and chief artist of the television series *Cosmos*.

Brown Betty Tea Rooms   The Toronto Writers Club, founded in 1923, acquired a private room five years later in the Brown Betty Tea Rooms, located opposite the King Edward Hotel on King Street East, for its luncheon and dinner functions. The Club president was Sir Charles G. D. Roberts; Charles Comfort headed the art committee. In *Literary Friends* (1980), writer and journalist Wilfrid Eggleston recalls hearing such speakers as drama critic Hector Charlesworth, Macmillan publisher Hugh Eayrs, and expatriate novelist Arthur Stringer. Active members included William Arthur Deacon, Merrill Denison, Frederick Griffin, Arthur Heming, Raymond Knister, D. M. LeBourdais, and E. J. Pratt.

Cabbagetown   The area of downtown Toronto bounded by Parliament Street on the west, Gerrard Street on the north, the Don River on the east, and Queen Street on the south is known as Cabbagetown. It is called Old Cabbagetown these days, to mark its rebirth as a desirable residential district which combines renovated houses and the Regent Park public housing development. The writer most identified with the Cabbagetown area is Hugh Garner (1913-1979), who made the area particularly his own in his realistic novel *Cabbagetown* (1950, 1968), which dramatizes how poverty may blight the lives of his idealistic hero Ken Tilling and his friend Myrla Patson. Garner wrote the novel in Cabbagetown; for further details see his biographical entry.

"Canada First" Movement   There is a plaque, mounted outside the National Club, 303 Bay Street, to commemorate the "Canada First" movement, founded in Ottawa, in 1868, with a Toronto branch headed by Goldwin Smith (1823-1910). Meant to spark a national consciousness, it influenced a generation of poets, including Charles Mair, Sir Charles G. D. Roberts, Bliss Carman, W. W. Campbell, Archibald Lampman, and Duncan Campbell Scott. The movement was named by James D. Edgar, patriot and father of Pelham Edgar who distinguished himself at Victoria College, University of Toronto.

Canadian Broadcasting Corporation   The head offices and principal radio and television production centres

The CBC's Radio Building, 354 Jarvis Street, Toronto. [Mark Fortier]

This vintage photograph recalls the Golden Days of Canadian Radio. Gathered around the microphone in one of the Jarvis Street radio studios are: Lister Sinclair, writer and broadcaster; Andrew Allan, producer and director; and actress Alice Hill. [CBC]

for the Canadian Broadcasting Corporation's English-language operations are located at 354 Jarvis Street. The white building immediately north is the executive headquarters and is known locally as "the Kremlin." As the Corporation has more than twenty offices and studios scattered throughout the city, there are plans to consolidate all operations in a single building to be erected on the Harbourfront in the late 1980s.

The Radio Building is the neo-gothic structure once occupied by Havergal College, the well-known girls school which was named after Frances Ridley Havergal (1836-1879), the English writer of hymns and other religious verse. The halls of this building reverberate with the sounds of the Golden Age of radio — such stirring syllables as Andrew Allan, John Drainie, Essa W. Ljungh, Lucio Agostini, Morris Surdin, Mavor Moore, Lister Sinclair, and Lorne Greene. Those were the years (generally dated from 1940 to 1955) of literate radio drama, lively discussions, and significant public-affairs programming.

Literary programming is associated with the broadcast career of the editor Robert Weaver (b. 1921) who initiated "CBC Wednesday Night" as the one evening each week when listeners across the country could hear cultural programming, including stories and poems, originally introduced by broadcaster and polymath James Bannerman. Staff, contract, or freelance authors who have worked in the offices and studios at "354" are legion. No account could ever ignore such names as Lister Sinclair, Nathan Cohen, Ronald Hambleton, and Morley Callaghan.

John Reeves (b. 1928), producer of musical programs, committed murder here — in the pages of *Murder by Microphone* (1978). Another "murderer" is program organizer Howard Engel (b. 1931), author of the Benny Cooperman mysteries. George Jonas (b. 1935), co-author of *By Persons Unknown* (1977), a study of the Demeter murder case, is also a radio producer.

Towering over "354" is the CBC's broadcast tower. As Jarvis Street was at one time more known as a red-light district than as a broadcast centre, the tower was called "the biggest erection on Jarvis Street." The Corporation itself was described as "the only non-profit making business on the street."

Canadian National Exhibition   There is little of literary interest at the CNE, the world's largest and longest-running annual exhibition, begun in 1846. But visitors to the CNE Grounds may be interested in two quasi-literary sites. The first is Scadding Cabin, the oldest standing house in Toronto, built of logs in 1794 by John Scadding whose youngest son, Henry Scadding (1813-1901), became the city's pioneer historian. (The son's house still stands in Trinity Square, off Yonge Street.)

The second quasi-literary site is the Garden of the Greek Gods. Visitors will want to review their Bulfinch's *Mythology* (1855) before viewing these twenty stone sculptures of such mythological figures as Pan, Orpheus, Hercules, and Medusa. They were sculpted lifesize in stone by E. B. Cox. The Garden was opened in 1979.

Casa Loma   This architectural fantasy and folly of a castle was built for the financier and royalist Sir Henry Pellatt in 1911-14. Northrop Frye described its twin towers, done in different architectural styles, as seventeenth-century Scotch baronial and 20th Century-Fox. The rumour during the Second World War was that Pope Pius XII was to establish the Vatican in Casa Loma for the duration of the war. (King George VI was to move Buckingham Palace to the Chateau Frontenac in Quebec City, and the incarcerated Nazi leader Rudolf Hess was to occupy an entire wing of Fort Henry in Kingston.)

In the literary vein, Raymond Souster (b. 1921) has written at least two poems about Casa Loma; in *Alligator Pie* (1974), Dennis Lee (b. 1939) has a poem which runs: "Wiggle to the Laundromat, / Waggle to the sea; / Skip to Casa Loma / And you can't catch me!"

Southeast of the castle, on Glen Edith Drive, there once grew "the old apple tree" which inspired the Toronto composer Harry Williams (1879-1922) to write the words of the popular song "In the Shade of the Old Apple Tree" (1905), with music by Egbert Van Alystyne. Williams is remembered as the author of the words of the World War I marching song, "It's a Long Way to Tipperary" (1908). It is believed he once lived on Glen Edith Drive.

Some distance northeast of the Castle is Ernest Seitz Park on Foxbar Road, near the intersection of Avenue Road and St. Clair Avenue. It honours the pianist Ernest Seitz, who lived nearby in Apartment 7, Bradgate Arms, in 1918 when, with Gene Lockhart, he wrote the popular song "The World is Waiting for the Sunrise."

Cemeteries   A number of writers and other notable figures are buried in two Toronto cemeteries.

In Mount Pleasant Cemetery, 375 Mount Pleasant Avenue, are the family plots of the Eatons, the Masseys, and the Westons. Near W. L. Mackenzie King (1874-1950) lies Alexander Muir (1830-1906), the composer of "The Maple Leaf Forever." Also buried here are Egerton Ryerson (1803-1882), Sir Charles G. D. Roberts (1860-1945), E. J. Pratt (1882-1964), and John Coulter (1888-1980). In an unmarked grave lie the remains of the pulp writer Thomas P. Kelley (1905-1982).

Funerals take place in this cemetery in at least two novels. "Fred Thompson" is buried in *It's Never Over* (1930) by Morley Callaghan (b. 1903), and "Auntie Muriel" in *Life before Man* (1979) by Margaret Atwood (b. 1939). Raymond Souster was inspired by the gravestones to write the poem "In Mount Pleasant Cemetery" (1962) with the lines: "Even the blackest tombstone shouts / 'Impossible, impossible!'"

In the Toronto Necropolis, 200 Winchester Street, are buried the athlete Ned Hanlan, as well as three publishers and one philosopher. The philosopher is George P. Young (1810-1889); the publishers are William Lyon Mackenzie (1795-1861) of the *Colonial Advocate*, George Brown (1818-1880) of the *Globe*, and John Ross Robertson (1841-1918) of the *Telegram*. Also buried here are Samuel Lount and Peter Matthews who were executed for taking part in the Rebellion of 1837. Raymond Souster (b. 1921) has written a moving poem about them called "Separate Inscriptions for the Graves of Lount and Matthews" (1974).

The Clarke Institute of Psychiatry   The Clarke Institute of Psychiatry was named after Charles Kirk Clarke, distinguished psychiatrist and dean of Medicine at the University of Toronto in 1908-20. The modern building at 250 College Street is sometimes called "the Inn on the Clarke." It is the setting for the play *You're Gonna Be Alright Jamie Boy* (1974) by David Freeman (b. 1947), the playwright better known for his drama about cerebral palsy, *Creeps* (1972).

CN Tower   The city's most popular tourist attraction is the CN Tower, which is described in the *Guinness Book of World Records* as the world's tallest free-standing structure, being in height 553 metres (1,815 feet). It was opened in 1976 but has yet to impress writers, although the Vancouver poet bill bissett (b. 1939) has recreated its shape in a "typescape," and mystery-story writer Tim Heald has made it the background of his "Simon Bognor" novel *Murder at Moose Jaw* (1982). As well, Sparkles, the rotating restaurant atop the CN Tower, is the setting of a central scene in *Palm Print* (1980), a police-procedural novel by the British novelist James Barrett (b. 1929).

Crest Theatre   The Crest Theatre, 551 Mount Pleasant Avenue, was operated as a repertory theatre by Murray and Donald Davis from 1954 to 1966. Since then it has reverted to its original status as a movie theatre. So impressed with the Davis brothers and their sister Barbara Chilcott was the English writer J. B. Priestley (1894-1984) that he wrote a play for them. *The Glass Cage* had its world premiere here on March 5, 1957. It was set in Toronto in 1906 and traced the effects of hatred on an old family.

Don Jail   The old Don Jail, on Gerrard Street East, overlooking the Don River, has been a Toronto landmark since 1859. It awaits new tenants. The Boyd Gang made good its escape from the Don Jail on September 8, 1952. One book, one TV film, and one poem (by Peter Miller) dramatize the jail break masterminded by the bankrobber Edwin Alonzo Boyd.

Folklorist Edith Fowke has collected "The Banks of the Don," a local version of a traditional song dating back to the 1890s. It begins, "On the banks of the Don there's a dear little spot, / A boarding house proper where you'll get your meals hot. . . ." The song is unpublished but may be heard on Fowke's *Folk Songs of Ontario* (Folkways, 1958).

The most noted temporary inmate of Don Jail was the Irish playwright Brendan Behan (1923-1964) who

Gordon Pinsent played the daring bank robber in The Life and Times of Edwin Alonzo Boyd *which was seen on the* CTV Network in 1982. [Canadian film Institute]

spent one night here in 1961 after assaulting two Metro detectives who were summoned to a Willowdale hotel after the playwright had repeatedly demanded a bottle be sent to his room. This was the occasion on which he maintained: "Ireland will put a shillelagh into orbit, Israel will put a matzoh ball into orbit, and Lichtenstein will put a postage stamp into orbit — all before you Canadians put up a mouse."

Perhaps the entry on the Don Jail is the appropriate one in which to secrete some information on James Earl Ray (b. 1928), the assissin. After shooting Martin Luther King, Jr., in Memphis, Tenn., Ray slipped across the border and took cover in Toronto in April and May 1968, where he employed a variety of aliases, including Eric Stavro Galt. As Paul Bridgman he rented a room at 102 Ossington Ave.; as George Sneyd he lived eight blocks away at 962 Dundas Street West. Then he took a plane to Europe and was caught. Research has shown that, as Eric S. Galt, he lived in Montreal, at the Har-K Apartments, 2586 Notre Dame Street East, in July 1967, some nine months before the assassination of the Black leader.

Don Mills   Canada's first planned community, Don Mills, was built northeast of the City of Toronto on land assembled by E. P. Taylor and initially completed in 1955. The novelist Hugh Garner (1913-1979) moved from the city's core to a house and then a flat in Don Mills in the 1960s, claiming the daughters of the women who set their hair in pincurls in Cabbagetown now set their hair in pincurls in Don Mills. It is the setting of his police-procedural novel *Death in Don Mills* (1975).

Forest Hill   This residential district grew out of the Village of Forest Hill and it is half Jewish and half Gentile. It was studied by a group of sociologists, headed by John R. Seeley (b. 1913), who published their findings as *Crestwood Heights* (1956). The words "Forest Hill" did not appear in the study. The authors toyed with other titles — Interwalden, Uppertown, Richview Heights, Woodmount — before settling on Crestwood Heights.

Among the few depictions of life in Forest Hill are those in the trilogy about West Indians in Toronto by Austin Clarke (b. 1932), the Barbadian-born author who lives in the Annex area. The trilogy consists of *The Meeting Point* (1967), *Storm of Fortune* (1973), and *The Bigger Light* (1975). The novels are rich in urban reference — O'Keefe Centre, Park Plaza, Yorkville, Toronto General Hospital, Union Station, Huron Street Public School, Colonial Tavern, Ontario Science Centre, Eaton's, etc. — and some events described take place in a Forest Hill apartment on "Marina Avenue" near Eglinton Avenue.

Grand Opera House   The Grand Opera House was owned by the millionaire Ambrose Small. He became

Ambrose Small's fate inspired Peter Whalley to draw this unpublished cartoon. [Whalley Collection]

A garden party on the grounds of The Grange, about 1880, the time when Matthew Arnold was a house guest and Algernon Blackwood and Sir Charles G.D. Roberts were visitors. Also shown is the entrance hall and staircase of The Grange, which was built in 1817 and is now restored to the period of 1835. The Boulton family coat of arms is visible in the stained-glass window. [Art Gallery of Ontario]

Canada's most famous missing person in the late afternoon of December 2, 1919, when he left the House, located at 9-15 Adelaide Street West, on the south side between Bay and Yonge, and walked south. He simply vanished, leaving his fortune intact. The Small case was written up by Charles Fort (1874-1932) in his collection of oddities called *Wild Talents* (1932). Noting the disappearance of the American writer Ambrose Bierce in Mexico in 1914, and Ambrose Small in Toronto five years later, Fort came to the conclusion that someone was collecting Ambroses.

The Grange The most distinguished occupant of The Grange, the mansion built in 1817 and restored in 1973 as part of the Art Gallery of Ontario, was Goldwin Smith (1823-1910) who held court here from 1871 to his death. He was a celebrated essayist who published the *Bystander* and *The Week*, the latter with the help of Sir Charles G. D. Roberts. Among his house guests were Matthew Arnold, Jefferson Davis, and John Morley. Indeed, as Katherine Hale wrote in *Canadian Houses of Romance* (1926): "Few visitors of importance to Toronto for the next three decades failed to call upon the sage of The Grange, and the conversations which here took place were probably as interesting as any book that Mr. Goldwin Smith ever wrote."

Stephen Leacock (1869-1944) wrote in *Canada: The Foundations of Its Future* (1941) that Smith was "the

patronizing patron of Canadian culture." "Goldwin Smith stood one day at his drawing-room window, overlooking the grounds of the Grange, musing on the reported strikes and violence at Cripple Creek. 'Why can't people be content,' he murmured, 'with what they have?' Why not? He himself, in property and investments, had close to a million."

The journalist E. J. Hathaway, writing in "Canadian Literary Homes," *The Canadian Magazine*, January 1908, declared The Grange to be "unquestionably the most interesting of Canadian literary homes." He went on to say: "From its earliest days it has played an important part in the social life of the city. It would be difficult to imagine a more delightful environment for a man of letters than his stately old vine-covered house, surrounded by its acres of noble trees and extensive lawns, in the very heart centre of the city. Everything is today as nearly as possible in its original condition, except that the present ample grounds are but a part of the former acreage. The spacious rooms and corridors are filled with rare and interesting treasures, and the walls of the dining-room are flanked with Cromwellian portraits — a worthy setting to a board which has numbered among its guests from time to time some of the most distinguished figures in the public and literary life of the day."

Greenwich Gallery The old Greenwich Gallery, located at 742 Bay Street, was the centre for poetry readings in Toronto before the appearance of the

The Grange, with historic plaque (to the left), in winter. [Mark Fortier]

Bohemian Embassy and the Harbourfront. The Gallery was operated by Avrom Isaacs between 1955 and 1961 when it was renamed the Isaacs Gallery and relocated at 832 Yonge Street. Here the "Contact Reading Series" was organized by Raymond Souster with an assist from Peter Miller and Kenneth McRobbie and later John Robert Colombo. A joint reading by Irving Layton and Louis Dudek is the subject of "Letter to Two Poets" (1955) by Raymond Souster. "Gallery Opening" (1962) and "Michele Lalonde, Reading" (1962) by the same poet describe the new premises. The American poet Charles Olson read at both the Greenwich and the Isaacs Galleries.

Irving Layton, Milton Acorn, and Eli Mandel the evening that Acorn was proclaimed "The Peoples's Poet." [Concordia University Library, Layton Collection]

Grossman's Tavern   At this tavern, at 379 Spadina Avenue, many painters with studios in lofts in the district relax. It was said to be the favourite "watering hole" in Toronto of the anarchist Emma Goldman. Poets have been known to frequent the premises, and one memorable evening in 1970, the poet Milton Acorn (b. 1923) was presented with an elaborate medal, inscribed "The People's Poet," when one of his books was not selected for the Governor General's Award.

The Guild Inn   The Guild Inn is a country inn set amid beautiful grounds that overlook Lake Ontario at the Scarborough Bluffs. The 106-room inn, built in 1914, was acquired by Rosa and H. Spencer Clark in 1932 and operated as The Guild of All Arts. The setting has been popular with painters, sculptors, performing artists, and authors (including Grey Owl and Wilson MacDonald). On the grounds are the Log Cabin, erected in 1791 and the oldest standing structure in Scarborough, once lived in by the *Telegram* journalist Lucy Doyle (d. 1971), and the Summer Cottage where Lorne Pierce (1890-1961) resided while writing his biography of William Kirby, published in 1929. Pierce dedicated the statue of St. Francis and the Wolf on September 30, 1956. Wallace Havelock Robb donated the granite sculptural portrait of

The Guild Inn boasts Canada's only Greek Theatre. It was built from eight Corinthian columns from the old Bank of Toronto building. Also part of the Spencer Clark Collection of Historic Architecture on the Guild grounds are the pediment and crest of the Oxford University Press building on University Avenue. Red Rowley designed the Guild's crest in 1933. [Spencer Clark]

wildlife artist Robert Holmes when he closed his farm near Kingston called Abbey Dawn in 1962. The grounds rival Kingsmere in the Gatineau for architectural "ruins." Some of the sixty-odd fragments of old buildings have some literary associations, notably carved panels from the 1938 William H. Wright Building that housed *The Globe and Mail*, art-deco ornaments from the *Toronto Star* building of 1929, and the pediment and crest from the old Oxford University Press building at 480 University Avenue demolished in 1964. Among the bas-relief carvings from various structures are those of composer Healey Willan, conductor Sir Ernest MacMillan, not to mention Benjamin Franklin, Molière, Sir Walter Scott, plus keystone images of Aaron, Moses, and Bacchus. There is also the fireplace from the Medical Sciences Building, where Banting and Best worked, as well as columns billed as "the only Greek Theatre in Canada." The Guild Inn has been acquired by the Ontario government.

ombo. Under the directorship of the poet Greg Gatenby (b. 1950), the Harbourfront series grew to national importance with year-round readings, and in October 1980 to global stature with the first of the annual International Writers Festivals which have brought Mary McCarthy, Stephen Spender, John Cheever, Andrei Voznesensky, and Czeslaw Milosz to Toronto, often for the first time. Doris Lessing gave her first public reading here in 1984. The Harbourfront reading series and international festivals are Canada's window on the world of literature.

High Park   High Park, in the city's west end, has a statue to the poet Lesya Ukrainka (1871-1913), called "the Greatest Ukrainian Poetess." It was sculpted and cast in bronze by Mykhailo Chereshniovsky and erected in 1975 by the Women's Committee of the Ukrainian-Canadian Committee. It is the favourite spot in the city of the Ukrainian dissident historian, Valentyn Moroz (b. 1936), author of *Report from the Beria Reserve* (1974), who settled in Toronto in 1981 after thirteen years in Soviet detention centres.

Dennis Lee has written about the "difficult sanities" in his poem "High Park, by Grenadier Pond" in *Civil Elegies and Other Poems* (1972). Raymond Souster, in his poem "Death of the Grenadiers" (1958), tells the story of the "lonely soldiers" who drowned when the ice cracked on the park's Grenadier Pond: "And girls have told me / they've felt that someone / was looking up their legs / as they skated the pond."

Harbourfront has become the most important centre for literary readings in Canada and one of the leading venues world-wide. More authors, both Canadian and foreign, have read at its York Quay Centre than anywhere else in the country. Margaret Atwood takes the podium as part of the regular reading series. Mary McCarthy, the American writer, reads from an unpublished autobiography as part of the International Writers Festival. Engaged in a discussion are Czeslaw Milosz, booked months before he became a Nobel laureate, and Greg Gatenby, Harbourfront's tireless and talented literary co-ordinator. [Harbourfront Corporation]

Statue of Lesya Ukrainka, "the Greatest Ukrainian Poetess," High Park. [Mark Fortier]

Harbourfront   The Harbourfront cultural complex, at York Quay Centre, 235 Queen's Quay West, with its Literary Reading Series on Tuesday evenings, has sponsored readings by most of the country's poetry and fiction writers, from the best known to the least known. Readings began here in June 1974 with a revival of Don Cullen's Bohemian Embassy, hosted by John Robert Col-

Hospitals   The Toronto General Hospital is described by Alice Munro (b. 1931) in the title story of *The Moons of Jupiter* (1982). Immediately south, on University Avenue, is the Hospital for Sick Children which was erected on the site of the childhood home of Gladys Mary Smith, better known as Mary Pickford (1893-1979). A plaque and small sculpture, by the Finnish artist Eino, mark the spot and identify her as the cinema's first "superstar." Toronto Western Hospital, 399 Bathurst Street, is mentioned in passing by Henry Kreisel in his novel *The Rich Man* (1948). Here died the noted economist and historian, Karl Polanyi (1886-1964), author of *The Great Transformation* (1957). Although born in Hungary, he spent his last years with his wife Ilona in Pickering, Ont. Their daughter Kari Levitt is the author of *Silent Surrender* (1970).

Kensington Market   The Kensington Market area, west of Spadina Avenue and south of College Street, was once Jewish and is now mainly Spanish, Portuguese, and East Asian. "O those lovely black corrupt olives," exclaimed one-time Toronto resident Irving Layton (b. 1912). "Nowhere else have I seen such generous ones winking at me with the moist eyes of a thousand Fatimas. I lost my heart to them on my first visit and haunt the place ever since. Fondly I gaze at them and the crowds diverse as the maps of the world. They also hunger for sensations only this fabulous realm can gratify. Wordsworth was turned on by daffodils. My flowers are the faces I pluck from Kensington's pavements: Oriental, Jamaican, Slovak, Jewish, Italian, Wasp. Nothing so moves me as their varied hues."

Mackenzie House   There are memorials to William Lyon Mackenzie (1795-1861) throughout the city. Mackenzie House, at 82 Bond Street, was purchased through public subscription and presented to him in 1859. He lived here until his death, and there are persistent reports that his spirit walks the halls. The two-storey stone dwelling is now a museum with many of his possessions, including the hand-operated printing press on which copies of his newspaper the *Colonial Advocate* were printed. The building has inspired at least two poems: "Mackenzie's House" (1965) by Raymond Souster, and Dennis Lee's "1838" from *Nicholas Knock* (1974) with the refrain: "Mackenzie, come again!" James Reaney (b. 1926) writes about Mackenzie as a printer in his children's book, *The Boy with the R in His Hand* (1965).

Maclean's Magazine   Until recently, 481 University Avenue was the most recognized address in the history of Canadian journalism and literature. Here could be found the head offices of Maclean-Hunter Limited, publishers of *Maclean's* as well as a slew of successful trade magazines. (The only address to rival "481" was 80 King Street West, the location of the *Toronto Star*, but while *Maclean's* enjoyed a national reputation, the *Star's* was principally southern Ontario.)

The graystone building standing at "481" was erected by Maclean-Hunter in the early 1950s and occupied until 1983. The red-brick building at Edward Street and the grey building on Dundas Street as well as "481" served as offices in the long history of the magazine, which goes back to 1905, the editors being: W. A. Craik, Roger Fry, Thomas B. Costain (who turned to novel-writing), J. Vernon McKenzie, H. Napier Moore, W. Arthur Irwin

(who was appointed an ambassador and married the poet P. K. Page), Ralph Allen, Blair Fraser (correspondent), Ken Lefolii, Borden Spears, Charles Templeton (broadcaster, evangelist, novelist), Peter Gzowski (broadcaster), Peter C. Newman (biographer), and Kevin Doyle. Contributors to the magazine are legion; household names include Pierre Berton and Scott Young. Doris Anderson is identified with *Chatelaine,* published since 1928. Trade-magazine editors with national reputations included Tom Patterson (founder of the Stratford Festival) and Arthur Hailey (later the novelist). In April 1983, "481" gave way to "777," when Maclean-Hunter Limited moved into its own thirty-story office building at 777 Bay Street.

Massey Hall   This concert hall, built in 1894 and officially opened by the young Vincent Massey (1887-1967), was the "one serious centre" of the city's cultural life, according to Ernest Jones writing in *Free Associations* (1959), at least until 1983 when the Roy Thomson Hall was opened.

Accounts differ but when William Butler Yeats (1865-1939) gave a poetry recital in Massey Hall in 1932, he outraged the audience by walking out during the ceremonial playing of "God Save the King." Questioned about his action, the tone-deaf Irish nationalist is said to have replied: "Is *that* what they were playing?"

Metropolitan Toronto Library   The Metropolitan Toronto Library, 789 Yonge Street, was designed with an impressive yet gracious atrium by Raymond Moriyama. The building was opened in 1977 and is perhaps the most pleasing library building in the country. The history department has in the Baldwin Room the John Ross Robertson collection of early pictures and maps. The literature department houses a special collection of more than sixty editions in various languages of Hémon's novel *Maria Chapdelaine* (1913).

The Sir Arthur Conan Doyle Collection is also part of the literature department. It brings together some five thousand items, ranging from books to memorabilia, devoted to Sir Arthur Conan Doyle (1859-1930), the creator of Sherlock Holmes. There is even material relating to Doyle's many visits to Canada. The collection is housed in the Conan Doyle Room which recreates Holmes's study at 221B Baker Street (down to the Persian slipper mentioned in one of the stories). On occasion, the Bootmakers of Toronto have met here. This is the Canadian counterpart of the Baker Street Irregulars whose name recalls the passage in *The Hound of the Baskervilles* (1902) in which Doyle describes a boot as bearing the mark "Meyers, Toronto." Here, in 1982, the Crime Writers of Canada formed, an association of mystery writers and aficionados.

The following tribute to "Metro Central" was proferred by Norris McWhirter who, with his brother Ross, established the *Guinness Book of World Records:*

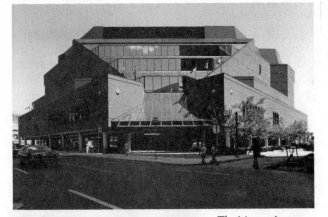

The Metropolitan Toronto Library was superbly designed by Raymond Moriyama who created an atrium as an area common to the five floors of "Metro Central." The elevators offer the best free ride in the city. [Metropolitan Toronto Library]

Sherlock Holmes's study at 221B Baker Street is recreated in the Arthur Conan Doyle Room of the Metropolitan Toronto Library. [Metropolitan Toronto Library]

"In my opinion the Metropolitan Library on Yonge Street, north of Bloor, is one of the finest in the world. It's magnificent! And most of the year it stays open until the civilized hour of 9:00 p.m. I really wish I had time to take a two-week holiday in Toronto and just luxuriate in that superb library."

Moss Park   Moss Park, south of Cabbagetown, is the locale described and depicted in maps in Hugh Garner's *The Sin Sniper* (1970). Detective Inspector Walter McDumont, head of the Metropolitan Toronto Police homicide squad, investigates a series of murders in this area of public housing. It was filmed in 1980 as *Stone Cold Dead.*

New City Hall   Toronto's past and present are represented in the Old City Hall, erected in 1899, and the New City Hall, built in 1964. To painter and essayist Harold Town, the old building, with its clock tower, is predominantly male, while the new building, with its oval, is predominantly female. The Russian poet Andrei Voznesnesky was attracted to the new building with its two shells: "It seems the air between them will hum at any moment."

In Nathan Phillips Square there is a plaque to commemorate William Lyon Mackenzie (1795-1861), first Mayor of Toronto and vigorous journalist. There is also a statue of Sir Winston Churchill (1874-1965), cast in bronze by Oscar Nemon and erected in 1977; it recalls Nemon's statue in Dover, England. A favourite is Henry Moore's sculpture "Three Way Piece No. 2 (The Archer)" erected in 1966.

An impressionistic novel in which Nathan Phillips Square is described is *Civic Square* (1969) by Scott Symons (b. 1933). The Square is singled out by Dennis Lee (b. 1939) in the title poem of *Civil Elegies and Other Poems* (1972) as: "A place, a making, / two towers, a teeming, a genesis, a city."

New Play Society   Not all the productions of the New Play Society, which was founded by Dora Mavor Moore (mother of man-of-the-theatre Mavor Moore) in 1946, were staged in the ROM Theatre in the basement of the Royal Ontario Museum but many of the important ones were. The annual revue *Spring Thaw* got its start here. The auditorium is now reserved for museum purposes. The NPS premiered plays by Morley Callaghan, Fletcher Markle, Len Peterson, John Coulter, and Lister Sinclair. Its founding fulfilled in essence the prophecy made by the English poet Rupert Brooke in Toronto in 1913: "It can scarcely be doubted that the first Repertory Theatre in Canada will be founded in Toronto, some thirty years hence, and will very daringly perform *Candida* and *The Silver Box.*" The NPS performed "daringly" but it never did stage those two plays. The New Play Society grew out of a group called the Village Players which originally met in an old barn, built in 1815 but since demolished, at 8 Ridelle Avenue, off Bathurst Street.

Newspapers   From the turn of the century the number — and some say the quality — of daily newspapers published in the city has steadily declined. From a high of eight, the city now has two (some say three by including the tabloid the *Toronto Sun*) significant dailies.

The Toronto Star, founded in 1894, was located at 18 King Street West in its halcyon days, when it was owned by Joseph (Holy Joe) Atkinson and managed by his son-in-law, Harry Hindmarch. Ernest Hemingway was on staff in 1923-24, alongside Greg Clark, Morley Callaghan, Wilfrid Eggleston, Fred Griffin, Gordon Sinclair, and other talented journalists, authors, and editors. The offices were moved farther west, into the new skyscraper at 80 King Street West, in 1929, the year Hugh Garner worked as a copy boy. Later years were never as halcyon, at least in retrospect, though during the 1950s and 1960s, editors, reporters, and columnists included Nathan Cohen, Pierre Berton, Charles Templeton, Peter C. Newman, Gary Lautens, and Peter Gzowski. The *Star* moved into its new corporate offices at One Yonge Street in 1971, and the old building made way for First Canadian Place in 1972. It remains what it was meant to be: an urban newspaper with progressive principles.

The Globe and Mail was born in 1936 of a merger of *The Globe,* founded in 1844, and *The Mail and Empire,* founded in 1895 of a merger of *The Mail* (founded in 1872 and *The Empire* (founded in 1887). With the 1936 merger it moved into its new William H. Wright Building of modernist design at King and York streets (now First Canadian Place). Beginning with *The Mail and Empire* in 1928, William Arthur Deacon (1890-1977) served as literary editor of *The Globe and Mail* until 1960, a remarkable reign. With the demise of *The Toronto Telegram* in 1971, the G&M moved into the *Tely*'s new building at 444 Front Street West, retaining the distinctive metal entranceway from the modernist building. The featured book columnist since 1960 has been William French (b. 1926). The G&M rightly regards itself as "Canada's National Newspaper."

The brick home, built in 1875-76, of George Brown (1818-1880), a Father of Confederation and a founder of *The Globe* in 1844, is still standing at 186 Beverley Street.

The Toronto Telegram, from its founding in 1876 to its folding in 1971, has had but three publishers: John Ross Robertson, the historian; George C. McCullagh, the speculator; and John W. Bassett, the television magnate. During the 1960s its literary editor was Barry Callaghan (b. 1937). Many of those who worked on the old *Tely* formed the new tabloid, *The Toronto Sun,* edited in turn by Peter C. Worthington and Barbara Amiel.

Park Plaza Hotel A favourite "watering hole" for the media crowd, especially writers with *Maclean's* and producers with the CBC, is the Roof Terrace of the Park Plaza Hotel, at Bloor Street and Avenue Road. There is a good description of the Roof Terrace in *A Fine and Private Place* (1975) by Morley Callaghan (b. 1903).

Publishing Houses Toronto has long been the hub of English-language publishing. While the Yellow Pages list almost one hundred book publishers, only a handful have a reputation for quality literary publishing. Of that handful here are five, one of which no longer exists as an independent imprint.

The Ryerson Press, once known as "the Mother Publishing House," was acquired by an American pub-

The editorial offices, printing plant, and warehouse of The Ryerson Press once occupied this building at 299 Queen Street West. [Mark Fortier]

lishing company in 1970 and became McGraw-Hill Ryerson Limited. The Ryerson Press occupied the Gothic-style building at 299 Queen Street West, from 1915 to its acquisition, and its imprint goes back to 1829. The early publisher, William Briggs (1879-1922), discovered Robert W. Service who was having his book of verse printed. Briggs was succeeded by Lorne Pierce (1890-1961) who, from a third-floor office with walls covered with framed photographs of distinguished authors, was at the editorial helm from 1920 to his retirement in 1960. A frequent visitor was Thoreau MacDonald (b. 1901), whose line drawings illuminated many a Ryerson book in the 1940s and 1950s. Ryerson issued volumes by such poets as Sir Charles G. D. Roberts, Bliss Carman, and Earle Birney, not to mention "The Ryerson Poetry Chap-Books" and even a monograph by Wyndham Lewis. The premises at 299 are currently occupied by Charlton International Inc., a stamp and coin operation which issues catalogues in far greater quantity than Ryerson issued poetry and fiction. In recent years A Space and commercial design and photography studios have rented suites here.

Sixty-Eight Publishers, the most specialized house

Josef Skvorecky, distinguished novelist, professor at the University of Toronto's Erindale College, is also a publisher of note. [Thomas Victor]

in the country, was founded by *émigré* Czech novelist Josef Skvorecky (b. 1924) and his wife Zdena Salivarova in 1971, three years after they escaped from Czechoslovakia. Their editorial, typesetting, and distribution offices are located in the building at 112 Avenue Road which once housed the Old Vienna Book Shop. Sixty-Eight Publishers was named after the year of the Soviet invasion of Czechoslovakia. The house has been called the most important contemporary Czech publishing house in the world. It issues books in Czech by writers who cannot publish in Czechoslovakia.

The Macmillan Co. of Canada Ltd. occupied this building at 70 Bond Street. Now it houses the offices of Saturday Night *magazine. [Mark Fortier]*

The familiar Grey Owl plaque, a symbol of the Macmillan company, followed the editorial staff when it moved to new offices at 146 Front Street East. [Mark Fortier]

Macmillan of Canada, a division of Gage Publishing Limited, occupies editorial offices on the sixth floor of 146 Front Street East. It was not ever thus. The Macmillan Company of Canada was founded in 1905 and prospered under the presidency of Hugh Eayrs (1894-1940) who added authors like Grey Owl to the list. Visitors to the house at 70 Bond Street, erected by the company in 1907, south of Mackenzie House, recall the tiny lobby, the plaque with the head of Grey Owl (which one rubbed for good luck), and the rickety elevator. The plaque followed Macmillan in its move in the early 1980s to its present location. The offices at 70 Bond Street are occupied by a number of enterprises including the magazine *Saturday Night*.

It was during Eayrs' presidency that the notorious Deeks vs. Wells case was heard. Florence Amelia Deeks, a Toronto spinster, sued H. G. Wells (1866-1946), alleging that the English author had plagiarized her unpublished manuscript "The Web." She had submitted this historical study to Macmillan in Toronto; she maintained the Toronto office had forwarded it to the London office where it was shown to Wells, a Macmillan author, who pirated it for his popular study *The Outline of History* (1920). The action dragged on for years, court after court, but was ultimately thrown out, with Wells bearing his own costs, as by then Deeks was destitute.

Under John Morgan Gray (1907-1978), who became manager in 1946 and president from 1956 to his retirement in 1973, the firm added to its list such authors as Morley Callaghan and Donald G. Creighton. Gray's memoirs appeared as *Fun Tomorrow* (1978), the year the firm passed from British into Canadian corporate ownership.

McClelland and Stewart Limited is variously known as "M&S," "The Canadian Publishers," and (to Al Purdy at least) "McStew." Its office and main warehouse are located at 25 Hollinger Road, as if in hiding in an industrial parkland in Scarborough. The firm, founded in 1906, has been headed since 1954 by J. G. (Jack) McClelland (b. 1922) whose promotional schemes often make better copy than his writers'. The firm has a reputation for aggressive promotion and includes on its list such top-selling quality writers as Margaret Atwood, Pierre Berton, Leonard Cohen, Irving Layton, Farley Mowat, Peter C. Newman, and Mordecai Richler.

Harlequin Books is the world's largest publisher of romantic fiction. The company was founded in Winnipeg in 1949 as a mass-market reprint house. Now it occupies a four-storey building, Harlequin Enterprises, 225 Duncan Mill Road, Don Mills, and the majority shareholder is Torstar, the holding company that also owns *The Toronto Star*. It issues about twenty Harlequin books a month. These appeal to women, especially older women, who like their romantic encounters to take place in hospitals or castles.

The Warehouse Building is the name in common use for the old but reconditioned warehouse, located between The Esplanade and Front Street, which is owned by publisher Michael de Pencier and employed by him as the offices of various of his publishing operations. It has a number of street addresses. Published from 56 The Esplanade is *Quill & Quire*, the tabloid of the book trade. From 70 The Esplanade comes *Canadian Business Magazine* and *The Canadian Forum*. Two magazines for children, *Chickadee* and *Owl*, appear from 51 Front Street East. Finally, *Toronto Life* magazine and Key-Porter Books both are approached from 59 Front Street East.

Queen Street Asylum   There has been an asylum for the insane or a mental hospital on the grounds of 999 Queen Street West since the Toronto Asylum opened in 1850. The present facility is located at 1001 Queen Street West.

Susanna Moodie (1803-1885) described in *Life in the Clearings* (1853) the conditions at the Toronto Asylum when she visited Grace Marks, the Irish serving girl who was found guilty of abetting the murder of her masters. Incarcerated in the Kingston Penitentiary until overcome by insanity, she was transferred to the Toronto Asylum.

Gwendolyn MacEwen (b. 1941) has a poem "Lines for 999 Queen Street" in *The Fire-Eaters* (1976) which begins: "A world where fear is normal and one seldom dares to love. . . ."

The Ontario Legislature, Queen's Park, in winter. [Hawkshead Services]

Queen's Park   The main Parliament Building, erected on the site of a lunatic asylum, was designed in Romanesque Revival style in 1893. It attracted the eye of John Updike (b. 1932), the visiting American novelist, who described the building in one of his "Bech" stories, "Australia and Canada" (1975), as "brick valentines posted to a distant dowager queen." To the west of the Parliament Building there is a memorial to William Lyon Mackenzie and to those who fell in the Rebellion of 1837.

"In 1885 the Ontario government finally tore down the old lunatic asylum in Queen's Park and resolutely set out to erect Canada's ugliest legislative building. It stands there still, squinting a little, like a huge red toad, peering through the trees and a couple of flagpoles at the traffic on Toronto's University Avenue." This is the opinion of the historian Desmond Morton (b. 1937) in his essay in *Government and Politics of Ontario* (1980), edited by Donald C. MacDonald.

Rochdale College   Rochdale College was a "free university" at 346 Bloor Street West which opened September 1968 and closed September 1975, when the last of the

Once known as Rochdale College, this building is now the Senator David A. Croll Apartments for Senior Citizens. [Mark Fortier]

tenants were evicted. The eighteen-storey building is now known as the Senator David A. Croll Apartments for Senior Citizens. The literary associations of Rochdale go deeper than the fact that Senator Croll supposedly wrote the Senate's Report on Poverty, which occasioned a backlash called *The Real Poverty Report* (1971) written by Ian Adams (b. 1937) and others.

A group of young writers, including Dennis Lee (b. 1939), Matt Cohen (b. 1942), and Victor Coleman (b. 1944), lived here in the early years. Judith Merril (b. 1923), who resided here from 1968 to 1971, established her Spaced Out Library on the premises before its administration was taken over by the Toronto Public Libraries. The League of Canadian Poets held its inaugural meeting here in 1968, chaired by F. R. Scott (b. 1899).

Both Coach House Press, the underground publishing house established by Stan Bevington and others in 1965, and Theatre Passe Muraille, the alternative theatrical collective founded by Tim Gerrard and Paul Thompson in 1968, had strong Rochdale links. Many of those associated with these operations lived in the College, some in the so-called Kafka Suites in the East Wing. Over the seven years, some seven thousand people lived for some time in Rochdale, which was named after the birthplace in Lancashire, England, of the cooperative movement.

It is surprising, considering all the literary talent associated with the College in its heyday, that virtually no poetry or fiction has been published that illuminate "the Rochdale experience."

Rosedale   Rosedale is a desirable residential district in downtown Toronto, a motley amalgam of rooming houses and mansions, of ethnics and WASPS, of old wealth and new money, that awaits its Balzac. There are set pieces descriptive of old Rosedale in the poetic novel *Civic Square* (1969) by Scott Symons (b. 1933). The district of settled ways comes alive in the comic novel *The Rosedale Hoax* (1977) by Rachel Wyatt (b. 1929). It makes a gloomy backdrop for mad melodrama in *The Rebel Angels*

This scene is from The Wars, *based on the novel by Timothy Findley. Mrs. Ross (played by Martha Henry), while conversing with her son Robert (Brent Carver), keeps a watchful eye on the guests in her Rosedale mansion.* [Ontario Film Institute]

(1981) by Robertson Davies (b. 1913). Morley Callaghan (b. 1903) has made fine use of Rosedale in his novel *A Fine and Private Place* (1975). He is a long-time resident of South Rosedale; his home, frequently pointed out to tourists, is located at 20 Dale Avenue. It is described by Hugh Hood (b. 1928) in "Where the Myth Touches Us," a short story included in *Flying a Red Kite* (1962).

Dennis Lee (b. 1939) has an amusing poem "When I Went Up to Rosedale" which concludes: "When I came down from Rosedale / I could not school my mind / To the manic streets before me / Nor the courtly ones behind."

No list of writers, broadcasters, and publishers who live in Rosedale could ever be complete. But here are the names of some who reside, or have resided, in South Rosedale: Doris Anderson, Morley Callaghan, Stephen Clarkson, David Cobb, Arnold Edinborough, Stephen Godfrey, William Kilbourn, Christina McCall Newman, Norman DePoe, Richard Rohmer, Alexander Ross, C. P. Stacey, Kenneth Thomson.

Royal Alexandra Theatre   This handsome Edwardian theatre, opened on King Street West in 1907 and refurbished in 1963, is the setting of one of the most gripping scenes in the novel *Fifth Business* (1970) by Robertson Davies (b. 1913). During Magnus Eisengrim's magic show, someone in the audience yells out a question for the Brazen Head to answer. The question is, "Who killed Boy Staunton?" The Head replies that among those responsible was "the inevitable fifth," at which revelation Dunstan Ramsay suffers a heart attack.

Royal Ontario Museum   Inscriptions flank the main entrance to the Royal Ontario Museum on Queen's Park Crescent. To the left: THE RECORD OF NATURE THROUGH COUNTLESS AGES; to the right: THE ARTS OF MAN THROUGH ALL THE YEARS. The imposing words are considered to be the inspiration of Charles Trick Currelly (1876-1957), first curator and author of *I Brought the Ages Home* (1956), edited by Northrop Frye.

Margaret Atwood (b. 1939) has written an intriguing poem "A Night in the Royal Ontario Museum," and Lesje, the heroine of her novel *Life before Man* (1979), works in the Vertebrate Evolution Department. "When she was much younger she used to believe, or try hard to believe, that at night when the Museum was closed the things inside it carried on a hidden life of their own."

Adjoining the Museum is the McLaughlin Planetarium which opened in 1968. "The auditorium is a dome," thinks one of the characters in *Life before Man;* "it's like being inside a breast." Other thoughts occur to the main character in the title story of *The Moons of Jupiter* (1982) by Alice Munro (b. 1931). The satellites of the fifth planet from the sun make their appearance in a light show described in the story.

Royal York Hotel   This Toronto landmark, across from Union Station, with its famous Imperial Room, is described briefly by Dorothy Livesay in the final sequence of her poem "'Queen City'" (1930s), with references to a "gold braced bell boy" and a "dark chambermaid."

Ryerson Polytechnical Institute   There is a statue of Egerton Ryerson (1803-1882) on the campus of the Ryerson Polytechnical Institute in downtown Toronto. Ryerson has been called "the father of education in Ontario," and the Institute named after him has a notable school of journalism and radio and television arts. Writers who have been associated with Ryerson include the poet George Swede, mystery-story author Eric Wright, and novelist Constance Beresford-Howe.

St. James Town   What life is like in the highrise apartment complex called St. James Town, on Sherbourne Street, north of Carlton Street, is described by Richard B. Wright in his novel *Final Things* (1980).

Selby Hotel   The Selby Hotel, at 592 Sherbourne Street, is more than a century old. The renovated Victorian mansion was originally owned by Henry Gooderham of the Gooderham and Worts distillery. It served as a woman's residence and hostel before it became

Residents of the Selby Hotel, 592 Sherbourne Street, included Ernest Hemingway and Wyndham Lewis. [Mark Fortier]

a hotel. Ernest Hemingway and his wife Hadley rented Room 25, the corner suite overlooking Sherbourne Street, for three weeks in 1923 before moving into a flat at the Cedarvale Mansions. Two decades later Wyndham Lewis and his wife stayed here briefly, following the fire that forced them out of the Tudor Hotel, farther south on Sherbourne Street. The hotel obtained its first liquor licence in 1950. The basement bar is a meeting place for poets and fiction writers.

Spadina Avenue   Chinese shops thrive where Jewish stores once did business on Spadina Avenue. The street attracted Isaac Bashevis Singer (b. 1904), the Nobel Prize novelist, in 1936. Unable to apply for an American visa while living in the United States, the Polish-born Yiddish writer crossed the border at Windsor and entered Canada illegally. He checked into the King Edward Hotel and immediately headed for the garment district, which in his autobiography, *Lost in America* (1981), he calls "Spodina Avenue." As soon as his visa was accepted, he returned to New York. Here is his description of the Avenue: "I was told that Spodina Avenue was the centre of Yiddishism in Toronto, and there we went. I again strolled on Krochmalna Street — the same shabby buildings, the same pushcarts and vendors of half-rotten fruit, the familiar smells of the sewer, soup kitchens, freshly baked bagels, smoke from the chimneys. I imagined that I heard the singsong of cheder boys reciting the Pentateuch and the wailing of women at a funeral. A little rag dealer with a yellow face and a yellow beard was leading a cart harnessed to an emaciated horse with short legs and a long tail. A mixture of resignation and wisdom looked out of its dark eyes, as old and as humble as the never-ending Jewish Exile."

The Spadina Expressway   This expressway, which runs from Highway 401 to Eglinton Avenue West, was halted by urban humanists, like Jane Jacobs, in the 1960s. In *Nicholas Knock* (1974), Dennis Lee has a poem "Spadina" about the stopping of the expressway, now known officially as the William R. Allen Road.

Sunnyside   The amusement park at Sunnyside, along the Lakeshore in the west end, made way for the Gardner Expressway, but not in the sentiments and memories of Torontonians. One of Raymond Souster's most popular poems, "Flight of the Roller-Coaster" (1955), describes how one of the carriages could fly free of the coaster, fly over "Spook's Castle," and "disappear all too soon behind a low-flying flight of clouds."

The Theosophical Society   At 52 Isabella Street, where a modern apartment building now stands, a three-storey brick residence housed from 1920 to 1970 the Theosophical Society of Canada, with its 400-seat hall and its library of over 5,000 volumes of occult literature. It was a meeting place and study centre for scientists (Frederick Banting), spiritualists (Albert Durrant Watson), suffragettes (Emily Stowe), socialists (Phillips Thompson), directors (Roy Mitchell), artists (Lawren Harris), and writers (Wilson MacDonald, Algernon Blackwood, Albert E. Smythe, Bertram Brooker, and William Arthur Deacon). The first and largest in Canada, the Toronto lodge was chartered by H.P. Blavatsky in New York a few months before her death in 1891. Its journal, *The Canadian Theosophist*, founded in 1920, published articles that combined occult thought and a sense of nascent nationalism. Since 1970, the Theosophical Society has occupied quarters in a gloomy Baptist Church building at 12 Macpherson Ave.

Toronto International Airport   Toronto International Airport handles the largest volume of air traffic of any airport in the country. It was renamed Lester B. Pearson International Airport, January 1, 1984. Opened at Malton in 1938, it became an international airport in 1964. Arthur Hailey (b. 1920) conducted research here for his thriller *Airport* (1968).

An aerial photograph of the airport is part of the inventory of sights and sounds of Earth included on the Interstellar Record fastened to the two Voyager spacecraft which were launched into outer space in 1977. In fact the airport's photograph is the only reference to Canada in the entire inventory. As the life expectancy of the Voyager Interstellar Record is one billion years, an image of Toronto International Airport will outlast the airport and perhaps the planet Earth. The full story is told in Carl Sagan's *Murmurs of Earth* (1978).

The Toronto Islands   The thirteen islands in Toronto Bay are used for recreational purposes, and two of them — Ward's Island and Algonquin Island — benefit by having small residential communities.

Gwendolyn MacEwen (b. 1941) lived at 3 Second Street on Ward's Island in 1962 and 1963. She wrote a group of poems about the Island experience and these appeared in *Earth Light* (1982). In "Animal Syllables" she wrote: "There is no key to this place and, in a sense, no

Kite-flying on Toronto Island, with the city, including the CN Tower, in the background. Robert Sward has hands on kite, Earle Birney has hands on belt. [Robert Sward]

door. There is free passage in and out. Already small weeds shoot up between the floor and the wall."

Another Ward's Island resident was Robert Fulford (b. 1932) who lived in the early 1960s at 10 Lakeshore, a rambling gingerbread house with a somewhat wild garden. The poet Victor Coleman (b. 1944) has a cottage at 25 Third Street on the same island.

Robert Sward (b. 1933), the poet and author of *The Toronto Islands* (1983), lives at 3 Wyandot Avenue on Algonquin Island in a two-storey green house with a view of one of the Island's lagoons, Snake Island, and the Royal Canadian Yacht Club.

During earlier periods, Sir Charles G. D. Roberts (1860-1945) spent weekends canoeing in the lagoons. It was while living on Hanlan's Point in 1927 that Raymond Knister (1899-1932) completed his novel *White Narcissus* (1929). Hugh Garner (1913-1979) lived here for three years in the 1950s when the Island community during the summer was ten thousand strong. Raymond Souster has a lovely poem, "Lagoons, Hanlan's Point" (1952), about a small boy "moving with wonder / through the antechamber / of a slowly waking world." And the Italian-American writer Arturo Vivante has evoked the slow pace of island life in his story "The Stream" in *The New Yorker*, January 12, 1963.

Toronto Workshop Productions Founded in 1959 by the director George Luscombe, Toronto Workshop Productions is located at 12 Alexander Street, off Yonge. Actors first performed in a warehouse setting in the west end of the city, then moved into the 320-seat theatre in 1968. TWP has been consistently experimental, with productions ranging from an adaptation of Barry Broadfoot's *Ten Lost Years* to Rick Salutin's *Les Canadiens*, a play that took place on ice.

TWP is not the only experimental or alternative theatre in the city with a reputation for the commissioning of new Canadian plays. Two others are Theatre Passe Muraille and Tarragon Theatre.

A scene from the Toronto Workshop Productions of Ten Lost Years, based on the bestselling oral history by Barry Broadfoot. Actors listening to the radio in foreground (left to right) are: Diane Douglass, Peter Hillard, Ross Skene (on floor), Grant Roll, Rosemary Dunsmore (on floor). [TWP]

Historic Scadding House in Trinity Square, complete with historic plaque (and modern air conditioner). [Mark Fortier]

Trinity Square The first rector of the Church of the Holy Trinity, consecrated in 1847, in Trinity Square, near Dundas and Yonge streets, was Henry Scadding (1813-1901), antiquarian and author of *Toronto of Old* (1873). It was his father, John Scadding, who erected Scadding Cabin, now on the CNE Grounds. Henry's rectory, No. 10 Trinity Square, may be visited.

Despite the fact that Trinity Square is dwarfed by the modernistic buildings around it, the Square retains an atmosphere of its own, a sense of place described by Blodwen Davies in *Storied York* (1931): "But in Trinity Square you enter a little pool of dusk and tranquillity. The old brick walls, with their little turrets and groined windows and buttresses, have a quality of perpetual peace. The prayers of a more leisurely age still linger here.

"Some one has said that it should always be Christmas in Trinity Square, that there should always be lights in the old stained glass windows and snow as soft as eiderdown falling about its venerable walls. It has that sort of an air."

The bucolic charm of the campus of the University of Toronto is caught by Eric Aldwinckle in this illustration for Morley Callaghan's The Varisity Story (1948). [Macmillan of Canada]

The University of Toronto "The University is the glory of Toronto," wrote Anthony Trollope in *North America* (1862). The country's largest academic institution is set in the centre of downtown Toronto. Writers and scholars abound.

The approach to the main campus from College Street is north on King's College Road. To the left a pillar commemorates the creation of Standard Time by Sir Sandford Fleming in 1879. The observatory, once here, was moved farther north in 1908. To the right is the building in which Banting and Best conducted their research which led to the discovery of Insulin in 1921. Straight ahead is University College which Trollope described as "a manly noble structure, free from false decoration, and infinitely creditable to those who projected it."

The main entrance to University College, University of Toronto, was much admired by Oscar Wilde in 1882. [Mark Fortier]

University College This academic building was constructed in the Gothic manner in 1857-58 and restored following the fire of 1890. It is considered one of the finest pieces of architecture in the city; indeed, its Norman gates were praised by Oscar Wilde on his visit of 1882. It is even said to be haunted, though no poems or stories celebrate the deadly rivalry between Ivan Reznikoff and Paul Diabolos, gargoyle-carvers, said to date from the summer of 1858. Eileen Sonin tells the story in *Especially Ghosts* (1970). University College is non-denominational. In the 1940s and 1950s the English Department, headed by Milton scholar A.S.P. Wodehouse, was specially notable. The English academic Douglas Grant and the poet James Reaney were among the instructors. Robert Finch taught French here. Douglas LePan, poet and novelist, was Principal of University College in the 1960s.

Trinity College Trinity College is affiliated with the Anglican Church and was founded by Bishop John Strachan in 1852. The present building, with its Gothic Revival architecture, dates back to 1925. Writers who have taught here include Philip Child, Dennis Duffy, Dave Godfrey, and Milton Wilson, one-time editor of *The Canadian Forum.*

Archibald Lampman (1861-1899) was a student in residence at the old Trinity College, located at Trinity-Bellwoods, near 999 Queen Street West, in the spring of 1880, when he read *Orion and Other Poems,* published earlier that year by Charles G. D. Roberts (1860-1943). Lampman read it "in a state of wildest excitement" for here was a book of poems "written by a Canadian, by a young man, one of ourselves." To the student it was "like a voice from some new paradise of art, calling us to be up and doing." The gates of the old College are still standing, and at the beginning of the fall term Trinity students made a ceremonial trek from the new College to the site of the old.

The Victoria College complex: The main college building (top), built in 1892, is shown here prior to the erection of the E.J. Pratt Library (middle) and the Northrop Frye Hall (bottom). [University of Toronto; Victoria University / Dr. Barry Toyonaga]

Victoria College Affiliated with the United Church of Canada, Victoria College dates back to 1836. The present building of Victorian Gothic design was completed in 1892. "Vic" has a long history of involvement with Canadian letters, attaining something of an imaginative apotheosis in the academic career of Northrop Frye as chairman of the English Department in 1952, principal in 1959, University Professor in 1967, and Chancellor in 1978, all the while contributing mightily to literary theory. The New Academic Building was named Northrop Frye Hall in 1983.

Portraits of E.J. Pratt and Northrop Frye hang in Victoria University's E.J. Pratt Library. Kenneth Forbes painted the poet in oil in 1944, Douglas Martin caught the literary critic in midair in acrylic in 1972. The Frye portrait gives rise to speculation. [Victoria University; Victoria University / Dr. Barry Toyonaga]

The decisive influence on the Department of English was that of Pelham Edgar (1871-1948), son of James D. Edgar who named the "Canada First" movement. Edgar joined the department in 1897 and retired as head in 1938. He appointed E. J. Pratt in 1920 and Northrop Frye joined in 1939. Frye edited *Across My Path* (1952), Edgar's memoirs, in which he explained: "When he was born, Canadian literature was nothing much. Today, it's not bad. He had a lot to do with making the difference." *Acta Victoriana*, the student literary magazine, perhaps the oldest still published in the country, has appeared since 1878.

The E.J. Pratt Library, so named in 1969, has a notable collection of books and manuscripts devoted to the poet and longtime professor of English. Other authors collected include Raymond Knister, Northrop Frye, Francis Sparshott, Pelham Edgar, Duncan Campbell Scott, Marjorie Pickthall, and Bliss Carman. It also has some letters written by Samuel Beckett and the holograph of Samuel Taylor Coleridge's *Christabel* (1797). Among the papers of the missionary James Evans will be found the *Cree Syllabic Hymn Book* which the industrious man typeset, printed, and bound at Norway House in 1841. Not to be overlooked are two notable portraits on the main floor. There is Kenneth Forbes's romantic-looking painting of Pratt, as well as Robert Martin's remarkable and highly imaginative depiction of Northrop Frye sitting in mid-air, defying gravity.

The influence of Edgar, Pratt, and Frye may be seen, perhaps, in the work of two talented undergraduates of the 1960s who attended Victoria College: Dennis Lee and Margaret Atwood. Other members of the faculty who should be mentioned are the poet Jay Macpherson and Kathleen Coburn, the renowned Coleridge scholar. The present principal is John Robson, humorist and authority on J. S. Mill.

St. Michael's College St. Michael's College, founded in 1852, is affiliated with the Roman Catholic Church. The Pontifical Institute of Mediaeval Studies, which dates back to 1927, was founded here, largely through the efforts of the French Thomist, Etienne Gilson (1884-1978). In 1949, Gilson lived at 8 Elmsley Place, now Gilson House, a student residence. Gilson was responsible for introducing a raft of distinguished lecturers, including Jacques Maritain (1882-1973). The French writer is the "M" in the dedication Morley Callaghan gave his novel *Such Is My Beloved* (1934): "To those times with M. in the winter of 1933."

Marshall McLuhan (1911-1980), who join the Department of English in 1946, published *The Mechanical*

Wycliffe College is a theological college with residence facilities run by the Anglican Church. William Faulkner resided briefly on the second floor during the First World War. [Mark Fortier]

In this coachouse on the grounds of St. Michael's College, Marshall McLuhan founded his Centre for Culture and Technology. His work continues, under Derrick de Kerckhove, as the McLuhan Program in Culture and Technology. [Mark Fortier]

Bride (1951), *The Gutenberg Galaxy* (1964), and other books here. He also edited *Explorations* (1953-59) which, along with *Cité Libre* (1950-66) founded by Pierre Elliott Trudeau and others, was one of the country's two most influential "little magazines."

McLuhan established in 1963 the Centre for Culture and Technology which explored "the psychic and social consequences of technology and media." The Centre operated out of the Coach House, 39A Queen's Park Crescent, south of the Library of St. Michael's College. Its interdisciplinary courses and seminars drew students and professors, artists and writers, from across the campus, the city, and the world. On Monday evenings there were open sessions characterized by the free play of intellect and intuition. The Centre did not survive McLuhan's death, but his ideas, or "probes," remain as provocative as ever. In 1983, the McLuhan Program in Culture and Technology was established.

In a sense the Centre's work is carried on by the Celtic Studies Program, established after thirteen years of work in 1981 by the Newfoundland-born academic Robert O'Driscoll (b. 1938), author of *The Celtic Consciousness* (1982). McLuhan's Centre was concerned with the most contemporary manifestations of technology. The Celtic Studies Program is concerned with an investigation of

"the oldest living continuum of civilization in Europe." There are some sixty-five million people of Celtic descent in North America; the Celts may be said to be the main founding people of modern Canada, as Brittany is basic to both Britain and France. William Irwin Thompson (b. 1938), the author of a number of books on the relationship of metaphor to tradition and modern man, joined the Program in 1984. The Program holds annual conferences, and makes its home in Carr Hall.

Library Sculpture Without question the Library Sculpture in front of the John M. Kelly Library of St. Michael's College, 113 St. Joseph Street, is the most intriguing piece of public sculpture in the city and one of the most intelligent in the country. It takes the form of a free-standing frieze of figures and was conceived by William McElcheran (who also created ACTRA's Nellie). On the street side it depicts an anonymous crowd of pedestrians; on the Library side it shows a select number of thinkers as if in conversation. The faces are of James Joyce, Stephen Leacock, T. S. Eliot, Geoffrey Chaucer, Marshall McLuhan, Dante, Madame de Staël, George Bernard Shaw, George Sand, Leo Tolstoy, William Shakespeare, Sigmund Freud, Jean-Paul Sartre, René Descartes, Etienne Gilson, Søren Kierkegaard, G. W. F. Hegel, Immanuel Kant, Eugène Ionesco, Jacques Maritain, St. Thomas Aquinas, Isaac Newton, St. Teresa of Avila, St. Augustine, Albert Einstein, Eldridge Cleaver, Cardinal Newman, Barbara Ward, Karl Marx, Charles Darwin, Mohandas K. Gandhi, and Herman Kahn.

The front of the celebrated Library Sculpture is admired by writer Mark Fortier and his young daughter Charlotte. The back is decorated in light relief with the faces of famous thinkers of the past and present. [Graziela Pimentel]

Massey College A residential institution for senior scholars within the University of Toronto, Massey College was designed by Ron Thom and opened in 1963. The name recalls that of Vincent Massey (1887-1967), the ambience that of Robertson Davies (b. 1913), the man of letters who served as Master of Massey College from 1963 to 1981, whose bust (sculpted by Almuth Lutkenhaus) rests on a plinth outside the Lower Library which now bears his name. At the annual Christmas "gaudy," Davies told an original ghost story, and these appear in *High*

View of the quadrangle of Massey College, University of Toronto. [University of Toronto / Jack Marshall]

The aristocratic air of Robertson Davies has been caught in this portrait by Barker Fairley. It is owned by the journalist Alan Walker. [Barker Fairley]

Spirits (1982). "University College has a ghost, of which it is justifiably proud, and doubtless there are others around the University which have not yet found their chroniclers," explained the author. "Massey College is a building of great architectural beauty, and few things become architecture so well as a whiff of the past, and a hint of the uncanny. Canada needs ghosts, as a dietary supplement, a vitamin taken to stave off that most dreadful of modern ailments, the Rational Rickets." Davies has contributed eighteen spectres to haunt the halls.

Among the authors who have lived or worked at the College are: Earle Birney, J.M.S. Careless, Donald Creighton, Robert Finch, Northrop Frye, Margaret Laurence, Dorothy Livesay, Douglas LePan, Douglas Lochhead, W. O. Mitchell, C. P. Stacey, J. Tuzo Wilson, and Adele Wiseman.

Other Colleges The three newer colleges are Innis College, Woodsworth College, and (inevitably) New College. The first was named after Harold Adams Innis (1894-1952), the renowned scholar; the second, J. S. Woodsworth (1874-1942), the founding leader of the CCF.

Cécile Cloutier, the poet, teaches in the French Department of the University of Toronto. The poet Suniti Namjoshi teaches on the Scarborough campus, and the novelist Josef Skvorecky (b. 1924) at the Erindale campus, which he calls "Edenvale College" in his novel *The Engineer of Human Souls* (1984).

Hart House Outside Hart House, the student union of the University of Toronto, stands Sorel Etrog's bronze sculpture "Survivors are Not Heroes." Erected in 1965, it is better known (after its slit-like aperture) as "The Letterbox."

Hart House was built in "collegiate Gothic" by Vincent Massey in honour of his grandfather, the founder of the Massey-Harris farm implement firm, and opened on Armistice Day 1919. The first director of Hart House Theatre was the innovative Roy Mitchell (1919-21), and the first dramaturge was the talented writer Merrill Denison. Many famous authors have read or declaimed from the stage of this Theatre, including William Butler Yeats.

The Great Hall, in its mediaeval splendour, catches everyone unaware. As Thomas H. Raddall (b. 1903) wrote in his autobiography *In My Time* (1976): "The Great Hall of Hart House, always an impressive place, where portraits of bygone college dignitaries look down on you and a long quotation from *Areopagitica* runs around the walls." The passage from Milton's 1644 work begins: "I HAVE SEEN A NOBLE AND PUISSANT NATION. . . ." Two of the sculptured dignitaries that gaze down upon the dining scholars bear the faces of Vincent Massey and his wife Alice.

The Robarts Library The John P. Robarts Research Library was named after the late Ontario premier and opened in 1973. Students know it as "the John" and "Fort Book." Indeed, its fortress-like exterior inspired the poet George Faludy (b. 1910) to criticize it in a poem included in *East and West* (1978). It has a capacity of 4.7 million volumes. The correspondence of Emile Zola, the collected writings of John Stuart Mill, the works of Erasmus, the letters of William Arthur Deacon, and a Dictionary of Old English are among the research projects currently underway at the Robarts.

The Thomas Fisher Rare Book Library forms the southern wing of the Robarts Library. It has numerous notable collections. The Shakespeare collection includes the four folios. It houses the papers of Jacob Bronowski (1908-1974) and of Drs. Banting and Best. The Padlock Series collects works by Czech authors denied publication in their homeland. There is manuscript material by Susanna Moodie, Archibald Lampman, and Duncan Campbell Scott. The library houses the papers of Mazo de la Roche and William Arthur Deacon. Contemporary

The John P. Robarts Research Library resembles, in this photograph at least, a prehistoric beast, its head the tower of the Thomas Fisher Rare Book Library, its body the stacks and offices. [Mark Fortier]

authors collected include Margaret Atwood, Earle Birney, Ernest Buckler, Leonard Cohen, Mavis Gallant, Dennis Lee, Gwendolyn MacEwen, John Newlove, Joseph Skvorecky, and Raymond Souster. Other collections range from Louis Blake Duff's rare books, through the New Play Society's archives, to the papers of Graphic Publishers which flourished in Ottawa in 1925-32. Unusually interesting acquisitions include manuscripts of Jean-Jacques Rousseau and D. H. Lawrence's own annotated copy of *Women in Love,* with some comments by his wife Frieda.

University of Toronto Press   The administrative and editorial offices of the University of Toronto Press, one of the world's largest academic publishing houses, are located above the yellow-brick bookstore. The printing division is located in Downsview, Ont. Founded in 1901, the UTP, especially under Marsh Jeanneret in the 1960s and Harald Bohne in the 1970s, has become an outstanding publisher of scholarly books and journals, with titles ranging from *Late Archaic Chinese* to Karsh's *Portraits,* not to mention scholarly editions of the works of Erasmus of Rotterdam and John Stuart Mill. The UTP also publishes the *Dictionary of Canadian Biography,* which is edited from the fourth floor of the Radio College of Canada building at 243 College Street. Between 1959 and 1984 the editors have issued eight large volumes of biographies. When complete, the *DCB* will cover Canadian biography from the year 1000 to 1900 in twelve volumes. Many of the entries in the *DCB* are thrilling life stories as well as superb scholarship. The UTP issues a raft of scholarly journals including the *University of Toronto Quarterly* (from 1931) with its annual survey called "Letters in Canada."

Upper Canada College   Upper Canada College, a private boys' school, was founded in 1829 and has occupied its present location on Lonsdale Road since 1891. William Lawson Grant (1872-1935) was headmaster at UCC for the last eighteen years of his life. A distinguished historian and educator, he was the son of George M. Grant

(1877-1902), principal of Queen's University, and the father of George P. Grant (b. 1918), author of *Lament for a Nation* (1965). Stephen Leacock (1869-1944) was a boarder at UCC in 1882-87 and a teacher in 1889-99. He wrote about his somewhat unhappy years here in the essay "My Memories and Miseries as a Schoolmaster."

Winchevsky Centre   Once located at Brunswick Avenue and College Street, now at 585 Cranbrooke Avenue, the Winchevsky Centre is a primary and secondary school run by Jewish labour groups. It was named after Morris Winchevsky (1856-1932), a Yiddish-language poet who wrote declamatory odes on behalf of justice and socialism in New York.

Wychwood Park   A private residential area, west of Bathurst Street and south of St. Clair Avenue, Wychwood Park was founded in 1874 as a wealthy artist's colony. The founder was Marmaduke Matthews, the artist, who lived in the residence at No. 6. Other prosperous professionals included the architect Eden Smith and the painter George Reid. In the 1940s, writer Margaret Bullard lived here with her husband, a physicist at the University of Toronto; she drew on her experiences here in *Wedlock's the Devil* (1951), a satiric novel in which Toronto figures as "New Glasgow." In recent years, Wilson Woodside has lived here as has the late Marshall McLuhan, at No. 3, perhaps the Park's most celebrated resident.

Yonge Street   Yonge Street, Toronto's principal thoroughfare, begins at Queen's Quay and proceeds north for 18 kilometres to reach the northern boundary of Metropolitan Toronto. The statement that it is "the longest street in the world" is based on the fact that it turns into Highway 11 and ends at Rainy River. From Queen's Quay to Rainy River the distance is 1,178.3 miles (1,896.3 kilometres). Indeed, the Highway Book Shop, in Cobalt, has advertised itself as being located at 200,000 Yonge Street! The longest-street statement was popularized by George Augustus Sala (1828-1895), an English journalist, about 1867. It has been accepted as such by the *Guinness Book of World Records.*

York University   York University was established in 1959 and became independent six years later. Bethune College, on its Downsview campus, was named after Dr.

Michael Ondaatje, poet and playwright. [Performing Arts]

195

Norman Bethune, the medical missionary. A slew of writers are associated with York, including Barry Callaghan, Eli Mandel, Miriam Waddington, Don Coles, Hédi Bouraoui, Clark Blaise, Bharati Mukerjee, Michael Ondaatje, and folklorist Edith Fowke. Among York-originated publications are *Waves* (founded in 1972) and *Essays in Canadian Writing* and *CTR: Canadian Theatre Review* (which both date from 1974).

York University's Scott Library has personal and literary papers of George Borrow, Roy Campbell, Federico Garcia Lorca, and the Sitwells (Dame Edith, Sir Osbert, and Sir Sacheverell). Canadian writers collected include bill bissett, Margaret Laurence, Norman Levine, Roy Mitchell, Mavor Moore, Herman Voaden, and Miriam Waddington. The Library also has scripts of the Canadian Film Development Corporation, CBC-TV, and the papers of the Canadian Speakers' and Writers' Service.

People

Margaret Atwood (b. 1939), although born in Ottawa, grew up in the quiet Moore Park area of the city. She attended Victoria College, University of Toronto, where one of her fellow students was Dennis Lee (b. 1939), and after graduate work, teaching stints, and a period of residency on a farm near Alliston, Ont., she and Graeme Gibson (b. 1934) acquired a largish house on Sullivan Street, off Spadina above Queen, not far from the publishing house of Lester & Orpen Dennys. Here she has been most productive, writing poems, plays, articles, stories, and novels with equal facility.

Atwood's fiction is fastened to locale. *The Edible Woman* (1969) is replete with references to the Park Plaza, the Brentview Apartments, the Royal Ontario Museum, even the Don Valley Parkway. *Surfacing* (1972) is set in an unnamed location in "Northern Quebec" close to the Ontario border where one may "go native." *Lady*

Oracle (1976) moves around: Italy, Toronto, London, Quebec City, with Toronto references to the CNE Coliseum, Braeside High School, Royal York Hotel, Queen's Park, Riverdale Zoo, Toronto Reference Library, and such streets as Charles, Spadina, and Avenue Road. *Life Before Man* (1979) makes its major setting the Royal Ontario Museum, but there are excursions to Queen's Park, Selby Hotel, Yorkville, Victoria College, St. Michael's College, the Planetarium, Fran's Restaurant, the Pilot Tavern, Eaton's College Street, Maple Leaf Gardens, and Mount Pleasant Cemetery. Specific streets are too numerous to mention. *Bodily Harm* (1981), with references to Fenton's and the *Toronto Star*'s offices, takes place here and on the Caribbean Island of "St. Antoine." Some Ontario towns and cities are mentioned in passing in the stories collected in *Dancing Girls* (1977) and *Bluebeard's Egg* (1983), but their locales are not always specified. The same is true of the poems as well as the evocative fictions that comprise *Murder in the Dark* (1983) which, however, does include one piece called "The Victory Burlesque" (a reference to a striptease house on Spadina Avenue no longer in operation).

John Wilson Bengough (1851-1923), cartoonist and author of *A Caricature History of Canadian Politics* (1886) among other volumes, is honoured with a plaque mounted at 82 Bond Street, the site of his birthplace. He founded, edited, and illustrated the humorous weekly *Grip* in 1873.

Earle Birney (b. 1904), the poet, has spent time in pretty well every province and major city in the country. He has made Toronto his home since the mid-1960s, and lives in a highrise at 200 Balliol Street, near Mount Pleasant Avenue. He was a graduate student at the University of Toronto before the First World War, and a lecturer at Victoria College following the war. He lived in a fourth-floor flat at 40 Hazelton Avenue when, inspired by the name of the street and a lady friend, he wrote

Margaret Atwood as photographed by Graeme Gibson for the jacket of Bluebeard's Egg. [McClelland & Stewart / Graeme Gibson]

A still from the NFB documentary Earle Birney: Portrait of a Poet. *[NFB]*

"From the Hazel Bough" (1945). It begins: "I met a lady / on a lazy street / hazel eyes / and little plush feet." Also written in Toronto was *David* (1942), his best-known poem, in 1940.

Algernon Blackwood (1869-1951), the English horror-story writer, spent two youthful but formative years (1890-92) in Toronto. Like a remittance man, he lost his capital; unlike a remittance man, he gained valuable experience in dealing with the world, salting away impressions he would later recall in such short stories as "The Wendigo" (1910) set in the Kenora area. The only building associated with Blackwood that is still standing is the warehouse of China Resource Products, 291 College Street, which in 1891 was the office he rented for the Islington Jersey Dairy, an ill-fated venture. He wrote about it in *Episodes before Thirty* (1923).

William Hume Blake (1861-1924), lawyer and author, lived in the large house at 35 Woodlawn Avenue which was built about 1830. He is principally remembered as the translator of Hémon's *Maria Chapdelaine* (1921).

Morley Callaghan (b. 1903), more than any other author, has written about Toronto and Torontonians with sympathy and understanding. He was born in the city, he attended St. Michael's College in the University of Toronto, and while still a student he worked alongside Ernest Hemingway, Greg Clark, and others at the *Toronto Star.* He graduated from Osgoode Hall and was called to the bar in 1928. Except for that eight-month-long summer of 1928 in Paris with Hemingway, Fitzgerald, and others, and a brief sojourn in Montreal, he has made Toronto his home as well as the subject of the majority of novels and stories. Conversations with Jacques Maritain at the Pontifical Institute of Medieval Studies are said to have deepened his faith in man's redemptive powers. For many years he has lived with his wife in the commodious house at 20 Dale Avenue in Rosedale. He was visited here by the literary critic Edmund Wilson who, in *O Canada* (1965), wondered about the incapacity of compatriots and others "for believing that a writer whose work may be mentioned without absurdity in association with Chekhov's and Turgenev's can possibly be functioning in Toronto."

Callaghan has called Toronto "my tiger city," and while Toronto is not always so identified in his fiction, it seems to be the setting of the majority of his novels. Here is a list of his books with some specific locales. The action is generally contemporaneous with the writing.

Strange Fugitive (1928), his first novel, is set in downtown Toronto. There is a wealth of local reference, including Queen's Park, Hart House, the Old City Hall, the Y.M.C.A., the Olympia Burlesque, Osgoode Hall, Exhibition Park, the Royal Alexandra Theatre, and "the Cathedral" (probably St. Michael's). Streets specifically named include Yonge, Albert, Queen, Church, Bay, Carlton, Chestnut, Bloor, Adelaide, King, Richmond,

Art photograph of Morley Callaghan, pipe in hand. [Nigel Dickson]

Simcoe, University Avenue, St. Clair Avenue, and Avenue Road.

It's Never Over (1930) is centred around a funeral in Mount Pleasant Cemetery — "in the cemetery with pretentious tombstones and the fine vaults on the flatland at the top" — with references to Massey Hall, High Park, and Bond Street.

No Man's Meat (1931, 1978), a novella, takes place in what is called "Cottage Country" on "Echo Lake," probably code words for Muskoka.

A Broken Journey (1932) abounds in references to Queen's Park, Bloor Street, Windermere Hotel, Spadina, and again "the Cathedral."

Such Is My Beloved (1934), about a troubled priest, has more to say about "the Cathedral" which is described as "an old, soot-covered, imitation Gothic church that never aroused the enthusiasm of a visitor to the city. It had been in that neighbourhood for so long it now seemed just a part of an old city block."

They Shall Inherit the Earth (1935), set in an unnamed city and a lake area, mentions Barrie by name. The city is patently Toronto, and the reference to Lakewood recalls Collingwood.

More Joy in Heaven (1937), obviously set in the city, concerns an apparently reformed bank robber modelled on Norman (Red) Ryan who died in a hail of bullets in Sarnia, May 24, 1936.

The Varsity Story (1948) is a semi-fictionalized work about life at the University of Toronto. It mentions the Banting and Best Institute, the Connaught Labs, University College, Victoria College, St. Michael's College, etc., in telling the story of the warden of Hart House.

Lake Baldwin's Vow (1948) was written for young readers and abounds in references to Georgian Bay. It is set in Collingwood.

The Loved and the Lost (1951), considered by many to be the author's principal novel, is set in a richly depicted Montreal. Much of the action takes place in the Black section of the day, St. Antoine Street, but there are references to St. Catherine, Dorchester, St. James, Peel, Crescent, and other streets, as well as to the Château Apartments near the Ritz, the Chalet Restaurant, the Canadian Club, Phillips Square, Windsor Station, Sun Life Building, Café Martin, Dominion Square, Ogilvy's, McGill, Wolgast's Bar, etc. The *pièce de résistance* is the account of the hockey game between the Rangers and the Canadiens at the Montreal Forum where all classes, religions, and ethnic groups "had found a way of sitting together, yelling together. . . ."

Morley Callaghan's Stories (1959) — which collects his popular stories from *A Native Argosy* (1929) to *Now that April's Here* (1936) — is a publication with no fixed abode except "Callaghan country." This description embraces a medium-sized metropolitan area with many unnamed Canadian towns (like the setting of his everpopular "Two Fishermen").

The Many Coloured Coat (1960), another Montreal novel, is replete with references to the Mount Royal Hotel, the Ritz, Morgan's, Dorfman's Bar, Stillman's Gym, Windsor Hotel, and such streets as Peel, St. Lawrence, etc.

A Passion in Rome (1961) is set in "the Eternal City" at the time of the death in 1958 of Pope Pius XII.

That Summer in Paris (1963) is the memoir of an eight-month-long "summer" in "the City of Light," with a celebrated account of the boxing match with Hemingway at the gym of the American Club in June 1929.

A Fine and Private Place (1975), one of his sharpest novels, is set close to home. There are memorable descriptions of the English student Al Delaney drinking atop the Park Plaza Hotel: "At the roof bar of the Park Plaza the doors to the terrace overlooking downtown had been swung open. In the new, bright sunlight the city seemed to be all trees," etc. The object of his interest is Eugene Shore, the world-famous writer who lives in South Rosedale: "Eugene Shore and his wife lived in a big house near the footbridge over a ravine. The ravine protected the Shores' affluent neighbourhood from the swarming apartment life and busy subway entrance on the other side," etc. The title comes from Andrew Marvell's poem "To His Coy Mistress" ("The grave's a fine and private place / But none I think do there embrace").

Close to the Sun Again (1977), an international novel, is set aboard a ship in the North Atlantic during the Second World War; in São Paulo and London; and in Toronto, with references to Nathan Phillips Square, Queen's Park, the York Club, etc.

The Enchanted Pimp (1978) is a novella in which the main character Jay Dubuque has an office on the twentieth floor of the Olympic Trust Building, which at least sounds like a real building. Dubuque was born in Cabbagetown.

A Time for Judas (1983) is set in biblical times, though the prologue takes place in the present and in an unnamed Canadian city.

Hector Charlesworth (1872-1945), journalist and critic, wrote the first of three volumes of autobiography, *Candid Chronicles* (1925), while living at 105 Summerhill Avenue, off Yonge Street.

Greg Clark (1892-1977), journalist and author of twenty-odd collections of light humour, never owned a home of his own. He was born at 56 McKenzie Crescent; then moved a block away with his family to 9 McKenzie Crescent. He spent his formative years at 66 Howland Avenue, these being from 1899 to World War I. He served in the war and then occupied the third-floor flat at 147 Indian Road. In the 1920s he lived at 90 Woodside Avenue, then moved to 3 Baby Point Road and on to 47 Baby Point Road (which backed onto the lot at 47 Humbercrest Boulevard, home of his cartoon collaborator Jimmy Frise). He occupied 19 Indian Grove from 1938, and 119 Crescent Road from 1954 to 1966, when he moved to the King Edward Hotel, where he was a permanent guest, entertaining reporters and others in Room 683, a small suite in the northeast corner of this well-known hostelry. In 1963, he estimated that he had written 10,653,000 words for newspaper publication. Ernest Hemingway, who admired him, maintained "there is too much India rubber in him."

Thomas B. Costain (1885-1965), best-selling novelist, lived in the Tudor-style house at 22 Lytton Boulevard from 1915 to 1920 when he was editor of *Maclean's*. He then joined the *Saturday Evening Post*, Twentieth Century-Fox, and finally Doubleday. Mainly remembered for *The Black Rose* (1945), an historical romance that was filmed, he was working on two projects when he died in his Riverside Drive apartment in New York — a fictionalized biography of Benjamin Franklin and a novel about the Hudon's Bay Company.

Isabella Valancy Crawford (1850-1887), the poet, accompanied by her mother and sister, moved from Peterborough to Toronto about 1880, where she attempted to support the family with her pen. The family lived in 1882 in rented rooms at 180 Adelaide Street W. From 1885 to her death, she lived in poverty and obscurity above the grocery store at 57 John Street. This building is still standing, immediately west of Roy Thomson Hall, at the corner of John and King streets. She is buried in Little Lake Cemetery, Peterborough.

Donald G. Creighton (1902-1979), the historian and biographer of Sir John A. Macdonald, was born in the large house at 262 Concord Avenue. In later years he lived in a larger Victorian house in Brooklin, near Pickering, where he added two new wings for "writing rooms." His wife Luella Creighton (b. 1901) is the author of *High Bright Buggy Wheels* (1951) and other books.

"Here then is Donald at his severest, or not far from it," noted Barker Fairley of his oil on masonite portrait of the historian Donald G. Creighton. [Barker Fairley]

Robertson Davies (b. 1913), the first Master of Massey College, is the author of novels with fully realized settings. There is the so-called Salterton Trilogy — *Tempest-Tost* (1951), *Leaven of Malice* (1954), *A Mixture of Frailties* (1958) — set in the fictional university town modelled on Kingston. The so-called Deptford Trilogy — *Fifth Business* (1970), *The Manticore* (1972), *World of Wonders* (1975) — is more cosmopolitan, moving from "Deptford," a village on the Thames in Southwestern Ontario in 1908, to Toronto, Montreal, France, London, Antwerp (in the first novel); Deptford to Toronto and Zurich (in the second); and Deptford to Switzerland (in the third). *The Rebel Angels* (1981), set in an unnamed Canadian City, has a college of St. John and the Holy Ghost (rather Masseyish) and a district called Rosedale (which resembles the real Rosedale).

Mazo de la Roche (1879-1961), the creator of the most celebrated country home in Canadian literature, was herself something of a homeless wanderer. Her novel *Jalna* (1927), and its fourteen sequels, are a paean to rootedness, of which the author knew little.

She was born in Newmarket, Ont. There is a plaque in Wesley Brooks Conservation Park commemorated to her life and work. It seems the Roche family moved to Toronto and lived at 113 John Street from 1885 to 1891. Then the family moved to Galt and Orillia from 1891 to 1895. They returned to Toronto in 1895 and lived at 157 Dunn Avenue until 1900. From 1900 to 1911, the family resided in a house on Jarvis Street. The house number is not mentioned in the author's autobiography, *Ringing the Changes* (1957), but the building is described: "It stood in what was at that time one of the most spacious and fashionable streets in Toronto. I do not remember when it began to degenerate but its downhill trend has been steady. In my youth it represented solid dignity and peaceful permanence." It was while living here that Mazo attended the Ontario School of Art and the University of Toronto.

From 1911 to 1915, the family lived at Foxleigh Farm, Cudmore Road and Highway 2, near Bronte. "It was a lovely spot. A rugged bluff fronted the lake below the house. An old wind-bent tree grew on its highest point. This bluff had withstood so many years of battering by the waves that it seemed invincible, yet, when I revisited the farm some years later, it had entirely disappeared and an unimpressive slope had taken its place." With the death of her father in 1915, Mazo and the family returned to Toronto and lived in a succession of residences.

Mazo and her cousin, Caroline Clement, built a small summer cottage in a wooded area near Clarkson, not far from the cottage where Dorothy Livesay grew up. They knew each other, and it was through the Livesays that Mazo acquired her knowledge of "Benares," the English-style country home still standing at 1503 Clarkson Road North. It had been built in 1854-58 by Captain James B. Harris, late of India, who named it after the city in which he had served. To both the novelist and the poet, "Benares" epitomized gracious living. As Livesay's mother was Harris's daughter, Livesay was invited to high tea at "Benares." There is no proof Mazo ever set foot inside this home which she transformed into "Jalna."

Mazo summered at Clarkson and wintered in Toronto in a second-floor flat at 86 Yorkville Avenue, now an avenue of boutiques, then a residential street. She completed *Jalna* here and learned the liberating news that the novel had won the $10,000 *Atlantic Monthly* prize. "Jalna," with its Art Deco ring so characteristic of the period, was selected from a list of British posts in India. There are many descriptions of "Jalna" in the fifteen novels. The original, "Benares," is privately owned by a descendant of the original Harris, but is deeded to the Ontario Heritage Foundation, destined to be a museum. Exterior shots of "Benares" were featured on the CBC-TV series *Whiteoaks of Jalna.*

With the success of *Jalna,* and its stage adaptation, Mazo lived abroad. For some years she occupied Vale House, Windsor, England. She returned to Toronto in 1939 and until 1945 lived in the four-bedroom, fieldstone house that overlooked the Don Valley at the corner of Bayview and Steeles Avenue. She called it "Windrush

Mazo de la Roche and her terrier from The Canadian Magazine, *May 1927. [C-5482 / Public Archives Canada]*

Hill." In 1945 she moved into a large house at 307 Russell Hill Road, in Forest Hill. Her last residence was 3 Ava Crescent, opposite the house designed and occupied by Lawren Harris. She died here, working on another "Jalna" book.

She is buried in the same cemetery as Stephen Leacock. This is St. George's Cemetery, Sutton. Her biographer, Ron Hambleton, called Mazo do la Roche in her fiction "the chief mourner for the dying English influence in Canada."

William Arthur Deacon (1890-1977), the country's first full-time book reviewer, served as literary editor of *The Globe and Mail* from 1928 to 1960. The $100 he received from Macmillan's as his advance for the *A Literary Map of Canada*, a beautifully drawn poster issued in October 1936, permitted him to make the down payment for the house at 66 Parkhurst Boulevard which he occupied from 1937 to 1945. Earlier he had lived at 36 Dilworth Crescent; later he resided at 48 Killdeer Crescent.

The idea of preparing a map to illustrate Canadian literary places came to Deacon as early as 1928, but it was not until eight years later that he was able to convince a publisher to commission it. He drew up lists of places associated with authors' lives and works and wrote to leading literary figures, both English and French. He asked them questions about locales, and Frederick Philip Grove, Arthur Stringer, Arthur Heming, and Adjutor Rivard were among those who replied in detail. In the fall of 1936, Macmillan issued *A Literary Map of Canada* "as compiled by William Arthur Deacon" and "drawn and embellished by Stanley Turner." A large and handsome four-colour affair, it retailed for $2.50. Sales were minimal, the author acquired unsold copies, and the revised map that Deacon hoped to prepare never materialized.

In fact, it was not until 1979 that its successor appeared. This was *A Literary Map of Canada* which was compiled by two writers, Morris Wolfe and David Macfarlane, designed and drawn by Graham Pilsworth, and issued by Hurtig Publishers. The writers were indebted to Deacon for much of their basic information and did not move far afield in their research. The way is still open for an artist and a writer to collaborate on a poster that will "put Canadian literature on the map."

George H. Doran (1869-1956), co-founder of the Doubleday publishing house, now the largest in the United States, was born in Toronto of Irish background. In his autobiography *Chronicles of Barabbas* (1935, 1952) he does not identify the street on which he was born, but he describes his first job with the Toronto Willard Tract Depository Limited on Yonge Street. He settled in Chicago in 1892. Fifteen years later he established George H. Doran, Limited in Toronto. Frank Swinnerton noted in *The Bookman's London* (1951): "I always felt that Doran, with his fine figure and presence, would have made a good ambassador; and he loved entertaining."

Pelham Edgar (1871-1948), educator and author, was head of the English Department at Victoria College. Northrop Frye edited his memoirs, *Across My Path* (1952). During the 1920s, the Edgars entertained as house guests the American poet Vachel Lindsay (1879-1931) and his bride who were fresh from a visit to Niagara Falls. The Edgars were alarmed when water from the upstairs bathroom began to cascade down the staris. Rushing up, they discovered Lindsay and his bride, both naked, cavorting in the bathroom with balloons, oblivious of the overflow.

Marian Engel, author of Bear, The Glassy Sea, Lunatic Villas, etc., and first chairperson of the Writers' Union. [McClelland & Stewart]

Marian Engel (b. 1933), the novelist, while born in Toronto, was raised in Galt, Sarnia, and Hamilton. She and her husband Howard Engel (b. 1931) lived in an apartment at 114 Pembroke Street when she wrote *No Clouds of Glory* (1968; reissued under its original title *Sara Bastard's Notebook*, 1974). It was while living in the house at 338 Brunswick Avenue that she wrote her popular novella *Bear* (1976). She now lives on Marchmount Road.

Barker Fairley caught in his studio by the well-known photographer Reg Innell. [Reg Innell]

Barker Fairley (b. 1887), a man of many parts, has lived for many years in a comfortable house at 90 Willcocks Street, west of the University of Toronto where from 1915 to 1957 he taught in the German Department. He has distinguished himself as a scholar, essayist, poet, painter, and early apologist for the Group of Seven. There is a small head of his late wife, Margaret Fairley (1885-1968), editor and writer, in Margaret Fairley Park, at the corner of Brunswick Avenue and Ulster Street, presented to the city in 1973 by friends. In 1922, he wrote the widely admired short poem "The Rock" which, while evocative of all Precambrian formations, was directly inspired by Head Island, north of Parry Sound. Since the late 1950s, he has painted his characteristic portraits in the second-storey front room. Here many famous writers, including Northrop Frye and Robertson Davies, have come to sit and talk and be painted.

William Faulkner (1897-1961) was an unlikely Toronto resident during the last year of the First World War. The American novelist enlisted in June 1918 with the Royal Air Force in New York. On July 9, he reported to the recruits' depot at Jesse Ketchum School where he remained for two weeks. He then trained with the RAF in Long Branch in the west end of the city. On September 20, he moved into a second-floor room at Wycliffe College, University of Toronto, overlooking Hoskin Avenue, as the building was being used for the School of Military Aeronautics. The First World War ended on November 11, and Faulkner was demobilized on January 4, 1919, when he returned to the United States and commenced his career which culminated in his acceptance of the Nobel Prize for Literature in 1949.

Northrop Frye (b. 1912), the famous literary critic, had his address and telephone number delisted following the publication of his study of the Bible. Apparently the public did not impose on the author of *Fearful Symmetry*

(1947) but felt the author of *The Great Code* (1982) was fair game. He has lived for many years in a pleasant house on Clifton Avenue in the residential Moore Park area. In 1939 he began his long association with Victoria College which culminated in 1983 in the naming of the New Academic Building the Northrop Frye Hall. He is now a University Professor with an office at Massey College. He has identified his "personal heroes" as his seniors at Victoria College: Pelham Edgar, John Robins, and E. J. Pratt. He paid tribute to Edgar and Pratt and also to ROM curator Charles T. Currelly by editing their memoirs and poems. He has defined his general attitude to life as being "that of a liberal bourgeois intellectual, which I consider the flower of humanity" and has claimed that "Toronto is an excellent town to mind one's business in."

The essential Hugh Garner was caught by the pen of Don Evans (who signs his work Isaac Bickerstaff). [Special Collections, University of Calgary Libraries]

Hugh Garner (1913-1979) in stories and novels chronicled the lives of the city's lower classes, just as Morely Callaghan described middle-class Torontonians, and Robertson Davies cocked a snook at the upper classes. Garner was born in Yorkshire, England, but brought here when he was six. In his autobiography, *One Damn Thing After Another* (1973), he described his first home "as rather large old slum house on Ontario Street just north of King" long since demolished. Then the family occupied a "two-room flat on Wascana Avenue in old Cabbagetown." Indeed, Wascana Avenue and Blevins Place to the north are transformed into "Timothy Place" in his novel *Cabbagetown* (1950, 1968). The family moved and occupied flats or houses on Sumach, Metcalf, Wellesley, Berkeley, and 42 Lewis Street in lower Rosedale. All have been torn down. In his childhood and youth he hated two things — "bedbugs and social workers" — and enjoyed the Riverdale Zoo (now the Riverdale Farm), particularly the monkeys, and especially "an exhibitionist masturbating Chacma baboon who always played with himself when he smelled females in his audience."

When he turned sixteen he quit school and became a

Northrop Frye as consummate academician, drawn by Isaac Bickerstaff (artist Don Evans). [Special Collections, University of Calgary Libraries]

copy boy for the *Toronto Star*. This was in 1929 and he lasted less than a year, taking to the road as a hobo. He picked tobacco in Simcoe and the experience provided him with a number of stories. In a room on the second floor of the old residence at 8 St. Joseph Street, which he occupied in 1946-47, he began *Cabbagetown*, finishing it some four years later. He went about it methodically, each evening penning one fifteen-page chapter.

A favourite spot was the Bathurst Street Bridge where one Sunday morning in the summer of 1948 "a serendipity thing happened." Out of the blue came the titles and themes of three short stories. As the stories are "One, Two, Three Little Indians," "Our Neighbours the Nuns," and "the Yellow Sweater," which he wrote that evening and over the next few days, this was quite a revelation on a blackened steel bridge that spans the railroad yards.

For a time in 1948 he occupied a room in the old Warwick Hotel, the centre of the red-light district on the northwest corner of Jarvis and Gerrard. For the byline of the hack novel *Waste No Tears* (1950), which he wrote at this time, he took the name of the hotel and the name of the street and signed it "Jarvis Warwick."

In 1951-53 he lived in a furnished flat on Centre Island with "about 5,000 hardy Bohemians." Here, to pay the rent one month, he wrote "A Trip for Mrs. Taylor," which was sold to *Chatelaine*. He drank at the Manitou Hotel on "The Drag," when he was not consorting with Jack Kent Cooke, the publisher, for whom he worked as a publicity agent, or making scenes at the Toronto Men's Press Club, then on Yonge north of King. Cooke, who began in business with Roy Thomson and later left for Los Angeles, appears as "Alex Hurd" in the novel *A Nice Place to Visit* (1970). When Cooke acquired Consolidated Press, Garner acquired an office in the Graphic Arts Building, corner of Richmond and Sheppard streets, where he contributed to *Saturday Night*, then published by Consolidated as a weekly. Such stories as "The Backward Glance" and "Another Time, Another Place, Another Me" date from this period.

Garner and his wife moved to Don Mills where they occupied a two-storey maisonette, then a third-floor apartment. His last residence in Toronto was an apartment on Erskine Avenue. He is buried in York Cemetery, Willowdale. His single memorial, aside from stories and novels, is the Hugh Garner Housing Cooperative Inc., a 181-unit development at 550 Ontario Street, opened in 1983. There is talk of erecting a statue of the man in the adjacent park.

Emma Goldman (1869-1940), the Russian-born anarchist, spent the last fourteen months of her life in Toronto. She rented a third-floor flat above Switzer's Delicatessen, 322 Spadina Avenue. On May 14, 1940, she died of a cerebral haemorrhage in the Toronto General Hospital and is buried in Chicago.

Such at least is the traditional wisdom. Paul Kennedy, the researcher, maintains that it is a red herring that she ever resided above Switzer's. At the time of her fatal stroke she boarded with friends in their residence (still standing) at 295 Vaughan Road. She lay in state in the old Labour Lyceum where Salem Bland delivered the eulogy. According to Kennedy she bought her sour cream in Kensingon Market and drank beer at Grossman's Tavern.

As a lecturer she visited Toronto on a number of occasions. In *Living My Life* (1931), she noted: "The Public and University libraries in Toronto were lacking in modern works on the social, education, and psychologic problems occupying the best minds. 'We do not buy books we consider immoral,' a local librarian was reported as saying." Carol Bolt (b. 1941), the playwright, wrote *Red Emma* (1974) about this intriguing woman.

Igor Gouzenko (1919-1982), the cypher clerk who defected from the Russian Embassy in Ottawa in 1945, lived for many years incognito (as "Mr. Peter Brown") "somewhere in Mississauga." He lies buried under an assumed name somewhere in the western part of the greater Toronto area. His autobiography *This Was My Choice* (1948) was filmed later that year as *The Iron Curtain*, with Dana Andrews as Igor. He also published a novel, *The Fall of a Titan* (1953), about life under a Stalin-like dictator, which won the Governor General's Award for Fiction. His wife Svetlana, who survives him, wrote *Before Igor* (1960). He appeared from time to time on television wearing a white hood.

Ernest Hemingway (1899-1961), who received the Nobel Prize for Literature in 1954, has a short but nonetheless significant association with the city. In the preface to an edition of his short stories, he listed Toronto among the places that were good ones in which to write. But it is doubtful that one could go as far as David Donnell, the poet, who maintained that his residency in Toronto contributed to the evolution of his characteristically clipped manner of writing.

Hemingway resided here at two points in his early career. He arrived for the first time in the autumn of 1919 at the invitation of Ralph Connable, an influential American who was general manager of the Woolworth chain in Canada. Hemingway was Connable's house guest at his residence, 153 Lyndhurst Avenue, to be a tutor for Connable's lame son. The residence is a handsome white building with a green tile roof. There is a Connable Drive which runs off Lyndhurst.

With his advertising and editorial connections, Connable arranged for Hemingway's introduction to Greg Clark of the *Toronto Star*. As Hemingway had newspaper credits — he worked on the *Kansas City Star* — he was able to sell short features to the *Daily Star* and the *Star Weekly*. These have since been collected by William White in 1967. Hemingway asked and was made the *Star's* Paris correspondent. That he was not greatly excited about Toronto may be gleaned from this

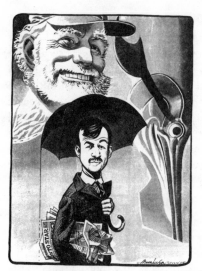

There are no known photographs of Ernest Hemingway in Toronto, but this cartoon by Duncan Macpherson appeared in the Toronto Star on May 30, 1981. It perfectly captures the youthful journalist who used copies of the Star to wrap up fish, and the older, rugged fisherman. [The Toronto Star]

Ernest Hemingway with his wife and their new-born son lived in a flat in the rear of this apartment building at 1599 Bathurst Street. [Mark Fortier]

Ernest Hemingway resided here as a tutor on his first visit to Toronto. The mansion is located at Lyndhurst Avenue and Connable Drive. [Mark Fortier]

exerpt from the letter he wrote to a friend on Dec. 20, 1919: "This Toronto thing looks like the original Peruvian Doughnuts." It is not known precisely when he left the city.

When Hemingway came for the second time it was from Paris with his pregnant wife Hadley at the insistence of the *Star*. They arrived in the fall of 1923 and rented a room for three weeks at the Selby Hotel and then an apartment at the Cedarvale Mansions, 1599 Bathurst Street, north of St. Clair Avenue, not far north of the Connable residence. The apartment number is not known but it was a one-bedroom flat with a sunroom that looked out onto the ravine in three directions, north, east, and south. Today the still-handsome building is known as the Bathurst Park Apartments. Their son John Hadley (called Mr. Bumby) was born in Toronto on October 10, 1923. They left the Cedarvale Mansions and returned to Paris in January 1924.

He wrote to Gertrude Stein on Oct. 11, 1923, expressing his feelings about living in Toronto. "However we have . . . a corking new apt. on a ravine where the town leaves off into country sunny, a fine stretch of fine country, a hill that you can ski down or rather I can ski down, if the snow comes, and if I come home from the office. . . ." To Ezra Pound, two days later, he confessed: "Things get worse here. I am now undertaking the show on a day by day basis. Get through today. Then get through tomorrow. Like 1918." (Scuttlebut has it that Pound's letters to Hemingway were addressed to Hemingway at "Tomato, Can.") To Sylvia Beach, on Nov. 6, he claimed "the people are all merde . . . we are the only nice people in Canada."

During his stay in the city he wrote a free-verse poem "I Like Canadians" which runs: "I like Canadians. / They are so unlike Americans. / They go home at night. / Their cigarets don't smell bad. / Their hats fit. / They really believe that they won the war. / They don't believe in Literature. / They think Art has been exaggerated. / But they are wonderful on ice skates."

Hemingway worked as a general reporter for the *Star* in its old editorial offices at 18 King Street West. His salary was $75 a week.

The memoirs and reminiscences of Morley Callaghan, Frederick Griffin, Greg Clark, Wilfrid Eggleston, Gordon Sinclair, J. H. Crandon, and others tell various tales about Hemingway and his feuds with Harry C. Hindmarch, the managing editor; his taste for cinnamon toast; his lunches at Old Angelo's Spaghetti House; his drinking at the Selby Hotel; his dancing at Bucket o' Blood night club on Yonge Street; his writing desk and its provenance when the Hemingways left their apartment, back rent owing, or so the story goes.

Hugh Hood (b. 1928), the novelist, was raised in the house that stands at 430 Summerhill Avenue near the top of Rosedale. (Watch for the sign that says Hutone Cleaners.) The novelist is blessed with a total-recall memory so that a lost Toronto could be recreated from his fiction the way postwar Warsaw was reconstructed using old maps and prints. Hood attended De LaSalle-Oaklands and the University of Toronto, and since 1961 has taught English at the Université de Montréal. An essay could be written on the use he has made of Toronto sites in his many stories and novels; a few sites follow. There is a breathtaking, impressionistic journey up Yonge Street in "The End of It," the final story in *Flying a Red Kite* (1962). The collection of essays called *The Governor's Bridge Is Closed*

This drawing by Lawren Harris appeared on the title page of the first edition of Hugh Hood's The Swing in the Garden *(1975) [National Gallery of Canada]*

(1973) takes its title from a sign that once appeared over the Glen Road Bridge in Rosedale. "One block to the east, in an attic flat on top of a Dale Avenue house, I met my wife for the first time," the author has explained. "I couldn't possibly forget that particular bridge because by walking across it I walked into a lifelong love, a marriage and four children, a whole life." Noreen, his wife, an artist in her own right, was then a student living in the top-floor flat in the residence of Morley Callaghan at 20 Dale Avenue, the ambience of which Hood described in his story "Where the Myth Touches Us," included in *Flying a Red Kite*. These are but scattered references; sustained metaphors appear in the published volumes of the projected twelve-volume series called "The New Age." So certain was Hood that he would complete the series in an orderly fashion that he listed the upcoming titles and years of publication in *Colombo's Canadian References* (1978). The series will not be complete until the year 1999, but it has already earned him the sobriquet "the Proust of Toronto" for the associative manner of writing and the documentation and dramatization of Canadian social history for a period of seventy-five years. *The Swing in the Garden* (1975) is set in an unnamed, middle-class residential district of the city in the 1930s. *A New Athens* (1977) takes place around Brockville in the 1950s and 1960s. *Reservoir Ravine* (1979) returns to Toronto and describes in the 1920s and 1930s such sites as University College (notably the Cloisters), Rosedale Ravine between Mount Pleasant and Yonge, South Drive, Summerhill Avenue, Jakes Avenue, and St. Clair Avenue East. *Black and White Keys* (1982), set in the 1940s, mentions the Hollywood Theatre, Maple Leaf Gardens, etc. Fulfilling the scenario, "The New Age" will unfold with the publication of *The Scenic Art* (1984), *The Motor Boys in Ottawa* (1986), *Property and Value* (1988), *Tony's Book* (1991), *Be Sure to Close Your Eyes* (1993), *Dead Men's Watches* (1995), *Great Realizations* (1997), and a title yet to be announced (1999).

Walter Huston (1884-1950), the actor, was born in Toronto and raised in a late Victorian house, at 11 Major Street, near Kensington Market. At the age of sixteen he made his stage début at Massey Hall. Although not a writer, he is associated with highly literate roles and with Kurt Weill's "September Song." He is the father of the director John Huston. Both father and son received Academy Awards for their contributions to *The Treasure of Sierra Madre*, the 1948 Hollywood film. The Toronto Film Society unveiled a plaque at 11 Major Street on June 3, 1984.

Harold Adams Innis (1894-1952), the economic historian, joined the University of Toronto's Department of Political Economy in 1920. He lived in the red brick residence, now painted grey, at 92 Dunvegan Road, in Forest Hill. He showed in his books that Canada exists because of — and not despite — its geography. Innis College, on St. George Street, was named in his honour in 1976. Donald Creighton called Innis "Canada's greatest national historian."

Anna Jameson (1794-1860), traveller and author, was a recognized literary figure (with seven published books to her credit) when, with considerable reluctance, she agreed to join her husband, Robert Jameson, Attorney General of Upper Canada, in the fledgling community at Toronto. She arrived in winter in 1836 and left for good some eight months later. Life in Toronto was rude by her standards, yet she resided in a large house and her needs were met by three servants. The house was located on the south side of Wellington Street, west of Spadina Avenue. At a later date the house became part of the Lyndhurst estate and then part of Loretto Abbey which was demolished in 1961. She described Toronto as "a little ill-built town on low land" and made use of summer to travel (alone) throughout Upper Canada. She recorded her experiences in her classic *Winter Studies and Summer Rambles in Canada* (1838). She visited and described the sites and inhabitants of Oakville, Stony Creek, St. Catharines, Niagara Falls, Hamilton, Brantford, the Grand River, Paris, Woodstock, London, Talbot County, St. Thomas, Chatham, Mackinac, Manitoulin Island, Penetanguishene, Lake Simcoe, Holland Landing, and Toronto again. She then returned to England. When she

C. W. Jefferys is shown sketching in his barn studio, Hogg's Hollow, York Mills, in 1939. [Robert Stacey]

visited the Manitowaning reserve on Manitoulin Island, she was inducted into the Ojibway tribe as Was-sa-je-wun-e-qua, or "Woman of the Bright Stream."

C. W. Jefferys (1869-1952), the historical artist, is mainly remembered for *The Picture Gallery of Canadian History* (1942-1950). His line drawings of life in the past which appeared in this three-volume set have illuminated innumerable textbooks. He lived from 1910 to his death in the red-brick farmhouse at 4111 Yonge Street, north of York Mills Road. The farmhouse dates from the 1820s. His studio was in the barn, since demolished. His achievement is also acknowledged by a plaque on the campus of the University of Toronto.

Ernest Jones (1879-1958), neurologist and first biographer of Sigmund Freud, taught at the University of Toronto from 1908 to 1913. He lived in the comfortable house at 407 Brunswick Avenue. An unconventional and controversial figure by the Toronto standards of the day, he noted in the dreams of his patients the ambivalent imagery of Niagara Falls; he commented publicly on the connection between oral sex and Holy Communion; and he paid $500 to a female patient who was blackmailing him by alleging sexual abuse. He left the city under a cloud, yet he wrote warmly about the city in his autobiography, *Free Associations* (1959): "Life in Toronto was in many ways rather pleasant." He then joined Freud's circle in Vienna and wrote the three-volume study *Sigmund Freud: Life and Work* (1953-57). Freud himself spent time on Canadian soil, viewing Niagara Falls; this was during his single trip to America to lecture at Clark University, Worchester, Mass., in 1909. Freud's younger brother, Alexander Freud, was a furrier, who lived with his wife in Toronto in the 1950s.

Wyndham Lewis (1882-1957), British writer and painter, claimed a Canadian connection on the basis of his father's nationality (Canadian) and his birthplace — on his father's yacht off Amherst, N.S. But any sentimental attachment he had to his country of birth (or berth) was undercut by his enforced residence in Toronto during the Second World War. He was visiting in New York with his wife when the war broke out, and unable to return to England he settled in Toronto. The Lewises took a room for $14 a week at the Tudor Hotel on Sherbourne Street, south of Bloor. In his novel *Self Condemned* (1954), in which Toronto is satirized as "Momaco," he depicted the Tudor Hotel as the Blundell Hotel, and when the Tudor burnt in February, 1943, he described the conflagration. (He referred to this time as his "Tudor Period.") Thereupon the Lewises rented a room at the nearby Selby Hotel, which is still standing. Lewis also rented a bed-sitting room farther south on Sherbourne, which he used as a studio for his portrait and other painting. Douglas LePan (b. 1914) recalled in *Bright Glass of Memory* (1979) posing for him here in the summer of 1941. At one point he rented a studio at

22 Grenville Street. Lewis supported himself by painting "wealthy Methodists," including Lorne Pierce, and by writing for *Saturday Night* and CBC Radio. In letters he described Toronto as a "sanctimonious ice-box," a "bush-metropolis," and a "zero-land." Torontonians were "solemn yokels" and the city was "not a good place to be an intellectual in." He satirized it in *Self Condemned* and in the outline of an unwritten novel "Hill 100." He was relieved to be invited to join the faculty of Assumption College in Windsor (which, in *Self Condemned*, is called "The College of the Sacred Heart"). After the war he left Canada as soon as transportation could be arranged. *Self Condemned* was written in London when he was in his seventies and blind. It is considered his greatest literary work, and T. S. Eliot spoke of it as "a book of almost unbearable spiritual agony." He was obviously writing about himself when he described the sufferings of Professor René Harding who, with his wife Hester, lived in the Blundell Hotel. The novel was reissued in 1983 with nineteen of the author's illustrations.

Beatrice Lillie (b. 1903), the vaudeville and revue entertainer, was born at 68 Dovercourt Road and attended Gladstone School. She enjoyed a brilliant stage career and through marriage became Lady Peel, fifth Viscountess Peel. In her autobiography *Every Other Inch a Lady* (1972) she wrote: "A little bit of heaven had fallen down from the skies one day onto the shores of Lake Ontario. So they sprinkled it with stardust, and it became Irish Toronto."

Wilson MacDonald (1880-1967) was so popular a versifier in the 1920s that his fame eclipsed that of Robert Service and Pauline Johnson. Today he is remembered mainly for "Exit" and "The Song of the Ski" from *Out of the Wilderness* (1926) which went into ten editions. When verse fell out of fashion he published his own poems and sold them at recitals in high-school auditoriums across the country. He was the one poet a generation or two of Canadian students had ever seen or heard. From 1953 he was sustained by the Wilson MacDonald Poetry Society. His last years were spent in Apartment No. 6, 34 Oakburn Place, just east of Yonge Street, Downsview. There is a museum devoted to his work in his birthplace of Cheapside, Ont.

Gwendolyn MacEwen (b. 1941), the poet and novelist, grew up in the house that once stood at 38 Keele Street, on the northwest corner of the intersection of Bloor, the site of the Keele subway station. Especially dear to her are imaginative memories of High Park, just across the street, and Sunnyside, especially the ruin-like waterfront baths described in a work in progress called "Noman's Land." She has lived intermittently on Centre Island.

Marshall McLuhan (1911-1980), the theorist of media, joined the English Department of St. Michael's College,

University of Toronto, in 1946. He founded in 1963 the university's Centre for Culture and Technology in the Coach House on Queen's Park Crescent. He and his family lived in a house, now torn down, at 81 St. Mary's Street, then in a modest residence at 29 Wells Hill Avenue. In 1968 the McLuhans moved a few blocks west into a more imposing home (Number 3) in the enclave known as Wychwood Park. He is buried in Holy Cross Cemetery, 8361 Yonge Street, Thornhill. His plaque reads: "The Truth Shall Make You Free."

Vincent Massey (1887-1967), patrician Governor General, was born in Toronto and raised in the mansion at 519 Jarvis Street, as was his younger brother, the actor Raymond Massey. In 1921, in one of these large Victorian rooms, Raymond announced to Vincent that he planned to try his luck on the English stage. Vincent replied, "What name are you going to use?" Raymond tells the story in the first volume of his autobiography, *When I Was Young* (1976).

L. M. Montgomery (1874-1942), the author of the much-loved "Anne" books, spent her last years in Toronto. When her husband retired from the ministry in 1935, they moved from the manse in Norval, Ont., to the large house, which they called "Journey's End," at 210 Riverside Drive, then in the Village of Swansea. Here she wrote her last three novels: *Anne of Windy Poplars* (1936), *Jane of Lantern Hill* (1937), and *Anne of Ingleside* (1939). She died here in 1942, her husband two years later. They lie buried side by side at Cavendish, P.E.I. The Toronto house is privately owned but a plaque has been erected in a nearby park which bears the name Lucy Maud Montgomery Park.

Susanna Moodie (1803-1885), chronicler of pioneer life, moved to Toronto following the death of her husband in Belleville in 1869, to live with her daughter, Mrs. John Vickers, at 152 Adelaide Street West. She spent part of each year with her sister, Catharine Parr Traill, in Peterborough.

Alexander Muir (1830-1906), composer of "The Maple Leaf Forever," was inspired to compose this once-popular song when a leaf from a silver maple tree brushed against his sleeve one evening in 1867. The patriotic song was so popular it became something of an anthem (though its pro-British sentiments have doomed it since the 1960s). The silver maple tree still thrives. It is located at 6 Laing Street, in the east end, and the site was first marked by a plaque erected in 1937. The plaque currently in place was raised in 1958 by the Grand Orange Lodge of British America. At the time of composition Muir was principal of nearby Leslieville Public School; in later years he was principal of Gladstone Street School and a resident of McKenzie Crescent, his neighbour being the young Greg Clark who recalled his appearance: "He was, I clearly recollect, a tall man with a large, rugged, creative head who walked leaning forward as if into a high wind."

Following his death the Alexander Muir Memorial Gardens in Lawrence Park were named in his honour.

John Wilson Murray (1840-1906), Chief Inspector of the Ontario Criminal Justice Department and author of *Memoirs of a Great Detective* (1904), lived on Brunswick Avenue, at old No. 82, demolished to make way for Margaret Fairley Park. Douglas Campbell portrayed Murray in the CBC-TV series *The Great Detective*.

Douglas Campbell created the role of John Wilson Murray for the television series The Great Detective. [CBC / Norman Chamberlin]

Mary Pickford (1893-1979), the film star, was born in a small, two-storey house at 211 University Avenue. The house was demolished after World War II to make way for the Hospital for Sick Children. She told the story of her early years in her autobiography, *Sunshine and Shadows* (1955). There is a plaque to mark the spot, augmented by a sculptured head executed by Eino, dedicated in 1983. The inscription describes her as cinema's first "superstar."

Marjorie Pickthall (1883-1922), the poet, was brought to Toronto when she was six. She attended Bishop Strachan School and lived in the family home, which is still standing, at 537 Euclid Avenue. With the death of

Photograph and specimen signature of Marjorie Pickthall, from Lorne Pierce's Marjorie Pickthall: A Book of Remembrance (1925). [Terry Keough]

her mother in 1910, she became a librarian at Victoria College. She died in Victoria, B.C., but is buried, at her father's request, in St. James' Cemetery. A granite cross marks her grave which adjoins her mother's. She arranged to have buried with her mother those manuscripts of stories and poems her mother particularly appreciated.

E. J. Pratt (1882-1964), with roots in Newfoundland and residence in Toronto, is a "national poet." He was known throughout the English-speaking world for his narrative poems, and although he spent his adult life in Toronto he wrote nothing specifically about the city. He taught in the English department of Victoria College from 1920 to 1953, and its E. J. Pratt Library was named in his honour. His manuscripts and other memorabilia are on display in the Library's Pratt Room. With his wife Viola and their daughter, the writer and editor Claire, the Pratt family occupied three houses in the northern part of the city. Between 1922 and 1932, they lived in the house at 25 Tullis Drive, where among their guests were Frederick Philip Grove and Laurence Binyon. From 1932 to 1953, they lived in the three-storey house at 21 Cortleigh Boulevard, the scene of fabled parties, with such guests as Sir Charles G.D. Roberts, Christopher Morley, Louis Broomfield, Leopold Infeld, Northrop Frye, Lovat Dickson, and Wyndham Lewis. (Morley, the American man of letters, added in the 1940s the following limerick, with its allusion to editor H. Napier Moore, to Claire's scrapbook: "If I don't get drunk in Toronto / It's not because I don't want to / For Napier and Ned / Can put me to bed / So give me another drink pronto!") From 1953 to 1960, they occupied the house at 47 Glencairn Avenue, which attracted such visitors as Ralph Gustafson, Arthur Phelps, and Lorne Pierce. The final residence was an apartment at 5 Elm Avenue, off Mount Pleasant Avenue. The poet is buried in Mount Pleasant Cemetery.

E. J. Pratt and his daughter Claire pose for the photographer in this snapshot taken in the summer of 1934 in the backyard of their home at 21 Cortleigh Boulevard. [Viola and Claire Pratt]

Robert L. Ripley (1893-1949), the American cartoonist of "Believe It or Not!" fame, visited Toronto to address the Canadian Club on October 5, 1932. While in the city he was entertained by Clifford Sifton Jr. and his wife at their spacious residence at 318 Lawrence Avenue East, at Bayview Avenue, now part of the Toronto French School. Gordon Sinclair claimed that Ripley and Sifton were sitting on the balcony overlooking the ravine when Mrs. Sifton joined them, exclaiming, "Here are the two biggest liars in the world!"

Sir Charles G. D. Roberts (1860-1943), who has been called the first English-Canadian man of letters, assisted Goldwin Smith at The Grange as an editor of *The Week* in 1883-84. Spending most of his productive years in New York and London, he returned to Canada in 1935 and occupied the top floor apartment at No. 25, Ernescliffe, at 197 Wellesley Street, at the corner of Sherbourne. He died here and was buried in Mount Pleasant Cemetery. One of his weekend pleasures in later years was canoeing around the Toronto Islands.

Marshall Saunders (1861-1947), the author of *Beautiful Joe* (1894), and other popular animal stories, spent her last years in Toronto. She lived at 62 Glengowan Road in the Lawrence Park area.

Ernest Thompson Seton (1860-1946), the author and artist, was brought to Canada by his parents in 1866, settling in Toronto in 1870. The family lived on Elizabeth Street. Seton roamed the Don Valley in his youth, and built himself a cabin there. He took the gold medal of the Ontario College of Art in 1879, after which he led a roving life which took him to Carberry, Man., and then to Santa Fe, New Mexico, where he established the Seton Institute. Three stories in *Wild Animals I Have Known* (1898) have Toronto locales. "Silversport, The Story of a Crow" takes place in the pine-clad grove around Castle Frank, on the Danforth. The Don Valley is the habitat of the last of the copper-ruffled partridges in "Redruff, The Story of the Don Valley Partridge." In the western reaches of the city, in the Erindale Woods, was set the tale of "The Springfield Fox." The naturalist is recalled today in the naming of Ernest Thompson Seton Park. He is said to have briefly lived in the conservation area in Mississauga called the Rattray Marsh.

Gordon Sinclair (1900-1984), broadcaster and journalist, was born in a rented house on Carlton Street "50 yards from Riverdale Zoo, on June 3, 1900 . . . a Victorian." So he wrote in the first volume of his autobiography, *Will the Real Gordon Sinclair Please Stand Up* (1966). The family lived on Howland Road from 1904 to 1913. Young Sinclair joined the Toronto *Star* in 1929 and became a globe-hopping feature writer during the Depression. After the war he became a popular radio commentator and newscaster, then a regular on *Front Page Challenge*. The second volume of autobiographical reminiscences is called *Will Gordon Sinclair Please Sit Down* (1975). He lived for many years in Islington.

Raymond Souster   (b. 1921), to whom belongs the appellation "the poet-laureate of Toronto," was born in the city and has lived in its west end ever since then (aside from those years spent in service in Europe during the Second World War). He works as a securities custodian at the Canadian Imperial Bank of Commerce, in the Queen and Bay financial district, and he lives on Baby Point Crescent, near Brulé Gardens, where he has been engaged in publishing his four-volume *Collected Poems*.

Souster compensates in his poems for the neglect of the city in the poetic works of Sir Charles G. D. Roberts and E. J. Pratt. Almost all his poems are set in the city in the period from the mid 1940s to the late 1970s. He sees the city clearly and his own position in regard to it. As he wrote in "The City Called a Queen" (1954): "Strange city, / cold, hateful city, / that I still celebrate and love. . . ."

Raymond Souster skates on thin ice in this drawing by Don Evans as Isaac Bickerstaff. [Special Collections, University of Calgary Libraries]

Souster operated Contact Press out of his home at 28 Mayfield Avenue, in the district of Swansea, from 1952 to 1967. The Contact imprint appeared on a mimeographed magazine and a series of books beginning with *Cerberus* (1952), an anthology of poems by Souster, Louis Dudek, and Irving Layton. An offshoot of Contact Press was the Contact Poetry Reading Series held regularly at the old Greenwich Gallery on Bay Street in the late 1950s. Souster's poem "Moving Day" (1967) expresses his sentiments on saying goodbye to all that.

C. P. Stacey   (b. 1906), the military historian, mentions in his autobiography, *A Date with History* (1983), that he was born opposite the University of Toronto, at 161 College Street. He finds this appropriate, as until his recent retirement he was University Professor at the university and Senior Fellow at Massey College. He now lives and continues to write at his apartment at 21 Dale Avenue in Rosedale.

Vincent Starrett   (1886-1974), the Chicago bookman, noted in his autobiography, *Born in a Bookshop* (1965): "I was born in a bookshop or so close to it as to be able to claim the distinction. It was the early morning of Tuesday, October 26, 1886, and the scene was No. 26 Oxford Street in the City of Toronto. In its prime it was a handsome enough middle-class dwelling, I have been told, but I have no particular affection for it. I saw it consciously for the first time about thirty years ago and was not impressed." Starrett contributed the popular "Books Alive" column to the *Chicago Tribune* and, with Christopher Morley and others, was one of the original Baker Street Irregulars. Oxford Street runs off Spadina Avenue in the Kensington market area. The "bookshop" seems to be the Upper Canada Bible and Tract Society, then located on the west side of Spadina Avenue not far from No. 26 Oxford Street.

A. E. van Vogt   (b. 1912), the contributor to the Golden Age of Science Fiction, lived for two years in the newly built house at 997 Briar Hill Avenue. He resided here with his wife, the writer E. Mayne Hull (1905-1975), and wrote some of his most powerful stories before leaving for Los Angeles in November 1944. Here he completed the original version of his classic novel *Slan* (1946).

Albert Durrant Watson   (1850-1926), a once-popular poet, essayist, spiritualist, and physician, lived at 10 Euclid Avenue, where he conducted séances. The evening of February 17, 1919, he contacted the spirits of Walt Whitman and the American poet's chief disciple, Richard Maurice Bucke, both of whom dictated detailed messages from "the Twentieth Plane" to Flora Macdonald Denison and others. His *Poetical Works* (1924) goes unread, but his books on spiritualism make marvellous reading, for on other occasions he was in contact with the shades of Tennyson, Shakespeare, Milton, Carlyle, etc. Lorne Pierce wrote an appreciation of the man, privately printed in an edition of two hundred copies in 1924.

Walt Whitman   (1819-1892), the great American poet, passed through Toronto on his way to spend the summer with his friend Richard Maurice Bucke (1837-1902) in London, Ont. In his diary for June 26-7, 1880, he recorded his elation at being in Toronto beside "blue Ontario's waters." He rode on "the omnibus with the driver" and "the city made the impression on me of a lively dashing place." He concluded his description in this way: "We are off, off into Toronto Bay (soon the wide expanse and cool breezes of Lake Ontario). As we steam out a mile or so we get a pretty view of Toronto from the blue foreground of the waters, — the whole rising spread of the city, groupings of roofs, spires, trees, hills in the background. Goodbye, Toronto, with your memories of a very lively and agreeable visit."

Oscar Wilde   (1856-1900), the Anglo-Irish writer, visited Toronto in May 1882 on a lecture tour. He toured the University of Toronto grounds on May 25 and much admired the wrought-iron gates of University College. His lecture that evening was described the following day by the *Evening Telegram* in these terms: "Miss Oscar Wilde seems to be a charming young lady, although her costume is rather unfeminine." On May 27 he was the dinner guest of Henry Pellatt, not yet a baronet or the builder of Casa Loma, but a twenty-two-year-old financier and anglophile.

Sir John S. Willison (1856-1927), the journalist and author, became in 1913 the first Canadian journalist to be made a knight bachelor. He edited successively the *Globe* and the *News* and then became Canadian correspondent of *The Times* of London. There is a memorial window in his honour in St. Paul's Church, Bloor Street East. The window depicts in the main the Good Shepherd and the Sermon on the Mount, but the lower left-hand panel shows William Caxton reading proofs of the first book to be published in England, and the lower right-hand panel reproduces the masthead and front page of *The Times* with the words "In memory of Sir John Willison, Journalist, Publicist, Patriot" and then a line from Chaucer: "He was a very perfect, gentle knight."

Larry Zolf (b. 1934), media guru or gadfly, lives in the Beaches area at 42 Balsam Avenue. The third floor of his "Balmy Beach Summer Mansion" (as he calls it) is devoted to his immense library.

The Group of Seven The Group of Seven was the most important school of artists in the country's history, but it was also a group of writers. Many of the original Seven, and the extended Eleven, wrote poetry and prose. Indeed, there has seldom been so literary-minded a collection of painters. The Group was brought together following a showing of J. E. H. MacDonald's sketches at the Arts and Letters Club in 1911, but it did not exhibit collectively until May 1920. Here is a limited amount of information on the principal residences or studios in the Toronto area of original and subsequent members of the Group.

The Studio Building, 25 Severn Street: The Studio Building of Canadian Art, in Rosedale Ravine, visible from the Yonge Street subway, was designed in a spartan, Modernist style by architect Eden Smith and built by artist Lawren Harris and art patron Dr. James MacCallum in 1913-14. It was intended as working and living quarters for like-minded artists, some of whom exhibited as members of the Group of Seven. Among artists associated with the Studio Building are Harris, writer and illustrator Arthur Heming, A. Y. Jackson, J. E. H. MacDonald, and Tom Thomson. Jackson and Thomson shared a studio until Thomson moved into a shack behind the building — relocated at the McMichael Canadian Collection in Kleinburg — and Jackson moved out only in 1955. The Studio Building is privately owned. With ateliers here now are artist Harold Town and art critic Paul Duval.

St. Anne's Church, 270 Gladstone Avenue, was built

St. Anne's Church is a Byzantine-style building decorated by artists, including members of the Group of Seven. This sketch was made by Dorothy Clark McClure in 1973. [St. Anne's Church]

in the Byzantine style and dedicated in 1908. This church was beautifully decorated in 1923 by ten artists and two sculptors working in modern styles to interpret scenes from the New Testament. There is a nativity by F. H. Varley, an Adoration of the Magi by Franklin Carmichael, a Raising of Lazarus by Thoreau MacDonald, a Crucifixion by J. E. H. MacDonald, with sculptures of the Four Evangelists — Matthew as an angel, Mark as a Lion, Luke as an ox, John as an eagle — by Frances Loring and Florence Wyle, etc.

Franklin Carmichael (1890-1945), born in Orillia, spent his last years painting in the studio behind his home at 23 Cameron Avenue, Willowdale.

A. J. Casson (b. 1898), born in Toronto, joined the Group in 1926. He has lived and painted for many years at 43 Rochester Avenue, in the Lawrence Park area.

LeMoine FitzGerald (1890-1956), who joined the Group in 1932, lived all his life in Winnipeg and was principal of the College of Art. He is the only member of the extended Group who had no Toronto address.

Lawren Harris (1885-1970), born in Brantford, had the modernistic white stucco residence, at 2 Ava Crescent, built to his specifications by architect Alexandra Birivkova. He lived here from 1930 to 1934 when he moved to the United States. His last years were spent in his home on Belmont Drive, Vancouver. His ashes are buried at the McMichael Gallery.

Edwin H. Holgate (1892-1977), born in Allandale, Ont., joined the Group in 1930. He lived in various unspecified residences in Toronto before moving to Morin Heights, Que., where his neighbour was Peter Whalley (b. 1921), the cartoonist and illustrator.

A. Y. Jackson (1882-1974), born in Montreal, worked in the Studio Building, being the last to leave in 1955. He moved to Manotick, then to Ottawa, where he resided on MacLaren Avenue. In his final years he was artist-in-residence at the McMichael Gallery, where he is buried.

Frank H. Johnston (1888-1949), born in Toronto,

grew up at 121 Shaw Street in a house since demolished, resigned from the Group in 1924, changed his first name to Franz, and lived his last years in the fine home at 135 St. Germain Avenue. He is buried at the McMichael Gallery.

Arthur Lismer (1885-1969), born in England, began painting in 1913, one year after renting the three-storey house at 306 Delaware Avenue. He moved to Montreal in 1940, joining the Montreal Museum of Fine Arts and living on Rue Fort. He is buried at the McMichael Gallery.

J. E. H. MacDonald (1873-1932), born in England, from 1910 resided in the ten-room, clapboard house located at 121 Centre Street, Thornhill. In the backyard he painted "The Tangled Garden" in 1916. The name of the painting was chosen by Paul Duval as the title of his 1978 illustrated biography of the painter. MacDonald's son, Thoreau MacDonald (b. 1901), who illustrated many books published by the Ryerson Press, lived here most of his life. J. E. H. MacDonald is buried in Prospect Cemetery, Toronto.

Tom Thomson (1877-1917), born at Claremont, Ont., was the spiritual founder of the Group. He lived and painted in the shack behind the Studio Building; in 1962, the shack was moved from the Rosedale Ravine to the McMichael Canadian Collection.

Frederick Varley (1881-1969), born in England, lived with friends in the house at 13 Lowther Avenue, and when they moved to Unionville in 1957, he accompanied them, living at 197 Main Street. He is buried at the McMichael Gallery.

For the entry on the McMichael Canadian Collection, see KLEINBURG.

Trollope Lake

Trollope Lake, north of Kirkland Lake, was named in honour of the English novelist, Anthony Trollope (1815-1882).

Tuck Lake

In Quetico Provincial Park, southeast of Atikokan, is Tuck Lake. It was named after Friar Tuck of Robin Hood fame in 1930 by Robert Douglas, secretary of the Geographic Board of Canada, who chose the name to replace the common name Caribou Lake. It was Douglas who from his wide knowledge of literature assigned names like Mercutio, Waverley, Geraint, and Marmion to other features in northwestern Ontario.

Utopia

Utopia is west of Barrie. The name derives from the Latin literary work Utopia (1516) written by Sir Thomas More (1478-1535).

Valjean Lake

Valjean Lake, north of Atikokan, was called after the convict Jean Valjean in the romantic novel Les Misérables (1862) by Victor Hugo (1802-1885).

Verse Lake   See NOKOMIS LAKE.

Vienna

In St. Luke's Cemetery in Vienna, southeast of St. Thomas, is buried the poet Wilson MacDonald (1880-1967). "The greatest thing I found in Canada was Wilson MacDonald," Albert Einstein once claimed.

Virgil

The community of Virgil, near Niagara-on-the-Lake, was named for the Latin poet Virgil (70-19 B.C.), who figures as the guide in Dante's Divine Comedy.

Walden

This small community, southwest of Sudbury, may bring to mind the famous book Walden, or Life in the Woods (1854). Yet the mining community was not named after the book by Henry David Thoreau. The town's name was derived, acronymically, from letters taken from the names of three amalgamated communities — Waters, Lively, and Denison.

Walden Pond

South of Bon Echo is located Walden Pond, which was named after Walden (1854) by Henry David Thoreau (1817-1862). The original Walden Pond, where Thoreau built his cabin, is near Concord, Massachusetts.

Wallacetown

Born on a farm near Wallacetown, a village between London and Chatham, was Robert Barr (1850-1912), a once-popular Anglo-American novelist. With Stephen Crane (1871-1900) he wrote the picaresque novel The O'Ruddy (1903).

Waterloo

Waterloo and its "twin city" of Kitchener are located northeast of London. Waterloo is well known as the home of the University of Waterloo, incorporated in 1959, which has an outstanding computer science faculty. The poet Earle Birney (b. 1904) has written a satire called "1984 Minus 17 & Counting at the U of Waterloo Ontario" (1967) in which he contrasts the "mathamen" and the "artsies" who apparently comprise the "communiternity." The University of Waterloo has hosted the biennial Elizabethan Theatre Conference since 1968 when it was established by David Galloway of the English department.

The University of Waterloo will become the repository of sixty million words when the university computerizes the Oxford English Dictionary (1928). The University of Waterloo and the Oxford University Press announced plans in 1984 to integrate and electronically file the OED's thirteen volumes and four supplements plus additional data. This computerization will make available on an on-line basis the contents of what is being called the "Super OED."

Whitby

Of dubious literary distinction but of some cinematic significance is the fact that May Irwin (1862-1938), the silent-film actress, was born in Whitby. She starred in the first movie condemned on moral grounds: *The Kiss* (1896), a short feature, which consisted of nothing more than an elongated osculation.

Wiarton

Wiarton is northeast of Owen Sound in the picturesque Georgian Bay area. The poet William Wilfred Campbell (1858-1918) arrived here as a young man in 1872. Here he wrote his first poem "Shadowy White." The house in which the Campbell family lived is extant, though altered, at the northwest corner of Mary and Gould Streets. A cairn in Blue Water Park, originally erected in 1937 and re-erected in 1967, has carved into an opened stone book the opening lines of his best-known poem "Indian Summer": "Along the line of smoky hills / The crimson forest

The Wiarton home of the youthful William Wilfred Campbell. [Terry Keough]

The cairn erected in memory of William Wilfred Campbell in the park at Wiarton, bears two inscriptions, as well as the opening lines of his poem "Indian Summer." The first inscription celebrates "the contribution of his poetic genius to Canadian letters. . .as an expression of affectionate regard for his lofty character and generous spirit." The second inscription of 1937 runs: "Who in boyhood roamed these shores / Who forever glorified in verse / "This magic region of blue waters throbbing." [Terry Keough]

stands." The cairn's inscription reads: "Memorial to William Wilfred Campbell, poet, who in boyhood roamed these shores, who forever glorified in verse 'This magic region of blue waters throbbing.'"

Northeast of Wiarton is Purple Valley where Campbell taught school (for $250 a year) in 1879. The school in question is now a community hall. A short distance down the road from it is the farm once owned by Charles Watchorn at which Campbell boarded.

Campbell's "Indian Summer" is amusingly parodied by Francis Sparshott (b. 1926) in his collection *The Naming of the Beasts* (1979). "Wasp Winter" begins: "Along the line of smoggy streets / The crimson neon glows, / And all day long the Dj bleats / From teenage radios." It ends: "Rich birds are flying south."

Wiarton is not far from the Cape Croker Reserve, 560 acres of which have been turned into a park. The author and ethnologist Basil H. Johnston (b. 1929) was born and raised on the reserve.

Wikwemikong Reserve See MANITOULIN ISLAND.

Windsor

The most southern city in the country, Windsor is located on the Detroit River south of Detroit, Michigan. It may

John Richardson drew on his military experience for such novels as Wacousta. He was, as he wrote about one of his heroes, "endowed with a susceptibility which rendered him unable to endure even the shadow of slight or insult." [Metropolitan Toronto Library]

This unsigned sketch of Assumption College, now Assumption University and part of the University of Windsor, dates from the 1940s. [Assumption University / Michael Power]

be said to enter into the annals of Canadian literature with the description of the vista from Amherstburg, to the south, written by Major John Richardson (1796-1852) in his novel *The Canadian Brothers* (1840).

Lewis at Assumption Associated with Assumption College, founded by the Basilian Fathers in 1857 but part of the University of Windsor since 1953, was the writer and artist Wyndham Lewis (1882-1957) who taught English and visual art in 1943-44. Lewis rented an apartment in the Royal Apartments, still standing at the northeast corner of Ellis and Ouellette Avenue, from which he admired the view down Ouellette of the Detroit skyline. Later he moved into a first-floor apartment with a western exposure in a building at 1805 Sandwich Street, now 1805 Riverside Drive West, which has since been demolished.

Pencil sketch of Marshall McLuhan done by Wyndham Lewis at Assumption College, 1944. [Assumption University / Michael Power]

This portrait of Wyndham Lewis was taken by a press photographer at St. Louis, Missouri, in 1943-44. [Cornell University Library]

Lewis delivered a lecture at the Vanity Theatre on Ouellette Avenue in the Christian Culture Series, founded in the 1930s by Father J. Stanley Murphy and still continuing. Other lecturers over the years included Etienne Gilson, Marshall McLuhan, Jacques Maritain, Fulton J. Sheen, Allen Tate, and Evelyn Waugh. Another speaker was A. M. Klein who gave his last public lecture at Assumption College in October 1956, his subject being the poetry of Gerard Manley Hopkins.

Lewis was commissioned to paint portraits, based on existing photographs, of earlier President Superiors of Assumption. He was paid $45 apiece for these canvases which now hang in the first-floor corridor of Assumption University, 400 Huron Church Road. He also painted the portrait of the wife of Paul Martin, in exchange for legal services provided by the prominent lawyer and future public figure. Assumption College is called "the College of the Sacred Heart" in Lewis's novel *Self Condemned* (1954).

Lewis was a faculty member in 1943-44, and this closely coincided with the tenure here of Marshall McLuhan (1911-1980). The two became fast friends and McLuhan was much affected by Lewis's rhetorical style. In fact, McLuhan's *Counterblast* (1969) echoes Lewis's magazine *Blast* (1914-15). The literary critic Hugh Kenner (b. 1923) taught here in 1946-48.

As a Catholic institution, Assumption College (now Assumption University) has had a particular appeal for Morley Callaghan (b. 1903) who has spent extended periods of time on the campus.

University of Windsor Assumption University is affiliated with the University of Windsor whose English Department expanded in the 1960s and 1970s to include writers. The *University of Windsor Review* was founded in 1965. The most prominent — and prolific — member of this department in the 1970s was Joyce Carol Oates (b. 1938), the American novelist (whose name, Gore Vidal quipped, sounds like a new kind of American breakfast food). While on campus she founded *The Ontario Review,* which she currently publishes from Princeton, N.J.

Evelyn Waugh was photographed following his lecture at Walkerville Collegiate, February 2, 1949, as part of the Christian Culture series, Assumption College. [Assumption University / Michael Power]

Major General Richard Rohmer: the type of man for whom the title "Sir" was conferred. [McClelland & Stewart / Ron McGough]

Numerous veiled references to Windsor occur in Oates's fiction of the period. The satiric collection *The Hungry Ghosts* (1975) is dedicated to "those fictitious and ghostly colleagues whose souls haunt this book" and the locale is "Hilberry University," which hardly differs from the University of Windsor. There are local references in many stories collected in *Crossing the Border* (1976), notably "Customs" which recreates the ordeal of crossing the Ambassador Bridge and facing border guards, and "An Incident in the Park" which accurately describes Jackson Park (calling it "Phillips Park"): "Beds and beds of roses, arranged in an immense circle, half the size of a city block. Tourists from the United States taking snapshots. Red roses, yellow roses, pink, white, peach-colored, pink edged with yellow. Pale roses, blood-red roses, dark blood-red roses. At the center of the rose garden was an airplane, on a pedestal. Hard to believe. Yes, but there it was, Evan had seen it once before, he and Renee had stared at it one Sunday a few months ago, had made a few jokes. Relic from World War II. A bomber with four propellers, 'historic,' painted with dim blue-green spots meant to be camouflage. A brass plaque explained it. *Liberator.*"

Authors associated with the University in the past or present include: Alexandre L. Amprimoz, John Ditsky, Dorothy Farmiloe, Len Gasparini, Alistair MacLeod, Eugene McNamara, Peter Sevens, and Tom Wayman (who became fascinated with the city's auto workers). On the editorial side of the *Windsor Star* are novelist Paul Vasey and C. H. (Marty) Gervais, poet and publisher of Black Moss Press. Also associated with the city is Paul Martin, the career politician, who lives on Riverside Drive. He was known to address gatherings around the world with these words: "Is there anyone here from Windsor?"

Wacousta   Across the river from Windsor is Detroit, Michigan. In a quirk of geography, the American city lies due north, not south, of the Canadian city; the location underlies the fact that Detroit's history is linked with Canada's. Detroit was founded as Fort Pontchartrain by the French in 1701 on today's Jefferson Avenue. Taken by the British in 1760, it was laid siege during the Conspiracy of Pontiac from May 9 to October 12, 1760. The siege is vividly described in *Wacousta; or, The Prophecy* (1832), a melodramatic novel by John Richardson (1796-1852), the first native-born novelist (who died destitute). The fort changed hands many times. It was surrendered to General Brock on August 16, 1812, and briefly occupied. *Wacousta's* sequel was called *The Canadian Brothers; or, The Prophecy Fulfilled* (1840). James Reaney (b. 1926) dramatized the first novel in 1978.

Wingham

The novelist and short-story writer Alice Munro (b. 1931) was born at Wingham, northeast of Goderich. In some respects the fictitious town of "Jubilee," where Del Jordan grows up in the 1940s in *Lives of Girls and Women* (1971), is modelled on Wingham. There are innumerable references to a Wingham-like town in the stories that comprise her other collections: *The Dance of the Happy Shades* (1968), *Something I've Been Meaning to Tell You* (1974), *Who Do You Think You Are?* (1978), and *The Moons of Jupiter* (1982). There is a plaque to mark the founding of Wingham, which is dated from 1851, at the Wingham Museum, Josephine Street.

Woodstock

Oscar Wilde (1856-1900) visited Woodstock, northeast of London, on May 29, 1882. He stayed at the O'Neill House and lectured on aesthetic matters in the old town hall, built in 1851-52. Restored to the condition in which he left it, the Italianate building houses the Oxford Museum. A native of Woodstock, who frequently writes about the region in his poems, is Don Coles (b. 1928), author of *Sometimes All Over* (1975) and other collections.

Blenheim Swamp, on the outskirts of Princeton, half way between Woodstock and Paris, was the scene of an internationally reported murder. Here, on February 21, 1890, J. Reginald Birchall killed and hid the body of F. C. Benwell, a remittance man. The case was solved by John Wilson Murray (1840-1906) and reported in his *Memoirs of a Great Detective* (1904).

Yum Yum Lake

In the Atikokan area are geographical features with names derived from Gilbert and Sullivan's comic opera *The Mikado* (1885). In addition to Yum Yum Lake, there is Poohbah Lake and Koko Falls.

Two views of the inspired memorial to Arctic explorer Vilhjalmur Stefansson at Arnes, his birthplace. [Travel Manitoba]

Manitoba

Allegra

This small community, north of Beauséjour, was named in 1918 by the first school teacher to arrive in the Bonar Law School District. It was called after a character in *The Children's Hour* (1859), a poem by Henry Wadsworth Longfellow (1807-1882).

Altamont

Altamont is a small town in the Pembina Hills south of Portage la Prairie. In *The Road Past Altamont* (1966), by Gabrielle Roy (1909-1983), the mother and daughter share a secret love of trips through the hilly country "past" Altamont. In 1927, the novelist, then a young school-teacher, taught in the village of Cardinal, north of Altamont.

Arnes

The Arctic explorer Vilhjalmur Stefansson (1879-1962) was born at Arnes, on Lake Winnipeg, north of Gimli. An imposing memorial has been erected in Stefansson Memorial Park to this controversial figure who led three expeditions to the Arctic. The memorial consists of his statue and a giant inukshuk inscribed with the following words: "I know what I have experienced, and I know what it has meant to me." The words come from his autobiography *Discovery* (1964) and appear in three languages: English, French, and Icelandic.

Barloe

A young farm labourer named Arthur George Street (1892-1966) left his native England and emigrated to Canada in 1911, settling on a quarter-section near Barloe, in northwest Manitoba. Here he worked the land for three years and experienced the mystique of the soil so often described by homesteaders but seldom as well as Street did in *Farmer's Glory* (1934), his autobiography, the first of more than thirty books about farming life. "Possibly this rhapsody on ploughing will seem absurd to many people," he wrote, "but no one can doubt my competence to sing on so noble a theme. If there be any such doubting Thomas, I would refer him to that quarter-section of land in North-West Manitoba. There have I written my signature with the plough, a signature that will stand when I am long forgotten, a signature of which I shall never be ashamed."

Boissevain See INTERNATIONAL PEACE GARDEN.

Brandon

Brandon is situated on the Assiniboine River and is the oldest prairie city west of Winnipeg. Born in Brandon was E. Mayne Hull (1905-1975), the one-time secretary to farm leader Henry Wise Wood who went on to marry A. E. van Vogt and publish a number of science-fiction stories in California. Born in Norway but educated in Brandon was the novelist Martha Ostenso (1900-1963). She taught high school in the lake district about one hundred miles northwest of Brandon. While living in Minnesota she wrote *Wild Geese* (1925) which is set in the farming community of "Oeland," Man., presumably based on the farming life northwest of Brandon.

Carberry

East of Brandon is Carberry which is the gateway to the region of Spruce Woods Provincial Park. This wilderness area is identified with the author and artist Ernest Thompson Seton (1860-1946). Seton homesteaded on his brother's farm near Carberry in 1882-85. Appointed Provincial Naturalist to the Manitoba Government in 1892, he laid out some of the Spruce Woods nature trails and wrote studies of the province's birds and mammals.

He set the novel *The Trail of the Sandhill Stag* (1899)

Ernest Thompson Seton sketched the log cabin that was the Seton homestead near Carberry in the 1880s. He called the drawing "My first Home in the West." [Estate of Julia M. Seton]

and parts of *Wild Animals I Have Known* (1898) in the region. The latter collection, probably the first thorough-going attempt to depict an animal's life in story form, inspired Rudyard Kipling, who read the stories in magazines prior to their book publication, to undertake his popular *Jungle Books* (1894-95). The animal tales also influenced Sir Charles G. D. Roberts' nature tales. In Spruce Woods Provincial Park, a bridge across the Assiniboine River near Kiche Manitou Campground bears Seton's name, as does Seton Wayside Park along the Trans-Canada Highway east of Carberry.

In 1930, Seton settled in Santa Fe, New Mexico. His estate and library formed the basis of the Seton Institute which remains devoted to his twin interests: woodcraft and wildlife.

Ernest Thompson Seton, the naturalist and author, was forty-one years old in 1901 when this photograph was taken. It first appeared in By a Thousand Fires *(1967) by Julia M. Seton. [Estate of Julia M. Seton]*

Carman

The town of Carman, southwest of Winnipeg, was named after the Methodist Bishop Arthur Carman and not after the poet Bliss Carman. The town has for many years been the home of Paul Hiebert (b.1892), who lives on a small farm on the town's edge, near the Carman Golf Course. Hiebert is the author of *Sarah Binks* (1947) and its sequel *Willows Revisited* (1967). These classics of tongue-in-cheek humour that satirize prairie life, art, and social pretentions are set in the fictitious community of "Willows" which is modelled on the town of Speyer, Sask. Hiebert was born at Pilot Mound, southwest of Carman.

Cartwright

Southwest of Pilot Mound, near the North Dakota border, is the town of Cartwright. When he was two the future novelist Robert Stead (1880-1959) was brought here by his parents who were homesteaders. At the age of eighteen, Stead founded the *Southern Manitoba Review* and the Crystal City *Courier,* two weeklies that he ran until 1919 when he opened an automobile agency. In 1919 he left the region which he called "Plainville" in such novels as *The Homesteaders* (1916) and *Grain* (1926). As he wrote in the latter novel, "Who knows Romance when he meets her in the daily round?"

Chaucer

Chaucer was a former CNR station, southeast of Brandon, named in honour of the great English poet Geoffrey Chaucer (1340-1400).

Churchill

Fort Prince of Wales, located at Churchill, where the Churchill River enters Hudson Bay, has been partially restored as a National Historic Park. It was commanded at one point by Samuel Hearne (1745-1792), who surrendered the Fort to the French in 1782.

Hearne explored the Barren Lands and found the Coppermine River. He became the first white man to reach the Arctic Ocean overland. A boulder near the fort bears his signature and the date, July 1, 1767 — perhaps the earliest Canadian graffiti. His famous *Journal,* published in 1795, has remained one of the most readable accounts of travels in the North.

The locale of *The Living Forest* (1925), by naturalist Arthur Heming (1870-1940), is the Churchill River which empties into Hudson Bay. In September 1936, Heming wrote to William Arthur Deacon who was then researching *A Literary Map of Canada:* "As to *The Living Forest,* it covers a certain district in the most minute and exact way and the region is that of the Churchill River. You may put your cross on the Churchill between North Indian Lake and South Indian Lake." He went on to say, "Although the plot is fiction the book is an absolutely true description of that district — the trees, scrubs, flowers, fruit, animals, birds, fish, flies, rivers, lakes, hills, rocks, marshes, everything to the most minute detail."

The richness and the remoteness of the region inspired Stephen Leacock (1869-1944), who wrote in *Canada: The Foundations of Its Future* (1941): "Such was the land of desolation that till yesterday God seemed to have forgotten. Beside its hidden wealth of today all the vineyards of France are as nothing."

Samuel Hearne inscribed his name and the date July 1, 1767, on a boulder near Fort Prince of Wales, the most northerly fort on the continent, Churchill. [Parks Canada / Photo Services]

"Dyer and Prentice"

William Somerset Maugham (1874-1965), the English novelist and playwright, created these rural Manitoba communities out of whole cloth for the setting of *The Land of Promise,* the three-act comedy he wrote for the actress Irene Vanbrugh. The play takes place in Dyer and Prentice but also in the very real town of Tunbridge Wells, England, where Maugham has his characters debate the pros and cons of prairie life. Marsh says, "This was the dumping ground for all the idlers, drunkards and scallywags in England." Norah disagrees, "I thought I hated the prairie through the long winter months, and yet somehow it has caught hold of me." Taylor concludes, "I guess we all hate the prairie sometimes, but when you've once lived in it, it ain't easy to live anywhere else." *The Land of Promise,* premiered in 1914, was filmed later that year. It appears in Maugham's *Collected Plays* (1931).

Emerson

The town of Emerson, located south of Winnipeg almost on the American border, was named after the American literary figure Ralph Waldo Emerson (1803-1882).

Falcon Lake

Falcon Lake is located close to the Trans-Canada Highway near the Ontario border. It was named in honour of Pierre Falcon (1783-1876), the Métis singer called "the Bard of the Plains." The post office here is named Falcon Beach.

Flin Flon

Located north of The Pas, on the border with Saskatchewan, Flin Flon is the single site in the world named after the hero of a dime novel. The mining community, founded in 1913, was called Flin Flon after the nickname of Josiah Flintabbatey Flonatin, hero of *The Sunless City* (1905), a novel from the prolific pen of the British adventure-story author J. E. Preston-Muddock (1842-1934). The novel tells how Flin Flon explores a world beneath the prairies where he finds a fabulous "sunless city" (ruled over by women) and valuable mineral deposits. Finding a dog-eared copy of the novel north of here, a prospector felt the novel accurately described the mineral wealth of the area and so named it Flin Flon. There is a copy of the novel in the Flin Flon Public Library. In 1962, to celebrate the fiftieth anniversary of the creation of northern Manitoba, a six-metre-high likeness of Flin Flon, designed by the American cartoonist Al Capp (1909-1979), was erected on a rocky promontory.

Fort Garry   See WINNIPEG.

The Norse settlements on the shore of Lake Winnipeg are symbolized in the stolid statue of a Viking, unveiled by the president of Iceland at Gimli in 1967. [*Travel Manitoba*]

Gimli

Gimli, on the west shore of Lake Winnipeg, is the centre of the country's Icelandic community, the largest outside Iceland. The Icelandic Festival, held in late summer, includes readings of poems in Old Norse, in which language "Gimli" means "Home of the Gods." As a centennial project, to commemorate the arrival of the first Icelandic settlers in 1875, the city erected a fifteen-foot Viking statue, designed by Gissur Eliasson.

Miriam Waddington (b. 1917) has a poem called "Gimli" in *Driving Home* (1972). Dave Arnason (b. 1940), the writer and editor, was born here. The Arctic explorer Vilhjalmur Stefansson (1879-1962) was born in nearby Arnes which has a monument there in his honour.

Although born in Winnipeg, W. D. Valgardson (b. 1939) was raised in Gimli. He assesses his Icelandic background in the stories collected in *Bloodflowers* (1973), *God Is Not a Fish Inspector* (1975), and *Red Dust* (1978). He teaches at the University of Victoria.

Gladstone

Frederick Philip Grove (1879-1948) taught at the high-school in Gladstone, northwest of Portage la Prairie, in 1917. His wife taught and resided in the small Falmouth School, seven miles west of Amaranth, so Grove com-

Al Capp designed this fiberglass figure of Professor Josiah Flintabbatey Flonatin, hero of the dime novel The Sunless City. [*Bill Brooks*]

Frederick Philip Grove, 17¢ stamp, 1979.
[Canada Post Corporation]

The Falmouth
Teacherage in 1976,
home of the Groves in
1917-19, called
"Plymouth" in Grove's
writing. [Manitoba
Department of Cultural
Affairs and Historical
Resources]

muted on weekends the thirty-five miles between Gladstone and Amaranth. Out of these travels came his first English-language book, *Over Prairie Trails* (1922), with its meditations on man and nature and lyrical evocation of the landscape. On his travels Grove could choose between two "prairie trails." The western route took him past the farm on which he modelled Lindstedt's in *Settlers of the Marsh* (1925); the eastern route took him by the one described in *The Yoke of Life* (1930). Both farms are in the Big Grassy Marsh district by Lake Manitoba.

Gretna

On a farm about five miles east of the farming village of Gretna, which is close to the North Dakota border, was born A. E. van Vogt (b. 1912), the celebrated science-fiction writer. The farm was owned by his grandfather, John Buhr, and his parents, then resident in Neville, Sask., travelled to Gretna for the birth. He was raised in the town of Morden, northwest of Gretna, as he later explained in a letter: "In Morden, Man., we lived in the large stone castle, built in 1905, by an M.D. — it's still there, occupied now — I understand — by an uncle of mine — a brother of my mother's named Henry Buhr." Eventually the family moved to Winnipeg. It is not difficult to imagine that the prairie vision, which so informed the poems of the Imagists, imparted to the youthful Alfred Elton van Vogt a sense of the "infinite spaces" he has conveyed in the *Voyage of the Space Beagle* (1950).

Ingelow

This small community, northeast of Brandon, was named in honour of Jean Ingelow (1820-1897), a once-popular English poet.

International Peace Garden

The world's largest garden dedicated to peace, the International Peace Garden is located on the Canadian-American border, at Boissevain, south of Brandon, not far from the geographic centre of North America (which coincides with Rugby, North Dakota). The garden, opened in 1938, is dedicated "To God in His Glory...we two nations dedicate this garden and pledge ourselves that as long as men shall live we shall not take up arms against one another." Engraved on the stone walls of the Chapel of Peace are sixty inspiring quotations from Canadian and world figures. The Canadians quoted are Alexander Graham Bell, Tim Bentley (identified as a "young Canadian — '67"), Elizabeth Kilbourn, Sir John A. Macdonald, Sir William Osler, Vincent Massey, and Lester B. Pearson. The Americans run the gamut from George Washington to Richard Nixon. Among authors represented with statements are: Albert Camus, Dante, Fyodor Dostoyevsky, Oliver Wendell Holmes, Henry Wadsworth Longfellow, Plutarch, John Ruskin, George Bernard Shaw, Robert Louis Stevenson, Jean-Paul Sartre.

La Rivière

The Archibald Historical Museum at La Rivière, northwest of Manitou, includes two buildings associated with the early life of feminist and writer Nellie L. McClung (1873-1951). The first is the log cabin in which she lived as a pioneer teacher, now refurnished according to the description of it in *Clearing in the West* (1936). The second is the two-storey home, moved here from Manitou, which she and her husband built.

"Little Water Hen River" See SAINTE-ROSE-DU-LAC.

Here is the house built by Wesley and Nellie L. McClung at Manitou. It was moved, along with their 1879 house, which she occupied when she started teaching at Hazel School, to the grounds of the Archibald Historical Museum, at La Rivière. [Manitoba Archives]

Lynn Lake

Lynn Lake, north of Flin Flon, near the Saskatchewan border, is home base for the cartoonist Lynn Johnston and her family. "For Better or for Worse," her family-situation comic strip, has been syndicated to 140 or so newspapers since September 1979. It is enjoyed each day by some forty million readers. Book-length collections of her strip include *David, We're Pregnant* (1975), *Hi Mom! Hi Dad!* (1977), *Do They Ever Grow Up?* (1978), and *It Must Be Nice to Be Little* (1983).

"Manawaka"   See NEEPAWA.

Neepawa

A small farming community set amid the rolling hills and smooth-flowing rivers of Manitoba, Neepawa is located northwest of Portage la Prairie. It is also firmly set in the imagination of the novelist Margaret Laurence (b. 1926), who was born here and lived here for eighteen years. In major novels like *The Stone Angel* (1964), *A Jest of God* (1966), *The Fire-Dwellers* (1969), and *The Diviners* (1974), and in the stories that make up *A Bird in the House* (1970), it is identified as "Manawaka." Yet, as the novelist explained in "A Place to Stand On" (1970), included in *Heart of a Stranger* (1976): "The name Manawaka is an invented one, but it had been in my mind since I was about seventeen or eighteen, when I first began to think about writing something set in a prairie town. Manawaka is not my hometown of Neepawa — it has elements of Neepawa, especially in some of the descriptions of places, such as the cemetery on the hill or the Wachakwa valley through which ran the small brown river which was the river of my childhood. In almost every way, however, Manawaka is not so much any one prairie town as an amalgam of many prairie towns. Most of all, I like to think it is simply itself, a town of the mind, my own private world. . .which one hopes will ultimately relate to the outer world which we all share."

The Davidson Memorial in Neepawa's Riverside Cemetery is said to be the inspiration for The Stone Angel. [Viscount Cultural Council / Neepawa Press]

The youngster was played by James Olson and the schoolteacher by Joanne Woodward in Rachel, Rachel, *the screen version of* A Jest of God. *Margaret Laurence's novel was set in Manitoba; the movie, directed by Paul Newman, in an unspecified New England town.* [Ontario Film Institute]

A still from the NFB documentary — Margaret Laurence — First Lady of Manawaka. [NFB]

As she explained in "Where the World Began" (1972), included in the same collection: "A strange place it was, that place where the world began. A place of incredible happenings, splendours and revelations, despairs like multitudinous pits of isolated hells. A place of shadow-spookiness, inhabited by the unknowable dead. A place of jubilation and of mourning, horrible and beautiful. It was, in fact, a small prairie town."

More prosaically, the imaginary place name includes syllables from "Manitoba" and "Neepawa." The influence of the town on the author is the burden of *The Manawaka World of Margaret Laurence* (1975) by Clara Thomas. Every July in Neepawa, a two-week Holiday Festival of the Arts draws painters, sculptors, and musicians from many parts of the country and the neighbouring United States.

Margaret Laurence's early years in Neepawa have been described in detail in a brochure called *Margaret Laurence: A Prairie Person at Heart* issued in 1983 by the Viscount Cultural Council, Neepawa. Her first home was at the northeast corner of Mountain and Vivian, her second at 312 First Avenue. She attended Neepawa Central School (a cairn marks the site) and the Neepawa Collegiate (now called Viscount School). In the summer of 1943 she worked as a reporter on the *Neepawa Press*. She was baptized, attended Sunday school, and married at the Neepawa United Church. The Davidson Memorial in the Riverside Cemetery is believed to have inspired *The Stone Angel*. (This is local tradition based on a literal reading of the following line from the novel: "She was doubly blind, not only stone but unendowed with even a pretense of sight." When Margaret Laurence visited Neepawa in 1976, she expressed surprise to find that the statue, erected for the pioneering family of the Hon. John Andrew Davidson in 1903, was being singled out for comment. She replied, "But Hagar is the Stone Angel.") The town declared October 6, 1975, "Margaret Laurence Day," and in 1983 the Margaret Laurence Room was opened in the Neepawa Building. In the 1979 NFB film *Margaret Laurence — First Lady of Manawaka* (which made use of the Davidson memorial) the novelist declared herself to be "a prairie person."

Most of Laurence's fiction is set in Manawaka. *The Stone Angel* (1964) takes place here and in an unnamed city on the West Coast that resembles Vancouver. The single novel set entirely in Manawaka is *A Jest of God* (1966), although the film version, starring Joanne Woodward and directed by Paul Newman in 1968, is located in a New England town. *The Fire-Dwellers* (1969) has Manawaka as its locale and also a city that is described as "the jewel of the Pacific Northwest," Vancouver again. The stories in *A Bird in the House* (1970) are set in Manawaka. *The Diviners* (1974), which was written in part in the Peterborough area, has many locales, including Manawaka, Winnipeg, Toronto, Vancouver, London, and "McConnell's Landing," Ont.

Also born in Neepawa is the poet Dale Zieroth (b. 1946) whose poems evoke his prairie childhood.

Nokomis Lake

Nokomis Lake (and South Nokomis Lake) are found southeast of Sherridon, which is northeast of Flin Flon. Nokomis is daughter of the moon and step-mother of Hiawatha in *The Song of Hiawatha* (1855) by Henry Wadsworth Longfellow (1807-1882).

Norway House

Norway House, the trading post on Playgreen Lake near the north end of Lake Winnipeg, was the administrative headquarters of the Hudson's Bay Company from 1821. It is now partly restored. Here the Cree Syllabic alphabet was devised in the 1840s by the missionary James Evans (1801-1846), who first adapted Pitman shorthand notation to the needs of the Indians at Rice Lake, Keene, Ont., in the 1820s. Denied type and printing press at Norway House, he devised his own syllabic alphabet (still in use among the Cree and, with adaptation later, among the Inuit), cast his own type, and built his own printing

The Rev. James Evans, inventor of the Cree syllabic system of writing, is shown in this engraving made about 1840 and signed J. E. Laughlin. [United Church Archives, Victoria University]

This photograph depicts Norway House in 1928. [Manitoba Archives]

press. He handprinted a *Cree Syllabic Hymn book* in 1841 (reissued in facsimile form in 1954). His ashes were scattered at nearby Rossville, where there is a James Evans Memorial United Church. The Cree called him "the man who made birchbark talk."

From 1868 to 1888, another Methodist missionary, Egerton Ryerson Young (1840-1909), administered to the Crees. He is the author of *Stories from Indian Wigwams and Northern Camp-Fires* (1893).

Oberon

The hamlet of Oberon, south of Neepawa, bears the name of the King of the Fairies. He is the mischief-maker in Shakespeare's *A Midsummer Night's Dream* (1594).

Pendennis

A rail siding on a former line northwest of Brandon, and south of Rivers, Pendennis was named for the novel *Pendennis* (1848-50) by the English novelist and journalist William Makepeace Thackeray (1811-1863).

"Plainville" See CARTWRIGHT.

Ponemah

A locality in Dunnottar on the southwest shore of Lake Winnipeg, Ponemah was named after a spirit named in *The Song of Hiawatha* (1855) by Henry Wadsworth Longfellow (1807-1882).

Poplar Point

Here, northeast of Portage la Prairie, the novelist and artist Bertram Brooker (1888-1955) spent part of his teenage years. He calls the community "Poplar Plains" in his novel *Think of the Earth* (1936) which is about the plight of a mystic-minded man in a farming community. The novel has the distinction of being the first to be singled out for the Governor General's Award for Literature.

Rapid City

Northwest of Brandon is Rapid City, the prairie community the novelist Frederick Philip Grove (1879-1948) most favoured. In the southwest corner of the Rapid City Burial Ground there stands a solid block of black granite on a base of grey granite; it bears the following inscription: FREDERICK PHILIP GROVE / 1872-1948. (There is disagreement over his year of birth.) Beside his burial site is that of his beloved daughter, Phyllis May Grove (1915-1927), which bears the inscription: "She is a portion of the loveliness which once she made more lovely."

The Grove family lived in this home in Rapid City where he was principal of the High School in 1921-24. Over Prairie Trails, *the first of his books in English, appeared while he was living here. The Groves left Rapid City for Ottawa and the literary life.* [Estate of Desmond Pacey]

The gravestone of Frederick Philip Grove in the cemetery at Rapid City. [Manitoba Archives]

Before he acquired a following as a novelist, Grove taught in a succession of Manitoba high schools. Between 1912, the year he arrived from the United States, and 1929, when he left Manitoba for Ottawa, he taught in schools in Haskett, Winkler, Virden, Gladstone, Leifur, Ferguson, Eden, Ashfield, and Rapid City. He lived in Rapid City from 1922 to 1929, and showed a marked preference for this town which is located on the Minnedosa River and derives its name from the rapids on the river, not from the rapidity of its growth. It is likely that it served as the model for the town in *Settlers of the Marsh* (1925). A plaque at the Rapid City Museum and Cultural Centre honours its most celebrated resident.

Setting to one side Grove's German-language novels and *Consider Her Ways* (1947) — the latter is a satire which follows a colony of sentient worker ants from Venezuela, up Central America, and across the United States to the New York Public Library — his major creative works are firmly planted in Canadian soil.

Over Prairie Trails (1922) takes the reader on seven trips over Manitoba trails between Gladstone and Falmouth and back in 1917-18. The setting is the Big Grassy Marsh area, described elsewhere. *The Turn of the Year* (1923) has the same setting. The sketches mention specifically Lake Manitoba and Falmouth. *Settlers of the Marsh* (1925) is a novel set in the Big Grassy Marsh area at the turn of the century. *A Search for America* (1927), as a novel not unlike Kerouac's *On the Road*, rambles around the United States and Canada, specifically Montreal and Toronto (Johnson's Café on Yonge Street). *Our Daily Bread* (1928) describes "bare hill after hill" and "flat, treeless, wild prairie" in Southern Saskatchewan and Manitoba, with references to Swift Current, Winnipeg, Brandon, Rapid City, and southern Manitoba. *The Yoke of Life* (1930) is set in 1912-19 in Manitoba on "the prairies" near "the lake." The setting is on purpose generalized. *Fruits of the Earth* (1933), set in 1900-21, is located near the village of Morley in the municipality of Somerville, Man. *Two Generations* (1939), subtitled "A Story of Present-Day Ontario," is set in 1928-29 in the Simcoe, Ont., region where the author then lived. *The Master of the Mill* (1944) goes from 1896 to 1938 and is set in the village of "Langholm," really Langham, Sask. *In Search of Myself* (1946) is a fictionalized autobiography, or a work of autobiographical fiction, and describes "my life as a writer in Canada." Published posthumously, *Tales from the Margin* (1971) brings together stories written in the 1920s with prairie settings — Pas-de-Calais, Ashfield, Winnipeg, Banff, etc.

Red River

The Red River was discovered by the La Vérendrye party in 1732-33 and doubtless named for the reddish brown silt that it carries. It rises in western Minnesota and joins Lake Winnipeg. "Before I became acquainted with the Red, I shared the general belief that it was the dullest river in Canada," wrote Hugh MacLennan (b. 1907) in *The*

Rivers of Canada (1961). "It is not, of course. It is the most surprising river we have in the whole land. It is unlike any other I know."

The valley of the Red River, south of Winnipeg, has been immortalized in the traditional lyrics of "The Red River Valley," the most-loved of the prairie folk songs. Edith Fowke, who reproduces the words and music in *The Penguin Book of Canadian Folks Songs* (1973), maintains it dates back to the Red River Rebellion of 1870 and is the lament of an Indian or half-breed girl for the departure of her white lover, a soldier under Colonel Wolseley. The chorus runs: "Come and sit by my side if you love me, / Do not hasten to bid me adieu, / But remember the Red River Valley / And the girl who has loved you so true."

Riding Mountain National Park

Riding Mountain National Park, north of Brandon, is where the naturalist and author Grey Owl (1888-1938) encouraged the growth of the beaver population. He arrived from Témiscouata in Northern Quebec in 1931 and resided in a cabin, which is still standing, at Beaver Lodge Lake, northeast of Wasagaming. *Pilgrims of the Wild* (1934) and *The Adventures of Sajo and Her Beaver People* (1935) are based in part on experiences and lessons learned here and elsewhere in the wild. He left in 1935 for Prince Albert National Park in Saskatchewan.

Grey Owl's stamping ground in Riding Mountain National Park was Beaver Pond. [Bill Brooks]

St. Boniface   See WINNIPEG.

St. Claude

To St. Claude, south of Portage la Prairie, came Maurice Constantin-Weyer (1881-1961) as a settler. He began to raise cattle in 1903 and remained until 1914 when he returned to his native France where he became a journalist. He never returned to Canada but captured in a series of novels something of the prairie experience. They include *A Man Scans His Past* (1929) and *The Half-Breed* (1930), to give the titles in their English translations.

There is an Indian legend that a great white horse roams the plains near St. François Xavier, so a life-size statue was raised to recall the legend. [Travel Manitoba]

Sainte-Rose-du-Lac

This is the name of one of the larger villages, located southeast of Dauphine Lake, in what Gabrielle Roy (1909-1983) calls "Water Hen Country" or "Little Water Hen Country." As a young woman in the late 1920s and early 1930s, she taught in Métis schools at Sainte-Rose-du-Lac and in nearby Portage-des-Prés. In her novel *Where Nests the Water Hen* (1950) she evokes this lake-strewn region by telling stories of the Toussignant family and describing "life as it might have been, or could have been, or could be." She also taught school in villages in southern Manitoba, notably Marchand, southwest of St. Boniface, and Cardinal, west of Carman and north of Altamont. Waterhen Lake, which sounds like it should be in "Water Hen Country," is too far north of the Interlake district — in fact, north of Lake Manitoba. She discusses her experiences in *The Fragile Lights of Earth* (1982), a collection of articles and memoirs. The Waterhen Reserve is located at the south end of Waterhen Lake, east of Lake Winnipegosis.

Selkirk   See WINNIPEG.

Shelley

Located east of Winnipeg on the main CP line, Shelley was named in 1877 for the English poet Percy Bysshe Shelley (1792-1822).

Souris

This town, southwest of Brandon, is called Mouse Bluffs by Patricia Blondal (1926-1959) in her novel *A Candle to Light the Sun* (1960). So steamy was the novel that *Maclean's* headed its review "Is it Canada's *Peyton Place?*"

Spruce Woods Provincial Park   See CARBERRY.

Stonewall

The artist William Kurelek (1927-1977) was raised on the family's farmstead north of Stonewall, a village just north of Winnipeg. He lived here with his parents and family from 1934 to 1947. All the original buildings have since then burnt down.

Tolstoi

The community of Tolstoi, located southeast of Winnipeg, was known until 1911 as Oleskiw, after the man who managed the estate of Count Leo Tolstoy (1828-1910) and who encouraged Russian peasants to emigrate to Western Canada. That year it was renamed for the great Russian novelist who earmarked the royalties from his novel *Resurrection* (1899) for this emigration.

Treherne

The farming village of Treherne, southwest of Portage la Prairie, is the setting of *Sowing Seeds in Danny* (1908), a collection of evangelical stories of community life in the guise of a novel, the first sustained work of fiction by Nellie L. McClung (1873-1951). It was immensely successful and sold over 100,000 copies.

"Water Hen Country"   See SAINTE-ROSE-DU-LAC.

Willows   See SPEYER, Sask.

Winnipeg

Winnipeg, the principal city and capital of Manitoba, has played a national role in the literary life of the country. The French district is known as St. Boniface. Yet the most telling comment on the city is Hugh MacLennan's observation in 1959 when he titled an essay "A Boy Meets a Girl in Winnipeg and Who Cares?" Travellers from 1890 to 1958 have struck their blows. "My only other memory of Winnipeg is the sensation of having felt for a moment what life in the arctic regions must be," noted Lafcadio Hearn (1850-1904), the American essayist who wrote about his "A Winter's Journey to Japan," *Harper's*, November 1890.

The English poet Rupert Brooke (1887-1915), visiting in 1913, had a lot to say about the city and its citizens in *Letters from America* (1916): "The people have something of the free swing of Americans, without the bumptiousness; a tempered democracy, a mitigated independence of bearing. The manners of Winnipeg, of the West, impress the stranger as better than those of the East, more friendly, more hearty, more certain to achieve graciousness, if not grace. There is, even, in the architecture of Winnipeg, a sort of gauche pride visible. It is hideous, of course, even more hideous than Toronto or Montreal; but cheerily and windily so."

"A good way I have found to get to know a place is to get lost in it," wrote Norman Levine (b. 1924), in the Winnipeg section of *Canada Made Me* (1958, 1979). "And for the next few days I walked through the streets, to the outskirts, to the hinterland, the suburbs, along railway tracks, by bridges, to the place where the two muddy rivers meet. My first impression of width, greyness, loose sand blowing, did not change."

It is not the travellers but the natives who have found the heart of the city. James Reaney (b. 1926), although born in Stratford, Ont., taught in the English Department of the University of Manitoba from 1949 to 1961. He wrote "A Message to Winnipeg" (1951-60) which does much to mitigate the surface impressions and mythologize the city. The same could be maintained of the authors discussed below.

Near Seven Oaks House, the oldest standing residence in Winnipeg, is a limestone monument to mark where, on June 19, 1816, the Battle of Seven Oaks took place, an event celebrated by Métis bard Pierre Falcon. [Travel Manitoba]

Seven Oaks House   A stone shaft has been erected at the southeast corner of Main Street and Rupertsland Avenue to mark the site of the Battle of Seven Oaks. The battle took place on June 19, 1816, between the rival traders of the Hudson's Bay Company and the North West Company. It was celebrated in song by the Métis bard, Pierre Falcon (1783-1876). One verse of "The Battle of Seven Oaks," in the translation of Alexandre L. Amprimoz, runs: "And who wrote this victory song? / Your own poet — Pierre Falcon, / A song to praise our noble band / On the day they saved our land. / All join in to tell this story / Of the Scorched Wood people's glory." The novelist Rudy Wiebe (b. 1934) has made Falcon the narrator of his historical novel *The Scorched-Wood People* (1977). The large, two-storey squared-log house known as Seven Oaks House was built in 1851 and is the oldest habitable house in Manitoba. It is located on Rupertsland and maintained as a museum.

Fort Garry   Today Fort Garry is a borough of Winnipeg. The original Fort Garry was a Hudson's Bay fur-trade post built in 1817-22. It was succeeded by Lower Fort Garry, a new post erected farther down the Red River in 1831-33. This post, in turn, was succeeded by Upper Fort Garry, built near the site of the original post in 1835.

The northern gateway is all that remains of Upper Fort Garry. The stone gate is located on Main Street, opposite the CNR station. Here one may dream of the romantic excitement of the past. . .when, say, the poet Charles Mair (1838-1927) was made a prisoner (like

Today children climb over the cannon at Lower Fort Garry, built by the North West Company in 1831. It is located at Selkirk. [Travel Manitoba]

This gate, in downtown Winnipeg, is all that remains of Upper Fort Garry, the fur trade post built by the Hudson's Bay Company in 1835. [Travel Manitoba]

This photograph of William Francis Butler, soldier and writer, was taken about 1875 by William Notman of Montreal. [Glenbow Archives, Calgary, Alberta]

the portals of the setting sun...lies the Great Lone Land."

Lower Fort Garry, at Selkirk, is the only stone fort of the fur-trade era still intact in North America. Here, north of Winnipeg, the visitor will find the restoration of the Big House, the Fur Loft, the Sales Shop, the South-West Bastion, a Red River Settler's House, a Blacksmith's Shop, and other buildings restored to recreate the 1830's. One thinks of such historical novels about the fur trade as *Lords of the North* (1900), *Heralds of Empire* (1902), and *Pathfinders of the West* (1904), by Agnes Laut (1871-1936) who, although born in Stanley, Ont., was educated at the University of Manitoba and served as an editorial writer for the Manitoba *Free Press* before settling in the United States.

Louis Riel   The public life of Louis Riel (1844-1885) has eclipsed this strange man's private life, which is only now coming to light in the publication, examination, and translation of his poems and journals. The University of Alberta Press has undertaken the publication of his complete writings; with the completion of this project, new light will be shed on this "prophet of the new world" and "founder of Manitoba."

Two sites in Winnipeg are of particular importance in

Thomas Scott) of Louis Riel in the days of the Rebellion of 1869-70.

Or one may trek across the Northwest in the company of Sir William Francis Butler (1838-1910), who was dispatched from Upper Fort Garry on a winter journey of 2,700 miles, which he described so vividly in *The Great Lone Land* (1872). A subsequent trek took him to Lake Athabasca and across the Peace River Pass to the Pacific, evoked in memorable language in *The World North Land* (1873). These two classics of wilderness travel describe a region of grandeur and a sense of solitude for "far away at

Louis Riel (played by Raymond Cloutier) is threatened by Mrs. Schultz (Brenda Donohue) in the CBC-TV production of Riel. This is a ruse to help her husband and Thomas Scott to escape. [Ontario Film Institute]

Riel House looks today much as it did when Louis Riel's family lived here. [Bill Brooks]

the Riel story. Riel House is located at 330 River Road, St. Vital. Although Riel never lived here, he was once taken here by his parents and following his execution in Regina his body lay in state in the main room for two days in December 1885. His wife Marguerite died here the following year, and the Riel family owned the house until 1968 when it was restored as a museum and memorial to Riel and the Lagimodière families.

The other site is the burial place of Riel in the churchyard of St. Boniface Basilica, 190 avenue de la Cathédrale, St. Boniface. Here a brown granite tombstone, inscribed "Riel / 16 Novembre 1885," marks his final resting place. (Or is said to do so, for the tradition persists that Riel's body was secretly buried elsewhere, to avoid desecration, and that only two or three living Métis know its present whereabouts.) The present monument, which replaces a simple wooden cross, was erected in 1891.

Night shot of Riel's Tombstone, St. Boniface. [Travel Manitoba]

Legislative Building The Manitoba Legislative Building, a neo-classical structure, was completed in 1920. Atop the 240-foot high dome stands (on one foot) the graceful figure of the Golden Boy. This four-metre-high statue is a personification of youth and has a torch in one hand and a sheaf of wheat in the other. It was created by Charles Gardet of Paris. The guilded bronze figure caught

the eye of Jack Ludwig (b. 1922), the Winnipeg native and novelist, who noted: "Golden Boy seems eternal, almost immortal." Since 1970, the torch in his hand has been electrically illuminated.

Arranged on the grounds around the Legislative Building are numerous statues, five of which are of literary significance. The statue of Robert Burns (1759-1796), the Scots poet, sculpted by G. A. Lawson, is a copy of the one at Ayr, Scotland. The bust of Sir George-Etienne Cartier (1814-1873), Father of Confederation and song writer, was donated by Montreal's Cartier Centenary Committee when it was discovered that it had on its hands a duplicate of the one commissioned for Cartier's birthplace, St. Antoine sur Richelieu, Que. In the House of Commons, on the occasion of the creation of the Province of Manitoba, Cartier exclaimed: "May the new province of Manitoba always speak to the North West the language of reason, truth, and justice."

The Manitoba Legislative Building is a Winnipeg landmark. Atop the building, high above the city of Winnipeg and the prairies, stands Golden Boy, the embodiment of the Spirit of Youth. [Travel Manitoba]

Three traditional statues and one modernistic one on the grounds of the Legislative building in Winnipeg hold literary interest. The Scots poet Robert Burns (top left) is honoured, as are the great Ukrainian poet and patriot Taras Shevchenko (top right), and the Icelandic littérateur Jon Sigurdsson (bottom left). The fourth statue, the Riel Monument (bottom right), of more recent vintage, honours the Métis leader, Louis Riel. [Travel Manitoba; Bill Brooks; Travel Manitoba; Bill Brooks]

The modernistic statue of Louis Riel (1844-1885) depicts the poet and controversial founder of Manitoba as a bound prisoner. The contributions of the province's Ukrainians are acknowledged by the statue of Taras Shevchenko (1814-1861), the poet and patriot of Ukraine who spent much of his life in peonage or prison. The contributions of citizens of Icelandic descent are noted by the statue of Jon Sigurdsson (1811-1879), Icelandic writer and public figure, a replica of his monument at Reykjavik, Iceland.

Winnipeg Free Press Building   This imposing building, at 300 Carlton Street, recalls the era when the *Winnipeg Free Press* exerted not only provincial but also national and international influence. This was under the editorship (1901-44) of John W. Dafoe (1866-1944), Western spokesman, staunch Liberal, and committed internationalist. A plaque commemorates his contribution. A second plaque honours E. Cora Hind (1861-1942), suffragette, temperance leader, and longtime agricultural editor of the paper. She wrote two books of reminiscences, *My Travels and Findings* (1939) and *Seeing for Myself* (1947).

"The life of a newspaper reporter in Winnipeg most of the time was about as exciting as the life of an elevator man or a men's-room attendant," wrote James H. Gray (b. 1906) who in 1935 joined the news department of the *Free Press*. In *The Boy from Winnipeg* (1970) he evokes the city he knew as a child. In *Troublemaker* (1978) he reminisces about Dafoe, the Siftons, George Ferguson, Archie Dale, J. B. (Hamish) McGeachy, and others

The Walker Theatre   The old Walker Theatre, at Market and Main, is now a movie theatre. The evening of January 28, 1914, the so-called Women's Parliament was convened here. A group of suffragettes staged a mock parliament to ridicule the provincial premier into granting equal rights to women. An important event — and grand entertainment — it was written up twice by Nellie L. McClung (1873-1951) who took the part of the premier. She dealt with it fictionally in her novel *Purple Springs* (1921) and autobiographically in *The Stream Runs Fast* (1945).

This vintage photograph of 1911 shows the Walker Theatre which once stood near the intersection of Portage and Main. On its stage Nellie McClung and other feminists staged their Women's Parliament, January 28, 1914. [Manitoba Archives]

Nellie McClung, the pioneer writer and feminist, is shown at her desk in this photograph taken sometime between 1910 and 1918. [Glenbow Arhives, Calgary, Alberta]

Portage and Main   The intersection of Portage Avenue and Main Street, the city's principal *carrefour*, is said to be the windiest corner in all of Canada. This statement has yet to be immortalized in any literary work.

226

A. H. Reginald Buller, poetaster, is recalled in the F.D.A. Building on the campus of the University of Manitoba. The memorial consists of his portrait and plaque and his personal library of biological texts. Poet Alexandre L. Amprimoz, shown here, has made a study of his work. [Sante Viselli]

The Administration Building of the University of Manitoba. This university is the oldest in Western Canada. [Tourism Manitoba]

Faculty members at St. John's College, left to right: Kenneth J. Hughes, literary and art critic; Alexandre L. Amprimoz, poet and philologist; Dave Arnason, writer and editor; and Dennis Cooley, poet and critic. The College, part of the University of Manitoba, specializes in Canadian studies. [Sante Viselli]

Perhaps Mordecai Richler (b. 1931) was standing at this intersection when he noted in "Pages from a Western Journal" (1970) in *Home Sweet Home* (1984): "In North America's only socialist province, the sky belongs to the people. The rest, mostly to members of the Manitoba Club."

University of Manitoba The oldest university in Western Canada, the University of Manitoba, which is located in the borough of Fort Garry, dates back to 1877.

There is an unusual memorial to a man of varied accomplishments in the federal Department of Agriculture's Laboratory Building on the university campus. Encased in a copper urn and sealed within a bronze plaque, fastened to the wall of the Library, are the ashes of A. H. Reginald Buller (1874-1944). Although never on the faculty, he worked alongside its agriculturalists and donated his valuable collection of books to the Library. The memorial was erected in 1958. Buller is, of course, the author of the most famous of all "clean" limericks. It is called "Relativity" and it first appeared in *Punch*, December 19, 1973: "There was a young lady named Bright / Whose speed was far faster than light; / She set out one day / In a relative way / And returned on the previous night."

Authors who teach at the University of Manitoba, or have done so in the immediate past, are: George Amabile, Alexandre L. Amprimoz, Dorothy Livesay, Chester Duncan, Dave Arnason, Robert Kroetsch, David Williams, and Carol Shields. Closely connected with members of the English Department, though not part of the university, is Turnstone Press. This literary publishing operation has been described as "the largest and most active literary press between Toronto and Vancouver." The university has published *Mosaic* since 1967.

The Elizabeth Dafoe Library of the University of Manitoba takes pride in the Grove Register, an extensive collection of Frederick Philip Grove's personal papers. The collection includes the manuscripts of twelve unpublished novels (some titles are "Heart's Desire," "The House of Stene," "Murder in the Quarry") and four dozen

unpublished short stories (some titles being "Achievement," "Maid of All Work," "Alien Enemy," "Canadianization," "Fog," "The Mystery of the Pond," "Radio Broadcast," "Hidden Sun"). Other authors whose papers reside in the Library are Heather Robertson, John W. Dafoe, Bertram Brooker, and Charles W. Gordon (Ralph Connor). The papers of Stephan G. Stephansson and Guttormur J. Guttormsson are part of the Icelandic Collection. The Archives also houses the papers and spirit photographs of T. Glendenning Hamilton.

Robert Kroetsch Robert Kroetsch (b. 1927) is a Professor of English at the University of Manitoba. He cherishes place as much as others love people, so locale is of vital importance to his work. *But We Are Exiles* (1965) roams over the Mackenzie River, Great Slave Lake, Norman Wells, Fort Simpson, Bear Island, Franklin Mountains, Gull Lake, and Swift Current. *The Words of My Roaring* (1966) is set in the author's fictional region of "Coulee Hill" and nearby "Notikeewin," Alta. "Coulee Hill" is also the locale of *The Studhorse Man* (1969), but so too are the following places: Edmonton (Legislative Building, Jasper Avenue, 101st Street, Exhibition Grounds, McDougall Church, Woodward's, Royal George Beer Parlour), Cree River Valley, and Wildfire Lake. *Gone*

Indian (1973) returns to "Coulee Hill" and "Notikeewin," also Edmonton and its International Airport. *Badlands* (1975) is set in the Badlands of Alberta, and is concerned with the hunt for dinosaur bones in 1916. *What the Crow Said* (1978) concerns the town of "Bigknife" on the Saskatchewan-Alberta border.

Manitoba Theatre Centre   The first of the regional theatres, the Manitoba Theatre Centre was founded in 1958 by arts administrator Tom Hendry and director John Hirsch. It moved into its present building at 174 Market Avenue in 1970.

Ivan Franko Museum   Located at 603 Pritchard Avenue, the Ivan Franko Museum is devoted to the life and writings of Ivan Franko (1856-1916), Ukrainian poet and nationalist. On display are first editions of his books of prose and poetry as well as paintings and handicrafts that evoke his life in Ukraine. The Ukrainian Public Library is housed in the basement.

The North End   The North End is that part of the city of Winnipeg that is north of Main Street at Portage Avenue. Between the two World Wars it was predominately Jewish and lower middle-class. The quarter has produced more than its quota of writers.

Miriam Waddington as an infant in her Winnipeg home in 1918. [Miriam Waddington]

Miriam Waddington (b. 1917) has written movingly in a number of poems about her early years as a "north Winnipeg girl." Although a native of Hungary, John Marlyn (b. 1912) was raised in the North End. He set his novel *Under the Ribs of Death* (1957) in the "howling wilderness" of Henry Avenue, and a critical scene takes place on Salter Street bridge. Jack Ludwig (b. 1922) has set stories and novels in the North End, including *Confusions* (1963) and *A Woman of Her Age* (1973). Local references are rife in *Corner Store* (1976) and *Malke, Malke* (1977), two novels by Bess Kaplan (b. 1927). The touchstone novel of the conflict among Jews of different generations is *The Sacrifice* (1956), by Adele Wiseman (b. 1928), which evokes a strong sense of "the crowded,

downhill area." Her novel *Crackpot* (1974) is also set in the North End.

Like John Marlyn, John Hirsch (b. 1930) is a native of Hungary who was raised in the North End. Hirsch cofounded the Manitoba Theatre Centre in 1958 and became a playwright and prominent director. The story of how Hirsch succeeded Robin Phillips as director of the Stratford Festival was told by Martin Knelman (b. 1943), another North End native, in *The Stratford Tempest* (1982). Two political commentators from the North End are the late Max Freedman, an adviser to U.S. President Lyndon B. Johnson, and Larry Zolf (b.1934), author of the imaginative tract, *Dance of the Dialectic* (1973), who was born and raised at 100 Aikins Avenue, near Selkirk Avenue.

Sondra Gotlieb: Not all books about Winnipeg are about North Winnipeg. [McClelland & Stewart]

Not all Jewish writers from Winnipeg come from the North End. Sondra Gotlieb (b. 1936), novelist and wife of a career diplomat, was born outside the area. Yet her upbringing in the city's Jewish community is the subject of her amusing memoir, *True Confections or How My Family Arranged My Marriage* (1978), which commences with these words: "Once upon a time in a flat cold city, colder than Moscow or Propoisk, it was believed that all people should marry."

Charles W. Gordon / Ralph Connor   Although born and buried in Ontario's Glengarry County, Charles W. Gordon (1860-1937) is identified with the West and with Winnipeg in particular. As well as being one of the country's leading novelists (using the pen name Ralph Connor), he was one of its leading churchmen and Presbyterian minister and pastor of St. Stephen's Church from 1894 to 1924. This church building fell victim to a fire in 1968, but there is a memorial plaque to Gordon in its successor, St. Stephen's (Broadway) Church.

The University Women's Club of Winnipeg has maintained the C. W. Gordon House at 54 Westgate for many years. This substantial, red-brick residence was built by Gordon and occupied by him from 1914 to his death. It is now used for educational and social purposes

Ralph Connor, Chaplain, 43rd Cameron Highlanders of Canada, 1917. From Postscript to Adventure (1938). [C-19115 / Public Archives Canada]

The Charles W. Gordon residence, 54 Westgate, now the University Women's Club. [Bill Brooks]

and the Women's Club maintains a library of Gordon's thirty or so novels. Three of these deal directly with social problems in Winnipeg. They are: *The Foreigner* (1909), concerned with the plight of unskilled immigrants from Central Europe; *To Him that Hath* (1921), an examination of the capitalist underpinnings of industrial democracy; and *The Arm of Gold* (1932), which probes the causes of the Crash of 1929.

"Dr. Gordon's home is in the bustling city of Winnipeg, where he is the working pastor of St. Stephen's Presbyterian Church," wrote the journalist E. J. Hathaway in "Canadian Literary Homes" in *The Canadian Magazine*, January 1908. "The house, which was built for his bride on their marriage, is in one of the best residential sections of Winnipeg. It was remodelled a couple of years

ago, and with its spacious verandahs, its neatly trimmed grassy lawns and its surrounding hedge of wild roses, which in the early summer is covered with bloom, is much more suggestive of the sunny south than of a Western Canadian city."

Gabrielle Roy   The distinguished novelist, Gabrielle Roy (1909-1983), was born in the predominantly French suburb of Winnipeg called St. Boniface, in the family home at 375 Rue Deschambault. This rambling, wood-frame house in the east quarter was built in 1905 and owned by the family until 1936. Roy attended L'Académie Saint-Joseph and later taught at L'Ecole Provencher, both in St. Boniface. She described the district in human terms in her novel, *Street of Riches* (1957), the original French title of which is *Rue Deschambault*, and her love of the district and the place in her heart this street of her childhood and youth held is its most endearing quality.

Here is a review of ten major works by Gabrielle Roy. English titles are given; when two years appear, the first is for the French edition, the second for the English translation; when one year appears, the translation followed later that year.

The Tin Flute (1945, 1947) is set in the Montreal slum of Saint-Henri with almost one hundred specified locales, including the Cartier Theatre, the Palace Theatre, the Princess Theatre, the Lachine Canal, St. Joseph's Oratory, Saint-Zotique Church, and such streets as Notre-Dame, St. Ambroise, St. Catherine, Atwater, etc.

Where Nests the Water Hen (1950) looks back "twenty years ago" to rural Manitoba. Named features are Little Water Hen River, Big Water Hen River, Water Hen Lake, Portage des Prés, Rorketon, Sainte-Rose-du-Lac, all within or near the Interlake district where the author once taught school.

Street of Riches (1955, 1957) describes in nostalgic detail life on Rue Deschambault, on which the author was raised, in the St. Boniface suburb of Winnipeg. Provencher Bridge, Rue Desmeurons, Saint Anne-des-Chênes Convent, and the Red River are some specific sites named.

The Cashier (1955) is set in Montreal in 1947-49. There are not many specific references, although Mount Royal is referred to, as is Lac Vert in the Laurentians.

The Hidden Mountain (1961, 1962) has three settings, following the artist hero around the Northwest Territories (Mackenzie River, Fort Renunciation, Churchill River, Lake Caribou, Muskrat Portage); Northern Quebec (Ungava, Knob Lake); and across the Atlantic to Paris.

The Road Past Altamont (1966) is set in a region of reminiscence, notably the community of Altamont with references to Lake Winnipeg, Winnipeg Beach, etc.

Windflower (1970) takes the reader to Fort Chimo, on the Koksoak River in the Ungava Bay area of Northern Quebec. The new name of Fort Chimo is Kuujuak.

Enchanted Summer (1972, 1976) has as its locale Charlevoix County, northeast of Quebec City. There are

Gabrielle Roy was born and raised in the wood frame house depicted in this historic photograph. The house, built in 1905 and sold by the family in 1936, is still standing at 375 Rue Deschambault, St. Boniface. (The child shown in the photograph is believed to be the author.) Roy once told an interviewer: "At the city end of the street I was in Canada and at the other end I was in God's world." [La Société Historique de Saint-Boniface]

Gabrielle Roy in the bloom of womanhood. [Basil Zarov]

Dust jacket of the first edition of Gabrielle Roy's novel Rue Deschambault (1955), translated into English as Street of Riches (1957). [Librarie Beauchemin Ltée]

references to Petite-Rivière-Saint-François, Baie-Saint-Paul, Grande-Pointe, Sainte-Anne-de-la-Pocatière, Ile d'Orléans, Ile aux Coudres, Montmagny, etc.

Garden in the Wind (1975, 1977) is collection of stories set in small Prairie communities like Horizon and Veregin, Sask.

Children of My Heart (1977, 1979) returns the reader to the Prairies and the Winnipeg slums of the 1930s, regions forever fixed in readers' minds with Gabrielle Roy.

Other Authors

Dorothy Livesay (b. 1909) was born, as she notes in Winnipeg Childhood (1973), in a house on Lipton Street, south of Portage, opposite Luxton School. Here was her "heart planted then / and never transplanted," she wrote in her poem "Roots" (1966).

Nellie L. McClung (1873-1951), the author and early feminist, studied at the Collegiate Institute in 1893-95 and the following year married a pharmacist. The McClungs lived between 1911 and 1914 in the substantial stucco house at 97 Chestnut Street, and Nellie was active as a social reformer, being largely responsible for the Women's Parliament at the Walker Theatre. The McClungs moved to Edmonton in 1914.

Laura Goodman Salverson (1890-1970), the novelist, was born in Winnipeg. Her parents had emigrated from Iceland three years earlier. Her novels, like The Viking Heart (1923), treat with understanding the plight of the Icelandic emigrants who settled around Gimli. She discusses the Winnipeg of her youth in Confessions of an Immigrant's Daughter (1939). George Salverson (b. 1916), the television writer, is her son.

A. E. van Vogt (b. 1912), one of the principal contributors to the Golden Age of Science Fiction, was born on a farm near Gretna. In Winnipeg he lived with his parents at 116 Furby Street, now a shopping centre, and attended Kelvin Technical High School. Throughout the 1930s he was a borrower of books from the main branch of the Winnipeg Public Library, at 380 William Avenue, now a district branch. In this Carnegie building, erected of stone in 1905, the youthful Van Vogt did his early writing — pulp romances, radio dramas, trade-magazine articles, and science fiction. He married in 1939 Brandon-born E. Mayne Hull (1905-1975), one-time secretary to Henry Wise Wood and writer in her own right, and they moved to Ottawa, Toronto, and Los Angeles. Before leaving for California in 1944, he completed some 600,000 words of fantastic fiction, including the notable story "Black Destroyer" (1939) and the classic mutant novel Slan (1946).

Miriam Waddington (b. 1917), who describes herself as a north Winnipeg girl in "Things of the World" in Driving

Home (1972), was born in the pleasant house at 106 Selkirk Avenue. The family moved to larger quarters on St. John's Avenue, first No. 372 and then No. 469.

George Woodcock (b. 1912), the man-of-letters long resident in Vancouver, was born on Portage Avenue and taken by his parents within the year to England, so he has no memory of his Winnipeg "childhood." Nonetheless he felt himself to be a Canadian, and in 1949 returned to Western Canada.

J. S. Woodsworth (1874-1942), as national leader of the CCF and the country's chief spokesman for democratic socialism, is remembered more as a public figure than as a literary figure. Yet his personality and ideas influenced many subsequent writers who knew him personally or through his pioneering sociological studies, *Strangers within Our Gates* (1909) and *My Neighbour* (1911). He had three main residences in Winnipeg. He lived intermittently in the family home at 60 Mayland Street (in 1909, 1913-14, 1916, and from 1930 to his death); at 464 Stella Avenue (as superintendent of All Peoples' Mission, 1910-12), and at 76 Chestnut Street (his sister's home, 1926-29).

New Horizons The first of the great prairie cities encountered by travellers moving from the East to the West is Winnipeg. Although the place name means "murky water" in Cree, perhaps this is the point at which to pause to consider some imaginative reactions to the prairies.

For agreeing to write an article about his CPR journey across Canada, Lafcadio Hearn (1850-1904) received a complimentary pass from Sir W. C. Van Horne. The American writer first experienced the prairies on his train journey to the West Coast, whence he departed for Japan where he made his mark as an essayist. The article he wrote, called "A Winter's Journey to Japan," appeared in *Harper's* in November 1890: "At immense intervals a farm, a ranch, outlines its buildings and fences against sky and snow. You wonder about the lives of those who dwell there, always ringed in by the naked horizon, — seeing always the same round of land level to the edge of heaven....But this will not endure; for all along this great highway to the Orient, the country is being rapidly settled; and these solitary farms in a few years more will have grown into villages and cities."

The vision of the prairies had a more pronounced and literary effect on the British critic T. E. Hulme (1883-

Mavor Moore adapted Russian dramatist Nikolai Gogol's The Inspector-General *to Western Canadian conditions and called it* The Ottawa Man. *Gogol's 1836 satiric masterpiece is about an impecunious imposter who is mistaken for a government inspector and treated accordingly. It is an exposé of injustice. Moore's version ridicules bureaucracy in Canada. Frances Hyland directed the Festival Lennoxville production in 1972, with Douglas Rain, Mia Anderson, Roger Blay, and Sandy Webster.* [Performing Arts / Paul Lindell]

Sinclair Lewis's Mantrap, *an adventure novel set in northern Manitoba, was made into a silent film in 1926, with Clara Bow and Ernest Torrence. The cinematographer James Wong Howe shot some scenes in the province.* [*Ontario Film Institute*]

1917) who spent eight months in Western Canada in 1906-7. "Speaking of personal matters, the first time I ever felt the necessity or inevitableness of verse, was in the desire to reproduce the peculiar quality of feeling which is induced by the flat spaces and wide horizons of the virgin prairie of western Canada." After his experience Hulme returned to England where he played a leading role in the birth of the literary movement called Imagism.

Central Manitoba is the setting of the romantic adventure novel *Mantrap* (1926) written by Sinclair Lewis (1885-1951) after a trip made through Northern Saskatchewan and Manitoba in 1924. Victor Fleming directed Clara Bow in the silent film version later that year.

Perhaps the most sensitive soul to respond to the prairie experience in non-fiction prose form was Rupert Brooke (1887-1915). The young English poet wrote articles, collected in *Letters from America* (1916), that reveal much about himself and about the need of humans to find associations in the landscape even when it appears to be a *tabula rasa*. He made the following observation about the landscape north of Winnipeg. At the time he was north of Milner *en route* to Lake George, August 1913: "It is that feeling of fresh loneliness that impresses itself before any detail of the wild. The soul — or the personality — seems to have indefinite room to expand. There is no one else within reach, there never has been anyone; no one else is *thinking* of the lakes and hills you see before you. They have no tradition, no names even; they are only pools of water and lumps of earth, some day, perhaps, to be clothed with loves and memories and the comings and goings of men, but now dumbly waiting their Wordsworth or their Acropolis to give them individuality, and a soul. In such country as this there is a rarefied clean sweatness."

Saskatchewan

Ajawaan Lake See PRINCE ALBERT NATIONAL PARK.

Ardath
This community, southwest of Saskatoon, was named after a character in the novel *Ardath* (1891) by the English romantic novelist Marie Corelli (1855-1924).

Avonlea
The village of Avonlea, southwest of Regina, was named in 1911 after the fictional community of Avonlea created by L. M. Montgomery (1874-1942) in *Anne of Green Gables* (1908). Montgomery modelled the literary Avonlea on Cavendish, P.E.I.

Batoche
Here, south of Prince Albert, on the South Saskatchewan River, was located Riel's headquarters. The Métis settlement was the site of the last battle in the North West Rebellion. It fell on May 12, 1885. It is now a National Historic Site, and has inspired historians and poets. Among the latter is Al Purdy (b. 1918) who wrote "The Battlefield at Batoche," a fine elegy included in *Being Alive: Poems 1958-78* (1978).

Northeast of Batoche, in the Minichinis Hills, is the copse where Almighty Voice (1874-1897) made his last stand. (The story of this Cree hero is told in the Duck Lake entry.)

Among those buried at Batoche, the unofficial capital of Louis Riel's Métis nation, was Riel's general, Gabriel Dumont. [Saskatchewan Tourism]

Gabriel Dumont, the Métis general, was played by Actor Roger Blay in the CBC-TV production of Riel. [Ontario Film Institute]

"More poems have been written about Batoche than any other village," according to the poet Glen Sorestad. A short list of memorable poems that depict the Métis village must include: Elizabeth Brewster's "At Batoche," Mick Burrs' "Towards an Epic of the Rebellion," Terence Heath's "Lament for Madeleine Dumont," John Newlove's "Crazy Riel," Glen Sorestad's "Archaeologists at Batoche," and Andrew Suknaski's "Abandoned Métis Church." Other poets who have written on the subject are E. D. Blodgett, George Bowering, R. G. Everson, Patrick Lane, Dorothy Livesay, Raymond Souster, and George Woodcock.

Blewett
Blewett, southeast of Weyburn, was named in honour of Jean Blewett (1862-1934), the once-popular, Toronto-based author of patriotic poems and stories.

Briercrest
Briercrest, southeast of Moose Jaw, is associated with Edna Jaques (1891-1978), the author of homespun verses about the simple life. When she was ten, her family homesteaded near here. In her verses she celebrated the rural virtues and pleasures. She found an international audience for her "reply" to the famous poem "In Flanders Fields" in which John McCrae (1872-1918) warned that "If ye break faith with us who die / We shall not sleep. . . ." Her "reply" is called "In Flanders Now"

(1918), and it was first read in 1918 at the unveiling of the Tomb of the Unknown Soldier, Arlington Cemetery, Washington, D.C. It begins: "We have kept faith, ye Flanders' dead. . . ."

Browning

This community, northeast of Estevan, was named to commemorate the English poet Robert Browning (1812-1889).

Bryant

Bryant, north of Estevan, bears the last name of William Cullen Bryant (1794-1878), American poet and journalist once popular in the West.

Carlyle

This community, north of Oxbow, was named in honour of Thomas Carlyle (1795-1881), the Anglo-Scottish author.

Cowper

A former CN grain shipping point, northeast of Estevan, Cowper was named after the English poet William Cowper (1731-1800), best remembered for his ballad "The Diverting History of John Gilpin" (1785).

Robert Ryan starred as a North West Mounted Policeman (who wore fur hats in summer) in The Canadians, *the 1961 Hollywood film set in the Cypress Hills. Supposedly concerned with the 1873 massacre here, it introduces Sitting Bull and his Sioux warriors (who arrived three years later). [Ontario Film Institute]*

"Crocus" See HIGH RIVER, Alta.

Cullen

Cullen, north of Estevan, was given the middle name of William Cullen Bryant (1794-1878), a once-popular American poet and journalist.

Duck Lake

At Duck Lake, southwest of Prince Albert, was fought, on March 26, 1885, the first engagement of the North West Rebellion. The site is marked.

The jail from which Almighty Voice (1874-1897) escaped has been restored and may be visited. The Cree

Cecil B. DeMille's first Technicolor feature film was Northwest Mounted Police, *for which he reconstructed Fort Carlton on the Paramount backlot. He also reconstructed history, for in his version of the Battle of Duck Lake it was the Métis and not the NWMP detachment that had the Gatling gun. The 1940 film starred Gary Cooper and Paulette Goddard. [Ontario Film Institute]*

led the NWMP on a 19-month manhunt which ended in the Minichinis Hills, northeast of Batoche, where he took his last stand on May 30, 1897. As a symbol of Indian resistance to arbitrary white authority, Almighty Voice has attracted much interest. There is the play *Almighty Voice* (1970) by Len Peterson (b. 1917), and the title story by Rudy Wiebe (b. 1934) in *Where Is the Voice Coming From?* (1974). Donald Sutherland played the pursuing Mountie in the Hollywood film *Alien Thunder*, released in 1973.

Buffalo Child Long Lance (1890-1932), the self-styled Indian spokesman and author, said that the Minichinis Hills region "marks the spot where the North American Indian made his last stand against the white man."

Eastend

Eastend, southwest of Swift Current, takes its name from its location in regard to the Cypress Hills region of Saskatchewan. In the works of the American writer Wallace Stegner (b. 1909), the small farming community is called "Whitemud." Between 1914 and 1921, he lived here with his family who homesteaded the land before moving on to Salt Lake City. "The 49th parallel ran directly through my childhood, dividing me in two," Stegner wrote. He treats the experience in such novels and fictionalized memoirs as *On a Darkling Plain* (1940), *The Big Rock Candy Mountain* (1943), and *Wolf Willow* (1962). "What I remember are low bars overgrown with wild roses, cutbank bends, secret paths through the willows, fords across the shallows, shallows in the clay banks, days of indolence and adventure where space was as flexible as the mind's cunning and where time did not exist. That was at the heart of it, the sunken and sanctuary river valley. Out around, stretching in all directions from the benches to become coextensive with the disk of the cold, went the uninterrupted prairie."

Esterhazy

The community of Esterhazy, located in eastern Saskatchewan about midway between Yorkton and Moosomin, is known for its potash reserves. It is, as well, the birthplace of Guy Vanderhaeghe (b. 1951), whose autobiographical stories appear in *Man Descending* (1982).

Estevan

Estevan, a small town close to the American border, is the hometown of Eli Mandel (b. 1922), the poet, who has written about prairie life in poems like those in *Stony Plain* (1973).

The so-called Poets Line, built by the CPR in 1911, extended from Maryfield in the east to Estevan in the west. Active stations on the line named after writers include: Ryerson, Mair, Parkman, Service, Carlyle, Wordsworth, Browning, and Lampman. Closed stations named after writers include: Cowper, Cullen, and Bryant. The concentration of writers' names is unique; in fact, only three stations on the line (Kingsford, Willmar, and Bienfait) are without their literary counterparts.

Eli Mandel, Canadian Crusoe from Estevan, caricatured by Don Evans who signs his work Isaac Bickerstaff. [Special Collections, University of Calgary Libraries]

Fairholme

Born in a Mennonite community located close to Fairholme, which is northwest of North Battleford, was the novelist Rudy Wiebe (b. 1934). He attended high school in Coaldale, east of Lethbridge, Alta., and enrolled at the University of Alberta in 1953, where he has taught English since 1967. His parents were immigrants from the Soviet Union, which fact may account for the epic and prophetic strain to his prairie fiction.

Fort Pitt

Leading the attack on Fort Pitt, northwest of Lloydminster, in April 1885 was the Cree chief Big Bear. The defender was NWMP Inspector Francis Dickens, son of the novelist Charles Dickens. The HBC fort, which fell to the Cree, has been partly reconstructed.

This incident in the North West Rebellion of 1885 has been described in *The Temptations of Big Bear* (1973) by Rudy Wiebe (b. 1934). The balance of Wiebe's novel is set elsewhere: at Frog Lake, just north of the North Saskatchewan River, scene of the Frog Lake Massacre on April 2; Fort Carlton, just north of the juncture of the north and south branches of the Saskatchewan River, abandoned during the Rebellion; and Sand Hills, south of the South Saskatchewan River, between Lethbridge and Swift Current, 1885-88.

Garrick

Located northwest of Nipawin, northern Saskatchewan, the community of Garrick was named to commemorate David Garrick (1717-1779), the celebrated English actor.

Hardy

The community of Hardy, located southwest of Weyburn, bears the last name of the English novelist Thomas Hardy (1840-1928).

"Horizon" See PRINCE ALBERT.

Ibsen

Ibsen, southeast of Moose Jaw, is a former CP shipping point that bears the name of the Norwegian dramatist Henrik Ibsen (1828-1906).

Ituna

West of Yorkton is Ituna, a small community with the Celtic name for Solway Firth, apparently mentioned in a literary work by Rudyard Kipling (1865-1936).

Kipling

The community of Kipling, which is west of Moosomin, bears the name of Rudyard Kipling (1865-1936), the British author who was so popular in Western Canada. He crossed the country by private CPR coach, arranged by Sir W. C. Van Horne, on at least three occasions. It is presumed but by no means certain that he stopped off at Kipling. His imagination was ever on the alert for drama out of the ordinary. Once from his coach window he saw a simple scene that set his mind awhirl. He described it in *Letters to the Family* (1908): "Once, while we halted a woman drove straight down at us from the sky-line, along a golden path between black ploughed lands. When the horse, who managed affairs, stopped at the cars, she nodded mysteriously, and showed us a very small baby in the hollow of her arm. Doubtless she was some exiled Queen flying North to found a dynasty and establish a country. The Prairie makes everything wonderful."

Lampman

Lampman, northeast of Estevan, was so named to honour the nature poet Archibald Lampman (1861-1899).

Langham

The village of Langham, on the North Saskatchewan River, northwest of Saskatoon, is the setting of *The Master of the Mill* (1944), the novel by Frederick Philip Grove (1879-1948). In the novel the community on "the North River" is described in these terms: "a small village, the village of Langholm, the sole reason for the existence of which consisted in the rambling, wooden mill at the foot of the rapids." The novel moves from 1896 to 1938; the Master is Senator Samuel Clark. The mill itself is said to be inspired by one at Keewatin, Ont.

Lilac

The town of Lilac, southeast of North Battleford, has been called the "Jewel of the Wheat Belt." The person doing the calling is Clement Watkins, Jr., reporter with *The Lilac Advance:* the author behind both of these imaginary creations is the columnist George Bain (b. 1920), who satirized federal politics from the vantagepoint of his *Letters from Lilac* (1978), which originally appeared in *The Globe and Mail* between 1963 and 1973. In this collection by the "Prairie Pepys," he shows that "the affairs of the world don't rest easily on Lilac."

Lumsden

The small town of Lumsden is located northwest of Regina. Here was born and educated Illingworth Kerr (b. 1905), a contributor of stories to *Blackwood's Magazine* and an instructor in art at the Vancouver School of Art and the Provincial Institute of Technology and Art, in Calgary. The stories in *Gay Dogs and Dark Horses* (1946) are set in the fictional prairie community of "Pronghorn," probably modelled on Lumsden.

Also born in Lumsden was Edith Fowke (b. 1913), the folklorist, who is the author of *Folklore of Canada* (1976), the first anthology to present a cross-section of the country's oral traditions drawn from authentic sources, and two delightful children's books, *Sally Go Round the Sun* (1969) and *Ring Around the Moon* (1977).

Mair

Mair, located south of Moosomin, is a small community named to honour the poet associated with the Red River Rebellion, Charles Mair (1838-1927).

Masefield

South of Swift Current, near the Montana border, Masefield was named in honour of the English poet John Masefield (1878-1967).

Minnehaha

Minnehaha, north of North Battleford, is a locality that bears the name of Hiawatha's bride in *The Song of Hiawatha* (1855) by Henry Wadsworth Longfellow (1807-1882).

Moose Jaw

Moose Jaw is located west of Regina. Moose Jaw Creek, which gave its name to the city, was first recorded on a map in 1857. But civilization here is much older than that, for as the novelist Edward McCourt (1907-1972) observed in *The Road Across Canada* (1965): "Troy town rose and fell ten times on the hill Hissarlik above the Hellespont; the Indian village sited a few miles west of Moose Jaw went Troy three better — thirteen distinct cultural levels have been uncovered in the Mortlach 'midden,' first stumbled upon by a local farmer who observed an unusual number of arrowheads in a pasture cowpath."

A Moose Jaw native is Ken Mitchell (b. 1940) who,

Here are two views of folklorist Edith Fowke. She was only two in 1915 when this snap was taken of her on the porch of the family home, which is still standing, in Lumsden. Almost seventy years later she posed for a photograph under the tree on the lawn of her Toronto home. [Edith Fowke]

Moose Jaw is the province's third city in size. "All citizens of the British Empire," noted poet Vachel Lindsay in 1926, "seem all to be citizens of that sacred Indian city called Moose Jaw." Pictured here is its Main Street. [Saskatchewan Tourism]

in novels like *Wandering Rafferty* (1972), rhapsodizes prairie life. Other writers associated with Moose Jaw and the South Hill district include Robert Currie, Gary Hyland, Jim McLean, Barbara Sapergia, and Geoffrey Ursell. Born elsewhere was M. T. Kelly (b. 1947) who worked for the *Moose Jaw Times-Herald* in 1975-76 and called the community "Elk Brain" in his first novel *I Do Remember the Fall* (1977).

Max Braithwaite laughs as easily as the readers of his novels. [McClelland & Stewart]

Samantha Eggar played the visiting teacher and Bud Cort the inquiring student in the movie Why Shoot the Teacher, based on the novel by Max Braithwaite, which effectively evokes the prairie setting. [Ontario Film Institute]

Alfred Lord Tennyson from The Dominion Illustrated, *November 28, 1891.* [PAC C 121099]

Moosomin

The nephew of Alfred Lord Tennyson lived in Moosomin, the town in southern Saskatchewan near the border with Manitoba. Here, in 1896, M. Bertram Tennyson (who died about 1903) published *The Land of Napioa and Other Essays in Prose and Verse*. The nephew was a poetaster at best and no rival to the poet-laureate. Here is a sample of his verse about the West: "The world is fair in this new land, and yet I envy you, / For we have not the primrose pale, and though 'tis just as blue, / The violet in exile here, throws out a scentless bloom; / The rose is fair as England's rose, but has not its perfume."

Nokomis

The small town of Nokomis, southeast of Saskatoon, was named after Old Nokomis, who teaches Hiawatha the legends of her race in Longfellow's *The Song of Hiawatha* (1855). Born in Nokomis was Max Braithwaite (b. 1911) who was raised in the towns of Aberdeen and Vonda, both located northeast of Saskatoon. Experiences in all three communities are described in Braithwaite's popular prairie trilogy: *Why Shoot the Teacher* (1965) is set in "Bleke"; *Never Sleep Three in a Bed* (1969) in Nokomis, Prince Albert, and Saskatoon; *The Night We Stole the Mountie's Car* (1971) in "Wannege." *Why Shoot the Teacher* was filmed in 1976.

North Battleford

The best-known poem about the Mounties is "The Riders of the Plains" which was published anonymously in 1878 in the September 23 issue of the *Saskatchewan Herald*.

This was the first newspaper in Western Canada, and the press that printed it is on display in a small museum outside the palisaded North West Mounted Police fort, established in 1876, now part of Battleford National Historic Park. The last verse of the poem runs: "Our mission is to plant the right / Of British freedom here — / Restrain the lawless savages, / And protect the pioneer. / And 'tis a proud and daring trust / To hold these vast domains / With but three hundred mounted men — / The Riders of the Plains."

Oxbow

The old CPR station at Oxbow, east of Estevan and southeast of Regina, was turned into the Ralph Allen Memorial Museum, where memorabilia associated with the newspaper and writing career of Ralph Allen (1913-1966) are displayed. Allen was born in Winnipeg but raised in Oxbow. The Allen family lived in the railway station from 1923 to 1930 for his father was the dispatcher. The station was turned into a museum in 1972. Allen left Oxbow at the age of sixteen to pursue a distinguished career in journalism, which included editorship of *Maclean's* (1950-60) and authorship of such novels as *The Chartered Libertine* (1954) and *Peace River Country* (1958). Christina Newman edited a selection of his writings called *The Man from Oxbow* (1967).

The old CPR station at Oxbow became the Ralph Allen Memorial Museum in 1972. The journalist and author, shown here in World War II uniform, was raised in Oxbow. In 1930, at the age of sixteen, he left from this station to make his mark in the world of journalism. [Ralph Allen Memorial Museum]

Parkman

Northeast of Oxbow is the community of Parkman; the name recalls that of the distinguished Boston historian who wrote about the French in America, Francis Parkman (1823-1893).

Piapot Reserve

On this reserve, west of Fort Qu'Appelle, was born Buffy Sainte-Marie (b. 1941), the folksinger. She was raised by adoptive parents in Wakefield, Massachusetts, and acquired a wide following for her protest songs, notably "Universal Soldier" composed in 1963 which became a quasi-anthem of those against American involvement in Vietnam.

Pickthall

A former grain shipping point on the CP line south of Assiniboia, Pickthall bore the name of Marjorie Pickthall (1883-1922), the poet who wrote "Resurgam." The elevator at Pickthall was torn down in 1964 and little remains. Even the name has been rescinded from the list of current nomenclature.

Plato

The community of Plato, southwest of Rosetown, was named after Plato, Minnesota. Presumably the latter was named in honour of the Greek philosopher Plato (427-347 B.C.).

Prince Albert

The short-story writer and novelist Sinclair Ross (b. 1908) was born in Prince Albert. His best-known novel, *As for Me and My House* (1941), is set in the isolated community of "Horizon." Its Main Street has a single row of "smug, false-fronted stores" built to resemble two-storey buildings. Despite its name, Horizon is a constricting place. There may well be elements of Prince Albert found in Horizon, or vice-versa. The same may be true of "Upward," the small community that serves Sinclair Ross as the setting of *Sawbones Memorial* (1974), which is concerned with the members of the community who await the opening of the local hospital which has been named after the local doctor, or "sawbone."

Prince Albert Penitentiary is a maximum-security institution on the outskirts of the city. Ron Marken, an English professor at the University of Saskatchewan, encouraged the inmates to write poems and stories about their experiences. These were published in *Don't Steal This Book* (1974). One inmate was Anthony Apakark Thrasher (b. 1937) who wrote *Thrasher: Skid Row Eskimo* (1976) while behind bars. This is the story of his childhood and youth, culminating in a conviction of manslaughter for beating a man to death in a rooming house in Calgary. Thrasher wrote, "Even the summer breezes knew enough to stay out of Prince Albert Penitentiary."

Sinclair Ross is reading from a good book and the Good Book in this drawing by Isaac Bickerstaff (artist Don Evans). [Special Collections, University of Calgary Libraries]

Prince Albert National Park

Prince Albert National Park, northwest of Prince Albert, is identified with Grey Owl (1888-1938), the naturalist and author, who arrived here from Riding Mountain National Park in Manitoba in 1935 and lived in a log

Grey Owl came into his own at Prince Albert National Park. He is shown feeding a baby beaver (top). Beaver Cabin (middle) overlooks Ajawaan Lake. Close by is his gravesite (bottom), with a plaque inscribed "Grey Owl Died April 1938." [Parks Canada / Photo Services; Saskatchewan Tourism; Saskatchewan Government Photograph]

cabin, Beaver Lodge, which still stands beside Ajawaan Lake and is now a museum. *Tales of an Empty Cabin* (1936) was directly inspired by his experiences here. He is buried on the shore of Ajawaan Lake. After his death, Greg Clark, the journalist, broke the story that he was not Indian-born but an Englishman named George S. Belaney. Yet his message, that man must learn to live with nature, was unaffected by the revelation.

Qu'Appelle Valley

This deep, verdant valley in southeastern Saskatchewan takes its name from the Qu'Appelle River — French for "who calls," derived from the Cree *Kah-tep-was*, "the river which calls." At Lebret, near Fort Qu'Appelle, is a marker which tells how an Indian brave, returning by canoe, hears his name. He shouts, "Who calls?" The only reply is the echo of his words. Arriving home, he discovers his sweetheart died calling out his name. Pauline Johnson (1861-1913) gave memorable expression to "The Legend of Qu'Appelle Valley" in *Flint and Feather* (1912).

Linked with the area is Captain Stanley Harrison (1885-1978), horseman and versifier, who is the subject of the biography by Grant MacEwan (b. 1902), *The Rhyming Horseman of the Qu'Appelle* (1978). One of Harrison's poems ends "I know great horses live again."

Red Pheasant Reserve

Born on the Red Pheasant Reserve, south of North Battleford, is the native artist Allen Sapp (b. 1929). He depicts his early life in words and pictures in his autobiographical work *A Cree Life* (1977).

Regina

The original name of Regina, the capital of the province, was Wascana, which means "pile of bones." This etymology is the basis of the outrageous conceit of F. R. Scott (b. 1899). In his poem "Trans Canada" (1943), he described the sensation of taking off from Regina Airport. The plane took off "and dropped Regina below like a pile of bones."

Wascana Park There are notable points of interest in Wascana Park, a parkland of 2,000 acres. On the grounds of the Legislative Building, erected in English Renaissance style in 1908-12, there is John Nugent's statue of Louis Riel (1844-1885) that gives agonized expression to the burdens borne by the leader of two rebellions executed for treason in Regina.

Here is a detail view of the Louis Riel monument in Wascana Park, Regina. [Bill Brooks]

The Diefenbaker Homestead is a tourist attraction at its new home in Wascana Park. [Bill Brooks]

Although largely forgotten as a literary man, Nicholas Flood Davin (1843-1901) was a respected politician and journalist in his day. He founded in 1883 the *Regina Leader*, predecessor of the *Regina Leader-Post*. Disguised as a priest, he gained admission to the Regina prison cell in which Riel was being held and succeeded in conducting a remarkable interview on the eve of Riel's execution which included "his parting message to mankind." There is a tablet in Davin's honour in the Speaker's Corner of the Legislative Building.

One of the focal points of Wascana Centre is the Diefenbaker Homestead, the three-room frame house once the home of John G. Diefenbaker (1895-1979), later Prime Minister of Canada. It was moved in 1967 to its present location from Borden where it was occupied in 1905-10 by the Diefenbaker family.

Louis Riel Canada's equivalent of Austria's Oberammergau Passion Play is *The Trial of Louis Riel,* a one-act play written by John Coulter (1888-1980). Staged thrice weekly throughout July and August by local citizens in the restored Government House, former home of the Lieutenant-Governor, it dramatizes the trial for treason of Louis Riel (1844-1885), Métis leader, minority spokesman, and poet.

Pencil drawing of Louis Riel, 1885, by Lt.-Col. Irwin. [PAC C 22242]

Louis Riel is played by a citizen of Regina in the re-enactment of the Métis leader's trial for treason which took place in 1885. The Trial of Louis Riel by John Coulter has been staged each summer since 1967. [Saskatchewan Tourism]

Globe Theatre Regina's professional theatre was founded by Ken and Sue Kramer in 1966 to tour children's plays. Since 1981 it has had permanent quarters at the Old City Hall, 1801 Scarth Street. The resident playwright is Rex Deverell (b. 1941) who specializes in docu-dramas on controversial subjects, like *Black Powder,* about the Estevan riots of 1931, with music and lyrics by Geoffrey Ursell, premiered in September 1981.

RCMP Depot Division Regina's history parallels the activities of the Royal Canadian Mounted Police. The Centennial Museum, at the Force's Depot Division, has many displays of historical, social, and cultural interest. Among the hundreds of books about the "Mounties," none is more appealing than *Susannah, A Little Girl with the Mounties* (1936), a children's novel about a nine-year-old girl who "joins" the North West Mounted Police in Regina in 1896. It was written by Winnipeg-born Muriel Denison (1885-1954) who added three sequels to the saga: *Susannah of the Yukon* (1937), *Susannah at Boarding School* (1938), and *Susannah Rides Again* (1940). The 1936 novel was filmed as *Susannah of the Mounties* in 1939, staring Shirley Temple as the adventurous heroine.

The lone Mountie remains to this day an enduring symbol of Canada. Hollywood took hold of the image of the lone law-enforcement officer and firmly fixed it in the context of the Western — a Canadian Western, to be sure. Edison released the first Mountie movie in 1910, and since then a whole detachment of virile American actors played members of the Force, including Tom Mix,

An aerial view of the RCMP's "Depot" Division with its Centennial Museum, Regina. [RCMP]

The stained-glass windows are a unique feature of the little RCMP Chapel at "Depot" Division. [RCMP]

Ralph Connor's novel Corporal Cameron (1912) inspired Ernest Shipman's production Cameron of the Royal Mounted released in 1921. Directed by Henry MacRae, it starred Vivienne Osborne, Gaston Glass, and Irving Cummings. [PAC / National Film, Television and Sound Archives]

In Rose Marie, the 1936 movie version of Friml's operetta about the Mounties, Nelson Eddy played Sergeant Bruce and Jeanette MacDonald played the lovely Marie De Flor. The film was shot near Lake Tahoe on the California-Nevada border. [Ontario Film Institute]

In this still from the 1939 Hollywood movie Susannah of the Mounties, Randolph Scott is addressing Shirley Temple, the little girl "adopted" by the Force. [Ontario Film Institute]

William S. Hart, Robert Ryan, Alan Ladd, George Segal, Robert Preston, Errol Flynn, Howard Keele, and Nelson Eddy. These and many more donned the scarlet and stetson for the cameras, as Pierre Berton noted in Hollywood's Canada (1975).

The hit of the 1924 Broadway season was the operetta Rose-Marie, with music by Rudolf Friml and lyrics by Otto Harbach and Oscar Hammerstein II. It has been filmed three times. In 1928, Joan Crawford starred in a silent version. The most memorable version, produced in 1936, featured Jeanette MacDonald and Nelson Eddy. The most recent version, with Anne Blyth and Howard Keel, was released in 1954. The MacDonald-Eddy version may well be the best-known and most popular movie ever made with a Canadian theme or setting. To this day a soft assignment within the Force is known as "a Rose Marie posting."

The popularity of the Mountie extended to the "funny papers." When Zane Grey (1875-1939) felt the pinch of the Depression, he created "King of the Royal Mounted" as a newspaper comic strip in 1935. The strip featured a Constable King, said to be modelled on Constable Alfred King who hunted down the Mad Trapper. "King of the Royal Mounted" was written not by Grey himself but by his son, being drawn by Allen Dean.

School-age children enjoyed "Sergeant Preston of the Yukon" which was heard on radio from 1947 to 1955 when it moved to television. On television it was sponsored by Quaker Oats Company which promoted the program by distributing, as premiums, deeds to the Klondike "Big Inch" (discussed in the entry on Dawson, Y.T.). One of the least memorable of American flirtations with the Force is the twelve-part serial, *Canadian Mounties vs. Atomic Invaders,* released by Republic Pictures in 1953.

There are innumerable histories of the Force, memoirs by former commissioners, and exposés by former members. But two books more than most others capture the mystique of the Mounties. These are *Wake the Prairie Echoes* (1973), a selection of verse about the Force made by the Saskatchewan History and Folklore Society, and *Best Mounted Police Stories* (1978), edited by Dick Harrison.

Then there is Sergeant Renfrew and his dog Cuddles, creations of comedian Dave Broadfoot (b. 1925). This Mountie who "never gets his man" lives in "a log cabin on the fourteenth floor of Mountie headquarters."

Dave Broadfoot as Sergeant Renfrew, mobile if not mounted. [CBC / Norman Chamberlin]

Regina Public Library The Regina Public Library, which occupies a new building on the site of the old Carnegie building, is one of the few public libraries in the country (Saskatoon's is another) which has a writer-in-residence. In 1978-79, for instance, Eli Mandel (b. 1922) served in this capacity. The poems he wrote and portions of his diary appear in *Life Sentences* (1981). One poem, dedicated to fellow prairie poet Andrew Suknaski, includes the lines: "We write ourselves into existence / on these plains."

Ridpath

The small community of Ridpath, southwest of Rosetown, was named after the once-popular American historian, John Clark Ridpath (1840-1900).

Robinhood

The community of Robinhood is located north of North Battleford. It was first called Robin, but it became confused with Roblin, Man., and in 1939 was named Robinhood, which recalls the outlaw of English lore and legend, Robin Hood of Sherwood Forest.

Robsart

Robsart, a village south of Maple Creek, bears the last name of Amy Robsart, the heroine in *Kenilworth* (1821), the novel by Sir Walter Scott (1771-1832).

Rokeby

The community of Rokeby, southeast of Yorkton, bears the name of the Knight of Rokeby in the poem *Rokeby* (1813) by Sir Walter Scott (1771-1832).

Ryerson

This small community, south of Moosomin, bears the last name of the educator, Egerton Ryerson (1803-1882).

Saskatchewan River

The largest and most important of the prairie rivers, the Saskatchewan River has two branches. The North branch rises near Banff, flowing through Edmonton; the South branch rises in south Alberta. The two branches meet just east of Prince Albert to flow into Cedar Lake and then Lake Winnipeg. Hugh MacLennan (b. 1907) in *The Rivers of Canada* (1961) wrote that "of all the major rivers of this continent, the Saskatchewan seems to me the loneliest looking."

Bliss Carman (1861-1929) recorded a vision "on the bank of the river that runs by Saskatoon." In his poem "A Mirage of the Plains" he describes how, on the bank of the South Saskatchewan River he "looked Northward / As far as the eye could range" and "saw the incredible happen." The "incredible" is a vision of future cities and the fulfilment of the spirit of man.

Saskatoon

Saskatoon is the province's second-largest city, after the provincial capital of Regina. The city is briefly but effectively evoked by Dorothy Livesay (b. 1909) in her poem "Roots" (1966) where the city offers the poet a "green welcome."

"Granny's Laddie"

One of the most moving songs of the Great War was composed in Saskatoon. Sir Harry Lauder (1870-1950), the Scots singer and entertainer, wrote the words and music of "Granny's Laddie" during a blizzard that engulfed the city in 1918. The song tells the story of the lad from Falkirk who, although but seventeen, had fought on the Front for two years and yearned only to see his granny again. The refrain runs: "His hair was fair and his eyes were blue." Sir Harry's best-known lyric is "I Love a Lassie."

Saskatoon Public Library This institution is one of the few in the country to establish the position of writer-in-residence, which it did in 1981. Since then the position has been held by Anne Szumigalski, Patrick Lane, and Guy Vanderhaeghe. Writers-in-residence are expected to continue with their writing but also to make themselves accessible to members of the community with problems in writing or (more likely) in publishing their work.

An early chief librarian of the Saskatoon Public Library was Angus Mowat, sometime writer and father of Farley Mowat (b. 1921). Although born in Belleville, Ont., Farley Mowat was raised in Saskatoon. He attended Nutana Collegiate and then the University of Toronto. Saskatoon is the locale of two of his most popular books of light humour. These are *The Dog Who Wouldn't Be* (1957) and *Owls in the Family* (1961).

Students stroll past one of the newer buildings on the campus of the University of Saskatchewan at Saskatoon. [Saskatchewan Tourism]

University of Saskatchewan On the campus of the University of Saskatchewan, created in 1907, there is a plaque to honour A. S. Morton (1870-1945). It was raised in 1958 to honour this clergyman, historian, archivist, and author of numerous historical publications, including *Under Western Skies* (1937), *A History of the Canadian West* (1939), and *Sir George Simpson* (1944), a biography of the governor of the Hudson's Bay Company.

Edward McCourt (1907-1972) taught in the English department from 1944 until his death. His fiction is set on the prairies, and his novel *The Wooden Sword* (1956) is about an English professor at an unnamed prairie university. His other contributions include *The Canadian West in Fiction* (1949, 1970) and his cultural travel book, *The Road Across Canada* (1965).

Elizabeth Brewster (b. 1922), the novelist and poet, has been a member of the English Department since 1972.

The Main Library of the University of Saskatchewan

houses diverse special collections, including some correspondence of Max Jacob (1876-1944), the French surrealist, and Roy Campbell (1901-1957), the South African poet. There is a complete collection of manuscripts and works of J. M. O. A. Lebel (1879-1955), the prolific Fransaskois author who published under the pseudonym Jean Féron. Among the poets are the papers of Irving Layton, Al Purdy, Ralph Gustafson, and Peter Stevens. In 1975, Paul Hiebert donated the typescripts of his two classic works, *Sarah Binks* (1947) and *Willows Revisited* (1967).

Saskatoon Airport It is 4:20 a.m. and Norman Levine (b. 1924), writing in *Canada Made Me* (1958, 1979), is being driven to the airport out of town. "Then the drive, half asleep, a purple film around the city like that around a newborn child that has just been pushed out. We came to the airport. I don't know anything quite so lonely as airports, especially in the early morning, stuck miles from the city, in a flat waste of land. I was the only passenger and I waited by the glass front wall watching for the airplane to come from the East and seeing a duck fly across, and the sun come up."

Service
Service is a shipping point on the CN line northeast of Estevan. It was named after the poet Robert W. Service (1874-1958).

Southey
The village of Southey, located north of Regina, was called after the English poet Robert Southey (1774-1843). Its main street is named Keats; other streets are named Burns, Frost, Byron, Cowper, and Browning.

Speyer
This area of sand hills, now farmed, is the setting of *Sarah Binks* (1947) and *Willows Revisited* (1967), humorous works by Paul Hiebert (b. 1892). Sarah Binks, the "Sweet Songstress of Saskatchewan," made her home at "Willows," modelled on the region of Speyer, north of Maple Creek, and south of Leader, where as a young educator Hiebert taught in a one-room school.

Swinburne
A former grain shipping point northwest of Unity, which in turn is southwest of North Battleford, Swinburne was named after the English poet, Algernon Swinburne (1837-1909).

Thackeray
Located southwest of North Battleford, Thackeray was named after the English novelist William Makepeace Thackeray (1811-1863).

Tribune
A village on the CP line west of Estevan and south of

Weyburn, Tribune was so named in 1913, presumably because the *Winnipeg Tribune* gave the CP extensive and favourable coverage.

"Upward" See PRINCE ALBERT.

Veregin

The lands around Veregin, northeast of Yorkton, were settled in 1899 by the Doukhobors from Russia. The Russian novelist Leo Tolstoy (1828-1910) assisted them to immigrate to Saskatchewan by donating the royalties from his novel *Resurrection* (1899) to their cause. At Veregin today may be seen the prayerhouse the Doukhobors built in 1917 for their spiritual leader, Peter Vasilovich Verigin, called Peter the Lordly. (His name is spelled with an *i*, the village's with an *e*.) He lived on the second floor; the first floor, once a church, is now a museum. Verigin was the victim of an assassin and died at Brilliant, B.C. The prayerhouse is evoked by John Newlove (b. 1938) in *Moving in Alone* (1965).

Warman

The town of Warman, north of Saskatoon, bears the name of Cy Warman (1855-1914), the American journalist and song-writer who was raised in Canada. He wrote about prairie railroading in *Frontier Stories* (1898). *Songs of Cy Warman* (1911) includes the lyrics of "Sweet "Marie" (1893) which gave the chocolate bar its name.

Weyburn

Weyburn, southeast of Regina, is sometimes identified with "Crocus," the fictional community of "Jake and the Kid." The identification is made because W. O. Mitchell (b. 1914), the author of the popular radio series, was born here. But "Crocus" is closer to High River, Alta., where the author lived when he wrote the scripts than it is to Weyburn. Yet there are elements of Weyburn in the unnamed prairie town that is the locale of Mitchell's classic prairie novel, *Who Has Seen the Wind* (1947), which was filmed in 1977. Some scenes of *How I Spent My Summer Holidays* (1982), an autobiographical novel, take place at the Weyburn Psychiatric Hospital.

Research at the Weyburn Psychiatric Hospital led to the coining of the word "psychedelic," for mind-expanding. Two psychiatrists — Humphrey Osmond and Abram Hoffer — studied the effects of hallucinogenic drugs on humans. Dr. Osmond was director of psychiatric research in the department of public health in Saskatoon, and Dr. Hoffer was professor of psychiatry at the University of Saskatchewan. Dr. Osmond administered mescaline, a natural form of LSD, to Aldous Huxley, who described the experience in *The Doors of Perception* (1954). "Psychedelic" first appeared in print in a technical article by Osmond on psychotomimetic agents in 1957.

"Whitemud" See EASTEND.

Wilcox

Here, south of Regina, at the beginning of the Great Depression, was founded Notre Dame College. It was founded by Father Athol Murray and is now known as Athol Murray College of Notre Dame. An anteroom of Varsity Hall has been turned into the Rex Beach Repository, a memorial to the American journalist and author Rex Beach (1877-1949) who took a long-time interest in the College and found it "good copy." He called it the "Miracle College of Saskatchewan" in *Cosmopolitan* in 1934. The bronze plaque salutes Beach as "architect of hemispheric friendliness and unity . . . explorer of Klondike gold . . . big game hunter . . . foremost novelist of America." The Repository includes autographed first editions of Beach's novels plus other memorabilia.

Also on campus is the Tower of God, built of stone, 55 feet high, which includes symbols of the Christian, Hebrew, and Islamic religions. The story of how Athol Murray, a Roman Catholic priest, came to impress Rex Beach and how he built this ecumenical Tower is told by Jack Gorman in *Père Murray and the Hounds* (1977). The film, *The Hounds of Notre Dame,* was released in 1980.

Wood Mountain

The village of Wood Mountain, southwest of Regina, is the birthplace of Andrew Suknaski (b. 1942). In *Wood Mountain Poems* (1976) and later collections, the poet writes about this wooded region with its 3,300-foot mountain and its population of Indians, Ukrainians, and others. The critic George Woodcock coined the term "geopoetry" to define Suknaski's use of the region. The NFB released *Wood Mountain Poems* in 1978.

Wordsworth

Northeast of Estevan, the community of Wordsworth was so named in honour of the English poet William Wordsworth (1770-1850).

Yorkton

The Yorkton International Film Festival, established in 1950 in Yorkton, in the eastern part of the province, specializes in documentary films.

The literary critic Leon Edel (b. 1907) was born in Pittsburgh, Pennsylvania, and brought here in 1912. He was educated at McGill and the Sorbonne, and went on to write an outstanding five-volume life (1953-72) of Henry James.

Yorkton is not named in *The Wind Our Enemy* (1939); indeed, no specific prairie community is depicted in this well-known poem about Dust Bowl conditions by Anne Marriott (b. 1913). But the descriptions of material and spiritual drought in the Dirty Thirties apply to Yorkton as much as to any prairie farming community. The long poem is full of evocations of the wind ("filling the dry mouth with bitter dust") and the wheat ("the wheat in spring was like a giant's bolt of silk / Unrolled over the earth").

Alberta

Aldersyde

The small community of Aldersyde, north of High River, bears the name of a fictitious Scottish community, based on a story of the Border country written by Annie S. Swan, a Scottish author who in the 1880s grew up in the Midlothian area of Scotland.

Anthony Creek See ZENDA CREEK.

Antonio

The locality of Antonio, between Lethbridge and Medicine Hat, was named after one of Shakespeare's two Antonios — either the merchant in *The Merchant of Venice* (1595) or the rightful heir in *The Tempest* (1611).

Athabasca Landing

No one passing through Athabasca Landing, on the Athabasca River, north of Edmonton, is likely to forget the observation made by Robert (Bob) Edwards (1864-1922) in the *Eye Opener*, October 25, 1911: "Westward the course of empire takes its way, veering slightly to the north in the direction of Athabasca Landing."

Athabasca Landing is part of the old District of Athabasca of the Northwest Territories which existed between 1882 and 1905 when most of the territory was

"This was the 'jumping off point' for the vast northland," reads the inscription on this marker at Athabasca Landing. [Alberta Photograph Library]

divided between the provinces of Alberta and Saskatchewan. The district in the summer of 1880 is the strange setting of the action of the novel *Tay John* (1939) by Howard O'Hagan (b. 1902) who was born in Lethbridge but raised in the Yellowhead Pass area of the District of Athabasca. Here is O'Hagan's account of the country where his half-Shuswap, half-white hero is born: "Athabasca Valley, near its head in the mountains, and along the other waters falling into it, and beyond them a bit, over Yellowhead Pass, to the westward, where the Fraser, rising in a lake, flows through wilderness and canyon down to the Pacific."

Athabasca River

Although Arthur Heming (1870-1940) in his writings generalized the experiences that occurred to him, setting them in "the vast northern woods," the naturalist and author knew intimately the region of the Athabasca River in northern Saskatchewan. Much of *The Drama of the Forest* (1921) is set here in the 1890s. Of this book, Arthur Stringer has written: "Some day when the North as we know it has passed, when the wheatfields of Canada stretch far up into the sub-Arctics, and the caribou is a zoo curiosity, the moose a memory, we will go back to Heming for our record of things as they were, and we will realize that our debt to him is greater than we dreamed."

Athabasca Tar Sands See FORT McMURRAY.

Balzac

The town of Balzac, north of Calgary, was named after the French novelist Honoré de Balzac (1799-1850).

Banff

Banff is the scenic and administrative centre of Banff National Park, the first of the national parks to be established. Since the town is located on parkland, there is no ownership of land; all land is leased for periods of forty-two years from the Park authorities. The English poet Rupert Brooke (1887-1915) spent a few days at the Banff Springs Hotel in August 1913 and wrote: "It is the most beautiful place in the world. Just sheer beauty. So I eat and chatter and roam and look." In a letter he confessed

Cascade Mountain is the backdrop for Banff and its main street. [Dept. of Regional Industrial Expansion]

The famed Banff Springs Hotel in Banff National Park. [Parks Canada / Ted Grant]

that he had ideas for seven poems but was too busy to write them. "I am just one of the idle rich. Tra! la!"

Ralph Connor   Associated with Banff was Charles W. Gordon (1860-1937), clergyman and author, who published his popular novels as Ralph Connor. William Arthur Deacon asked him about these early years when he was researching *A Literary Map of Canada*. Gordon replied in a letter, September 21, 1936: "During my three years missionary experience in the Rocky Mountains my Headquarters were Banff. My own Field reached from Field on the west to the Gap on the east. I was Clerk of the Calgary Presbytery, then the largest presbytery in the world. It extended from Revelstoke in the west to Swift Current in the east and from Edmonton to the United States Borderline." Gordon went on to mention the names of Nelson, Revelstoke, Medicine Hat, Edmonton, and MacLeod. He added that *The Sky Pilot* (1899) "extended over the foothill country north and south of Calgary."

Following his ordination as a Presbyterian minister, Charles William Gordon was sent to Banff. He served as a travelling missionary from 1890 to 1894, assisting miners and lumbermen in camps that extended from Nelson, B.C., to Swift Current, Sask. Out of these experiences he fashioned his first novel, *Black Rock: A Tale of the Selkirks* (1898), published under the pen name Ralph Connor. The lonely life of the settler on the prairie informs *The Sky Pilot: A Tale of the Foothills* (1899). His novels were written not in Banff but in Winnipeg following his appointment as pastor of St. Stephen's Church.

Earle Birney   The two-storey frame house in which the poet Earle Birney (b. 1904) lived as a youngster in 1912-14 is still standing. Located at 308 Squirrel Street, it was built by his father who painted the tongue-in-cheek sign "Kwitcherkik-In," still visible on the cabin from the back yard. The house would make a suitable memorial to the poet and his homesteading parents.

"Tarry-a-While"   "Tarry-a-While" is the name painted on the unnumbered house at the foot of Grizzly Street which was built in 1913 by the husband of the writer Mary T. S. Schaffer Warren, the author of *Old Indian Trails of the Canadian Rockies* (1911, 1980), considered by many to be the quintessential book of Rockies lore.

Among those who value this work is the writer and publisher Jon Whyte (b. 1941) whose mother was attracted to Banff by the presence here of Mary T. S. Schaffer Warren. Whyte is the author of the epic poem

Still standing in Banff is the Birney homestead, erected by the father of the poet Earle Birney in 1912. It is shown here (top) in 1912. The log cabin (bottom), erected by Birney Senior behind the homestead, is also standing. It was rented by tourists, two of whom are shown here in 1922. The sign above the door reads KWITCHERKIK-IN. [Birney Collection, Thomas Fisher Rare Book Library, University of Toronto]

Earle Birney was eight years old when this photograph of him wearing his Sunday school suit and Christie hat was taken in Banff in 1912. [Birney Collection, Thomas Fisher Rare Book Library, University of Toronto]

Homage (1981), *Henry Kelsey* (1981) and other works on the mystique of mountains, including the text to two photo collections, *The Rockies* (1978) and *Lake Louise* (1982). He is a director of the Peter Whyte Foundation.

Banff Centre The Banff Centre for continuing education offers summer courses in arts and year-round courses in a number of disciplines. It goes back to 1933 when it was organized as a summer extension program by the University of Alberta. Many writers and poets, such as Margaret Laurence and Al Purdy, have given readings and conducted writers' workshops at the Banff Centre.

Monument to John Murray Gibbon, folklorist, novelist, and CPR publicist, on the grounds of the Banff Centre. [Bill Brooks]

Behind the Administration Building there is a plaque that commemorates the work of John Murray Gibbon (1875-1952). A man of many parts, Gibbon was employed as publicity director for the CPR from 1913 to his retirement in 1945. He sponsored fourteen major folk festivals in CP hotels across the country during the years 1927-30. He was a founder of the Canadian Authors' Association and he published, in addition to novels and collections of traditional songs and poems, an important multicultural study, *Canadian Mosaic: The Making of a Northern Nation* (1938). He also established the "Trail Riders of the Canadian Rockies" at Banff. He lies buried in the Banff Cemetery beneath a headstone which depicts a packhorse in the foreground with trees and mountain peaks in the background.

In 1983, the Banff Centre opened the Leighton Artist Colony. Named after David Leighton, a Centre president, the colony consists of eight studios reserved for the exclusive use of established artists. Each was designed by a leading architect. There are two visual arts studios, three composers' studios, and three writers' studios (designed by Richard Henriquez, Peter Hemingway, and Michael E. Evamy).

The poet Eli Mandel (b. 1922) kept a journal while at the Banff Centre and published portions of it in *Life Sentences* (1981) where he explained: "The school's location is truly extraordinary: the steadily changing mountains all around, now familiar, their slow mountain thoughts obscure: geologic thought, stratas of feeling."

247

Bindloss

The hamlet of Bindloss, north of Medicine Hat and close to the Saskatchewan border, recalls the past popularity of Harold Bindloss (1866-1945), the English novelist who spent some years in the Canadian West. His novel *The Wilderness Patrol* (1925) begins: "A soft chinook wind blew from the Rockies. . . ."

Blackfoot Crossing See GLEICHEN.

Blood Reserve See STAND OFF.

The skyline of Calgary is dominated by the Calgary Tower. [Dept. of Regional Industrial Expansion]

Calgary

Splendidly located within sight of the Rocky Mountains, Calgary is Alberta's first city in terms of civic pride and its second city (after Edmonton) in size. It has a number of literary associations yet it is the thesis of writer and poet Jon Whyte that Calgary exists in the pages of literature as the jumping-off point for Banff where all the sex and intrigue take place. In his article "The Place Where Nothing Happens" in *Calgary Magazine,* May 1983, he asks the rhetorical question, "Whoever Keystone-Kopped it on the Crowfoot Trail?" His answer is in the negative and his conclusion is: "Calgary is a poorer city for the failure of authors to bring it alive. It's difficult to love a city authors have ignored." He adds: "Until a community becomes a stage it is difficult for its denizens to imagine themselves as even bit players in its drama. Until they become part of the drama, they lack the love that makes a place particular, special, and unique."

Calgary Eye Opener Forever associated with the city of Calgary is the career of the satirist and publisher, Robert (Bob) Edwards (1864-1922). It was here that the itinerant, hard-drinking, Scots-born publisher of the *Eye Opener* settled down and married. Indeed, he is buried in the city and his satiric paper is still known as the Calgary *Eye Opener.* His broad, irreverent humour seems to suit the city.

Photograph of Bob Edwards, editor of the Eye Opener, in Calgary. [Glenbow Archives, Calgary, Alberta]

Calgary's sole memorial to its famous humourist: Some faculty and students pose on the steps of Bob Edwards Junior High School, 4424 Marlborough Drive, Calgary. [Alberta Photography Library]

Between 1897, when he arrived in Canada, and 1911, when he settled in Calgary, Edwards worked as a journalist in Wetaskiwin, Calgary, Winnipeg, Leduc, Strathcona, Wetaskiwin again, High River, Toronto, Montreal, and Port Arthur. He launched his *Eye Opener* from High River in 1902 and published it until the year of his death.

He wrote in the *Eye Opener* on February 4, 1905: "Edmonton now estimates that it has a population of over 4,000. Estimates are easy to make. Calgary with her bona fide population of 11,000 is seriously thinking of estimating her population at 25,000 just to prove that its imagination is not inferior to Edmonton's."

It is surprising there is still no plaque, marker, or memorial to Edwards in his adopted city. But perhaps the best memorial of all is *The Best of Bob Edwards* (1975), edited by Hugh A. Dempsey.

Arthur Stringer Arthur Stringer (1874-1950) specified the setting of his novel *The Prairie Wife* (1915) in a letter written on September 20, 1936, to William Arthur Deacon who was in the process of compiling *A Literary Map of Canada* (1936). The novel — part of a trilogy that included *The Prairie Mother* (1920) and *The Prairie Child*

(1923) — was set on a ranch, then owned by Stringer, seventeen miles southwest of Calgary. He added the information that there were plans to issue the three novels in one volume as "The Prairie Stories." He concluded with a reference to Franklin Pierce Adams, the New York journalist: "F. P. A. once asked in his column why I didn't do 'The Prairie Dog' and then I'd have the whole damned family."

This photograph shows the Calgary Public Library in 1912. The next year Rupert Brooke praised it as "a very neat and carefully kept building." It is now the Memorial Park Branch. [Calgary Public Library]

Calgary Public Library   It was Rupert Brooke's observation that as one travelled from east to west in Canada, the quality of the public libraries improved. The best library he found in the country in 1913 was the Calgary Public Library, a Beaux-Arts Carnegie building that is still standing today: "In Calgary, you find a very neat and carefully kept building, stocked with an immense variety of periodicals, and an admirably chosen store of books, ranging from the classics to the most utterly modern literature. Few large English towns could show anything as good. Cross the Rockies to Vancouver, and you're back among dirty walls, grubby furniture, and inadequate literature again. There's nothing in Canada to compare with the magnificent libraries little New Zealand can show. But Calgary is hopeful."

Calgary Stampede   This internationally famous annual exhibition of rodeo events, amusements, and livestock shows, held for ten days each July in Stampede Park, was established in 1912 and is advertised as "the greatest outdoor show on earth." The Stampede Grounds are mentioned in at least two novels. In *The Con Man* (1979), Ken Mitchell (b. 1940) has his protagonist sell souvenirs that contain two caps of heroin. Herbert Harker has his central character in *Goldenrod* (1972) win a bronco-riding championship at the Stadium. In a third work, the Stampede Grounds are the probable location of the "Cow Palace" in the novel *Copperhead* (1971) by James Henderson (b. 1934).

Nellie L. McClung   The pioneer feminist and writer

Nellie L. McClung (1873-1951) moved to Alberta in 1914 and settled in Calgary. She sat in the Legislature from 1921 to 1926 and spent her last years in Victoria, B.C. A number of novels, including *Purple Springs* (1921) and *Painted Fires* (1925), appeared while she lived in Calgary. The house in which she lived — at 803 15th Street S.W. — has been a provincial historic site since 1978.

Shaarey Tzedec Synagogue   There is a "family Torah" in the Shaarey Tzedec Synagogue, 107-17th Avenue, S.W. The story of how this Scroll of the Law got from Russia to Canada is full of human interest and has been told in *The Reader's Digest,* February 1976, by Morris C. Shumiatcher (b. 1917), the prominent Regina jurist and author of *The Man of Law* (1979). The "family Torah," the prized possession of the Lubinsky family of Poland and Russia, had been commissioned in 1914 on the advice of the Rabbi of Slonim to help Nathan Lubinsky control his grief following the murder of his son Mendel in Siberia. The Torah remained with the family through thick and thin. It was brought wrapped in a bedsheet from Moscow to Calgary in 1974 by Zalman Lubinsky and deposited with the Shaarey Tzedec Synagogue.

Zalman Lubinsky is shown in the Shaarey Tzedec Synagogue studying the Torah he brought from Moscow to Calgary. [Morris C. Shumiatcher]

Glenbow Centre   A major social, educational, cultural, and artistic resource, the Glenbow Centre goes back to 1954 and was founded to collect Western Canadiana in order to tell the story of the West from prehistoric to modern times. The Centre is located at 9th Avenue and 1st Street S.E., and operates a major museum and library and archives. Visitors are always impressed by "Aurora Borealis" in the foyer. This is James Houston's four-storey-high chandelier of more than one thousand acrylic prisms. In addition to books, periodicals, newspapers, maps, and government documents, the library has a number of special collections, including a major collection of photographs. The well-known writer on Western Subjects, Hugh A. Dempsey (b. 1929), is associated with the Centre.

Exterior view of the Glenbow Centre and view of James Houston's sculpture "Aurora Borealis." [*Glenbow Archives, Calgary, Alberta*]

T. Lobsang Rampa The most controversial author ever to have lived in Calgary has to be T. Lobsang Rampa (1911-1981), the British writer of some two dozen occult books who claimed to be a Tibetan lama whose pineal gland had been activated surgically. Following the notoriety generated by his so-called autobiography, *The Third Eye* (1954), he emigrated to Canada, living successively in Tecumseh (near Windsor), Fort Erie, Prescott, Saint John, Montreal (in Habitat), Vancouver, and Calgary where he died of heart failure. His dedication of *As It Was!* (1976) has to be unique in the annals of literature: "Dedicated to the City of Calgary, where I have had peace and quiet and freedom from interference in my personal affairs. Thank you, City of Calgary." The last seven years of his life he spent in Apartment 2808, O'Neil Towers, 700 9th Street S.W. The two-bedroom apartment overlooks the downtown area and lacks a view of the Rockies. In failing health, he had a motorized wheelchair which he used on 8th Avenue S.W., particularly on the weekend when there was little downtown traffic. His body was cremated so there is no burial site.

Other Authors A long-time resident of Calgary is James H. Gray (b. 1906), the popular historian of prairie social life. His first book was the autobiographical work,

The Winter Years (1966). He examined prairie prostitution in *Red Lights on the Prairies* (1971) and the temperance movement in *Booze* (1972). From the top of the Calgary Tower he showed the city to the British travel writer Jan Morris.

Kevin Major (b. 1949), the writer from Newfoundland, set part of his novel *Too Far from Shore* (1980) in Calgary.

Perhaps the most colourful author to live in Calgary and write for the Calgary Herald was Buffalo Child Long Lance, who was born Sylvester Clarke (1890-1932) of mixed native and Black background in the United States. He joined the *Herald* in 1919 and wrote features for the next three years. It was in Alberta that he retroactively established his credentials as a Blood Indian. The story of this remarkable man is told by Donald B. Smith in *Long Lance: The Story of an Impostor* (1982).

University of Calgary The University of Calgary, established in 1945 and autonomous in 1966, is located on a campus in the northwest section of the city. Among the authors on the faculty of the university are the poet Christopher Wiseman and the novelist W. P. Kinsella. The review *Ariel* has apeared since 1970.

The University of Calgary Library is one of the largest repositories of authors' manuscripts. The holdings in foreign writers (John Middleton Murry, John Cowper Powys, Kathleen Raine) are slim, but the Canadian authors collected are legion. Represented are Earle Birney, Clark Blaise, George Bowering, David Bromige, Michael Cook, Cliff Faulknor, Joanna Glass, John Gray, Christie Harris, Harold Horwood, Bruce Hutchison, Patricia Joudry, Robert Kroetsch, André Langevin, J. W. Grant MacEwan, Hugh MacLennan, John Metcalf, W. O. Mitchell, Brian Moore, Alice Munro, Alden Nowlan, Claude Péloquin, Len Peterson, Mordecai Richler, Sinclair Ross, George Ryga, and Rudy Wiebe. In addition, the collection boasts musical scores of R. Murray Schafer and Morris Surdin; the literary caricatures of Isaac Bickerstaff (the artist Don Evans); and the archives of Coach House Press, Hancock House, ECW Press, and *Tish* magazine.

Canmore

A cairn at Canmore, southeast of Banff, pays tribute to Charles W. Gordon (1860-1937), the missionary and author. As a missionary, he ministered to the miners and farmers of this area; as an author, who published his best-selling books under the pen-name Ralph Connor, he wrote such novels as *The Sky Pilot* (1899) and *Corporal Cameron* (1912). There is the Ralph Connor Memorial United Church, originally erected in 1891.

Carvel

The community of Carvel, west of Edmonton, was named in 1911 after *Richard Carvel* (1899), the novel by the American writer, Winston Churchill (1871-1947),

There are at Canmore two memorials to Charles W. Gordon, the Methodist minister who reached a wide public through the fiction he published as Ralph Connor. The handlettered sign identifies the Ralph Connor Memorial United Church, erected by Gordon in 1890-1. The plaque attached to the Charles W. Gordon Memorial describes its subject as "Pioneer Presbyterian Minister. . . Canadian Author . . . Minister of This Church." [Bill Brooks]

whose works were often mistakenly attributed to the British Prime Minister, Sir Winston S. Churchill.

Consort

Consort, the community south of Wainwright, is the stomping ground of R. Ross Annett (b. 1895), author of the "Babe and Little Joe" stories which appeared in the *Saturday Evening Post.* Seventy-two of these prairie tales about the five-year-old kid and the widower were published in the magazine from 1937 to its demise in 1962. The first thirteen were collected in *Especially Babe* (1978).

Annett taught at Consort Consolidated School in the early 1920s, but he maintained the setting of the stories was the community of Jenner, northeast of Brooks. After years of residence in Edmonton, Annett returned to Consort. The earliest of the tales, "It's Gotta Rain Sometime," is about the kid's discovery that there is such a thing as rain. In his afterword to *Especially Babe,* Rudy Wiebe (b. 1934) commented on the importance of place in human life. "After all, New York is a place, but Consort is a place too."

"Crocus"   See HIGH RIVER.

Edmonton's Jasper Avenue outside rush hours. [Dept. of Regional Industrial Expansion]

Edmonton

There may be witches in Edmonton, Alta., but *The Witch of Edmonton* is about none of them. Instead it is about one Elizabeth Sawyer who was hanged as a witch at Tyburn in 1621. Her story was "immortalized" by three playwrights — Thomas Dekker, John Ford, and William Rowley — in a tragi-comedy called *The Witch of Edmonton* which was premiered in London in 1623. Edmonton is a district of Metropolitan London, as well as the capital and largest city of Alberta. Dorothy Livesay (b. 1909), in her poem "The Pied Piper of Edmonton" (1971), referred to it as "O glitter city," and it does have a special radiance at night. Earle Birney (b. 1904) flew across the country on a TCA *North Star* and recorded his impressions in the long poem "North Star West" (1951). According to Birney, from the air "Edmonton grows like a puzzled frown." The Polish *émigré* poet Waclaw Iwaniuk (b. 1915) has a description of Edmonton and the effect of the prairies on him in *Evenings on Lake Ontario* (1981): "I broke out in a sweat / staring at the enormous plains, with the enormous sky."

Janey Canuck   Emily Murphy (1868-1933), the crusader for women's rights and author who employed the pen name "Janey Canuck," settled in Edmonton in 1907 and nine years later was appointed first woman magistrate in the British Empire. She found vitality in Edmonton, for as she wrote in *Janey Canuck in the West* (1910): "I would like to write more about Edmonton, this place of fascinations where Cree, Christian, and cowboy, trader and trapper, governor and judge, senator and soldier, engineer and explorer, priest, professor, and pioneer, each is doing his best to build up a great city high on the banks of the Saskatchewan. And it will be a great city; but, to my way of thinking, never more interesting than today, when each man is individualistic and stands alone."

Emily Murphy Park, on the south side of the Saskatchewan River, east of Groat Bridge, was named in her honour. The plaque in the park, unveiled in 1960, calls her "a crusader for social reform and for equal status for women." Born in Cookstown, Ont., she died in Edmonton where she is buried.

Jasper Avenue and 101st Street   Hazard Lepage, the cowboy hero of *The Studhorse Man* (1969) by Robert Kroetsch (b. 1927), causes eight hundred horses to stampede at the intersection of Jasper Avenue and 101st Street in downtown Edmonton. Other sites visited in the lively novel include the Legislative Building and the McDougall Church, now a museum.

Hurtig Publishers   Hurtig Publishers, located at 10560 - 105 Street, was founded in 1967 by Mel Hurtig (b. 1932), an Edmonton bookseller, who publishes books of both Western and national interest. It was Hurtig who conceived the notion of *The Canadian Encyclopedia,* now being edited from two houses on the campus of the University of Alberta. It will appear in three volumes in the fall of 1985.

University of Alberta   The University of Alberta was founded in 1906 and located on the south bank of the North Saskatchewan River. Such is the prosaic truth. Stephen Leacock (1869-1944) expressed the facts more fancifully in *Canada: The Foundations of Its Future* (1941): "The University of Alberta emerged from Fort Edmonton as complete as Minerva from the head of Jove. It is a hidden secret, known only inside colleges, but unsuspected even by college trustees, that the most distinguished university in all the world can be made overnight by gathering to it the most distinguished scholars of all the world."

In the 1920s the English Department was headed by the inspired teacher E. K. Broadus (1876-1936), author of the autobiographical *Saturday and Sunday* (1935). His star pupil was Lovat Dickson (b. 1902) who enrolled in 1923 as a mature student, graduated in 1927, and then taught briefly as a lecturer. Dickson would have continued in academia except that an Edmonton millionaire took a shine to him, offering him the editorship of the *English Review,* the journal published in London, England, which he had just then acquired. Dickson tells the improbable story of how he became a London magazine and book publisher in *The Ante-Room* (1959) and its sequel *The House of Words* (1963).

The tradition of Broadus continues. Among the writers with a past or present association with the English department are Henry Kreisel, Wilfrid Watson, Sheila Watson, Doug Barbour, Stephen Scobie, and Rudy Wiebe. Kreisel's novel *The Betrayal* (1964) makes convincing use of the city as locale.

Of national interest is the University of Alberta's Riel

View of the campus of the University of Alberta in Edmonton. [*Alberta Photograph Library*]

Project, which will issue a four-volume critical edition of the writings of Louis Riel (1844-1885), the Métis leader and visionary. Publication is planned to coincide with the centennial of the North West Rebellion of 1885. The general editors are George F. G. Stanley, author of *Louis Riel* (1963), and Thomas E. Flanagan, author of three books about the man, including *Riel and the Rebellion* (1983).

Grant MacEwan   A familiar figure in the halls of the Legislative Building in Edmonton was J. W. Grant MacEwan (b. 1902). From 1966 to 1974 he served as the Lieutenant-Governor of Alberta. He shares with James H. Gray the knack of writing popular Western Canadian histories. Two of his notable books are *Fifty Mighty Men* (1958) and its sequel *And Mighty Women Too* (1975). He has written an entire book on Stanley Harrison, "Poet of the Qu'Appelle Valley."

Don Evans (who signs his work Isaac Bickerstaff) has drawn author Grant MacEwan directing an old-style tractor. [*Special Collections, University of Calgary Libraries*]

Aritha van Herk, Rudy Wiebe, and Marian Engel at Strawberry Creek, April 22, 1978. Wiebe has a cabin and large log lodge at Strawberry Creek, fifty miles from Edmonton. Van Herk, who had just won the Seal $50,000 first novel award, was Wiebe's graduate student at the University of Alberta where Engel was writer-in-residence. [Rudy Wiebe]

Rudy Wiebe   Rudy Wiebe (b. 1934) has taught in the Department of English of the University of Alberta since 1967. Setting is of signal significance in his fiction. *Peace Shall Destroy Many* (1962) is set in the 1930s and 1940s in a Mennonite community at Wapiti in Northern Saskatchewan. *First and Vital Candle* (1966) has as its locale a prairie place called Frozen Lake as well as Winnipeg. *The Blue Mountains of China* (1970) follows the Mennonites on their migrations; prairie locales include Swift Current, Winnipeg, Gretna, Schoenbach, Altona, Hague, etc. *The Temptations of Big Bear* (1973) is set in the 1880s at Frog Lake, Fort Pitt, Fort Carlton, Sand Hills, etc. The short stories collected in *Where Is the Voice Coming From?* (1974) range over the prairies; the title story is about the death of Almighty Voice. *The Scorched-Wood People* (1977) concerns the Riel Rebellions at Fort Garry, Batoche, Winnipeg, etc. *The Mad Trapper* (1980) follows Albert Johnson around the West:

A meeting of the editorial board of NeWest Press, September 18, 1982. Members are from Edmonton, unless otherwise stated, and identified from left to right. Standing: Mort Ross, Rudy Wiebe, Robert Kroetsch (Winnipeg), Andrea Spalding, Aritha van Herk (Calgary), Don Kerr (Saskatoon), Henry Kreisel, Paul Hjartarson, Shirley Neumann, Larry Pratt. Seated: Joe Fafard (Pense, Sask.), Doug Barbour, Myrna Kostash, Smaro Kambourelli (Winnipeg), Jack Lewis, Diane Bessai, Jorge Frascara. [Rudy Wiebe]

Edmonton, Eagle River, Fort McPherson, Peel River, Rat River, Ogilvie Mountains, Aklavik, etc. *My Lovely Enemy* (1983), set in contemporary Edmonton, mentions the Cameron Library at the University of Alberta as well as the North Saskatchewan River, the Glenbow Centre, All Saints Church, the University Mall, the High Level Bridge, etc.

Ermineskin Reserve   See HOBBEMA.

Fedorah
Fedorah, the community north of Edmonton, was named after the once-popular melodrama *Fédora* (1882) written by the French dramatist Victorien Sardou (1831-1908) as a vehicle for Sarah Bernhardt.

Fort McLeod
The town of Fort McLeod, west of Lethbridge, is the birthplace of Joni Mitchell (b. 1944), the folksinger who rose to fame with such songs as "Both Sides Now" (1968) and "Woodstock" (1969). Lines from the latter hit include: "We are stardust / We are golden / And we've got to get ourselves / Back to the garden."

Fort McMurray
Fort McMurray is the gateway to the Athabasca Tar Sands in northeastern Alberta. Oil production from the tar sands commenced in 1967. Much has been written about the world's largest known oil deposits here, little of it literary. One exception is the title story of *The Angel of the Tar Sands and Other Stories* (1982) by Rudy Wiebe (b. 1934), in which earth-moving equipment uncovers in the bituminous sand a six-winged angelic being.

"Fu-Sang"   See WRITING-ON-STONE PROVINCIAL PARK.

Gleichen
Crowfoot, the last of the great chiefs, died at Blackfoot Crossing on April 25, 1890, and is buried overlooking the

The words on the cross above Crowfoot's grave at Gleichen read: "Father of His People." [Bill Brooks]

Bow River at the town of Gleichen, southeast of Calgary. The dying words attributed to him by John Peter Turner in *The North-West Mounted Police* (1950) are the essence of popular poetry: "A little while and I will be gone from among you, whither I cannot tell. From nowhere we came, into nowhere we go. What is life? It is a flash of a firefly in the night. It is a breath of a buffalo in the winter time. It is as the little shadow that runs across the grass and loses itself in the sunset."

Heisler

In the small farming community of Heisler, southeast of Camrose, was born the novelist Robert Kroetsch (b. 1927) who lived here until his seventeenth year when he enrolled at the University of Alberta.

The boy on the cart is Robert Kroetsch. The family farm was southwest of Heisler. "The horse being led is a studhorse," mused the author. "Perhaps this experience inspired The Studhorse Man!*" [Robert Kroetsch]*

Robert Kroetsch is caught in an uncharacteristic pose by Isaac Bickerstaff (pen name of caricaturist Don Evans). [Special Collections, University of Calgary Libraries]

Heldar

Northwest of Edmonton, the community of Heldar was named after Dick Heldar, the hero of *The Light that Failed* (1890), the novel by Rudyard Kipling (1865-1936).

High River

High River, south of Calgary, has the distinction of being the town in which Bob Edwards (1864-1922), satirist and publisher, launched his tabloid, the *Eye Opener*, March 4, 1902. In its day it was the most loved — and hated —

publication in the country. "Hope for the best," Edwards once wrote, "and then hustle for it."

The writer and raconteur, W. O. Mitchell (b. 1914), has lived in High River off and on since the 1940s. By association this town has become "Crocus" — the fictional setting for Mitchell's radio series "Jake and the Kid," popular on CBC Radio throughout the 1950s. Some of the scripts were published in story form as *Jake and the Kid* (1961). According to various scripts, "Crocus, Sask." had a population in the 1940s of 739. It was set variously "on the CPR line" or "on the CNR line"; one aficionado of the radio series claimed it was located "on the banks of the Broken Shell River in the heart of the bald-headed prairie, deep in the imagination of W. O. Mitchell." It is difficult not to believe that someday there will be a memorial to Mitchell — and perhaps to the fictional hired man Jake — in High River.

Since the early 1970s, High River has been associated with former Prime Minister Joe Clark, and also with Smallville, Superman's second home. (His first home was on the planet Krypton.) The small-town sequences of *Superman: The Movie*, *Superman II*, and *Superman III* were shot on location in High River (and, for good measure, in Calgary).

Something about the High River area gives rise to tall tales. Southwest of the town, in the upper reaches of the Highwood River, or south in the Livingstone Range, is said to lie the Lost Lemon Mine. The many legends about this lost gold mine date from about 1870. As Hugh Dempsey wrote in *The Lost Lemon Mine* (1962): "Whether it is fact or fiction will probably never be known but as long as adventure and dreams of sudden wealth stir the imagination of man there will be those who will be going in search of the fabulous Lost Lemon Mine in the Rocky Mountains of Western Canada."

Hobbema

The Ermineskin Reserve, near Hobbema south of Wetaskiwin, is nationally known as the locale of the short stories of W. P. Kinsella (b. 1935). The tales of Cree reservation life are told in dialect for comic and sometimes tragic effect. They appear in the following collections: *Dance Me Outside* (1977), *Scars* (1978), *Born Indian* (1981), and *The Moccasin Telegraph* (1983).

Innisfree

Southeast of Vegreville, the community of Innisfree was named after the ideal retreat described by William Butler Yeats (1865-1939) in his famous poem "The Lake Isle of Innisfree."

Jasper

The resort town of Jasper is the administrative centre for Jasper National Park. The author Howard O'Hagan (b. 1902) was born near Crow's Nest Pass but grew up north of there on Yellowhead Lake. Later he was a guide and packer in Jasper National Park. His fiction includes the

One of the best-liked writers in the country, W. O. Mitchell, from the NFB documentary W. O. Mitchell — Novelist in Hiding. [NFB]

William Kurelek prepared pen-and-ink drawings for the 1976 edition of W. O. Mitchell's Who has Seen the Wind. [Macmillan of Canada]

Even as a youngster Superman was capable of prodigious feats. Here he amazes his foster father, played by actor Glenn Ford, in Superman: The Movie. The scene, set in "Smallville, U.S.A.," was shot in High River, Alta. [Ontario Film Institute]

Who Has Seen the Wind tells the story of a sensitive boy growing up on the prairies. W. O. Mitchell's novel was filmed by Allan King, with José Ferrar as Old Ben and Brian Painchaud as a namesake, Young Brian. [Ontario Film Institute]

mythic novel Tay John (1939), the short stories in The Woman Who Got on at Jasper Station (1963) and The School Marm Tree (1977).

Kicking Horse Pass

This well-known pass through the Rocky Mountains northwest of Banff, named when a geologist with the Palliser expedition was kicked by his own horse, inspired Bliss Carman (1861-1929) to write the poem "Song of the Kicking Horse" included in Bliss Carman's Poems (1931).

Lake Louise

"But Lake Louise — Lake Louise is of another world," wrote Rupert Brooke (1887-1915), the English poet, who rested for a few days at the Château Lake Louise in Banff National Park in August 1913. He tried to describe this "beauty-spot" in personal letters and in the articles that were later collected under the title Letters from America (1916), but he found it difficult, for he sensed here and in other "forests and wild places" in Canada what he called "a strangeness." As an Englishman, he found the Orient to be "too luxuriantly fetid"; the West suffered the opposite fault, for it was "an empty land" that lacked "the dreadful pressure of immortals." Between the two was England — "the immaterial soil of England is heavy and fertile" and benefits from "the friendly presence of ghosts." Thus he concluded: "The forests and wild places are windswept and empty. That is their charm, and their terror."

Brooke's poetic response to the landscape, with its lack of human association, is germain to any consideration of literary landmarks. He found no mystery in the wilderness. "The maple and the birch conceal no dryads, and Pan has never been heard amongst these reed-beds. Look as long as you like upon a cataract of the New World, you shall not see a white arm in the foam. A godless place. And the dead do not return. That is why there is nothing lurking in the heart of the shadows, and no human mystery in the colours, and neither the same joy nor the kind of peace in dawn and sunset that older lands know. It is, indeed, a new world.

"The land is virginal, the wind cleaner than elsewhere, and every lake new-born, and each day is the first day. The flowers are less conscious than English flowers, the breezes have nothing to remember, and everything to promise. There walk, as yet, no ghosts of lovers in Canadian lanes. This is the essence of the grey freshness and brisk melancholy of this land. And for all the charm of those qualities, it is also the secret of a European's discontent. For it is possible, at a pinch, to do without gods. But one misses the dead."

Robert Kroetsch (b. 1927), the novelist, has the heroine in his novel *Badlands* (1975) begin her spiritual quest for the source of the Red Deer River at Lake Louise. She follows the trail to Skoki Lodge and along the way visits Halfway Hut, which according to local tradition is believed to be haunted. John Porter, in "The Legend of Halfway Hut," included in *Timberline Tales* (1977), edited by Jim Deegan and John Porter, tells the story of that haunting.

Lethbridge

Lethbridge, in southern Alberta, according to James H. Gray (b. 1906) in *Red Lights on the Prairies* (1971), had the largest brothel in Western Canada in the Twenties and Thirties. It seems not to have affected the country's fiction or poetry. Bootlegging in Lethbridge and Calgary is the subject of *Good Night, Sammy Wong* (1982), a satiric novel by Michael Cullen (b. 1948).

Here is Stephansson House at Markerville on the day it was officially opened, August, 7, 1982. Stephan G. Stephansson was the "farmer-poet" of Alberta who became poet-laureate of Iceland. [Alberta Photography Library; Alberta Culture]

Makepeace

The community of Makepeace, southwest of Calgary, bears the middle name of the English novelist, William Makepeace Thackeray (1811-1863).

Markerville

Southwest of Red Deer is the town of Markerville, and just north of Markerville is the homestead of Stephan G. Stephansson (1853-1927), national poet of Iceland and Canada's leading Icelandic-language writer. Born in Northern Iceland, Stephansson emigrated to the United States, and then to Alberta in 1889. The Stephansson homestead has been restored and refurnished to suggest the man and the heritage.

The Republic of Iceland donated $10,000 for the restoration of the Stephansson House at Markerville, Alta. The rest was provided by the Historic Sites Service of Alberta Culture, and the home of the Alberta "farmer-poet" who became poet-laureate of Iceland was officially opened on August 7, 1982. The exterior of the house is seen here as it appeared between 1899 and 1927 when Stephansson died. He is buried close by at Christiansson Cemetery, and an impressive cairn was raised in his honour near the Icelandic capital of Reykjavik.

Here he wrote voluminously in traditional Icelandic forms, expressing an affection for both his native land and his adopted land. "No other Canadian poet in any language presents a comparable picture of Western Canada," wrote one of his translators, Watson Kirkconnell. Translations by Kirkconnell and others appear in *Stephan G. Stephansson: Selected Translations from Andvokur* (1982), published by the Stephansson Homestead Restoration Committee. In "The Exile," he wrote: "Never could my foster mother / Take my mother's place; / Always there was something lacking, / She could not replace."

Mazeppa

This community, northeast of High River, bears the same name as Mazeppa, Cossack Prince of the Ukraine, the hero of a once widely read poem *Mazeppa* (1819) by Lord Byron (1788-1824). Alexander Pushkin (1799-1837) also told the Prince's story in his long poem *Pultowa* (1829).

Medicine Hat

Medicine Hat is located southeast of Calgary, though Stephen Leacock once quipped that Medicine Hat is halfway between London and Peking. It was named in 1894 after the Blackfoot *saamis*, "the headdress of a medicine man."

Rudyard Kipling paused here on his continental tour of 1907. "The only commonplace thing about the spot was its name — Medicine Hat, which struck me instantly as the only name such a town could carry." Nevertheless there was agitation to change the name to a more usual one. In 1910, Francis F. Fatt, the postmaster and leader of the retentionists, wrote to Kipling as "the Father Confessor of the Empire" to enlist his aid in an attempt to halt

Globetrotting photographer Roloff Beny was a native of Medicine Hat. He is shown here in Athens. After his death in Rome in 1984, his ashes were flown to Medicine Hat for burial. [McClelland & Stewart / Nigel Kennell]

the revisionists whom Fatt called "the sons of Belial." Kipling replied from Sussex, England, on December 9, 1910, writing "as a citizen of the Empire and as a lover of Medicine Hat." "Believe me, the very name is an asset, and as years go by will become more and more of an asset. It has no duplicate in the world; it makes men ask questions. . . it has the qualities of uniqueness, individuality, assertion, and power." He concluded: "What, then, should a city be rechristened that has sold its name? Judasville." Kipling's letter saved the day for the retentionists.

Midnapore

The town of Midnapore, south of Calgary, lacks literary significance, except that it was satirized by Bob Edwards (1864-1922). Writing in the *Eye Opener*, he created out of whole cloth the Midnapore *Gazette* which was published by Peter J. McGonigle, gentleman and drunk and frequenter of the Nevermore House. The *Gazette* supposedly published the letters written back home by the English remittance man, Albert Buzzard-Cholomondeley. So popular were Edwards' satires on Midnapore that an actual Midnapore *Gazette* was launched in 1910-11.

Mirror

The village of Mirror was named not for any reflective quality but for *The Daily Mirror,* the popular London newspaper, in 1911. The newspaper had earlier made a survey of the area and had informed its readers of the opportunities awaiting them in Alberta.

Morley

Near Morley, a town located northwest of Calgary, Frederick Philip Grove (1879-1948) set the wheat farm of Abe Spalding in his novel *Fruits of the Earth* (1933). The precise location is "southwest corner of section five in the township beginning four miles north of Morley," although in one of his letters Grove admitted, "In one word, the hero of *Fruits of the Earth* is the Prairie."

Morningside

Located north of Red Deer, on the railway line between Lacombe and Ponoka, Morningside has the distinction of being named after a district in Scotland with an asylum called Morningside. In this small community, the poet Earle Birney (b. 1904) spent the first seven years of his life. The youngster kept a diary which has been published. As the poet reminisced in *Spreading Time* (1980): "[I spent] my first seven years on a remote ranch in the Alberta bush. That shaped me to be at home with 'Nature' — animals, flowers in the summer sun, the vast snows of winter — and to be shy of humans. A Wordsworthian infant but precociously literate. Everything happened within a radius of ten miles. The villages of Ponoka, Lacombe, glimpsed once or twice on the rim. Morningside flag station a half-hour weekly buggy ride from the ranch-house, the centre. A world without cars, phones, planes, tractors, electricity, plumbing. . . ."

Mount Meda

Mount Meda, which rises in an outer range of the Rocky Mountains east of Maligne Lake in Jasper National Park, was named for the heroine of the poem "The Meda Maiden" (1877), written by the Earl of Southesk (1827-1905) who travelled in the Northwest and published *Saskatchewan and the Rocky Mountains* (1875). Mount Balinshard was named for another work of the literary-minded earl. Other related features are Southesk River, Southesk Lake, Southesk Cairn (a mountain), and Southesk Pass.

"Notikeewin" See WETASKIWIN.

Okotoks

Okotoks, in Algonkian, means "lots of stones." Lots of satiric barbs were thrown at this small community, south of Calgary, by Bob Edwards (1864-1922) in the *Eye Opener*. "In Okotoks," he wrote in 1906, "where no village official has ever yet been accused of graft, the inhabitants are wondering whether they are better than other people or only duller." In 1922, he observed: "The Okotoks Methodist Ladies' Aid will give a bean supper from 6 to 8, to be followed by a musical program." One assumes "Edwards" is a bad word in Okotoks.

Onoway

The village of Onoway, northwest of Edmonton, was named in 1904 after the Ojibwa word "onaway" found in *The Song of Hiawatha* (1855) by Henry Wadsworth Longfellow (1807-1882). It is presumed the spelling is in error for the Ojibwa word for "awake" from the marriage hymn which begins: "Onaway! Awake beloved! / Thou the wild flower of the forest, / Thou the wild bird of the prairie. . . !"

Peace River Country

No one has paid a finer tribute to the pioneers who settled the fertile valley of the Peace River of northern Alberta and British Columbia than John Buchan (1875-1940), Governor General Lord Tweedsmuir. "Where do you find the pioneer," he asked in his autobiographical *Memory Hold-the-Door* (1940)? "At his best, I think, I have found him as a newcomer in Canada, where he is pushing north into districts like the Peace River, pioneering in the old sense. By what signs is he to be known? Principally by the fact that he is wholly secure, that he possesses his soul, that he is the true philosopher. He is one of the few aristocrats left in the world. He has a right sense of the values of life, because his cosmos embraces both nature and man. I think he is the most steadfast human being now alive."

North of Dunvegan, by the Peace River, a plaque marks the point from which headwaters in the mountains of British Columbia flow through the Peace River Valley on their way to the Arctic. On the banks of this river a peace treaty was concluded between warring Cree and Beaver Indians, as noted in 1793 by Sir Alexander Mackenzie (1764-1820).

The journalist Ralph Allen (1913-1966) wrote a novel, *Peace River Country* (1958), inspired by the land and its settlers.

Poe

Southeast of Edmonton is the community of Poe which bears the last name of the American poet and writer Edgar Allan Poe (1809-1849).

Red Deer

Almost mid-way between Edmonton and Calgary is Red Deer, the gateway to Alberta's Badlands, a desert-like area rich in dinosaur fossils. The prehistorical landscape caught the eye and sparked the imagination of the novelist Robert Kroetsch (b. 1927) who describes in *Badlands* (1975) passage through the region about 1916.

Kerry Wood (b. 1907), the writer for children, was raised and lives in Red Deer. West of the city the Stoney Indians hunted; the region is described in his novel *Samson's Long Ride* (1965).

The Rocky Mountains

Renowned for their beauty, the Rocky Mountains extend from the Liard River in the north into the United States in the south and are bordered by the Foothills of Alberta in the east and the Rocky Mountain Trench of British Columbia in the west. There are a great many descriptions of their effect upon travellers. The American essayist Lafcadio Hearn (1850-1904) described them in "A Winter's Journey to Japan," *Harper's*, November 1890: "Unlike anything ever seen before is this first spectacle of the Rockies to me; — this vision of a world shell rifted and wrinkled by infinite forces unknown; — mile-thick jagged fragments of it pitched up at all angles." And in August 1913, the English poet Rupert Brooke (1887-1915) found the peaks "unmemoried": "These unmemoried heights are inhuman — or rather, irrelevant to humanity. No recorded Hannibal has struggled across them; their shadow lies on no remembered literature."

Lord Lorne It is generally believed that the first sight of the Rocky Mountains inspired Lord Lorne (1845-1914), Governor General of Canada from 1878 to 1883, to write the popular hymn which begins "Unto the hills around do I lift up / My longing eyes," basing it on Psalm 121 and the stately melody of C. H. Purdy. The inspiration is generally dated 1872, though this is six years before Lorne visited the West.

Crawford's Pass Isabella Valancy Crawford (1850-1887) never saw the Rocky Mountains, yet she wrote a realistic poem in cowpuncher's dialect about a cattle stampede through a fictitious pass. The narrative poem is called "Old Spookses' Pass" (1884).

David While a number of peaks bear names familiar to readers of books — there is Mount Erasmus (named after a guide and interpreter) and Winston Churchill Range, to give two instances — it is other peaks that are most familiar to readers of Canadiana. The most powerful work of literature inspired by the Rocky Mountains remains *David*, the narrative poem written by Earle Birney (b. 1904) in 1940 while he was living in Toronto but based on extensive experience climbing these mountains. The setting of the poem is the Sawback Range in the Rockies; the locales are a mixture of real and imagined places.

Here are some correspondences. Inglismaldie and Assiniboine refer to actual mountains. "Mount Gleam" is modelled on Mount Alymer; "Rampart's arête" (not the Jasper mountain of this name) on Mount Edith Cavell; "The Fortress" on Castle Mountain. "The Spray" is a reference to the Spray River which joins the Bow at Banff. "Sundance" identifies the canyon, not Sundance Peak. Here the correspondences end.

Or do they? Birney imagined a mountain with a chimney-like extension and named it "the Finger." In the poem, David and the narrator scale this imaginary peak. A decade or so later, a group of alpinists decided to locate "the Finger," believing the poem to be based on a real climb. About ten kilometres northwest of Banff they found the spur of an unnamed peak (with an elevation of 9,040 feet) in the Sawback Range that seemed to meet all

DAVID
and other Poems by
EARLE BIRNEY

The Ryerson Press · Toronto
1942

Above is The Finger, a mountain in Banff National Park, and to the left is the title page of Earle Birney's David. The drawing is by Thoreau MacDonald. Birney rejected MacDonald's first mountain peak, directing the artist to depict it as "the Finger." [Parks Canada; Metroplitan Toronto Library]

Earle Birney scaled Goat Mountain the summer of 1922. He is shown here after he and two companions erected a cairn on its peak. In the background to the left is Cascade Mountain. [Birney Collection, Thomas Fisher Rare Book Library, University of Toronto]

though he had never scaled this mountain, he had seen it in the distance. Its chimney-like extension had been visible to him when, years earlier, he had experienced a near-accident at Sheep's Cave in Hole-in-the-Wall Mountain — an incident that led to the writing of the poem in the first place. Thus when writing the poem his imagination had mined his memory for useable images and had come up with the memory of the sight in the distance of "the Finger," the mountain identified by the alpinists.

Contemporary Poets At least three contemporary poets were so inspired by the sight of the Rocky Mountains that they published book-length collections of poems descriptive of the peaks and valleys. Ralph Gustafson (b. 1909) is the author of *Rocky Mountains Poems* (1960) which treats the grandeur of the Rockies with the respect the poet reserves for the great works of art of Europe. George Bowering (b. 1935) evoked the depths and heights in *Rocky Mountain Foot* (1968), notably Tunnel Mountain, Mount Norquay, and nearby Calgary. In one poem he wrote: "nobody / belongs anywhere, / even the / Rocky Mountains / are still / moving." The love of nature and its splendour is evident in the poems that make up *Headwaters* (1973) and the prose descriptions of *Men for the Mountains* (1978) by Sid Marty (b. 1944), the poet and writer who has worked as a warden in Yoho, Jasper, Prince Albert, and Banff National Parks.

Left: Poet Ralph Gustafson and his wife Betty at the Plain of Six Glaciers, Lake Louise, in 1980. Right: Sid Marty, poet and naturalist. [Gustafson Collection; McClelland & Stewart / Bruno Engler]

the requirements of the poem. Indeed, from the south, "the Finger" could be seen as a prominent spire, like the one described in the poem, and to a generation of alpinists this was "David's mountain." Tourists are told the same thing, and there is a movement to have the unnamed peak officially designated The Finger, or Finger Mountain.

Birney returned to Banff in 1981, and after visiting his childhood home he decided to take a look at "David's mountain." He was greatly surprised to realize that, al-

St. Paul

This town, northeast of Edmonton, is the site of Alberta's sole UFO landing pad and one of the few anywhere in the world. The 12-metre-long platform was erected as a centennial project and decorated with provincial and territorial flags. The site contains a time capsule to be opened June 3, 2067. A close reading of *UFO: Sightings, Landings and Abductions: The Documented Evidence* (1979) by Yurko Bondarchuk (b. 1949) fails to disclose any sightings or abnormal activity in the airspace above St. Paul.

This UFO landing pad was one of St. Paul's centennial projects. The "Closed" signs advise earthlings to "Use South Gate." [Travel Alberta]

Indian days at the Kainai Blood Reservation, Stand Off. [Dept. of Regional Industrial Expansion]

Sharrow

Located between Empress and Bindloss, Sharrow was named for the novel *Sharrow* (1912) written by Baroness von Hutten, an American-born, British writer (whose full named appears in reference works as: Baroness Bettina von Hutten Zum Stolzenberg).

Stand Off

Near Stand Off, southwest of Lethbridge, lies the Blood Reserve which, at 349,618 acres, is the largest Indian reserve in the country. Here the traditional Sun Dance

John Buchan, Governor General Lord Tweedsmuir, as Chief Eagle Head, photographed by Yousuf Karsh. [Copyright (c) Karsh, Ottawa / Miller Services Ltd.]

ceremony is held for two weeks each summer. Of literary interest is the custom the Kainai Chieftainship of the Blood Indian Tribe (Blackfoot Confederacy) has of awarding honourary chieftainships. There may be no more than forty living members. Honorary chiefs of the past include (with English names and years): The Prince of Wales (Red Crow, 1919, 1977); Sylvestre Long Lance (Buffalo Child, 1922); Lord Tweedsmuir (Eagle Head, 1936); Vincent Massey (Running Antelope, 1952). Among the current honourary chiefs are: J. W. Grant MacEwan (Owns Many Horses, 1967); Hugh A. Dempsey (Flying Chief, 1967); Pierre Berton (Big Plume, 1973).

Stony Reserve

There are actually two Stony Reserves, one west of Calgary, the other northwest of the city. As a composite they are the setting of *The Vanishing Point* (1973), the novel about the trials of an Indian agent among the Blood Indians, written by W. O. Mitchell (b. 1914).

Thoreau Creek   See ZENDA CREEK.

Wapiti

In the Mennonite farming community at Wapiti, southwest of Grand Prairie, is set the action of *Peace Shall Destroy Many* (1962), the novel about faith and doubt by Rudy Wiebe (b. 1934).

Waterton Lakes National Park

The lakes and mountains of this park in southern Alberta have been described and photographed in a succession of books by the naturalist, photographer, and writer Andy Russell (b. 1915). He explained the mystique of the landscape in *Tales of a Wilderness Wanderer* (1970): "As a boy I grew up in the shadows of the Rockies here in southwest Alberta, where the plains come uninterrupted by hills to go swooping up to the spectacular skyline in front of my door."

Westward Ho

The small community of Westward Ho, located northwest of Calgary, was named after *Westward Ho!* (1855), an historical novel by the English novelist Charles Kingsley (1819-1875). Kingsley was aware that the Elizabethan dramatists, Thomas Dekker and John Webster, were the joint authors of two plays — *Westward Ho!* and *Northward Ho!* — in 1604; and that Ben Johnson, George Chapman, and John Marston collaborated on *Eastward Ho!* in 1605. No one seems to have written *Southward Ho!* but Samuel Beckett (b. 1906) called a short prose work *Worstward Ho* (1983). It concludes, laconically: "Enough. Sudden enough."

Wetaskiwin

Wetaskiwin, south of Edmonton, may well be the model for "Notikeewin," the prairie community that serves as the setting of such novels as *The Words of My Roaring* (1966) and *Gone Indian* (1973) by Robert Kroetsch (b. 1927).

Whitford

The artist and writer, William Kurelek (1927-1977), was born in a one-room cabin, which burnt down, and raised in a two-room shack, which also burnt down, on farmland near Whitford, northeast of Edmonton, When he was seven years old the family moved to Stonewall.

In later years Kurelek depicted the way of life of the Ukrainian farmers of the prairies he knew in his childhood. He did so in his paintings but also in the extended captions he wrote for them when they were exhibited or reproduced in some two dozen books. His autobiography, *Someone with Me*, appeared in 1973. On the basis of the availability of his work in book form, he is easily the most popular Canadian artist at home and abroad.

He worked literally and systematically, producing many series of paintings. One hundred and sixty paintings make up "The Passion of Christ." This series is exhibited at the Niagara Falls Art Gallery and Museum and at the time of his death he was engaged in illustrating the Four Gospels. He set himself the task of depicting the lives of the multicultural groups of Canada. He completed the series on Ukrainians, Jews, Eskimos, Irish, French Canadians, Polish — many of which resulted in separate book publication — but death intervened before he could tackle the next group, the Germans.

"Wildrose"

The floral emblem of Alberta may be the Wild Rose, but there is no community known as "Wildrose" in that province (though there is a Wild Rose in Saskatchewan). W. O. Mitchell (b. 1914) is the author of the radio and television play *The Black Bonspiel of Wullie MacCrimmon*, which became a stage play at Festival Lennoxville in 1980. A harnessmaker from the "foothills town of Wildrose" in the 1930s challenged the devil, in the guise of Judas Iscariot, to a bonspiel — and won. The play is published in *Dramatic W. O. Mitchell* (1982).

Winston Churchill Range

The Winston Churchill Range of mountains, northwest of Lake Louise, was named in 1956 after Sir Winston Churchill (1874-1965), Prime Minister of Great Britain during the Second World War and Nobel Laureate in Literature for 1953.

Writing-on-Stone Provincial Park

Although they lack specific literary associations, the petroglyphs of Writing-on-Stone Provincial Park, located

There are weird geological formations at Writing-on-Stone Provincial Park. [Travel Alberta]

south of Lethbridge, leave the literary-minded visitor appreciative of the fact that this form of "writing" may forever be indecipherable. What the carvings on the sandstone cliffs on both banks of the Milk River are meant to preserve or convey may never be known. The intriguing designs are as indecipherable as Minoan Linear B before Michael Ventris.

Or are they? Perhaps the rock art is a record of the presence of Asiatics in North America in pre-Columbian times. Such at least is the view of Henriette Mertz, an American lawyer and student of "unsolved mysteries." Writing in *Pale Ink: Two Ancient Records of Chinese Exploration in America* (1953, rev. 1972), she notes that in two classical Chinese texts there are detailed references to voyages across a wide, Pacific-like sea to a broad and mountainous land rather like western North America. The two texts are "Classic of Mountains and Sea," compiled by Yu at the request of Emperor Shun, traditionally dated to 2250 B.C.; and "Fu-Sang," written by Hwui Shan (or Hoei Shin), a Buddhist monk who left the Court of China for "the West" — to him it was "the East" — traditionally in 499 A.D. As conjectural as the reading and the dates may be, Mertz is enthusiastic. Indeed, an earlier work of hers sets out to prove that Ulysses voyaged along the coast of North America. Yet the rock art at Writing-on-Stone Provincial Park, which Mertz specifically mentions in drawing the routes taken in the interior of North America by the author of "Classic of Mountains and Sea," remain enigmatic and the texts remain inscrutable. If Hwui Shan was a Chinese Buddhist monk who proselytized and explored in North America, as did the Jesuits more than a millennium later, then his descriptions of towering mountains and gigantic trees could perhaps be related to West Coast geography. In fact, the name he gives the new continent, Fu-Sang, has already been translated "Fir tree."

Yellowhead Pass See ATHABASCA LANDING.

Zenda Creek

Zenda Creek in the Persimmon Range of the Rocky Mountains, northwest of Jasper, was so named to recall the romantic adventure novel *The Prisoner of Zenda* (1894) and its sequel *Rupert of Hentzau* (1898) by Sir Anthony Hope Hawkins (1863-1933) who wrote as Anthony Hope. It was so named in 1955, perhaps to continue the tradition of naming geographical features in the area after this author and his popular works. Anthony Creek and Phroso Creek were named after the English author and a reference in one of his books in 1920. Other literary names east of Phroso Creek are Pope Creek and Thoreau Creek.

British Columbia

Alberni

Indian rock carvings of mythological beasts are found in Sproat Lake Provincial Park, in the vicinity of Alberni and Port Alberni on Vancouver Island. The Nootka artist and writer, George Clutesi (b. 1905), lives on the nearby Sheshaht Reserve. His two books, *Son of Raven, Son of Deer* (1967) and *Potlatch* (1969), preserve the traditions of his Tse-shaht People.

The ethnologist Edward Sapir (1884-1939) made field trips to Alberni in 1910 and 1913-14 to collect materials for his publications *Nootka Texts* (1939) and *Songs of the Nootka Indians* (1955). The ethnomusicologist Ida Halpern recorded the songs on her *Nootka* Folkways Album of 1974 at Port Alberni in 1965-72.

Claude Lévi-Strauss (b. 1908), the celebrated French anthropologist, has expressed considerable excitement for West Coast Indian art. In 1943, he stated: "This art is not unequal to the greatest." He devoted a book to the Swihwé masks of the Coast Salish, published in English as *The Way of the Masks* (1982).

George Clutesi (right) took the part of the shaman who assists a young boy, played by Ian Tracey (centre), and his mute friend, acted by Jacques Hubert (left) in the CBC production of Dreamspeaker. *[Ontario Film Institute]*

Alert Bay

This village, on Cormorant Island off the northeast coast of Vancouver Island, is known for its striking array of totem poles. Franz Boas (1858-1942), the anthropologist, made field trips here in 1886, 1889, 1900, and 1931, latterly with his native informant George Hunt, to collect the stories that appeared in the various editions of his *Kwakiutl Tales* (1910, 1935, 1943). Marius Barbeau (1883-1969) collected material on totem poles here in 1947.

Atavist Mountain

Atavist Mountain, southeast of Bella Coola, was named in 1960 after a poem by Robert W. Service (1874-1958). The name has a somewhat sinister ring to it, as do the names of nearby mountains: Ogre Mountain, Ember Mountain, Mount Satan, Mount Azazel, Mount Belial, Mount Beelzebub, Styx Mountain, and Purgatory Ridge.

Ayesha Peak

Ayesha Peak is located in the Rocky Moutains of British Columbia, west of Alberta's Bow Lake. Ayesha is the name of the beautiful, immortal woman in such novels as *She* (1887) and *Ayesha* (1905) by the English novelist, Sir Henry Rider Haggard (1856-1925). The name was proposed in 1908 and the reason given was the peak's appearance: "The crest of the mountain resembles a beautiful female face turned upwards, and, owing to the wild surroundings, suggested the name." Sir Henry crossed Western Canada by train in 1916 and had the additional honour of having three more geographical features named after him and his creations. (See also Haggard Glacier.)

Bella Coola

On a boulder situated at the point where the Bella Coola River empties into the Pacific Ocean, the explorer Sir Alexander Mackenzie (1764-1820), to mark his historic overland trek from the forks of the Peace and Smoky rivers, wrote the most historic graffiti in the country: "I now mixed up some vermilion in melted grease, and inscribed, in large characters, on the South-East face of the rock on which we had slept last night, this brief memorial — 'Alexander Mackenzie, from Canada, by land, the twenty-second of July, one thousand seven hundred and ninety-three.'" Weather has erased the inscription but Mackenzie's words have been embedded with red cement in the rock believed to be Mackenzie's. It is part of Sir Alexander Mackenzie Provincial Park.

Sir Alexander Mackenzie's celebrated inscription, Dean Channel, B.C. [*Government of B.C. Photo*]

Aerial view of Simon Fraser University, Burnaby, B.C., designed by Arthur Erickson. [*Tourism B.C.*]

Stories and songs of the Bella Coola Indians were collected at the reserve on numerous field trips. Franz Boas (1858-1942) visited in 1897 and 1923 with his native informant George Hunt, who helped with the compilation and analysis of *The Mythology of the Bella Coola Indians* (1898). Their visit probably overlapped with that of the Canadian anthropologist T. F. McIlwraith (1899-1964) who lived in 1922-24 with the natives and wrote *The Bella Coola Indians* (1948).

Boccaccio Creek
A small stream northeast of 100 Mile House, Boccaccio Creek was named in 1977 after Giovanni Boccaccio (1313-1375), the Italian who wrote the hundred stories of *The Decameron* (1351).

Bowen Island
On this island in Howe Sound, Earle Birney (b. 1904) spent days, weeks, and months in creative work between 1946 and 1973. He stayed at "Lieben," the cliff-side cottage (since demolished) of the sculptor Einar Neilson, where he wrote many of the poems of *The Strait of Anian* .(1948) and much of the novel *Turvey* (1949), not to mention later works. The poem "Driftwood Sculptor" is dedicated to Neilson.

Burnaby
Burnaby is located east of Vancouver, and atop Burnaby Mountain, with its commanding view, is Simon Fraser University, which opened in 1965. Some well-known poets teach in the English Department, including Robin Blaser, Lionel Kearns, and George Bowering. The university has published the *West Coast Review* since 1966.

The W.A.C. Bennett Library of Simon Fraser University has a Contemporary Literature Collection which "expresses a basic and implicit faith in the quality, the integrity, and the significance of post-war experimental and avant-garde poetry." It includes books, magazines,

and manuscripts, especially of the Black Mountain movement, the San Francisco Renaissance, the Beats, the New York School, and the Tish group. There is correspondence with Ezra Pound and the complete archives of poets Michael McClure and Frank Davey, plus manuscript material from bp Nichol.

Capitol Hill in Burnaby and Lytton served Ethel Wilson (1888-1980) as settings for her novel *Swamp Angel* (1954).

In North Burnaby is located Oakalla Maximum Security Prison. Here and at Haney Correctional Centre, Pine Ridge Camp, and Stave Lake Camp, the writer Andreas Schroeder (b. 1946) served a drug-related sentence and wrote his "prison memoir" published as *Shaking It Rough* (1976).

Burns Lake
Burns Lake, northwest of Prince George, lies in the heart of the lake district of the interior of British Columbia. Near Burns Lake are two sites associated with authors: the Ethel F. Wilson Memorial Park, named after the novelist Ethel Wilson (1888-1980), and Tweedsmuir Provincial Park, named after Governor General Lord Tweedsmuir, better known as the novelist John Buchan (1875-1940).

Campbell River
The Campbell River on the east coast of Vancouver Island is known as "the salmon fishing capital of the world." It attracted Roderick Haig-Brown (1908-1976) who settled on a farm on the river's edge and became an avid angler as well as a magistrate and judge of the juvenile court. Among his many publications about nature are the seasonal quartet *Fisherman's Spring* (1951), *Fisherman's Winter* (1954), *Fisherman's Summer* (1959), and *Fisherman's Fall* (1964). He dealt with the months of the year in *Measure of the Year* (1950). His twenty-acre farm, "Above Tide," is now a colony for writers and conservationists.

The scenery at Seymour Narrows in the Campbell River area recalls the art of Toni Onley. [Bill Brooks]

Historic photograph of the driving of the Last Spike, 9:30 a.m., November 7, 1885. [PAC (C 3693)]

Site of the Last Spike Ceremony, Craigellachie, B.C. [Bill Brooks]

Cariboo Country

Cariboo Country is located on the Chilcotin Plateau in the interior, north of Vancouver. It is a familiar ranching region to viewers of the CBC-TV series *Cariboo Country* shown in 1968-72. The series was written by Paul St. Pierre (b. 1923), who created the fictional community of "Namko" and wrote the novel *Breaking Smith's Quarter Horse* (1966), the basis of the 1969 Walt Disney movie *Smith*. St. Pierre lives in Fort Langley.

At 100 Mile House in Cariboo Country, Al Purdy (b. 1918) wrote the title poem of his important collection *The Cariboo Horses* (1965).

Churchill Peak See MOUNT WINSTON.

Cowichan Bay

On a farm in the vicinity of Cowichan Bay, near Duncan, the youthful Robert W. Service (1874-1958) worked as a labourer. He wrote one of his first verses "The Old Log Cabin" here in 1902, before moving to Victoria, Kamloops, and thence to fame and fortune in the Yukon. The farm buildings are long gone, but the land is still being worked. A provincial plaque marks the spot.

Craigellachie

Craigellachie is located on the CPR line west of Revelstoke where the historic plaque reads, in part: "Here on November 7, 1885, a plain iron spike welded East to West. . . . A nebulous dream was a reality: an iron ribbon crossed Canada from sea to sea."

The events that happened here are the apex of *Towards the Last Spike* (1952), the narrative poem by E. J. Pratt (1882-1964). "No flags or bands announced this ceremony, / No Morse in circulation through the world, / And though the vital words like Eagle Pass, / Craigellachie, were trembling in their belfries, / No hands were on the ropes."

A satiric footnote was added to the narrative poem by F. R. Scott (b. 1899) who, in a poem of his own "All the Spikes but the Last" (1954), asked: "Where are the coolies in your poem, Ned?" Gordon Lightfoot, the singer, celebrated the achievement in his popular song "Canadian Railroad Trilogy" (1967).

A memorable description of the Last Spike ceremony appears in *The Last Spike* (1971), by Pierre Berton (b. 1920), the second volume in the series that began with *The National Dream* (1970). Still, as the playwright Bernard Slade (b. 1930) once noted: "Something has to be wrong with a country whose national dream is a railroad."

Crescent Beach

Here, on Boundary Bay, close to the American border, the youthful Earle Birney (b. 1904) wrote "Slug in Woods" (1928), a masterful poem about the ecology that is the habitat of a "greentipped" slug that sleeps and "so spends a summer's jasper century."

Creston Valley

This region of the Kootenays in the southeastern part of the province had a strong influence on Earle Birney (b. 1904) who between fourteen and sixteen lived on the

Earle Birney was raised on this fruit ranch near Erickson. The ranch house was built by his father and is shown here in the spring of 1920. It was still standing in 1981. [Birney Collection, Thomas Fisher Rare Book Library, University of Toronto]

family fruit ranch near Goat Mountain above the village of Erickson. He reminisced in *Spreading Time* (1980): "All that summer and the next two, we three worked dawn to dusk raising berries, treefruits, vegetables, chickens, pigs, calves; fighting droughts, killing frosts, plant pests, Spanish flu, monopoly express charges, rapacious wholesalers; and through two winters of stumping, slashing, wood bucking, ploughing, repairing, and generally sweating to keep abreast of the mortgage. I don't remember finding energy, in all that time, to read a new book that wasn't on the school curriculum. Nor can I recall where I would have found one, since in the whole forty-mile valley there wasn't a bookstore or a magazine stand, or a library, public or lending."

The hero of his picaresque novel *Turvey* (1949) comes from the fictitious community of Skookum Falls (the

Sheila Watson in nun's robe with double hook of pen nibs, drawn by Don Evans as Isaac Bickerstaff. [Special Collections, University of Calgary Libraries]

name was suggested by the actual community named Skookumchuck). Birney caught the speech rhythms of the farmers in the Kootenays in his story "Big Bird in the Bush" (1948).

Dog Creek

Dog Creek, on the Fraser River, is northwest of Kamloops. The young Sheila Watson (b. 1909) taught elementary school here from 1935 to 1937, absorbing the influences necessary for the writing of her now-classic novel, *The Double Hook* (1959), actually composed while attending the University of Calgary in 1952-54. Considering the influence of that novel, it is likely there will some day be a memorial to the author and her parable-like work, and in what village would it more appropriately stand than in Dog Creek?

Dollarton

Dollarton, on the north shore of Burrard Inlet, bears the name of a rich American named Robert Dollar who owned land here. In the 1940s and 1950s the region was undeveloped except for a collection of waterfront shacks erected illegally by holiday-makers. The shacks have since been demolished and Dollarton has been incorporated into the Municipality of North Vancouver.

Scenic view of Dollarton Beach, Vancouver, not far from the site of Malcolm Lowry's squatter's shack. [Bill Brooks]

On and off between 1940 and 1954, the novelist Malcolm Lowry (1909-1957) and his wife Margerie Bonner occupied, as squatters, a one-room shack at Dollarton. Here Lowry wrote of "the very immediacy of the eternities" and worked sporadically on his Mexican-locale masterpiece, *Under the Volcano* (1947). He commenced but never completed such powerful works as *Hear Us O Lord from Heaven Thy Dwelling Place* (1961) and *October Ferry to Gabriola* (1970), both published posthumously. Indeed, the latter work is concerned with the future destruction of the squatter's colony. In one of his letters, Lowry confessed that he was so poor that he could not afford to buy a radio to hear his poems which were being broadcast on CBC Radio.

Malcolm Lowry

Under the Volcano

Reynal & Hitchcock, New York

Title page of the first edition of Malcolm Lowry's masterpiece Under the Volcano *(1947). [Estate of Malcolm Lowry]*

Photograph of Malcolm Lowry at his Dollarton shack from the NFB film Volcano, *directed by Donald Brittain.* [NFB]

When Lowry was not living at Dollarton, he entrusted the door key to Earle Birney (b. 1904) who wrote his poem "Pacific Door" here in 1947. Birney presented the key to Dorothy Livesay (b. 1909) in 1948. She wrote parts of her long poem *Call My People Home* (1950) here "in Malcolm Lowry's cabin, with an orange August moon rising directly before me over the soft-soughing sea."

Following the destruction of the waterfront colony, Lowry returned to England. He is buried in the churchyard in the village of Ripe, East Sussex. Along the Upper Burrard Inlet today there is a cairn on Malcolm Lowry Walk in Cates Park to mark the presence here of an artist of great power and imagination.

Enderby

Enderby, north of Vernon, was named in 1887 after a reference in the poem "The High Tide on the Coast of Lincolnshire" by the English versifier and novelist, Jean Ingelow (1820-1897). The reference is to an English folksong called "The Brides of Enderby."

Errington

The community of Errington, northwest of Nanaimo, shares its name with the Northumberland village where the Border wars with the Scots were fought. The village figures in the poem "Jock of Hazeldean" by Sir Walter Scott (1771-1832) which runs: "Young Frank is chief of Errington / And Lord of Langley-dale. . . ."

Field

West of Lake Louise, on the Kicking Horse River, the town of Field has "snow-draped" mountains which were so described by Dorothy Livesay (b. 1909) in her poem "Roots" (1966). The young minister Charles W. Gordon (1860-1937), not yet the novelist who signed his books Ralph Connor, was stationed at Field. His missionary work took him far afield and this experiences informed his first novels.

Fort St. John

North of Dawson Creek in the northeast part of the province is the town of Fort St. John. Here the irrepressible pioneer journalist, Margaret "Ma" Murray (1888-1982), published *The Alaska Highway News* in the 1940s and 1950s, before relocating at Lillooet in the southern interior of the province. She was always a source of "good copy." She once told an interviewer: "I'm the editor of the dinkiest newspaper in British Columbia. The place I live in is so isolated you gotta scrape the bottom of the barrel. My God, there isn't a week I don't have slivers in my fingers scrapin' up the news."

Forty-five miles outside Fort St. John is the community known as Mile 18. It is well known to readers of children's literature for Mary Blades (b. 1947) once taught here and made it the setting of her well-known book

Pioneer newspaperwoman Margaret Murray, as played to perfection by Joy Coghill in Eric Nicol's Ma. [CBC]

Mary of Mile 18 (1971). In words and drawings Blades captures the loneliness of life on an isolated ranch off the Alaska Highway. It was filmed by the NFB in 1981.

Fraser River

The leading river of British Columbia, the Fraser rises in the Rocky Mountains near the Yellowhead Pass, flows northwest, then south, then west again to the coast. Between Lytton and Yale it runs through a deep canyon; here is found Hell's Gate. Discovered by Alexander Mackenzie, it was mapped by Simon Fraser. "This is the savagest of all the major rivers of America," claimed Hugh MacLennan (b. 1907) in *The Rivers of Canada* (1961). "It is probably the savagest in the world." He then noted: "If a river could flow on the moon, it would probably look like this." An outstanding book about the river and its history is *The Fraser* (1950) by Bruce Hutchison (b. 1901).

"Fu-Sang"   See WRITING-ON-STONE PROVINCIAL PARK, Alta.

Furry Creek

On the beach at Furry Creek, in Howe Sound, north of Vancouver, on October 13, 1975, was found the body of the poet Pat Lowther (1935-1975). She had been murdered in her prime. Published posthumously was her collection *A Stone Diary* (1977).

Gibsons

The community of Gibsons overlooks Howe Sound, northwest of Vancouver. This is logging country, and the practices of the foresters and lumberjacks have been well described in poetic form by Robert Swanson in the 1940s and 1950s, and by Peter Trower (b. 1930) in such collections as *Between the Sky and the Splinters* (1974), *Bush Poems* (1978), and *Moving through the Mystery* (1969).

Golden

This town, northeast of Revelstoke, with its "sun-fevered hills," is evoked effectively by Dorothy Livesay (b. 1909) in her poem "Roots" (1966).

Greenwood

A ghost town west of Trail, Greenwood was designated a Japanese "Relocation Centre" in 1943, and 1,203 evacuated Japanese lived here in appalling circumstances. After the War, Dorothy Livesay (b. 1909) visited Greenwood and based sections of her long poem *Call My People Home* (1950) on what she learned here of the ordeal.

Gulf Islands

The relaxed lifestyle on the Gulf Islands, in the Strait of Georgia between Vancouver and Victoria, has attracted both transients and residents, writers as well as artists. There are over one hundred islands between the main-

Scenic view of one of the Gulf Islands with ferry. [Bill Brooks]

land and Vancouver Island. Islands identified strongly with individual writers are Gabriola (Malcolm Lowry), Galiano (Dorothy Livesay, Jane Rule, Audrey Thomas), Mayne (Cathy Ford), Pender (William Deverell), and Saltspring (Sean Virgo, Phyllis Webb). It was on Pender Island that Elizabeth Smart (b. 1914) wrote her classic poetic prose narrative, *By Grand Central Station I Sat Down and Wept* (1945), while pregnant with her first child, fathered by the British poet George Barker. Malcolm Lowry (1909-1957) never lived on Gabriola Island, and indeed may never have actually visited it. In his unfinished novel, *October Ferry to Gabriola* (1970), he describes the trip that he and his wife made in 1946 by boat from Vancouver to Victoria, by bus from Victoria to Nanaimo, and by ferry from Nanaimo to Gabriola Island. The purpose was to inspect a sea captain's house with a view to purchasing it, but for various reasons the ferry had to turn back. The aborted trip is through time and experience as well as space. Jane Rule (b. 1931) has set a number of her works on Galiano Island, including *The Young in One Another's Arms* (1977).

Haggard Glacier

Haggard Glacier and Mount Rider, in the Rocky Mountains of British Columbia, west of Alberta's Bow Lake, were named in honour of Sir Henry Rider Haggard (1856-1925). Sir Henry so impressed a local Grand Trunk railway official that the official forced the hand of the Surveyor-General to have the glacier and the mountain so named. He went further and arranged for the railway station and siding, northwest of McBride, to be called Rider.

Sir Henry was in Calgary in July 1916 when he learned of the honour. As he wrote in a letter home, "Here they give my name to a towering Alp. In Norfolk, they would not bestow it upon the smallest pightle." (In Norfolk, where he lived, a small field or enclosure is known as a "pightle.")

Haggard Glacier, Mount Rider, and Rider recall the author. Ayesha Peak, named eight years earlier, recalls one of his imaginative creations. (See also Ayesha Peak.)

Harrison Hot Springs

Near this resort area with its mineral springs will be found the Bigfoot Campgrounds and Sasquatch Provincial Park. The Sasquatch has yet to make its debut in a work of adult fiction. Ted Ashlee (b. 1914) has written a children's book about an encounter with the wild man of the woods called *Night of the Sasquatch* (1973).

Hazelton

The 'Ksan Indian Village was opened in 1969 near Hazelton which is located at the junction of the Skeena and Bulkley rivers in the interior of the province. Here the arts and crafts of the Gitksan and Carrier people are kept alive. Marius Barbeau (1883-1969) retold the legend of Temlaham, the ancestral paradise, in *The Downfall of Temlaham* (1928). From the Skeena and Nass River region came *Visitors Who Never Left: The Origin of the People of Damelahamid* (1974), preserved by Chief Kenneth B. Harris and Frances M. P. Robinson. It tells of a utopian paradise that lies between the Nass and Skeena Rivers. The writer for young people, Christie Harris (b. 1907), made use of such legends in *Sky Man on the Totem Pole* (1975) which establishes a cosmic context for native tradition.

The 'Ksan Indian Village at Hazelton. [*Tourism B.C.*]

The 'Ksan Trademark is the stylized representation of an upright hand. It guarantees the workmanship and authenticity of each article produced by craftsmen and women of the Today House of the Arts and the Carving House of All Times at the village of 'Ksan, near Hazelton. ['Ksan Association]

Iago

Iago, Jessica, Juliet, Lear, Othello, Portia, and Romeo were all names of sidings on the CP line leading from Hope up the Coquihalla River Valley. The Shakespearian names were rescinded in 1968.

Former stunt-man Richard Farnsworth played the resourceful robber Bill Miner in The Grey Fox, which also starred Jackie Burroughs. Key scenes take place in Kamloops where the film was shot. [*Ontario Film Institute*]

Kamloops

Robert W. Service (1874-1958) came from Victoria to Kamloops, northwest of Kelowna, to work here at the branch of the Canadian Bank of Commerce. He served as a clerk from July to November 1904, when he accepted a transfer to Whitehorse where he was inspired to write verses about the Yukon.

The name Kamloops — which is Indian for "the meeting of the waters" — has been immortalized by Dennis Lee (b. 1939) in his poem "In Kamloops" (1974) which begins: "In Kamloops / I'll eat your boots."

While travelling by train between Kamloops and Nelson in 1911, the young British actor William Pratt decided his career in the theatre would be helped by a name change. Then and there he adopted the stage name Boris Karloff.

East of Kamloops a plaque marks the spot where Bill Miner, the "Great Train Robber," stopped the wrong CPR train and stole only fifteen dollars. *The Grey Fox*, a feature film about Miner, was released in 1983.

Kingcome Inlet

This little Kwakiutl village, on the west coast, south of Bella Coola, is the setting of the popular novel *I Heard the Owl Call My Name* (1967), written by the American author Margaret Craven (b. 1901). Filmed in 1974, it tells the story of a young vicar at the Anglican Church in the village who painfully comes to accept the inevitability of his own death.

Kingcome Inlet has a strong oral tradition. Stories and legends told by Kwakiutl school children were collected and published in *Tales from the Longhouse* (1973).

Kootenay   See NELSON.

Ladysmith

The town of Ladysmith is located southeast of Nanaimo. It is the birthplace of two writers, Gladys Hindmarch (b. 1940) and Ken Cathers (b. 1951).

Lillooet

West of Kamloops, Lillooet is the town in which Margaret "Ma" Murray (1888-1982), the outspoken pioneering publisher, established her newspaper when she left Fort St. John in the 1950s. She called it *Bridge River–Lillooet News* and boasted: "This week's circulation 1769, and every bloody one of them paid for." The full story is told by Georgina Keddell in *The Newspapering Murrays* (1967).

Lulu Island

This small island in the Fraser Delta was visited by Dorothy Livesay (b. 1909), who wanted to learn how Japanese fishermen made their living for her long poem *Call My People Home* (1950) about the evacuation of the Japanese. "This memory remained with me, strongly. It was the basis for the part of the poem called 'A Young Nisei,' one of the first sections I wrote. . . ."

"Lyndon" See PRINCE GEORGE.

Lytton

Lytton, north of Hope, is the setting of the early pages of *Hetty Dorval* (1947), the novel by Ethel Wilson (1888-1980).

Merritt

Merritt, northwest of Penticton, is the heart of "cow country." Here was raised the newspaperman Bruce Hutchison (b. 1901). He returned to the community, imaginatively at least, in *Uncle Percy's Wonderful Town* (1981), twelve sketches of small-town life. The town is identified as "Emerald Vale," and the stories are narrated by a fourteen-year-old lad.

Mile 18 See FORT ST. JOHN.

Mission City

Mission City, east of New Westminster, is identified with the writer Andreas Schroeder (b. 1946) who lives in the house on Erickson Road he built with his own hands.

Monte Cristo Mountain

This mountain, near Trail, was named after the popular adventure novel *The Count of Monte Cristo* (1844) by Alexandre Dumas (1802-1870).

Mount Artaban

Mount Artaban, north of Vancouver, was so named in 1929. Close by was located the Church of England's Camp Artaban. The name derives from a once-popular pietistic fantasy, *The Story of the Other Wise Man* (1896), by Henry Van Dyke (1852-1933), a Professor of English at Princeton and a Presbyterian minister.

Mount Beowulf

Mount Beowulf and Mount Grendel are features of the Selkirk Mountains, southeast of Revelstoke. The names, approved in 1948, recall the hero and the monster from the marshes described by an unknown bard in the Anglo-Saxon epic *Beowulf* which dates from the eighth century.

Mount Erasmus

This peak was named in honour of Desiderius Erasmus (1466-1536), the Dutch scholar and humanist of the Renaissance, best known as the author of *In Praise of Folly*. He figures in the once-popular historical novel *The Cloister and the Hearth* (1861) by the English author Charles Reade (1814-1884).

Mount Gandalf

Mount Gandalf, Mount Aragorn, and Mount Shadowfax are features in the Coast Mountains, north of Pemberton and west of Lillooet. The names, approved in 1979, derive from *The Lord of the Rings* (1968), epic fantasy by the scholar and writer J.R.R. Tolkien (1892-1973).

Mount Macbeth

There are two mountains in British Columbia named after Shakespeare's tragic hero.

Mount Macbeth, Macbeth Icefield, Mount Lady Macbeth, Mount Macduff, Mount Banquo, and Mount Fleance are all features of the Purcell Mountains west of Invermere and northwest of Cranbrook. They were so named in 1960 after the characters in Shakespeare's play, *Macbeth* (1606).

Mount Macbeth, Mount Iago, and Mount Benvolio are peaks in Garibaldi Provincial Park, east of Whistler. They were given these Shakespearian names in 1965.

Mount Moby Dick

The following are features in the Selkirk Mountains, southeast of Revelstoke: Mount Moby Dick, Mount Ahab, Mount Billy Budd, Claggart Peak, Vere Summit, Pequod Mountain, Omoo Peak, Typee Mountain, Benito Cereno Mountain, and White Jacket Mountain. The names of these features were derived from *Moby Dick* (1851) and other fictional works by the American novelist Herman Melville (1819-1891). The names were approved in 1963.

Mount Nemo

Mount Nemo and Nautilus Mountain are features in the Selkirk Mountains, southeast of Revelstoke, approved in 1948. They were named after the mysterious Captain Nemo and his submarine *Nautilus* in the popular novel *Twenty Thousand Leagues Under the Sea* (1870) by Jules Verne (1828-1905).

Mount Rider See HAGGARD GLACIER.

Mount Romeo

Mount Romeo and Mount Juliet are the names of mountains on Vancouver Island northwest of Campbell River. The names, which come from Shakespeare's play *Romeo and Juliet* (1597), were approved in 1933. Two streams draining the mountains are called Montague Creek and Capulet Creek, after the family names of the two lovers.

Mount Scarlett O'Hara

The red rocks of this mountain, near Radium Hot Springs, inspired the namer, Curt Wagner of Marshall, Minnesota, to recall the raven-haired heroine of Margaret Mitchell's novel *Gone With the Wind* (1936) and the movie based on it. The name was officially recognized in 1972. Nearby is Tara Lake, an expansion of Irish Creek, named after Tara, the mansion and plantation of the novel and movie.

Mount Van Winkle

Mount Van Winkle, southeast of Prince George, appears on a map of 1861 as "Mount Van Wrunkle" but in its present form was authorized in 1922. The name recalls the folktale of the Dutch colonist, Rip Van Winkle, who falls asleep in the Catskill Mountains and awakens twenty years later to find an independent United States. The tale is told in the *Sketch Book* (1819) by Washington Irving (1783-1859).

Winston Churchill is shown here on the grounds of Government House, Victoria, September 6, 1929. [Provincial Archives of British Columbia]

Mount Winston

In the central interior of the province there are two geographical features that honour Sir Winston Churchill (1874-1965), British leader during the Second World War and recipient of the 1953 Nobel Prize for Literature. Churchill Peak was named in 1944, Mount Winston in 1951.

"Namko"   See CARIBOO COUNTRY.

Novelist Jack Hodgins from the NFB documentary Jack Hodgins' Island. *[NFB]*

Nanaimo

Nanaimo is a city on the east coast of Vancouver Island. Jack Hodgins (b. 1938), the novelist, was born in the logging and farming community of Merville, in the Comox Valley, along the east coast of Vancouver Island. For some years he lived in Lantzville and taught high school at nearby Nanaimo. He often writes about the imaginary community of "Rutherford Heights," said to be modelled on Nanaimo. The title story of *Spit Delaney's Island* (1976) refers to the Wooden Nickel, an antique store at Qualicum Beach, and the title character owns a gas station somewhere along the Island's main highway.

Hodgins has set "The Revelations Colony of Truth" near an unnamed town in *The Invention of the World* (1977). Donal Keneally, the founder of the religious sect, recalls Edward Arthur Wilson who, as "The Brother, XII," established his Aquarian Foundation on Gabriola Island in 1927. The real-life colony thrived and spilled over to Cedar-by-the-Sea on the east coast of Vancouver Island near Nanaimo as well as to Valdes Island and the De Courcey Islands.

The Resurrection of Joseph Bourne (1979) is set in "Port Annie." Hodgins explained: "Though Port Annie shares some of its geography and a little of its history with actual towns in the northern region of Vancouver Island, it is a product of the imagination." The town is said to resemble Port Alice. Finally, *The Barclay Family Theatre* (1981) is set in what might be called "Hodgins' Hinterland" — the region round Nanaimo — and elsewhere in Canada and the world.

Barry Broadfoot (b. 1926), a native of Winnipeg, is a resident of Nanaimo. He pioneered the use in Canada of oral history, finding a ready market for four books: *Ten Lost Years* (1973), *Six War Years* (1974), *The Pioneer Years* (1976), and *Years of Sorrow, Years of Shame* (1977). Even his autobiography — *My Own Years* (1983) — was done by the oral-history method.

Nelson

Nelson is located in the Kootenay region in the southeastern corner of the province. Here, at the David Thompson University Centre, the poet Fred Wah (b. 1939) established a School of Writing in 1979. Faculty members have included Tom Wayman, David McFadden, Margaret Hollingsworth, John Newlove, Colin Browne, Sean Virgo, Paulette Jiles, Fraser Sutherland, Lorraine Johnson, and Patrick Walsh. Among the writers-in-residence are Clark Blaise and Audrey Thomas. The provincial Ministry of Education announced the closure of the School of Writing, effective May 1, 1984.

The founder, Fred Wah, is a native of Swift Current, Sask., who grew up in Nelson. In such books as *Pictograms from the Interior of B.C.* (1975) and *Loki Is Buried at Smoky Creek* (1980), he catches the flavour of the mountainous region. "I live in the 'interior' of British Columbia and such a qualification affects my particular sense of what the world looks like," he says in the latter collection. "We go, 'down' to the coast, which is the exterior, the outside, the city. The spaces between here and there are part of a vast similarity. The towns become predictable in their activities and appearances. Castlegar and Prince George, though specifically themselves, share certain aspects of distance, colour, and taste. One feels at home nearly anywhere there are rivers, pulp mills, trucks, the mysterious gravel roads further inward, and similar 'local' inhabitants."

New Denver

New Denver, north of Castlegar, is now a ghost town. It was designated a Japanese "Relocation Centre" during the second World War. In 1943, 1,701 evacuated Japanese lived in New Denver and neighbouring Roseberry under deplorable conditions. One internee was Takeo Ujo Nakano (b. 1903), the Japanese-born poet, who helped to establish a Haiku Club at New Denver. Detainees met to read their haiku and tanka and even to print them in limited editions, as Nakano recalls in his memoir, *Within the Barbed Wire Fence* (1980). Nakano was an adult, but Shizuye Takashima (b. 1928) was only a child; many years later she wrote and drew her memories in *A Child in a Prison Camp* (1971).

New Westminster

Southeast of Vancouver, New Westminster is one of the places visited by Maggie Vardoe, the main character in *Swamp Angel* (1954), the novel by Ethel Wilson (1890-1980). She begins in Victoria and travels through New Westminster, Hope, and Kamloops.

Conditions in the British Columbia Penitentiary, located here, are described in vivid detail by Anthony Apakark Thrasher (b. 1937) in his autobiography, *Thrasher: Skid Row Eskimo* (1976).

The novelist Sheila Watson (b. 1909) was born in New Westminster. Her father was superintendent of the Pro-

Title-page spread of Sheila Watson's The Double Hook, *designed by Frank Newfeld.* [McClelland & Stewart]

vincial Mental Hospital, so she lived on the grounds of the institution as a child until his death in 1922. Perhaps this experience prepared her for some of the insights she expressed in her novel *The Double Hook* (1959).

There is an odd connection between New Westminster and the English poet A. E. Housman (1859-1936). The link is Moses Jackson, an intimate college friend of Housman's, who married, left England, and in 1911 acquired a farm at Aldergrove, near New Westminster. When the English poet learned that Jackson was dying of stomach cancer in a Vancouver hospital, he recalled their close friendship. Between March 30 and April 9, 1922, he wrote fifty-seven pages of poems. These were included in *Last Poems* and published later that year. A copy was rushed to Jackson who read them in hospital in October, a few months before his death early in 1923.

Nicola

Among the Interior Salish along the banks of the Nicola River, at Shulus, near Nicola, north of Merritt, the anthropologist Douglas Leechman (b. 1890) collected in the late 1940s the lovely legend that tells how the loon acquired its distinguishing neckband. He wrote the script of the short film *The Loon's Necklace* released in 1950, and published the legend in popular form in *Native Tribes of Canada* (1955).

Nootka Sound

This inlet on the west coast of Vancouver Island was discovered by Captain Cook in 1778. Here in 1803 the Boston sailor, John R. Jewitt (1783-1821), was taken prisoner by Maquinna, chief of the Nootkas, who held him captive for two years. Jewitt recounted his experiences in his *Journal* (1807), which was used by the novelist James Houston (b. 1921) as the basis of *Eagle Song: An Indian Saga Based on True Events* (1983). The novel is a fictional retelling of the captivity narrative from the point of view of Siam, Maquinna's brother-in-law.

Okanagan Valley

In the Okanagan valley, in the interior of the province, lies Okanagan Lake, habitat of the celebrated lake monster, Ogopogo, whose palindromic name was acquired from an English music hall song, as Mary Moon explains in *Ogopogo: The Okanagan Mystery* (1977). North of Penticton a plaque identifies "Ogopogo's Home."

Penticton is the home of Edith Lambert Sharp (b. 1917), author of *Nkwala* (1958), about a Salish boy of the Spokan tribe in the region. In nearby Summerland lives playwright and novelist George Ryga (b. 1932). Born in Deep Creek, Alta., he is best known for his play *The Ecstasy of Rita Joe*, about an Indian prostitute in Vancouver. It premiered at the Vancouver Playhouse in 1967 and a ballet based on the story was subsequently staged by the Royal Winnipeg Ballet.

Bliss Carman (1861-1929) was impressed with the region, as he was by almost all the regions he visited, and wrote "In the Okanagan" in *Bliss Carman's Poems* (1931), a poem in which he refers to the fruit-bearing valley as "This Eden of the North."

The playwright George Ryga was caught in an uncharacteristic moment (one hopes) by artist Don Evans (who signs his work Isaac Bickerstaff). [Special Collections, University of Calgary Libraries]

Peace Arch Park

Peace Arch Park is set on the International Boundary between Canada and the United States on lands maintained by the Province of British Columbia and the State of Washington. It is near White Rock and Crescent Beach, southeast of New Westminster.

The unique park was dedicated on September 6, 1921, to commemorate the lasting peace that exists between the two countries. The centrepiece of the park is the Peace Arch, a reinforced concrete structure thirty metres in height. On the American side it is inscribed "Children of a Common Mother"; on the Canadian side "Brethren Dwelling Together in Unity." There are inscriptions on the two iron gates that lead from one country to the other. On the Atlantic side appear the words "May These Gates Never Be Closed"; on the Pacific side "1814 — Open for One Hundred Years — 1914."

When the American singer and peace advocate Paul Robeson was denied permission to enter Canada to perform at a peace concert in Vancouver, the concert was rescheduled at Peace Arch Park. He performed on the American side on May 18, 1952, but was heard by an immense crowd on the Canadian side. The total attendance was estimated at forty thousand.

Peace River Country   See PEACE RIVER COUNTRY, Alta.

Port Alberni   See ALBERNI.

Prince George

Located in the interior of British Columbia, Prince George figures as "Lyndon" in three novels written by Robert Harlow (b. 1923) who was born here but raised in the port city of Prince Rupert. The novels are *Royal Murdoch* (1962), *A Gift of Echoes* (1965), and *Scann* (1972).

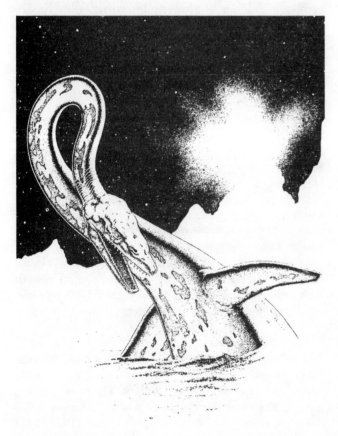

Ogopogo resembles a plesiosaur in this drawing by Martin Springett for Mary Moon's Ogopogo: The Okanagan Mystery *(1977). [J. J. Douglas Ltd.]*

J. Michael Yates, full-time poet and part-time logger, atop a load of spruce, Juskatla Division, MacMillan Bloedel Logging Claim, Moresby Island, Queen Charlotte Islands, 1972. [National Library of Canada, Literary Manuscripts Collection]

James Houston, northern renaissance man, is a sometime resident of the Queen Charlotte Islands. [James Houston]

Queen Charlotte Islands

The Queen Charlotte Islands, a chain of islands off the northern Pacific coast, figure prominently on the Surrealist's Map of the World, prepared by Belgian and French surrealists in 1929 to identify regions productive of audacious art. The artists who drew the map had in mind the Haida who, at Masset on Graham Island, produced monumental poles and fine argillite carvings.

An area rich in Indian lore, the Islands have been studied by generations of anthropologists. John R. Swanton (1873-1958) did field work here in 1900-1 on *Haida Songs* (1912). The American photographer, Edward Curtis (1868-1952), explored the Islands in 1910-14 for his record in words and pictures in his series "The North American Indians," the relevant volumes being published in 1913-16. As well, Marius Barbeau (1883-1969) worked here in 1939 and 1947 on the study of local lore and design, culminating in his *Totem Poles* (1950).

Raven's Cry (1966), by Christie Harris (b. 1907), is a fictionalized history of the Haida from the arrival of Captain James Cook in 1775 to the present. It takes place in the Haida village of Kiusta on Cloak Bay.

From 1971 to 1974, the poet J. Michael Yates (b. 1938) was a resident of Port Clements. Here he wrote such poetic sequences as "The Abstract Beast" and "The Queen Charlotte Island Meditations," and issued books with the Sono Nis imprint.

Other writers who have inhabited the Islands include Matt Cohen (b. 1942) who resided here briefly, writing his novel *Wooden Hunters* (1975) which he set on the Islands. Sean Virgo (b. 1940), the poet, lived here in 1971-75 and wrote *Deathwatch on Skidegate Narrows* (1979). The novelist James Houston (b. 1921) divides his time between his cottage on the Islands and his farm at Escoheag, Rhode Island. Although the poet Susan Musgrave (b. 1951) was born in California (of parents from British Columbia), she regards the Queen Charlottes as her "spiritual home," with Masset playing the part of the hearth. She lives on an island farther south, at Curteis Point, near Sidney, where she occupies a small log house and writes about the natural world.

Rider See HAGGARD GLACIER.

Roberts Creek

The small community of Roberts Creek, on the coast northwest of Vancouver, is associated with Hubert Evans (b. 1892) who, although born at Vankleek Hill, Ont., and raised in Galt, has lived here intermittently since 1927. He writes about the interaction of nature and man in his best-known book, *Mist on the River* (1954), and tells his own story in *O Time in Your Flight* (1979).

Ruskin

The community of Ruskin, north of Mission City, was named in honour of the English writer John Ruskin (1819-1900) by the original settlers, a group of communal-minded farmers.

"Rutherford Heights" See NANAIMO.

St. Nicholas Peak

This peak, northwest of Lake Louise, was named in 1908 for a rock formation said to resemble Santa Claus.

Sechelt

Here, overlooking the Strait of Georgia, northwest of Vancouver, Dorothy Livesay (b. 1909) wrote two sensitive sonnets. Collectively titled "At Sechelt" (1956), they contrast "the earth's warm silences" with "the loquacious solace of the sea."

Peter Trower (b. 1930), the logging poet, works in the Sechelt Peninsula area. He has written about its forests in such collections as *Moving through the Mystery* (1969) and *Between the Sky and the Splinters* (1974).

Selkirk Mountains

The Selkirk Mountains, which extend from the international boundary north to the Columbia River, were named after the colonist Lord Selkirk. The mining region is the setting of *Black Rock: A Tale of the Selkirks* (1898), the first-published novel of Ralph Connor (1860-1937) who knew the conditions of life here as a missionary.

"These mountains I had long wished to see," wrote the Western American writer Hamlin Garland (1860-

1940) in his travel account *The Trail of the Gold Seekers* (1899), "and they were in no sense a disappointment. Desolate, death-haunted, they pushed their white domes into the blue sky in savage grandeur. The little snow-covered towns seemed to cower at their feet like timid animals lost in the immensity of the forest. All day we rode among these heights, and at night we went to sleep feeling the chill of their desolate presence."

Shelley

The CN station of Shelley, northeast of Prince George, was named in 1913 for the poet Percy Bysshe Shelley (1792-1822).

Susan Musgrave, the poet, lives outside Sidney. She is shown here leaning against a signpost on the road outside Great Musgrave, Cumberland, Northern England. [Musgrave Collection]

Sidney

Located in Sidney, north of Victoria, is Gray's Publishing, which has issued among its many titles two books by George Clutesi (b. 1905), *Son of Raven, Son of Deer* (1967) and *Potlatch* (1969). Among writers resident in Sidney are Susan Musgrave (b. 1951), the poet, and Michael G. Coney (b. 1932), the science-fiction author.

Skeena Valley

A small Gitskan village, situated in the Skeena Valley near Hazelton, is the setting of *Mist on the River* (1954), a moving study of Indians caught between two worlds, by Hubert Evans (b. 1892). The ethnologist Marius Barbeau (1883-1969) made field trips here in 1920-26, gathering lore for *The Downfall of Temlaham* (1928).

Slocan

This ghost town, north of Nelson, was designated a Japanese "Relocation Centre" during the Second World War. It became the largest of the six camps in the province (the others were Greenwood, Kaslo, New Denver, Sandon, and Tashme) and, in 1943, 4,764 Japanese lived in Slocan Valley (which included Slocan City, Bay Farm, Popoff, and Lemon Creek). Here Joy Kogawa (b. 1935) was raised. Some poems in *A Choice of Dreams* (1974) deal with her childhood experiences.

Aerial view of Slocan. [Tourism B.C.]

"But the Slocan that we knew in the forties was no longer there, except for the small white community which had existed before we arrived and which watched us come with a mixture of curiosity and fear. Now, down on the shore of the Slocan Lake, on the most beautiful part of the sandy beach, where we used to swim, there was a large new sawmill owned by someone who lived in New York," she wrote in her autobiographical work *Obasan* (1981). "In Sandon, Tashme, Kaslo, Greenwood, Slocan, Bayfarm, Popoff, Lemon Creek, New Denver, we lived in tents, in bunks, in skating rinks, in abandoned hotels. Most of us lived in row upon row of two-family, three-room huts, controlled and orderly as wooden blocks. There was a tidy mind somewhere."

Soda Creek

Here, south of Prince George, Mary Augusta Tappage (b. 1888) was raised. This Shushwap woman's memories of life on the Soda Creek Reserve were skilfully edited into a sequence of found poems by Jean E. Speare and published as *The Days of Augusta* (1973).

Sooke

Sooke is a small farming community on the southwest coast of Vancouver Island. Returning to Canada after many years in England, George Woodcock (b. 1912) and his wife Ingeborg lived in semi-isolation at Sooke, combining the life of labour and literature. He has written warmly about these years, from 1949 to 1956, which ended when he joined the University of British Columbia and then launched its quarterly publication, *Canadian Literature*.

Steveston

This small community had a large population of Japanese who worked as fish canners prior to the evacuation in the Second World War. Daphne Marlatt (b. 1942) has made the community particularly her own with her poetic portrait, *Steveston* (1974), and her oral history, *Steveston Recollected: Japanese-Canadian History* (1975).

Tara Lake   See MOUNT SCARLETT O'HARA.

Thrums

The small community of Thrums, southwest of Nelson, was named after the fictional Scottish community of Thrums in *A Window in Thrums* (1889) by Sir James M. Barrie (1860-1936), best remembered as the creator of Peter Pan. Barrie's Thrums was modelled on Kirriemuir, Forfarshire, Scotland.

Tweedsmuir Provincial Park

Tweedsmuir Provincial Park, the largest park in British Columbia, is located southwest of Burns Lake. It was named after John Buchan (1875-1940), Lord Tweedsmuir, who served from 1935 to his death as the 15th Governor General. Buchan is widely admired for thrillers such as *The Thirty-Nine Steps* (1915), but he also wrote *Sick Heart River* (1941), a psychological adventure novel set in the Nahanni Valley. It was during his period of office that the Governor General's Awards for Literature were established. Lord Tweedsmuir, a great outdoorsman, travelled extensively by float aircraft and horseback in the park in August 1937. "I have now travelled over most of Canada and have seen many wonderful things," he exclaimed, "but I have seen nothing more beautiful and more wonderful than the great park which British Columbia has done me the honour to call by my name."

Aerial view of Hunlen Falls in Tweedsmuir Provincial Park. The Park was named after John Buchan, Governor General Lord Tweedsmuir. [Tourism B.C.]

Vancouver

"To describe the beauties of this region will, on some future occasion, be a very grateful task to the pen of a skilled panegyrist," wrote Captain George Vancouver (1757-1798) in the spring of 1792 in his account, *A Voyage of Discovery* (1798). A handful of poets but hardly any novelists have taken up the task. Captain Vancouver makes an appearance in *The Damnation of Vancouver* (1977), a comic play written by Earle Birney (b. 1904) in verse for broadcast as "Trial of a City" on CBC Radio in 1952, in which the city is weighed on the scales of justice and found wanting. The Good Captain makes a surprising reappearance in *Burning Water* (1980), a poetic novel by George Bowering (b. 1935).

Rupert Brooke (1887-1915), a distinguished visitor in 1913, wrote back to his mother: "It's a queer place, rather different from the rest of Canada. More oriental." Another distinguished visitor, the Russian poet Andrei Voznesensky (b. 1933), while here in 1973 to read poems at Simon Fraser University, wrote a major long poem which was published in English as *Story Under Full Sail* (1974). It is about the love of a Russian sea captain for a Spanish-American girl in California, and became the basis of the first Soviet rock opera, *Junon and Avos*, which premiered in Moscow in 1981. Voznesensky toured the country from West to East and visualized it as "a comparatively narrow strip above the American border... like a layer of cream on a jug of milk." He noted that "the sky is ever-sensed above Canada, untamed nature to the pole — green sky of summer and white of winter."

Chief Dan George played the old shaman in Shadow of the Hawk, *a psychological horror film directed by George McCowan. One sequence takes place on the Capilano Suspension Bridge. [Ontario Film Institute]*

Burrard Reserve   Chief Dan George (1899-1981), the Indian spokesman and leader, was born and lies buried at the Burrard Reserve in North Vancouver. He worked as a logger and then as a longshoreman on the Vancouver docks, gradually emerging as a spokesman on behalf of his Squamish band, the Indians of Canada, and the first nations of North America. In the 1960s he played the part of Ol' Antoine in the CBC-TV series *Cariboo Country*. He played the part of the aged Cheyenne chief Old Lodge Poles in the movie *Little Big Man* (1970). He narrated the ballet and television versions of *The Ecstasy of Rita Joe* (1970) and wrote the lovely lyrics collected in *My Heart Soars* (1974). He was a great orator, combining poetry and power with authority and a sense of continuity and community.

Davie Street   The novelist Malcolm Lowry (1909-1957) once lived on this street, as mentioned by Dorothy Livesay (b. 1909) in her poem "Roots" (1966), which runs: "He lived in the west end once / on Davie Street / a house indifferent to strangers."

Deep Cove   Dorothy Livesay (b. 1909) was moved by Deep Cove to write in the 1930s her lovely poem "Deep Cove: Vancouver" which begins: "But we, who love to lie here hushed. . . ."

Duthie Books   Duthie Books is the place where the Vancouver *literati* acquire their books. The Main Store and Paperback Cellar, 919 Robson Street, has an excellent section devoted to Canadiana and avant-garde literature. The store, one of a number, was opened in 1957 by bookseller Bill Duthie. One book the store always stocks is an *omnium gatherum* of city lore called *The Vancouver Book* (1976) compiled by Chuck Davis.

English Bay   The beauty of English Bay has inspired innumerable poets. There is Bliss Carman (1861-1929) who in his poem "Vancouver" in *Bliss Carman's Poems* (1931) wrote: "Tyre and Sidon, where are they? / Where is the trade of Carthage now? / Here is Vancouver on English Bay, / With tomorrow's light on her brow!"

In her poem "At English Bay: December, 1937" (1937), Dorothy Livesay (b. 1909) has suggested that the water here "has washed the coasts of China." Earle Birney (b. 1904) has written a number of fine poems about the beach here, including "Dusk on English Bay" (1941) and "November Walk Near False Creek Mouth" (1961).

Grouse Mountain   From the vantagepoint of Grouse Mountain plateau, with its sweeping view of Vancouver, Earle Birney (b. 1904) wrote "Vancouver Lights," which begins: "On this mountain's brutish forehead with terror of space / I stir. . . ." Dorothy Livesay (b. 1909) sought a similar perch for her meditation on dock workers in "West Coast: 1943" (1943).

Hastings Park   The Exhibition Grounds of Hastings Park served as a temporary shelter and clearing house for the Japanese, both native and naturalized Canadians, evacuated from the coastal areas in 1942. The relocation centre is mentioned in the long poem *Call My People Home* (1950) by Dorothy Livesay (b. 1909).

Among the evacuees was the poet, Takeo Ujo Nakano (b. 1903), who spent five days in March in the Livestock Building. He was en route between his home in the company town of Woodfibre, north of Vancouver, and the Road Camp at Yellowhead. He wrote a tanka about the experience, later translated and published in *Within the Barbed Wire Fence* (1980): The five-line poem runs: "Reek of manure, / Stench of livestock, / And we are hearded / Milling — / Jumble of the battlefield."

Hotel Vancouver   The Hotel Vancouver is something of a landmark in downtown Vancouver with its steeply sloping, green mansard roofs. No doubt a number of

George Segal plays a Mountie in Russian Roulette, *based on Tom Ardies' novel* Kosygin Is Coming. *The climax occurs on the roof of the Hotel Vancouver.* [Ontario Film Institute]

dramas have been enacted in the rooms and suites of the hotel, but none was more dramatic than the one that took place in the espionage novel *Kosygin Is Coming* (1974) by Tom Ardies (b. 1931) which concerns a plot to assassinate Alexei Kosygin. (The Soviet Premier was assaulted on October 19, 1971, on Parliament Hill, Ottawa.) The key scene of the novel is a gun-battle on the roof of the Hotel Vancouver. It is a highpoint in *Russian Roulette*, the 1975 movie based on the novel, starring George Segal as the RCMP corporal.

Spanish Banks   Here, where Captain Vancouver held colloquy with the admiral of the Spanish fleet, Earle Birney (b. 1904) wrote his well-known satirical poem "Can. Lit." (1947) which concludes: "no Whitman wanted / it's only by our lack of ghosts / we're haunted."

Stanley Park   The sites of literary interest in Stanley Park, which was established in 1889, are associated with the Mohawk poetess, Pauline Johnson (1861-1913). There is a Memorial to her erected at Siwash Rock, near Ferguson Point. The Rock is a naturally formed symmetrical column of grey stone, in the vicinity of which were scattered her ashes. From Chief Joseph Capilano she learned the legend of the origin of the Rock. It seems it was once a brave Indian who sacrificed his life for that of his wife and unborn child. She retold the legend in romantic form in *Legends of Vancouver* (1911). Near the Rock is Lost Lagoon, about which she wrote a popular poem; once it was a tidal pool, now a causeway seals it off from the sea. At Prospect Point, which looks out over Lions Gate Bridge and the North Shore of Vancouver, towering over the stand of totem poles, will be found the personal pole of Chief Capilano, the Squamish leader who befriended the poetess and told her the traditional tales of his people. He carved it himself in the 1930s to commemorate the meeting of Captain Vancouver with the Squamish in 1792. The name Capilano, an honoured

Legends swirl around Siwash Rock in Vancouver's Stanley Park. [Vancouver Public Library]

Pauline Johnson 5¢ stamp, 1961. [Canada Post Corporation]

one in Vancouver, has been affixed to a canyon, cemetery, golf course, lake, park, river, road, salmon hatchery, suspension bridge (the world's longest), and a literary magazine.

Two other poets are honoured in Stanley Park. At the Georgia Street entrance stands on a high stone plinth a statue of Robert Burns (1759-1796), the Scottish poet and patriot. England's national poet and dramatist, William Shakespeare (1564-1616), is depicted in bas-relief on the monument erected in his honour in the area of the park designated Shakespeare Gardens.

University of British Columbia A good many writers were or are associated with the English Department and the Creative Writing Department of the University of British Columbia which was founded in 1899 and is located at West Point Grey. From the English Department, George Woodcock (b. 1912) launched the critical quarterly *Canadian Literature* in 1959; the same year, from within the Creative Writing Program, Jacob Zilber and others launched *Prism* which became *Prism International* five years later. In 1965, Earle Birney (b. 1904) established and headed the first Creative Writing Department — as distinct from a Program — in the country, with the University of Victoria following suit

Earle Birney appears in the NFB documentary film Aloud / Bagatelle. [NFB]

eight years later. Warren Tallman (b. 1921), the critic, has been a strong influence within the English Department. At various times in the English or Writing departments instructors have included Michael Bullock, Joan Haggerty, Robert Harlow, J. Michael Yates, Audrey Thomas, Ian Slater, Jane Rule, to name a handful.

Literary papers relating to a number of authors, mostly from British Columbia, are housed in the Special Collections Division of the University of British Columbia Library. Among these are manuscripts by Malcolm Lowry, Roderick Haig-Brown, Audrey Thomas, Ethel Wilson, Ronald Hambleton, George Bowering, Pat Lane, Raymond Hull, Nellie McClung, and Frederick Niven. The most notable collection is Lowry's, for it consists of papers from many sources, including manuscripts rescued from his Dollarton shack before it was levelled. Earle Birney and the widow, Margerie Bonner Lowry, helped gather together papers from Lowry's associates, and it is from this collection that almost all his posthumously published works have been derived. Included in the extensive collection are several drafts of *Under the Volcano* (1947) and *October Ferry to Gabriola* (1970), to name but two well-known works.

Tourists chat amid the totem poles at the Museum of Anthropology, designed by Arthur Erickson, University of British Columbia, Vancouver. [Dept. of Regional Industrial Expansion]

Vancouver Art Gallery The Vancouver Art Gallery, founded in 1931, moved into the neo-classical Provincial Courthouse, on Robson Square, October 15, 1983. Every reader who tours the gallery, designed by F. M. Rattenbury and renovated by Arthur Erickson, will be impressed by the Emily Carr Gallery, an area of 5,000 square feet that is devoted exclusively to the paintings and drawings of Emily Carr (1871-1945) who left her distinctive mark on both the art and the literature of the country.

Vancouver East Cultural Centre The Vancouver East Cultural Centre, 1895 Venables Street, was established in 1973 as an intimate, multi-purpose space for professional performing arts. It is located in an old church. *Billy Bishop*

The new home of the Vancouver Art Gallery with its Emily Carr wing.
[Tourism B.C.]

Goes to War was premiered here in November 1978, and there have been two revivals of *The Ecstasy of Rita Joe*, originally premiered in the Queen Elizabeth Playhouse. The VECC is the home of the Tamahnous Theatre, Vancouver Playhouse Blue Series, and musical and craft group shows. The *Globe and Mail* called VECC's offerings "eclectic and off the wall."

Vancouver International Airport   The novelist Arthur Hailey (b. 1920) got his start with *Flight into Danger*, an hour-long play commissioned by CBC-TV and telecast on April 3, 1956. The drama concerns a TCA flight between Winnipeg and Vancouver. The question is whether or not, with the pilot and copilot sick, a passenger with limited flight experience can land the plane safely at Vancouver International Airport.

Writers   No list of the writers and authors, journalists and editors, who live in the Greater Vancouver area could ever be complete. What follows is incidental information that has come to hand on some well-known writers of the past and present.

Pauline Johnson (1861-1913), exhausted from crossing and recrossing the country to give recitals of her

Eric Peterson is dressed as the "Air Ace" in the one-man revue, Billy Bishop Goes to War. [CBC]

Photograph of Pauline Johnson in her theatrical costume. [Vancouver Public Library]

empassioned poems on whatever platform or stage presented itself, settled in Vancouver in 1909. She lived in Suite 2, 1117 Howe Street, and a vivid picture of her last years, spent as a semi-invalid, is presented by Betty Keller in her biography *Pauline* (1981). Here she met with her long-time friend, Joe Capilano, chief of the Squamish Band, and she preserved some of his tales in *Legends of Vancouver* (1911). After a protracted illness she died at Bute Street Hospital and the funeral service was held at Christ Church Cathedral. Her ashes were buried or scattered at Ferguson Point, Stanley Park.

Eric Nicol (b. 1919), the well-known humorist, has written: "I am astonished that my house, and study, could be of interest to anyone but a carpenter ant with a gourmet taste for unfinished cedar." He was born in Kingston, Ont., but brought to Vancouver at the age of six. He attended the University of British Columbia and contributed a column to the campus newspaper. He is a columnist for the *Vancouver Province* and the author of many books, collections of columns, and plays. His collaboration with cartoonist Peter Whalley (b. 1921), of Morin Heights, Que., produced *An Uninhibited History of Canada* (1959) and other titles. He has written affectionately about his city in *Vancouver* (1970, 1978). "I have lived and done most of my writing in my present house, at 3993 West 36th Ave., in the South Dunbar district of Vancouver. I bought the house in 1957. It is one block from the University of British Columbia Endow-

This sketch of Eric Nicol with interloper was prepared by Peter Whalley who illustrated many of the Vancouver humorist's books. [Peter Whalley]

ment Lands, a natural wilderness that has been a second home for me since my parents moved into the area about fifty-five years ago."

George Woodcock (b. 1912) and his wife the photographer Ingeborg Woodcock have lived in the comfortable house at 6429 McCleery Street in Vancouver since April 1959. From his study — "my study is approximately 12 ft. by 16 ft.; I'm a stickler for the old measurements" — he has produced a mountain of prose — prefaces, interviews, articles, poems, plays, anthologies, and critical studies. "People who've visited me here? They include A. J. M. Smith, Earle Birney, Margaret Laurence, Margaret Atwood, Al Purdy, Bob Fulford, Bob Weaver, Hugh Garner (a disastrous visit, that!), P. K. Page, Dorothy Livesay, Roy Daniells, Audrey Thomas, Jane Rule, Phyllis Webb, Doug

George Woodcock rows his way across a sea of books in this drawing by Isaac Bickerstaff, pen name of Don Evans. [Special Collections, University of Calgary Libraries]

Fetherling, David Helwig, and, of course John Robert Colombo, together with wandering English writers like V. S. Pritchett, Julian Symons, Alex Comfort, and Malcolm Muggeridge."

Woodcock continued: "After leaving Sooke in 1953, we lived for some time in a cabin on Capitol Hill near Jack Shadbolt's house, and from 1956-57, while the Shadbolts were in Europe, we lived in their house. Northrop Frye visited us there, and when I took him out on the deck to show him the really splended view of the North Shore mountains, Frye went a little pale, turned and walked back into the house, saying: 'Those mountains make my blood run cold!' We also lived a few months in 1955 in the basement of Birney's house on West 3rd Avenue, Vancouver, and for several months in 1955-56 in an apartment on Lonsdale Avenue, North Vancouver (I forget the number), where we were visited by Herbert Read, Norman Levine (who mentions the meal Inge gave him then in *Canada Made Me*) and Allen Ginsberg, who gave me a grubby preview of 'Howl' in a typescript he pulled from somewhere inside his shirt; I remember being unflattering, and have had no cause to regret my lack of enthusiasm. I still think it is one of the worst poems foisted on the century."

Woodcock is the author of more than fifty books. The range of his writing is suggested by *A George Woodcock Reader* (1980) edited by Doug Fetherling. As Peter Hughes noted in *George Woodcock* (1974), Woodcock has written more books than most people have read.

Allan Fotheringham (b. 1932), columnist and author, is known as the Wicked Wit of the West for his irreverent sallies and similes on provincial and federal politicos and other matters published on the final page of *Maclean's* and in numerous books, beginning with the drolly titled *Collected and Bound* (1972), where he reprints a newspaper column published in 1961 in which he states: "If Vancouver were loaned to Italy for two years there would be a restaurant hanging out over the cliff at Prospect Point, flower sellers would soften the brittle neon glare of Granville and there would be more noise everywhere." Fotheringham self-defined himself as "a flamboyant introvert."

Victoria

No visitor to Victoria leaves this capital of British Columbia, on the southern tip of Vancouver Island, unimpressed. Rudyard Kipling (1865-1936) was suitably moved when he wrote in *Letters to the Family* (1908): "Canada possesses two pillars of Strength and Beauty in Quebec and Victoria. The former ranks by herself among those Mother-cities of whom none can say 'This reminds me.' To realize Victoria you must take all that the eye admires most in Bournemouth, Torquay, the Isle of Wight, the Happy Valley of Hong Kong, the Doon, Sorrento, and Camps Bay; add reminiscences of the Thousand Islands, and arrange the

There are more statues of Robert Burns in Canada than of any other literary figure. (There are probably more Burns memorials in Canada than in Scotland.) This engraving of the Scots poet by Alf. Sandham was printed in 1892. [PAC C 22242]

whole round the Bay of Naples, with some Himalayas for the background." Sir John A. Macdonald is said to have observed of Victoria: "The day was always in the afternoon." All of this belies the veracity of the quip that Victoria is the home of "the newly wed and the nearly dead."

Rupert Brooke   It seems appropriate that Victoria appealed to Rupert Brooke (1887-1915), the most English of poets, who arrived here in September 1913 at the end of his cross-Canada tour, which he described in poetic detail in *Letters from America* (1916). He stayed at the Dallas Hotel on the seaside and was in a contemplative frame of mind when he scribbled the following sentence on a postcard mailed on September 12: "I'm sitting, wildly surmising, on the edge of the Pacific, gazing at mountains which are changing colour every two minutes in the most surprising way. Nature here is half Japanese."

He could have been fretful for, somewhere in British Columbia, perhaps on Vancouver Island, he had lost his notebook which "contained 2 months' notes on my travels and unfinished sonnets, and all sorts of wealth. . . ." Instead of fretting, he was philosophical. In an unfinished essay titled "Victoria" which was published only in 1978 he described how he sat on the beach and pondered the future of Canada: "I watched the children and the mountains and thought of Canada. I thought of her possibilities, and of her wealth and corruption and individualism and ugliness. I thought of all the people I had met and talked with, their simplicity and friendliness, the lack of charm of many, the loneliness of some, the dullness and absence of ideal in the young, the strength and beauty of heart and queer purity of mind in certain men and women I had come to know. I wondered what was to be the future of the land."

Victoria's Beacon Hill Park features a monument to Robert Burns (left), which depicts the Scottish poet with his lady love. (According to the inscription, it was erected to "Scotia's Immortal Bard" by "His Admirers" in 1900.) The pebblestone bridge (below) was erected in memory of Emily Carr, "Canadian Artist and Writer. [Greater Victoria Visitors Information Centre: Tourism B.C.]

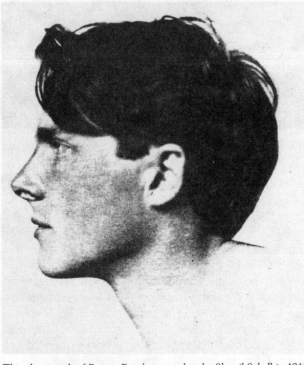

This photograph of Rupert Brooke was taken by Sherril Schell in 1915, two years after the poet and traveller recorded his Canadian impressions in essays and letters. [Sedgwick & Jackson]

Beacon Hill Park   Among the points of interest in this park in downtown Victoria are the monument to the Scots poet Robert Burns (1759-1796) and the small pebblestone bridge dedicated to the painter and writer Emily Carr (1871-1945) by her sister Alice M. Carr.

Canadian Bank of Commerce   Before he reached the Yukon and achieved fame as a versifier, Robert W. Service (1874-1958) secured a clerkship at the Victoria branch of the Canadian Bank of Commerce, where he worked from October 1903 to July 1904 when he was transferred to the branch at Kamloops.

Emily Carr Gallery   Officially opened in July 1977 as an extension of the Provincial Archives of British Columbia is the Emily Carr Gallery, 1107 Wharf Street, devoted to the documentation of the life and work of the painter and writer Emily Carr (1871-1945). The gallery has an extensive collection of letters, manuscripts, articles, books, photographs, films, sketches, and paintings. Among the short films produced about Carr's life and work is one with the appropriate title: *Little Old Lady on the Edge of Nowhere*, produced by CBC-TV in 1975.

Emily Carr's House, Victoria. [*Bill Brooks*]

Sketch of Emily Carr in front of one of her paintings by Isaac Bickerstaff (artist Don Evans). [*Special Collections, University of Calgary Libraries*]

Emily Carr's House   Emily Carr (1871-1945), the painter and writer who drew her inspiration from the native way of life she saw in North Vancouver and the Queen Charlotte Islands, was born and raised in this two-storey frame house, built in 1863, at 207 Government Street. She was an outstanding writer as well as painter and described her early life in *The Book of Small* (1942). She published two other collections during her life — *Klee Wyck* (1941) and *The House of All Sorts* (1944) — and at least five more drawn from her talks and journals have appeared subsequently. A book of poems inspired by the artist's vision was called *Emily* (1975) by the poet Florence McNeil (b. 1940).

The Empress Hotel   High tea at the Empress Hotel, overlooking the city's Inner Harbour, is a West Coast tradition. This famous hostelry, designed by F. M. Rattenbury (whose non-architectural affairs caused a scandal in Victoria and resulted in a book of its own), was one of the last of the CPR's Chateau-style hotels, built in 1908.

The Empress Hotel and the Inner Harbour, Victoria. [*Dept. of Regional Industrial Expansion*]

"I went and had some tea in the Empress Hotel," wrote Norman Levine (b. 1924) in *Canada Made Me* (1958, 1979). "It was difficult to believe that one wasn't back in a hotel in Bideford or another one I remember in Harrogate. The Edwardian high-backed sofas, settees, tall chairs; the elderly ladies with kind faces, the thick carpets, the pillars, the piano and the cello playing in one corner of the room. Oil paintings of four generations of the Royal Family on the walls, above the fireplaces, flowers on the tables. Old men with canes. The small lights from the candelabra. Candlesticks over the fireplace. Ferns in vases. Wealth and the retired and good manners talking quietly, while the cello and the piano continued to make a noise in the corner."

A recreaion of Anne Hathaway's cottage is part of the Tudor village on the grounds of the Olde England Inn. Esquimalt. [Tourism B.C.]

English Village Students of English literature may well be delighted to walk along Chaucer Lane and admire replicas of Anne Hathaway's cottage, the birthplace of William Shakespeare, etc. The commercial attraction is located on the grounds of the Olde England Inn at 429 Lampton Street in Esquimalt.

Munro's Books Munro's Books is an institution in Victoria. The principal store was at 669 Fort Street, the satellite store at 168 Market Square. The main store was founded on Yates Street as a paperback shop in 1963 by James Munro and his wife, novelist Alice Munro (b. 1931). The Market Square branch was opened in 1976. In 1980, the Yates Street location was moved to much larger premises in a heritage building at 669 Fort Street. In October 1984, Munro's Books closed these stores and opened in the former Royal Bank building, 1108 Government Street.

Malahat The drive around Malahat Mountain on the east coast of Vancouver, overlooking Victoria, is celebrated for its scenic beauty. It inspired Bliss Carman (1861-1929) to write "Malahat," in *Bliss Carman's Poems* (1931), with its conclusion that here is "a glimpse of heaven from Malahat." The mountain lent its name to *The Malahat Review*, published by the University of Victoria from 1967. The offical name of the geographical feature is Malahat Ridge. The Cowichan word is said to mean "place of bait."

The Parliament Buildings Near the impressive Parliament Buildings, seat of the provincial government, is Heritage Court, a complex of museums, galleries, and archives centred around Colombo Place, named after the Italian navigator Christoforo Colombo, where may be viewed important paintings by Emily Carr (1871-1945).

University of Victoria The University of Victoria was established in 1903 and has both an English Department and a Department of Creative Writing. Some writers with full-time or part-time association with the University are Robin Skelton, Robert Sward, W. D. Valgardson, Derk Wynard, and Sean Virgo. Skelton, with novelist John Peter, established *The Malahat Review* as "an inter-national quarterly of life and letters" in 1967, naming it after Malahat Mountain. Writer-in-residence from December 1981 to March 1982 was Saul Bellow (b. 1915), Lachine-born, Chicago novelist.

The Library of the University of Victoria has notable holdings in unpublished materials by George Barker, John Betjeman, Lawrence Durrell, T. S. Eliot, Robert Graves, Ted Hughes, Ezra Pound, Sir Herbert Read, Laura Riding, Muriel Spark, Dylan Thomas, and W. B. Yeats, among other British authors. It also has manuscripts by Robin Skelton and Robert Sward, not to mention a collection devoted to Henry Miller.

Writers Victoria has served as the home — and the retirement home — of any number of authors. The following names suggest the range of writers who chose to live here for varying lengths of time.

L. Adams Beck (d. 1931), a name now forgotten, an author with no books currently in print, was of British birth and settled here in 1919 to begin a literary career. She wrote some thirty books of historical fiction, occult stories, eastern tales, etc. These appeared under her own name and also under the names E. Barrington and Louis Moresby. She died in Kyoto, Japan, in 1931.

David Belasco (1853-1931), the playwright and theatrical producer, was born in San Francisco but raised in Victoria from 1858 to 1865. His father kept a tobacco shop on Yates Street, and David attended the Catholic school called The Collegiate. While still a youngster he acted at the Victoria Theatre Royal. Then the family returned to San Francisco. In later years Belasco enjoyed a Broadway career. It was he who induced Gladys Smith to change her name to Mary Pickford.

Raymond Chandler (1888-1959), the American detective-story writer, enlisted with the Canadian Gordon Highlanders, a kilted regiment, in August 1917 and trained for three months in Victoria. He served with the Canadian Expeditionary Force in France but later transferred to the Royal Flying Corps. He was discharged in Vancouver on February 20, 1919, having served for eighteen months. "It was still natural for me to prefer a British uniform," he later explained. (Although born in Chicago he had been raised in England.) He did not think much of Victoria, which he described as "dullish, as an English town would be on a Sunday, everything shut up, churchy atmosphere and so on." Yet in 1949 he wrote in a letter to the writer Alex Barris that he had settled in La Jolla, California, which was "almost as dull as a Victoria afternoon in February."

Alan Crawley (1887-1975), a Winnipeg-born lawyer who was blind after 1933, became a mentor to poets and the publisher of *Contemporary Verse* which appeared in 1941-52. It was revived the year of his death as *CV/II* by Dorothy Livesay in Winnipeg.

Bruce Hutchison (b. 1901), the newspaperman, was born in the family home at the corner of Dibble and Edward streets in Prescott, Ont. He was taken as an infant to Cranbrook, B.C., and raised there and in Merritt before the family moved to Victoria, where he lived in a bungalow on Wilmer Street which is depicted in Hutchison's autobiography, *The Far Side of the Street* (1976). He later lived with his parents and his wife in a nearby house. Now retired from a life of authorship and journalism — which saw him as editor of the *Winnipeg Free Press*, the *Victoria Times*, and the *Vancouver Sun* — he lives in Victoria. He created quite a splash with the sentimental patriotism of *The Unknown Country* (1943) and the unabashed enthusiasm for W. L. Mackenzie King in *The Incredible Canadian* (1952). *Uncle Percy's Wonderful Town* (1981) is a series of sketches about small-town life in "Emerald Vale," modelled on Merritt.

Nellie L. McClung (1873-1951), writer and early feminist, spent her last years in Victoria, having worked her way across the country from Ontario to Manitoba to Alberta to British Columbia. With her pharmacist husband, she retired in 1935 to Gordonhead, near Victoria, their retirement home being "Lantern Lane," at 1861 Ferndale Road. Far from retiring, she continued to write and served on the CBC's Board of Governors and was named delegate to a League of Nations conference in Geneva. She wrote *Leaves from Lantern Lane* (1936) and *More Leaves from Lantern Lane* (1937) as well as two volumes of autobiography: *Clearing in the West* (1936) and *The Stream Runs Fast* (1945). She was buried in the cemetery of St. Aidan's United Church at Mount Tolmie.

P. K. Page (b. 1916), the poet, though born in England, was brought at the age of three to Red Deer, Alta. She was educated at Calgary and she worked in Saint John, N.B., and Montreal. In 1950, she married W. A. Irwin, NFB Commissioner, and subsequently *Maclean's* editor, and Ambassador to Australia, Brazil, and Mexico from 1953 to 1964, when the Irwins settled in Victoria.

Marjorie Pickthall (1883-1922), the poet, always wanted to see the West Coast. In 1920 she left her mother behind in Toronto and settled into a small cottage near Victoria. She ultimately wrote two major collections of

Robin Skelton, man of letters, leaning against one of the twenty-two pillars of his house at 1255 Victoria Avenue, Victoria, a gathering place for writers and artists. [Marcia Willis]

poems, five novels, and two hundred stories. She died following an operation in a Vancouver hospital, April 1922, and is buried in Toronto.

Robin Skelton (b. 1925), the man of letters, was born in England but immigrated to Canada and joined the Department of English at the University of Victoria in 1963, where he presided over the birth of the Department of Creative Writing and *The Malahat Review*. He lives with his wife in a large Victorian house at 1255 Victoria Avenue. His affection for his adopted land is shown in his marvellous and mellifluous longer poem "Night Poem, Vancouver Island," *Selected Poems* (1968).

White Rock   See PEACE ARCH PARK.

Yale

Some eight thousand construction workers laying track along the Fraser River, near Yale, went on strike on March 27, 1912. The workers were organized by the IWW whose bard, the semi-legendary Joe Hill (1879-1915), appeared on the scene. At Yale he composed "Where the Fraser River Flows" (to be sung to the tune "Where the River Shannon Flows"). The chorus runs: "Where the Fraser River flows, each fellow worker knows, / They have bullied and oppressed us, but still our Union grows. / And we're going to find a way, boys, for shorter hours and better pay, boys! / And we're going to win the day, boys; where the Fraser River flows."

Yellowhead

The Yellowhead Pass through the Rocky Mountains, west of Jasper, Alta., was named in 1814 after François Decoigne, a Nor'wester in charge of Jasper House, who being fair-haired was nicknamed Tête-Jaune, or Yellowhead. The community of Yellowhead, located on the British Columbia side of the border, was the site of a detention camp for Japanese evacuees during World War II. The poet Takeo Ujo Nakano (b. 1903) was interned here and at the road camp farther east in Decoigne from late March to late July 1942. Here he wrote tanka, five-line poems, which were translated and published in *Within the Barbed Wire Fence* (1980), his reminiscences of the war years.

Yoho National Park

The word Yoho, which is Cree for "how wonderful," identifies a station, a glacier, a lake, a mountain, a pass, a river, a valley, and a national park. Yoho National Park is described in *Men for the Mountains* (1978), an account of the mountain mystique written by Sid Marty (b. 1944), the poet, who was born in England but raised in Medicine Hat and Calgary. He became a park warden in 1966 and worked at Yoho, Jasper, Prince Albert, and Banff national parks. Mountains stand out in his collections of poems, *Headwaters* (1973) and *Nobody Danced with Miss Rodeo* (1981). He lives at Lundbreck, in the southwestern corner of Alberta and is a consultant to the Banff Centre.

Yukon Territory

Chilkoot Pass

The year 1896 saw the Klondike Gold Rush and thousands of prospectors making their slow way over the Chilkoot Pass in the Coast Mountains. They had left Skagway, Alaska, behind and were seeking their fortunes in the gold fields of the Yukon. The route they took is memorably described by Pierre Berton (b. 1920) in *Klondike* (1958) and is now counted a Yukon Historic Site.

Michael Ambrose Mahoney was more muscular than most prospectors and claimed he carried a piano over the Chilkoot Pass. Merrill Denison (1893-1975) describes the feat in his biography of the audacious character, *Klondike Mike* (1943). Denison went on to maintain that Mahoney and his exploits supplied Jack London (1876-1916), the American novelist then in the Yukon, with incident, colour, and character for the classic short story "Burning Daylight" (1910). Denison quotes Mahoney as maintaining that the prospector witnessed the event that inspired "The Shooting of Dan McGrew" in the Malamute Saloon. Others have suggested that the boastful prospector was the original Jimmy Mahoney in *Rise and Fall of the City of Mahogany* (1927), the opera with words by Bertolt Brecht and music by Kurt Weill.

Dawson

Dawson, on the east bank of the Yukon River at the confluence of the Klondike River, sprang up following the discovery of gold on nearby Bonanza Creek in 1896, and as Dawson City it boasted a population of 25,000 at the peak of the Klondike Gold Rush. Today's population is under one thousand permanent residents. It is the site of restored Gold Rush buildings.

Canadian Bank of Commerce   Robert W. Service (1874-1958) was a teller at the Canadian Bank of Commerce in 1908-9. He worked in the Gold Room on the second floor of Bank, located on First Avenue (Front Street) at Queen Street. The Gold Room is open to visitors during the tourist season.

Robert W. Service's Cabin   Throughout the tourist season there are readings of the rousing ballads of Robert W. Service (1874-1958) in his restored cabin. The two-room

Charles Chaplin, dressed as the Tramp, is shown here on the set of The Gold Rush. *The 1928 silent film may be set in Alaska but it recreates the experiences of Yukon prospectors.* [Ontario Film Institute]

cabin, with moose antlers hanging above the doorway and a hammock slung across the porch, was moved here from Whitehorse. Service resided in the cabin when it was located in Whitehorse for two periods of time, in 1908-9 and 1911-12.

Here Robert Service wrote his rhymes in charcoal letters on coarse rolls of wallpaper which he pinned to the cabin wall. "Then I would pace back and forth before them, studying them, repeating them, trying to make them perfect. I wanted them to appeal to the eye as well as to the ear," he recalled in his autobiography.

This is the cabin in which Robert W. Service wrote many of his famous poems during his residency in the Klondike. It is now open during the summer months and actors declaim "The Shooting of Dan McGrew" for the tourists. [Tourism Yukon]

In this building Robert W. Service worked as a teller in 1909-12. One of the original buildings left from the Gold Rush days, it is used as a bank to this day. [Tourism Yukon]

Robert W. Service, bank employee. [PA-110158 / Public Archives Canada]

Living in the cabin with his cat and bearhound, he wrote his two most famous ballads. These are "The Shooting of Dan McGrew" (1904) which told how "the Dangerous Dan McGrew" was shot by "the lady that's known as Lou" in "the Malamute saloon" (there was no saloon so named in Dawson City) and "The Cremation of Sam McGee" (1906) which takes place on "the marge of Lake Labarge." Both appear in his first collection, *Songs of a Sourdough* (1907). Within these walls Service also wrote *Ballads of a Cheechako* (1909) and his first novel, *The Trail of Ninety-Eight* (1910).

He left Dawson city in 1909 to sample the fruits of his fame, but returned via the Old Edmonton Trail. Wintering here in 1911-12, he wrote *Rhymes of a Rolling Stone* (1912). Then he left the Yukon for good and lived in sunny Monaco, as far away as possible from the snows of the Yukon. In retirement he wrote the two volumes of his autobiography, *Ploughman of the Moon* (1945) and *Harper of Heaven* (1948). He is buried not in the North but at Lancieux, Brittany, France.

Two of his works were filmed in Hollywood. *The Shooting of Dan McGrew*, loosely based on the ballad, was a silent film released in 1924 starring Lew Cody. *The Trail of Ninety-Eight*, subtitled "A Northland Romance," was filmed in 1928 as *The Trail of '98*, starring Dolores del Rio and Harry Carey.

Jack London's Cabin The cabin occupied in 1897-98 by Jack London (1876-1916), the American novelist, stood on the Left Fork of Henderson Creek. Dick North, the journalist, headed the White Pass & Yukon Expedition of March-April 1965 in quest of the Cabin, rediscovered it, and arranged for its removal to Dawson, where it stands close by Robert W. Service's Cabin. The original site of the cabin is the setting of London's classic story "To Build a Fire" (1908). The story is about man's endurance against overwhelming odds. It brought comfort to Lenin on his deathbed, according to Krupskaya who read it to him at his request.

London's best known novel, *The Call of the Wild* (1903), tells of a dog pressed into service as a sledge dog only to become leader of a wolf pack. It is set in the Yukon and Alaska and has been filmed and dramatized any number of times. "It was in the Klondike I found myself," London wrote in the introduction to his novel *The Star Rover* (1915). "There nobody talks. Everybody does things. You get your true perspectives. I got mine." Throughout the tourist season, readings from his novels and stories are given in the cabin. In the 1960s there was a movement to name one of the neighbouring mountain peaks in his honour, but the request was denied as it was felt, curiously, London had little connection with the Yukon.

Other Gold Rush Authors In addition to Jack London, two American novelists are associated with the Klondike Gold Rush in the Yukon and Alaska. Rex Beach (1877-1949) is the author of a trilogy set in Alaska

Jack London's Cabin on the day it was rediscovered on the left fork of Henderson Creek, Y.T., April 1, 1965, by Dick North (centre) with Victor Henry (left) and Joe Henry (right). The photo was taken by trapper Robin Burian. [Dick North]

Jack London's log cabin was moved from Henderson Creek to Dawson in 1965. It is shown here in its new location but before restoration work turned it into a tourist attraction. [Yukon Tourism]

— Pardner (1905), The Spoilers (1906), The Barrier (1907) — reprinted in an omnibus volume called Alaska Adventures (1933). There is no memorial to Beach in the Yukon, but there is the Rex Beach Repository in Wilcox, Sask. There is no memorial anywhere in Canada to James Oliver Curwood (1878-1927) who spent time in the region and set works of fiction here. Other American authors drawn to the gold fields in person or in imagination include Zane Grey (1872-1939), Joaquin Miller (1841-1913), and Owen Wister (1860-1938).

"City of Gold" So literate is the script of the NFB short feature, City of Gold, released in 1957, it should be regarded as a work of literature. The script was written and narrated by Pierre Berton (b. 1920), a native of Whitehorse and an authority on the Klondike. Through the use of verbal and visual images (from old stills), the author conveys what it was like to live in Dawson when it was Dawson City and the "City of Gold."

"Big Inch" Twelve miles north of Dawson there is a

Pierre Berton wrote and narrated the NFB short feature, City of Gold. It combined vintage photographs, like this Dawson City shot, with views of Dawson today. [Ontario Film Institute]

plot of land on the bank of the Yukon River which was acquired by the Quaker Oats Company in 1955 and used as a premium. Quaker arranged for the Klondike Big Inch Land Co. Inc., of Illinois, to divide the 19.11 acre tract into 21 million square-inch plots. Each plot was numbered and listed on a Deed of Land included as a premium in a box of Quaker Puffed Rice or Quaker Puffed Wheat. Twenty-one million deeds were distributed as part of this unique advertising campaign. The cereal company described the land as being located in "the heart of Sergeant Preston country," as it was the sponsor of the "Sergeant Preston" TV series. One collector amassed 10,000 deeds and requested ownership of the combined area; his request was denied, as nowhere on the Deed of Land did it state that the square inches were adjacent. Eventually the land was reclaimed by the Crown for $37 in back taxes. This amusing episode in premium history is told in Significa (1983) by Irving Wallace, David Wallechinsky, and Amy Wallace.

Lake Laberge

Lake Laberge is located on the Dawson Trail north of Whitehorse. It was "on the marge of Lake Labarge" — so spelled in the poem — that the bizarre event described by Robert W. Service (1874-1958) in "The Cremation of Sam McGee" (1906) took place. In the poem McGee emerged unscathed from the fiery furnace — the boiler of the steamship Casca, still visible on the shore.

Mount Adney

Mount Adney, northeast of Dawson, was named in 1979 for Tappan Adney (1868-1950), author of The Klondike Stampede (1900). The one-time prospector and writer was born in New Brunswick.

Mount Leacock

Mount Leacock, a mountain 10,200 feet high in the Saint

Even the signpainter had problems spelling the name of Lake Laberge, just north of Whitehorse. [Dept. of Regional Industrial Expansion]

Here is picturesque Lake Laberge, which was so memorably mentioned by Robert W. Service in "The Cremation of Sam McGee." [Tourism Yukon]

Elias Range, was named in 1970 in honour of Stephen Leacock (1869-1944). This is the pinnacle of Canadian humour.

Mount Robert Service

This mountain, near the head of the North Klondike River, honours Robert W. Service (1874-1958), "The Poet of the Yukon." It was so named in 1968. It is located in the same range and vicinity as Mount McGee and Mount McGrew which recall the sentimental ballads "The Cremation of Sam McGee" and "The Shooting of Dan McGrew" from the author's first and most important collection, *Songs of a Sourdough* (1907).

The Indian village of Old Crow, on the bank of the Porcupine River, is about seventy-five miles north of the Arctic Circle. It has a population of approximately 250 and is the Yukon's most northerly community. [Tourism Yukon]

Old Crow

Old Crow is situated north of the Arctic Circle and is the most northern settlement in the Yukon Territory. In 1976 it had a population of 221. Old Crow is home to Edith Josie (b. 1921), the Loucheux Indian who acts as special correspondent for the *Whitehorse Star*. She reports on community events in a vivid, laconic, ungrammatical style. "It is the very small village here at Old Crow but the news is getting better ever week," she explained in *The Best of Edith Josie* (1963). Often her reports begin: "Here are the News." Sometimes they end: "Everything Good Now."

Porcupine River

Robert W. Service (1874-1958) composed the popular Yukon song "When the Ice-Worm Nests Again" while sailing the Porcupine River between Rampart and Dawson in 1911. He was *en route* between Edmonton and Dawson over the Old Edmonton Trail. The song was published the following year in *Rhymes of a Rolling Stone* (1912), his collection of verses inspired not by the Yukon but by the Mackenzie River and the Arctic. Various versions of the song are sung today.

The trip from Edmonton to Dawson supplied Service with many experiences, only a few of which found expression in his stories and poems. As he wrote in *Ploughman of the Moon* (1945): "We visited a score of forts and met many Factors who hailed from the Hebrides. Highlandmen make the best officers of the Company, because they are hardy, used to loneliness and good traders. It is a saturnine life that takes men of determined sanity to endure it. These Hudson's Bay posts were a mine for the story-teller, but the grim men who manned them had no sense of the romance of destiny."

Robert Service Creek

This creek, which was named in honour of the poet

Robert W. Service (1874-1958), is a tributary of the North Klondike River.

Whitehorse

Whitehorse has been the capital of the Yukon Territory since 1952. It came into being in 1898 as a stopping point for prospectors on their way to the Klondike gold-fields. Today it is the largest city in the Territory.

Log Church   In this little log church, next door to Christ Church Cathedral in Whitehorse, will be found the vestry minutes. These were kept by the poet Robert W. Service (1874-1958) while resident in Whitehorse (1904-8).

Today there are parking meters in front of the Log Church in downtown Whitehorse. This Anglican church, attended by Robert W. Service, was one of the first permanent structures in the district. [Tourism Yukon]

Robert W. Service   Robert W. Service (1874-1958) worked as a teller at the Whitehorse branch of the Canadian Bank of Commerce from 1904 to 1908, when he was transferred to the branch at Dawson. As he recalls in his autobiography *Ploughman of the Moon* (1945), he wrote his earliest ballads about "the men who moiled for gold" in a two-room log cabin on a hill overlooking the Yukon River. This cabin has been moved to Dawson and restored. Service arrived in the Klondike as a bank clerk, not a prospector, half a decade after the Gold Rush which he immortalized in his ballads.

Sam McGee   It is unlikely that Sam McGee and Robert Service ever met. The sourdough prospector never relished the fame given him by the rhymester in his famous ballad "The Cremation of Sam McGee" (1906). Service found McGee's name in the bank ledger and simply appropriated it, no doubt because of its rhythmical and rhyming potential.

The log cabin occupied by Sam McGee on Lake Laberge (the locale of the ballad) has been moved to the McBride Museum where it may be seen as a cabin typical of the 1898 period. The house in town occupied by McGee and his wife and three children still stands at 501 Wood Street. The house was constructed in 1907 of

Sam McGee, the prospector, lived in this cabin, now a tourist attraction in Whitehorse. He had never met the poet Robert W. Service when the latter used his name in his famous ballad "The Cremation of Sam McGee." [Tourism Yukon]

squared logs, but these have since been stuccoed over. Sam McGee left the Yukon in 1923 and died at Beiseker, Alta., on September 11, 1940. As the saying goes, he may be dead but the name lingers on.

Muirhead House   The house at 507 Wood Street was occupied by the Berton family from 1919 to 1921. Here Pierre Berton (b. 1920) was born. It was later owned by a Mr. Muirhead, hence its present name.

Berton has made extensive use of his Yukon background. Articles about the region appear in *The Mysterious North* (1956). *Klondike* (1958) is an exceptionally well written history of the Gold Rush. He scripted and narrated the 1957 NFB film *City of Gold*, which has won innumerable international awards, and he wrote the words and music of *Paradise Hill*, a musical based on an incident that took place during the Gold Rush when a prospector attempted to buy a dancehall girl for her weight in gold. Choreographed by Alan Lund, it opened at the Charlottetown Summer Festival on July 3, 1967.

Wearing his characteristic bow tie is Pierre Berton, chronicler of the North and of all things Canadian. [CBC]

Author Farley Mowat, on location for Never Cry Wolf, *is flanked by actor Charles Martin Smith (left) and producer Lewis Allen (right). Mowat's book is set in the Barrens, Allen's movie in the district north of Whitehorse and in Nome, Alaska. The movie's credits thank the people of Atlin, B.C.* [Ontario Film Institute]

"If you can't get something you need take it from the other guy," Clark Gable tells Loretta Young as Jack Oakie looks on. The 1935 film Call of the Wild *was shot in California's San Fernando Valley. The snow, according to Pierre Berton, is gypsum.* [Ontario Film Institute]

To Berton the Klondike represented — and continues to represent — adventure. "The Klondike experience had taught all these men that they were capable of a kind of achievement they had never dreamed possible. It was this, perhaps more than anything else, that set them apart from their fellows."

Never Cry Wolf   The popular book *Never Cry Wolf* (1963) by Farley Mowat (b. 1921) was set in the Barren Lands of the Northwest Territories, but the 1983 film version of the novel was photographed north of Whitehorse. In addition to the wolves and the young American actor Charles Martin Smith, it starred two Inuit from the Northwest Territories — the elderly shaman, played by Zachary Ittimangnaq of Pelly Bay on the Gulf of Boothia; and the young hunter, played with a sense of comic timing by Samson Jorah of Baker Lake. Ittimangnaq, a movie veteran, starred in the NFB's "Netsilik Series" of twenty-six anthropological films. The landscape north of Whitehorse is lovingly photographed in *Never Cry Wolf.*

Northwest Territories

Aklavik

Buried at Aklavik, by the mouth of the Mackenzie Delta, is Albert Johnson, "The Mad Trapper of Rat River." His body lies in unconsecrated ground outside the cemetery. Johnson killed two Mounties, and following a massive manhunt — well described by Dick North in *The True Story of Rat River* (1972) — he died in a shoot-out in the Eagle River area, February 17, 1932. Rudy Wiebe (b. 1934) has given the incident some symbolic value in "The Naming of Albert Johnson," a short story included in *The Angel of the Tar Sands* (1982). *The Mad Trapper* (1980) is Wiebe's novel about the man. *Trapper* (1981) is what Thomas York (b. 1940) called his novel. Herbert T. Schwarz has a poem called "To Fred Firth" written at the Mad Trapper's gravesite; it appears in Schwarz's *Tuktoyaktuk 2-3* (1975). Some scenes involving oil exploration at Aklavik appear in *Where the High Winds Blow* (1960), a novel by David Walker (b. 1911).

An Inuit elder, played by Simonie Kopapik, teaches a marooned whaler, played by Timothy Bottoms, about the facts of life on Baffin Island, in the film version of James Houston's novel The White Dawn. [Ontario Film Institute]

land, Frobisher Bay, Gandolf Head, Pangnirtung, Pond Inlet, and Thackeray Point.

A small boat of sailors from an English whaling vessel landed on West Baffin Island in 1897. The sailors' lives were saved by the Sikusalingmiut people who were too proud to allow the sailors and their ways to disrupt and ultimately destroy their traditional ways. The tragic consequences led James Houston (b. 1921) to write *The White Dawn* (1971), perhaps the most powerful of the novels of the North. It was filmed to fine effect in 1974.

Robert Kroetsch with three women and a deckhand, Aklavik, 1950. "I was purser on the M.V. Richard E., which is visible (the pilothouse) in the background. The three women are Eskimo women who came aboard the barge to visit us. The deckhand is the man who was killed in an explosion on the barge and whose death led to my writing of But We Are Exiles." *[Robert Kroetsch]*

Baffin Island

This is the largest and the most eastern of the Arctic Islands, and it has a permanent population of about 3,500. Baffin Island has numerous literary associations, and these are discussed in entries for the following coastal settlements and adjacent islands: Blacklead Island, Bylot Island, Byron Bay, Cape Dorset, Cape Dyer, Cape Tennyson, Charles Dickens Point, Danish Is-

Baker Lake

This small community is situated on the south shore of

Armand Tagoona, minister and author, Baker Lake. [Indian & Northern Affairs]

Baker Lake in the Keewatin District. The Inuit writer and artist Armand Tagoona (b. 1926), who was born at Repulse Bay, on the south coast of Melville Peninsula, was ordained an Anglican priest in 1960 and nine years later settled at Baker Lake. In the words and images of his book *Shadows* (1975), he recreates the traditional world of his Inuit ancestors.

Barren Lands

It was the explorer Samuel Hearne (1745-1792) who referred to this great expanse of tundra as "The Barren Ground." In general terms, the triangle-like boundaries are the Arctic Coast to the north, the western shore of Hudson Bay to the east, and an imaginary line drawn from the port of Churchill, Man., to Coronation Gulf on the Arctic Ocean.

John Hornby (1880-1927), the English trapper and explorer, called it "the land of feast and famine." It was famine for Hornby, his young cousin Edgar Christian (1908-1927), and their friend Harold Adlard. An RCMP officer found that the trio had starved to death in their cabin on the Thelon River. George Whalley (1915-1983) told Hornby's story in *The Legend of John Hornby* (1962), and Christian's diary has been published as *Unflinching: A Diary of Tragic Adventure* (1937). Hornby's sad heroism inspired Thomas York (b. 1940) to write his novel *Snowman* (1976).

Famine was the familiar foe of the Ihalmiut people whose fate was the subject to two moving memoirs of life among them in 1947-48 by Farley Mowat (b. 1921) in *People of the Deer* (1952) and *Desperate People* (1959). Locales mentioned in the two volumes, subsequently combined as *Death of a People*, include Ootek's Lake, Angkuni Lake, and Henik Lake.

The photographer Richard Harrington, appalled at the condition in which he found the Inland Eskimo, recorded their poverty and way of life in a series of photographs for *Life* magazine which, in effect, commenced their rescue. These poignant photos later appeared, with a text, in *The Inuit: Life As It Was* (1981).

Also set in the Barrens is *Never Cry Wolf* (1963),

Farley Mowat lived for two years in the Barrens and has written about the region in books of fiction and non-fiction. He is specially sensitive to the plight of the native people. [McClelland & Stewart]

Mowat's vivid account of a wolf family in the wild and man's misunderstanding of the animal. The setting is a cabin some 300 miles northwest of Churchill, Man. Although located in the Northwest Territories, the novel was filmed in the Yukon Territory, north of Whitehorse. The movie was released in 1983. Mowat is no stranger to the Barrens (or to most other regions of the country). His frequent pronouncements on northern lifestyles have earned him the sobriquet "Barely Know It."

The Barren Lands are the backdrop for two of Mowat's adventure novels for younger readers. *Lost in the Barrens* (1956) begins at The Pas, north of Winnipeg, but moves on to the tundra where two boys, Jamie and Awasin, get lost over the winter and almost starve. Some of the action takes place on the banks of the Kazan River. The same setting and characters appear in the sequel, *The Curse of the Viking Grave* (1966).

Bathurst Inlet

This settlement at the southernmost extremity of Coronation Gulf on the mainland is the area inhabited by the Krangmalit people in *Ayorama* (1956), a novel by Raymond De Coccola (b. 1912) and Paul King (b. 1912).

Manager in the 1960s of the HBC store at Umingmaktok, near Bathurst Inlet, was Scottish-born Duncan Pryde (b. 1937), who wrote about his experiences in an uninhibited manner in *Nunaga* (1972).

Belcher Islands

The most famous Eskimo in the world came from the Belcher Islands, an island group in Hudson Bay located off the east shore of Quebec near the mouth of the Great Whale River. The Eskimo was Nanook who appeared as himself in *Nanook of the North*, the world's first feature-length documentary film, directed by Robert Flaherty (1884-1951) and released in 1922. The film itself was shot in the Ungava region of northern Quebec in 1921-22. Nanook (the name means polar bear) died of starvation in his prime in the year of the film's release. Flaherty wrote two novels about his northern experiences, *The Captain's Chair* (1938) and *White Master* (1939). There was even a novelization of *Nanook of the North* (1935), done by Julian William Bilby, complete with stills in the "photoplay edition."

The Belcher Islands serve as the setting of *The Story of Comock the Eskimo* (1968), a true story told by Comock to Flaherty in 1912, edited by Edmund Carpenter.

Cape Hope Island, in James Bay, is the birthplace of Minnie Aodla Freeman (b. 1936), an Inuit who came south to work as a government translator. She was twenty at the time and wrote memorably of her experiences in the play "Survival in the South," produced by CBC Radio. In her autobiography, *Life among the Qallunaat* (1978), she wrote: "On arrival in the south, I suddenly found myself in a totally new world, and had to start learning from the beginning once again how to survive each day."

A *still from* Nanook of the North, *the first feature-length documentary film, photographed by Robert Flaherty in Ungava and on the Belcher Islands.* [Ontario Film Institute]

The Rev. E. J. Peck adapted the Cree syllabic system for Eskimo use. [General Synod Archives, Anglican Church of Canada]

Bernard Harbour

In a wooden shack in the isolated settlement of Bernard Harbour, on the southern coast of Victoria Island, Vilhjalmur Stefansson (1879-1962) established the headquarters of the Canadian Arctic Expedition of 1913-18. Here the ethnologist Diamond Jenness (1886-1969) set up a primitive recording studio and preserved on wax cylinders the moody and meditative songs of the Eskimos. With transcriptions by Helen H. Roberts, the words and music in Inuktitut and English were published as *Songs of the Copper Eskimo* (1925). One of the lyrics from Bernard Harbour begins: "There is joy in / Feeling the warmth / Come to the great world. . . ."

This photograph of Vilhjalmur Stefansson was taken by G. H. Wilkins of the Canadian Arctic Expedition, September 1914. [Indian & Northern Affairs]

Blacklead Island

E. J. Peck, the Anglican minister who adapted James Evans's Cree syllabic system to the needs of the Inuit, made his translations of the Scriptures into syllabics at Blacklead Island, Cumberland Sound, eastern Baffin Island. He undertook this work in 1894, employing innovations introduced into Evans's orthography by John

Horden and E. A. Watkins who worked at Moose Factory, Ont.

Blackwood Point

Blackwood Point, on Queen Maud Gulf, was named in 1839 for William Blackwood (1776-1834), the Scottish publisher, and for the popular periodical, *Blackwood's Magazine,* which he founded in Edinburgh in 1817. It is still being published.

Bloody Falls

Bloody Falls is the name given by Samuel Hearne (1745-1792) to the site on the Coppermine River where, on July 16, 1771, his Indian guides, coming upon an Eskimo encampment, raided the tents and slaughtered the "Poor Esquimaux." Hearne was horror-struck, but helpless to restrain his guides he remained "neuter in the rear." His account of the massacre, which appears in *Journey from the Prince of Wales's Fort* (1795), is one of the most vivid passages in the literature of atrocity.

Bylot Island

Located off the north coast of Baffin Island, Bylot Island was the locale chosen by Nicholas Monsarrat (1910-1979), the South African-born novelist then resident in Ottawa, for his novel *The Time before This* (1962). This short, cautionary novel tells how an old prospector stumbles across an immense, artificially constructed cavern in which are preserved artifacts from a civilization previous to man's, one that attained the use of the atom but then succumbed to its destructive potential.

Byron Bay

Byron Bay, on the south coast of Victoria Island, was named for Lord Byron (1788-1824), the English poet, whose father served at Louisbourg, N.S.

Cape Dorset

A settlement on the south coast of Baffin Island's Foxe

Peninsula, Cape Dorset is famed for its fine arts and crafts. These have been collectively sold since 1959 through the West Baffin Eskimo Co-operative. James Houston (b. 1921), arts administrator, artist, and novelist, settled here in 1951 and organized the first of the successful Eskimo co-operatives.

Cape Dorset is identified with three Pitseolaks. The celebrated artist Pitseolak Ashoona (b. 1900), as well as preparing graphic art, has written her autobiography, *Pitseolak: Pictures Out of My Life* (1971), which contrasts the old and the new Inuit ways. Her brother, Peter Pitseolak (1902-1973), was a carver of realistic images, sketcher of fantastic images, and a photographer of haunting images. His work appears in *People from Our Side* (1975) and *Peter Pitseolak's Escape from Death* (1977), both edited by Dorothy Eber. Also relevant is *Pitseolak: A Canadian Tragedy* (1980) by David F. Raine, about the younger Pitseolak (1945-1969), an artist of talent who died before his power could prove itself.

Aerial view of Cape Dorset. [*Economic Development & Tourism*]

Cape Dyer

This cape, on the northeastern coast of Baffin Island, may well be the site of the Norse landfall of A.D. 1001. Such at least is the opinion of Helge Ingstad, the Norwegian archaeologist who identified Cape Dyer with the Helluland (or Flatstone Land) of *The Greenlanders' Saga*, the Icelandic prose narrative written by an unknown author. In the translation by George Johnston made in 1976, Leif the Lucky declares: "I shall give a name to this land and call it Flatstone Land."

Cape Tennyson

Cape Tennyson, on the southeast coast of Ellesmere Island, was named in 1853 in honour of the English poet Alfred Lord Tennyson (1809-1892) who, three years earlier, had been appointed Poet-Laureate.

Charles Dickens Point

Charles Dickens Point is on the southeastern coast of Prince of Wales Island. It was named by the Arctic explorer Francis Leopold M'Clintock in 1852-53 in honour of the English novelist Charles Dickens (1812-1870).

Nineteenth-century authors like Alfred Lord Tennyson (left) and Charles Dickens (right) were popular enough to have their names attached to geographical features and fledgling communities. [C 106780 and PA 99809 / Public Archives Canada]

M'Clintock also named Thackeray Point, which is nearby, as is Swinburne Point.

On the southwest coast of Victoria Island, on Dolphin and Union Strait, is another landmark named after the novelist: Dickens Point.

Chesterfield Inlet

Chesterfield Inlet, on the west coast of Hudson Bay, was named about 1749 for Philip Stanhope (1694-1773), the fourth Earl of Chesterfield. The diplomat and wit is remembered for two volumes of letters of sensible instruction respectively addressed to his son and grandson and published in 1774 and 1890. Some of his fatherly and grandfatherly advice was considered scandalous. ("Women are much more like each other than men: they have, in truth, but two passions, vanity and love; these are their universal characteristics.") He is less-favourably recalled as the non-patron of Dr. Johnson's *Dictionary* (1775), for as the impecunious lexicographer noted of Chesterfield's commendation: "Had it been early, it had been kind; but it has been delayed till I am indifferent, and cannot enjoy it." Finally, Chesterfield is recalled has having lent his name to a kind of overcoat and a kind of couch.

Coppermine River

On the bank of the Coppermine River, which flows into Coronation Gulf, the explorer Samuel Hearne (1745-1792), the first white man to reach the Arctic overland from Hudson Bay, witnessed a massacre of the Inuit by the Indians. The bloody event of July 1771 so affected him that in retirement, when he wrote his famous *Journey from Prince of Wales's Fort in Hudson's Bay to the Northern Ocean* (1795), he shuddered: "Even at this hour I cannot reflect on the transactions of that horrid day without shedding tears." He named the site Bloody Falls.

Hearne tells also of the "strange tradition" among the Yellowknife Indians of the origin of copper in this region. It seems a native woman discovered the deposits but was so ill-treated by her companions that she sank into the ground taking the copper, which formerly lay on the surface, beneath the earth.

C. W. Jefferys' drawing of Samuel Hearne on his journey to the Coppermine, 1770. [C 70250 / Public Archives Canada]

Members of the famous Fifth Thule Expedition pose for the camera. Knud Rasmussen, the youthful-looking leader, is in the front row, second from left. [Indian & Northern Affairs]

Hearne built the HBC's first inland post at Cumberland House in present-day Saskatchewan, the setting of "Samuel Hearne in Wintertime" (1968), a sensitive poem by John Newlove (b. 1938).

Danish Island

There is a plaque on Danish Island, off Foxe Peninsula, Baffin Island, to mark the site of the headquarters in 1921-24 of the important Fifth Thule Expedition. It was headed by Knud Rasmussen (1879-1933), the Danish explorer and ethnologist who was himself part Eskimo. Rasmussen collected many of the traditional lyrics of the Copper and other Eskimos that are so widely reprinted in anthologies. He wrote *Across Arctic America* (1927) and until his death supervised the publication of the expedition's ten-volume *Report* (1931-34). The expedition identified the culture of the Eskimos of the period A.D. 900 to 1450, employing Rasmussen's term "Thule" to describe it. He took the word from the Greek reference to the most northern land.

Dickens Point   See CHARLES DICKENS POINT.

Ellesmere Island

The most northerly island in the Canadian Arctic, Ellesmere Island, lies in the extreme northeastern Arctic. Much of its surface is permanently ice-covered. Although Earle Birney (b. 1904) has travelled widely in the world, he has never visited Ellesmere Island. This did not stop him from writing two amusing poems about the Arctic island. In "Ellesmereland I" (1952), he claims that "no man is settled on that coast." In "Ellesmereland II" (1965), he observed that "there is talk of growth."

Fort McPherson

Only thirty-five miles south of Fort McPherson, District of Mackenzie, members of the so-called Lost Patrol succumbed to hunger and cold on February 5, 1911. Four members of the RNWMP, headed by Inspector Francis J. Fitzgerald, had attempted to cross from Dawson City to Fort McPherson by dogsled in winter. This epic of endurance has yet to receive poetic or fictional treatment. The standard account is *The Lost Patrol* (1978) by Dick North. The Dempster Highway, which is the only road into the Arctic, was named after RNWMP Corporal W. J. D. Dempster who led the successful search for the bodies of his comrades. The 460-mile gravel highway roughly follows the corporal's route.

Fort Reliance

Fort Reliance, on McLeod Bay in the Mackenzie District, is the departure point for the expedition to establish "Fort Hope" off "Cape Bathurst" on the Arctic coast in *The Fur Country* (1874), a sensational adventure novel by Jules Verne (1828-1905). No sooner is the trading post set up than it is found to be built not on the coast but on a giant ice-pan which begins to float away and melt.

It was a settlement like Fort Reliance that was in the back of the mind of the Belgian novelist Georges Simenon (b. 1908) when he wrote in his autobiography *When I Was Old* (1971): "Lying down for a short nap, a flash of

F. R. Scott, his rapier wit ever at the ready, drawn by Isaac Bickerstaff (caricaturist Don Evans). [Special Collections, University of Calgary Libraries]

the kind of place for which I have most nostalgia came to me. There aren't many left in the world. Thirty years ago in Equatorial Africa, in the South Seas, it was called a general store. I know they have changed since. One still finds a few, under the name of Trading Posts, in some obscure corners of the United States and Canada."

Fort Smith

Fort Smith is located on the Slave River less than a mile from the Alberta border. Here the Northern Life Museum, opened in 1972, displays the printing press brought north in 1873 and the manuscript of John Testo's autobiography, *Trapping Is My Life* (1964). "Flying to Fort Smith" (1958) is a fine poem by the Montreal poet F. R. Scott (b. 1899) which includes these lines so evocative of the North: "An arena / Large as Europe / Silent / Waiting the contest."

Frobisher Bay

The most prolific of contemporary Inuit writers is Alootook Ipellie (b. 1951) whose poems, stories, and articles appear regularly in northern publications. He grew up in the settlement of Frobisher Bay, in the southern part of Baffin Island. He writes mostly about the old, nomadic way of life characteristic not of himself but of his grandfather. His work is included by Robin Gedalof in *Paper Stays Put: A Collection of Inuit Writing* (1980), which Ipellie illustrated with line drawings.

Aerial view of Frobisher Bay. [Economic Development & Tourism / Don Worrall]

William Tagoona of the Makivik Corporation and Alootook Ipellie, artist and author, at Frobisher Bay Airport in 1981. [Inuit Today]

Gandolf Head

This point of land, on the northeast coast of Baffin Island, was named, not for Tolkien's wizard, but for a reference to an onion stone in a poem by Robert Browning (1812-1889). It appeared that the head of land was scaling, like an onion.

J. Michael Yates on the shore of Great Bear Lake with a lake trout, summer 1968. [National Library of Canada, Literary Manuscripts Collection]

Great Bear Lake

The fourth largest lake on the continent, the Great Bear Lake drains into the Mackenzie River. At the eastern extremity, on McTavish Arm, is Port Radium established following the discovery of pitchblende here on May 16, 1930, by Gilbert LaBine. "How far north will the mind consent?" asked the poet J. Michael Yates (b. 1938) in *The Great Bear Lake Meditations* (1970). "I'm alive because I wonder how far things can go. Anything that survives its original purpose becomes a record. Anything that survives."

"Headless Valley"   See NAHANNI NATIONAL PARK.

Igloolik

Igloolik is a settlement and a co-operative on the northeastern coast of Melville Peninsula. It has associations with Rasmussen's Fifth Thule Expedition and was the home of the American woman who calls herself Georgia (b. 1928), whom the Inuit call Nayanguaq ("The One Who Is Like a Nun"). She moved from "down South" to Alaska in 1964, and to the Northwest Territories in 1970. She is the author of *Georgia: An Arctic Diary* (1982).

Inuvik

Located on the Mackenzie River delta, Inuvik is the first settlement designed and built for permanent residence in

Aerial view of Inuvik. [Dept. of Regional Industrial Expansion]

the Far North. Two writers who are associated with Inuvik, which means "the place of man," are Anthony Thrasher (b. 1937), the author of *Trasher: Skid Row Eskimo* (1976), and Bob Cockney (1895-1966), better known by his Inuit name, Nuligak. Cockney, the first Inuit to write an autobiography, prepared the manuscript in syllabics; it was published in Inuktitut in magazine form and then translated into both English and French by Father Maurice Metayer. The English version is titled *I, Nuligak* (1966).

King William Island

It was off King William Island, southwest of Boothia Peninsula, that Sir John Franklin, the famous Arctic explorer, and his two ominously named vessels, the *Terror* and the *Erebus*, disappeared in 1846. A cairn was found thirteen years later at Victory Point which contained a note giving the date of Franklin's death and other details of the ill-fated third Arctic expedition in search of the elusive Northwest Passage. Some forty search parties failed to rescue him or his men. The sense of mystery surrounding the fate of Franklin has been well caught in *Terror and Erebus* (1974), the play for voices, written by the poet Gwendolyn MacEwen (b. 1941), which treats of the theme "where the passage lies / Between conjecture and reality."

Laurentian Shield

Exposed throughout most of the Northwest Territories, the Laurentian Shield is an expanse of rock, forest, and water that covers 42 per cent of the land area of Canada. The population of the Laurentian, Precambrian, or Canadian Shield is less than 10 per cent of the Canadian total.

Of all the poets and naturalists who have been struck by the great age and extent of this region, perhaps only F. R. Scott (b. 1899) has caught its immensity in "Laurentian Shield" (1945). The poem begins: "Hidden in wonder and snow, or sudden with summer, / This land stares at the sun in a huge silence / Endlessly repeating something we cannnot hear. / Inarticulate, arctic. . . ."

Little Whale River

Little Whale River is situated on the east coast of Hudson Bay somewhat north of Great Whale River. The Rev. E. J. Peck established his Anglican mission here in 1877, translating some Scriptures into syllabics prior to moving north to Blacklead Island in 1894.

Mackenzie River

The Mackenzie River, Canada's longest river, is navigable from Great Slave Lake northwesterly to the Beaufort Sea in the Arctic Ocean. About this mighty river and the country around it, F. R. Scott (b. 1899) has written "Mackenzie River" (1963) which refers to it as: "A river so Canadian / it turns its back / on America," concluding: "In land so bleak and bare / a single plume of smoke / is a scroll of history."

"Of all the places I have ever been in my life, I still remember the delta of the Slave — or rather, of the Peace — as the loneliest. Here is loneliness on a scale awe-inspiring, and increased by your knowledge of having seen no habitation for so long." So wrote Hugh MacLennan (b. 1907) of this immense artery in *The Rivers of Canada* (1961). He went on to make a prediction about this river's valley. "Though I do not expect that anyone a hundred years hence will be reading these words, it amuses me to send them on through time with this prophecy. In the year 2061 there will be at least three million people living in the Mackenzie Valley. There will be hospitals, schools, and at least two universities established on sites overlooking that cold, clean river. After all, it was little more than a century ago that the money of a friend of Alexander Mackenzie himself was used to establish the first university on the banks of the St. Lawrence."

Poet and folklorist Herbert T. Schwarz has collected a number of traditional tales told by natives of the Mackenzie Delta region. These have been published as *Elik and Other Stories of the Mackenzie Eskimos* (1970).

The stretch of the Mackenzie from Yellowknife to the Beaufort Sea is navigated by the captain and crew aboard the *Nahanni Jane* in the exuberant comic novel *But We Are Exiles* (1965) by Robert Kroetsch (b. 1927).

Aerial view of the maze of muskeg, Mackenzie Delta. [Dept. of Regional Industrial Expansion]

A hiker on Albert Faille Portage Trail admires Virginia Falls, Nahanni National Park. According to lore and literature, somewhere in the Park, which is one of UNESCO's World Heritage Sites, will be found mysterious "Headless Valley" and the healing waters of "Sick Heart River." The Park is accessible by plane from Fort Simpson. [Parks Canada / Mike Beedell]

Nahanni National Park

Remote and awesome in its grandeur, Nahanni National Park was established in 1972. It was listed by UNESCO as a World Heritage Site in 1978. The valley of the mighty Nahanni River amid the Mackenzie Mountains, in the southwest corner of the Territories, has become a valley of mystery. Mineral springs gave rise to the legend of "Tropical Valley," a veritable Shangri-La amid the impassable snows, according to Pierre Berton in *The Mysterious North* (1956). The discovery of the headless bodies of two prospectors in 1908 resulted in legends of a lost gold mine in "Headless Valley." There are even legends of wild mountain men ruled by a White Queen. The region abounds in sinister names: Deadmen Valley, Headless Range, Broken Skull River, Funeral Range, etc.

The principal literary treatment of the legend of the lost valley is an impressive and moving one: *Sick Heart River* (1941). It was dictated to his secretary in Rideau Hall by John Buchan (1874-1940), Governor General Lord Tweedsmuir, who was, like the novel's hero, Sir Edward Leithen, dying. It tells how Leithen, in quest of a missing man and in search of his own salvation, finds it in the valley of "Sick Heart River."

Here is a place beyond time. "Now he suddenly saw the valley of the Sick Heart as a marvellous thing. This gash in the earth, full of cold, pure sunlight, was a secret devised by the Great Artificer and revealed to him and to him only. There was no place for life in it — there could not be; but neither was there room for death. This peace was beyond living and dying."

Leithen is a minor character in a number of Buchan's adventure novels. *Sick Heart River* marks his debut as a principal and his finale. Buchan himself died shortly after finishing the novel which was published posthumously.

Norman Wells

Norman Wells, a small town on the Mackenzie River just south of the Arctic Circle, was the first oil-producing centre in the Northwest Territories. Production commenced in 1920. There is a satiric poem called "Norman Wells" (1956) by F. R. Scott (b. 1899) about the use man has made of the wealth of this region.

Pangnirtung

Many of the elderly Inuit in this hamlet of 839, located on Baffin Island's Cumberland Peninsula, moved from the "bone age" to the atomic age in a matter of decades. There is a sadness and a sameness to the accounts of their lives, as is evident in *Stories from Pangnirtung* (1976), illustrated by Germaine Arnaktauyok. As Josephee Sowdloapik, a sixty-year-old former hunter of caribou, concluded his tale: "This is the end of my stories, and all of them are true. I used to be a brave man."

The poet Al Purdy (b. 1918) received a Canada Council grant in 1965 to travel in the Arctic and write poems about his experiences. He made "Pang" his home base and wrote the poems collected in *North of Summer: Poems from Baffin Island* (1967), illustrated by A. Y. Jackson. At Pangnirtung, he wrote such poems as "Eskimo Graveyard," "Trees at the Arctic Circle," "Arctic Rhododendrons," "H.B.C. Post," and "The Sculptors." On the more isolated Kikastan Islands, he wrote "Tent Rings" and "Eskimo Hunter," among others. About these poems Purdy noted: "They seem to me like a set of binoculars thru which you can view the Arctic from several thousand miles away. I'd prefer that the reader felt them to be an extension of his or her own eyes and mind. What I'm doing here is providing my own particular kind of optic glass."

A view of Pangnirtung, the hamlet of 839 people on Cumberland Sound, Baffin Island. [Indian & Northern Affairs]

Pelly Bay

Here in 1923 in the Gulf of Boothia the Danish explorer Knud Rasmussen (1879-1933), leader of the Fifth Thule Expedition, encountered the most impressive and powerful of the Eskimo singers, Orpingalik, leader of the Netsilik (People of the Seal). About the same age as Rasmussen, Orpingalik was a skilled hunter, archer, and kayakman. He fathered twenty-one children and sang more traditional songs than Rasmussen could record in pen and ink and later publish in translation as Volume VIII of his Report: *The Netsilik Eskimos* (1931). "All my being is song," Orpingalik explained, "and I sing as I draw breath." A selection of his songs — which he called "comrades in solitude" — appears in *Poems of the Inuit* (1981), edited by John Robert Colombo.

Pond Inlet

Pond Inlet, on the northeastern coast of Baffin Island, is the home of the Toonooik-Sahoonik Co-operative. It is also the home of the Inuit writer Simon Arnaviapik (b. 1915), the author of "Remembering Old Times," *Inuktitut* magazine, Fall 1974. Doug Wilkinson (b. 1919) recorded the way of life of the Inuit in this area in *Land of the Long Day* (1953).

Aerial view of Pond Inlet, Baffin Island, with name and RCMP crest visible on the slope of the hill. [NFB]

Rankin Inlet

On the west coast of Hudson Bay, in the Keewatin District, Rankin Inlet is the site of the Kissarvik Co-operative. It was the home of John Ayaruaq (1907-1969), who is the author of the first book written by a Canadian Inuit to be published in syllabics. *The Autobiography of John Ayaruaq* (1968) is currently being translated into English.

Resolute

Resolute is located on the south shore of Cornwallis Island not far from the North Magnetic Pole. Although born at Port Harrison in northern Quebec, the Inuit writer Markoosie (b. 1943) was raised at Resolute, often called "Crossroads of the Arctic," and here he became the first Inuit to hold a commercial pilot's licence. *Harpoon of the Hunter* (1970), a work of fiction with strong autobiographical elements, is the first novel published by an Inuit in the English language.

"Sick Heart River" See NAHANNI NATIONAL PARK.

Spence Bay

A good sense of what life is like among the Inuit and whites at Spence Bay, a settlement on the southern coast of Boothia Peninsula, can be had by reading the poems that make up *North Book* (1975), written by the Alberta-born poet Jim Green (b. 1943), who in the 1960s was an administrator in the area, which is the northernmost extension of the North American mainland. Green wrote in "Everybody Knows about the Arctic": "There's the tundra, / the sea and the islands; / northern lights / caribou and permafrost." He concluded: "Nobody knows much about the Arctic."

Swinburne Point

Swinburne Point, on the southern tip of Prince of Wales Island, was named by a Captain Young of the M'Clintock Expedition for a Rear-Admiral Swinburne, not for the English poet Algernon Swinburne (1837-1909).

Thackeray Point

This point, on the southwest coast of Prince of Wales Island, was named by Francis Leopold M'Clintock, the Arctic explorer, in 1859, after the English novelist William Makepeace Thackeray (1811-1863). M'Clintock must have been a reader of current fiction, for he also named Dickens Point.

"Tropical Valley" See NAHANNI NATIONAL PARK.

Tuktoyaktuk

Tuktoyaktuk, in the Mackenzie Delta region on the Beaufort Sea, is identified with Bob Cockney (1895-1966) who, as Nuligak, was the first Inuit to write his autobiography, in 1956. It was translated from the Inuktitut by Maurice Metayer and published as *I, Nuligak* (1966). Nuligak lived his early life on Herschel Island in the Beaufort Sea. The Nanuk Co-operative is located at Tuktoyaktuk.

In the 1970s the physician and author Herbert T. Schwarz lived at "Tuk." As well as collecting and publishing traditional Inuit tales, he wrote several volumes of verse which capture the quality of life in the Far North. His best-known collection is *Tuktoyaktuk 2-3* (1975). Schwarz once said that as a doctor on the DEW Line he had "the longest practice in the world, from Alaska to Greenland!"

Washington Irving Island

This island, off the east coast of Ellesmere Island, was named in 1876 after the American author Washington Irving (1783-1859).

Yellowknife

Yellowknife has been the capital of the Northwest Territories since 1967. The city is the home of René Fumoleau, theologian, photographer, anthropologist, and author of *As Long as This Land Shall Last* (1973). The city's story is told by Ray Price (b. 1931), the journalist, in *Yellowknife* (1968), but it has yet to produce its poets and novelists. The American science-fiction writer, Fritz

Contemporary engraving of Jules Verne whose imagination embraced the remotest regions of Canada. [Metropolitan Toronto Library]

Leiber (b. 1910), renamed it Amarillo Cuchillo in *A Spectre Is Haunting Texas* (1969) for in the future it has become part of an enlarged Texas as "Canada is a gone land, like Sumeria or Burgundy or Vietnam." The construction of the Northern Arts and Cultural Centre was sponsored by *The Globe and Mail* on "a dream and a dare." It became the first theatre "north of sixty" in 1984.

The North Pole

Although few if any readers of this book will ever visit the North Pole, some will fly over this northern end of the earth's axis on the "great circle" route from Western Canada to Europe. Here latitude and longitude, fact and fiction, meet. The co-ordinates are: Latitude 90°, Longitude 0°.

Situated on a polar ice cap north of Ellesmere Island, the North Pole is an imaginary point first reached (the technical term is "attained") by two claimants, Frederick A. Cook in 1908 and/or Robert E. Peary in 1909. When asked to describe the Polar Region, the Arctic explorer Vilhjalmur Stefansson would state that he had never been there. He would add: "I am not a tourist."

The North Pole is the traditional site of Santa's Toy Factory (the Postal code is H0H 0H0) and of Superman's Fortress of Solitude. Dozens of fantasy-adventure novels, like Edgar Rice Burroughs' *Tarzan at the Earth's Core* (1929), are set in the interior of the Earth, access to which is through the "polar opening." The Hollow Earth is illuminated by a Central Sun and peopled by a Lost Race. Such writers give new meaning to the phrase "the land of the midnight sun."

In Jules Verne's novel *The Adventures of Captain Hatteras* (1866), the North Pole is discovered to be an active volcano on an island amid a circumpolar sea.

The climax of the novel is the eruption of the volcano, which leaves Captain Hatteras (a kind of British Captain Nemo) insane from the "magnetic lava."

The most dramatic use of the North Pole as a fictional setting was made by Mary Shelley (1797-1851) in *Frankenstein, or The Modern Prometheus* (1818). She puts the following words into the mouth of the Frankenstein monster. "I shall. . .seek the most northern extremity of the globe; I shall collect my funeral pile, and consume to ashes this miserable frame. . . ." The words are addressed to Captain Walton who heads an English expedition to attain the Pole. True to his words, Frankenstein immolates himself on the roof of the world. (Hollywood should take note.) The single dramatic version of the Frankenstein story to retain Shelley's original finale is the play *Frankenstein* (1976) written by Walter Learning and Alden Nowlan (1933-1983).

The North Pole is stationary; it is the Earth that turns. The North Pole is not to be confused with the North Magnetic Pole which "wanders." The Arctic explorer Sir James C. Ross was the first person to attain the North Magnetic Pole. He did so in 1831 when it was located near Boothia Peninsula, and Ross's discovery is marked by a plaque erected at Spence Bay in 1979. Today the North Magnetic Pole is located somewhat north of Erskin Inlet, Bathurst Island, N.W.T.

All the compasses of the world point to Canada.

Dr. Frankenstein's monster died many different deaths in Hollywood movies. Not one of them recreated the fate reserved for him by Mary Shelley. In her classic novel of 1818 he immolates himself at the North Pole. In the 1932 movie Frankenstein, the monster was played by the English actor William Pratt who, in 1911, on a train between Kamloops and Nelson, B.C., decided on the stage name Boris Karloff. [Ontario Film Institute]

Index

McCulloch, Thomas
Pictou, N.S., 35
Macdonald, Alastair
St. John's, Nfld., 24
Macdonald, Brian
Gaspé, Que., 59
MacDonald, Donald C.
Toronto, Ont., 187
Macdonald, Flora
Windsor, N.S., 38
Milton Station, P.E.I., 53
MacDonald, J. E. H.
Algonquin Park, Ont., 104
Lake Superior Provincial Park, Ont., 131
Toronto, Ont., 209, 210
Macdonald, Sir John A.
Kingston, Ont., 126
International Peace Garden, Man., 218
Victoria, B.C., 281
MacDonald, M. A.
Saint John, N.B., 47
Macdonald, Ross
Kingsville, Ont., 129
Kitchener, Ont., 130
Macdonald, Roy
Montreal, Que., 83
London, Ont., 135
MacDonald, Thoreau
Toronto, Ont., 185, 209, 210
The Rocky Mountains, Alta., 259
MacDonald, Wilson
Callander, Ont., 111
Cheapside, Ont., 113
Kingston, Ont., 128
Morpeth, Ont., 140
Toronto, Ont., 181, 189, 205
Vienna, Ont., 210
McDonough, John
Asbestos, Que., 55
MacDougall, Dr. John G.
Halifax, N.S., 32
McDougall, Robert L.
Ottawa, Ont., 155
MacEwan, J. W. Grant
Qu'Appelle Valley, Sask., 239
Calgary, Alta., 250
Edmonton, Alta., 252
Stand Off, Alta., 260
MacEwen, Gwendolyn
Kingsmere, Que., 61
Niagara Falls, Ont., 142
Toronto, Ont., 176, 187, 189, 195, 205
King William Island, N.W.T., 297
McFadden, David
The Great Lakes, Ont., 121
Hamilton, Ont., 124
Nelson, B.C., 272
Macfarlane, David
Preface, 11
Toronto, Ont., 200
McFarlane, Leslie
Haileybury, Ont., 123
McGee, Thomas D'Arcy
Montreal, Que., 66, 79, 87
Ottawa, Ont., 151, 154
MacGillie-Eathain, Iain
See MacLean, John
McGregor, Mary Esther
See Keith, Marion
McIlwraith, T. F.
Bella Coola, B.C., 264
McIntyre, James
Ingersoll, Ont., 124
Stratford, Ont., 170
Mackenzie, Sir Alexander
Peace River Country, Alta., 258
Bella Coola, B.C., 263, 264
Fraser River, B.C., 268
Mackenzie River, N.W.T., 297
McKenzie, J. Vernon
Toronto, Ont., 183
McKenzie, R. Tait
Almonte, Ont., 105
Ottawa, Ont., 152
Mackenzie, Roy

River John, N.S., 36
Mackenzie, William Lyon
Navy Island, Ont., 140
Niagara Falls, Ont., 141
Queenston, Ont., 163
Toronto, Ont., 174, 178, 183, 184, 187
McKinnon, Catherine
Dartmouth, N.S., 27
McLachlan, Alexander
Erin, Ont., 118
Orangeville, Ont., 145
McLaren, Norman
Montreal, Que., 72
McLean, Jim
Moose Jaw, Sask., 237
MacLean, John
Antigonish, N.S., 26
Pictou, N.S., 35
MacLennan, Hugh
Preface, 8, 11
Glace Bay, N.S., 27
Halifax, N.S., 31
St. John River, N.B., 47
Eastern Townships, Que., 58
Lièvre River, Que., 63
Montreal, Que., 65, 69, 79-80, 81, 87-8
Quebec City, Que., 92
St. Lawrence River, Que., 98
Gravenhurst, Ont., 121
Niagara Falls, Ont., 140
Ottawa River and Valley, Ont., 158
Red River, Man., 221
Winnipeg, Man., 223
Saskatchewan River, Sask., 242
Calgary, Alta., 250
Fraser River, B.C., 268
Mackenzie River, N.W.T., 297
MacLeod, Alistair
Windsor, Ont., 213
McLuhan, Marshall
Hamilton, Ont., 123
Ottawa, Ont., 153
Toronto, Ont., 192-93, 195, 205-6
Windsor, Ont., 212
MacMechan, Archibald
Halifax, N.S., 32
Kitchener, Ont., 130
McMichael, Robert
Kleinburg, Ont., 130
Manitoulin Island, Ont., 136
Macmillan, Cyrus
Cape Blomidon, N.S., 26
MacMurchy, Archibald
Rockwood, Ont., 165
McNamara, Eugene
Windsor, Ont., 213
McNeil, Florence
Victoria, B.C., 282
MacPhail, Sir Andrew
Orwell Cove, P.E.I., 53
McPherson, Aimee Semple
Ingersoll, Ont., 124
Macpherson, Jay
Ottawa, Ont., 153
Toronto, Ont., 192
MacRae, James
Alexandria, Ont., 103
McRobbie, Kenneth
Toronto, Ont., 181
McWhirter, Norris
Manitoulin Island, Ont., 136
Toronto, Ont., 183
Mad Trapper, The
See Johnson, Albert
Maheu, Pierre
Montreal, Que., 78
Maheux, Arthur
Quebec City, Que., 96
Maillet, Antonine
Buctouche, N.B., 39
Mair, Charles
Lanark, Ont., 133
Thamesville, Ont., 172
Toronto, Ont., 177
Winnipeg, Man., 224

Estevan, Sask., 235
Mair, Sask., 236
Major, André
Montreal, Que., 78, 79
Major, Kevin
Calgary, Alta., 250
Mallarmé, Stéphane
Ottawa, Ont., 157
Malraux, André
Ottawa, Ont., 157
Mandel, Eli
Toronto, Ont., 181, 196
Estevan, Sask., 235
Regina, Sask., 242
Banff, Alta., 247
Manny, Louise
Newcastle, N.B., 45
Mansfield, Grace Yarrow
Sally's Cove, Nfld., 24
March, Vernon
Orillia, Ont., 147
Ottawa, Ont., 151
Marcotte, Gilles
Montreal, Que., 81
Marguerite d'Angoulême
Ile des Demons, Que., 60
Maritain, Jacques
Toronto, Ont., 192, 193, 197
Windsor, Ont., 212
Marken, Ron
Prince Albert, Sask., 238
Markle, Fletcher
Toronto, Ont., 184
Markoosie
Inukjuaq, Que., 60
Ottawa, Ont., 152
Resolute, N.W.T., 299
Marlatt, Daphne
Steveston, B.C., 275
Marlyn, John
Winnipeg, Man., 228
Marmion, Lord
Marmion, Ont., 136
Marriott, Anne
Yorkton, Sask., 244
Marryat, Captain Frederick
Bay Fortune, P.E.I., 49
Marshall, Bruce
Niagara-on-the-Lake, Ont., 144
Marshall, Tom
Kingston, Ont., 127, 128
Martigny, Paul de
Montreal, Que., 66
Martin, Claire
Ottawa, Ont., 152
Martin, Paul
Windsor, Ont., 212, 213
Marty, Sid
The Rocky Mountains, Alta., 259
Victoria, B.C., 284
Marx, Karl
Toronto, Ont., 193
Masefield, John
Ottawa, Ont., 155
Masefield, Sask., 236
Mason, F. Van Wyck
Louisbourg, N.S., 33
Massey, Raymond
Cobourg, Ont., 116
Port Hope, Ont., 162
Toronto, Ont., 206
Massey, Vincent
Ottawa, Ont., 153
Port Hope, Ont., 162
Toronto, Ont., 183, 193, 194, 206
International Peace Garden, Man., 218
Stand Off, Alta., 260
Matthews, Marmaduke
Toronto, Ont., 195
Maugham, W. Somerset
Fredericton, N.B., 42
"Dyer and Prentice," Man., 217
Maupassant, Guy de
Ottawa, Ont., 157